A User's Guide to Data Protection

The University of Law
incorporating The College of Law

D0808855

INLP
Lam
Std

Dedication

To Everett and Family
Astra

A User's Guide to Data Protection

Second edition

Dr Paul Lambert BA, LLB, LLM, CTMA

Adjunct Lecturer, Lawyer, Consultant, PhD

Bloomsbury Professional

Bloomsbury Professional Ltd, Maxwelton House, 41–43 Boltro Road, Haywards Heath, West Sussex, RH16 1BJ

© Bloomsbury Professional Ltd 2016

Bloomsbury Professional is an imprint of Bloomsbury Publishing plc

A CIP Catalogue record for this book is available from the British Library.

ISBN 978 1 78451 249 1

Typeset by Compuscript Ltd, Shannon
Printed and bound in Great Britain by CPI Group (UK) Ltd, Croydon, CR0 4YY

Contents

Contents

Contents

Contents

Contents

Contents

Contents

'Technology has ... altered the way we work. It is no longer really necessary to go into "an office" to make viable contribution to an organisation. We can work at home, in coffee bars, in airports, on trains using wifi and 3G telephone services utilising an increasingly diverse range of devices from laptops to tablet computers to smart phones in order to access emails and "attend" online meetings.'[1]

'[P]ersonal data ... are more and more processed and archived.'[1]

The importance of consent[2] cannot be overestimated.

'There is an inherent security issue with many of these online exchanges which if often overlooked. Emails are not particularly secure.'[3]

'A blog [or social networking post] is a bit like a tattoo: a good idea at the time but you might live to regret it.'[4]

1 Davies, C, Editorial, *Communications Law*, (2012)(17), pp 38–39.
2 Costa, L., and Poullet, Y, 'Privacy and the Regulation of 2012,' *Computer Law & Security Review*, (2012)(28), pp. 254–262, at 256.
3 Ferretti, F, 'A European Perspective on Data Processing Consent Through the Re-Conceptualiation of European Data Protection's Looking Glass After the Lisbon Treaty: Taking Rights seriously,' *European Review of Private Law*, (2012)(20), pp. 473–506.
4 Davies, C, Editorial, *Communications Law*, (2012)(17), pp. 38–39.

Abbreviations

These abbreviations shall be used throughout.

DPA: UK Data Protection Act 1998;

DPD: EU Data Protection Directive 1995 (Directive
                95/46/EC of the European Parliament and of the
                Council of 24 October 1995 on the protection of
                individuals with regard to the processing of personal
                data and on the free movement of such data);

GDPR: EU General Data Protection Regulation;

                Regulation (EU) 2016/679 of the European
                Parliament and of the Council of 27 April 2016
                on the protection of natural persons with regard
                to the processing of personal data and on the free
                movement of such data, and repealing Directive
                95/46/EC (General Data Protection Regulation)
                (Text with EEA relevance) OJ L 119, 4.5.2016,
                p 1–88;

                (Original Commission version: Proposal for a
                Regulation of the European Parliament and of the
                Council on the protection of individuals with regard
                to the processing of personal data and on the free
                movement of such data (General Data Protection
                Regulation) COM(2012) 11 final);

                (The GDPR replaces the DPD and is directly
                effective throughout the EU without the need for
                separate sets of national implementing legislation);

                There is a two year implementation deadline from
                the date of official publication, in May 2016;

Abbreviations

ePD:	Directive 2002/58/EC of the European Parliament and of the Council of 12 July 2002 concerning the processing of personal data and the protection of privacy in the electronic communications sector (Directive on privacy and electronic communications). This is also known as the ePrivacy Directive (ePD);
WP29:	EU Article 29 Working Party on Data Protection (replaced by EDPR);
EDPB:	European Data Protection Board;
Personal data:	Any data or information identifying or relating to the individual data subject (see DPD and DPR detailed definitions below);
Data Subject:	The individual who the personal data relates to (see DPD and DPR detailed definitions below);
Data Controller:	The organisation collecting, processing and holding the personal data (see DPD and DPR detailed definitions below);
Data Processor:	An outsourced third party organisation or related entity carrying out certain defined outsourced activities for and on behalf of the main data controller with the personal data eg outsourced payroll, outsourced direct marketing, etc. (see DPD and DPR detailed definitions below);
DPO:	Data Protection Officer;
ICO:	Information Commissioner's Office ie the main UK data protection regulator or supervisory authority;
Member State:	means a member State of the European Union (EU);
PECR:	Privacy and Electronic Communications (EC Directive) Regulations 2003;
PECR:	Privacy and Electronic Communications
Amendment:	(EC Directive) (Amendment) Regulations 2011;
Commission:	means the EU Commission;
EEA:	means the European Economic Area, comprising the EU plus Iceland, Liechtenstein and Norway. (Note, Switzerland has a similar type arrangement with the EU.)

List of Statutes

A more detailed Table of Statutes, with references to the text, can be found at p. xlv

Access to Health Records Act 1990
Access to Justice Act 1999
Access to Medical Reports Act 1988
Access to Personal Files Act 1987
Adoption Act 1976
Anti-terrorism, Crime and Security Act 2001
Banking and Financial Dealings Act 1971
Broadcasting Act 1990
Broadcasting Act 1996
Business Names Act 1985
Charities Act 1993, 2006
Charities Act (Northern Ireland) 2008
Children Act 1989
Communications Act 2003
Companies Act 1985
Computer Misuse Act 1990
Communications Act 2003
Constitutional Reform Act 2005
Consumer Credit Act 1974
Copyright, Designs and Patents Act 1988
Coroners and Justice Act 2009
Courts and Legal Services Act 1990
Crime and Disorder Act 1998
Crime (International Co-operation) Act 2003
Crime and Security Act 2010
Criminal Damage Act 1971
Criminal Justice Act 1988, 2003
Criminal Justice and Courts Services Act 2000
Criminal Justice and Immigration Act 2008
Criminal Justice and Police Act 2001
Criminal Justice and Public Order Act 1994
Data Protection Act 1984

List of Statutes

Data Protection Act 1998
Data Retention and Investigatory Powers Act 2014
Defamation Act 1996
Digital Economy Act 2010
Disability Discrimination Act 1995
Education Act 1996
Education Reform Act 1988
Employers Liability (Compulsory Insurance) Act 1969
Employment Act 2002
Employment Rights Act 1996
Enterprise Act 2002
Equality Act 2010
Finance Act 1998
Financial Services Act 1986
Financial Services and Markets Act 2000
Football Spectators Act 1989
Fraud Act 2006
Freedom of Information Act 2000
Freedom of Information (Scotland) Act 2002
Further and Higher Education Act 1992
Gas Act 1986
Health and Safety at Work Act 1974
Health and Social Care Act 2001, 2008
Health and Social Care (Community Health and Standards) Act 2003
Health and Social Services and Social Security Adjudications Act 1983
Housing Act 1985
Housing Act 1988
Human Fertilisation and Embryology Act 1990
Human Rights Act 1998
Human Tissue Act 2004
Immigration, Asylum and Nationality Act 2006
Information Acts
Interception of Communications Act 1985
Interpretation Act 1978, 1889
Insurance Companies Act 1982
Interception of Communications Act 1985
Interpretation Act 1978
Jobseekers Act 1995
Local Authority Social Services Act 1970
Local Government Act 1972
Local Government Act 2000
Malicious Communications Act 1988
Medical Act 1983

Mental Capacity Act 2005
National Health Service Act 1977
National Health Services Act 2006
National Health Service and Community Care Act 1990
Office of Communications Act 2002
Official Secrets Act 1989
Opticians Act 1989
Osteopaths Act 1993
Pension Schemes Act 1993
Personal Files Act 1987
Pharmacy Act 1954
Police Act 1996, 1997
Police and Criminal Evidence Act 1984 (PACE)
Police and Justice Act 2006
Powers of Criminal Courts (Sentencing) Act 2000
Prison Act 1952
Probation Service Act 1993
Proceeds of Crime Act 2002
Professions Supplementary to Medicine Act 1960
Protection from Harassment Act 1997
Protection of Children Act 1978
Protection of Freedoms Act 2012
Protection of Vulnerable Groups (Scotland) Act 2007
Public Records Act 1958
Race Relations Act 1976
Race Relations (Amendment) Act 2000
Regulation of Investigatory Power Act 2000
Regulation of Investigatory Power (Scotland) Act 2000
Rehabilitation of Offenders Act 1974
Representation of the People Act 1983
Representation of the People Act 2000
Safeguarding Vulnerable Groups Act 2006
School Standards and Framework Act 1998
Serious Crime Act 2007
Serious Organised Crime and Police Act 2005
Sex Discrimination Act 1975
Social Security Act 1989
Social Security Administration Act 1992
Social Security Contributions and Benefits Act 1992
Statistics and Registration Act 2007
Superannuation Act 1972
Taxes Management Act 1970
Terrorism Act 2000

List of Statutes

Theft Act 1968
Trade Union and Labour Relations (Consolidation) Act 1992
Transfer of Undertakings (Protection of Employment)
Tribunal of Inquiries Act 1992
Value Added Tax Act 1994
Video Recordings Act 2010

List of Statutory Instruments

A more detailed Table of Statutory Instruments, with references to the text, can be found at p. xlix

List of Statutory Instruments

Data Protection (Notification and Notification Fees) Regulations 2000

Data Protection (Notification and Notification Fees) (Amendment) Regulations 2001

Data Protection (Notification and Notification Fees) (Amendment) Regulations 2009

Data Protection (Processing of Sensitive Personal Data) Order 2000, 2006, 2009, 2012

Data Protection (Processing of Sensitive Personal Data) (Elected Representatives) Order 2002

Data Protection (Processing of Sensitive Personal Data) (Elected Representatives) (Amendment) Order 2002, 2010Data Protection Registration Fee Order 1991

Data Protection (Subject Access Modification) (Education) Order 2000

Data Protection (Subject Access Modification) (Health) Order 2000

Data Protection (Subject Access Modification) (Social Work) Order 2000

Data Protection (Subject Access Modification) (Social Work) Amendment Order 2011

Data Protection Registration Fee Order 1991

Data Protection (Subject Access) (Fees and Miscellaneous Provisions) Regulations 2000

Data Protection (Subject Access) (Fees and Miscellaneous Provisions) (Amendment) Regulations 2001

Data Protection (Subject Access Modification)(Social Work) (Amendment) Order 2005

Data Protection Tribunal (Enforcement Appeals) Rules 2000

Data Protection Tribunal (National Security Appeals) Rules 2000

Data Protection Tribunal (National Security Appeals) (Telecommunications) Rules 2000

Data Retention (EC Directive) Regulations 2007, 2009

Education (School Records) Regulations 1989

Education (Special Educational Needs) Regulations 1994

Electronic Commerce (EC Directive) Regulations 2002

Electronic Communications (Universal Service) Order 2003

Environmental Information (Fees and Appropriate Limits) Regulations 2004

Environmental Information Regulations 2004

Family Proceedings Courts (Children Act 1989) Rules 1991

Family Proceedings Rules 1991

Freedom of Information and Data Protection (Appropriate Limit and Fees) Regulations 2004

Health Professions Order 2001

Health Service (Control of Patient Information) Regulations 2002

Information Tribunal (Enforcement Appeals) Rules 2005

Information Tribunal (Enforcement Appeals)(Amendment) Rules 2002

Information Tribunal (Enforcement Appeals)(Amendment) Rules 2005

Information Tribunal (National Security Appeals) Rules 2005

INSPIRE Regulations

Insurance Companies (Third Insurance Directives) Regulations 1994

Investigatory Powers Tribunal Rules

List of Statutory Instruments

Telecommunications (Lawful Business Practice) (Interception of Communications) Regulations 2000

Transfer of Undertakings (Protection of Employment) Regulations 246/2006

Unfair Terms in Consumer Contracts Regulations 1999

Waste Electrical and Electronic Equipment Regulations 2006

List of European/International Legislation

More detailed Tables of EU, EC and International Material can be found at p. liii

Aarhus Convention on Access to Information, Public Participation in Decision making and Access to Justice in Environmental Matters 1998

Charter of Fundamental Rights of the European Union 2009

CIS Convention on the Use of Information technology for Customs Purposes 1995

Commission Decision 2004/91 of December 7, 2004 amending Decision 2001/497 as Regards the Introduction of an Alternative Set of Standard Clauses for Transfer of Personal Data to Third Counties

Commission decision 2004/535 on the Adequate Protection of Personal Data Contained in Passenger Name Record of Air Passengers Transferred to the United States Bureau of Customs and Border Protection

Convention for the Processing of Individuals with Regard to the Automatic Processing of Personal Data 1981 (Council of Europe Convention 1981)

Convention on Mutual Assistance between Customs Administrations 1967

Convention on Mutual Assistance in Criminal Matters 2000

Council of Europe Convention for the Protection of Individuals with Regard to the Automatic Processing of Personal Data (Treaty 108) 1981

Council Decision 2004/496 on the Agreement Between the European Community and the United States of America on the Processing and Transfer of PNR Data by Air carriers to the United States of America on the Transfer and processing of PNR data by Carriers to the United States Department of Homeland Security, Bureau of Customs and Border Protection

Council Directive 73/148 (Council Directive 73/148/EEC of 21 May 1973 on the abolition of restrictions on movement and residence within the Community for nationals of Member States with regard to establishment and the provision of services)

Council Directive 89/552 ()Council Directive 89/552/EEC of 3 October 1989 on the coordination of certain provisions laid down by Law, Regulation or Administrative Action in Member States concerning the pursuit of television broadcasting activities

Council Directive 95/46 (Directive 95/46/EC of the European Parliament and of the Council of 24 October 1995 on the protection of individuals with regard to the processing of personal data and on the free movement of such data) (DPD95)

Council Directive 1997/7/EC (Directive 97/7/EC of the European Parliament and of the Council of 20 May 1997 on the protection of consumers in respect of distance contracts – Statement by the Council and the Parliament re Article 6 (1) – Statement by the Commission re Article 3 (1), first indent) (Distance Selling Directive)

Council Directive 97/66 (Directive 97/66/EC of the European Parliament and of the Council of 15 December 1997 concerning the processing of personal data and the protection of privacy in the telecommunications sector)(Telecoms Data Protection Directive)

Council Directive 98/34 (Directive 98/34/EC of the European Parliament and of the Council of 22 June 1998 laying down a procedure for the provision of information in the field of technical standards and regulations and of rules on Information Society services)

Council Directive 98/48 (Directive 98/48/EC of the European Parliament and of the Council of 20 July 1998 amending Directive 98/34/EC laying down a procedure for the provision of information in the field of technical standards and regulations)

Council Directive 99/5 (Directive 1999/5/EC of the European Parliament and of the Council of 9 March 1999 on radio equipment and telecommunications terminal equipment and the mutual recognition of their conformity)

Council Directive 2000/31(Directive 2000/31/EC of the European Parliament and of the Council of 8 June 2000 on certain legal aspects of information society services, in particular electronic commerce, in the Internal Market ('Directive on electronic commerce') (eCommerce Directive)

Council Directive 2002/21 Directive 2002/21/EC of the European Parliament and of the Council of 7 March 2002 on a common regulatory framework for electronic communications networks and services (Framework Directive)

Council Directive 2002/22 (Directive 2002/22/EC of the European Parliament and of the Council of 7 March 2002 on universal service and users' rights relating to electronic communications networks and services (Universal Service Directive)

Council Directive 2002/58 (Directive 2002/58/EC of the European Parliament and of the Council of 12 July 2002 concerning the processing of personal data and the protection of privacy in the electronic communications sector (Directive on privacy and electronic communications))(ePD or ePrivacy Data Protection Directive)

Council Directive 2003/98 (Directive 2003/98/EC of the European Parliament and of the Council of 17 November 2003 on the re-use of public sector information)

Council Directive 2009/136/EC (Directive 2009/136/EC of the European Parliament and of the Council of 25 November 2009 amending Directive 2002/22/EC on universal service and users' rights relating to electronic communications networks and services, Directive 2002/58/EC concerning the processing of personal data and the protection of privacy in the electronic communications sector and Regulation (EC) No 2006/2004 on cooperation between national authorities responsible for the enforcement of consumer protection laws)

Council Regulation (EC) 2299/89 (Council Regulation (EEC) No 2299/89 of 24 July 1989 on a code of conduct for computerized reservation systems)

Council Regulation 1035/97 (Council Regulation (EC) No 1035/97 of 2 June 1997 establishing a European Monitoring Centre on Racism and Xenophobia)

Council Regulation 2725/2000 (Council Regulation (EC) No 2725/2000 of 11 December 2000 concerning the establishment of 'Eurodac' for the comparison of fingerprints for the effective application of the Dublin Convention)

Council Regulation 2424/2001 (Council Regulation (EC) No 2424/2001 of 6 December 2001 on the development of the second generation Schengen Information System (SIS II)

Council Regulation 2580/2001 (Council Regulation (EC) No 2580/2001 of 27 December 2001 on specific restrictive measures directed against certain persons and entities with a view to combating terrorism)

Council Regulation 45/2001 (Regulation (EC) 45/2001 of the European Parliament and of the Council of 18 December 2000 on the Protection of Individuals with Regard to the processing of personal data by the Community Institutions and Bodies and on the Free Movement of Such Data)

Council Regulation 2252/2004 (Council Regulation (EC) No 2252/2004 of 13 December 2004 on standards for security features and biometrics in passports and travel documents issued by Member States)

Council Regulation 871/2004 (Council Regulation (EC) No 871/2004 of 29 April 2004 concerning the introduction of some new functions for the Schengen Information System, including in the fight against terrorism)

Cybercrime Convention

Decision 2001/497 of June 15, 2001 on Standard Contractual Clauses for the Transfer of Personal Data to Third Countries under Directive 95/46

Directive 95/46 on the Protection of Individuals with Regard to the Processing of Personal Data and on the Free Movement of the Data (Directive on Data Protection)(DPD95)

Directive on the Protection of Individuals with Regard to the Processing of Personal Data [2013], draft

Directive 97/7 on the Protection of Consumers in Respect of Distance Contracts

Directive 97/66 Concerning the Processing of Personal Data and the Protection of Privacy in the Telecommunications Sector (Telecommunications Directive)

Directive 98/48 amending Directive 98/34 (Directive 98/48/EC of the European Parliament and of the Council of 20 July 1998 amending Directive 98/34/EC laying down a procedure for the provision of information in the field of technical standards and regulations)

Directive 99/67 amending Directive 93/49 (Commission Directive 1999/67/EC of 28 June 1999 amending Directive 93/49/EEC setting out the schedule indicating the conditions to be met by ornamental plant propagating material and ornamental plants pursuant to Council Directive 91/682/EEC)

Directive 2002/59/EC Establishing a Community Vessel Traffic Monitoring and Information System

Directive 2002/19 on Access to and Interconnection of Electronic Communications Networks and Associated Facilities

Directive 2002/21 on a Common Regulatory Framework for Electronic Communications Networks and Services

Directive 2002/22 on Universal Service and Users' Rights Relating to Electronic Communications Networks and Services

Directive 2002/58 Concerning the Processing of Personal Data and the protection of Privacy in the Electronic Communications Sector Privacy and Electronic Communications Directive

Directive 2002/96 on Waste Electrical and Electronic Equipment (WEEE)

Directive 2003/4 Public Access to Environmental Information

Directive 2005/18 on the Retention of Data Generated or processing in Connection with the Provision or Publicly Available Electronic Communications Services or of Public Communications Networks

Directive 2006/24 on the Retention of Data Generated or Processed in Connection with the Provision of Publicly Available Electronic Communications Services or of Public Communications Networks and Amended Directive 2002/58

Directive 2009/136/EC Relating to Electronic Communications Networks and Services

Draft Regulation on the Protection of Individuals with Regard to the Data Protection [2013]

Draft Directive on the Protection of Individuals with Regard to the Processing of Personal Data [2013]

Dublin Convention 1990 (Convention determining the State responsible for examining applications for asylum lodged in one of the Member States of the European Communities – Dublin Convention)

EC Treaty

Eurodac Convention 1996

Europol Convention on the Establishment of a European Police Force

European Convention for the Protection of Human Rights and Fundamental Freedoms 1950 (European Convention on Human Rights)

Europol Convention

Lisbon Treaty 2009

Mutual Assistance Convention

Nice Charter of Fundamental Rights 2000

Organisation for Economic Co-operation and Development (OECD) Guidelines Concerning the Protection of Privacy and Trans-border Flows of Personal Data

Proposed Regulation on the Protection of Individuals with Regard to the Data Protection [2013], draft

Proposed Directive on the Protection of Individuals with Regard to the Processing of Personal Data [2013], draft

Regulation 515/97 on Mutual Assistance Between Administrative Authorities of the Member States

Regulation 45/2001 on the Protection of Individuals with Regard to the Processing of Personal Data by the Community Institutions and Bodies and on the Free Movement of Such Data

Regulation (EU) 2016/679 of the European Parliament and of the Council on the protection of individuals with regard to the processing of personal data and on the free movement of such data (General Data Protection Regulation) (GDPR) [27 April 2016]

Regulation 343/2003 (Dublin II Regulation)

Regulation 1987/2006 (Schengen II/SIS II)
Rome EC Treaty 1957
Single European Act 1987
Strasbourg Convention
Treaty 108 of the Council of Europe Convention for the Protection of Individuals
  with Regard to Automatic Processing of Personal Data 1981
Treaty of Amsterdam
Treaty on European Union
Treaty on European Union consolidated (TEU)
Treaty on the Functioning of the European Union (TFEU)
UNCITRAL Model Law on Electronic Commerce
Universal Declaration of Human Rights 1948

WP29 (replaced by the EDPB)

Update of Opinion 8/2010 on applicable law in light of the CJEU judgment in *Google Spain* (WP 179 update) (16 December 2015)

Statement on the implementation of the judgment of the Court of Justice of the European Union of 6 October 2015 in the *Maximilian Schrems v Data Protection Commissioner* case (C-362-14)

Opinion 02/2015 on C-SIG Code of Conduct on Cloud Computing

Opinion 01/2015 on Privacy and Data Protection Issues relating to the Utilisation of Drones

Explanatory Document on the Processor Binding Corporate Rules, Revised version May 2015 – WP 204

Cookie sweep combined analysis 2015

Guidelines on the implementation of the Court of Justice of the European Union judgment on 'Google Spain and Inc v Agencia Española de Protección de Datos (AEPD) and Mario Costeja González' c-131/121

Opinion 9/2014 on the Application of Directive 2002/58/EC to Device Fingerprinting

Opinion 8/2014 on the Recent Developments on the Internet of Things

Statement on Statement of the WP29 on the impact of the development of big data on the protection of individuals with regard to the processing of their personal data in the EU, 2014

Statement on the ruling of the Court of Justice of the European Union which invalidates the Data Retention Directive, 2014

Statement on the role of a risk-based approach in data protection legal framework, 2014

Opinion 06/2014 on the 'Notion of Legitimate Interests of the Data Controller under Article 7 of Directive 95/46/EC'

Opinion 05/2014 on Anonymisation Techniques

Working document 01/2014 on Draft ad hoc contractual clauses 'EU data processor to non-EU sub-processor'

Opinion 03/2014 on Personal Data Breach Notification

Opinion 02/2014 on a Referential for requirements for Binding Corporate Rules submitted to national Data Protection Authorities in the EU and Cross Border Privacy Rules submitted to APEC CBPR Accountability Agents

Opinion 07/2013 on the Data Protection Impact Assessment Template for Smart Grid and Smart Metering Systems ('DPIA Template') prepared by Expert Group 2 of the Commission's Smart Grid Task Force

Working Document 02/2013 providing guidance on obtaining consent for cookies, 2013

Opinion 04/2013 on the Data Protection Impact Assessment Template for Smart Grid and Smart Metering Systems ('DPIA Template') prepared by Expert Group 2 of the Commission's Smart Grid Task Force

Explanatory Document on the Processor Binding Corporate Rules, WP 204 Revised version, 2013

Opinion 03/2013 on Purpose Limitation

Opinion 02/2013 on Apps on Smart Devices

Opinion 06/2012 on the draft Commission Decision on the measures applicable to the notification of personal data breaches under Directive 2002/58/EC on privacy and electronic communications

Opinion 05/2012 on Cloud Computing

Working Document 02/2012 Setting up a table with the elements and principles to be found in Processor Binding Corporate Rules

Recommendation 1/2012 on the Standard Application form for Approval of Binding Corporate Rules for the Transfer of Personal Data for Processing Activities

Opinion 04/2012 on Cookie Consent Exemption

Opinion 03/2012 on Developments in Biometric Technologies

Opinion 02/2012 on Facial Recognition in Online and Mobile Services

Opinion 01/2012 on the Data Protection Reform Proposals

Opinion 16/2011 on EASA/IAB Best Practice Recommendation on Online Behavioural Advertising

Opinion 15/2011 Consent

Opinion 13/2011 on Geolocation Services on Smart Mobile Devices

Working Document 01/2011 on the current EU personal data breach framework and recommendations for future policy developments

Opinion 12/2011 on Smart Metering

Opinion 9/2011 on the Revised Industry Proposal for a Privacy and Data Protection Impact Assessment Framework for RFID Applications (and Annex: Privacy and Data Protection Impact Assessment Framework for RFID Applications)

Opinion 8/2010 on Applicable Law (WP29 adds as follows: 'In its judgment in Google Spain the Court of Justice of the European Union decided upon certain matters relating to the territorial scope of Directive 95/46/EC. The WP29 commenced an internal analysis of the potential implications of this judgment on applicable law and may provide further guidance on this issue during the course of 2015, including, possibly, additional examples.')

Opinion 5/2010 on the Industry Proposal for a Privacy and Data Protection Impact Assessment Framework for RFID Applications

Opinion 4/2010 on the European Code of Conduct of FEDMA for the Use of Personal Data in Direct Marketing

Opinion 3/2010 on the Principle of Accountability

Opinion 2/2010 on Online Behavioural Advertising

Opinion 8/2001 on the Processing of Personal Data in the Employment Context

Opinion 7/2003 on the Re-use of Public Sector Information and the Protection of Personal Data

Opinion 4/2007 on the Concept of Personal Data

Opinion 1/2010 on the Concepts of 'Controller' and 'Processor'

Opinion 2/2010 on online behavioural advertising

Article 29 working party opinion on the processing of personal data in the employment context 8/2001

Opinion 3/2009 on the Draft Commission Decision on standard contractual clauses for the transfer of personal data to processors established in third countries, under Directive 95/46/EC (data controller to data processor)

FAQs in order to address some issues raised by the entry into force of the EU Commission Decision 2010/87/EU of 5 February 2010 on standard contractual clauses for the transfer of personal data to processors established in third countries under Directive 95/46/EC 2010

Opinion 3/2002 on the Data Protection Provisions of a Commission proposal for a Directive on the Harmonisation of the Laws, Regulations and Administrative Provisions of the Member States Concerning Credit for Consumers

Working document on the surveillance of electronic communications in the workplace 2002

Recommendation 1/2001 on Employee Evaluation Data 2001

Recommendation 1/2007 on the Standard Application for Approval of Binding Corporate Rules for the Transfer of Personal Data

The Future of Privacy Joint contribution to the Consultation of the European Commission on the legal framework for the fundamental right to protection of personal data 2009

Table of Cases

Table of Cases

Table of Cases

Table of Statutes

Table of Statutes

Table of Statutory Instruments

Table of Statutory Instruments

Table of Statutory Instruments

Table of European Regulations

Table of European Regulations

Table of European Directives

Table of Treaties and Conventions

Part I
Data Protection

How to Comply with the Data Protection Regime

Chapter 1

Data Protection

What is Data Protection?

1.01 Data protection aims to protect the privacy and personal information of individuals. It provides a regulatory protection regime around personal informational privacy, or personal data. Personal data is data or information which relates to or identifies, directly or indirectly, an individual.

The data protection legal regime governs when and how organisations may collect and process personal data.

This applied to all sorts of personal information, from general to highly confidential and sensitive. Examples of the later include sensitive health data and details of criminal convictions.

The data protection regime is twofold in the sense of: (a) providing obligations (which are inward-facing and outward-facing, see below) which organisations must comply with; and (b) providing individuals or Data Subjects as they are known, with various data protection rights which they or the Information Commissioner's Office (ICO) can invoke or enforce as appropriate. Significantly, recent measures expand the ability to invoke the data protection rights to privacy groups and collective non-governmental type organisations (see the EU General Data Protection Regulation (GDPR), replacing the DPD). The GDPR brings 'comprehensive reform'[1] to the EU and UK data protection regime.

Certain specific sections of industry and certain specific activities (eg data transfers abroad, direct marketing, cookies), also have additional data protection compliance rules.

In terms of individuals, they can invoke their rights directly with organisations, with the ICO and also via the courts in legal proceedings. Compensation can also be awarded. In addition, criminal offences can be prosecuted. Data protection compliance is therefore very important.

---

1 In Brief, *Communications Law* (2012) (17) 3.

As regards implementing compliance frameworks, an organisation must have defined structures, policies and teams in place to ensure that it knows what personal data it has, for what purposes, ensure that it is held fairly, lawfully and in compliance with the data protection regime, and that it is safely secured against damage, loss and unauthorised access. The cost of loss, and of security breach, can be significant both financially and publicly. The IBM Cost of Data Breach Study (2015) puts the average cost at $3.8m. The TalkTalk data breach is estimated as costing £35m. The Target data breach was estimated as costing €162m plus a 5.3 per cent drop in sales. Breaches which are criminal offences can be prosecuted. In addition, personal liability can attach to organisational personnel separate and in addition to the organisation itself.

The Importance of Data Protection

1.02 One Editorial notes that '[p]rivacy and data protection issues are never far from the horizon at the moment. There are waves of discussion in this area ... and currently that wave is riding high.'[2] The increasing 'centralisation of information through the computerisation of various records has made the right of privacy a fundamental concern.'[3] Data protection is important, increasingly topical and an issue of legally required compliance for all organisations. More importantly it is part of management and organisational best practice. Individuals, employees and customers expect that their personal data will be respected by organisations. They are increasingly aware of their rights, and increasingly they enforce said rights.

1.03 The coverage of data protection has also increased in the mainstream media. This is due in part to a large number of recent data loss and data breach incidents. These have involved the personal data of millions of individuals being lost by commercial organisations, but also trusted government entities.

Even more recently the issue of online abuse, which involves amongst other things privacy and data protection, has also been hitting the headlines. Tragically, such online abuse can, and does, result in and contribute to actual suicide. This is a particular concern in relation to children and teenagers.

It is also in the headlines because of public and official data protection Supervisory Authority (eg ICO in UK) concerns with the problem of the damage of permanent data online. The EU Court of Justice in the light

---

2   Editorial, S Saxby, *Computer Law & Security Review* (2012) (28) 251–253, at 251.
3   'Personal Data Protection and Privacy,' Counsel of Europe, at http://www.coe.int/en/.

of such concerns issued an important decision in the *Google Spain* case and the Right to be Forgotten (see later) directing that certain personal data online had to be deleted, following a complaint, from search engine result listings.[4]

The EU Court of Justice also pronounced on the often contentious area of official data retention. This is the obligation placed by countries on internet service providers (ISPs) to retain certain customer data in relation to telephone calls, internet searches, etc, so that (certain) official agencies can ask to access or obtain copies of such data in the future. Debate frequently surrounds whether this should be permitted at all, if so, when and under what circumstances, how long ISPs must store such data, the cost of retaining same, etc. The strongest argument for an official data retention regime may relate to the prevention or investigation of terrorism. Serious crime might come next. There are certainly legitimate concerns that the privacy and data protection costs are such that official data retention, if permitted, should not extend to 'common decent crime'. On one end of the spectrum is the EU Court of Justice decision in *Digital Rights Ireland* striking down the EU Data Retention Directive as invalid.[5] By implication this also undermined the Regulation of Investigatory Powers Act 2000 (RIPA 2000) in the UK. The government proposed a new amending regulation entitled the Data Retention and Investigatory Powers Act 2014 (DRIPA 2014). However, two MPs (David Davis and Tom Watson), successfully challenged the DRIPA 2014 in the High Court. The court held that ss 1 and 2 of the DRIPA 2014 breached rights to respect for private life and communications and to the protection of personal data under Articles 7 and 8 of the EU Charter of Fundamental Rights.[6] The decision gave the government until March 2016 to rectify the DRIPA 2014 problems. The Queen's speech has also promised a 'snooper's charter' which would replace the DRIPA 2014.[7]

---

4   See Google Spain SL, *Google Inc v Agencia Española de Protección de Datos (AEPD)*, Mario Costeja González, Court of Justice (Grand Chamber), Case C-131/12, 13 May 2014.

5   Judgment in Joined Cases C-293/12 and C-594/12, *Digital Rights Ireland and Seitlinger and Others*, Court of Justice, 8 April 2014. Directive 2006/24/EC of the European Parliament and of the Council of 15 March 2006 on the retention of data generated or processed in connection with the provision of publicly available electronic communications services or of public communications networks and amending Directive 2002/58/EC (OJ 2006 L105, p 54). J Rauhofer and D Mac Sithigh, 'The Data Retention Directive Never Existed,' (2014) (11:1) SCRIPTed 118.

6   In relation to data protection as a fundamental right, see, for example S Rodata, 'Data Protection as a Fundamental Right,' in S Gutwirth, Y Poullet, P de Hert, C de Terwangne and S Nouwt, Reinventing Data Protection? (Springer, 2009) 77.

7   See T Whitehead, 'Google and Whatsapp will be forced to hand messages to MI5,' *Telegraph*, 27 May 2015, at www.telegraph.co.uk/news/politics/queens-speech/11634567/Google-and-Whatsapp-will-be-forced-to-hand-messages-to-MI5.html.

Since then a draft of the Communications Data Bill has been issued. No doubt argument, debate and research will ensue. It remains to be seen how challenges to the DRIPA 2014 may transpire, and how courts and policymakers will react. This remains, if anything, a contentious issue. The various Snowden revelations and their ripple effects also lean against the data retention regime, or at least an overly broad and over-reaching one.

However, every time there is a terror related event, and at the time of writing we are in the immediate aftermath of the Brussels, Paris, Egypt, Palestine and Mali attacks, the calls and arguments for data retention/extended data retention are at their strongest. Prime Minister Cameron has made statements to advance data retention proposals, in particular the Communications Data Bill, labelled by some as a 'snooper's charter'. Critics also increasingly suggest that research indicates that data retention does not work. However, official sources in various jurisdictions refer to terror attacks being prevented and that retained data is invaluable in this process. The link or proof of positive effect is not necessarily specified. This debate also crosses over with issues of unauthorised access or tapping by official agencies of technology companies and their customers' data, and public and industry arguments that official access must be regulated, transparent and proportional.

While the issues of official data retention are important, it is a separate subject to data protection. This work focuses on data protection alone.

A further reason as to why data protection is important, and increasingly the focus of press attention, is that organisations are increasingly using security and respect for data protection as a commercial differentiator in the marketplace. Apple has repeatedly announced that it does not operate on a user-data-intrusive model collecting user data. In fact, it has even criticised some of its technology competitors. Microsoft has for many years promoted the data protection and privacy friendly policy of Data Protection by Design (DPbD) (see later). Post Snowden, many US technology companies have been heavily lobbying the US administration for a roll back of certain activities and practices, particularly those felt to be extra-judicial and extra-legal, on the basis that it will disadvantage the US based cloud industry. Many non-US cloud companies have been highlighting that they are not US based.

1.04 All organisations collect and process personal data. Whether they are big or new start-ups, they need to comply with the data protection regime. It should also be borne in mind that even a new technology start-up can scale relatively quickly to millions of users. Many issues enhance the importance of getting organisational data protection understanding and compliance right from day one. These include legal obligations, director, board and officer obligations, investigations, fines, prosecutions, being ordered to *delete* databases, adverse publicity, commercial imperatives and even commercial advantages. If one also considers some of the recent large scale data breach incidents, there are examples of chief technology officers as well as managing directors/ CEOs, losing their positions as a result of the incident.

1.05 In addition, organisations often fail to realise that data protection compliance is frequently an issue of dual compliance. They need to be looking both *inward* and *outward*. Internally, they have to be data protection compliant in relation to all of their employees' (and contractors') personal data, which traditionally may have related to HR files and employee contracts, but now includes issues of electronic communications, social media, internet usage, filtering, monitoring abuse, on-site activity, off-site activity, etc.

1.06 Separately, organisations have to be concerned about other sets of personal data, such as those relating to persons outside of the organisation, eg customers, prospects, etc. Comprehensive data protection compliance is also required here. The consequences are significant for non compliance.

1.07 Substantial fines have been imposed in a number of recent cases. In some instances also, organisations have been ordered to delete their databases. In a new internet or technology start-up situation, this can be the company's most valuable asset. Even in an established organisation, it can be a valuable asset.

1.08 Up until recently the issue of data loss was a small story. More recently, however, the loss of personal data files of tens of millions of individuals in the UK – and from official governmental sources – makes UK data loss a front page issue. There is increased scrutiny from the ICO, and others, and increasing regulation of data security issues, preparedness and reactivity. Organisations must look at security issues with increasing rigour. Organisations can face liability issues in breach incidents but also in the aggravating situation where a vulnerability may have already been highlighted internally but not acted upon, thus contributing to the breach incident. As well as an official investigation, fine and sanction, organisations also face liability issues to users and in some instances potentially to banks and financial intermediaries.

1.09 In the UK and elsewhere there are enhanced obligations to report all data losses; as well as potentially enhanced financial penalties, and in some instances personal director responsibility for data loss. The need for compliance is now a boardroom issue and an important issue of corporate compliance. Proactive and complete data protection compliance is also a matter of good corporate governance, brand loyalty and a means to ensuring user and customer goodwill.

1.10   The frequency and scale of breaches of security eg TalkTalk, Target, Sony's Playstation (70 million individuals' personal data[8] in one instance, and 25 million in another[9]) make the topicality and importance of data security compliance for personal data ever more important. The Revenue and Customs loss of discs with the names, dates of birth, bank and address details involved 25 million UK individuals.[10]

1.11   There are many UK cases involving substantial fines for data protection breaches. The Brighton and Sussex University Hospitals NHS Trust had a fine of £325,000 imposed by the ICO in relation to a data loss incident.[11] Zurich Insurance was fined £2.3m for losing data in relation to 46,000 individual customers.[12] Sony was fined £250,000.

Apart from data loss incidents, two Spam texters were fined a total of £440,000 in respect of text Spam their marketing company had sent.[13] The size of the penalty is significant. However, possibly more significant is that it involves director liability. In a further significant development, the ICO has also issued a substantial data fine in relation to breach of the data protection regime by way of incorrect storage and processing when the financial data and files of individual customers were mixed up. Potentially, a customer could have suffered financial loss and adverse consequences. This was the ICO case of Prudential. Prudential was fined £50,000.

In another case, a health trust was fined £225,000 in relation to third party unauthorised access to files held at a disused building.[14] A Barclays

---

8   See, for example, G Martin, 'Sony Data Loss Biggest Ever,' *Boston Herald*, 27 April 2011.

9   See, for example, C Arthur, 'Sony Suffers Second Data Breach With Theft of 25m More User Details,' *Guardian*, 3 May 2011.

10 See, for example, 'Brown Apologises for Record Loss, Prime Minister Gordon Brown has said he "Profoundly Regrets" the Loss of 25 Million Child Benefit Records,' *BBC*, 21 November 2007, at http://news.bbc.co.uk/2/hi/7104945.stm.

11 See, for example, 'Largest Ever Fine for Data Loss Highlights Need for Audited Data Wiping,' *ReturnOnIt*, at http://www.returnonit.co.uk/largest-ever-fine-for-data-loss-highlights-need-for-audited-data-wiping.php.

12 See, for example, J Oates, 'UK Insurer Hit With Biggest Ever Data Loss Fine,' *The Register*, 24 August 2010, at http://www.theregister.co.uk/2010/08/24/data_loss_fine/. This was imposed by the Financial Services Authority (FSA).

13 *ICO v Christopher Niebel and Gary McNeish* (2012). ICO, 'Spam Tecters Fines Nearly Half a Million Pounds' at https://ico.org.uk. However, note that this was appealed.

14 Belfast Health and Social Care (BHSC) Trust. ICO, 'Belfast Trust Fines 22,5000 After Leaving Thousands of Patient Records in Disused Hospital,' at https://ico.org.uk.

bank employee was fined in a court prosecution for unauthorised access to bank records for personal reasons under s 55 of the DPA 1998.[15]

1.12   National data protection authorities are increasingly pro-active and undertake audits of data protection compliance frameworks, as well as incidents of breaches.[16] The ICO also investigated some of the personal data issues in the Leveson Inquiry press phone hacking scandal,[17] entitled Operation Motorman.[18]

The Data Protection Regime

1.13   Personal data protection is enshrined in the EU DPD of 1995 and the DPA 1998 in the UK, and now the EU GDPR. (The DPA implements the DPD in the UK, as does respective national legislation in the other EU Member States.) The GDPR is directly effective and applicable in each EU Member State without having to wait on national implementing legislation in each country.

Outward-Facing Data Protection Compliance

1.14   The data protection regime creates legal obligations which organisations must comply with when collecting and processing the personal data of individuals. '[I]f someone can be distinguished from other people, data protection legislation is applicable.'[19] This applies to customers and prospective customers, hence there are outward-facing obligations. It can also apply to non-customers who may be using a particular website but are not a registered customer, if their personal data are being collected.

Inward-Facing Data Protection Compliance

1.15   The data protection regime also applies to the organisation in its dealings regarding the personal data of its employees. Equally, where the organisation is engaging third party independent contractors but is collecting, processing and using their personal data, the data protection

---

15   She was fined at Derby Crown Court. ICO, 'Bank Employee Fined for Reading Partners Ex Wife Statements' at https://ico.org.uk.
16   Facebook was audited by one of the EU data protection authorities. See https://dataprotection.ie. Note also Europe Against Facebook, at http://europe-v-facebook.org/EN/en.html.
17   At http://www.levesoninquiry.org.uk/.
18   For more details see 'Operation Motorman – Steve Whittamore Notebooks,' ICO website, at https://www.ico.org.uk.
19   L Costa and Y Poullet, 'Privacy and the Regulation of 2012,' *Computer Law & Security Review* (2012) (28) 254–262, at 256.

regime will also apply. Hence, the data protection regime in relation to organisations is inward-facing.

1.16 As well as creating legal compliance obligations for organisations, the data protection regime enshrines certain rights or data protection rights for individuals in terms of ensuring their ability to know what personal data are being collected, to consent – or not consent – to the collection of their personal data, and to control the uses to which their personal data may be put. There is also a mechanism through which individuals can complain to Controllers holding their personal data, the ICO and also via the courts directly.

Information Commissioner

1.17 In order to ensure that the duties are complied with, and the rights of individuals vindicated, there is an official SA established in each Member State to monitor and act as appropriate in relation to compliance with and the efficient operation of the data protection regime. This role is fulfilled in the UK by the ICO.

Why Data Protection?

1.18 Why have a data protection regime? We have a data protection regime because of the legal and political recognition that society respects the personal privacy and informational privacy of individuals. In the context of data protection, that means respect for, control of, and security in relation to informational personal data. The DPA 1998 protects personal data relating to individuals, which includes employees, contractors, customers and users.

Data protection exists in order to ensure:

- protection and regulation of the collection, use, processing and transfer of personal information;
- protection in relation to personal information;
- the consent of individuals is obtained to collect and process personal data;
- security in respect for the right to privacy and personal information;
- protection against privacy and informational privacy abuse;
- protection against privacy theft and identity theft;
- protection against unsolicited direct marketing (DM);
- remedies are available to individual Data Subjects.

The threats to personal data and informational privacy have increased as the ease with which personal data can be collected and transferred electronically. This has increased further with digital technology, computer processing power and the rise of Internet 2.0 and social media.[20]

Summary Data Protection Rules

1.19 Controllers must comply with a number of data protection issues, perhaps the foremost of which relate to:

- fairness;
- transparency;
- consent;
- accuracy;
- security;
- proper procedures for processing;
- proportionality of the need and use of personal data;
- risk assessments.

The collecting, use and onward transfer of personal data must be fair, legitimate and transparent.

Transparency (and access to a person's personal data) is increasingly being emphasised in importance in relation to the internet and social media sphere. While this is beginning to be examined and there have been improvements with some websites, there is still a long way to go. Some have more improvements to make, even including the implementation of privacy policies and statements, reporting mechanisms and procedures. These also need to be assessed at the front and back end. In the *Prudential* case where a fine of £50,000 was issued, there was potential financial loss to the Data Subject.

The personal data must be correct and accurate. The reason is that damage or harm to the individual Data Subject can be a consequence of inaccurately held personal data. For example, a credit rating could be adversely affected through incorrect or wrong personal data records regarding personal payment histories.

There is a general obligation in terms of safeguarding personal data. Organisations must assess and implement security measures to protect personal data. Increasingly, this is also being considered in relation to the developing cloud environment and the increasing use of Processors and third parties.[21]

---

20 Note generally, comments of the ICO in relation to Privacy by Design (PbD), and the report *Privacy by Design*, at https://www.ico.org.uk.

21 In relation to cloud generally, see *W Kuan Hon and Christopher Millard*, 'Data Export Cloud Computing – How Can Personal Data be Transferred Outside the EEA? The Cloud of Unknowing,' SCRIPTed (2012) (9:1), at http://script-ed.org/?page_id=302;

There is also an obligation on Controllers to register or notify the ICO as regards their data processing activities.

If personal data is permitted to be transferred to third countries, it must qualify under a specific exemption, as well as the general security conditions. (Note that the issue of the EU-US Safe Harbour exemption mechanism is a matter of particular contention and import at this time given that the Court of Justice has invalidated this mechanism[22] – known as the EU-US Safe Harbour Agreement – and the EU and US are presently negotiating a new replacement mechanism to legitimise the controlled transfer of EU data to the US, known as the EU-US Privacy Shield.)

Controllers can have a duty of care to individuals as regards their personal data being processed by the organisation, particularly if loss or damage arises.

Controllers and Processors have obligations in certain circumstances to have legal contracts in place between them. Processors process and deal with personal data for, and on behalf of, a Controller in relation to specific defined tasks, eg activities such as outsourced payroll, HR, marketing, market research, customer satisfaction surveys, etc. Additional issues and considerations arise for cloud services and data protection compliance. From an organisational perspective, it sometimes is considered that organisational customers have less opportunity to negotiate clauses in cloud service provider contracts, including Processor and security related contracts. There is therefore a greater obligation to be satisfied with the cloud service provider, where data is located and the security measures and security documentation available.

General Criteria for Data Processing

1.20 Generally, in order to lawfully collect and process personal data, a Controller should be aware that:

- the individual Data Subject must consent to the collection and processing of their personal data;

G Singh and S Mishra, 'Cloud Computing Security and Data Protection: A Review,' International Journal of Computers & Technology (2015) (14:7) 5887; F Pfarr, T Buckel and A Winkelmann, 'Cloud Computing Data Protection – A Literature Review and Analysis,' 2014 47th Hawaii International Conference on System Sciences (2014) 5018.

22   *Schrems v Commissioner*, Court of Justice, Case C-362/14, 6 October 2015, at http://curia.europa.eu/juris/document/document.jsf?text=&docid=169195&pageIndex=0&doclang=en&mode=req&dir=&occ=first&part=1&cid=113326. The case technically related to Prism and Facebook Europe and transfers to the US. However, the wider import turned out to be the entire EU-US Safe Harbour Agreement and data transfers to the US. As such, this is one of if not the most important case decided by the Court of Justice to date.

- the Data Subject may say that they object to processing or continued processing;
- legal data protection requirements are complied with;
- the prior information requirements, Data Protection Principles, Legitimate Processing Conditions, Sensitive Personal Data Legitimate Processing Conditions (in the case of sensitive personal data), and security obligations are required to be complied with;
- the rights and interests of the individual Data Subject must be respected and complied with.

The interests of the Controller can sometimes be relevant in particular instances in deciding what data processing is necessary and permitted.

Data Protection Overview

1.21   The GDPR and DPA 1998 (implementing the DPD), set out a number of structures, obligations, rights and implementing criteria which are together the basis of the legal data protection regime in the UK.

The main criteria and obligations to be respected and complied with in order to be able to legally collect and process personal data include:

- the definitions of personal data and the data protection regime;
- the Data Protection Principles, also known as the 'data quality principles';
- the Legitimate Processing Conditions;
- the requirement that processing of personal data be 'legitimate' under at least one of the Legitimate Processing Conditions;
- recognising the two categories of personal data covered by the data protection regime, namely, *sensitive* personal data and *non-sensitive* general personal data;
- in the case of sensitive personal data, complying with the additional Sensitive Personal Data Legitimate Processing Conditions;
- ensuring the fair obtaining of all personal data collected and processed;
- taking and ensuring appropriate security measures in relation to all processing activities;
- implementing formal legal contracts when engaging or dealing with third party Processors (eg outsourcing data processing tasks or activities);
- complying with the separate criteria in relation to *automated decision making processes* or *automated decisions*;
- complying with the legal criteria for direct marketing (DM);
- a duty of care can exist in relation to the individual Data Subjects whose personal data the organisation is collecting and processing;

- the transfer of personal data outside of the EEA is strictly controlled. Personal data may not be transferred outside of the EEA unless specifically permitted under the data protection regime;
- access requests, or requests by individuals for copies of their personal data held by the organisation, must be complied with (with limited exceptions);
- registration obligations by organisations must be complied with;
- implementing internal privacy policies and terms;
- implementing outward facing privacy policies for customers, etc;
- implementing outward facing website privacy statements (generally a data protection policy covers organisation-wide activities, whereas a website privacy statement governs only the online collection and processing of personal data);
- implementing mobile, computer and internet usage policies;
- implementing data loss, data breach, incident handling and incident reporting policies and associated reaction plans;[23]
- keeping abreast of the increasing trend towards sector/issue specific rules eg Spam; direct marketing (DM); industry codes of conduct[24] in relation to personal data, etc;
- complying with new legal developments.

The EEA is wider than the EU Member States and includes Iceland, Liechtenstein and Norway. Switzerland has a similar type arrangement with the EU. EU data protection law frequently refers to the EEA generally meaning the EU Member States plus the EEA countries.

Legitimate Processing

1.22 There is a prohibition on the collection and processing of personal data and sensitive personal data unless:

- the processing complies with the Data Protection Principles; and
- the processing comes within one of a limited number of specified conditions (the Legitimate Processing Conditions);
- the processing must also comply with the security requirements.

---

23 Note, for example, the ICO PECR security breach notifications – guidance for service providers, at https://www.ico.org.uk.
24 The DPA and the EU data protection regime provide for codes of conduct being agreed with national data protection authorities such as the ICO in relation to specific industry sectors.

Definitions

1.23 The DPA 1998 contains a number of key definitions. These are central to understanding the data protection regime, and ultimately complying with it. These are essentially the building blocks of the data protection regime. While these can be 'complex concepts,'[25] organisations need to fully understand them. Some examples of the matters defined include:

● Data Subject;
● Controller;
● Processor;
● personal data;
● processing;
● relevant filing system;
● sensitive personal data.

The definitions are found in greater detail in Chapter 3.

---

25   D Hallinan, M Friedewald and P McCarthy, 'Citizens' Perceptions of Data Protection and Privacy in Europe,' *Computer Law & Security Review* (2012) (28) 263–272, at 263.

Chapter 2

Sources of Data Protection Law

Introduction

2.01   Organisations and individuals need to consider a number of sources of the law and policy underpinning the data protection regime. In addition, there are a growing number of sources of interpretation and understanding of data protection law. Reliance on the GDPR or DPA 1998 alone can, therefore, be insufficient. Data protection is therefore arguably quite different from many other areas of legal practice. In order to fully understand the data protection regime, one has to look beyond the text, or first principles, of the GDPR and DPA 1998.

What are the sources of data protection law and policy?

UK DPA 1998

2.02   Primarily, the data protection regime in the UK is governed by the DPA 1998 and the GDPR (and previously the DPD of 1995). In addition, it is also necessary to have regard to a number of other sources of law, policy and the interpretation of the data protection regime. It is also necessary to look out for any amendments to same.

UK Secondary Legislation

2.03   In addition to the DPA 1998, various statutory instruments need to be considered, which include:

- Adoption Agency Regulations 1983;
- Adoption Rules 1984;
- Banking Coordination (Second Council Directive) Regulations 1992;

- Civil Procedure Rules 1998;
- Consumer Credit (Credit Reference Agency) Regulations 1977;
- Consumer Credit (Credit Reference Agency) Regulations 2000;
- Consumer Protection (Contracts Concluded by Means of Distance Communications) Regulations 2000;
- Data Protection Act 1998 (Commencement) Order 2000;
- Data Protection Act 1998 (Commencement No 2) Order 2000;
- Data Protection Act 1998 (Commencement No 2) Order 2008;
- Data Protection (Corporate Finance Exemption) Order 2000;
- Data Protection (Conditions under paragraph 3 of Part II of Schedule 1) Order 2000;
- Data Protection (Crown Appointments) Order 2000;
- Data Protection (Designated Codes of Practice) Order 2000;
- Data Protection (Designated Codes of Practice) (No 2) Order 2000;
- Data Protection (Fees under section 19(7)) Regulations 2000;
- Data Protection (Functions of Designated Authorities) Order 2000;
- Data Protection (International Cooperation) Order 2000;
- Data Protection (Miscellaneous Subject Access Exemptions) Order 2000;
- Data Protection (Miscellaneous Subject Access Exemptions) (Amendment) Order 2000;
- Data Protection (Monetary Penalties) (Maximum Penalty and Notices) Regulations 2010;
- Data Protection (National Security Appeals) Regulations 2000;
- Data Protection (Notification and Notification Fees) Regulations 2000;
- Data Protection (Notification and Notification Fees) (Amendment) Regulations 2001;
- Data Protection (Notification and Notification Fees) (Amendment) Regulations 2009;
- Data Protection (Processing of Sensitive Personal Data) Order 2000;
- Data Protection (Processing of Sensitive Personal Data) Order 2006;
- Data Protection (Processing of Sensitive Personal Data) Order 2009;
- Data Protection (Processing of Sensitive Personal Data) (Elected Representatives) Order 2002;
- Data Protection (Processing of Sensitive Personal Data) (Elected Representatives) (Amendment) Order 2002;
- Data Protection Registration Fee Order 1991;
- Data Protection (Subject Access Modification) (Health) Order 2000;
- Data Protection (Subject Access Modification) (Education) Order 2000;
- Data Protection (Subject Access Modification) (Social Work) Order 2000;
- Data Protection (Processing of Sensitive Personal Data) Order 2000;

- Data Protection Registration Fee Order 1991;
- Data Protection (Subject Access) (Fees and Miscellaneous Provisions) Regulations 2000;
- Data Protection (Subject Access) (Fees and Miscellaneous Provisions) (Amendment) Regulations 2001;
- Data Protection (Subject Access Modification) (Social Work) (Amendment) Order 2005;
- Data Protection Tribunal (Enforcement Appeals) Rules 2000;
- Data Protection Tribunal (National Security Appeals) Rules 2000;
- Data Protection Tribunal (National Security Appeals) (Telecommunications) Rules 2000;
- Data Retention (EC Directive) Regulations 2007;
- Education (School Records) Regulations 1989;
- Education (Special Educational Needs) Regulations 1994;
- Electronic Commerce (EC Directive) Regulations 2002;
- Electronic Communications (Universal Service) Order 2003;
- Environmental Information (Fees and Appropriate Limits) Regulations 2004;
- Environmental Information Regulations 2004;
- Family Proceedings Courts (Children Act 1989) Rules 1991;
- Family Proceedings Rules 1991;
- Freedom of Information and Data Protection (Appropriate Limit and Fees) Regulations 2004;[1]
- Health Professions Order 2001;
- Health Service (Control of Patient Information) Regulations 2002;
- Information Tribunal (Enforcement Appeals) Rules 2005;
- Information Tribunal (Enforcement Appeals) (Amendment) Rules 2002;
- Information Tribunal (Enforcement Appeals) (Amendment) Rules 2005;
- Information Tribunal (National Security Appeals) Rules 2005;
- INSPIRE Regulations;[2]
- Insurance Companies (Third Insurance Directives) Regulations 1994;
- Investment Services Regulations 1995;
- Magistrates Courts (Adoption) Rules 1984;
- Magistrates Courts (Children and Young Persons) Rules 1992;
- Magistrates Courts (Criminal Justice (Children)) Rules 1992;

---

1 The Freedom of Information and Data Protection (Appropriate Limit and Fees) Regulations 2004, at http://www.legislation.gov.uk/uksi/2004/3244/contents/made.
2 The INSPIRE Regulations, 2009, at http://www.legislation.gov.uk/uksi/2009/3157/contents/made.

- Open Ended Investment Companies (Investment Companies with Variable Capital) Regulations 1996;
- Parental Orders (Human Fertilisation and Embryology) Regulations 1994;
- Pharmacists and Pharmacy Technicians Order 2007;
- Police Act 1997 (Criminal Records) Regulations 2002;
- Police Act 1997 (Criminal Records) (Amendment) Regulations 2007;
- Privacy and Electronic Communications (EC Directive) Regulations 2003 (PECR);[3]
- Privacy and Electronic Communications (EC Directive) (Amendment) Regulations 2004;
- Privacy and Electronic Communications (EC Directive) (Amendment) Regulations 2011 (PECR Amendment Regulations);
- Privacy and Electronic Communications (EC Directive) Regulations 2003;
- Regulations of Investigatory Powers (Interception of Communications: Code of Practice) Order 2002;
- Regulation of Investigatory Powers (Communications Data) Order 2003;
- Regulation of Investigatory Powers (Communications Data) (Additional Functions and Amendment) Order 2006;
- Rehabilitation of Offenders (Exceptions) (Amendment) Order 2001;
- Rehabilitation of Offenders (Exceptions) (Amendment) (No 2) Order 2001;
- Representation of People (England and Wales) Regulations 2001;
- Representation of People (England and Wales) (Amendment) Regulations 2001;
- Representation of People Regulations 1986;
- Telecommunications (Data Protection and Privacy) (Direct Marketing) Regulations 1998;
- Telecommunications (Data Protection and Privacy) Regulations 1999;
- Telecommunications (Data Protection and Privacy) Regulations 2000;
- Telecommunications (Data Protection and Privacy) (Amendment) Regulations 2000;
- Telecommunications (Lawful Business Practice) (Interception of Communications) Regulations 2000;
- Transfer of Undertakings (Protection of Employment) Regulations 2006;

---

3   The Privacy and Electronic Communications (EC Directive) Regulations, 2003, at http://www.legislation.gov.uk/uksi/2003/2426/contents/made

- Unfair Terms in Consumer Contracts Regulations 1999;
- Waste Electrical and Electronic Equipment Regulations 2006.

It is also necessary to look out for any amendments to same.

EU Data Protection Law

2.04   The main sources of EU data protection law include:

- GDPR;
- DPD;
- EPD;
- new Directive (once enacted);
- Directive 2002/58 on Privacy and Electronic Communications (ePrivacy Directive) amended by Directive 2009/136 (Cookie Regulation Directive);
- Regulation (EC) No 45/2001on the protection of personal data by EU institutions.[4]

It is also necessary to constantly keep abreast of all amendments to same.

The EU review of the DPD and the update of the DPD via the draft GDPR (and associated Directive) are arguably the most important developments in EU and UK data protection since 1995 (see Part 4). There will be significant implications for organisations and data protection practice.

Case Law

2.05   Increasingly data protection cases (and cases which involve direct or indirect reference to personal data and information impacting the data protection regime) are coming to be litigated and determined before the courts.

One of the reasons is that individuals are increasingly aware of and concerned about their rights under the data protection regime. A further reason is technological developments have enhanced the potential abuse of personal data, from Spam, unsolicited direct marketing (DM), hacking and data loss, phishing, email and internet scams, online abuse, data transfers, access to personal data, etc and litigation related to personal data.

---

4   Regulation (EC) No 45/2001 of the European Parliament and of the Council of 18 December 2000 on the protection of individuals with regard to the processing of personal data by the EU institutions and bodies and on the free movement of such data, Regulation (EC) No 45/2001, OJ L 8, 12.1.2001.

The case law which is relevant, whether influential or binding, to applying and interpreting the UK data protection regime include:

- case studies and documentation from the ICO;
- case complaints adjudicated by the ICO and or Tribunal;
- cases in England and Wales;
- cases in Scotland;
- cases in Northern Ireland;
- EU Court of Justice cases (CJEU (previously ECJ));
- European Court of Human Rights (ECHR) cases;
- relevant cases in other EU Member States and or Common Law jurisdictions.

Some of the relevant cases are summarised and referenced herein.

ICO Guides

2.06   The ICO provides a number of guides and interpretations in relation to specific data protection issues and industry sectors. These include guides for:

- online and electronic devices;
- audits;
- CCTV;
- charity;
- construction blacklists;
- credit and finance;
- crime mapping;
- criminal, court and police records;
- data processing;
- data sharing;
- data protection – general;
- deletion;
- Driver and Vehicle Licensing Agency (DVLA);
- drones;
- education;
- electoral register;
- electronic communications and marketing;
- employment;
- environmental information;
- finance;
- health;

- health records;
- housing;
- identity theft;
- identity scanning;
- international transfer;
- marketing;
- media;
- monetary penalties;
- MPs, political parties and elected officials;
- nuisance calls;
- notification;
- online;
- online and electronic devices;
- Operation Motorman;
- personal data;
- privacy and electronic communications – general;
- Data Protection by Design (DPbD);
- privacy notice;
- relevant filing system;
- RFID tags;
- schools, universities and colleges;
- security;
- spam;
- spatial information;
- Data Subject access;
- telecommunications.[5]

ICO Determinations

2.07   In addition, there is a body of decided decisions in relation to complaints filed by individuals with the ICO on various issues. These include the ICO's Office in England and Wales[6] and the ICO's Office in Scotland.[7] They can assist in considering identical and similar situations regarding issues of data protection compliance.[8]

---

5   See, for example, ICO, Data Protection and Privacy and Electronic Communications, at https://ico.org.uk.
6   At https://ico.org.uk/.
7   At https://ico.org.uk/about_us/our_organisation/scotland.aspx.
8   In relation to the ICO and National Authorities generally regarding data protection not DPD95; and also Greenleaf, G, 'Independence of Data Privacy Authorities (Part 1): International Standards,' *Computer Law & Security Review* (2012) (28) 3–13.

Legal Textbooks

2.08 There are an increasing number of data protection legal textbooks and guides. Frequently also, IT legal textbooks will have chapters or sections dedicated to data protection. Some examples of the former include:

- *Data Protection Law and Practice*, Rosemary Jay (2012);
- *Data Protection Law and Practice*, First Supplement, Rosemary Jay (2014);
- *Data Protection Strategy*, Richard Morgan and Ruth Boardman (2012);
- *Data Protection Compliance in the UK: A Pocket Guide*, Rosemary Jay and Jenna Clarke (2008);
- *Data Protection: Law and Practice*, Rosemary Jay and Angus Hamilton (2007);
- *Data Protection Law*, David Bainbridge (2005);
- *Data Protection Toolkit*, Alison Matthews (2014);
- *Reforming European Data Protection Law (Law, Governance and Technology Series/Issues in Privacy and Data Protection)*, Serge Gutwirth and Ronald Leenes (2014);
- *Protecting Privacy in Private International and Procedural Law and by Data Protection: European and American Developments*, Burkhard Hess (2015);
- *Market Integration Through Data Protection: An Analysis of the Insurance and Financial Industries in the EU (Law, Governance and Technology Series)*, Mario Viola de Azevedo Cunha (2015);
- *The Foundations of EU Data Protection Law*, Dr Orla Lynskey (2015);
- *Data Protection for Photographers: A Guide to Storing and Protecting Your Valuable Digital Assets*, Patrick H Corrigan (2014);
- *Data Protection on the Move: Current Developments in ICT and Privacy/Data Protection*, Serge Gutwirth and Ronald Leenes (2015);
- *The Emergence of Personal Data Protection as a Fundamental Right of the EU*, Gloria González Fuster (2014);
- *Privacy in the Age of Big Data: Recognizing Threats, Defending Your Rights, and Protecting Your Family*, Hon Howard A Schmidt and Theresa M Payton (2015);
- *Data Protection and the Cloud: Are the Risks Too Great?*, Paul Ticher (2015);
- *Data Protection: A Practical Guide to UK and EU Law*, Peter Carey (2015);
- *Property Rights in Personal Data, A European Perspective*, Nadezhda Purtova (2012);
- *Data Protection: Legal Compliance and Good Practice for Employers*, Lynda AC Macdonald (2008);

- *Data Protection in the Financial Services Industry*, Mandy Webster (2006);
- *Data Protection and Compliance in Context*, Stewart Room (2007);
- *European Data Protection Law: Corporate Compliance and Regulation*, Christopher Kuner (2007);
- *Data Protection for Financial Firms: A Practical Guide to Managing Privacy and Information Risk*, Tim Gough, ed (2009);
- *Data Protection for Voluntary Organisations*, Paul Ticher (2009);
- *Data Protection for Virtual Data Centers*, Jason Buffington (2010);
- *Effective Data Protection: Managing Information in an Era of Change*, Mandy Webster (2011);
- *Data Protection & Privacy: Jurisdictional Comparisons*, general editor: Monika Kuschewsky (2012);
- *Implementation of the Data Protection Directive in Relation to Medical Research in Europe*, D Beyleveld *et al* (2005);
- *Research Ethics Committees, Data Protection and Medical Research in European Countries*, D Beyleveld, D Townend and J Wright (2005);
- *Data Protection and Employment Practices*, Susan Singleton (2005);
- *Data Protection: A Practical for Employers*, Engineering Employers' Federation (2005);
- *The New Data Protection Liabilities & Risks for Direct Marketers: Handbook*, Rosemary Smith, and Jenny Moseley (2005);
- *Data Protection in the NHS*, Murray Earle (2003);
- *Data Protection Strategy, Implementing Data Protection Compliance*, Richard Morgan and Ruth Boardman (2012);
- *Data Protection & the Pensions Industry: Implications of the Data Protection Act*, Clare Fawke & Louise Townsend (2002);
- *Data Protection Law: Approaching its Rationale, Logic and Limits*, Lee A Bygrave (2002);
- *Regulating Spam: A European Perspective After the Adoption of the E-Privacy Directive*, L Asscher, and SA Hoogcarspel (2006);
- *Information and Decisional Privacy*, Madeleine Schachter (2003);
- *Privacy on the Line, The Politics of Wiretapping and Encryption*, Whitfield Diffie and Susan Landau (1998);
- *European Data Protection Law: Corporate Regulation and Compliance*, Christopher Kuner (2007).
- *First Report on the Implementation of the Data Protection Directive (95/46/EC)* (ie the DPD);
- *Encyclopaedia of Data Protection*.

Some examples of the latter include:

- *Face Detection and Recognition: Theory and Practice*, Asit Kumar Datta and Madhura Datta (2015);

- *Information Technology Law*, Diane Rowland and Uta Kohl (2016);
- *International Handbook of Social Media Laws*, Paul Lambert (2014);
- *E-Commerce and Convergence: A Guide to the Law of Digital Media*, Mike Butler ed (2012);
- *Information Technology Law*, Ian J Lloyd (2014);
- *Information Technology Law: The Law and Society*, Andrew Murray (2013) (chapters 18 and 19);
- *Concise European IT Law*, Alfred Büllesbach *et al* (2010);
- *Information Technology Law: The Law and Society*, Andrew Murray (2013);
- *The EU Regulatory Framework for Electronic Communications Handbook*, Michael Ryan (2010);
- *Law and the Internet*, Lilian Edwards and Charlotte Waelde eds (2009) (chapters 14–21);
- *Introduction to Information Technology Law*, David Bainbridge (2008);
- *Internet Law and Regulation*, Graham JH Smith (2016) (chapter 7);
- *Information Technology Law*, Diane Rowland, Elizabeth Macdonald (2005);
- *Computer Law: The Law and Regulation of Information Technology*, Chris Reed and John Angel, eds (2007) (chapters 10 and 11);
- *Outsourcing – The Legal Contract*, Rachel Burnett (2005);
- *Outsourcing IT: The Legal Aspects: Planning, Contracting, Managing and the Law*, Rachel Burnett (2009);
- *A Business Guide to Information Security: How to Protect Your Company's IT Assets, Reduce Risks and Understand the Law*, Alan Calder (2005);
- *The New Legal Framework for E-Commerce in Europe*, L Edwards, ed (2005);
- *Communications Law Handbook*, Mike Conradi, ed (2009);
- *Government and Information: The Law Relating to Access, Disclosure and their Regulation*, Birkinshaw and Varney (2012).

Legal Journals

2.09 There are also relevant learned journals and articles published in relation to data protection compliance and developing data protection issues. Some examples include:

- *Data Protection Law and Practice*;
- *Communications Law*;
- *Journal of Information Law and Technology* (JILT);
- *Computers and Law* from the Society of Computers and Law, at www.scl.org;

- *SCRIPTed*;
- *Computer Law and Security Review*.

EDPB

2.10   In terms of the interpretation and understanding of the data protection regime in the UK, the European Data Protection Board (EDPB) (established under Article 68 of the GDPR) is also required to be consulted. (Previously this was effectively the Article 29 Working Party of the EU (WP29).[9]) This is an influential body in relation to addressing and interpreting the data protection regime as well as problem areas in data protection practice. It is also influential as it is comprised of members from the respective data protection authorities in the EU, including the ICO.

WP29 issued working papers, opinions and related documentation, at:

- http://ec.europa.eu/justice/data-protection/article-29/documentation/opinion-recommendation/index_en.htm.

The EDPB will also make documents available online in due course.

European Data Protection Supervisor

2.11   The European Data Protection Supervisor is also worth consulting and is arguably increasing in prominence and importance. Details are at:

- http://www.edps.europa.eu/EDPSWEB/edps/EDPS.

Council of Europe

2.12   There are various important reference materials in relation to data protection and privacy emanating from the Council of Europe (with 47 Member States), such as:

- Council of Europe Convention on data protection, No 108 of 1981;
- Recommendation R(85) 20 on Direct Marketing;
- Recommendation R(86) 1 on Social Security;
- Recommendation R(97) 1 on the Media;
- Recommendation R(97) 5 on Health Data;

---

9   WP29 was established under Article 29 of the DPD.

- Recommendation CM/Rec (2014)4 on electronic monitoring;
- Democratic and effective oversight of national security services (2015);
- Etc.

These and other documents are available at: http://www.coe.int/t/dghl/ standardsetting/dataprotection/Documents_TPD_en.asp.

The Council of Europe Convention on data protection[10] of 1981 pre-dates the DPD and GDPR and is incorporated into the national law of many EU and other states (40 plus) prior to the DPD. The Council of Europe is also reviewing and updating the Convention.[11]

Other Data Protection Authorities

2.13   Issues which may not yet be decided or formally reported on in the UK can sometimes have been considered elsewhere. It can therefore be useful to consider the decisions and logic behind decisions, reports and opinions of:

- Data protection authorities of other EU Member States and EEA Member States;
- Data protection authorities of other states eg Canada.

The European Data Protection Supervisor provides links to the data protection authorities in the EU at:

- http://ec.europa.eu/justice/policies/privacy/nationalcomm/index_ en.htm.

Other Official Sources

2.14   Related issues can sometimes arise under freedom of information legislation.

10   Convention for the Protection of Individuals with regard to Automatic Processing of Personal Data, Council of Europe (1982), at http://conventions.coe.int/Treaty/en/ Treaties/Html/108.htm. 'Draft Convention for the Protection of Individuals with Regards to Automatic Processing of Personal Data,' *International Legal Materials* (1980) (19) 284–298.

11   See S Kierkegaard et al, '30 Years On – The Review of the Council of Europe Data Protection Convention 108,' *Computer Law & Security Review* (2011) (27) 223–231; G Greenleaf, 'Modernising Data Protection Convention 108: A Safe Basis for a Global Privacy Treaty,' *Computer Law & Security Review* (2013) (29) 430–436; P de Hert and V Papakonstantinou, 'The Council of Europe Data Protection Convention Reform: Analysis of the New Text and Critical Comment on its Global Ambition,' *Computer Law & Security Review* (2014) (30:6) 633.

Tribunals can also be relevant, such as the Leveson Inquiry, particularly in terms of protection for personal data, security, deliberate breaches, hacking, etc, and the ICO and Operation Motorman. The report and recommendations of the Leveson Inquiry are of interest from a data protection perspective (see below, Part 4).

Key/Topical Issues

2.15 Some of the key developments and issues which also influence the data protection regime and how it is interpreted include:

- data transfers, Safe Harbours and other data transfer legitimising mechanisms;
- data breach incidents;
- insurance for data breach incidents;
- preparedness and team preparations for incidents arising;
- risk assessments;
- privacy impact assessments;
- mandated Data Protection Officers (DPOs) in organisations;
- deletion, take down and the Right to be Forgotten;
- security requirements for business;
- employee monitoring and consent;
- spam and direct marketing;
- the relationship between the Controller and the Processor, and which relationship needs to be formalised in contract pursuant to the DPA 1998 and GDPR;
- disposal of computer hardware. Particular care is needed when considering the disposal of IT hardware, equipment and software. They may still contain personal data files. This can continue to be the case even when it appears that files have been wiped or deleted. There are many examples accessible personal data still being available even after it is believed to have been deleted and the device handed over to a third part, or worse sold on. The new recipient could be able to access the original personal data and records. This could quite easily be a breach of a number of principles in the data protection regime. It is always advised to take professional legal, IT and or forensic advice when considering disposing of computer devices;
- websites and social media compliance with the data protection regime;
- online abuse;
- Internet of Things (IoT) and devices;
- the ongoing ripples from the Snowden disclosures.

Data Protection Websites and Blogs

2.16   There are number of privacy and data protection websites and blogs, such as Datonomy, available at http://www.datonomy.eu/, the Data Protection Forum at www.dpforum.org.uk and the Society of Computers and Law at www.scl.org.

Other Laws

2.17   Other laws can also be relevant in considering personal data and privacy.[12] Examples include:

- IT law;
- contract law;
- consumer law;
- eCommerce law;
- financial services law;
- health and medical law and related obligations;
- computer crime and theft laws;
- abuse and harassment laws;
- insurance law;
- travel, accommodation and hospitality law;
- motoring law;
- vehicle and taxi law;
- succession law;
- developing drone laws, licensing and regulations.

Conferences

2.18   There are a variety of conferences, annual events and training organisations related to data protection. Some will be organised by professional conference firms while others are non-profit technology, legal or related organisations.

Reference

2.19   Useful reference material is available as set out below.

The DPA 1998 is at: http://www.legislation.gov.uk/ukpga/1998/29/section/2

---

12   See review of particular laws in R Delfino, 'European Union Legislation and Actions,' *European Review of Contract Law* (2011) (7) 547–551, which includes reference to data protection law.

The ICO is at: https://ico.org.uk/

The EU Commission is at: http://ec.europa.eu/justice/data-protection/index_en.htm

The WP29 (now replaced by the EDPB) is at: http://ec.europa.eu/justice/data-protection/article-29/documentation/opinion-recommendation/index_en.htm

The European Court of Justice website is at: http://europa.eu/about-eu/institutions-bodies/court-justice/index_en.htm

Court of Justice (previously ECJ and CJEU) cases[13] are at: http://curia.europa.eu/juris/recherche.jsf? language=en

The ECHR website is at: http://echr.coe.int/Pages/home.aspx?p=home

---

13 M Tzanou, 'Balancing Fundamental Rights, United in Diversity? Some Reflections on the Recent Case Law of the European Court of Justice on Data Protection,' *CYELP* (2010) (6) 53–74.

Chapter 3
Definitions

Introduction

3.01 It is critical to understanding the data protection regime to know and appreciate the definitions of key terms which underpin the legal measures implementing the data protection regime. The definitions are the building blocks for the data protection regime. They are contained in the DPA 1998, the DPD and now the GDPR. The definitions in the GDPR (the Regulations for the new EU data protection regime) should be considered in detail as these update the EU data protection legal regime. The GDPR will also be the main EU data protection legal measure for many years to come.

The various definitions are referred to below.

DPA Definitions

3.02 Section 1 of the DPA 1998 sets out the following definitions:

'data'   means information which,

    (a) is being processed by means of equipment operating automatically in response to instructions given for that purpose,

    (b) is recorded with the intention that it should be processed by means of such equipment,

    (c) is recorded as part of a relevant filing system or with the intention that it should form part of a relevant filing system,

    (d) does not fall within paragraph (a), (b) or (c) but forms part of an accessible record as defined by s 68; or

    (e) is recorded information held by a public authority and does not fall within any of the above;

'data controller'	means, subject to sub-s (4), a person who (either alone or jointly or in common with other persons) determines the purposes for which and the manner in which any personal data are, or are to be, processed;
'data processor'	in relation to personal data, means any person (other than an employee of the [C]ontroller) who processes the data on behalf of the [C]ontroller;
'Data Subject'	means an individual who is the subject of personal data;
'personal data'	means data which relate to a living individual who can be identified,

- from those data, or

- from those data and other information which is in the possession of, or is likely to come into the possession of, the [C]ontroller,

and includes any expression of opinion about the individual and any indication of the intentions of the [C]ontroller or any other person in respect of the individual;

'processing'	in relation to information or data, means obtaining, recording or holding the information or data or carrying out any operation or set of operations on the information or data, including,

- organisation, adaptation or alteration of the information or data,

- retrieval, consultation or use of the information or data,

- disclosure of the information or data by transmission, dissemination or otherwise making available, or

- alignment, combination, blocking, erasure or destruction of the information or data;

'public authority'	means a public authority as defined by the Freedom of Information Act 2000 or a Scottish public authority as defined by the Freedom of Information (Scotland) Act 2002;
'relevant filing system'	means any set of information relating to individuals to the extent that, although the information is not processed by means of equipment operating automatically in response to instructions given for that purpose, the set is structured, either by reference to individuals or by reference to criteria relating to individuals, in such a way that specific information relating to a particular individual is readily accessible;
'obtaining' or 'recording'	in relation to personal data, includes obtaining or recording the information to be contained in the data;
'using' or 'disclosing'	in relation to personal data, includes using or disclosing the information contained in the data.

In determining for the purposes of the DPA 1998 whether any information is recorded with the intention:

- that it should be processed by means of equipment operating automatically in response to instructions given for that purpose; or
- that it should form part of a relevant filing system,

it is immaterial that it is intended to be so processed or to form part of such a system only after being transferred to a country or territory outside the EEA.

Where personal data are processed only for purposes for which they are required by or under any enactment to be processed, the person on whom the obligation to process the data is imposed by or under that enactment is for the purposes of the DPA the Controller.

In paragraph (e) of the definition of 'data' in sub-s (1), the reference to information 'held' by a public authority shall be construed in accordance with s 3(2) of the Freedom of Information Act 2000 or s 3(2), (4) and (5) of the Freedom of Information (Scotland) Act 2002.

Where:

- s 7 of the Freedom of Information Act 2000 prevents Parts I to V of that Act; or
- s 7(1) of the Freedom of Information (Scotland) Act 2002 prevents that Act from applying to certain information held by a public authority, that information is not to be treated for the purposes of paragraph (e) of the definition of 'data' in sub-s (1) as held by a public authority.

Section 2 of the DPA 1998 also sets out the following definition of sensitive personal data. It is personal data consisting of information as to:

- the racial or ethnic origin of the Data Subject;
- their political opinions;
- their religious beliefs or other beliefs of a similar nature;
- whether they are a member of a trade union (within the meaning of the Trade Union and Labour Relations (Consolidation) Act 1992);
- their physical or mental health or condition;
- their sexual life;
- the commission or alleged commission of any offence; or
- any proceedings for any offence committed or alleged to have been committed, the disposal of such proceedings or the sentence of any court in such proceedings.

Sensitive personal data contains higher compliance obligations and conditions.

DPD Definitions

3.03 Article 2 of the DPD sets out the following definitions:

'personal data'	shall mean any information relating to an identified or identifiable natural person ('Data Subject'); an identifiable person is one who can be identified, directly or indirectly, in particular by reference to an identification number or to one or more factors specific to his physical, physiological, mental, economic, cultural or social identity;
'processing of personal Data' ('processing')	shall mean any operation or set of operations which is performed upon personal data, whether or not by automatic means, such as collection, recording, organisation, storage, adaptation or alteration, retrieval, consultation, use, disclosure by transmission, dissemination or otherwise making available, alignment or combination, blocking, erasure or destruction;
'personal data filing system' ('filing system')	shall mean any structured set of personal data which are accessible according to specific criteria, whether centralised, decentralised or dispersed on a functional or geographical basis;
'Controller'	shall mean the natural or legal person, public authority, agency or any other body which alone or jointly with others determines the purposes and means of the processing of personal data; where the purposes and means of processing are determined by national or EU laws or regulations, the controller or the specific criteria for his nomination may be designated by national or EU law;
'Processor'	shall mean a natural or legal person, public authority, agency or any other body which processes personal data on behalf of the [C]ontroller;
'third party'	shall mean any natural or legal person, public authority, agency or any other body other than the Data Subject, the [C]ontroller, the data Processor and the persons who, under the direct authority of the [C]ontroller or the data Processor, are authorised to process the data;
'recipient'	shall mean a natural or legal person, public authority, agency or any other body to whom data are disclosed, whether a third party or not; however, authorities which may receive data in the framework of a particular inquiry shall not be regarded as recipients;
'the Data Subject's consent'	shall mean any freely given specific and informed indication of their wishes by which the Data Subject signifies their agreement to personal data relating to them being processed.

GDPR Definitions

3.04 Article 4 of the new GDPR sets out the definitions for the new data protection regime as follows:

'Personal data'   means any information relating to an identified or identifiable natural person ('Data Subject'); an identifiable natural person is one who can be identified, directly or indirectly, in particular by reference to an identifier such as a name, an identification number, location data, an online identifier or to one or more factors specific to the physical, physiological, genetic, mental, economic, cultural or social identity of that natural person;

'processing'   means any operation or set of operations which is performed on personal data or on sets of personal data, whether or not by automated means, such as collection, recording, organisation, structuring, storage, adaptation or alteration, retrieval, consultation, use, disclosure by transmission, dissemination or otherwise making available, alignment or combination, restriction, erasure or destruction;

'restriction of processing'   means the marking of stored personal data with the aim of limiting their processing in the future;

'profiling'   means any form of automated processing of personal data consisting of the use of the personal data to evaluate certain personal aspects relating to a natural person, in particular to analyse or predict aspects concerning that natural person's performance at work, economic situation, health, personal preferences, interests, reliability, behaviour, location or movements;

'pseudonymisation'   means the processing of personal data in such a manner that the personal data can no longer be attributed to a specific Data Subject without the use of additional information, provided that such additional information is kept separately and is subject to technical and organisational measures to ensure that the personal data are not attributed to an identified or identifiable natural person;

'filing system'   means any structured set of personal data which are accessible according to specific criteria, whether centralised, decentralised or dispersed on a functional or geographical basis;

'Controller'   means the natural or legal person, public authority, agency or any other body which alone or jointly with others determines the purposes and means of the processing of personal data; where the purposes and means of processing are determined by EU law or Member State law, the Controller or the specific criteria for its nomination may be provided for by EU law or Member State law;

'Processor'   means a natural or legal person, public authority, agency or any other body which processes personal data on behalf of the Controller;

'recipient'   means a natural or legal person, public authority, agency or any other body, to which the personal data are disclosed, whether a third party or not. However, public authorities which may receive personal data in the framework of a particular inquiry in accordance with EU or Member State law shall not be regarded as recipients; the processing of those data by those public authorities shall be in compliance with the applicable data protection rules according to the purposes of the processing;

'third party'   means any natural or legal person, public authority, agency or body other than the Data Subject, Controller, Processor and persons who, under the direct authority of the Controller or the Processor, are authorised to process the data;

'the consent'   of the Data Subject means any freely given, specific, informed and unambiguous indication of the Data Subject's wishes by which the Data Subject, by a statement or by a clear affirmative action, signifies agreement to the processing of personal data relating to them;

'personal data breach'   means a breach of security leading to the accidental or unlawful destruction, loss, alteration, unauthorised disclosure of, or access to, personal data transmitted, stored or otherwise processed;

'genetic data'   means all personal data relating to the genetic characteristics of an individual that have been inherited or acquired, which give unique information about the physiology or the health of that individual, resulting in particular from an analysis of a biological sample from the individual in question;

'biometric data'	means any personal data resulting from specific technical processing relating to the physical, physiological or behavioural characteristics of an individual which allows or confirms the unique identification of that individual, such as facial images, or dactyloscopic data;
'data concerning health'	means personal data related to the physical or mental health of an individual, including the provision of health care services, which reveal information about his or her health status;
'main establishment'	means:

- as regards a Controller with establishments in more than one Member State, the place of its central administration in the EU, unless the decisions on the purposes and means of the processing of personal data are taken in another establishment of the Controller in the EU and the latter establishment has the power to have such decisions implemented, in this case the establishment having taken such decisions shall be considered as the main establishment;

- as regards a Processor with establishments in more than one Member State, the place of its central administration in the EU, and, if the Processor has no central administration in the EU, the establishment of the Processor in the EU where the main processing activities in the context of the activities of an establishment of the Processor take place to the extent that the Processor is subject to specific obligations under this Regulation;

'representative'	means any natural or legal person established in the EU who, designated by the Controller or Processor in writing pursuant to Article 25, represents the Controller or Processor, with regard to their respective obligations under this Regulation;
'enterprise'	means any natural or legal person engaged in an economic activity, irrespective of its legal form, including partnerships or associations regularly engaged in an economic activity;
'group of undertakings'	means a controlling undertaking and its controlled undertakings;

'binding corporate rules'	means personal data protection policies which are adhered to by a Controller or Processor established on the territory of a Member State of the EU for transfers or a set of transfers of personal data to a Controller or Processor in one or more third countries within a group of undertakings or group of enterprises engaged in a joint economic activity;
'supervisory authority'	means an independent public authority which is established by a Member State pursuant to Article 46 (SA);
'supervisory authority concerned'	means a supervisory authority which is concerned by the processing, because:

- the Controller or Processor is established on the territory of the Member State of that supervisory authority;
- Data Subjects residing in this Member State are substantially affected or likely to be substantially affected by the processing; or
- a complaint has been lodged to that supervisory authority;

'cross-border processing of personal data'	means either:

- processing which takes place in the context of the activities of establishments in more than one Member State of a Controller or a Processor in the EU and the Controller or Processor is established in more than one Member State; or
- processing which takes place in the context of the activities of a single establishment of a Controller or Processor in the EU but which substantially affects or is likely to substantially affect Data Subjects in more than one Member State;

'relevant and reasoned objection'	means an objection as to whether there is an infringement of this Regulation or not, or, as the case may be, whether the envisaged action in relation to the Controller or Processor is in conformity with the Regulation. The objection shall clearly demonstrate the significance of the risks posed by the draft decision as regards the fundamental rights and freedoms of Data Subjects and where applicable, the free flow of personal data within the EU;

'Information   means any service as defined by Article 1(2) of
Society service'   Directive 98/34/EC of the European Parliament and of
     the Council of 22 June 1998 laying down a procedure
     for the provision of information in the field of technical
     standards and regulations and of rules on Information
     Society services;

'international   means an organisation and its subordinate bodies
organisation'   governed by public international law or any other body
     which is set up by, or on the basis of, an agreement
     between two or more countries.

Two Categories of Personal Data

3.05 Organisations need to be familiar with two separate categories of personal data in relation to their data protection actions and compliance obligations. It also affects what personal data they may collect in the first instance.

The first is general personal data. Unless specified otherwise, all personal data falls into this category. The second category is sensitive personal data. The importance of sensitive personal data is that it triggers additional and more onerous obligations of compliance and initial collection conditions.

Why is there a distinction? Certain categories of personal data are more important, personal and sensitive to individuals over other categories of personal data. This is recognised in the data protection regime. Additional rules are put in place. Firstly, sensitive personal data is defined differently. Secondly, in order to collect and process sensitive personal data, an organisation must satisfy additional processing conditions, in addition to the Data Protection Principles and the general Legitimate Processing Conditions, namely complying with the Sensitive Personal Data Legitimate Processing Conditions.

Sensitive Personal Data

Sensitive Personal Data under the DPA 1998

3.06 Section 2 of the DPA 1998 defines Sensitive Personal Data as consisting of information as to:

- the racial or ethnic origin of the Data Subject;
- political opinions;
- religious beliefs or other beliefs of a similar nature;
- whether a member of a trade union (within the meaning of the Trade Union and Labour Relations (Consolidation) Act 1992);

- physical or mental health or condition;
- sexual life;
- the commission or alleged commission of any offence; or
- any proceedings for any offence committed or alleged to have been committed, the disposal of such proceedings or the sentence of any court in such proceedings.

Sensitive Personal Data under the DPD

3.07 Article 8 of the DPD refers to the processing of special categories of data. It states:

- Member States shall prohibit the processing of personal data revealing racial or ethnic origin, political opinions, religious or philosophical beliefs, trade-union membership, and the processing of data concerning health or sex life;
- the above Article 8(1) shall not apply where:
  - the Data Subject has given their explicit consent to the processing of those data, except where the laws of the Member State provide that the prohibition referred to in Article 8(1) may not be lifted by the Data Subject's giving his consent; or
  - processing is necessary for the purposes of carrying out the obligations and specific rights of the Controller in the field of employment law in so far as it is authorised by national law providing for adequate safeguards; or
  - processing is necessary to protect the vital interests of the Data Subject or of another person where the Data Subject is physically or legally incapable of giving their consent; or
  - processing is carried out in the course of its legitimate activities with appropriate guarantees by a foundation, association or any other non-profit-seeking body with a political, philosophical, religious or trade-union aim and on condition that the processing relates solely to the members of the body or to persons who have regular contact with it in connection with its purposes and that the data are not disclosed to a third party without the consent of the Data Subjects; or
  - the processing relates to data which are manifestly made public by the Data Subject or is necessary for the establishment, exercise or defence of legal claims;
- Article 8(1) above shall not apply where processing of the data is required for the purposes of preventive medicine, medical diagnosis, the provision of care or treatment or the management of health-care services, and where those data are processed by a health professional subject under national law or rules established by national competent

bodies to the obligation of professional secrecy or by another person also subject to an equivalent obligation of secrecy;

- Subject to the provision of suitable safeguards, Member States may, for reasons of substantial public interest, lay down exemptions in addition to those laid down in Article 8(2) (bullet 2) either by national law or by decision of the supervisory authority;

- Processing of data relating to offences, criminal convictions or security measures may be carried out only under the control of official authority, or if suitable specific safeguards are provided under national law, subject to derogations which may be granted by the Member State under national provisions providing suitable specific safeguards. However, a complete register of criminal convictions may be kept only under the control of official authority. Member States may provide that data relating to administrative sanctions or judgements in civil cases shall also be processed under the control of official authority.

Member States shall determine the conditions under which a national identification number or any other identifier of general application may be processed.

Sensitive Personal Data under the GDPR

3.08 Sensitive personal data are referred to in Recitals 10 and 51 of the new GDPR and special categories of personal data are referred to in Recitals 10, 51, 52, 53, 54, 71, 80, 91 and 97.

Article 9 of the new GDPR refers to processing of special categories of personal data. The processing of personal data, revealing racial or ethnic origin, political opinions, religious or philosophical beliefs, trade-union membership, and the processing of genetic data, biometric data in order to uniquely identify a person or data concerning health or sex life and sexual orientation shall be prohibited (Article 9(1)).

The above shall not apply if one of the following applies:

- the Data Subject has given explicit consent to the processing of those personal data for one or more specified purposes, except where EU law or Member State law provide that the prohibition referred to in paragraph 1 may not be lifted by the Data Subject; or

- processing is necessary for the purposes of carrying out the obligations and exercising specific rights of the Controller or of the Data Subject in the field of employment and social security and social protection law in so far as it is authorised by EU law or Member State law or a collective agreement pursuant to Member State law providing for adequate safeguards for the fundamental rights and the interests of the Data Subject; or

- processing is necessary to protect the vital interests of the Data Subject or of another person where the Data Subject is physically or legally incapable of giving consent; or
- processing is carried out in the course of its legitimate activities with appropriate safeguards by a foundation, association or any other non-profit-seeking body with a political, philosophical, religious or trade-union aim and on condition that the processing relates solely to the members or to former members of the body or to persons who have regular contact with it in connection with its purposes and that the data are not disclosed outside that body without the consent of the Data Subjects; or
- the processing relates to personal data which are manifestly made public by the Data Subject; or
- processing is necessary for the establishment, exercise or defence of legal claims or whenever courts are acting in their judicial capacity; or
- processing is necessary for reasons of substantial public interest, on the basis of EU or Member State law which shall be proportionate to the aim pursued, respect the essence of the right to data protection and provide for suitable and specific measures to safeguard the fundamental rights and the interests of the Data Subject; or
- processing is necessary for the purposes of preventive or occupational medicine, for the assessment of the working capacity of the employee, medical diagnosis, the provision of health or social care or treatment or the management of health or social care systems and services on the basis of EU law or Member State law or pursuant to contract with a health professional and subject to the conditions and safeguards referred to in Article 9(4); [h] or
- processing is necessary for reasons of public interest in the area of public health, such as protecting against serious cross-border threats to health or ensuring high standards of quality and safety of health care and of medicinal products or medical devices, on the basis of EU law or Member State law which provides for suitable and specific measures to safeguard the rights and freedoms of the Data Subject, in particular professional secrecy; or
- processing is necessary for archiving purposes in the public interest, or scientific and historical research purposes or statistical purposes in accordance with Article 83(1) based on EU or Member State law which shall be proportionate to the aim pursued, respect the essence of the right to data protection and provide for suitable and specific measures to safeguard the fundamental rights and the interests of the Data Subject (Article 9(2)).

Personal data referred to in Article 9(1) of the new GDPR may be processed for the purposes referred to in Article 9(2)(h) when those data are processed by or under the responsibility of a professional subject to the obligation of professional secrecy under EU or Member State law or rules established by national competent bodies or by another person also subject to an obligation of secrecy under EU or Member State law or rules established by national competent bodies (Article 9(4)).

Member States may maintain or introduce further conditions, including limitations, with regard to the processing of genetic data, biometric data or health data (Article 9(5)).

Article 10 of the new GDPR refers to processing of data relating to criminal convictions and offences. Processing of personal data relating to criminal convictions and offences or related security measures based on Article 6(1) may only be carried out either under the control of official authority or when the processing is authorised by EU law or Member State law providing for adequate safeguards for the rights and freedoms of Data Subjects. Any comprehensive register of criminal convictions may be kept only under the control of official authority.

Conclusion

3.09 It is important for organisations to distinguish, in advance of collecting personal data, whether the proposed data collection relates to general personal data or sensitive personal data. They also need to be able to confirm compliance procedures in advance of collecting and maintaining personal data and particularly sensitive personal data. The organisation could be asked to demonstrate at a future date that it obtained consent, and general compliance. If it cannot, it may have to delete the data, have committed breaches and offences, and potentially face fines and or being sued by the Data Subject. Depending on the circumstances, personal liability can also arise.

Chapter 4

History and EU Data Protection

Introduction

4.01   The legal discussion in relation to privacy is frequently linked to the Warren and Brandeis's legal article in 1890 entitled 'The Right to Privacy' published in the Harvard Law Review.[1] Arguably, data protection is the modern coalface of the debate in relation to privacy and privacy protection.[2] The EU data protection regime can be considered as setting standards in certain areas of informational privacy protection – which have come to be followed in other jurisdictions internationally beyond the EU.[3] There have also been calls for international level data protection rules.[4] Certainly, if this was to come to pass, it could add greater certainty for both organisations, industry and individual Data Subjects. Arguably the pressure for better and more international standards is increasing.

History of Data Protection

4.02   The growth of the processing of information relating to individuals in electronic computer data format from the 1970s onwards, led to

---

1   S Warren and L Brandeis, 'The Right to Privacy,' *Harvard Law Review* (1890) (IV) 193.
2   See JB Rule and G Greenleaf, eds, *Global Privacy Protection – The First Generation* (Cheltenham: Elgar, 2008).
3   See M Birnhack, 'The EU Data Protection Directive: An Engine of a Global Regime,' *Computer Law & Security Report* (2008) (2) 508, at 512.
4   On the topic of international data protection issues, see, for example, C de Terwangne, 'Is a Global Data Protection Regulatory Model Possible?' in S Gutwirth, Y Poullet, P de Hert, C de Terwange and S Nouwt, *Reinventing Data Protection?* (Springer, 2009), p 175; and C Kuner, 'Developing an Adequate Legal Framework for International Data transfers,' in S Gutwirth, Y Poullet, P de Hert, C de Terwange and S Nouwt, *Reinventing Data Protection?* (Springer, 2009), p 263.

ever increasing concerns regarding such processing. Existing laws were 'insufficient to deal with concerns about the amount of information relating to individuals that was held by organisations in electronic form.'[5] The purpose behind the DPA was largely to promote openness and transparency of information held about individuals in filing systems, whether manual or computerised, and to protect the privacy and data protection interests and rights of such individuals.[6]

The main EU data protection instrument was the DPD,[7] implemented in the UK by the DPA, now being replaced across the EU by the GDPR.

However, even prior to the 1995 Directive concern for informational privacy in the computer environment was recognised in an early data protection regime. The Council of Europe proposed and enacted the Convention for the Protection of Individuals with Regard to Automatic Processing of Personal Data Done at Strasbourg on the 28 January 1981.[8] The UK implemented the DPA 1984. Ultimately this was replaced with the DPA in 1998 to implement the DPD. It is also implemented in secondary legislation relating to data protection.[9]

There were also a number of official investigations and proposed bills regarding privacy and data protection. The Younger Committee on Privacy[10] proposed ten recommendations and principles regarding personal data. It proposed the following principles:

- information should be regarded as held for a specific purpose and should not be used, without appropriate authorisation, for other purposes;
- access to information should be confined to those authorised to have it for the purpose for which it was supplied;
- the amount of information collected and held should be the minimum necessary for the achievement of a specified purpose;

---

5 P Carey, *Data Protection, A Practical Guide to UK and EU Law* (Oxford: OUP, 2009) 1. Also, Bainbridge, D, *Data Protection* (CLT, 2000) 2.

6 L AC MacDonald, Lynda, *Data Protection: Legal Compliance and Good Practice for Employers* (Tottel, 2008), p 33.

7 RI D'Afflitto, 'European Union Directive on Personal Privacy Rights and Computerised Information,' *Villanova Law Review* (1996) (41) 305–324.

8 Council of Europe Convention for the Protection of Individuals with Regard to Automatic Processing of Personal Data Done at Strasbourg on the 28 January 1981, at http://conventions.coe.int/Treaty/en/Treaties/Html/108.htm. Also, 'Convention for the Protection of Individuals with Regard to Automatic Processing of Personal Data,' *International Legal Materials* (1981) (20) 317–325.

9 See generally P Carey, *Data Protection, A Practical Guide to UK and EU Law* (Oxford, OUP, 2009) chapter 1.

10 Younger Committee on Privacy, Cmnd 5012 (1972).

- in computerised systems handling information for statistical purposes, adequate provision should be made in their design and programs for separating identities from the rest of the data;
- there should be arrangements whereby a subject can be told about the information held concerning them;
- the level of security to be achieved by a system should be specified in advance by the user and should include precautions against the deliberate abuse or misuse of information;
- a monitoring system should be provided to facilitate the detection of any violation of the security system;
- in the design of information systems, periods should be specified beyond which the information should not be retained;
- data held should be accurate. There should be machinery for the correction of inaccuracy and updating of information;
- care should be taken in coding value judgements.

This was followed by the Lindrop Committee[11] on how best to protect privacy and personal data. The Committee uses the term 'data privacy' to mean the individual Data Subject's right to control the circulation of data about them.[12] While specific recommendations were made, these were not enacted. Ultimately, the DPA 1984 was enacted following on from the Council of Europe Convention 1981 relating to data processing. It is entitled 'Convention for the Protection of Individuals with regard to the Automatic Processing of Personal Data.' The Convention sets out the following principles and requirements, namely, that personal data must be:

- obtained and processed fairly and lawfully;
- stored for specified and legitimate purposes and not used in a way incompatible with those purposes;
- adequate, relevant and not excessive in relation to the purposes for which they are stored;
- accurate and, where necessary, kept up to date;
- preserved in a form which permits identification of the Data Subjects for no longer than is required for the purpose for which those data are stored.

In addition, the Convention provides that:

- personal data revealing racial origin, political opinions or religious or other beliefs, as well as personal data concerning health or sexual life, may not be processed automatically unless domestic law

---

11 Lindrop Committee, Cmnd 7341 (1978).
12 Referred to in P Carey, above, at 3.

provides appropriate safeguards. The same shall apply to personal data relating to criminal convictions;

- appropriate security measures shall be taken for the protection of personal data stored in automated data files against accidental or unauthorised destruction or accidental loss as well as against unauthorised access, alteration or dissemination;
- any person shall be enabled,
  - o to establish the existence of an automated personal data file, its main purposes, as well as the identity and habitual residence or principal place of business of the Controller of the file;
  - o to obtain at reasonable intervals and without excessive delay or expense confirmation of whether personal data relating to them are stored in the automated data file as well as communication to them of such data in an intelligible form;
  - o to obtain, as the case may be, rectification or erasure of such data if these have been processed contrary to the provisions of domestic law giving effect to the basic principles set out in Articles 5 and 6 of the Convention;
  - o to have a remedy if a request for confirmation or, as the case may be, communication, rectification or erasure are not complied with.[13]

Data Protection Act

4.03   The DPA 1998 implements the provisions of the EU DPD on the protection of individuals with regard to the processing of personal data and on the free movement of such data. The DPD ensured data protection and a common data protection regime across Member States in the EU. It is also extended to EEA Member States. The GDPR replaces the DPD. The DPA 1998 was commenced on 1 March 2000 in the UK.[14]

The DPA 1998, and the GDPR, have important implications for business and organisations which collect, process and deal in information relating to living individuals, and in particular customers and employees. They contain stringent data protection measures to safeguard personal informational privacy and to ensure that personal data is not misused or used for purposes that are incompatible with data protection legislation.

---

13   Convention Articles 5–8.
14   There was also a previous Data Protection Act in the UK, namely, the Data Protection Act 1984. The DPA of 1998 repealed the DPA of 1984. The DPA was passed into law on 1 March 2000 pursuant to the Data Protection Act (Commencement) Order 2000 (SI 2000/183).

Legal Instruments

4.04 The introduction or Recitals to the European legal instruments, while not legally binding like the main text of the provisions, are still influential in terms of interpreting the data protection regime, and also highlight some of the history, philosophy and policy behind particular data protections laws and provisions.

DPD Recitals

4.05 The DPD provides the overarching framework for data protection in the EU and EEA.[15] The Directive provides the Data Protection Principles, Legitimate Processing Conditions, security requirements, individual Data Subject rights, fair collection and processing rules, restriction of trans-border data flows or transfers of personal data and sensitive personal data rules. The DPD at a headline level also provides for:

- privacy and data protection;
- harmonisation of such measures throughout the EU.

Some of the pertinent Recitals to the DPD include the following themes which are also illustrative of the aims, intentions and implementation of the DPD. (Also note the Recitals for the final text of the GDPR.) These include:

- harmonisation (*Recital 1*);
- privacy/data protection/fundamental rights/sectors (*Recitals 2, 22, 23, 26, 27, 28, 30, 31, 33, 38, 39, 68*);[16]
- technology/increased processing (*Recitals 4, 5, 6 and 10*);
- barriers (*Recitals 7–9*);
- Convention (*Recital 11*);
- domestic exemption (*Recital 12*);
- political/economic policy (*Recitals 13, 71, 72*);
- definitions/structured data/automated (*Recital 15*);
- security/defence/criminal law (*Recital 16*);
- journalism (*Recital 17*);
- Member States/jurisdiction (*Recitals 18–19*);
- Third Party Controllers and EU Data Subjects (*Recital 20*);
- criminal exclusion (*Recital 21*);
- balance (*Recital 25*);
- security and technical security (*Recital 25*);

---

15 EU Member States plus Iceland, Liechtenstein and Norway.
16 In relation to data protection as a fundamental right, see, for example S Rodata, 'Data Protection as a Fundamental Right,' in S Gutwirth, Y Poullet, P de Hert, C de Terwangne and S Nouwt, *Reinventing Data Protection?* (Springer, 2009), p 77.

- historical, statistical or scientific purposes (*Recital 29*);
- official authority (*Recital 32*);
- public health and social protection (*Recital 34*);
- legal policy/religion (*Recital 35*);
- elections (*Recital 36*);
- journalism, art, etc (*Recital 37*);
- exemptions (*Recital 40*);
- access right to personal data (*Recital 41*);
- health data access (*Recital 42*);
- State interests, security, defence, safety, economy, criminal law (*Recital 43*);
- right to object to processing (*Recital 45*);
- security (*Recital 46*);
- transmission (*Recital 47*);
- specific processing risks (*Recitals 53–54*);
- court and judicial remedy (*Recitals 55*);
- data transfers/TBDFs (*Recitals 56, 57, 59, 60, 66*);
- consent (*Recital 58*);
- Information Commissioner/national authorities (*Recitals 62–64*);
- WP29 (replaced by the EDPB) (*Recital 65*).

GDPR Recitals

4.06   The Recitals to the *original* Commission proposal draft for GDPR are also instructive (and the final agreed version will be even more important given that the GDPR now will replace the DPD). The original version refers to:

- data protection/fundamental right (*Recitals 1 and 2*);[17]
- processing increase/technology/co-operation (*Recitals 4 and 5*);
- need for stronger data protection regime framework (*Recitals 6–12*);
- technologically neutral protection (*Recital 13*);
- exclusion (*Recital 14*);
- domestic (*Recital 15*);
- criminal exemption (*Recital 16*);
- ISPs (*Recital 17*);
- official documents (*Recital 18*);
- location/jurisdiction/processing (*Recitals 19–20*);
- monitoring (*Recital 21*);
- any information (*Recital 23*);

---

17   In relation to data protection as a fundamental right, see, for example S Rodata, 'Data Protection as a Fundamental Right,' in S Gutwirth, Y Poullet, P de Hert, C de Terwangne and S Nouwt, *Reinventing Data Protection?* (Springer, 2009), p 77.

- internet (*Recital 24*);
- consent (*Recital 25*);
- health (*Recital 26*);
- establishment (*Recital 26*);
- group companies (*Recital 28*);
- children (*Recital 29*);
- lawful processing (*Recitals 30–40*);
- consent (*Recitals 32–34*);
- sensitive personal data (*Recitals 41–42*);
- official processing/religion (*Recital 43*);
- elections (*Recital 44*);
- access (*Recital 45*);
- transparency/children (*Recital 46*);
- exercising rights (*Recitals 47, 51, 52*);
- prior information (*Recitals 49–50*);
- rectification (*Recital 53*);
  (Recital 53 *originally* stated that any person should have the right to have personal data concerning them rectified and a 'right to be forgotten' where the retention of such data is not in compliance with the Regulation. In particular, Data Subjects should have the right that their personal data are erased and no longer processed, where the data are no longer necessary in relation to the purposes for which the data are collected or otherwise processed, where Data Subjects have withdrawn their consent for processing or where they object to the processing of personal data concerning them or where the processing of their personal data otherwise does not comply with the Regulation. This right is particularly relevant, when the Data Subject has given their consent as a child, when not being fully aware of the risks involved by the processing, and later wants to remove such personal data especially on the Internet. However, the further retention of the data should be allowed where it is necessary for historical, statistical and scientific research purposes, for reasons of public interest in the area of public health, for exercising the right of freedom of expression, when required by law or where there is a reason to restrict the processing of the data instead of erasing them);
- enhancing Right to Be Forgotten (*Recital 54*);
  (Recital 54 *originally* stated that to strengthen the 'right to be forgotten' in the online environment, the right to erasure should also be extended in such a way that a Controller who has made the personal data public should be obliged to inform third parties which are processing such data that a Data Subject requests them to erase any links to, or copies or replications of that personal data. To ensure this information, the Controller should take all reasonable steps,

including technical measures, in relation to data for the publication of which the Controller is responsible. In relation to a third party publication of personal data, the Controller should be considered responsible for the publication, where the Controller has authorised the publication by the third party);

- electronic access (*Recital 55*);
- right to object (*Recital 56*);
- direct marketing (*Recital 57*);
- automated processing (*Recitals 58–59*);
- liability (*Recital 60*);
- policies and measures (*Recitals 61, 62, 65*);
- Third Countries (*Recitals 63–64*);
- security (*Recital 66*);
- data breach (*Recitals 67–69*);
  (Data breach reporting laws are arising 'in response to a growth in unauthorised disclosures of personal information by public and private sector organisations'[18]);
- registration/notification (*Recitals 70–71*);
- impact assessments (*Recitals 72–74*);
- public sector (*Recital 75*);
- industry codes (*Recital 76*);
- certification (*Recital 77*);
- global data protection/TBDFs/cross border transfers (*Recitals 79–81*);
- TBDFs, cross border transfers, white list, etc (*Recitals 82–91*);
- ICO/Supervisory Authorities (*Recitals 92–96*);
- processing in more than one Member State (*Recital 97*);
- one stop shop (*Recital 98–101*);
- data protection awareness (*Recitals 102–107*);
- enforcement (*Recitals 108–110*);
- complaints to ICO (*Recitals 111–112*);
- court remedies (*Recitals 113–117*);
- compensation (*Recital 118*);
- penalties (*Recital 119*);
- sanctions (*Recital 120*);
- journalism (*Recital 121*);
  (Member States should, as originally stated, classify activities as 'journalistic' for the purpose of the exemptions and derogations to be laid down under the Regulation if the object of these activities is the disclosure to the public of information, opinions or ideas,

---

18 Editorial, S Saxby, *Computer Law & Security Review* (2012) (28) 251–253, at 252.

irrespective of the medium which is used to transmit them. They should not be limited to media undertakings and may be undertaken for profit-making or for non-profit making purposes);
- health (*Recitals 122–123*);
- employment (*Recital 124*);
- research (*Recitals 125–127*);
- religious not effected (*Recital 128*);
- data protection rights and laws (*Recitals 129–130*).
  (These issues are becoming increasingly topical and important, both in terms of complying with the data protection regime, fines and penalties in the event of breach as well as civil remedies available to Data Subjects. Indeed, civil remedies already exist for Data Subjects under the DPD and DPA 1998);
- standards/forms (*Recital 131*);
- third countries (*Recitals 132–133*);
- DPD repeal (*Recital 134*);
- ePD amended (*Recital 135*);
- Schengen (*Recitals 136–138*);
- proportionality (*Recital 139*).

GDPR Recitals (Final Version)

4.07   The final version of the GDPR was agreed in December 2015 by the tripartite group and passed by the EU Parliament in April 2016. From the date of publication in the Official Journal (4 May 2016) there is a two year implementation period for organisations – and Member States in terms of any amendments required to national legislation. The final version Recitals include the following:

DPD Repealed

The DPD is repealed; Commission decisions based on the DPD remain until replaced (Recital 171); and Directive 2002/58/EC[19] is to be updated following the GDPR (Recital 173).

WP29/EDPB

Establishment of European Data Protection Board (EDPB) which is the effective equivalent of WP29 under the DPD (Recital 139).

---

19 Directive 2002/58/EC of the European Parliament and of the Council of 12 July 2002 concerning the processing of personal data and the protection of privacy in the electronic communications sector (Directive on privacy and electronic communications).

Background and Rationale

Personal data protection is (now) a fundamental right;[20] Article 8(1) of the Charter of Fundamental Rights of the EU and Article 16(1) of the Treaty (Recital 1); data processing should be designed to serve mankind; balanced with other fundamental rights; principle of proportionality (Recital 4); internal market and cross border transfers (Recital 6); rapid technological developments and challenges (Recital 6); developments require a strong and more coherent data protection framework (Recital 7); the DPD has not prevented fragmentation in how data protection is implemented (Recital 9); the need to ensure a consistent and high level of protection and to remove obstacles to data flows (Recital 10); the need for a consistent level of protection throughout the EU (Recital 13); the GDPR protects natural persons and their personal data (Recital 12); protections should be technologically neutral (Recital 15).

Obligations

Data processing must be lawful and fair (Recital 39); processing necessary for a contract (Recital 44); processing for a legal obligation (Recital 45); processing necessary to protect life (Recital 46); the legitimate interests of the Controller (Recital 47).

Security

Network and information security, Computer Emergency Response Teams (CERTs) and Computer Security Incident Response Teams (CSIRTs) (Recital 49); appropriate technical and organisational measures (Recitals 81, 87); security and risk evaluation (Recital 90); high risk (Recital 84); impact assessments (Recitals 84, 90, 91, etc); large scale processing operations (Recital 91); consultations (Recital 94); data breach and data breach notification (Recitals 85, 86); and Commission delegated acts.

Processing

Processing; pseudonymised data (Recitals 26, 28, 29); online identifiers (Recital 30); consent (Recitals 32, 38, 40, 42, 43, 44, 50) lawful processing and consent (Recital 40); principle of transparency (Recital 39, 58, 60, 71); children (Recital 38); processing for (additional) other purposes

20 In relation to data protection as a fundamental right, see, for example S Rodata, 'Data Protection as a Fundamental Right,' in S Gutwirth, Y Poullet, P de Hert, C de Terwangne and S Nouwt, *Reinventing Data Protection?* (Springer, 2009), p 77. It is necessary to reinforce its protection in order to make it effective and not conditioned by the asymmetries which characterise the relationship between Data Subject and data controllers.

(Recital 50); genetic data (Recital 34); health data (Recital 35); sensitive personal data (Recitals 51, 52, 53, 54); additional identifying information (Recital 57); processing and electoral activities (Recital 56); religious associations (Recital 55); processing and direct marketing (Recital 70); right not to be subject to a decision; automated processing (Recital 68, 71); profiling (Recitals 70, 72); restrictions on principles and rights (Recital 73); responsibility and liability of Controllers (Recital 74); risks (Recitals 75, 76, 83, 84, etc); Processors and Controllers (Recitals 79, 81, 82, etc); Codes of Conduct (Recital 98); transparency and certification mechanisms (Recitals 99, 100); penalties and fines (Recital 148); criminal sanctions (Recital 149); employee data (Recital 155); public authorities; processing in the public interest or official authority; processing and public interest, scientific and historical research purposes, statistical purposes, safeguards; archiving purposes; scientific research purposes; historical research purposes; medical research purposes; statistical purposes; religious organisations.

Rights

Data Subject rights (Recital 59); principles of fair and transparent processing (Recital 60); prior information requirements (Recital 61); right of access (Recital 63); right of rectification and right to be forgotten (RtbF) (Recital 65); right to complain (Recital 141); automated processing (Recital 68).

Proceedings

Proceedings against Controllers, Processors and jurisdiction (Recitals 145, 146); damages and compensation (Recital 146); the prevention, investigation, detection or prosecution of offences.

Establishment

Establishment (Recitals 22, 23, 36); groups of undertakings (Recital 37); establishment (Recital 36, etc).

Transfers

Cross border data transfers (Recital 101, etc).

ICO and Supervisory Authorities

Supervisory authorities such as the ICO (SAs) (previously called data protection authorities (DPAs) and the complete independence of SAs (Recitals 117, etc).

New Bodies

Data protection not-for-profit bodies, organisations and associations (Recital 142).

Notification/Registration Replaced

Replacement of 'general' notification/registration requirement (Recital 89).

Exceptions/Exemptions

The GDPR does not address national security (Recital 16); the GDPR should not apply to data processing by a natural person in the course of a purely personal or household activity and thus without a connection with a professional or commercial activity (Recital 18); without prejudice to eCommerce Directive[21] in particular eCommerce defences of Articles 12–15 (Recital 21); the GDPR does not apply to the data of the deceased (Recital 27).

Lawful Processing and Consent

Lawful processing and consent (Recital 40).

Online Identifiers

Online identifiers (Recital 30).

Sensitive Personal Data

Sensitive personal data and special categories of personal data (Recitals 10, 51, 53).

Children and Personal Data

Processing of children's personal data (Recitals 38, 58, 65, 71, 75).

Health Data

Health data processing (Recitals 35, 45, 52, 53, 54, 63, 65, 71, 73, 75, 91, 112, 155, 159).

DPD

General Provisions

4.08 Chapter I of the DPD contains the general provisions of the Directive. Article 1 refers to the object of the Directive. In particular Article 1(1) states that in accordance with the Directive, Member States shall protect the fundamental rights and freedoms of natural persons, and in particular their right to privacy with respect to the processing of personal data. Article 1(2) provides that Member States shall neither restrict

---

21 Directive 2000/31/EC.

nor prohibit the free flow of personal data between Member States for reasons connected with the protection afforded under Article 1(1).[22]

Scope

4.09   Article 3 relates to scope. Article 3(1) states that the DPD shall apply to the processing of personal data wholly or partly by automatic means, and to the processing otherwise than by automatic means of personal data which form part of a filing system or are intended to form part of a filing system.

It does not apply, however, according to Article 3(2), to the processing of personal data:

- in the course of an activity which falls outside the scope of EU law, such as those provided for by Titles V and VI of the Treaty on EU and in any case to processing operations concerning public security, defence, State security (including the economic well-being of the State when the processing operation relates to State security matters) and the activities of the State in areas of criminal law;
- by a natural person in the course of a purely personal or household activity.

National Laws

4.10   Article 4 relates to the national law applicable. Under Article 4(1) each Member State shall apply the national provisions it adopts pursuant to the Directive to the processing of personal data where:

- the processing is carried out in the context of the activities of an establishment of the Controller on the territory of the Member State; when the same Controller is established on the territory of several Member States, he must take the necessary measures to ensure that each of these establishments complies with the obligations laid down by the national law applicable;
- the Controller is not established on the Member State's territory, but in a place where its national law applies by virtue of international public law;
- the Controller is not established on EU territory and, for purposes of processing personal data makes use of equipment, automated or otherwise, situated on the territory of the said Member State, unless such equipment is used only for purposes of transit through the territory of the EU.

---

22   In relation to data protection as a fundamental right, see, for example S Rodata, 'Data Protection as a Fundamental Right,' in S Gutwirth, Y Poullet, P de Hert, C de Terwangne and S Nouwt, *Reinventing Data Protection?* (Springer, 2009), p 77.

Under Article 4(2) it is provided that in the circumstances referred to in paragraph 1 third bullet, the Controller must designate a representative established in the territory of that Member State, without prejudice to legal actions which could be initiated against the Controller itself.

Data Protection Principles (Data Quality Principles)

4.11 The Data Protection Principles are also known as the data quality principles, as referred to in the DPD. Section I relates to principles relating to data quality. Article 6(1) provides that Member States shall provide that personal data must be:

(a) processed fairly and lawfully;

(b) collected for specified, explicit and legitimate purposes and not further processed in a way incompatible with those purposes. Further processing of data for historical, statistical or scientific purposes shall not be considered as incompatible provided that Member States provide appropriate safeguards;

(c) adequate, relevant and not excessive in relation to the purposes for which they are collected and/or further processed;

(d) accurate and, where necessary, kept up to date; every reasonable step must be taken to ensure that data which are inaccurate or incomplete, having regard to the purposes for which they were collected or for which they are further processed, are erased or rectified;

(e) kept in a form which permits identification of Data Subjects for no longer than is necessary for the purposes for which the data were collected or for which they are further processed. Member States shall lay down appropriate safeguards for personal data stored for longer periods for historical, statistical or scientific use.

Article 6(2) provides that it shall be for the Controller to ensure that Article 6(1) is complied with.

Legitimate Data Processing Conditions

4.12 Section II refers to the criteria for making data processing legitimate.

Article 7 provides that Member States shall provide that personal data may be processed only if:

(a) the Data Subject has unambiguously given their consent; or

(b) processing is necessary for the performance of a contract to which the Data Subject is party or in order to take steps at the request of the Data Subject prior to entering into a contract; or

(c) processing is necessary for compliance with a legal obligation to which the Controller is subject; or

(d) processing is necessary in order to protect the vital interests of the Data Subject; or

(e) processing is necessary for the performance of a task carried out in the public interest or in the exercise of official authority vested in the Controller or in a third party to whom the data are disclosed; or

(f) processing is necessary for the purposes of the legitimate interests pursued by the Controller or by the third party or parties to whom the data are disclosed, except where such interests are overridden by the interests for fundamental rights and freedoms of the Data Subject which require protection under Article 1(1).[23]

GDPR

General Provisions

4.13 The initial provisions refer to the context of the GDPR, namely, the subject matter and objectives (Article 1); material scope (Article 2); and territorial scope (Article 3).

The GDPR applies to the processing of personal data wholly or partly by automated means, and to the processing other than by automated means of personal data which form part of a filing system or are intended to form part of a filing system (Article 2(2)). Matters not covered or included are referred to in Article 2(3).

Data Processing Principles

4.14 Chapter II refers to the Data Protection Principles. Article 5 of the new GDPR relates to principles relating to personal data processing.
Personal data must be:

(a) processed lawfully, fairly and in a transparent manner in relation to the Data Subject ('lawfulness, fairness and transparency');

(b) collected for specified, explicit and legitimate purposes and not further processed in a manner that is incompatible with those purposes; further processing for archiving purposes in the public interest, scientific or historical research purposes or statistical purposes shall, in accordance with Article 89(1), not be considered to be incompatible with the initial purposes ('purpose limitation');

(c) adequate, relevant and limited to what is necessary in relation to the purposes for which they are processed ('data minimisation');

---

23 In relation to data protection as a fundamental right, see, for example S Rodata, 'Data Protection as a Fundamental Right,' in S Gutwirth, Y Poullet, P de Hert, C de Terwangne and S Nouwt, *Reinventing Data Protection?* (Springer, 2009), p 77.

(d) accurate and, where necessary, kept up to date; every reasonable step must be taken to ensure that personal data that are inaccurate, having regard to the purposes for which they are processed, are erased or rectified without delay ('accuracy');

(e) kept in a form which permits identification of Data Subjects for no longer than is necessary for the purposes for which the personal data are processed; personal data may be stored for longer periods insofar as the data will be processed solely for archiving purposes in the public interest, scientific or historical research purposes or statistical purposes in accordance with Article 89(1) subject to implementation of the appropriate technical and organisational measures required by the Regulation in order to safeguard the rights and freedoms of the Data Subject ('storage limitation');

(f) processed in a manner that ensures appropriate security of the personal data, including protection against unauthorised or unlawful processing and against accidental loss, destruction or damage, using appropriate technical or organisational measures ('integrity and confidentiality') (Article 5(1)).

The Controller shall be responsible for and be able to demonstrate compliance with Article 5(1) ('accountability' principle) (Article 5(2)).

These can be *summarised* as:

- processed lawfully, fairly and in a transparent manner ('lawfulness, fairness and transparency');
- for specified, explicit and legitimate purposes and not further processed incompatibly with the purpose; (with carveout for archiving purposes in the public interest, scientific or historical research purposes or statistical purposes) ('purpose limitation');
- adequate, relevant and limited to what is necessary for the purposes ('data minimisation');
- accurate and, where necessary, kept up to date; every reasonable step must be taken to ensure that personal data that are inaccurate, having regard to the purposes for which they are processed, are erased or rectified without delay ('accuracy');
- kept in a form which permits identification for no longer than is necessary; (with carveout for archiving purposes in the public interest, or scientific and historical research purposes or statistical purposes subject to appropriate technical and organisational measures) ('storage limitation');
- appropriate security, including protection against unauthorised or unlawful processing and against accidental loss, destruction or damage, using appropriate technical or organisational measures ('integrity and confidentiality').

The Controller must demonstrate compliance ('accountability').

Legitimate Processing Conditions

4.15 Article 6 of the new DDPR refers to the lawfulness of processing. Article 6(1) provides that processing of personal data shall be lawful only if and to the extent that at least one of the following applies:

- the Data Subject has given consent to the processing of their personal data for one or more specific purposes;
- processing is necessary for the performance of a contract to which the Data Subject is party or in order to take steps at the request of the Data Subject prior to entering into a contract;
- processing is necessary for compliance with a legal obligation to which the Controller is subject;
- processing is necessary in order to protect the vital interests of the Data Subject or of another natural person;
- processing is necessary for the performance of a task carried out in the public interest or in the exercise of official authority vested in the Controller;
- processing is necessary for the purposes of the legitimate interests pursued by the Controller or by a third party, except where such interests are overridden by the interests or fundamental rights and freedoms of the Data Subject which require protection of personal data, in particular where the Data Subject is a child. This (bullet) shall not apply to processing carried out by public authorities in the performance of their tasks (Article 6(1)).

Member States may maintain or introduce more specific provisions to adapt the application of the rules of the GDPR with regard to the processing of personal data for compliance with Article 6(1)(c) and (e) by determining more precisely specific requirements for the processing and other measures to ensure lawful and fair processing including for other specific processing situations as provided for in Chapter IX (Article 6(2)).

The basis for the processing referred to in Article 6(1)(c) and (e) of must be laid down by: EU law, or Member State law to which the Controller is subject.

The purpose of the processing shall be determined in this legal basis, or as regards the processing referred to in Article 6(1)(e), shall be necessary for the performance of a task carried out in the public interest or in the exercise of official authority vested in the Controller. This legal basis may contain specific provisions to adapt the application of rules of the GDPR, *inter alia*, the general conditions governing the lawfulness of data processing by the Controller, the type of data which are subject to the processing, the Data Subjects concerned; the entities to, and the purposes for which the personal data may be disclosed; the purpose limitation; storage periods, and processing operations and processing procedures, including measures to ensure lawful and fair processing, such as those for other specific processing situations as provided for in Chapter IX. EU law or the law of the Member State must meet an objective of public interest and be proportionate to the legitimate aim pursued (Article 6(3)).

Where the processing for a purpose other than that for which the personal data have been collected is not based on the Data Subject's consent or on an EU or Member State law which constitutes a necessary and proportionate measure in a democratic society to safeguard the objectives referred to in Article 23(1), the Controller shall, in order to ascertain whether processing for another purpose is compatible with the purpose for which the personal data are initially collected, take into account, *inter alia*:

- any link between the purposes for which the personal data have been collected and the purposes of the intended further processing;
- the context in which the personal data have been collected, in particular regarding the relationship between Data Subjects and the Controller;
- the nature of the personal data, in particular whether special categories of personal data are processed, pursuant to Article 9 or whether data related to criminal convictions and offences are processed, pursuant to Article 10;
- the possible consequences of the intended further processing for Data Subjects;
- the existence of appropriate safeguards, which may include encryption or pseudonymisation (Article 6(4)).

Consent Conditions

4.16 Article 7 of the new GDPR refers to conditions for consent as follows. Where processing is based on consent, the Controller shall be able to demonstrate that the Data Subject has consented to the processing of their personal data (Article 7(1)).

If the Data Subject's consent is given in the context of a written declaration which also concerns other matters, the request for consent must be presented in a manner which is clearly distinguishable from the other matters, in an intelligible and easily accessible form, using clear and plain language. Any part of the declaration which constitutes an infringement of the GDPR shall not be binding (Article 7(2)).

The Data Subject shall have the right to withdraw their consent at any time. The withdrawal of consent shall not affect the lawfulness of processing based on consent before its withdrawal. Prior to giving consent, the Data Subject shall be informed thereof. It shall be as easy to withdraw consent as to give consent (Article 7(3)).

When assessing whether consent is freely given, utmost account shall be taken of the fact whether, inter alia, the performance of a contract, including the provision of a service, is conditional on consent to the processing of personal data that is not necessary for the performance of that contract (Article 7(4)).

Conclusion

4.17   Privacy and data protection are evolving in terms of how technology is changing how personal data are collected, used and processed. The current data protection legal regime is perceived as requiring updating. The DPD was enacted in 1995, prior to social media, cloud computing, mass data storage, data mining, electronic profiling, Web 2.0 and the threats to the data security surrounding personal data. This was even before the spotlight centred on abuse issues. Data protection needs to evolve to deal with, or at least more explicitly deal with, these issues. This is partly the reason for the new EU GDPR.

This is important for the issues it addresses as well as the current legal provisions it enhances. As a Regulation as opposed to a Directive, it means that it is directly applicable in the UK without the need for a Directive or national implementing legislation such as the DPA 1998. The law and practice of the UK will be changed as will many of the obligations of organisations. This will also differ more for organisations in particular sectors.

There must be better awareness and more hands on board management responsibility, planning and data protection assessment, and including risk assessment, in advance of product or service launch via the Data Protection by Design (DPbD) concept (see Part 4). There is explicit recognition of children under the data protection regime for the first time. Data protection compliance is now required to be much more considered, organised and planned.

Chapter 5

Data Protection Principles

Introduction

5.01 All organisations which collect and process personal data must comply with the obligations of the UK data protection regime. It is, therefore, very important to be familiar with the data protection regime. This is set out in the DPA 1998 (which commenced on 1 March 2000) and now the EU GDPR.

When Data Protection Provisions Apply

5.02 The circumstances in which UK data protection provisions apply are important. The data protection regime applies:

- to the collection and processing of personal data where the Controller is established in the UK (and the data are processed in the context of the establishment);
- to Controllers not established in UK or the EEA, or who make use of equipment situated in UK to process personal data (otherwise than for the purpose of transit to UK).

Fair Processing Requirements

5.03 The DPA 1998 provides details as to what constitutes fair processing and identifies the information that must be given to Data Subjects not only where the personal data is obtained directly from the Data Subjects but also when it is obtained indirectly. It also refers to the times at which this information needs to be given.

Organisations cannot collect and process personal data unless they:

- comply with the registration requirements;

- comply with the Data Protection Principles (also known as the data quality principles);
- ensure the processing is carried out in accordance with the Legitimate Processing Conditions (and the Sensitive Personal Data Legitimate Processing Conditions in the case of sensitive personal data);
- provide specific information to Data Subjects in advance of the collection and processing of personal data, known as the Prior Information Requirements;
- also comply with security requirements.

These all serve as pre-conditions to lawful data processing of personal data.

Data Protection Principles (also known as Data Quality Principles)

5.04   Schedule 1 Part 1 of the DPA 1998 sets out the Data Protection Principles. Personal data shall be processed fairly and lawfully and, in particular, shall not be processed unless at least one of the conditions in Sch 2 is met, and in the case of sensitive personal data, at least one of the conditions in Sch 3 is also met.

Schedule 2 contains the general personal data Legitimate Processing Conditions.

Schedule 3 contains the personal data Sensitive Personal Data Legitimate Processing Conditions.

These Data Protection Principles state that:

- personal data shall be obtained only for one or more specified and lawful purposes, and shall not be further processed in any manner incompatible with that purpose or those purposes;
- personal data shall be adequate, relevant and not excessive in relation to the purpose or purposes for which they are processed;
- personal data shall be accurate and, where necessary, kept up to date;
- personal data processed for any purpose or purposes shall not be kept for longer than is necessary for that purpose or those purposes;
- personal data shall be processed in accordance with the rights of Data Subjects under the DPA 1998;
- appropriate technical and organisational measures shall be taken against unauthorised or unlawful processing of personal data and against accidental loss or destruction of, or damage to, personal data (ie the security conditions);
- personal data shall not be transferred to a country or territory outside the EEA unless that country or territory ensures an adequate level of

protection for the rights and freedoms of Data Subjects in relation to the processing of personal data.

There are thus eight Data Protection Principles to be complied with by all Controllers. It can, therefore, be summarised that all personal data must be:

(1) fairly and lawfully processed;
(2) processed for limited purposes;
(3) adequate, relevant and not excessive;
(4) accurate and up to date;
(5) not kept for longer than is necessary;
(6) processed in line with Data Subject rights;
(7) secure; and
(8) not transferred to other countries without adequate protection.

Section 4(4) of the DPA 1998 states that 'it shall be the duty of a Controller to comply with the Data Protection Principles in relation to all personal data with respect to which [it] is the data Controller.'

Article 5 of the new GDPR sets out these principles as follows. Personal data must be:

● processed lawfully, fairly and in a transparent manner in relation to the Data Subject ('lawfulness, fairness and transparency');
● collected for specified, explicit and legitimate purposes and not further processed in a manner that is incompatible with those purposes; further processing for archiving purposes in the public interest, scientific or historical research purposes or statistical purposes shall, in accordance with Article 89(1), not be considered to be incompatible with the initial purposes ('purpose limitation');
● adequate, relevant and limited to what is necessary in relation to the purposes for which they are processed ('data minimisation');
● accurate and, where necessary, kept up to date; every reasonable step must be taken to ensure that personal data are inaccurate, having regard to the purposes for which they are processed, are erased or rectified without delay ('accuracy');
● kept in a form which permits identification of Data Subjects for no longer than is necessary for the purposes for which the personal data are processed; personal data may be stored for longer periods insofar as the data will be processed solely for archiving purposes in the public interest, scientific or historical research purposes or statistical purposes in accordance with Article 89(1) subject to implementation of the appropriate technical and organisational measures required by the GDPR in order to safeguard the rights and freedoms of the Data Subject ('storage limitation');

- processed in a manner that ensures appropriate security of the personal data, including protection against unauthorised or unlawful processing and against accidental loss, destruction or damage, using appropriate technical or organisational measures ('integrity and confidentiality').

The Controller must be responsible for and be able to demonstrate compliance with the above ('accountability').

Interpreting the Data Protection Principles

5.05 The DPA also contains certain guidance which assists in interpreting the Data Protection Principles. These are contained in Schedule 1, Part I.

First Data Protection Principle

5.06 The first Data Protection Principle states that personal data must be:

- fairly and lawfully processed.

The collection and processing must be fair and transparent. It must, therefore, be in a manner which is not covert or deceptive. The requirement incorporates an obligation that information must be provided to the individual Data Subject in relation to the Controller and the details of the collection and processing. The prior information requirement and conditions must be satisfied.

In relation to the first Data Protection Principle, Schedule 1 states, *inter alia*, that, in determining for the purposes of the first principle whether personal data are processed fairly, regard is to be had to the method by which they are obtained, including in particular whether any person from whom they are obtained is deceived or misled as to the purpose or purposes for which they are to be processed (Schedule 1, Part 1, s 1(1)).

Under Schedule 1, Part II, s 1(2) it is provided that subject to paragraph 2, for the purposes of the first principle, data are to be treated as obtained fairly if they consist of information obtained from a person who:

- is authorised by or under any enactment to supply it, or
- is required to supply it by or under any enactment or by any convention or other instrument imposing an international obligation on the UK.

Under Schedule 1, Part II, s 2(1) it is provided that subject to paragraph 3, for the purposes of the first principle, personal data are not to be treated as processed fairly unless:

- in the case of data obtained from the Data Subject, the Controller ensures so far as practicable that the Data Subject has, is provided with, or has made readily available to them, the information specified in sub-paragraph (3); and
- in any other case, the Controller ensures so far as practicable that, before the relevant time or as soon as practicable after that time, the Data Subject has, is provided with, or has made readily available to them, the information specified in sub-paragraph (3).

  Under Schedule 1, Part II, s 2(2) it is provided that the 'the relevant time' (in sub-paragraph 1(b) above) means:

  (a)   the time when the Controller first processes the data; or
  (b)   in a case where at that time disclosure to a third party within a reasonable period is envisaged,

- if the data are in fact disclosed to such a person within that period, the time when the data are first disclosed;
- if within that period the Controller becomes, or ought to become, aware that the data are unlikely to be disclosed to such a person within that period, the time when the Controller does become, or ought to become, so aware; or
- in any other case, the end of that period.

In addition, it states that the information referred to in sub-paragraph (1) is as follows, namely:

(a)   the identity of the Controller;
(b)   if he has nominated a representative for the purposes of the DPA, the identity of that representative;
(c)   the purpose or purposes for which the data are intended to be processed; and
(d)   any further information which is necessary, having regard to the specific circumstances in which the data are or are to be processed, to enable processing in respect of the Data Subject to be fair.

Under Schedule 1, Part II, s 3(1) it provides that paragraph 2(1)(b) does not apply where either of the primary conditions in sub-paragraph (2), together with such further conditions as may be prescribed by the Secretary of State by order, are met.

Under Schedule 1, Part II, s 3(2) it provides that the primary conditions referred to in sub-paragraph (1) are:

(a) that the provision of that information would involve a disproportionate effort; or
(b) that the recording of the information to be contained in the data by, or the disclosure of the data by, the Controller is necessary for compliance with any legal obligation to which the Controller is subject, other than an obligation imposed by contract.

The second to fifth Data Protection Principles relate to data quality.

Second Data Protection Principle

5.07 The second Data Protection Principle states that personal data must be:

• processed for limited purposes.

Therefore, the intended purposes must be enumerated and set out, both by the organisation, in the registration notification, and provided to the individual Data Subject in a transparent manner.

Third Data Protection Principle

5.08 The third Data Protection Principle states that personal data must be:

• adequate, relevant and not excessive.

This indicates that the processing must be adequate for the fair and lawful purpose; it must be relevant to that specific purpose; and must not be disproportionate or excessive in relation to that purpose.

Fourth Data Protection Principle

5.09 The fourth Data Protection Principle states that personal data must be:

• accurate and up to date.

The personal data must be correct and accurate. Given that personal data can become out of date, and consequently increase the risk of adverse consequences for the individual Data Subject, there is an obligation to ensure that the personal data is kept up to data. This means continually assessing the data and updating, correcting or deleting it as appropriate. It also implies a finite end to processing activities.

Fifth Data Protection Principle

5.10   The fifth Data Protection Principle states that personal data must be:

● not kept for longer than is necessary.

Once the purpose is accomplished, the need is over and there does not continue to be a current purpose continuing for to keep and process the personal data. It must be kept no longer than necessary in relation to the original collection and processing purpose. This is partly why it is important for the original purpose to be properly set out. Again, it implies a finite end to processing activities.

Sixth Data Protection Principle

5.11   The sixth Data Protection Principle states that personal data must be:

● processed in line with the Data Subject's rights.

The rights of Data Subjects can be summarised as including:

● right of access (DPA 1998, s 7);
● right to establish if personal data exists (DPA 1998, s 7(1)(a));
● right to be informed of the logic in automatic decision taking (DPA 1998, s 7(1)(d));
● right to prevent processing likely to cause damage or distress (DPA 1998, s 18);
● right to prevent processing for direct marketing (DPA 1998, s 11);
● right to prevent automated decision taking (DPA 1998, s 12);
● right in relation to exempt manual data (DPA 1998, s 12A);
● right to compensation (DPA 1998, s 13);
● right to rectify inaccurate data (DPA 1998, s 14);
● right to rectification, blocking, erasure and destruction (DPA 1998, s 14);
● right to complain to ICO (DPA 1998, s 42);
● right to go to court (DPA 1998, s 15).

There are exemptions in relation to the access right, such as in relation to repeat requests, confidentiality of references, sensitive business forecasting, negotiations, professional legal privilege, crime and taxation.

Exemptions also arise as regards the rights in relation to processing causing damage or distress, such as third party information interests, or serious harm arsing in the event of disclosure.

Seventh Data Protection Principle

5.12 The seventh Data Protection Principle states that personal data must be:

- secure.

This is critically important, and is increasingly emphasised with the significant number of official and commercial data breach and data loss incidents. In addition, there is an increasing emphasis that organisations should not only inform the ICO but also individual Data Subjects in the event of data breach. The latter can be justified if it would be necessary for individuals to change passwords, etc, in order to minimise damage, loss or distress from the misuse of the personal data the subject of the breach.

Organisations should also consider that it may be more difficult to explain a data breach incident if the security is lapse, nor to defend a claim for compensation if there was less than optimum security proportionate to the cost, organisation, types of data, and risks involved.

Security considerations also arise as regards outsourcing to Processors; transfers abroad; the new world of cloud computing; internet and website usage; online abuse; and social media websites. Sony was fined £250,000 for data breaches.

Eighth Data Protection Principle

5.13 The eighth Data Protection Principle states that personal data must:

- not be transferred to other countries without adequate protection.

Personal data, as a default position may, not be transferred outside of the EEA. In order to do so, there must be a situation of determined adequate protection arising as envisaged and provided under the data protection regime. This includes examples such as safe harbour, binding corporate rules, specific contract clauses, passenger records to US, etc. (However, that the EU-US Safe Harbour data transfer regime has to be replaced, given that the Court of Justice in the *Schrems* case[1] struck down the Safe Harbour regime as invalid. Note that negotiations have recently resulted in a replacement agreement entitled the EU-US Privacy Shield.)

---

1 *Schrems v Commissioner*, Court of Justice, Case C-362/14, 6 October 2015, at http://curia.europa.eu/juris/document/document.jsf?text=&docid=169195&pageIndex=0&doclang=en&mode=req&dir=&occ=first&part=1&cid=113326. The case technically related to Prism and Facebook Europe and transfers to the US. However, the wider import turned out to be the entire EU-US Safe Harbour Agreement and data transfers to the US. Note WP29 statement on the case, Statement on the implementation of the judgement of the Court of Justice of the European Union of 6 October 2015 in the *Maximillian Schrems v Data Protection Commissioner* case (C-362/14).

There are exemptions to the default ban, however. Schedule 4 to the DPA 1998 sets out cases where the eighth Data Protection Principle does not apply. It states:

- the Data Subject has given his consent to the transfer;
- the transfer is necessary:
  - for the performance of a contract between the Data Subject and the Controller; or
  - for the taking of steps at the request of the Data Subject with a view to his entering into a contract with the Controller;
- the transfer is necessary:
  - for the conclusion of a contract between the Controller and a person other than the Data Subject which:
    - (i)   is entered into at the request of the Data Subject; or
    - (ii) is in the interests of the Data Subject; or
  - for the performance of such a contract;
- the transfer is necessary for reasons of substantial public interest;
- the Secretary of State may by order specify:
  - circumstances in which a transfer is to be taken for the purposes of sub-paragraph (1) to be necessary for reasons of substantial public interest; and
  - circumstances in which a transfer which is not required by or under an enactment is not to be taken for the purpose of sub-paragraph (1) to be necessary for reasons of substantial public interest;
- the transfer:
  - is necessary for the purpose of, or in connection with, any legal proceedings (including prospective legal proceedings);
  - is necessary for the purpose of obtaining legal advice; or
  - is otherwise necessary for the purposes of establishing, exercising or defending legal rights;
- the transfer is necessary in order to protect the vital interests of the Data Subject;
- the transfer is part of the personal data on a public register and any conditions subject to which the register is open to inspection are complied with by any person to whom the data are or may be disclosed after the transfer;
- the transfer is made on terms which are of a kind approved by the Commissioner as ensuring adequate safeguards for the rights and freedoms of Data Subjects;
- the transfer has been authorised by the Commissioner as being made in such a manner as to ensure adequate safeguards for the rights and freedoms of Data Subjects.

Chapter 6

Ordinary Personal Data Legitimate Processing Conditions

Introduction

6.01 Organisations when obtaining and processing personal data must not mislead and must also provide a number of prior information requirements to the individual Data Subjects.

Without these it would be deemed that there is unfair obtaining and processing. In addition, organisations must satisfy and meet one of the Legitimate Processing Conditions.

General Legitimate Processing Conditions

6.02 The Legitimate Processing Conditions are required to be complied with, in addition to the Data Protection Principles. Schedule 2 to the DPA 1998 contains the general Legitimate Processing Conditions. In order to collect and process personal data, in addition to complying with the above Data Protection Principles, organisations must comply or fall within one of the following general personal data Legitimate Processing Conditions.

Schedule 2 to the DPA 1998 contains conditions relevant for the purposes of the first Data Protection Principle, in particular the processing of personal data. It states:

1   The Data Subject has given their consent to the processing.
2   The processing is necessary:
    (a)   for the performance of a contract to which the Data Subject is a party, or
    (b)   for the taking of steps at the request of the Data Subject with a view to entering into a contract.

3   The processing is necessary for compliance with any legal obligation to which the Controller is subject, other than an obligation imposed by contract.

4   The processing is necessary in order to protect the vital interests of the Data Subject.

5   The processing is necessary:
    (a) for the administration of justice,
    (aa) for the exercise of any functions of either House of Parliament,
    (b) for the exercise of any functions conferred on any person by or under any enactment,
    (c) for the exercise of any functions of the Crown, a Minister of the Crown or a government department, or
    (d) for the exercise of any other functions of a public nature exercised in the public interest by any personal.

6   (1) The processing is necessary for the purposes of legitimate interests pursued by the Controller or by the third party or parties to whom the data are disclosed, except where the processing is unwarranted in any particular case by reason of prejudice to the rights and freedoms or legitimate interests of the Data Subject.

     (2) The Secretary of State may by order specify particular circumstances in which this condition is, or is not, to be taken to be satisfied.

There are, therefore, six general Legitimate Processing Conditions. Frequently, an organisation would seek to fall within the legitimate interests condition above.

   These conditions might be summarised as follows:

- the Data Subject has given consent;
- the processing is necessary for performance of contract to which the Data Subject is a party;
- the processing is necessary to take steps at request of the Data Subject prior to entering into contract;
- the processing is necessary for compliance with a legal obligation (other than contractually imposed obligation);
- it is necessary to protect the vital interests of the Data Subject;
- it is necessary for the administration of justice, performance of statutory function or function of public nature;
- the processing is necessary for legitimate interests pursued by Controller except where unwarranted.

Sensitive Personal Data Legitimate Processing Conditions

6.03 In the case of sensitive personal data, an organisation must, in addition to complying with the Data Protection Principles, be able to comply or fall within one of the Sensitive Personal Data Legitimate Processing Conditions.

Schedule 3 to the DPA 1998 sets out the conditions relevant for the purposes of the first Data Protection Principle in particular in relation to the processing of sensitive personal data. It sets out the following provisions:

1 The Data Subject has given his explicit consent to the processing of the personal data.

2 (1) The processing is necessary for the purposes of exercising or performing any right or obligation which is conferred or imposed by law on the Controller in connection with employment.

   (2) The Secretary of State may by order:

     (a) exclude the application of sub-paragraph (1) in such cases as may be specified, or

     (b) provide that, in such cases as may be specified, the condition in sub-paragraph (1) is not to be regarded as satisfied unless such further conditions as may be specified in the order are also satisfied.

3 The processing is necessary:

   (a) in order to protect the vital interests of the Data Subject or another person, in a case where;

     (i) consent cannot be given by or on behalf of the Data Subject, or

     (ii) the Controller cannot reasonably be expected to obtain the consent of the Data Subject, or

   (b) in order to protect the vital interests of another person, in a case where consent by or on behalf of the Data Subject has been unreasonably withheld.

4 The processing:

   (a) is carried out in the course of its legitimate activities by any body or association which;

     (i) is not established or conducted for profit, and

     (ii) exists for political, philosophical, religious or trade-union purposes,

   (b) is carried out with appropriate safeguards for the rights and freedoms of Data Subjects,

    (c)   relates only to individuals who either are members of the body
          or association or have regular contact with it in connection with
          its purposes, and
    (d)   does not involve disclosure of the personal data to a third party
          without the consent of the Data Subject.
5   The information contained in the personal data has been made pub-
    lic as a result of steps deliberately taken by the Data Subject.
6   The processing:
    (a)   is necessary for the purpose of, or in connection with, any legal
          proceedings (including prospective legal proceedings),
    (b)   is necessary for the purpose of obtaining legal advice, or
    (c)   is otherwise necessary for the purposes of establishing, exer-
          cising or defending legal rights.
7   (1)   The processing is necessary:
          (a)   for the administration of justice,
          (aa) for the exercise of any functions of either House of
                Parliament,
          (b)   for the exercise of any functions conferred on any person
                by or under an enactment, or
          (c)   for the exercise of any functions of the Crown, a Minister
                of the Crown or a government department.
    (2)   The Secretary of State may by order:
          (a)   exclude the application of sub-paragraph (1) in such
                cases as may be specified, or
          (b)   provide that, in such cases as may be specified, the con-
                dition in sub-paragraph (1) is not to be regarded as satis-
                fied unless such further conditions as may be specified in
                the order are also satisfied.
7A (1)   The processing:
          (a)   is either:
                (i)   the disclosure of sensitive personal data by a per-
                       son as a member of an anti-fraud organisation or
                       otherwise in accordance with any arrangements
                       made by such an organisation, or
                (ii)   any other processing by that person or another per-
                       son of sensitive personal data so disclosed, and
          (b)   is necessary for the purposes of preventing fraud or a
                particular kind of fraud.
    (2)   In this paragraph 'an anti-fraud organisation' means any unin-
          corporated association, body corporate or other person which
          enables or facilitates any sharing of information to prevent
          fraud or a particular kind of fraud or which has any of these
          functions as its purpose or one of its purposes.

8   (1)   The processing is necessary for medical purposes and is undertaken by:

         (a)   a health professional, or

         (b)   a person who in the circumstances owes a duty of confidentiality which is equivalent to that which would arise if that person were a health professional.

     (2)   In this paragraph 'medical purposes' includes the purposes of preventative medicine, medical diagnosis, medical research, the provision of care and treatment and the management of health care services.

9   (1)   The processing:

         (a)   is of sensitive personal data consisting of information as to racial or ethnic origin,

         (b)   is necessary for the purpose of identifying or keeping under review the existence or absence of equality of opportunity or treatment between persons of different racial or ethnic origins, with a view to enabling such equality to be promoted or maintained, and

         (c)   is carried out with appropriate safeguards for the rights and freedoms of Data Subjects.

     (2)   The Secretary of State may by order specify circumstances in which processing falling within sub-paragraph (1)(a) and (b) is, or is not, to be taken for the purposes of sub-paragraph (1) (c) to be carried out with appropriate safeguards for the rights and freedoms of Data Subjects.

These sensitive personal data legitimate processing conditions may be summarised as follows:

- the individual who the sensitive personal data is about has given explicit consent to the processing;
- the processing is necessary to comply with employment law;
- the processing is necessary to protect the vital interests of:
  - the individual (in a case where the individual's consent cannot be given or reasonably obtained); or
  - another person (in a case where the individual's consent has been unreasonably withheld).
- the processing is carried out by a not-for-profit organisation and does not involve disclosing personal data to a third party, unless the individual consents. Extra limitations apply to this condition;
- the individual has deliberately made the information public;
- the processing is necessary in relation to legal proceedings; for obtaining legal advice; or otherwise for establishing, exercising or defending legal rights;

- the processing is necessary for administering justice, or for exercising statutory or governmental functions;
- the processing is necessary in relation to preventing fraud;
- the processing is necessary for medical purposes, and is undertaken by a health professional or by someone who is subject to an equivalent duty of confidentiality;
- the processing is necessary for monitoring equality of opportunity, and is carried out with appropriate safeguards for the rights of individuals.

Furthermore, regulations enacted also set out further obligations in relation to the processing of sensitive personal data.

Chapter 7

Processing Pre-Conditions: DPA Prior Information Requirements

Introduction

7.01 Organisations even prior to obtaining and processing personal data are generally obliged to provide certain information to individual Data Subjects. This is in order that Data Subjects can be properly informed, and can decide whether to consent or not, to the proposed data collection and data processing.

Prior Information Requirements under the DPA

7.02 The DPA 1998 in Sch 1, Part II provides as follows:

1 (1) In determining for the purposes of the first principle whether personal data are processed fairly, regard is to be had to the method by which they are obtained, including in particular whether any person from whom they are obtained is deceived or misled as to the purpose or purposes for which they are to be processed.

   (2) Subject to paragraph 2, for the purposes of the first principle data are to be treated as obtained fairly if they consist of information obtained from a person who:
      (a) is authorised by or under any enactment to supply it, or
      (b) is required to supply it by or under any enactment or by any convention or other instrument imposing an international obligation on the United Kingdom.

Directly Obtained Data

7.03   The DPA 1998 in Sch 1, Part II provides as follows:

2   (1)   Subject to paragraph 3, for the purposes of the first principle personal data are not to be treated as processed fairly
        unless:
        (a)   in the case of data obtained from the Data Subject, the
              Controller ensures so far as practicable that the Data
              Subject has, is provided with, or has made readily
              available to them, the information specified in sub-
              paragraph (3) ...
    (2)   In sub-paragraph (1)(b) 'the relevant time' means:
        (a)   the time when the Controller first processes the data, or
        (b)   in a case where at that time disclosure to a third party
              within a reasonable period is envisaged,
              (i)   if the data are in fact disclosed to such a person
                     within that period, the time when the data are first
                     disclosed,
              (ii)   if within that period the Controller becomes, or
                     ought to become, aware that the data are unlikely to
                     be disclosed to such a person within that period, the
                     time when the Controller does become, or ought to
                     become, so aware, or
              (iii) in any other case, the end of that period.
    (3)   The information referred to in sub-paragraph (1) is as follows,
          namely:
        (a)   the identity of the Controller,
        (b)   if he has nominated a representative for the purposes of
              the DPA 1998, the identity of that representative,
        (c)   the purpose or purposes for which the data are intended to
              be processed, and
        (d)   any further information which is necessary, having regard
              to the specific circumstances in which the data are or are
              to be processed, to enable processing in respect of the
              Data Subject to be fair.

Indirectly Obtained Data

7.04   The DPA 1998 in Sch 1, Part II provides as follows:

2   (1)   Subject to paragraph 3, for the purposes of the first principle
        personal data are not to be treated as processed fairly unless:
        (a)   ...
        (b)   *in any other case*, the Controller ensures so far as practicable that, before the relevant time or as soon as practicable

after that time, the Data Subject has, is provided with, or has made readily available to them, the information specified in sub-paragraph (3).

(2) In sub-paragraph (1)(b) 'the relevant time' means:

(a) the time when the Controller first processes the data, or

(b) in a case where at that time disclosure to a third party within a reasonable period is envisaged,

(i) if the data are in fact disclosed to such a person within that period, the time when the data are first disclosed,

(ii) if within that period the Controller becomes, or ought to become, aware that the data are unlikely to be disclosed to such a person within that period, the time when the Controller does become, or ought to become, so aware, or

(iii) in any other case, the end of that period.

(3) The information referred to in sub-paragraph (1) is as follows, namely:

(a) the identity of the Controller,

(b) if he has nominated a representative for the purposes of the DPA 1998, the identity of that representative,

(c) the purpose or purposes for which the data are intended to be processed, and

(d) any further information which is necessary, having regard to the specific circumstances in which the data are or are to be processed, to enable processing in respect of the Data Subject to be fair.

Prior Information Requirements under the DPD

Directly Obtained Data

7.05 Article 10 of the DPD provides for information in cases of collection of personal data from the individual Data Subject. It states that Member States shall provide that the Controller or its representative must provide a Data Subject from which data relating to them is collected with at least the following information, except where they already have it, namely:

- the identity of the Controller and of his representative, if any;
- the purposes of the processing for which the data are intended;
- any further information such as,
  - the recipients or categories of recipients of the data;

 ○ whether replies to the questions are obligatory or voluntary, as well as the possible consequences of failure to reply;

 ○ the existence of the right of access to and the right to rectify the data concerning them,

in so far as such further information is necessary, having regard to the specific circumstances in which the data are collected, to guarantee fair processing in respect of the Data Subject.

Indirectly Obtained Data

7.06 Article 11 of the DPD provides and distinguishes information where the data have not been obtained from the individual Data Subject. In this case, where the data have not been obtained from the Data Subject, Member States shall provide that the Controller or his representative must at the time of undertaking the recording of personal data or if a disclosure to a third party is envisaged, no later than the time when the data are first disclosed provide the Data Subject with at least the following information, except where he already has it:

- the identity of the Controller and of his representative, if any;
- the purposes of the processing;
- any further information such as,
  ○ the categories of data concerned;
  ○ the recipients or categories of recipients;
  ○ the existence of the right of access to and the right to rectify the data concerning them,

in so far as such further information is necessary, having regard to the specific circumstances in which the data are processed, to guarantee fair processing in respect of the Data Subject (Article 11(1)).

Article 11(2) of the DPD provides that Article 11(1) shall not apply where, in particular for processing for statistical purposes or for the purposes of historical or scientific research, the provision of such information proves impossible or would involve a disproportionate effort or if recording or disclosure is expressly laid down by law. In these cases Member States shall provide appropriate safeguards.

Prior Information Requirements under the GDPR

7.07 Articles 12, 13 and 14 of the new GDPR makes provision in relation to information available and provided to the Data Subject, including where personal data are collected, directly or indirectly.

Directly Obtained Data

7.08 Chapter III, Section 2 of the GDPR refers to data access. Article 13 refers to information to be provided where the data are collected from the Data Subject.

Where personal data relating to a Data Subject are collected from the Data Subject, the Controller shall, at the time when personal data are obtained, provide the Data Subject with the following information:

- the identity and the contact details of the Controller and, and where applicable, of the Controller's representative;
- the contact details of the DPO, where applicable;
- the purposes of the processing for which the personal data are intended as well as the legal basis for the processing;
- where the processing is based on Article 6(1)(f), the legitimate interests of the Controller or by a third party;
- the recipients or categories of recipients of the personal data, if any;
- where applicable, that fact that the Controller intends to transfer personal data to a third country or international organisation and the existence or absence of an adequacy decision by the Commission, or in case of transfers referred to in Article 46 or 47, or the second subparagraph of Article 49(1), reference to the appropriate or suitable safeguards and the means to obtain a copy of them or where they have been made available (Article 13(1)).

In addition to the information referred to in Article 13(1), the Controller shall, at the time when personal data are obtained, provide the Data Subject with the following further information necessary to ensure fair and transparent processing:

- the period for which the personal data will be stored, or if this is not possible, the criteria used to determine that period;
- the existence of the right to request from the Controller access to and rectification or erasure of the personal data or restriction of processing concerning the Data Subject or to object to processing as well as the right to data portability;
- where the processing is based on Article 6(1)(a) or Article 9(2)(a), the existence of the right to withdraw consent at any time, without affecting the lawfulness of processing based on consent before its withdrawal;
- the right to lodge a complaint to a supervisory authority;
- whether the provision of personal data is a statutory or contractual requirement, or a requirement necessary to enter into a contract, as well as whether the Data Subject is obliged to provide the data and of the possible consequences of failure to provide such data;

- the existence of automated decision-making including profiling, referred to in Article 22(1) and (4), and at least in those cases, meaningful information about the logic involved, as well as the significance and the envisaged consequences of such processing for the Data Subject (Article 13(2)).

Where the Controller intends to further process the data for a purpose other than that for which the personal data were collected, the Controller shall provide the Data Subject prior to that further processing with information on that other purpose and with any relevant further information as referred to in Article 13(2) (Article 13(3)).

Article 13(1), (2) and (3) shall not apply where and insofar as the Data Subject already has the information (Article 14(5)).

Indirectly Obtained Data

7.09   Article 14 refers to information to be provided where the personal data have not been obtained from the Data Subject.

Where personal data have not been obtained from the Data Subject, the Controller shall provide the Data Subject with the following information:

- the identity and the contact details of the Controller and, where applicable, of the Controller's representative;
- the contact details of the DPO, where applicable;
- the purposes of the processing for which the personal data are intended as well as the legal basis for the processing;
- the categories of personal data concerned;
- the recipients or categories of recipients of the personal data, if any;
- where applicable, that the Controller intends to transfer personal data to a recipient in a third country or international organisation and the existence or absence of an adequacy decision by the Commission, or in case of transfers referred to in Article 46 or 47, or the second subparagraph of Article 49(1), reference to the appropriate or suitable safeguards and the means to obtain a copy of them or where they have been made available (Article 14(1)).

In addition to the information referred to in Article 14(1), the Controller shall provide the Data Subject with the following information necessary to ensure fair and transparent processing in respect of the Data Subject:

- the period for which the personal data will be stored, or if this is not possible, the criteria used to determine that period;
- where the processing is based on Article 6(1)(f), the legitimate interests pursued by the Controller or by a third party;

- the existence of the right to request from the Controller access to and rectification or erasure of personal data or restriction of processing concerning the Data Subject and to object to the processing as well as the right to data portability;
- where the processing is based on Article 6(1)(a) or Article 9(2)(a), the existence of the right to withdraw consent at any time, without affecting the lawfulness of processing based on consent before its withdrawal;
- the right to lodge a complaint to a supervisory authority;
- from which source the personal data originate, and if applicable, whether it came from publicly accessible sources;
- the existence of automated decision-making, including profiling, referred to in Article 22(1) and (4) and, at least in those cases, meaningful information about the logic involved, as well as the significance and the envisaged consequences of such processing for the Data Subject (Article 14(2)).

The Controller shall provide the information referred to in Article 14(1) and (2):

- within a reasonable period after obtaining the personal data, but at the latest within one month, having regard to the specific circumstances in which the personal data are processed;
- if the personal data are to be used for communication with the Data Subject, at the latest at the time of the first communication to that Data Subject; or
- if a disclosure to another recipient is envisaged, at the latest when the data are first disclosed (Article 14(3)).

Where the Controller intends to further process the personal data for a purpose other than that for which the data were obtained, the Controller shall provide the Data Subject prior to that further processing with information on that other purpose and with any relevant further information as referred to in Article 14(2) (Article 14(4)).

Article 14(1) to (4) shall not apply where and insofar as:

- the Data Subject already has the information; or
- the provision of such information proves impossible or would involve a disproportionate effort, in particular for processing for archiving purposes in the public interest, scientific or historical research purposes or statistical purposes, subject to the conditions and safeguards referred to in Article 89(1) or in so far as the obligation referred to in Article 14(1) is likely to render impossible or seriously impair the achievement of the objectives of that processing. In such cases the Controller shall take appropriate measures to protect

the Data Subject's rights and freedoms and legitimate interests, including making the information publicly available;

- obtaining or disclosure is expressly laid down by EU or Member State law to which the Controller is subject and which provides appropriate measures to protect the Data Subject's legitimate interests; or
- where the data must remain confidential subject to an obligation of professional secrecy regulated by EU or Member State law, including a statutory obligation of secrecy (Article 14(5)).

Chapter 8

Exemptions

Introduction

8.01 In considering compliance obligations it is also important to consider the exemptions that may apply. In the context of the DPA 1998, these include exemptions applying in particular to the following:

- national security;
- crime and taxation;
- health;
- education;
- social work;
- regulatory activity;
- journalism, literature and art;
- research, history and statistics;
- public authority personnel records;
- public disclosure;
- corporate finance;
- examination marks;
- examination scripts;
- legal professional privilege;
- self incrimination;
- disclosures required by law;
- egal proceedings and advice;
- domestic purposes;
- confidential references;
- armed forces;
- judicial appointments, honours and dignities;
- crown employment or Ministerial appointments;
- management forecasts;

- negotiations;
- human fertilisation and embryology;
- adoption records and reports;
- special educational needs;
- parental records and reports;
- parliamentary privilege.

Part IV of the DPA 1998 refers to exemptions. Section 27(1) provides that references in any of the Data Protection Principles or any provision of Parts II and III to personal data or to the processing of personal data do not include references to data or processing which by virtue of this Part are exempt from that principle or other provision.

Section 27(2) states that in this Part 'the subject information provisions' means:

- the first Data Protection Principle to the extent to which it requires compliance with para 2 of Part II of Sch 1; and
- s 7.

Section 27(3) states that in this Part 'the non-disclosure provisions' means the provisions specified in sub-s (4) to the extent to which they are inconsistent with the disclosure in question.

Further, s 27(4) states that the provisions referred to in sub-s (3) are:

- the first data protection principle, except to the extent to which it requires compliance with the conditions in Schs 2 and 3;
- the second, third, fourth and fifth Data Protection Principles; and
- ss 10 and 14(1) to (3).

Section 27(5) states that except as provided by this Part of the DPA 1998, the subject information provisions shall have effect notwithstanding any enactment or rule of law prohibiting or restricting the disclosure, or authorising the withholding, of information.

There is a caveat, however, similar to the three specific eCommerce activity defences, in that just because a particular exemption exists does not always mean that it applies generally, universally and regardless of the factual situation. There can, on occasion be criteria and conditions applicable to meet, and to maintain, a particular exemption. When considering whether a particular exemption applies, the full text of the exemption needs to be considered.

Separately, it can also be noted that the Leveson Report in considering the journalism 'exemption' has suggested that it may have been too widely drafted, and also considered the history of the particular section. The Report has suggested that the DPA be amended to ensure a more balanced journalism exemption provision.

Exemptions under the DPA 1998

National Security

8.02 Section 28 of the DPA 1998 refers to national security. Section 28(2) provides that personal data are exempt from any of the provisions of:

- the Data Protection Principles;
- Parts II, III and V; and
- sections 54A and 55,

if the exemption from that provision is required for the purpose of safeguarding national security.

Section 28(2) states that subject to sub-s (4), a certificate signed by a Minister of the Crown certifying that exemption from all or any of the provisions mentioned in sub-s (1) is or at any time was required for the purpose there mentioned in respect of any personal data shall be conclusive evidence of that fact.

Section 28(3) states that certificate under sub-s (2) may identify the personal data to which it applies by means of a general description and may be expressed to have prospective effect.

Section 28(4) provides that any person directly affected by the issuing of a certificate under sub-s (2) may appeal to the Tribunal against the certificate.

Section 28(5) provides that if on an appeal under sub-s (4), the Tribunal finds that, applying the principles applied by the court on an application for judicial review, the Minister did not have reasonable grounds for issuing the certificate, the Tribunal may allow the appeal and quash the certificate.

Section 28(6) provides that where in any proceedings under or by virtue of the DPA it is claimed by a Controller that a certificate under sub-s (2) which identifies the personal data to which it applies by means of a general description applies to any personal data, any other party to the proceedings may appeal to the Tribunal on the ground that the certificate does not apply to the personal data in question and, subject to any determination under sub-s (7), the certificate shall be conclusively presumed so to apply.

Section 28(7) provides that on any appeal under sub-s (6), the Tribunal may determine that the certificate does not so apply.

Section 28(8) provides that document purporting to be a certificate under sub-s (2) shall be received in evidence and deemed to be such a certificate unless the contrary is proved.

Section 28(9) provides that document which purports to be certified by or on behalf of a Minister of the Crown as a true copy of a certificate issued by that Minister under sub-s (2) shall in any legal proceedings be evidence (or, in Scotland, sufficient evidence) of that certificate.

Section 28(10) provides that the power conferred by sub-s (2) on a Minister of the Crown shall not be exercisable except by a Minister who is a member of the Cabinet or by the Attorney General or the Lord Advocate.

Section 28(11) provides that no power conferred by any provision of Part V may be exercised in relation to personal data which by virtue of this section are exempt from that provision.

Section 28(12) provides that sch 6 shall have effect in relation to appeals under sub-s (4) or sub-s(6) and the proceedings of the Tribunal in respect of any such appeal.

Crime and Taxation

8.03 Section 29 of the DPA 1998 relates to crime and taxation. Section 29(1) provides that personal data processed for any of the following purposes:

- the prevention or detection of crime;
- the apprehension or prosecution of offenders; or
- the assessment or collection of any tax or duty or of any imposition of a similar nature,

are exempt from the first data protection principle (except to the extent to which it requires compliance with the conditions in sch 2 and 3) and s 7 in any case to the extent to which the application of those provisions to the data would be likely to prejudice any of the matters mentioned in this sub-section.

Section 29(2) provides that personal data which:

- are processed for the purpose of discharging statutory functions; and
- consist of information obtained for such a purpose from a person who had it in his possession for any of the purposes mentioned in sub-s (1),

are exempt from the subject information provisions to the same extent as personal data processed for any of the purposes mentioned in that sub-section.

However, under s 29(3) it is provided that personal data are exempt from the non-disclosure provisions in any case in which:

- the disclosure is for any of the purposes mentioned in sub-s (1); and,
- the application of those provisions in relation to the disclosure would be likely to prejudice any of the matters mentioned in that sub-section.

Section 29(4) provides that personal data in respect of which the Controller is a relevant authority and which:

- consist of a classification applied to the Data Subject as part of a system of risk assessment which is operated by that authority for either of the following purposes:
  - ○ the assessment or collection of any tax or duty or any imposition of a similar nature; or
  - ○ the prevention or detection of crime, or apprehension or prosecution of offenders, where the offence concerned involves any unlawful claim for any payment out of, or any unlawful application of, public funds; and
- are processed for either of those purposes,

are exempt from s 7 to the extent to which the exemption is required in the interests of the operation of the system.

Section 29(5) provides that in sub-s (4) – 'public funds' includes funds provided by any EU institution; 'relevant authority' means: (a) a government department, (b) a local authority, or (c) any other authority administering housing benefit or council tax benefit.

Health, Education and Social Work

8.04   Section 30 of the DPA 1998 relates to health, education and social work. Section 30(1) provides that the Secretary of State may by order exempt from the subject information provisions, or modify those provisions in relation to, personal data consisting of information as to the physical or mental health or condition of the Data Subject.

Section 30(2) provides that the Secretary of State may by order exempt from the subject information provisions, or modify those provisions in relation to:

- personal data in respect of which the Controller is the proprietor of, or a teacher at, a school, and which consist of information relating to persons who are or have been pupils at the school; or
- personal data in respect of which the Controller is an education authority in Scotland, and which consist of information relating to persons who are receiving, or have received, further education provided by the authority.

Section 30(3) provides that the Secretary of State may by order exempt from the subject information provisions, or modify those provisions in relation to, personal data of such other descriptions as may be specified in the order, being information:

- processed by government departments or local authorities or by voluntary organisations or other bodies designated by or under the order; and

- appearing to them to be processed in the course of, or for the purposes of, carrying out social work in relation to the Data Subject or other individuals,

but the Secretary of State shall not under this sub-section confer any exemption or make any modification except so far as he considers that the application to the data of those provisions (or of those provisions without modification) would be likely to prejudice the carrying out of social work.

Section 30(4) provides that an order under this section may make different provision in relation to data consisting of information of different descriptions.

Section 30(5) provides that in this section 'education authority' and 'further education' have the same meaning as in the Education (Scotland) Act 1980 ('the 1980 Act'), and 'proprietor':

- in relation to a school in England or Wales, has the same meaning as in the Education Act 1996;
- in relation to a school in Scotland, means:
  ○ in the case of a self-governing school, the board of management within the meaning of the Self-Governing Schools, etc, (Scotland) Act 1989;
  ○ in the case of an independent school, the proprietor within the meaning of the 1980 Act;
  ○ in the case of a grant-aided school, the managers within the meaning of the 1980 Act; and
  ○ in the case of a public school, the education authority within the meaning of the 1980 Act; and

in relation to a school in Northern Ireland, has the same meaning as in the Education and Libraries (Northern Ireland) Order 1986 and includes, in the case of a controlled school, the Board of Governors of the school.

Regulatory Activity

8.05 Section 31 of the DPA 1998 relates to regulatory activity. Section 31(1) provides that personal data processed for the purposes of discharging functions to which this sub-section applies are exempt from the subject information provisions in any case to the extent to which the application of those provisions to the data would be likely to prejudice the proper discharge of those functions.

Section 31(2) provides that sub-s (1) applies to any relevant function which is designed:

- for protecting members of the public against:

- ○ financial loss due to dishonesty, malpractice or other seriously improper conduct by, or the unfitness or incompetence
of, persons concerned in the provision of banking, insurance,
investment or other financial services or in the management of
bodies corporate;
- ○ financial loss due to the conduct of discharged or undischarged
bankrupts; or
- ○ dishonesty, malpractice or other seriously improper conduct by,
or the unfitness or incompetence of, persons authorised to carry
on any profession or other activity;
- for protecting charities or community interest companies against
misconduct or mismanagement (whether by trustees, directors or
other persons) in their administration;
- for protecting the property of charities or community interest companies from loss or misapplication;
- for the recovery of the property of charities or community interest
companies;
- for securing the health, safety and welfare of persons at work; or
- for protecting persons other than persons at work against risk to
health or safety arising out of or in connection with the actions of
persons at work.

Section 31(3) provides that in sub-s (2) 'relevant function' means:
(a) any function conferred on any person by or under any enactment,
(b) any function of the Crown, a Minister of the Crown or a government
department, or (c) any other function which is of a public nature and is
exercised in the public interest.

Section 31(4) provides that personal data processed for the purpose of
discharging any function which:

- is conferred by or under any enactment on:
  - ○ the Parliamentary Commissioner for Administration;
  - ○ the Commission for Local Administration in England or, the
Commission for Local Administration in Wales;
  - ○ the Health Service Commissioner for England or, the Health
Service Commissioner for Wales;
  - ○ the Public Services Ombudsman for Wales;
  - ○ the Assembly Ombudsman for Northern Ireland;
  - ○ the Northern Ireland Commissioner for Complaints; or
  - ○ the Scottish Public Services Ombudsman; and
- is designed for protecting members of the public against:
  - ○ maladministration by public bodies;
  - ○ failures in services provided by public bodies; or
  - ○ a failure of a public body to provide a service which it was a
function of the body to provide,

are exempt from the subject information provisions in any case to the extent to which the application of those provisions to the data would be likely to prejudice the proper discharge of that function.

Section 31(4A) provides that personal data processed for the purpose of discharging any function which is conferred by or under Part XVI of the Financial Services and Markets Act 2000 on the body established by the Financial Services Authority for the purposes of that Part are exempt from the subject information provisions in any case to the extent to which the application of those provisions to the data would be likely to prejudice the proper discharge of the function.

Section 31(4B) provides that personal data processed for the purposes of discharging any function of the Legal Services Board are exempt from the subject information provisions in any case to the extent to which the application of those provisions to the data would be likely to prejudice the proper discharge of the function.

Section 31(4C) provides that personal data processed for the purposes of the function of considering a complaint under the scheme established under Part 6 of the Legal Services Act 2007 (legal complaints) are exempt from the subject information provisions in any case to the extent to which the application of those provisions to the data would be likely to prejudice the proper discharge of the function.

Section 31(5) provides that personal data processed for the purpose of discharging any function which:

- is conferred by or under any enactment on the the Office of Fair Trading; and
- is designed:
  - for protecting members of the public against conduct which may adversely affect their interests by persons carrying on a business;
  - for regulating agreements or conduct which have as their object or effect the prevention, restriction or distortion of competition in connection with any commercial activity; or
  - for regulating conduct on the part of one or more undertakings which amounts to the abuse of a dominant position in a market,

are exempt from the subject information provisions in any case to the extent to which the application of those provisions to the data would be likely to prejudice the proper discharge of that function.

Section 31(5A) provides that personal data processed by a CPC enforcer for the purpose of discharging any function conferred on such a body by or under the CPC Regulation are exempt from the subject information provisions in any case to the extent to which the application of those provisions to the data would be likely to prejudice the proper discharge of that function.

Section 31(5B) provides that in sub-s (5A):

- 'CPC enforcer' has the meaning in s 213(5A) of the Enterprise Act 2002 but does not include the Office of Fair Trading;
- 'CPC Regulation' has the meaning in s 235A of that Act.

Section 31(6) provides that personal data processed for the purpose of the function of considering a complaint under s 113(1) or (2) or 114(1) or (3) of the Health and Social Care (Community Health and Standards) Act 2003, or s 24D, 26 or 26ZB of the Children Act 1989, are exempt from the subject information provisions in any case to the extent to which the application of those provisions to the data would be likely to prejudice the proper discharge of that function.

Section 31(7) provides that personal data processed for the purpose of discharging any function which is conferred by or under Part 3 of the Local Government Act 2000 on:

- the monitoring officer of a relevant authority;
- an ethical standards officer; or
- the Public Services Ombudsman for Wales,

are exempt from the subject information provisions in any case to the extent to which the application of those provisions to the data would be likely to prejudice the proper discharge of that function.

Section 31(8) provides that in sub-s (7), (a) 'relevant authority' has the meaning given by s 49(6) of the Local Government Act 2000, and (b) any reference to the monitoring officer of a relevant authority, or to an ethical standards officer, has the same meaning as in Part 3 of that Act.

Journalism, Literature and Art

8.06 Section 32 of the DPA 1998 relates to journalism, literature and art. Section 32(1) provides that personal data which are processed only for the special purposes are exempt from any provision to which this sub-section relates if:

- the processing is undertaken with a view to the publication by any person of any journalistic, literary or artistic material;
- the Controller reasonably believes that, having regard in particular to the special importance of the public interest in freedom of expression, publication would be in the public interest; and
- the Controller reasonably believes that, in all the circumstances, compliance with that provision is incompatible with the special purposes.

Section 32(2) provides that sub-s (1) relates to the provisions of:

- the data protection principles except the seventh Data Protection Principle;

- s 7;
- s 10;
- s 12; and
- s 14(1) to (3).

Section 32(3) provides that in considering for the purposes of sub-s (1)(b) whether the belief of a Controller that publication would be in the public interest was or is a reasonable one, regard may be had to its compliance with any code of practice which:

- is relevant to the publication in question; and
- is designated by the Secretary of State by order for the purposes of this subsection.

Section 32(4) provides that where at any time ('the relevant time') in any proceedings against a Controller under ss 7(9), 10(4), 12(8) or 14 or by virtue of s 13 the Controller claims, or it appears to the court, that any personal data to which the proceedings relate are being processed:

- only for the special purposes; and
- with a view to the publication by any person of any journalistic, literary or artistic material which, at the time twenty-four hours immediately before the relevant time, had not previously been published by the Controller,

the court shall stay the proceedings until either of the conditions in sub-s (5) is met.

Section 32(5) that those conditions are (a) that a determination of the ICO under s 45 with respect to the data in question takes effect, or (b) in a case where the proceedings were stayed on the making of a claim, that the claim is withdrawn.

Section 32(6) states that for the purposes of the DPA 'publish,' in relation to journalistic, literary or artistic material, means make available to the public or any section of the public.

Research, History and Statistics

8.07 Section 33 refers to research, history and statistics. Section 33(1) provides that in this section 'research purposes' includes statistical or historical purposes; 'the relevant conditions,' in relation to any processing of personal data, means the conditions:

- that the data are not processed to support measures or decisions with respect to particular individuals; and
- that the data are not processed in such a way that substantial damage or substantial distress is, or is likely to be, caused to any Data Subject.

For the purposes of the second Data Protection Principle, the further processing of personal data only for research purposes in compliance with the relevant conditions is not to be regarded as incompatible with the purposes for which they were obtained (s 33(2)).

Personal data which are processed only for research purposes in compliance with the relevant conditions may, notwithstanding the fifth Data Protection Principle, be kept indefinitely (s 33(3)).

Section 33(4) provides that personal data which are processed only for research purposes are exempt from s 7 if: (a) they are processed in compliance with the relevant conditions; and (b) the results of the research or any resulting statistics are not made available in a form which identifies Data Subjects or any of them.

Section 33(5) provides that for the purposes of sub-s (2) to (4) personal data are not to be treated as processed otherwise than for research purposes merely because the data are disclosed: (a) to any person, for research purposes only; (b) to the Data Subject or a person acting on his behalf; (c) at the request, or with the consent, of the Data Subject or a person acting on his behalf; or (d) in circumstances in which the person making the disclosure has reasonable grounds for believing that the disclosure falls within paragraph (a), (b) or (c).

Manual Data Held by Public Authorities

8.08 Section 33A refers to manual data held by public authorities. Section 33A(1) provides that personal data falling within paragraph (e) of the definition of 'data' in s 1(1) are exempt from:

- the first, second, third, fifth, seventh and eighth Data Protection Principles;
- the sixth Data Protection Principle except so far as it relates to the rights conferred on Data Subjects by ss 7 and 14;
- ss 10 to 12;
- s 13, except so far as it relates to damage caused by a contravention of s 7 or of the fourth Data Protection Principle and to any distress which is also suffered by reason of that contravention;
- Part III; and
- s 55.

Section 33A(2) provides that personal data which fall within paragraph (e) of the definition of 'data' in s 1(1) and relate to appointments or removals, pay, discipline, superannuation or other personnel matters, in relation to:

- service in any of the armed forces of the Crown;
- service in any office or employment under the Crown or under any public authority; or

- service in any office or employment, or under any contract for services, in respect of which power to take action, or to determine or approve the action taken, in such matters is vested in Her Majesty, any Minister of the Crown, the National Assembly for Wales, any Northern Ireland Minister (within the meaning of the Freedom of Information Act 2000) or any public authority,

are also exempt from the remaining Data Protection Principles and the remaining provisions of Part II.

Information Available to Public by or Under Enactment

8.09 Section 34 refers to information available to the public by or under enactment. Personal data are exempt from:

- the subject information provisions;
- the fourth Data Protection Principle and s 14(1) to (3); and
- the non-disclosure provisions,

if the data consist of information which the Controller is obliged by or under any enactment other than an enactment contained in the Freedom of Information Act 2000 to make available to the public, whether by publishing it, by making it available for inspection, or otherwise and whether gratuitously or on payment of a fee.

Disclosures Required by Law or Made in Connection with Legal Proceedings, etc

8.10 Section 35 refers to disclosures required by law or made in connection with legal proceedings, etc. Section 35(1) provides that personal data are exempt from the non-disclosure provisions where the disclosure is required by or under any enactment, by any rule of law or by the order of a court.

Section 35(2) provides that personal data are exempt from the non-disclosure provisions where the disclosure is necessary:

- for the purpose of, or in connection with, any legal proceedings (including prospective legal proceedings); or
- for the purpose of obtaining legal advice,

or is otherwise necessary for the purposes of establishing, exercising or defending legal rights.

Parliamentary Privilege

8.11 Section 35A refers to Parliamentary privilege. Personal data are exempt from:

- the first Data Protection Principle, except to the extent to which it requires compliance with the conditions in Schedules 2 and 3;

- the second, third, fourth and fifth Data Protection Principles;
- s 7; and
- ss 10 and 14(1) to (3);

if the exemption is required for the purpose of avoiding an infringement of the privileges of either House of Parliament.

Domestic Purposes

8.12   Section 36 refers to domestic purposes. Personal data processed by an individual only for the purposes of that individual's personal, family or household affairs (including recreational purposes) are exempt from the data protection principles and the provisions of Parts II and III.

Miscellaneous

8.13   Section 37 refers to certain miscellaneous exemptions. Schedule 7 (which confers further miscellaneous exemptions) has effect.

Powers to Make Further Exemptions by Order

8.14   Section 38 provides powers to make further exemptions by order. Section 38(1) provides that the Secretary of State may by order exempt from the subject information provisions personal data consisting of information the disclosure of which is prohibited or restricted by or under any enactment if and to the extent that he considers it necessary for the safeguarding of the interests of the Data Subject or the rights and freedoms of any other individual that the prohibition or restriction ought to prevail over those provisions.

Section 38(2) provides that the Secretary of State may by order exempt from the non-disclosure provisions any disclosures of personal data made in circumstances specified in the order, if he considers the exemption is necessary for the safeguarding of the interests of the Data Subject or the rights and freedoms of any other individual.

Exemptions under the DPD

8.15   Section VI of the DPD refers to the exemptions and restrictions. Article 13(1) provides that Member States may adopt legislative measures to restrict the scope of the obligations and rights provided for in Articles 6(1), 10, 11(1), 12 and 21 when such a restriction constitutes a necessary measures to safeguard:

- national security;
- defence;

- public security;
- the prevention, investigation, detection and prosecution of criminal offences, or of breaches of ethics for regulated professions;
- an important economic or financial interest of a Member State or of the European EU, including monetary, budgetary and taxation matters;
- a monitoring, inspection or regulatory function connected, even occasionally, with the exercise of official authority in cases referred to in (c), (d) and (e);
- the protection of the Data Subject or of the rights and freedoms of others.

Article 13(2) provides that subject to adequate legal safeguards, in particular that the data are not used for taking measures or decisions regarding any particular individual, Member States may, where there is clearly no risk of breaching the privacy of the Data Subject, restrict by a legislative measure the rights provided for in Article 12 when data are processed solely for purposes of scientific research or are kept in personal form for a period which does not exceed the period necessary for the sole purpose of creating statistics.

Exemptions under the GDPD

8.16 The GDPR does not address national security (Recital 16); the GDPR should not apply to data processing by a natural person in the course of a purely personal or household activity and thus without a connection with a professional or commercial activity (Recital 18); without prejudice to the eCommerce Directive[1] in particular eCommerce defences of Articles 12–15 (Recital 21); the GDPR does not apply to the data of the deceased (Recital 27). Certain Member States might also seek to apply exemptions in certain respects in relation to parts of the GDPR.

Conclusion

8.17 The exemptions are important when and where applicable. They will often be more relevant to particular sectors. Generally, the exemptions appear to be less litigated than other areas of data protection. It remains to be seen if the UK will enact specific derogations from aspects of the GDPR.

---

1   Directive 2000/31/EC.

Chapter 9

Individual Data Subject Rights

Introduction

9.01   The data protection regime provides, or enshrines, a number of rights to individuals in relation to their informational data and informational privacy. Transparency and consent are very important aspects of respecting and enabling such fundamental rights to be vindicated, utilised and enforced by Data Subjects. Individual Data Subjects have a right of access to personal data. There are also time limits to be complied with by a Controller in relation to replying to a Data Subject access request (ie a request to access or obtain a copy of their personal data that the organisation holds).

Individuals also have a right to prevent data processing for direct marketing (DM) purposes.

The individual Data Subject has a right to prevent processing likely to cause damage or distress.

A further right relates to automated decision taking, which relates to automated decisions being taken without human oversight or intervention. The traditional example often used is adverse credit decisions being taken automatically. However, it can equally encompass such adverse decisions and activities as so called neutral algorithmic processing and arranging of information and result outputs. Examples could include search rankings and priorities; search suggestions; search prompts; autosuggest; autocomplete; etc. Other examples could arise in relation to profiling and advertising related activities.

Importantly, individual Data Subjects have specific rights in relation to rectification, blocking, erasure and destruction and what is becoming known as the Right to be Forgotten (RtbF). This has added significance and attention following the Court of Justice decision in the RtbF landmark case of *Google Spain*.[1]

Individual Data Subjects are also entitled to compensation and damages, as well as being entitled to complain to the ICO and to the courts to obtain judicial remedies.

The DPD also refers to rights and states that whereas the object of the national laws on the processing of personal data is to protect fundamental rights and freedoms, notably the right to privacy, which is recognised both in Article 8 of the European Convention for the Protection of Human Rights and Fundamental Freedoms and in the general principles of EU law. The approximation of those laws must not result in any lessening of the protection they afford but must, on the contrary, seek to ensure a high level of protection in the EU.

The new GDPR Recitals refer to Data Subject rights; principles of fair and transparent processing; prior information requirements; right of access; right of rectification and right to be forgotten (RtbF); right to complain to single supervisory authority; automated processing.

Data Protection Principles

9.02 The eight Data Protection Principles require that personal data are:

(1) fairly and lawfully processed;
(2) processed for limited purposes;
(3) adequate, relevant and not excessive;
(4) accurate and up to date;
(5) not kept for longer than is necessary;
(6) processed in line with your rights;
(7) secure; and
(8) not transferred to other countries without adequate protection.

The new GDPR expresses the Principles as requiring that personal data are:

- processed lawfully, fairly and in a transparent manner in relation to the Data Subject ('lawfulness, fairness and transparency');
- collected for specified, explicit and legitimate purposes and not further processed in a way incompatible with those purposes; further

---

1 *Google Spain SL, Google Inc v Agencia Española de Protección de Datos (AEPD), Mario Costeja González*, Court of Justice (Grand Chamber), Case C-131/12, 13 May 2014. This relates to outdated search engine result listings.

processing for archiving purposes in the public interest, scientific and historical research purposes or statistical purposes shall, in accordance with Article 89(1), not be considered incompatible with the initial purposes ('purpose limitation');

- adequate, relevant and limited to what is necessary in relation to the purposes for which they are processed ('data minimisation');
- accurate and, where necessary, kept up to date; every reasonable step must be taken to ensure that personal data that are inaccurate, having regard to the purposes for which they are processed, are erased or rectified without delay ('accuracy');
- kept in a form which permits identification of Data Subjects for no longer than is necessary for the purposes for which the personal data are processed; personal data may be stored for longer periods insofar as the data will be processed solely for archiving purposes in the public interest, scientific or historical research purposes or statistical purposes in accordance with Article 89(1) subject to implementation of the appropriate technical and organisational measures required by the GDPR in order to safeguard the rights and freedoms of the Data Subject ('storage limitation');
- processed in a manner that ensures appropriate security of the personal data, including protection against unauthorised or unlawful processing and against accidental loss, destruction or damage, using appropriate technical or organisational measures ('integrity and confidentiality').

The Controller must be responsible for and be able to demonstrate compliance ('accountability').

Rights for Individual Data Subjects

9.03 The DPA 1998 contains a number of important rights for individuals in respect of their personal data, such as:

- the prior information that has to be given to them by Controllers;
- access to personal data;
- the right to object into processing;
- not being forced to make an access request as a condition of recruitment, employment or provision of a service;
- not being subjected to 'automated decision making processes.'

The rights are expanding and are becoming more explicit. It is important that organisations keep abreast of the expanding rights and obligations. The data protection rights enshrined in the data protection regime for individuals are set out in the Data Protection Principles and, in particular, in ss 7–15 of the DPA 1998. They include the following:

- individuals have a right to be informed by organisations as to their identity when they are collecting and processing the individual's personal data;
- the organisation must disclose to the individual the purpose for which it is collecting and processing the individual's personal data;
- if the organisation is forwarding on the personal data to third party recipients, it must disclose this to the individual as well as identify the third party recipients. If it is permitted to transfer the personal data outside of the county, the organisation must then also identify which third party country will be receiving the personal data;
- organisations must answer and comply with requests from the individual in relation to their data protection rights.

This includes requests for access to a copy of the personal data held in relation to the individual. This is known as a personal data access request.

The rights of Data Subjects can be summarised as including:

- right of access (DPA 1998, s 7);
- right to establish if personal data exists (DPA 1998, s 7(1)(a));
- right to be informed of the logic in automatic decision taking (DPA 1998, s 7(1)(d));
- right to prevent processing likely to cause damage or distress (DPA 1998, s 18);
- right to prevent processing for direct marketing (DPA 1998, s 11);
- right to prevent automated decision taking (DPA 1998, s 12);
- right to compensation (DPA 1998, s 13);
- right to rectify inaccurate data (DPA 1998, s 14);
- right to rectification, blocking, erasure and destruction (DPA 1998, s 14);
- right to complain to ICO (DPA 1998, s 42);
- right to go to court (DPA 1998, s 15).

Recipients of Right

9.04 The data protection rights apply generally in relation any individuals whose personal data are being collected and processed. Specifically, it can include:

- employees;
- other workers such as contractors, temps, casual staff;

- agency staff;
- ex-employees and retired employees;
- spouses and family members;
- job applicants, including unsuccessful applicants;
- volunteers;
- apprentices and trainees;
- customers and clients;
- prospective customer and clients;
- suppliers;[2]
- members;
- users;
- any other individuals.

Access Right under the DPA 1998

9.05   Part II of the DPA 1998 refers to the rights of Data Subjects and others. In particular, s 7 refers to the right of access to personal data. This applies to Data Subjects. It is a Data Subject right. Section 7(1) provides that subject to the following provisions of this section and to s 8, 9 and 9A, an individual is entitled:

- to be informed by any Controller whether personal data of which that individual is the Data Subject are being processed by or on behalf of that Controller;
- if that is the case, to be given by the Controller a description of,
  - ○ the personal data of which that individual is the Data Subject;
  - ○ the purposes for which they are being or are to be processed; and
  - ○ the recipients or classes of recipients to whom they are or may be disclosed;
- to have communicated to them in an intelligible form,
  - ○ the information constituting any personal data of which that individual is the Data Subject; and
  - ○ any information available to the Controller as to the source of those data; and
- where the processing by automatic means of personal data of which that individual is the Data Subject for the purpose of evaluating matters relating to them such as, for example, his performance at work, his credit worthiness, his reliability or his conduct, has constituted or is likely to constitute the sole basis for any decision significantly

---

2   L AC MacDonald, *Data Protection: Legal Compliance and Good Practice for Employers* (Tottel, 2008) 41.

affecting them, to be informed by the Controller of the logic involved in that decision-taking.

Section 7(2) provides that a Controller is not obliged to supply any information under sub-s (1) unless he has received:

- a request in writing; and
- except in prescribed cases, such fee (not exceeding the prescribed maximum) as he may require.

Section 7(3) provides that where a Controller:

- reasonably requires further information in order to satisfy them as to the identity of the person making a request under this section and to locate the information which that person seeks; and
- has informed them of that requirement,

the Controller is not obliged to comply with the request unless he is supplied with that further information.

Section 7(4) provides that where a Controller cannot comply with the request without disclosing information relating to another individual who can be identified from that information, he is not obliged to comply with the request unless:

- the other individual has consented to the disclosure of the information to the person making the request; or
- it is reasonable in all the circumstances to comply with the request without the consent of the other individual.

Section 7(5) provides that in sub-s (4) the reference to information relating to another individual includes a reference to information identifying that individual as the source of the information sought by the request; and that sub-section is not to be construed as excusing a Controller from communicating so much of the information sought by the request as can be communicated without disclosing the identity of the other individual concerned, whether by the omission of names or other identifying particulars or otherwise.

Section 7(6) provides that in determining for the purposes of sub-s (4)(b) whether it is reasonable in all the circumstances to comply with the request without the consent of the other individual concerned, regard shall be had, in particular, to:

- any duty of confidentiality owed to the other individual;
- any steps taken by the Controller with a view to seeking the consent of the other individual;
- whether the other individual is capable of giving consent; and
- any express refusal of consent by the other individual.

Section 7(7) provides that an individual making a request under this section may, in such cases as may be prescribed, specify that his request is limited to personal data of any prescribed description.

Section 7(8) provides that subject to sub-s (4), a Controller shall comply with a request under this section promptly and in any event before the end of the prescribed period beginning with the relevant day.

Section 7(9) provides that if a court is satisfied on the application of any person who has made a request under the foregoing provisions of this section that the Controller in question has failed to comply with the request in contravention of those provisions, the court may order them to comply with the request.

Section 7(10) also provides that in this section:

- 'prescribed' means prescribed by the Secretary of State by regulations;
- 'the prescribed maximum' means such amount as may be prescribed;
- 'the prescribed period' means forty days or such other period as may be prescribed;
- 'the relevant day,' in relation to a request under this section, means the day on which the Controller receives the request or, if later, the first day on which the Controller has both the required fee and the information referred to in sub-s (3).

Section 7(11) provides that different amounts or periods may be prescribed under this section in relation to different cases.

Section 7(12) provides that a person is a relevant person for the purposes of sub-s (4)(c) if he:

- is a person referred to in paragraph 4(a) or (b) or paragraph 8(a) or (b) of Sch 11;
- is employed by an education authority (within the meaning of paragraph 6 of Schedule 11) in pursuance of its functions relating to education and the information relates to them, or he supplied the information in his capacity as such an employee; or
- is the person making the request.

Section 7(12) provides that a person is a relevant person for the purposes of sub-s (4)(c) if he:

- is a person referred to in paragraph 1(p) or (q) of the Schedule to the Data Protection (Subject Access Modification) (Social Work) Order 2000; or
- is or has been employed by any person or body referred to in paragraph 1 of that Schedule in connection with functions which are or have been exercised in relation to the data consisting of the information; or

- has provided for reward a service similar to a service provided in the exercise of any functions specified in paragraph 1(a)(i), (b), (c) or (d) of that Schedule,

and the information relates to them or he supplied the information in his official capacity or, as the case may be, in connection with the provision of that service.

Section 8 refers to provisions supplementary to s 7. Section 8(1) provides that the Secretary of State may by regulations provide that, in such cases as may be prescribed, a request for information under any provision of sub-s (1) of s 7 is to be treated as extending also to information under other provisions of that sub-section.

Section 8(2) provides that the obligation imposed by s 7(1)(c)(i) must be complied with by supplying the Data Subject with a copy of the information in permanent form unless:

- the supply of such a copy is not possible or would involve disproportionate effort; or
- the Data Subject agrees otherwise;

and where any of the information referred to in s 7(1)(c)(i) is expressed in terms which are not intelligible without explanation the copy must be accompanied by an explanation of those terms.

Section 8(3) provides that where a Controller has previously complied with a request made under s 7 by an individual, the Controller is not obliged to comply with a subsequent identical or similar request under that section by that individual unless a reasonable interval has elapsed between compliance with the previous request and the making of the current request.

Section 8(4) provides that in determining for the purposes of sub-s (3) whether requests under s 7 are made at reasonable intervals, regard shall be had to the nature of the data, the purpose for which the data are processed and the frequency with which the data are altered.

Section 8(5) provides that s 7(1)(d) is not to be regarded as requiring the provision of information as to the logic involved in any decision-taking if, and to the extent that, the information constitutes a trade secret.

Section 8(6) provides that the information to be supplied pursuant to a request under s 7 must be supplied by reference to the data in question at the time when the request is received, except that it may take account of any amendment or deletion made between that time and the time when the information is supplied, being an amendment or deletion that would have been made regardless of the receipt of the request.

Section 8(7) provides that for the purposes of s 7(4) and (5) another individual can be identified from the information being disclosed if he can be identified from that information, or from that and any other information which, in the reasonable belief of the Controller, is likely to be in, or to come into, the possession of the Data Subject making the request.

It is important to consider that being informed only verbally may not always, or at all, be a proper vindication of the Data Subject's access right. This is particularly so where large sets of personal data, or complex details involving personal data, are involved. Generally, personal data is provided in hardcopy. However, in particular circumstances, certain Controllers prefer to furnish personal data in electronic format where large volumes of materials are involved. If a Controller was to refuse to furnish the personal data required, on the basis that it had verbally communicated same, this would jar with the accepted understanding of the data access right. It could also be argued that the Controller was not allowing access to the personal data to be effectively and properly given. Note, however, the case of *Durham County Council v Dunn* [2012] EWCA Civ 1654, which while acknowledging the legitimacy of copies of documents, appears to suggest that other avenues also arise. An organisation should be cautious in embarking in data access disclosures other than in a documented and written manner. It is clearly the case that an organisation has an obligation to be able to demonstrate its compliance with access requests which includes maintaining written procedures and records. Some would also query whether interpreting the data access right as some sort of a *data communicated right* as appears to be suggested in part of *Durham* as compatible with the DPA 1998, the DPD and now the GDPR (referring to electronic access).

Credit Reference Agencies

9.06   Section 9 refers to the application of s 7 where the Controller is a credit reference agency.

Section 9(1) provides that where the Controller is a credit reference agency, s 7 has effect subject to the provisions of this section.

Section 9(2) provides that an individual making a request under s 7 may limit his request to personal data, relevant to his financial standing, and shall be taken to have so limited his request unless the request shows a contrary intention.

Section 9(3) provides that where the Controller receives a request under s 7 in a case where personal data, of which the individual making the request is the Data Subject, are being processed by or on behalf of the Controller, the obligation to supply information under that section includes an obligation to give the individual making the request a statement, in such form as may be prescribed by the Secretary of State by regulations, of the individual's rights:

- under s 159 of the Consumer Credit Act 1974; and
- to the extent required by the prescribed form, under the Act.

Public Authorities

9.07 Section 9A relates to unstructured personal data held by public authorities. Section 9A(1) provides that in this section 'unstructured personal data' means any personal data falling within paragraph (e) of the definition of 'data' in s 1(1), other than information which is recorded as part of, or with the intention that it should form part of, any set of information relating to individuals to the extent that the set is structured by reference to individuals or by reference to criteria relating to individuals.

Section 9A(2) provides that a public authority is not obliged to comply with sub-s (1) of s 7 in relation to any unstructured personal data unless the request under that section contains a description of the data.

Section 9A(3) provides that even if the data are described by the Data Subject in his request, a public authority is not obliged to comply with subsection (1) of s 7 in relation to unstructured personal data if the authority estimates that the cost of complying with the request so far as relating to those data would exceed the appropriate limit.

Section 9A(4) provides that sub-s (3) does not exempt the public authority from its obligation to comply with paragraph (a) of s 7(1) in relation to the unstructured personal data unless the estimated cost of complying with that paragraph alone in relation to those data would exceed the appropriate limit.

Section 9A(5) provides that in sub-s (3) and (4) 'the appropriate limit' means such amount as may be prescribed by the Secretary of State by regulations, and different amounts may be prescribed in relation to different cases.

Section 9A(6) provides that any estimate for the purposes of the section must be made in accordance with regulations under s 12(5) of the Freedom of Information Act 2000.

Access Right

Access Right under the DPD

9.08 Article 12 of the DPD provides for the right of access, and states, Member States shall guarantee every Data Subject the right to obtain from the Controller:

- without constraint at reasonable intervals and without excessive delay or expense,
  - confirmation as to whether or not data relating to them are being processed and information at least as to the purposes of the processing, the categories of data concerned, and the recipients or categories of recipients to whom the data are disclosed;

○ communication to them in an intelligible form of the data under-going processing and of any available information as to their source;

○ knowledge of the logic involved in any automatic processing of data concerning them at least in the case of the automated deci-sions referred to in Article 15(1);

● as appropriate the rectification, erasure or blocking of data the pro-cessing of which does not comply with the provisions of the DPD, in particular because of the incomplete or inaccurate nature of the data (12(b));

● notification to third parties to whom the data have been disclosed of any rectification, erasure or blocking carried out in compliance with (b), unless this proves impossible or involves a disproportionate effort.

Intelligible form is generally meant and understood as including copies of the relevant personal data or document containing it. It could be often ineffective and difficult for an individual merely to receive verbal com-munications, particularly where large sets of personal data are involved. Less scrupulous Controllers could also seek to circumvent the spirit and letter of the data protection regime if actual copies were not required. In any event, the data protection regime provides that certain charges can be applied in relation to copies being provided to Data Subjects in com-pliance with their access rights.

In practice, websites are also developing tools in order to provide access to certain sets of personal data electronically as opposed to furnishing in hard copy format.

Access Right under the GDPR

9.09   Article 15 of the GDPR relates to the right of access for the Data Subject.

The Data Subject shall have the right to obtain from the Controller confirmation as to whether or not personal data concerning them are being processed, and where that is the case, access to the personal data and the following information:

● the purposes of the processing;
● the categories of personal data concerned;
● the recipients or categories of recipient to whom the personal data have been or will be disclosed, in particular recipients in third coun-tries or international organisations;
● where possible, the envisaged period for which the personal data will be stored, or, if not possible, the criteria used to determine that period;

- the existence of the right to request from the Controller rectification or erasure of personal data or restriction of the processing of personal data concerning the Data Subject or to object to such processing;
- the right to lodge a complaint with a supervisory authority;
- where the personal data are not collected from the Data Subject, any available information as to their source;
- the existence of automated decision making including profiling referred to in Article 22(1) and (4) and at least in those cases, meaningful information about the logic involved, as well as the significance and the envisaged consequences of such processing for the Data Subject (Article 15(1)).

Where personal data are transferred to a third country or to an international organisation, the Data Subject shall have the right to be informed of the appropriate safeguards pursuant to Article 46 relating to the transfer (Article 15(2)).

The Controller shall provide a copy of the personal data undergoing processing. For any further copies requested by the Data Subject, the Controller may charge a reasonable fee based on administrative costs. Where the Data Subject makes the request in electronic means, and unless otherwise requested by the Data Subject, the information shall be provided in a commonly used electronic form (Article 15(3)).

The right to obtain a copy referred to in paragraph 3 shall not adversely affect the rights and freedoms of others (Article 15(4)).

Dealing with Access Requests

9.10 One commentary[3] refers to the advisability of having a process flow chart in place. The main components referred to include:

- Data Subject calls or asks for personal data;
- Data Subject access request form issued;
- Data Subject access request form returned plus appropriate fee if requested);
- personal data located, whether by legal department, data protection personnel, etc;
- examining same in relation to whether any third party information; health data; exempt data;
- data reviewed by legal department;
- personal data copy issues to Data Subject.

---

3   R Morgan and R Boardman, *Data Protection Strategy* (Sweet & Maxwell, 2003) 252.

The ICO provides the following guidance or checklist:[4]

1 Is this a subject access request?
No – Handle the query as part of the normal course of business.
Yes – Go to 2.

2 Is there enough information to be sure of the requester's identity?
No – If the requester's identity is unclear, ask them to provide evidence to confirm it. For example, one may ask for a piece of information held in your records that the person would be expected to know, such as membership details, or a witnessed copy of their signature. Once satisfied, go to 3.
Yes – Go to 3.

3 Is any other information required to find the records they want?
No – Go to 4.
Yes – One will need to ask the individual promptly for any other information reasonably needed to find the records they want. One might want to ask them to narrow down their request. For example, if keeping all customers' information on one computer system and suppliers' information on another, one could ask what relationship they had with the organisation. Or, one could ask when they had dealings with the organisation. However, they do have the right to ask for everything held about them and this could mean a very wide search. The organisation has 40 calendar days to respond to a subject access request after receiving any further information one needs and any fee charged. Go to 4.

4 Are you going to charge a fee?
No – Go to 5.
Yes – If there is a fee one must ask the individual promptly for one. The maximum that can be charged is £10 unless medical or education records are involved (see guidance on our website). The 40 calendar days in which one must respond starts when one receives the fee and all necessary information to help one find the records. Go to 5.

5 Does the organisation hold any information about the person?
No – If one holds no personal information at all about the individual one must tell them this.
Yes – Go to 6.

---

4 *Data Protection Good Practice Note, Checklist for Handling Requests for Personal Information* (subject access requests), ICO, at https://ico.org.uk.

6   Will the information be changed between receiving the request and sending the response?

No – Go to 7.

Yes – One can still make routine amendments and deletions to personal information after receiving a request. However, one must not make any changes to the records as a result of receiving the request, even if one finds inaccurate or embarrassing information on the record. Go to 7.

7   Does it include any information about other people?

No – Go to 8.

Yes – One will not have to supply the information unless the other people mentioned have given their consent, or it is reasonable to supply the information without their consent. Even when the other person's information should not be disclosed, one should still supply as much as possible by editing the references to other people. Go to 8.

8   Is the organisation obliged to supply the information?

No – If all the information held about the requester is exempt, then one can reply stating that one does not hold any of their personal information required to be revealed.

Yes – Go to 9.

9   Does it include any complex terms or codes?

No – Go to 10.

Yes – One must make sure that these are explained so the information can be understood. Go to 10.

10   Prepare the response.[5]

DPA: Right to Prevent Data Processing Likely to Cause Damage or Distress

9.11   Section 10 of the DPA 1998 refers to the right to prevent processing likely to cause damage or distress.

Section 10(1) provides that subject to sub-s (2), an individual is entitled at any time by notice in writing to a Controller to require the Controller at the end of such period as is reasonable in the circumstances to cease, or not to begin, processing, or processing for a specified purpose or in

---

5   *Ibid.*

a specified manner, any personal data in respect of which he is the Data Subject, on the ground that, for specified reasons:

- the processing of those data or their processing for that purpose or in that manner is causing or is likely to cause substantial damage or substantial distress to them or to another; and
- that damage or distress is or would be unwarranted.

Section 10(2) provides that sub-s (1) does not apply:

- in a case where any of the conditions in paras 1 to 4 of Sch 2 is met; or
- in such other cases as may be prescribed by the Secretary of State by order.

Section 10(3) provides that the Controller must within twenty-one days of receiving a notice under sub-s (1) ('the Data Subject notice') give the individual who gave it a written notice,

- stating that he has complied or intends to comply with the Data Subject notice; or
- stating his reasons for regarding the Data Subject notice as to any extent unjustified and the extent (if any) to which he has complied or intends to comply with it.

Section 10(4) provides that if a court is satisfied, on the application of any person who has given a notice under sub-s (1) which appears to the court to be justified (or to be justified to any extent), that the Controller in question has failed to comply with the notice, the court may order them to take such steps for complying with the notice (or for complying with it to that extent) as the court thinks fit.

Section 10(5) provides that the failure by a Data Subject to exercise the right conferred by sub-s (1) or s 11(1) does not affect any other right conferred on them by this Part.

This may well have renewed importance and application in relation to online abuse and social media abuse.

Also note comments on the Right to be Forgotten (RtbF) below.

DPA: Right to Prevent Data Processing for Direct Marketing

9.12   Section 11 of the DPA 1998 relates to the right to prevent processing for purposes of direct marketing (DM).

Section 11(1) provides that an individual is entitled at any time by notice in writing to a Controller to require the Controller at the end of such period as is reasonable in the circumstances to cease, or not to begin, processing for the purposes of direct marketing personal data in respect of which he is the Data Subject.

Section 11(2) provides that if the court is satisfied, on the application of any person who has given a notice under sub-s (1), that the Controller has failed to comply with the notice, the court may order them to take such steps for complying with the notice as the court thinks fit.

Section 11(2A) provides that this section shall not apply in relation to the processing of such data as are mentioned in para (1) of reg 8 of the Telecommunications (Data Protection and Privacy) Regulations 1999 (processing of telecommunications billing data for certain marketing purposes) for the purposes mentioned in para (2) of that regulation.

Section 11(3) provides that in this section, 'direct marketing' means the communication (by whatever means) of any advertising or marketing material which is directed to particular individuals.

DPA: Automated Decision Taking/Making Processes

9.13 Controllers may not take decisions which produce legal effects concerning a Data Subject or which otherwise significantly affect a Data Subject and which are based solely on processing by automatic means of personal data and which are intended to evaluate certain personal matters relating to the Data Subject such as, performance at work, credit worthiness, reliability of conduct.

Section 12 provides for the rights in relation to automated decision-taking. Section 12(1) provides that an individual is entitled at any time, by notice in writing to any Controller, to require the Controller to ensure that no decision taken by or on behalf of the Controller which significantly affects that individual is based solely on the processing by automatic means of personal data in respect of which that individual is the Data Subject for the purpose of evaluating matters relating to them such as, for example, his performance at work, his creditworthiness, his reliability or his conduct.

Section 12(2) provides that where, in a case where no notice under sub-s (1) has effect, a decision which significantly affects an individual is based solely on such processing as is mentioned in sub-s (1):

- the Controller must as soon as reasonably practicable notify the individual that the decision was taken on that basis; and
- the individual is entitled, within twenty-one days of receiving that notification from the Controller, by notice in writing to require the Controller to reconsider the decision or to take a new decision otherwise than on that basis (12(2)(b)).

Section 12(3) provides that the Controller must, within twenty-one days of receiving a notice under sub-s (2)(b) ('the Data Subject notice') give the individual a written notice specifying the steps that he intends to take to comply with the Data Subject notice.

Section 12(4) provides that a notice under sub-s (1) does not have effect in relation to an exempt decision; and nothing in sub-s (2) applies to an exempt decision.

Section 12(5) provides that in sub-s (4) 'exempt decision' means any decision:

- in respect of which the condition in sub-s (6) and the condition in sub-s (7) are met; or
- which is made in such other circumstances as may be prescribed by the Secretary of State by order.

Section 12(6) provides that the condition in this sub-s is that the decision:

- is taken in the course of steps taken;
  - for the purpose of considering whether to enter into a contract with the Data Subject;
  - with a view to entering into such a contract; or
  - in the course of performing such a contract; or
- is authorised or required by or under any enactment.

Section 12(7) provides that the condition in this sub-s is that either:

- the effect of the decision is to grant a request of the Data Subject; or
- steps have been taken to safeguard the legitimate interests of the Data Subject (for example, by allowing them to make representations).

Section 12(8) provides that if a court is satisfied on the application of a Data Subject that a person taking a decision in respect of them (the 'responsible person') has failed to comply with sub-s (1) or (2)(b), the court may order the responsible person to reconsider the decision, or to take a new decision which is not based solely on such processing as is mentioned in sub-s (1).

Section 12(9) provides that an order under sub-s (8) shall not affect the rights of any person other than the Data Subject and the responsible person.

Section 12 of the DPA 1998 provides rights in relation to automated decision-taking. It states:

(1) An individual is entitled at any time, by notice in writing to any Controller, to require the Controller to ensure that no decision taken by or on behalf of the Controller which significantly affects that individual is based solely on the processing by automatic means of personal data in respect of which that individual is the Data Subject

for the purpose of evaluating matters relating to them such as, for example, his performance at work, his creditworthiness, his reliability or his conduct;

(2) Where, in a case where no notice under sub-s (1) has effect, a decision which significantly affects an individual is based solely on such processing as is mentioned in sub-s (1);

    (a) the Controller must as soon as reasonably practicable notify the individual that the decision was taken on that basis; and

    (b) the individual is entitled, within twenty-one days of receiving that notification from the Controller, by notice in writing to require the Controller to reconsider the decision or to take a new decision otherwise than on that basis;

(3) The Controller must, within twenty-one days of receiving a notice under sub-s (2)(b) ('the Data Subject notice') give the individual a written notice specifying the steps that he intends to take to comply with the Data Subject notice;

(4) A notice under sub-s (1) does not have effect in relation to an exempt decision; and nothing in sub-s (2) applies to an exempt decision;

(5) In subsection (4) 'exempt decision' means any decision,

    (a) in respect of which the condition in sub-s (6) and the condition in sub-s (7) are met; or

    (b) which is made in such other circumstances as may be prescribed by the Secretary of State by order;

(6) The condition in this sub–s is that the decision,

    (a) is taken in the course of steps taken;

        (i) for the purpose of considering whether to enter into a contract with the Data Subject;

        (ii) with a view to entering into such a contract; or

        (iii) in the course of performing such a contract; or

    (b) is authorised or required by or under any enactment;

(7) The condition in this sub–s is that either,

    (a) the effect of the decision is to grant a request of the Data Subject; or

    (b) steps have been taken to safeguard the legitimate interests of the Data Subject (for example, by allowing them to make representations);

(8) If a court is satisfied on the application of a Data Subject that a person taking a decision in respect of them ('the responsible person') has failed to comply with sub-s (1) or (2)(b), the court may order the responsible person to reconsider the decision, or to take a new decision which is not based solely on such processing as is mentioned in sub-s (1);

(9) An order under sub-s (8) shall not affect the rights of any person other than the Data Subject and the responsible person.

DPD: Right to Object

9.14 Section VII of the DPD refers to the Data Subject's right to object. Article 14 refers to the Data Subject's right to object. It provides that Member States shall grant the Data Subject the right:

- at least in the cases referred to in Article 7 (e) and (f), to object at any time on compelling legitimate grounds relating to his particular situation to the processing of data relating to them, save where otherwise provided by national legislation. Where there is a justified objection, the processing instigated by the Controller may no longer involve those data;
- to object, on request and free of charge, to the processing of personal data relating to them which the Controller anticipates being processed for the purposes of direct marketing, or to be informed before personal data are disclosed for the first time to third parties or used on their behalf for the purposes of direct marketing, and to be expressly offered the right to object free of charge to such disclosures or uses.

It also provides that Member States shall take the necessary measures to ensure that Data Subjects are aware of the existence of the right.

DPD: Right Against Automated Individual Decisions

9.15 Article 15 of the DPD refers to automated individual decisions. Article 15(1) provides that Member States shall grant the right to every person not to be subject to a decision which produces legal effects concerning them or significantly affects them and which is based solely on automated processing of data intended to evaluate certain personal aspects relating to them, such as their performance at work, creditworthiness, reliability, conduct, etc.

Article 15(2) provides that subject to the other Articles of the Directive, Member States shall provide that a person may be subjected to a decision of the kind referred to in para 1 if that decision:

- is taken in the course of the entering into or performance of a contract, provided the request for the entering into or the performance of the contract, lodged by the Data Subject, has been satisfied or that there are suitable measures to safeguard his legitimate interests, such as arrangements allowing them to put his point of view; or
- is authorised by a law which also lays down measures to safeguard the Data Subject's legitimate interests.

DPA: Rectification, Blocking, Erasure and Destruction Rights

9.16 Section 14 of the DPA 1998 provides user rights in relation to rectification, blocking, erasure and destruction.

Section 14(1) provides that if a court is satisfied on the application of a Data Subject that personal data of which the applicant is the subject are inaccurate, the court may order the Controller to rectify, block, erase or destroy those data and any other personal data in respect of which he is the Controller and which contain an expression of opinion which appears to the court to be based on the inaccurate data.

Section 14(2) provides that sub-s (1) applies whether or not the data accurately record information received or obtained by the Controller from the Data Subject or a third party but where the data accurately record such information, then:

- if the requirements mentioned in paragraph 7 of Part II of Schedule 1 have been complied with, the court may, instead of making an order under sub-s (1), make an order requiring the data to be supplemented by such statement of the true facts relating to the matters dealt with by the data as the court may approve (14(2)(a)); and
- if all or any of those requirements have not been complied with, the court may, instead of making an order under that sub-section, make such order as it thinks fit for securing compliance with those requirements with or without a further order requiring the data to be supplemented by such a statement as is mentioned in the above paragraph (a).

Section 14(3) provides that where the court:

- makes an order under sub-s (1); or
- is satisfied on the application of a Data Subject that personal data of which he was the Data Subject and which have been rectified, blocked, erased or destroyed were inaccurate,

it may, where it considers it reasonably practicable, order the Controller to notify third parties to whom the data have been disclosed of the rectification, blocking, erasure or destruction.

Section 14(4) provides that if a court is satisfied on the application of a Data Subject:

- that he has suffered damage by reason of any contravention by a Controller of any of the requirements of the DPA in respect of any personal data, in circumstances entitling them to compensation under s 13; and
- that there is a substantial risk of further contravention in respect of those data in such circumstances,

the court may order the rectification, blocking, erasure or destruction of any of those data.

Section 14(5) provides that where the court makes an order under sub-s (4) it may, where it considers it reasonably practicable, order the Controller to notify third parties to whom the data have been disclosed of the rectification, blocking, erasure or destruction.

Section 14(6) provides that in determining whether it is reasonably practicable to require such notification as is mentioned in sub-s (3) or (5) the court shall have regard, in particular, to the number of persons who would have to be notified.

Again, this can apply in relation to various forms of online and social media abuse.

DPD: Rectification, Erasure or Blocking

9.17   Article 12 of the DPD provides for the right of access, and states, Member States shall guarantee every Data Subject the right to obtain from the Controller:

(a)   ...
(b)   as appropriate the rectification, erasure or blocking of data the processing of which does not comply with the provisions of the DPD, in particular because of the incomplete or inaccurate nature of the data;
(c)   notification to third parties to whom the data have been disclosed of any rectification, erasure or blocking carried out in compliance with (b), unless this proves impossible or involves a disproportionate effort.

Also note comments on the RtbF below.

GDPR: Rectification and Erasure

9.18   Chapter III, Section 3 of the new GDPR refers to rectification and erasure.

Rectification Right

9.19   The new GDPR provides that the Data Subject shall have the right to obtain from the Controller without undue delay the rectification of inaccurate personal data concerning them. Taking into account the purposes of the processing, the Data Subject shall have the right to have incomplete personal data completed, including by means of providing a supplementary statement (Article 16).

Erasure Right/Right to be Forgotten

9.20 The new GDPR provides that the Data Subject shall have the right to obtain from the Controller the erasure of personal data concerning them without undue delay where one of the following grounds applies:

- the data are no longer necessary in relation to the purposes for which they were collected or otherwise processed;
- the Data Subject withdraws consent on which the processing is based according to Article 6(1)(a), or Article 9(2)(a), and where there is no other legal ground for the processing;
- the Data Subject objects to the processing pursuant to Article 21(1) and there are no overriding legitimate grounds for the processing, or the Data Subject objects to the processing pursuant to Article 21(2);
- the personal data have been unlawfully processed;
- the personal data have to be erased for compliance with a legal obligation in EU or Member State law to which the Controller is subject;
- the data have been collected in relation to the offering of information society services referred to in Article 8(1) (Article 17(1)).

Where the Controller has made the personal data public and is obliged pursuant to para 1 to erase the personal data, the Controller, taking account of available technology and the cost of implementation, shall take reasonable steps, including technical measures, to inform Controllers which are processing the personal data, that the Data Subject has requested the erasure by such Controllers of any links to, or copy or replication of that personal data (Article 17(2)).

Article 17(1) and (2) shall not apply to the extent that processing is necessary:

- for exercising the right of freedom of expression and information;
- for compliance with a legal obligation which requires processing by EU or Member State law to which the Controller is subject or for the performance of a task carried out in the public interest or in the exercise of official authority vested in the Controller;
- for reasons of public interest in the area of public health in accordance with Article 9(2)(h) and (i) as well as Article 9(3);
- for archiving purposes in the public interest, scientific or historical research purposes or statistical purposes in accordance with Article 89(1) in so far as the right referred to in para 1 is likely to render impossible or seriously impair the achievement of the objectives of that processing;
- for the establishment, exercise or defence of legal claims (Article 17(3)).

Synodinou[6] refers to the 'right to oblivion' and notes in relation to her research that media rights are not immune to the right to be forgotten. Examples are given where cases have been successful in preventing particular media stories dragging up past events long after they had occurred, including court cases.[7] Indeed, many countries already obscure party names from decisions and judgments so as to render them anonymous, such as in Germany, Austria, Greece, Finland, Belgium, Hungary, the Netherlands, Poland and Portugal.[8] The right to be forgotten has also been recognised in France and Belgium.[9] A UK case also granted anonymity to the Plaintiff,[10] as did the Canadian Supreme Court in an online abuse case.[11] To be successful, however, it can be important to change party initials.[12]

Right to Restriction of Processing

9.21   Article 18 of the new GDPR refers to the right to restriction of processing. The Data Subject shall have the right to obtain from the Controller the restriction of the processing where one of the following applies:

- the accuracy of the data is contested by the Data Subject, for a period enabling the Controller to verify the accuracy of the personal data;
- the processing is unlawful and the Data Subject opposes the erasure of the personal data and requests the restriction of their use instead;
- the Controller no longer needs the personal data for the purposes of the processing, but they are required by the Data Subject for the establishment, exercise or defence of legal claims;

---

6   Tatiana-Eleni Synodinou, 'The Media Coverage of Court Proceedings in Europe: Striking a Balance Between Freedom of Expression and Fair Process,' *Computer Law & Security Review* (2012) (28) 208–219, at 217.
7   *Ibid*, 218.
8   *Ibid*, 218 and fn 106, 218.
9   *Ibid*, 208–219, at 217.
10 See *XY v Facebook*, which also said that the website was a publisher. *XY v Facebook*, McCloskey J [2012] NIQB 96, 30 November 2012.
11 *AB v Bragg Communications*, 27 September 2012. At http://scc-csc.lexum.com/scc-csc/scc-csc/en/item/10007/index.do.
12 For example, while the parties and director defendants in a Berlin Facebook data protection case were reduced initials, reducing one party's name to 'MZ' may not have been fully effective. See *The Federal Association of Consumer Organisations and Consumer Groups, Federal Consumer Association, GB v Facebook Ireland Limited, MA, JB, DG, PT and the Chairman* [names redacted], [redacted].

- the Data Subject has objected to processing pursuant to Article 21(1) pending the verification whether the legitimate grounds of the Controller override those of the Data Subject (Article 18(1)).

Where processing has been restricted under Article 18(1), such personal data shall, with the exception of storage, only be processed with the Data Subject's consent or for the establishment, exercise or defence of legal claims or for the protection of the rights of another natural or legal person or for reasons of important public interest of the EU or of a Member State (Article 18(2)).

A Data Subject who obtained the restriction of processing pursuant to Article 18(1) shall be informed by the Controller before the restriction of processing is lifted (Article 18(3)).

Notification Obligation re Rectification, Erasure or Restriction

9.22 The new GDPR provides that the Controller shall communicate any rectification or erasure of personal data or restriction of processing carried out in accordance with Articles 16, 17(1) and 18 to each recipient to whom the personal data have been disclosed, unless this proves impossible or involves disproportionate effort. The Controller shall inform the Data Subject about those recipients if the Data Subject requests it (Article 19).

Right to Data Portability

9.23 The new GDPR provides that the Data Subject shall have the right to receive the personal data concerning them, which they have provided to a Controller, in a structured, commonly used and machine-readable format and have the right to transmit those data to another Controller without hindrance from the Controller to which the personal data have been provided, where:

- the processing is based on consent pursuant to Article 6(1)(a) or Article 9(2)(a) or on a contract pursuant to Article 6(1)(a); and
- the processing is carried out by automated means (Article 20(1)).

In exercising their right to data portability, the Data Subject has the right to have the personal data transmitted directly from Controller to Controller, where technically feasible (Article 20(2)).

The exercise of this right shall be without prejudice to Article 17. That right shall not apply to processing necessary for the performance of a task carried out in the public interest or in the exercise of official authority vested in the Controller (Article 20(3)).

The right referred to in para 1 shall not adversely affect the rights and freedoms of others (Article 20(4)).

Automated Individual Decision Making Right

9.24   Chapter III, Section 4 of the new GDPR refers to the right to object and automated individual decision making.

Right to Object

9.25   The new GDPR provides that the Data Subject shall have the right to object, on grounds relating to their particular situation, at any time to the processing of personal data concerning them which is based on Article 6(1)(e) or (f), including profiling based on those provisions. The Controller shall no longer process the personal data unless the Controller demonstrates compelling legitimate grounds for the processing which override the interests, rights and freedoms of the Data Subject or for the establishment, exercise or defence of legal claims (Article 21(1)).

Where personal data are processed for direct marketing purposes, the Data Subject shall have the right to object at any time to the processing of personal data concerning them for such marketing, which includes profiling to the extent that it is related to such direct marketing (Article 21(2)).

Where the Data Subject objects to the processing for direct marketing purposes, the personal data shall no longer be processed for such purposes (Article 21(3)).

At the latest at the time of the first communication with the Data Subject, the right referred to in Article 21(1) and (2) shall be explicitly brought to the attention of the Data Subject and shall be presented clearly and separately from any other information (Article 21(4)).

In the context of the use of information society services, and notwithstanding Directive 2002/58/EC,[13] the Data Subject may exercise their right to object by automated means using technical specifications (Article 21(5)).

Where personal data are processed for scientific and historical research purposes or statistical purposes pursuant to Article 89(1), the Data Subject, on grounds relating to their particular situation, shall have the right

---

13   Directive 2002/58/EC of the European Parliament and of the Council of 12 July 2002 concerning the processing of personal data and the protection of privacy in the electronic communications sector (Directive on privacy and electronic communications).

to object to processing of personal data concerning them, unless the processing is necessary for the performance of a task carried out for reasons of public interest (Article 21(6)).

Automated Individual Decision Making, Including Profiling

9.26 The new GDPR provides that Data Subjects shall have the right not to be subject to a decision based solely on automated processing, including profiling, which produces legal effects concerning them or similarly significantly affects them (Article 22(1)).

Article 22(1) shall not apply if the decision:

- is necessary for entering into, or performance of, a contract between the Data Subject and a Controller [a];
- is authorised by EU or Member State law to which the Controller is subject and which also lays down suitable measures to safeguard the Data Subject's rights and freedoms and legitimate interests; or
- is based on the Data Subject's explicit consent (Article 22(2)) [c].

In cases referred to in Article 22(2) (a) and (c) the Controller shall implement suitable measures to safeguard the Data Subject's rights and freedoms and legitimate interests, at least the right to obtain human intervention on the part of the Controller, to express their point of view and to contest the decision (Article 22(3)).

Decisions referred to in paragraph (2) shall not be based on special categories of personal data referred to in Article 9(1), unless Article 9(2)(a) or (g) apply and suitable measures to safeguard the Data Subject's rights and freedoms and legitimate interests are in place (Article 22(4)).

DPA: Compensation for Data Subjects

9.27 Section 13 of the DPA 1998 refers to compensation for failure to comply with certain requirements.

Section 13(1) provides that an individual who suffers damage by reason of any contravention by a Controller of any of the requirements of the DPA is entitled to compensation from the Controller for that damage.

Section 13(2) provides that an individual who suffers distress by reason of any contravention by a Controller of any of the requirements of the Act is entitled to compensation from the Controller for that distress if:

- the individual also suffers damage by reason of the contravention; or
- the contravention relates to the processing of personal data for the special purposes.

Section 13(3) provides that in proceedings brought against a person by virtue of this section it is a defence to prove that he had taken such care as in all the circumstances was reasonably required to comply with the requirement concerned.

This is an area which will continue to grow in importance. The facts in the *Prudential* case could have resulted in actual financial loss and damage to a Data Subject. While the ICO implemented a fine of £50,000, civil compensation could also have been a possibility.

In another case, a businessman successfully sued a company for Spamming.[14] Another victim of Spam also sued and received £750 for a single Spam message received.[15] Typically, a Spammer sends tens of thousands if not millions of Spam messages at a time, so per message fines can add up, even if only a small sample of them result in fines or awards.

In the US there have been cases by service providers, in addition to individual recipients of Spam. Microsoft successfully sued a Spam company in the UK and received £45,000.[16]

The trend in Spam laws appears to be to permitting recipients, service providers and a regulator to be able to sue Spammers. Indeed, Regulation 30(1) PECR Amendment provides that 'A person who suffers damage by reason of any contravention ... by any other person shall be entitled to bring proceedings for compensation from that person for that damage.'

Injunctions can be possible for Spam, as well as other areas involving data protection rights.

The ICO also fined the promoters behind a Spam company a total of £440,000.[17]

The area of compensation and civil litigation in vindication of data protection rights will continue to develop. While the scale of monetary claims, and awards, can differ as between the US and the UK, it is noted that one defendant was happy to settle one such case for approx $20 m.[18]

It is possible that Data Subjects, and indeed Data Subjects who have not suffered financial loss, can still suffer damage and be awarded compensation or damages.

---

14   H Hart, 'Cutting Down on Spam,' *Solicitors Journal*, 10 March 2005, 290.
15   T Young, 'Courts Put Price on Unsolicited Email,' *Computing*, 15 March 2007, 14.
16   *Microsoft v Paul Martin McDonald* [2006] EWHC 3410 (Ch).
17   *ICO v Niebel, McNeish and Tetrus Telecoms* (2012).
18   Facebook was willing to settle social media privacy and advertising litigation case for approx $20 million. This related to the unlawful use of personal data in relation to the Beacon project. Indeed, it appears that this figure could have risen significantly from that figure.

DPA: Requiring Data Disclosure

9.28 Appendix 2 s 57 refers to avoidance of certain contractual terms relating to organisation access to health records.

Appendix 2 s 57(1) provides that any term or condition of a contract is void in so far as it purports to require an individual:

- to supply any other person with a record to which this section applies, or with a copy of such a record or a part of such a record; or
- to produce to any other person such a record, copy or part.

Appendix 2 s 57(2) provides that this section applies to any record which:

- has been or is to be obtained by a Data Subject in the exercise of the right conferred by s 7; and
- consists of the information contained in any health record as defined by s 68(2).

Jurisdiction

9.29 Recital 22 of the new GDPR states that any processing of personal data in the context of the activities of an establishment of a Controller or a Processor in the Union should be carried out in accordance with the GDPR, regardless of whether the processing itself takes place within the EU. Establishment implies the effective and real exercise of activity through stable arrangements. The legal form of such arrangements, whether through a branch or a subsidiary with a legal personality, is not the determining factor in this respect.

Recital 23 of the new GDPR states that in order to ensure that natural persons are not deprived of the protection to which they are entitled under the GDPR, the processing of personal data of Data Subjects who are in the EU by a Controller or a Processor not established in the EU should be subject to the GDPR where the processing activities are related to the offering of goods or services to such Data Subjects irrespective of whether connected to a payment. In order to determine whether such a Controller or Processor is offering goods or services to Data Subjects who are in the EU, it should be ascertained whether it is apparent that the Controller or Processor envisages offering services to Data Subjects in one or more Member States in the EU. Whereas the mere accessibility of the Controller's, Processor's or an intermediary's website in the Union, of an email address or of other contact details, or the use of a language generally used in the third country where the controller is established, is insufficient to ascertain such intention, factors such as the use of a language or a currency generally used in one or more Member States with the possibility of ordering goods and services in that other language, or the mentioning of customers or users who are in the EU, may make it apparent that the controller envisages offering goods or services to such Data Subjects in the EU.

Section 15 of the DPA 1998 refers to jurisdiction and procedure. Section 15(1) provides that the jurisdiction conferred by ss 7 to 14 is exercisable by the High Court or a county court or, in Scotland, by the Court of Session or the sheriff.

Section 15(2) of the DPA 1998 provides that for the purpose of determining any question whether an applicant under sub-s (9) of s 7 is entitled to the information which he seeks (including any question whether any relevant data are exempt from that section by virtue of Part IV) a court may require the information constituting any data processed by or on behalf of the Controller and any information as to the logic involved in any decision-taking as mentioned in s 7(1)(d) to be made available for its own inspection but shall not, pending the determination of that question in the applicant's favour, require the information sought by the applicant to be disclosed to them or his representatives whether by discovery (or, in Scotland, recovery) or otherwise.

Complaints to ICO

9.30 Recital 141 of the new GDPR states that every Data Subject should have the right to lodge a complaint with a single supervisory authority, in particular in the Member State of their habitual residence, and the right to an effective judicial remedy in accordance with Article 47 of the Charter if the Data Subject considers that their rights under the Regulation are infringed or where the supervisory authority does not act on a complaint, partially or wholly rejects or dismisses a complaint or does not act where such action is necessary to protect the rights of the Data Subject. The investigation following a complaint should be carried out, subject to judicial review, to the extent that is appropriate in the specific case. The supervisory authority should inform the Data Subject of the progress and the outcome of the complaint within a reasonable period. If the case requires further investigation or coordination with another supervisory authority, intermediate information should be given to the Data Subject. In order to facilitate the submission of complaints, each supervisory authority should take measures such as providing a complaint submission form which can also be completed electronically, without excluding other means of communication.

Organisational Data Protection Group

9.31   Recital 142 of the GDPR states that where a Data Subject considers that their rights under the Regulation are infringed, they should have the right to mandate a not-for-profit body, organisation or association which is constituted according to the law of a Member State, has statutory objectives which are in the public interest and is active in the field of the protection of personal data to lodge a complaint on their behalf with a supervisory authority, exercise the right to a judicial remedy on behalf of Data Subjects or exercise if provided for in Member State law exercise the right to receive compensation on behalf of Data Subjects. A Member State may provide for such a body, organisation or association to have the right to lodge a complaint in that Member State, independently of a Data Subject's mandate, and the right to an effective judicial remedy where it has reason to consider that the rights of a Data Subject have been infringed as a result of the processing of personal data which infringes the Regulation. That body, organisation or association may not be allowed to claim compensation on a Data Subject's behalf independently of the Data Subject's mandate.

Indeed, there are an increasing number of data protection and privacy groups, both nationally and supra-nationally. Indeed, the Court of Justice case striking down the Data Retention Directive was taken by one such group.[19]

Court Remedies

9.32   Recital 143 of the GDPR states that each natural or legal person should have an effective judicial remedy before the competent national court against a decision of a supervisory authority which produces legal effects concerning that person. This is, inter alia, distinguished from other matters such as opinions and non legal effects.

Different Supervisory Authorities

9.33   One of the aims of the GDPR was originally to establish a single supervisory authority in respect of which organisations would have to deal with, a so called one-stop-shop, as opposed to dealing with data

---

19   Cases C-293/12 and C-594/12, *Digital Rights Ireland and Seitlinger and Others*, Court of Justice, 8 April 2014. Directive 2006/24/EC and amending Directive 2002/58/EC.

protection authorities in each Member State, there is recognition that circumstances can arise for other authorities to become involved.

Supervisory authorities may cooperate on specific matters.

Recital 144 of the GDPR states proceedings may be stayed or declined where there are similar or identical prior proceedings ongoing in another Member State.

Plaintiff Choice of Jurisdictions and Courts

9.34 Recital 145 of the new GDPR states that for proceedings against a Controller or Processor, the plaintiff should have the choice to bring the action before the courts of the Member States where the controller or processor has an establishment or where the Data Subject resides, unless the Controller is a public authority of a Member State acting in the exercise of its public powers.

Compensation

9.35 Recital 146 of the new GDPR states that the Controller or Processor should compensate any damage which a person may suffer as a result of processing that infringes the GDPR. The Controller or Processor should be exempt from liability if it proves that it is not in any way responsible for the damage. The concept of damage should be broadly interpreted in the light of the case law of the Court of Justice in a manner which fully reflects the objectives of the GDPR. This is without prejudice to any claims for damage deriving from the violation of other rules in EU or Member State law. Processing that infringes the GDPR also includes processing that infringes delegated and implementing acts adopted in accordance with the GDPR and Member State law specifying rules of the GDPR. Data Subjects should receive full and effective compensation for the damage they have suffered. Where Controllers or Processors are involved in the same processing, each Controller or Processor should be held liable for the entire damage. However, where they are joined to the same judicial proceedings, in accordance with Member State law, compensation may be apportioned according to the responsibility of each Controller or Processor for the damage caused by the processing, provided that full and effective compensation of the Data Subject who suffered the damage is ensured. Any Controller or Processor which has paid full compensation may subsequently institute recourse proceedings against other Controllers or Processors involved in the same processing.

Penalties

9.36 Recital 148 of the new GDPR states that in order to strengthen the enforcement of the rules of the GDPR, penalties including administrative fines should be imposed for any infringement of the GDPR, in addition to, or instead of appropriate measures imposed by the supervisory authority pursuant to the GDPR. In a case of a minor infringement or if the fine likely to be imposed would constitute a disproportionate burden to a natural person, a reprimand may be issued instead of a fine. Due regard should be given to the nature, gravity and duration of the infringement, the intentional character of the infringement, actions taken to mitigate the damage suffered, degree of responsibility or any relevant previous infringements, the manner in which the infringement became known to the supervisory authority, compliance with measures ordered against the Controller or Processor, adherence to a code of conduct and any other aggravating or mitigating factor. The imposition of penalties including administrative fines should be subject to appropriate procedural safeguards in accordance with the general principles of EU law and the Charter, including effective judicial protection and due process.

Sanctions

9.37 Recital 150 of the GDPR states that the in order to strengthen and harmonise administrative penalties for infringements of the GDPR, each supervisory authority should have the power to impose administrative fines. The GDPR should indicate infringements and the upper limit and criteria for setting the related administrative fines, which should be determined by the competent supervisory authority in each individual case, taking into account all relevant circumstances of the specific situation, with due regard in particular to the nature, gravity and duration of the infringement and of its consequences and the measures taken to ensure compliance with the obligations under the GDPR and to prevent or mitigate the consequences of the infringement. Where administrative fines are imposed on an undertaking, an undertaking should be understood to be an undertaking in accordance with Articles 101 and 102 TFEU for those purposes. Where administrative fines are imposed on persons that are not an undertaking, the supervisory authority should take account of the general level of income in the Member State as well as the economic situation of the person in considering the appropriate amount of the fine. The consistency mechanism may also be used to promote a consistent application of administrative fines. It should be for the Member States to determine whether and to which extent public authorities should be subject to administrative fines. Imposing an administrative fine or giving a warning does not affect the application of other powers of the supervisory authorities or of other penalties under the GDPR.

GDPR: Right to Portability

9.38   Article 20 of the new GDPR refers to the right to data portability. The Data Subject shall have the right to receive the personal data concerning them, which they provided to a Controller, in a structured, commonly used and machine-readable format and have the right to transmit those data to another Controller without hindrance from the Controller to which the data have been provided, where:

- the processing is based on consent pursuant to Article 6(1)(a) or Article 9(2)(a) or on a contract pursuant to Article 6(1)(b); and
- the processing is carried out by automated means (Article 20(1)).

In exercising their right to data portability pursuant to para 1, the Data Subject has the right to have the data transmitted directly from Controller to Controller, where technically feasible (Article 20(2)).

The exercise of this right shall be without prejudice to Article 17. That right shall not apply to processing necessary for the performance of a task carried out in the public interest or in the exercise of official authority vested in the Controller (Article 20(3)).

The right referred to in para 1 shall not adversely affect the rights and freedoms of others (Article 20(4)).

GDPR: Right to Object, Automated Decisions and Profiling

9.39   Chapter III, Section 4 of the GDPR refers to the right to object to processing, automated individual decisions and to profiling.

The Data Subject shall have the right to object, on grounds relating to their particular situation, at any time to the processing of personal data concerning them which is based on Article 6(1)(e) or (f), including profiling based on these provisions. The Controller shall no longer process the personal data unless the Controller demonstrates compelling legitimate grounds for the processing which override the interests, rights and freedoms of the Data Subject or for the establishment, exercise or defence of legal claims (Article 21(1)).

Where personal data are processed for direct marketing purposes, the Data Subject shall have the right to object at any time to processing of personal data concerning them for such marketing, which includes profiling to the extent that it is related to such direct marketing (Article 21(2)).

Where the Data Subject objects to processing for direct marketing purposes, the personal data shall no longer be processed for such purposes (Article 21(3)).

At the latest at the time of the first communication with the Data Subject, the right referred to in paras 1 and 2 shall be explicitly brought to the attention of the Data Subject and shall be presented clearly and separately from any other information (Article 21(4)).

In the context of the use of information society services, and notwithstanding Directive 2002/58/EC,[20] the Data Subject may exercise their right to object by automated means using technical specifications (Article 21(5)).

Where personal data are processed for scientific and historical research purposes or statistical purposes pursuant to Article 89(1), the Data Subject, on grounds relating to their particular situation, shall have the right to object to processing of personal data concerning them, unless the processing is necessary for the performance of a task carried out for reasons of public interest (Article 21(6)).

GDPR Automated Individual Decision Making, Including Profiling

9.40 The Data Subject shall have the right not to be subject to a decision based solely on automated processing, including profiling, which produces legal effects concerning them or similarly significantly affects them (see Article 22(1) and para **9.27** above).

Conclusion

9.41 The rights are very important for organisations to recognise and protect, and reflect in the documented processes, procedures and plans of the organisation. These need to be incorporated from day one, as it may not be possible to retrospectively become a complaint if the initial collection and processing was illegitimate. This is increasingly significant as data protection authorities and Data Subjects become more proactive and as the levels of fines and penalties increase. It is clear that the importance attached to data protection has increased significantly, and so too the obligation for organisational compliance.

---

20 Directive 2002/58/EC of the European Parliament and of the Council of 12 July 2002 concerning the processing of personal data and the protection of privacy in the electronic communications sector (Directive on privacy and electronic communications).

Cases to Consider

9.42 ICO complaints, cases and case studies which may be useful for organisations to consider:

- *ICO v Prudential;*[21]
- *Microsoft v Paul Martin McDonald;*[22]
- *McCall v Facebook;*[23]
- *ICO v Niebel, ICO v McNeish;*[24]
- *Rugby Football Union v Viagogo Limited;*[25]
- *Durham County Council v Dunn;*[26]
- *British Gas v Data Protection Registrar;*[27]
- *Brian Reed Beetson Robertson;*[28]
- *Campbell v MGM;*[29]
- *CCN Systems v Data Protection Registrar;*[30]
- *Lindqvist v Kammaraklagaren;*[31]
- *Commission v Bavarian Lager;*[32]
- *Common Services Agency v Scottish Information Commissioner;*[33]
- *Douglas v Hello!;*[34]
- *Halford v UK;*[35]
- *Von Hannover v Germany;*[36]
- *Mosley* (newspaper case);
- *Motion Picture Association v BT;*[37]
- *WP29 (now EDPB) and Data Protection Authorities/Google* (re Google policy change and breaches);
- Barclays/Lara Davies prosecution;[38]

21 *ICO v Prudential*, 'Prudential Fined £50,000 for Customer Account Confusion,' 6 November 2012.
22 [2006] EWHC 3410.
23 20 September 2012.
24 28 November 2012.
25 [2012] UKSC 55.
26 [2012] EWCA Civ 1654.
27 [1998] UKIT DA98 – 3/49/2, 4 March 1998.
28 [2001] EWHC Admin 915.
29 [2004] UKHL 22.
30 [1991] UKIT DA90.
31 Case C-101/01, ECR I-12971.
32 Case C-28/08.
33 [2008] UKHL 47.
34 [2005] EWCA Civ 595.
35 [1997] IRLR 47, ECHR.
36 10 February 2012.
37 28 July 2011.
38 *ICO v Lara Davies*, December 2012.

- *ICO v* Sony;[39]
- *Facebook Beacon* case (US);[40]
- *Digital Rights Ireland and Seitlinger and Others*;[41]
- *Schrems v Commissioner*;[42]
- *Tamiz v Google*;[43]
- *Google v Vidal-Hall*;[44]
- *Mosley v Google* (various);
- *Google Spain SL Google Inc v Agencia Española de Protección de Datos, Mario Costeja González*;[45]
- *Weltimmo v Nemzeti Adatvédelmi és Információszabadság Hatóság*;[46]
- *Bărbulescu v Romania*.[47]

39 July 2013.
40 *McCall v Facebook*, 20 September 2012.
41 Joined Cases C-293/12 and C-594/12, 8 April 2014.
42 Case C-362/14, 6 October 2015.
43 [2012] EWHC 449 (QB) 3 December 2012.
44 [2014] EWHC 13 (QB).
45 Case C-131/121.
46 Case C-230/14, 1 October 2015.
47 ECHR, Case No 61496/08, 12 January 2016.

Chapter 10

Notification and Registration

Introduction

10.01 Organisations are prohibited from carrying on data collection and processing without notification and registration. There are certain details and categories of information required to be registered. There are, however, certain exemptions available. The ICO maintains the register. If the organisation makes any changes to the registered details, these must then be updated in the register. Registrations also need to be reviewed and renewed. It was proposed during the legislative process of the GDPR that the requirement for notification or registration by organisations be discontinued. This would be in line with the proposed approach of a greater emphasis by organisations on risk assessments.

Under the new GDPR there is a replacement of 'general' notification/registration requirement (Recital 89). Organisations need to consider any changes to national data protection law – including the notification/registration requirements – as may occur consequent upon the new GDPR.

Organisation Registration

10.02 Organisations are obliged to register with the ICO. Section 17 of the DPA 1998 prohibits data processing without registration. It provides that:

(1) Subject to the following provisions of this section, personal data must not be processed unless an entry in respect of the Controller is included in the register maintained by the ICO under s 19 (or is treated by notification regulations made by virtue of s 19(3) as being so included).

(2) Except where the processing is assessable processing for the purposes of s 22, sub-s (1) above does not apply in relation to personal data consisting of information which falls neither within paragraph (a) of the definition of 'data' in s 1(1) of the DPA nor within paragraph (b) of that definition.

(3) If it appears to the Secretary of State that processing of a particular description is unlikely to prejudice the rights and freedoms of Data Subjects, notification regulations may provide that, in such cases as may be prescribed, sub-s (1) is not to apply in relation to processing of that description.

(4) Sub-section (1) does not apply in relation to any processing whose sole purpose is the maintenance of a public register.

Section 16 of the DPA 1998 also refers to registration and contains details of the 'registrable particulars' required in relation to a Controller when registering. The details which must be registered are:

- organisation name and address;
- if the organisation has nominated a representative for the purposes of the Act, the name and address of the representative, etc;
- a description of the personal data being or to be processed by or on behalf of the Controller and of the category or categories of Data Subject to which they relate;
- a description of the purpose or purposes for which the data are being or are to be processed;
- a description of any recipient or recipients to whom the Controller intends or may wish to disclose the data;
- the names, or a description of, any countries or territories outside the EEA to which the Controller directly or indirectly transfers, or intends or may wish directly or indirectly to transfer, the data;
- where the Controller is a public authority, a statement of that fact;
- in any case where,
  ○ personal data are being, or are intended to be, processed in circumstances in which the prohibition in sub-s (1) of s 17 is excluded by sub-s (2) or (3) of that section; and
  ○ the notification does not extend to those data, a statement of that fact, and
- such information about the Controller as may be prescribed under s 18(5A) (s 16(1)).

Section 16(2) refers to further definitions in this Part of the DPA 1998, namely:

'fees regulations'   means regulations made by the Secretary of State under s 18(5) or 19(4) or (7);

'notification regulations'	means regulations made by the Secretary of State under the other provisions of this Part;
'prescribed'	except where used in relation to fees regulations, means prescribed by notification regulations.

Section 16(3) of the DPA 1998 states that for the purposes of this Part of the Act, so far as it relates to the addresses of Controllers:

- the address of a registered company is that of its registered office; and
- the address of a person (other than a registered company) carrying on a business is that of its principal place of business in the UK.

Section 18 refers to notification by Controllers. Any Controller who wishes to be included in the register maintained under s 19 shall give a notification to the Commissioner under this section. A notification under this section must specify in accordance with notification regulations:

- the registrable particulars; and
- a general description of measures to be taken for the purpose of complying with the seventh Data Protection Principle (ie the required security measures).

Section 18(3) provides that notification regulations made by virtue of sub-s (2) may provide for the determination by the ICO, in accordance with any requirements of the regulations, of the form in which the registrable particulars and the description mentioned in sub-s (2)(b) are to be specified, including in particular the detail required for the purposes of s 16(1)(c), (d), (e) and (f) and sub-s (2)(b).

Under s 18(4) notification regulations may make provision as to the giving of notification:

- by partnerships; or
- in other cases where two or more persons are the Controllers in respect of any personal data.

Section 18(5) provides that the notification must be accompanied by such fee as may be prescribed by fees regulations. Section 26 of the DPA 1998 provides that the Secretary of State may make various fee regulations. Section 18(5A) provides that notification regulations may prescribe the information about the Controller which is required for the purpose of verifying the fee payable under sub-s (5). Section 18(6) provides that notification regulations may provide for any fee paid under sub-s (5) or s 19(4) to be refunded in prescribed circumstances.

Register of Notifications

10.03   The ICO is obliged, under s 19(1), to:

- maintain a register of persons who have given notification under s 18; and
- make an entry in the register in pursuance of each notification received by them under that section from a person in respect of whom no entry as Controller was for the time being included in the register.

Each entry in the register shall, under s 19(2), consist of:

- the registrable particulars notified under s 18 or, as the case requires, those particulars as amended in pursuance of s 20(4); and
- such other information as the ICO may be authorised or required by notification regulations to include in the register.

Section 19(3) provides that notification regulations may make provision as to the time as from which any entry in respect of a Controller is to be treated for the purposes of s 17 as having been made in the register.

Section 19(4) provides that no entry shall be retained in the register for more than the relevant time except on payment of such fee as may be prescribed by fees regulations.

Section 19(5) provides that in sub-s (4) 'the relevant time' means twelve months or such other period as may be prescribed by notification regulations; and different periods may be prescribed in relation to different cases.

Under s 19(6), the ICO:

- shall provide facilities for making the information contained in the entries in the register available for inspection (in visible and legible form) by members of the public at all reasonable hours and free of charge; and
- may provide such other facilities for making the information contained in those entries available to the public free of charge as he considers appropriate.

The ICO shall, in accordance with s 19(7), on payment of such fee, if any, as may be prescribed by fees regulations, supply any member of the public with a duly certified copy in writing of the particulars contained in any entry made in the register. Nothing in sub-s (6) or (7) applies to information which is included in an entry in the register only by reason of it falling within s 16(1)(h) (s 19(8)).

Duty to Notify Changes

10.04   There is also an obligation on Controllers to notify changes. Section 20 of the DPA 1998 provides for the duty to notify changes. Section 20(1) provides that for the purpose specified in sub-s (2), notification regulations shall include provision imposing on every person in respect of whom an entry as a Controller is for the time being included in the register maintained under s 19 a duty to notify to the ICO, in such circumstances and at such time or times and in such form as may be prescribed, such matters relating to the registrable particulars and measures taken as mentioned in s 18(2)(b) as may be prescribed.

There is an obligation to notify of any changes. Section 20(1) provides that for the purpose specified in sub-s (2), notification regulations shall include provision imposing on every person in respect of whom an entry as a Controller is for the time being included in the register maintained under s 19 a duty to notify to the ICO, in such circumstances and at such time or times and in such form as may be prescribed, such matters relating to the registrable particulars and measures taken as mentioned in s 18(2)(b) as may be prescribed.

Section 20(2) indicates that the purpose referred to in sub-s (1) is that of ensuring, so far as practicable, that at any time,

- the entries in the register maintained under s 19 contain current names and addresses and describe the current practice or intentions of the Controller with respect to the processing of personal data; and
- the ICO is provided with a general description of measures currently being taken as mentioned in s 18(2)(b).

Section 20(3) provides that sub-s (3) of s 18 has effect in relation to notification regulations made by virtue of sub-s (1) as it has effect in relation to notification regulations made by virtue of sub-s (2) of that section. Section 20(4) provides that on receiving any notification under notification regulations made by virtue of sub-s (1), the ICO shall make such amendments of the relevant entry in the register maintained under s 19 as are necessary to take account of the change notification.

Process of Organisation Registration

10.05   Where the organisation is required to register and notify, it must notify the ICO with details of:

- the name and identity of whom is the Controller;
- the purpose or purposes for which the personal data are being processed;

- to whom the personal data may be disclosed;
- where the organisation is engaged with TBDFs or transfers of personal data abroad, it must set out the details in the registration;
- the organisational security measures used.

More specifically, the notification and registration process requires even more specific detailed information on certain specific criteria. One example is the description of the individual Data Subjects to whom the personal data relates and whose personal data is to be used by the organisation. The ICO *Notification Handbook*[1] refers, for example to sections for:

- the name and address of the Controller;
- the company registration number (optional);
- contact details;
- general description of the processing of personal information being carried out by the Controller, including,
- the *purposes* for which personal information is being or is to be processed, eg debt collection or research;
- a description of the *Data Subjects* about whom data is or is to be held, eg employees or patients;
- a description of the *data classes*, eg employment details and financial details;
- a list of the *recipients* of data, eg Central Government and Financial Organisations; and
- information about whether data is transferred outside the EEA;
- security statement;
- trading names;
- statement of exempt processing;
- voluntary notification;
- representative name and address;
- fees; and
- the declaration.[2]

It provides that in relation to the general description of the processing of personal information, each notification must include a general description of the processing of personal information being carried out.[3] On the register this description is structured by reference to the purposes for which data is being processed.[4]

---

1 *ICO Notification Handbook*, ICO, at https://ico.org.uk.
2 *Ibid*.
3 *Ibid*, section 3.1.5.
4 *Ibid*.

The ICO provides the following 'purpose' example registration details:

Provision of Financial Services and Advice

Data Subjects are:
- customers and clients;
- complainants, correspondents and enquirers; and
- advisers, consultants and other professional experts.

Data classes are:
- personal details;
- family, lifestyle and social circumstances;
- employment details;
- financial details; and
- goods or services provided.

Recipients are:
- Data Subjects themselves;
- relatives, guardians or other persons associated with the Data Subject;
- business associates and other professional advisers;
- financial organisations and advisers; and
- ombudsmen and regulatory authorities.

Transfers:
- none outside the EEA.

It also refers to example 'business' purposes, such as:

Staff administration

Appointments or removals, pay, discipline, superannuation, work management or other personnel matters in relation to the staff of the Controller.

Advertising, marketing and public relations

Advertising or marketing the Controller's own business, activity, goods or services, and promoting public relations in connection with that business or activity, or those goods or services.

Accounts and records

Keeping accounts relating to any business or other activity carried out by the Controller or deciding whether to accept any person as a customer or supplier or keeping records of purchases, sales or other transactions for the purpose of ensuring that the requisite payments and deliveries are made or services provided by them or to them in respect of those transactions, or for the purpose of making financial or management forecasts to assist them in the conduct of any such business or activity.[5]

---

5   *ICO Notification Handbook,* ICO, at https://ico.org.uk.

It also refers to examples of other purposes:

Accounting and auditing

The provision of accounting and related services; the provision of an audit where such an audit is required by statute.

Administration of justice

Internal administration and management of courts of law or tribunals and discharge of court business.

Administration of membership records

The administration of membership records.

Advertising, marketing and public relations for others

Public relations work, advertising and marketing, including host mailings for other organisations and list broking.

Assessment and collection of taxes and other revenue

Assessment and collection of taxes, duties, levies and other revenue. You will be asked to indicate the type of tax or other revenue concerned.

Benefits, grants and loans administration

The administration of welfare and other benefits. You will be asked to indicate the type(s) of benefit you are administering.

Canvassing political support amongst the electorate

The seeking and maintenance of support amongst the electorate by the Controller.

Constituency casework

The carrying out of casework on behalf of individual constituents by elected representatives.

Consultancy and advisory services

Giving advice or rendering professional services. The provision of services of an advisory, consultancy or intermediary nature. You will be asked to indicate the nature of the services which you provide.

Credit referencing

The provision of information relating to the financial status of individuals or organisations on behalf of other organisations. This purpose is for use by credit reference agencies, not for organisations who merely contact or use credit reference agencies.

Crime prevention and prosecution of offenders

Crime prevention and detection and the apprehension and prosecution of offenders. This includes the use of most CCTV systems which are used for this purpose.

Debt administration and factoring

The tracing of consumer and commercial debtors and the collection on behalf of creditors. The purchasing of consumer or trade debts, including rentals and instalment credit payments, from business.

Education

The provision of education or training as a primary function or as a business activity.

Fundraising

Fundraising in support of the objectives of the Controller.

Health administration and services

The provision and administration of patient care.

Information and databank administration

Maintenance of information or databanks as a reference tool or general resource. This includes catalogues, lists, directories and bibliographic databases.

Insurance administration

The administration of life, health, pensions, property, motor and other insurance business. This applies only to insurance companies doing risk assessments, payment of claims and underwriting. Insurance consultants and intermediaries should use the provision of financial services and advice purpose.

Journalism and media

Processing by the Controller of any journalistic, literary or artistic material made or intended to be made available to the public or any section of the public.

Legal services

The provision of legal services, including advising and acting on behalf of clients.

Licensing and registration

The administration of licensing or maintenance of official registers.

Pastoral care

The administration of pastoral care by a vicar or other minister of religion.

Pensions administration

The administration of funded pensions or superannuation schemes. Controllers using this purpose will usually be the trustees of pension funds.

Policing

The prevention and detection of crime; apprehension and prosecution of offenders; protection of life and property; maintenance of law and order; also rendering assistance to the public in accordance with force policies and procedures.

Private investigation

The provision on a commercial basis of investigatory services according to instruction given by clients.

Processing for not-for-profit organisations

Establishing or maintaining membership of or support for a body or association which is not established or conducted for profit, or providing or administering activities for individuals who are either members of the body or association or have regular contact with it.

An organisation that is a body or association not established or conducted for profit may be exempt from notification provided that the processing meets specific criteria. If you are a not-for-profit organisation, please call the notification helpline for guidance on whether the exemptions cover your organisation's processing.

Property management

The management and administration of land, property and residential property and the estate management of other organisations.

Provision of financial services and advice

The provision of services as an intermediary in respect of any financial transactions including mortgage and insurance broking.

Realising the objectives of a charitable organisation or voluntary body

The provision of goods and services in order to realise the objectives of the charity or voluntary body.

Research

Research in any field, including market, health, lifestyle, scientific or technical research. You will be asked to indicate the nature of the research undertaken.

Trading/sharing in personal information

The sale, hire, exchange or disclosure of personal information to third parties in return for goods/services/benefit.[6]

Examples of the general types or classes of personal data, and which must be designated in processes, are also provided, as follows:

C200: Personal details

Included in this category is any information that identifies the Data Subject and their personal characteristics. Examples are name, address, contact details, age, sex, date of birth, physical description, and any identifier issued by a public body, eg National Insurance number.

C201: Family, lifestyle and social circumstances

Included in this category is any information relating to the family of the Data Subject and the Data Subject's lifestyle and social circumstances. Examples are details about current marriage and partnerships and marital history, details of family and other household members, habits, housing, travel details, leisure activities and membership of charitable or voluntary organisations.

C202: Education and training details

Included in this category is any information which relates to the education and any professional training of the Data Subject. Examples are academic records, qualifications, skills, training records, professional expertise, and student and pupil records.

C203: Employment details

Included in this category is any information relating to the employment of the Data Subject. Examples are employment and career history, recruitment and termination details, attendance records, health and safety records, performance appraisals, training records and security records.

C204: Financial details

Included in this category is any information relating to the financial affairs of the Data Subject. Examples are income, salary, assets and investments, payments, creditworthiness, loans, benefits, grants, insurance details and pension information.

---

6   *ICO Notification Handbook*, section 3.1.8.

C205: Goods or services provided

Included in this category is any information relating to goods and services that have been provided. Examples are details of the goods or services supplied, licences issued, agreements and contracts.[7]

Sensitive personal data classes are also referenced, as follows:

C206: Racial or ethnic origin;

C207: Political opinions;

C208: Religious or other beliefs of a similar nature;

C209: Trade union membership;

C210: Physical or mental health or condition;

C211: Sexual life;

C212: Offences (including alleged offences);

C213: Criminal proceedings, outcomes and sentences.[8]

The recipient details must also be included, where the personal data is furnished to third parties. This is particularly so where it is proposed to make transfers outside the EEA.

The details and types of individual security measures must be described.

First Notification Regulations

10.06   Section 25 refers to the functions of ICO in relation to making of notification regulations.

Section 25(1) provides that as soon as practicable after the passing of the DPA, the ICO shall submit to the Secretary of State proposals as to the provisions to be included in the first notification regulations.

Section 25(2) provides that the ICO shall keep under review the working of notification regulations and may from time to time submit to the Secretary of State proposals as to amendments to be made to the regulations.

Section 25(3) provides that the Secretary of State may from time to time require the ICO to consider any matter relating to notification

---

7   *ICO Notification Handbook.*
8   *Ibid.*

regulations and to submit to them proposals as to amendments to be made to the regulations in connection with that matter.

Section 25(4) provides that before making any notification regulations, the Secretary of State shall: (a) consider any proposals made to them by the ICO under sub-s (2) or (3), and (b) consult the Commissioner.

Conclusion

10.07   The important things for organisations are to be aware of what classes of personal data are being collected, and for what purposes and to notify these as part of the registration process. Any time that changes occur, including adding data collections or anticipating additional new purposed, updated registration details must be furnished (and new consents if required). As highlighted above, organisations will need to consider any national law changes as may occur in future and which may affect, or change, the notification regime.

Chapter 11

Time Limits for Compliance

Introduction

11.01 There are various time limits referred to in the data protection regime for the accomplishment of particular tasks. Depending on the task at hand, non-compliance with a time limit could amount to a breach and or offence.

Time Limits

11.02 The DPA 1998 time limits include the following:

- an access request must be complied with within 40 calendar days;
- the Controller must reply within 21 days of receiving it to explain whether it is going to comply with the s 10 notice;
- under the DPA 1998, s 11 an individual can request the Controller to cease using personal information for direct marketing, including junk mail, sales calls, or email and text messages. The ICO states that in normal circumstances electronic communications should stop within 28 days of receiving the notice, and postal communications should stop within two months;
- credit files should be supplied in seven calendar days.

Official Information (FOI and Environmental Information Regulations)

11.03 Organisations must reply to a request for official information within 20 working days.

Data Breach Notification

Notification of a Data Breach to Supervisory Authority

11.04 The Controller shall without undue delay and, where feasible, not later than 72 hours after having become aware of it, notify the personal data breach to the supervisory authority (Article 33(1) GDPR).

Communication of a Data Breach to Data Subject

11.05 When the personal data breach is likely to result in a high risk to the rights and freedoms of individuals, the Controller shall communicate the personal data breach to the Data Subject without undue delay (Article 34(1) GDPR).[1]

Conclusion

11.06 When an organisation fails to comply within the required timeframe, this in itself is another breach. It may be taken into consideration by the ICO and or a court.

1 Note, for example, P Wainman, 'Data Protection Breaches: Today and Tomorrow,' SCL *Computers and Law*, 30 June 2012. Also see M Dekker, Dr, C Christoffer Karsberg and B Daskala, *Cyber Incident Reporting in the EU* (2012).

Chapter 12

Enforcement and Penalties for Non-Compliance

Introduction

12.01 There are a series of offences set out in the DPA 1998. These are designed to ensure compliance with the data protection regime, from registration to fair use of personal data. Organisations must fully comply with their obligations. In addition to questions arising in relation to their continued use of personal data if it has not been collected fairly, investigations, prosecutions and financial penalties can also arise.

Organisations can be fined up to £500,000 by the ICO for unwanted marketing phone calls and emails in accordance with the updated and amended PECR.

Offences by organisation can include:

- failure of a Controller to notify (s 1(1));
- failure to notify of changes to the notified entry details (s 21(2));
- processing before the expiration of assessable processing time limits or receipt of assessable processing notice within such time (s 22(6)).

The GDPR sets out significant amendments to the prosecution and fines regime (see below).

Breaches, Offences and Penalties

12.02 The DPA and the data protection regime set out the rules with which Controllers must obey. Breaches of these rules sometimes involve offences which are punishable by fines. The offences set out in the data protection regime include the following:

- offences by Controllers who are required to register (s 17 and 21(1));

- offences by any person who fails to comply with the duty imposed by notification regulations (s 21(2));
- offences by any Controllers (not just those who are required to register);
- offences by employees or agents of Controllers;
- offences by Processors who are required to register;
- offences by any Processors (not just those who are required to register);
- offences by directors, etc, of organisations (s 61);
- penalties for offences under the DPA 1998;
- offences by direct marketers;
- penalties for offences under PECR and PECR Amendments;
- offences for breach of assessment/assessment procedure (s 22(6));
- offences for not making information available (s 24(4));
- offences in relation to unlawfully obtaining, disclosing or procuring the disclosure or procuring the disclosure to another person of personal data (s 55);
- offences of selling personal data if unlawfully obtained, disclosed or procured the disclosure or procured the disclosure to another person of personal data (s 55(4) and (5)).

See ICO penalties, fines and prosecutions details below.

Criminal Offences

12.03   The organisation can commit criminal offences in relation to its data processing activities, namely:

- unlawful obtaining or disclosure of personal data;
- selling and offering to sell personal data;
- enforcing individual Data Subject access;
- disclosure of information;
- obstructing or failing to assist in the execution of a warrant;
- processing without a register entry;
- failing to notify changes regarding registration;
- carrying on assessable processing;
- failing to make certain particulars available;
- failing to comply with a notice;
- making a false statement in response to a notice.

Other Consequences of Breach

12.04   Some of the other consequences of a breach of the data protection regime include:

- offences can be committed by the organisation and its officers;
- processing focused offences;
- access related offences;
- offences for non-compliance with ICO and ICO related powers (eg enforcement notices; assessments; information notices; entry and inspection);
- being sued by individual Data Subjects;
- potentially being sued by rights based organisations and or class action type cases (eg Google re Apple; *DRI* case; *Schrems* case) and which cases are likely to increase under the GDPR;
- publicity of an unwanted nature.

Prohibition on Processing Without Registration under the DPA

12.05   Section 17 refers to the prohibition on processing without registration. Section 17(1) states that subject to the following provisions of this section, personal data must not be processed unless an entry in respect of the Controller is included in the register maintained by the Commissioner under s 19 (or is treated by notification regulations made by virtue of s 19(3) as being so included). Section17(2) states that except where the processing is assessable processing for the purposes of s 22, sub-s (1) does not apply in relation to personal data consisting of information which falls neither within paragraph (a) of the definition of 'data' in s 1(1) nor within paragraph (b) of that definition. Section 17(3) states that if it appears to the Secretary of State that processing of a particular description is unlikely to prejudice the rights and freedoms of Data Subjects, notification regulations may provide that, in such cases as may be prescribed, sub-s (1) is not to apply in relation to processing of that description. Section 17(4) states that sub-s (1) does not apply in relation to any processing whose sole purpose is the maintenance of a public register.

Offences under the DPA

Offence of Prohibition on Processing Without Registration (s 21)

12.06   Section 21 of the DPA 1998 refers to offences.

Section 21(1) provides that if s 17(1) (prohibition on processing without registration) is contravened, the Controller is guilty of an offence.

Section 21(2) provides that any person who fails to comply with the duty imposed by notification regulations made by virtue of s 20(1) is guilty of an offence.

Section 21(3) provides that it shall be a defence for a person charged with an offence under sub-s (2) to show that he exercised all due diligence to comply with the duty.

Accordingly, Controllers who keep personal data, without meeting their requirement to register are liable to be prosecuted.

However, it should be noted that section does not say 'all reasonable due diligence.' Therefore, it is arguable that the obligation on organisations is much higher. The legislators decided not to incorporate a reasonableness standard.

Offences for Breach of Assessment/Assessment Procedure (s 22)

12.07 Section 22 refers to preliminary assessment by the Commissioner. Section 22(1) provides that in this section 'assessable processing' means processing which is of a description specified in an order made by the Secretary of State as appearing to them to be particularly likely:

- to cause substantial damage or substantial distress to Data Subjects; or
- otherwise significantly to prejudice the rights and freedoms of Data Subjects.

The ICO will give a notice to the Controller stating the extent to which the ICO is of the opinion that the processing is likely or unlikely to comply with the provisions of the Act.

Section 22(5) provides that no assessable processing in respect of which a notification has been given to the Commissioner shall be carried on unless either:

- the period of 28 days beginning with the day on which the notification is received by the Commissioner (or, in a case falling within sub-s (4), that period as extended under that sub-section) has elapsed; or
- before the end of that period (or that period as so extended) the Controller has received a notice from the Commissioner under sub-s (3) in respect of the processing.

Section 22(6) provides that where sub-s (5) is contravened, the Controller is guilty of an offence.

Offences Regarding Not Making Information Available (s 23)

12.08   Section 23 refers to a power to make provision for appointment of data protection supervisors.

Section 24 refers to a duty of certain Controllers to make certain information available. Section 24(1) provides that subject to sub-s (3), where personal data are processed in a case where:

- by virtue of sub-s (2) or (3) of s 17, sub-s (1) of that section does not apply to the processing; and
- the Controller has not notified the relevant particulars in respect of that processing under s 18,

the Controller must, within twenty-one days of receiving a written request from any person, make the relevant particulars available to that person in writing free of charge. Section 24(4) provides that any Controller who fails to comply with the duty imposed by sub-s (1) is guilty of an offence.

Offences for Failure to Comply With Notices (s 47)

12.09   Section 40 of the DPA 1998 indicated that the ICO can issue enforcement notices to organisations when it feels the organisation is contravening the Data Protection Principles, specifying and requiring compliance. The ICO can also issue information notices to organisations requesting information or compliance under s 43. Section 44 also refers to special information notices.

Section 47(1) provides that there are offences for failure to comply with enforcement notices, information notices, and or special information notices.

Offence of Knowingly or Recklessly Making a False Statement (s 47)

12.10   Section 47(2) refers to an offence of knowingly or recklessly making a false statement in relation to an information notice or special information notice.

Offence of Obstruction

12.11   Schedule 9 refers to powers of entry and inspection and warrants. There are offences of intentional obstruction of, or failure to give reasonable assistance in the execution of a warrant (Sch 9, para 12).

Offence Regarding Unlawful Obtaining or Procuring Personal Data (s 55)

12.12   Section 55 provides that it is an offence for a person, knowingly or recklessly, without the consent of the Controller, to:

- obtain or disclose personal data or the information contained in personal data;
- procure the disclosure to another person of the information contained in personal data.

This refers to 'a person' and therefore includes directors, employees, agents and any other person.

In one case there was successful convictions regarding blagging and unlawful access to the personal data relating to tenants. The case involved Philip Campbell Smith, Adam Spears, Graham Freeman and Daniel Summers. Amongst other things, the ICO again called for custodial sentences for breach of the data protection regime. This was also a theme in the Leveson recommendations.

The ICO states:

> 'The Department for Work and Pensions hold important information about each and every one of us. We are very pleased that a DWP staff member was alert to this attempt to blag information and that the call was halted before it was too late. The motive behind Mr Braun's action was financial. He knew that such an underhand method of obtaining the tenant's personal information was illegal but carried on regardless. This case shows that unscrupulous individuals will continue to try and blag peoples' details until a more appropriate range of deterrent punishments is available to the courts. There must be no further delay in introducing tougher powers to enforce the Data Protection Act beyond the current "fine only" regime.'[1]

The ICO also said:

> 'The scourge of data theft continues to threaten the privacy rights of the UK population. Whilst we welcome today's sentencing of the private investigator, Graham Freeman, and his three accomplices, the outcome of the case underlines the need for a comprehensive approach to deterring information theft. If SOCA had been restricted to pursuing this case solely using their powers under the Data Protection Act then these individuals would have been faced with a small fine and would have been able to continue their activities the very next day. This is not good enough. Unscrupulous individuals will continue to try and obtain peoples' information through deception until there are strong

---

1   'Private Detectives Jailed for Blagging: ICO Statement,' ICO, 27 February 2012, at https://ico.org.uk.

punishments to fit the crime. We must not delay in getting a custodial sentence in place for section 55 offences under the Data Protection Act.'[2]

Record Offences (s 56)

12.13   Section 56 provides that it is an offence for a person to require another person or a third party to:

* supply them or her with a relevant record; or
* produce a relevant record to them,

in connection with,

* the recruitment of that other person as an employee;
* the continued employment of that other person;
* any contract for the provision of services to them by that other person; or
* where a person is concerned with providing (for payment or not) goods, facilities or services to the public or a sector of the public, as a condition of providing or offering to provide any goods, facilities or services to that other person.

Again, this refers to any person.
    There are exceptions to liability, such that:

* the imposition of the requirement was required or authorised by the law; or
* in particular circumstances the imposition of the requirements was justified as being in the public interest.

Offences by Direct Marketers under PECR

12.14   Offences arise in relation to activities referred to under PECR (as amended). These include:

* sending unsolicited marketing messages to individuals by fax, SMS, email or automated dialing machine;
* sending unsolicited marketing by fax, SMS, email or automated dialing machine to a business if it has objected to the receipt of such messages;
* marketing by telephone where the subscriber has objected to the receipt of such calls;
* failing to identify the caller or sender or failing to provide a physical address or a return e-mail address;

---

2   'Private Decectives Jailed for Blagging: ICO Statement,' ICO, 27 February 2012, at https://ico.org.uk.

- failing to give customers the possibility of objecting to future email and SMS marketing messages with each message sent;
- concealing the identity of the sender on whose behalf the marketing communication was made.

Fines can be significant. Organisations can be fined up to £500,000 by the ICO for unwanted marketing phone calls and emails in accordance with the updated amended PECR. It is also envisaged that fines will increase significantly in potential under the proposed GDPR.

The ICO imposes significant fines in relation to Spamming, including sometimes the promoters and directors of the company engaged in Spamming. Similar examples arise in relation to private investigation firms engaged in breaches. The types of instances where personal liability for breaches arise will continue to increase.

ICO Monetary Penalties

12.15 The ICO is also empowered under the Criminal Justice and Immigration Act 2008 (CJIA 2008) to impose penalties of a monetary variety. Section 77 of the CJIA 2008 provides power to alter penalties for unlawfully obtaining, etc, personal data, as follows:

(1) The Secretary of State may by order provide for a person who is guilty of an offence under s 55 of the DPA (unlawful obtaining, etc, of personal data) to be liable:
    (a) on summary conviction, to imprisonment for a term not exceeding the specified period or to a fine not exceeding the statutory maximum or to both;
    (b) on conviction on indictment, to imprisonment for a term not exceeding the specified period or to a fine or to both;
(2) In sub-s (1)(a) and (b) 'specified period' means a period provided for by the order but the period must not exceed:
    (a) in the case of summary conviction, 12 months (or, in Northern Ireland, 6 months); and
    (b) in the case of conviction on indictment, two years;
(3) The Secretary of State must ensure that any specified period for England and Wales which, in the case of summary conviction, exceeds 6 months is to be read as a reference to 6 months so far as it relates to an offence committed before the commencement of s 282(1) of the Criminal Justice Act 2003 (c. 44) (increase in sentencing powers of magistrates' courts from 6 to 12 months for certain offences triable either way);

(4) Before making an order under this section, the Secretary of State must consult:
    (a) the Information Commissioner;
    (b) such media organisations as the Secretary of State considers appropriate; and
    (c) such other persons as the Secretary of State considers appropriate;
(5) An order under this section may, in particular, amend the DPA.

See examples of some of the recent ICO fines and monetary penalties referred to below.

GDPR Changes re Fines and Prosecution

12.16 As noted above, the new GDPR sets out significant amendments to the prosecution and fines regime (see below).

Right to Compensation and Liability

12.17 Any person who has suffered material or non-material damage as a result of an infringement of the GDPR shall have the right to receive compensation from the Controller or Processor for the damage suffered (Article 82(1)).

Any Controller involved in processing shall be liable for the damage caused by the processing which infringes the GDPR specifically directed to Processors or where it has acted outside or contrary to lawful instructions of the Controller (Article 82(2)).

A Controller or Processor shall be exempted from liability in accordance with Article 78(2) if it proves that it has not in any way responsible for the event giving rise to the damage (Article 82(3)).

Where more than one Controller or Processor, or both a Controller and a Processor are involved in the same processing and where they are, in accordance with Article 82(2) and (3), responsible for any damage caused by the processing, each Controller or Processor shall be held liable for the entire damage in order to ensure effective compensation of the Data Subject (Article 82(4)).

Where a Controller or Processor has, in accordance with Article 82(4), paid full compensation for the damage suffered, that Controller or Processor shall be entitled to claim back from the other Controllers or Processors involved in the same processing that part of the compensation corresponding to their part of responsibility for the damage in accordance with the conditions set out in Article 82(2) (Article 82(5)).

Court proceedings for the right to receive compensation shall be brought before the courts competent under the law of the Member State referred to in Article 79(2).

Court proceedings against a Controller or Processor can be brought in the Member State where they are established or in the Member State where the Data Subject resides (Article 79(2)).

General Conditions for Imposing Administrative Fines

12.18   Each supervisory authority shall ensure that the imposition of administrative fines pursuant to this Article in respect of infringements of the GDPR referred to in Article 83(4), (5), (6) shall in each individual case be effective, proportionate and dissuasive (Article 83(1)).

Administrative fines shall, depending on the circumstances of each individual case, be imposed in addition to, or instead of, measures referred to in Article 58(2) (a) to (h) and (j). When deciding whether to impose an administrative fine and deciding on the amount of the administrative fine in each individual case due regard shall be given to the following:

- the nature, gravity and duration of the infringement taking into account the nature, scope or purpose of the processing concerned as well as the number of Data Subjects affected and the level of damage suffered by them;
- the intentional or negligent character of the infringement;
- any action taken by the Controller or Processor to mitigate the damage suffered by Data Subjects;
- the degree of responsibility of the Controller or Processor taking into account technical and organisational measures implemented by them pursuant to Articles 25 and 32;
- any relevant previous infringements by the Controller or Processor;
- the degree of co-operation with the supervisory authority, in order to remedy the infringement and mitigate the possible adverse effects of the infringement;
- the categories of personal data affected by the infringement;
- the manner in which the infringement became known to the supervisory authority, in particular whether, and if so to what extent, the Controller or Processor notified the infringement;
- where measures referred to in Article 58(2), have previously been ordered against the Controller or Processor concerned with regard to the same subject-matter, compliance with these measures;
- adherence to approved codes of conduct pursuant to Article 40 or approved certification mechanisms pursuant to Article 42; and
- any other aggravating or mitigating factor applicable to the circumstances of the case, such as financial benefits gained, or losses avoided, directly or indirectly, from the infringement (Article 83(2)).

If a Controller or Processor intentionally or negligently, for the same or linked processing operations, infringes several provisions of the GDPR, the total amount of the fine shall not exceed the amount specified for the gravest infringement (Article 83(3)).

Infringements of the following provisions shall, in accordance with Article 83(2), be subject to administrative fines up to 10,000,000 EUR, or in case of an undertaking, up to two percent of the total worldwide annual turnover of the preceding financial year, whichever is higher:

- the obligations of the Controller and the Processor pursuant to Articles 8, 11, 25, 39 and 42 and 43;
- the obligations of the certification body pursuant to Articles 42 and 43;
- the obligations of the monitoring body pursuant to Article 41(4) (Article 83(4)).

Infringements of the following provisions shall, in accordance with Article 83(2), be subject to administrative fines up to 20,000,000 EUR, or in case of an undertaking, up to four percent of the total worldwide annual turnover of the preceding financial year, whichever is higher:

- the basic principles for processing, including conditions for consent, pursuant to Articles 5, 6, 7 and 9;
- the Data Subjects' rights pursuant to Articles 12–22;
- the transfers of personal data to a recipient in a third country or an international organisation pursuant to Articles 44–49;
- any obligations pursuant to Member State laws adopted under Chapter IX;
- non-compliance with an order or a temporary or definitive limitation on processing or the suspension of data flows by the supervisory authority pursuant to Article 58(2) or failure to provide access in violation of Article 58(1) (Article 83(5)).

Non-compliance with an order by the supervisory authority as referred to in Article 58(2) shall, in accordance with Article 83(2), be subject to administrative fines up to 20,000,000 EUR, or in case of an undertaking, up to 4 percent of the total worldwide annual turnover of the preceding financial year, whichever is higher (Article 83(6)).

Without prejudice to the corrective powers of supervisory authorities pursuant to Article 58(2), each Member State may lay down the rules on whether and to what extent administrative fines may be imposed on public authorities and bodies established in that Member State (Article 83(7)).

The exercise by the supervisory authority of its powers under this Article shall be subject to appropriate procedural safeguards in conformity with EU law and Member State law, including effective judicial remedy and due process (Article 83(8)).

Where the legal system of the Member State does not provide for administrative fines, Article 83 may be applied in such a manner that the fine is initiated by the competent supervisory authority and imposed by competent national courts, while ensuring that those legal remedies are effective and have an equivalent effect to the administrative fines imposed by supervisory authorities. In any event, the fines imposed shall be effective, proportionate and dissuasive. Those Member States shall notify to the Commission those provisions of their laws which they adopt pursuant to Article 83 (Article 83(9)).

Penalties

12.19   Member States shall lay down the rules on penalties applicable to infringements of the GDPR in particular for infringements which are not subject to administrative fines pursuant to Article 83, and shall take all measures necessary to ensure that they are implemented. Such penalties shall be effective, proportionate and dissuasive (Article 84(1)).

Each Member State shall notify to the Commission the provisions of its law which it adopts pursuant to Article 84(1), by 25 May 2018 and, without delay, any subsequent amendment affecting them (Article 84(2)).

Civil Sanctions under the DPA

12.20   This is an area which will continue to expand in future. Individual Data Subjects can also sue for compensation under the DPA 1998. Where a person suffers damage as a result of a failure by a Controller or Processor to meet their data protection obligations, then the Controller or Processor may be subject to civil sanctions by the person affected. Damage suffered by a Data Subject will include damage to reputation, financial loss and mental distress.

Section 13 of the DPA 1998 provides as follows:

- An individual who suffers damage by reason of any contravention by a Controller of any of the requirements of the DPA is entitled to compensation from the Controller for that damage;
- An individual who suffers distress by reason of any contravention by a Controller of any of the requirements of the DPA is entitled to compensation from the Controller for that distress if,
  - the individual also suffers damage by reason of the contravention; or

○   the contravention relates to the processing of personal data for the special purposes.
- In proceedings brought against a person by virtue of this section it is a defence to prove that one had taken such care as in all the circumstances was reasonably required to comply with the requirement concerned.

While there are certain conditions, the primary clause refers to 'any contravention' by the organisation. In terms of the defence, in order to be able to avail of it, an organisation will have to establish that it has 'taken such care as in all the circumstances was reasonably required.' This will vary from organisation to organisation, sector to sector, the type of personal data involved, the risks of damage, loss, etc, the nature of the security risks, the security measures and procedures adopted, the history of risk, loss and damage in the organisation and sector.

Certain types of data will convey inherent additional risks over others, such as loss of financial personal data. This can be argued to require higher obligations for the organisation.

One interesting area to consider going forward is online damage, such as viral publication, defamation, bulletin boards, discussion forums and websites (or sections of websites), and social media websites. Where damage occurs as a result of misuse or loss of personal data or results in defamation, abuse and threats, liability could arise for the individual tortfeasors as well as the website.

While there are three eCommerce defences in the eCommerce Directive, one should recall that the data protection regime (and its civil rights, sanctions, duty of care and liability provisions) are separate and stand alone from the eCommerce Directive legal regime. Indeed, even in terms of the eCommerce defences one should also recall that: (a) an organisation must first fall within an eCommerce defence, and not lose that defence, in order to avail of it; and (b) there is no automatic entitlement to an internet service provider (ISP) or website to a global eCommerce defence, as in fact there in not one eCommerce defence but three specific defences relating to specific and technical activities. Not all or every ISP activity will fall into one of these defences. Neither will one activity fall into all three defences.

It is also possible to conceive of a website which has no take down procedures, inadequate take down defences, or non-expeditious take down procedures or remedies, and which will face potential liability under privacy and data protection as well as eCommerce liability. For example, an imposter social media profile which contains personal data and defamatory material could attract liability for the website operator under data protection, and under normal liability if none of the eCommerce defences were unavailable or were lost. The later could occur if, for example, the false impersonating profile was notified to the website (or it was otherwise aware) but it did not do anything.[3]

As indicated above, the issue of civil liability and litigation by Data Subjects to enforce their rights will continue. This will in part be fuelled by increased awareness but also by the increasingly publicised instances of data loss, data breach, damage and instances of abuse which involve personal data. The *Facebook Beacon* settlement, while in the US, for approx. $20 million emphasises the import of individuals seeking to vindicate their privacy and personal data rights. In the UK, while *Prudential* was fined £50,000, it is not inconceivable that loss, damage and financial loss may have ensued. Consider, further that this example appears to have related to a small number of individuals. However, what if thousands of customer suffered financial loss, damage, stress, delay, missed payments, lost flights, lost contracts, etc, as a result of mixing up files, not completing files and transactions. These are all things which can occur, whether through process errors or software glitches. This is not at all far-fetched, as customers of RBS bank will confirm. Google was also sued re Apple breach.

While we are well aware of the press phone hacking scandal, the Leveson Inquiry and the ensuing litigation from many victims, as well as there being admissions, interception offences, etc, there are also personal data breach and data protection civil liability issues arising.

Director Liability and Offences

12.21 The potential for personal liability (DPA 1998, s 61) is also a significant issue for an organisation and those within positions of authority where the organisation is involved in offences.

Employees can also be liable for offences if they obtain, disclose or procure the personal data in the organisation for their own purposes.

Section 61 of the DPA 1998 refers to liability of directors, etc. Section 61(1) provides that where an offence under this Act has been committed by a body corporate and is proved to have been committed with the consent or connivance of or to be attributable to any neglect on the part of any director, manager, secretary or similar officer of the body corporate or any person who was purporting to act in any such capacity, he as well as the body corporate shall be guilty of that offence and be liable to be proceeded against and punished accordingly.

Section 61(2) provides that where the affairs of a body corporate are managed by its members sub-s (1) shall apply in relation to the acts and

---

3 This is a complex and developing area of law, common law, civil law, Directive, GDPR and case law, both in the UK and internationally. A full detailed analysis is beyond this current work.

defaults of a member in connection with his functions of management as if he were a director of the body corporate.

Section 61(3) provides that where an offence under the DPA 1998 has been committed by a Scottish partnership and the contravention in question is proved to have occurred with the consent or connivance of, or to be attributable to any neglect on the part of, a partner, he as well as the partnership shall be guilty of that offence and shall be liable to be proceeded against and punished accordingly.

One interesting case involves using initials in case names.[4]

Offences by Processors

12.22 Processors can also commit offences. These include:

- failure of a Processor to register;
- failure to notify the ICO of changes and change of address;
- provision of false or misleading information when applying for registration;
- failure to comply with notices;
- disclosure of personal data without authorisation of Controller.

Judicial Remedies, Liability and Sanctions under the DPD

Courts

12.23 Chapter III of the DPD refers to judicial remedies, liability and sanctions. Article 22 refers to remedies. It provides that without prejudice to any administrative remedy for which provision may be made, inter alia before the supervisory authority referred to in Article 28, prior to referral to the judicial authority, Member States shall provide for the right of every person to a judicial remedy for any breach of the rights guaranteed them by the national law applicable to the processing in question.

---

4   In a data protection related case in Berlin, not only was the company sued but the directors were also personally named and included in the case. One of the reasons specified was to ensure that the directors made sure that the Board of the company made the appropriate amendments to ensure the breaches were rectified and would not re-occur. A further interesting aspect of the case is that while the directors were included personally, their names were redacted to initials. One such set of initials was 'MZ'. See *The Federal Association of Consumer Organisations and Consumer Groups, Federal Consumer Association, GB v Facebook Ireland Limited, MA, JB, DG, PT and the Chairman MZ*, [names redacted], [redacted] Reach, [redacted] Quay, Dublin, Ireland.

Damages and Compensation

12.24 Article 23 of the DPD refers to liability. Article 23(1) provides that Member States shall provide that any person who has suffered damage as a result of an unlawful processing operation or of any act incompatible with the national provisions adopted pursuant to the Directive is entitled to receive compensation from the Controller for the damage suffered. Article 23(2) provides that the Controller may be exempted from this liability, in whole or in part, if he proves that he is not responsible for the event giving rise to the damage.

The increase in profiling, advertising and marketing, as well as the separate issue of online abuse, will continue to increase the potential instances where damages and compensation will arise.

Sanctions

12.25 Article 24 of the DPD refers to sanctions. It provides that the Member States shall adopt suitable measures to ensure the full implementation of the provisions of the Directive and shall in particular lay down the sanctions to be imposed in case of infringement of the provisions adopted pursuant to the Directive.

Remedies, Liability and Penalties under the GDPR

12.26 Chapter VIII refers to remedies, liability and penalties regarding data protection.

Right to Lodge Complaint with Supervisory Authority

12.27 Without prejudice to any other administrative or judicial remedy, every Data Subject shall have the right to lodge a complaint with a supervisory authority, in particular in the Member State their habitual residence, place of work or place of the alleged infringement if the Data Subject considers that the processing of personal data relating to them does not comply with the GDPR (Article 77(1)).

The supervisory authority with which the complaint has been lodged shall inform the complainant on the progress and the outcome of the complaint including the possibility of a judicial remedy pursuant to Article 78 (Article 77(2)).

Right to Judicial Remedy against Supervisory Authority

12.28 Without prejudice to any other administrative or non-judicial remedy, each natural or legal person shall have the right to an effective judicial remedy against a legally binding decision of a supervisory authority concerning them (Article 74(1)).

The supervisory authority with which the complaint has been lodged shall inform the complainant on the progress and the outcome of the complaint including the possibility of a judicial remedy pursuant to Article 78 (Article 77(2)).

Right to an Effective Judicial Remedy Against Controller or Processor

12.29   Without prejudice to any available administrative or non-judicial remedy, including the right to lodge a complaint with a supervisory authority under Article 77, each Data Subject shall have the right to an effective judicial remedy if they consider that their rights under this GDPR have been infringed as a result of the processing of their personal data in non-compliance with the GDPR (Article 79(1)).

Proceedings against a Controller or a Processor shall be brought before the courts of the Member State where the Controller or Processor has an establishment. Alternatively, such proceedings may be brought before the courts of the Member State where the Data Subject has his or her habitual residence, unless the Controller or Processor is a public authority of a Member State acting in the exercise of its public powers (Article 79(2)).

Representation of Data Subjects

12.30   The Data Subject shall have the right to mandate a not-for-profit body, organisation or association, which has been properly constituted according to the law of a Member State, has statutory objectives are in the public interest, and is active in the field of the protection of Data Subjects' rights and freedoms with regard to the protection of their personal data to lodge the complaint on their behalf, to exercise the rights referred to in Articles 77, 78 and 79 on their behalf and to exercise the right to receive compensation referred to in Article 82 on their behalf where provided for by Member State law (Article 80(1)).

Member States may provide that any body, organisation or association referred to in Article 80(1), independently of a Data Subject's mandate, has the right to lodge in that Member State, a complaint with the supervisory authority competent which is competent pursuant to Article 77 and to exercise the rights referred to in Articles 78 and 79 if it considers that the rights of a Data Subject have been infringed as a result of the processing (Article 80(2)).

Suspension of Proceedings

12.31   Where a competent court of a Member State has information on proceedings, concerning the same subject matter as regards processing by the same Controller or Processor, that are pending in a court in another Member State, it shall contact that court in the other Member State to confirm the existence of such proceedings (Article 81(1)).

Where proceedings concerning the same subject matter as regards processing by the same Controller or Processor are pending in a court in another Member State, any competent court other than the court first seized may suspend its proceedings (Article 81(2)).

Where those proceedings are pending at first instance, any court other than the court first seized may also, on the application of one of the parties, decline jurisdiction if the court first seized has jurisdiction over the actions in question and its law permits the consolidation thereof (Article 81(3)).

Right to Compensation and Liability

12.32 Person who has suffered damage as a result of an infringement of the GDPR shall have the right to receive compensation from the Controller or Processor for the damage suffered (Article 82(1)). (See para **12.17** above for more particular details.)

General Conditions for Imposing Administrative Fines

12.33 An organisation can have fines and penalties imposed for non-compliance. The fines regime is significantly updated under the new data protection regime. In particular the level of fines and penalties are increased. See para **12.18** above for further details.

Penalties

12.34 Member States shall lay down the rules on penalties applicable to infringements of the GDPR in particular for infringements which are not subject to administrative fines. Further details are referred to in para **12.19** above.

Fines and Remedy Levels

12.35 Article 83 relates to administrative fine sanctions. Each supervisory authority is empowered to impose administrative fines, which are meant to be effective, proportionate and dissuasive, and include reference to the nature, gravity and duration of the breach, amongst other factors.

Certain fines can be up to 10,000,000 EUR (or equivalent), or in case of an enterprise up to two percent of its annual worldwide turnover, whichever is higher. Other fines can amount to 20,000,000 EUR (or equivalent) or four percent of turnover, whichever is higher. Further details are referred to in para **12.18** above.

Powers and Functions of the ICO

12.36 The ICO has a number of registration, promotion, investigation and enforcement powers and functions under the DPA 1998. These include:

- the obligation to check each application for registration;
- to assess whether especially risky or dangerous types of processing are involved;
- to prepare and publish codes of practice for guidance in applying data protection law in particular areas;
- cases;
- investigations;
- complaints;
- audits;
- fines.

Preliminary Assessment

12.37 Section 22 refers to preliminary assessment by the ICO. Section 22(1) provides that in the section 'assessable processing' means processing which is of a description specified in an order made by the Secretary of State as appearing to them to be particularly likely:

- to cause substantial damage or substantial distress to Data Subjects; or
- otherwise significantly to prejudice the rights and freedoms of Data Subjects.

Section 22(2) provides that on receiving notification from any Controller under s 18 or under notification regulations made by virtue of s 20 the ICO shall consider:

- whether any of the processing to which the notification relates is assessable processing, and
- if so, whether the assessable processing is likely to comply with the provisions of the Act.

Section 22(3) provides that subject to sub-s (4), the ICO shall, within the period of twenty-eight days beginning with the day on which he receives a notification which relates to assessable processing, give a notice to the Controller stating the extent to which the ICO is of the opinion that the processing is likely or unlikely to comply with the provisions of the DPA 1998.

Section 22(4) provides that before the end of the period referred to in sub-s (3) the ICO may, by reason of special circumstances, extend that period on one occasion only by notice to the Controller by such further period not exceeding fourteen days as the ICO may specify in the notice.

Section 22(5) provides that no assessable processing in respect of which a notification has been given to the ICO as mentioned in sub-s (2) shall be carried on unless either:

- the period of 28 days beginning with the day on which the notification is received by the ICO (or, in a case falling within sub-s (4), that period as extended under that sub-section) has elapsed, or
- before the end of that period (or that period as so extended) the Controller has received a notice from the ICO under sub-s (3) in respect of the processing.

Section 22(6) provides that where sub-s (5) is contravened, the Controller is guilty of an offence.

Section 22(7) provides that the Secretary of State may by order amend sub-s (3), (4) and (5) by substituting for the number of days for the time being specified there a different number specified in the order.

Financial Penalties

12.38 The ICO can issue monetary penalty notices or fines.[5] This is where serious breaches occur which are deliberate and with knowledge or where there ought to be knowledge of the breach and of the likely damage. This is in accordance with the ICO's powers as per the Criminal Justice and Immigration Act of 2008. Organisations can be fined up to £500,000 by the ICO for unwanted marketing phone calls and emails in accordance with the updated amended PECR.

Inspections

12.39 The ICO may also undertake inspections of organisations. This is where the ICO suspects that there may be a breach of the DPA and it obtains a warrant to search the organisational premises. In such an instance the ICO may enter, search, inspect, examine, test equipment, inspect and seize documents, materials, etc. Obstructing such an inspection will be a criminal offence. Legal advices should be immediately sought in relation to such incidents.

---

5   In accordance with the powers of the ICO under the Criminal Justice and Immigration Act 2008.

Data Protection Supervisors under the DPA

12.40 Section 23 refers to a power to make provision for appointment of data protection supervisors.

Section 23(1) provides that the Secretary of State may by order:

- make provision under which a Controller may appoint a person to act as a data protection supervisor responsible in particular for monitoring in an independent manner the Controller's compliance with the provisions of the DPA; and
- provide that, in relation to any Controller who has appointed a data protection supervisor in accordance with the provisions of the order and who complies with such conditions as may be specified in the order, the provisions of this Part are to have effect subject to such exemptions or other modifications as may be specified in the order.

Section 23(2) provides that an order under the section may:

- impose duties on data protection supervisors in relation to the ICO; and
- confer functions on the ICO in relation to data protection supervisors.

Section 24 refers to a duty of certain Controllers to make certain information available.

Section 24(1) provides that subject to sub-s (3), where personal data are processed in a case where:

(a) by virtue of subs-s (2) or (3) of s 17, sub-s (1) of that section does not apply to the processing; and

(b) the Controller has not notified the relevant particulars in respect of that processing under s 18,

the Controller must, within 21 days of receiving a written request from any person, make the relevant particulars available to that person in writing free of charge.

Section 24(2) provides that in the section 'the relevant particulars' means the particulars referred to in paragraphs (a) to (f) of s 16(1).

Section 24(3) provides that the section has effect subject to any exemption conferred for the purposes of the section by notification regulations.

Section 24(4) provides that any Controller who fails to comply with the duty imposed by sub-s (1) is guilty of an offence.

Section 24(5) provides that it shall be a defence for a person charged with an offence under sub-s (4) to show that he exercised all due diligence to comply with the duty.

ICO Data Enforcement, Loss/Data Breaches, Fines and Convictions

12.41

Issue	Date	Party	Breach	Penalty
Data breach. Unlawful disclosure	4 May 2016	Blackpool Teaching Hospitals NHS Foundation Trust	Inadvertently published online workers' confidential data including their National Insurance number, date of birth, religious belief and sexual orientation.	£185,000
Nuisance calls	27 April 2016	Nevis Home Improvements Ltd	2.5 million recorded phone calls.	£50,000
Data breach/ Unlawful disclosure	21 April 2016	Chief Constable of Kent Police	Fined after sensitive personal details of woman who accused her partner of domestic abuse passed to the suspect.	£80,000
Trying to buy data without consent.	7 April 2016	David Barlow Lewis	Former LV employee David Barlow Lewis prosecuted at Bournemouth Magistrates' Court for attempting to commit a s 55 offence, by attempting to obtain personal data without the controller's consent. Pleaded guilty to trying to get an existing LV employee to sell him customer data.	Prosecution and fine.
Failure to comply with notice	5 April 2016	Keurboom Communications Limited and director Gregory Rudd	Both prosecuted at Luton Magistrates' Court for failing to comply with a third party information notice issued by the Commissioner in relation to an investigation for PECR breaches. The communication company pleaded guilty to the s 47 offence.	Prosecution of company and directors. Company fined £1,500, plus costs and director fined £1,000
Nuisance calls with fake number	1 April 2016	Advice Direct Ltd	Fined by ICO.	£20,000

Issue	Date	Party	Breach	Penalty
Failure to comply with breach notification rules	24 March 2016	TalkTalk Telecom Group Plc	Data breach and failure to comply with breach notification rules. Privacy and Electronic Communications (EC Directive) Regulations 2003.	£1,000 per reg 5C(2) of PECR
Nuisance calls	17 March 2016	FEP Heatcare	Spam calls. 2.6 m calls.	£180,000
Access request	29 March 2016	MI Wealth Management Ltd	Failure to comply with access request	Ordered to comply
Security of data	10 March 2016	Chief Constable Wiltshire Constabulary	Investigation file lost. Data breach.	Undertaking to comply with Seventh Principle
Nuisance calls	29 February 2016	Prodial Ltd	Spam calls. 46m calls.	£350,000
Spam texts	22 November 2015	UKMS Money Solutions Ltd (UKMS)	Spamming. 1.3m Spam texts.	£80,000
Spam calls	10 November 2015	Oxygen Ltd	Unsolicited automated marketing calls.	£120,000
Stolen laptops	4 November 2015	Crown Prosecution Service (CPS)	Stolen laptops with police interview videos of victims and witnesses, mostly for ongoing violent or sexual type cases.	£200,000
Spam texts	27 October 2015	Help Direct UK Ltd	Unsolicited marketing text messages.	£200,000
	20 October 2015	Pharmacy 2U Ltd	Online pharmacy sold details of more than 20,000 customers to marketing companies. No Consent. No notification to customers.	£130,000
Information notice	8 October 2015	Nuisance Call Blocker Ltd	Failing to respond to information notice.	Prosecuted
Automated marketing calls	30 September 2015	Home Energy & Lifestyle Management Ltd (HELM)	6m automated marketing calls. Breach of marketing call regulations.	£200,000
Unsolicited marketing calls	16 September 2015	Cold Call Elimination Ltd	Unsolicited marketing calls.	£75,000

Issue	Date	Party	Breach	Penalty
Enforcement notice Right to be Forgotten.	20 August 2015	Google Inc	Ordered to remove nine search results after ICO ruled the information linked was no longer relevant.	Enforcement notice
Nuisance calls	10 August 2015	Point One Marketing Ltd (previously Conservo Digital Ltd)	Nuisance calls.	£50,000
Lost data	6 August 2015	The Money Shop	Loss of computer equipment with significant amount of customer details.	£180,000
Non-notification	4 August 2015	Consumer Claims Solutions Ltd	Personal injury claims telemarketing company.	Prosecution. Guilty plea to the s17 non-notification offence
Loss of unencrypted DVDs	18 May 2015	South Wales Police	Fine for losing a video recording which formed part of the evidence in a sexual abuse case. Despite containing a graphic and disturbing account, DVDs were unencrypted and left in a desk drawer.	£160,000
Non-notification	16 April 2015	Lismore Recruitment Ltd	Failing to notify with the ICO.	Prosecution. Guilty plea
Spam calls	1 April 2015	Direct Assist Ltd	Direct marketing calls to people without their consent.	£80,000
Unauthorised disclosure	30 March 2015	Serious Fraud Office	Witness in a serious fraud, bribery and corruption investigation mistakenly sent evidence relating to 64 other people in case.	£180,000
Spam texts	24 March 2015	Sweet Media Ltd	Enforcement notice to stop sending nuisance Spam texts. ICO raid. SIM cards and computers seized. Sent over 4.5m texts.	Enforcement notice
Spam texts	17 March 2015	Help Direct UK	Order to stop Spam texts.	Enforcement notice

Issue	Date	Party	Breach	Penalty
Unlawful access	12 March 2015	Yasir Manzoor	Former customer service assistant at Lloyds Banking Group prosecuted for unlawfully accessing a former partner's bank account.	Prosecution
Unlawful access	26 February 2015	Bernard Fernandes	Former support clerk at Transport for London prosecuted for unlawfully accessing the oyster card records of family and neighbours.	Prosecution
Hack Security Breach	24 February 2015	Staysure.co.uk Ltd	IT security failings let hackers access customer records. More than 5,000 customers had their credit cards used by fraudsters after the attack on the online holiday insurance company. Hackers potentially accessed over 100,000 live credit card details, and customers' medical details. Credit card CVV numbers were also accessible despite industry rules that they should not be stored at all.	£175,000
Privacy Policy	30 January 2015	Google Inc	Google Inc signs undertaking committing to making further changes to its amalgamated Privacy Policy in order to ensure compliance with the first principle of DPA 1998.	Privacy Policy
Failure to respond to information notice	6 January 2015	Tivium Ltd	Failure to respond to information notice.	Prosecution. Fined £5000, plus compensation plus costs.
Spam texts	6 January 2015	Optical Express (Westfield) Ltd	Enforcement notice to stop Spam texts.	Enforcement notice

Issue	Date	Party	Breach	Penalty
Spam calls	27 December 2014	Kwik Fix Plumbers Ltd	Nuisance Spam calls targeting vulnerable victims. In several cases, the calls resulted in elderly people being tricked into paying for boiler insurance they did not need.	£90,000
Failure to report breach	19 December 2014	Vodafone	Failure to comply with the personal data breach reporting requirements under the Privacy and Electronic Communications (EC Directive) Regulations 2003.	£1,000
Spam texts	5 December 2014	Parklife Manchester Ltd	Unsolicited marketing texts. Text sent to 70,000 people bought tickets to last year's event, and appeared on recipients' mobile phone as sent by 'Mum'.	70,000
Enforcement notice Data breach	19 November 2014	Grampian Health Board (NHS Grampian)	ICO ordered NHS Grampian to ensure patients' information better protected. Six data breaches in 13 months where papers containing sensitive personal data were left abandoned in public areas of a hospital. In one case the data was found at a local supermarket.	Enforcement notice
Unlawful access	13 November 2014	Harkanwarjit Dhanju	Former West Sussex Primary Care Trust pharmacist prosecuted for unlawfully accessing medical records of family members, work colleagues and local health professionals.	Prosecution
Spam calls	12 November 2014	Hot House Roof Company	Enforcement notice to stop Spam calls.	Enforcement notice

Issue	Date	Party	Breach	Penalty
Company director	11 November 2014	Matthew Devlin	Company director Matthew Devlin fined after illegally accessing Everything Everywhere's (EE) customer database, to target them with services of his own telecoms companies.	Prosecution
Hack Security Breach	5 November 2014	Worldview Ltd	Serious data breach when vulnerability on company's site allowed hackers to access full payment card details of 3,814 customers.	£7,500
Spam email	21 October 2014	Abdul Tayub	Enforcement notice. Sending unsolicited marketing mail by electronic means without providing information as to his identity and without prior consent.	Enforcement notice
Spam calls	1 October 2014	EMC Advisory Services Ltd	Spam calls. Also failure to ensure persons registered with Telephone Preference Service (TPS), or who previously asked not to be contacted, were not called.	£70,000
Spam email	12 September 2014	All Claims Marketing Ltd	Enforcement notice. Spam email and without providing information as to its identity.	Enforcement notice
Spam calls	3 September 2014	Winchester and Deakin Limited (also trading as Rapid Legal and Scarlet Reclaim)	Enforcement notice. Spam calls. Included calls to people who had registered with the Telephone Preference Service (TPS), or who had asked not to be contacted.	Enforcement notice
Breach	24 August 2014	Ministry of Justice	Serious failings in the way prisons handed people's information.	£180,000
Unlawful access	22 August 2014	Dalvinder Singh	Santander banker fined for reading 11 colleagues' bank accounts, to see their salary and bonuses.	Prosecution

Issue	Date	Party	Breach	Penalty
Failure to notify with ICO	6 August 2014	A Plus Recruitment Limited	Failure to notify with ICO.	Prosecution
Failure to notify with ICO	5 August 2014	1st Choice Properties (SRAL)	Failure to notify with ICO.	Prosecution
Spam calls	28 July 2014	Reactiv Media Ltd	Spam calls. Calls to people who registered with Telephone Preference Service (TPS).	£50,000
Hack Security Breach	23 July 2014	Think W3 Limited	Online travel services company. Serious breach of DPA 1998. Thousands of people's data accessed by hacker.	£150,000
Company owner Failure to notify ICO of changes to his notification	15 July 2014	Jayesh Shah	Owner of a marketing company (Vintels) prosecuted for failing to notify ICO of changes to his notification.	Prosecution. Fined £4000, plus costs and victim surcharge
Failure to notify with ICO	14 July 2014	Hayden Nash Consultants	Recruitment company. Failure to notify with ICO.	Prosecution
Unlawful access Unlawful sale	10 July 2014	Stephen Siddell	Former branch manager for Enterprise Rent-A-Car prosecuted for unlawfully stealing the records of almost two thousand customers and selling them to a claims management company.	Prosecution
Failure to notify with ICO	9 July 2014	Global Immigration Consultants Ltd	Failure to notify with ICO.	Prosecution.
Spam calls	16 June 2014	DC Marketing Ltd	Enforcement notice. Spam calls.	Enforcement notice
Director Failure to notify with ICO	6 June 2014	Darren Anthony Bott	Director of pensions review company prosecuted for failure to notify with ICO.	Prosecution. Guilty plea
Failure to comply with information notice	5 June 2014	API Telecom	Failure to comply with information notice.	Prosecution

Issue	Date	Party	Breach	Penalty
Unlawful disclosure	29 May 2014	Wolverhampton City Council	Investigation into a data breach at the council that occurred in January 2012, when a social worker who had not received data protection training, sent a report to a former service user detailing their time in care. The social worker failed to remove highly sensitive information about the recipient's sister that should not have been included.	Enforcement notice
Failure to notify with ICO	13 May 2014	QR Lettings	Failure to notify with ICO.	Prosecution
Failure to notify with ICO	25 April 2014	Allied Union Ltd	Failure to notify with ICO.	Prosecution
Spam calls	3 April 2014		Unsolicited Spam calls to people who registered with Telephone Preference Service (TPS).	£50,000
Failure to notify with ICO	25 March 2014	Help Direct UK Ltd	Failure to notify with ICO.	Prosecution
Security Unlawful access	19 March 2014	Kent Police	Highly sensitive and confidential information, including copies of police interview tapes, were left in a basement at the former site of a police station.	£100,000
Directors and company Failure to notify with ICO	12 March 2014	Boilershield Limited	Failure to notify with ICO.	Prosecution. Both fined £1,200, plus costs and surcharge
Failure to notify with ICO	11 March 2014	Becoming Green (UK) Ltd	Failure to notify with ICO.	Prosecution
Spam calls	10 March 2014	Isisbyte Limited	Enforcement notice, Spam calls.	Enforcement notice
Spam calls	10 March 2014	SLM Connect Limited	Enforcement notice. Spam calls.	Enforcement notice

Issue	Date	Party	Breach	Penalty
Hack Security Breach	7 March 2014	British Pregnancy Advice Service (BPAS)	Hacker threatened to publish thousands of names of people who sought advice on abortion, pregnancy and contraception.	£200,000
Blagging	24 January 2014	ICU Investigations Ltd	Blagging. Six men who were part of a company that tricked organisations into revealing personal details about customers has today been sentenced for conspiring to breach the DPA.	Prosecution
Security Unlawful disclosure	11 January 2014	Department of Justice Northern Ireland	A monetary penalty notice has been served on Department of Justice Northern Ireland after a filing cabinet containing details of a terrorist incident was sold at auction.	£185,000
Spam texts	16 December 2013	First Financial (UK) Ltd	Millions of Spam texts.	£175,000
Security. Unlawful disclosure No encryption	29 October 2013	North East Lincolnshire Council	Loss of an unencrypted memory device containing personal data and sensitive personal data relating to 286 children.	£80,000
Security Unlawful disclosure	22 October 2013	Ministry of Justice	Failure to keep personal data securely, after spreadsheets showing prisoners' details were emailed to members of the public in error.	£140,000
Data breach	2 January 2013	Sony	Hack breach	£250,000
Unlawful access Customer financial data Bank employee	6 November 2012	Lara Davies	Bank employee obtained unlawfully access to bank statements of her partner's ex-wife. Court prosecution. Pleaded guilty to 11 DPA offences.	Court conviction. Fined. Lost job.

Issue	Date	Party	Breach	Penalty
Spam	28 November 2012	Christopher Niebel and Gary McNeish, joint owners of Tetrus Telecoms	An ICO monetary penalty was issued. The company had sent millions of unlawful spam texts to the public over the past three years. This case involved the prosecution of Directors.	£300,000 £140,000
Data Loss/ Data Breach Unlawful disclosure Sensitive data	22 November 2012	Plymouth City Council	An ICO monetary penalty issued for a serious breach of the seventh data protection principle. A social worker sent part of a report relating to family A, to family B due to printing issues. The photocopied report contained confidential and highly sensitive personal data relating to the two parents and their four children, including of allegations of child neglect in on-going care proceedings.	£60,000
Incorrect storage and processing Potential loss and damage Financial institution	6 November 2012	Prudential	An ICO monetary penalty issued after a mix-up over the administration of two customers' accounts led to tens of thousands of pounds, meant for an individual's retirement fund, ending up in the wrong account. This was the first case in relation to a fine for incorrect storage and processing.	£50,000
Data Loss/ Data Breach Unlawful disclosure Sensitive data	25 October 2012	Stoke-on-Trent City Council	An ICO monetary penalty issued following a serious breach of the Data Protection Act that led to sensitive information about a child protection legal case being emailed to the wrong person.	£120,000

Issue	Date	Party	Breach	Penalty
Data Loss/ Data Breach Police	16 October 2012	Greater Manchester Police	An ICO monetary penalty issued after the theft of a memory stick containing sensitive personal data from an officer's home. The device, which had no password protection, contained details of more than a thousand people with links to serious crime investigations.	£150,000
Data Loss/ Data Breach Charity	10 October 2012	Norwood Ravenswood Ltd	An ICO monetary penalty issued after highly sensitive information about the care of four young children was lost after being left outside a London home. This was a charity which was fined.	£70,000
Data Loss/ Data Breach	11 September 2012	Scottish Borders Council	An ICO monetary penalty issued after former employees' pension records were found in an over-filled paper recycle bank in a supermarket car park.	£250,000
Unlawful disclosure Sensitive data	6 August 2012	Torbay Care Trust	An ICO monetary penalty issued after sensitive personal information relating to 1,373 employees was published on the Trust's website.	£175,000
Unlawful disclosure Sensitive data	12 July 2012	St George's Healthcare NHS Trust	An ICO monetary penalty issued after a vulnerable individual's sensitive medical details were sent to the wrong address.	£60,000
Data Loss/ Data Breach	5 July 2012	Welcome Financial Services Ltd	An ICO monetary penalty issued following a serious breach of the Data Protection Act. The breach led to the personal data of more than half a million customers being lost.	£150,000

Issue	Date	Party	Breach	Penalty
Data Loss/ Data Breach Sensitive data	19 June 2012	Belfast Health and Social Care Trust	An ICO monetary penalty issued following a serious breach of the Data Protection Act. The breach led to the sensitive personal data of thousands of patients and staff being compromised. The Trust also failed to report the incident to the ICO.	£225,000
Unlawful disclosure Sensitive data	6 June 2012	Telford & Wrekin Council	An ICO monetary penalty issued for two serious breaches of the seventh data protection principle. A Social Worker sent a core assessment report to the child's sibling instead of the mother. The assessment contained confidential and highly sensitive personal data. Whilst investigating the first incident, a second incident was reported to the ICO involving the inappropriate disclosure of foster carer names and addresses to the children's mother. Both children had to be re-homed.	£90,000
Unlawful disclosure Sensitive data Security	1 June 2012	Brighton and Sussex University Hospitals NHS Trust	An ICO monetary penalty issued following the discovery of highly sensitive personal data belonging to tens of thousands of patients and staff – including some relating to HIV and Genito Urinary Medicine patients – on hard drives sold on an Internet auction site in October and November 2010.	£325,000

Issue	Date	Party	Breach	Penalty
Unlawful disclosure Sensitive data	21 May 2012	Central London Community Healthcare NHS Trust	An ICO monetary penalty issued for a serious contravention of the DPA, which occurred when sensitive personal data was faxed to an incorrect and unidentified number. The contravention was repeated on 45 occasions over a number of weeks and compromised 59 Data Subjects' personal data.	£90,000
Data Loss/ Data Breach Sensitive data	15 May 2012	London Borough of Barnet	An ICO monetary penalty issued following the loss of sensitive information relating to 15 vulnerable children or young people, during a burglary at an employee's home.	£70,000
Unlawful disclosure Sensitive data	30 April 2012	Aneurin Bevan Health Board	An ICO monetary penalty issued following an incident where a sensitive report – containing explicit details relating to a patient's health – was sent to the wrong person.	£70,000
Unlawful disclosure Sensitive data	14 March 2012	Lancashire Constabulary	An ICO monetary penalty issued following the discovery of a missing person's report containing sensitive personal information about a missing 15 year old girl.	£70,000
Unlawful disclosure Sensitive data	15 February 2012	Cheshire East Council	An ICO monetary penalty issued after an email containing sensitive personal information about an individual of concern to the police was distributed to 180 unintended recipients.	£80,000
Data Loss/ Data Breach Sensitive data	13 February 2012	Croydon Council	An ICO monetary penalty issued after a bag containing papers relating to the care of a child sex abuse victim was stolen from a London pub.	£100,000

Issue	Date	Party	Breach	Penalty
Unlawful disclosure Sensitive data	13 February 2012	Norfolk County Council	An ICO monetary penalty issued for disclosing information about allegations against a parent and the welfare of their child to the wrong recipient.	£80,000
Unlawful disclosure Sensitive data	30 January 2012	Midlothian Council	An ICO monetary penalty issued for disclosing sensitive personal data relating to children and their carers to the wrong recipients on five separate occasions. The penalty is the first that the ICO has served against an organisation in Scotland.	£140,000
Unlawful disclosure Sensitive data	6 December 2011	Powys County Council	An ICO monetary penalty issued for a serious breach of the Data Protection Act after the details of a child protection case were sent to the wrong recipient.	£130,000
Unlawful disclosure Sensitive data	28 November 2011	North Somerset Council	An ICO monetary penalty issued for a serious breach of the Data Protection Act where a council employee sent five emails, two of which contained highly sensitive and confidential information about a child's serious case review, to the wrong NHS employee.	£60,000
Unlawful disclosure Sensitive data	28 November 2011	Worcestershire County Council	An ICO monetary penalty issued for an incident where a member of staff emailed highly sensitive personal information about a large number of vulnerable people to 23 unintended recipients.	£80,000

Issue	Date	Party	Breach	Penalty
Unlawful disclosure Sensitive data	9 June 2011	Surrey County Council	An ICO monetary penalty issued for a serious breach of the Data Protection Act after sensitive personal information was emailed to the wrong recipients on three separate occasions.	£120,000
Unlawful disclosure Sensitive data Security	10 May 2011	Andrew Jonathan Crossley, formerly trading as solicitors firm ACS Law	An ICO monetary penalty issued for failing to keep sensitive personal information relating to around 6,000 people secure.	£1,000
Data Loss/ Data Breach Laptop Encryption	8 February 2011	Ealing Council	An ICO monetary penalty issued following the loss of an unencrypted laptop which contained personal information. Ealing Council breached the Data Protection Act by issuing an unencrypted laptop to a member of staff in breach of its own policies.	£80,000
Data Loss/ Data Breach Laptop Encryption	8 February 2011	Hounslow Council	An ICO monetary penalty issued following the loss of an unencrypted laptop which contained personal information. Hounslow Council breached the Act by failing to have a written contract in place with Ealing Council. Hounslow Council also did not monitor Ealing Council's procedures for operating the service securely.	£70,000

Conclusion

12.42 One comment on the above is that it is worrying how many problem issues arise with regard to health data, and which amounts to sensitive personal data.

It should also be noted that company directors (and other officers) can be personally prosecuted and fined.

If a request for information or other notice is received from the ICO it may be appropriate to seek immediate legal advice. The ICO can also issue enforcement notices. In addition, the ICO may also issue monetary penalty notices or fines.[6] It is important to note the emphasis now under the new GDPR regime on teams dealing with the nuanced respective data protection (and security) issues; DPOs; assessing data protection risks and dealing with them appropriately; and the related new rules. Organisations should ensure proper policies; awareness and ongoing training are in operation across all personnel whom have an impact and responsibility regarding data protection operations. It appears that fines, prosecutions and Data Subject damage and access litigation will increase.

---

6   In accordance with the powers of the ICO under the Criminal Justice and Immigration Act 2008.

Chapter 13

Security of Personal Data

Introduction

13.01 'Personally identifiable information (PII) data has become the prime target of hackers and cyber-criminals. It can be exploited in many ways, from identity theft, spamming and phishing right through to cyber-espionage.'[1] The data protection regime sets information and data security obligations on all Controllers, as well as Processors. These IT and personal data security requirements must be complied with. While security risks have increased with the internet,[2] security issues are not just limited to the organisation's internet.

The increasing instances of data security breach, including through inadequate security, as well as internet usage and social media, cloud computing and online abuse will all increase the attention on security and data protection. Sony, for example, was fined £250,000 in relation to a hacking data breach incident. Recently, telco Talk Talk and children's toy manufacturer Vtech were hacked. The MD of Talk Talk has said that 'cyber criminals are becoming increasingly sophisticated and attacks against companies which do business online are becoming more frequent.'

Appropriate Security Measures

13.02 There are specific requirements with regard to the security measures that need to be implemented under the DPA 1998.

Organisations and Controller must take appropriate security measures against unauthorised access to, or unauthorised alteration, disclosure or

---

1   Y Rozenberg, 'Challenges in PII Data Protection,' *Computer Fraud & Security* (2012) 5–9, at 5.
2   'Security of the Internet and the Known Unknowns,' *Communications of the ACM* (2012) (55) 35–37.

destruction of, the data, in particular where the processing involves the transmission of data over a network, and against all other unlawful forms of processing. As these risks grow,[3] so too must the effort of the organisation. It cannot be a case that one solution, on one occasion, will be sufficient.

The requirements regarding security of processing are contained in the seventh Data Protection Principle (DPA 1998, Sch 1, Pt I, para 7). The Controller must take appropriate technical and organisational measures against unauthorised or unlawful processing of personal data and against accidental loss or destruction of, or damage to personal data.

The Controller must ensure the following:

'*Appropriate technical* and *organisational* measures shall be taken against *unauthorised* or *unlawful* processing of personal data and against accidental *loss* or *destruction* of, or *damage* to personal data.'

The new GDPR places significant emphasis on risk and risk assessment. Organisations need to be compliant with these obligations.

Ensuring Appropriate Security Measures

13.03 What are security and 'appropriate technical and organisational measures'? What must the organisation do? In determining appropriate technical and organisational measures, a Controller may have regard to:

- the state of technological development and the cost of implementing any measures;
- the harm that might result from such unauthorised or unlawful processing or accidental loss, destruction or damage; and
- the nature of the data to be protected.

The seventh Data Protection Principle contained in Sch 1 to the DPA 1998 refers to security.

DPA 1998, Sch 1, Pt II, para 9 provides that having regard to the state of technological development and the cost of implementing any measures, the measures must ensure a level of security appropriate to:

- the harm that might result from such unauthorised or unlawful processing or accidental loss, destruction or damage as are mentioned in the seventh principle; and
- the nature of the data to be protected.

---

3   See, for example, 'The Cybersecurity Risk,' *Communications of the ACM* (2012) (55) 29–32.

Security under the DPA

Security Level

13.04   The eighth Data Protection Principle interpretative guidance contained in Sch 1 to the DPA 1998 refers to security.

DPA 1998, Sch 1, Pt II, para 13 provides that an adequate level of protection is one which is adequate in all the circumstances of the case, having regard in particular to:

- the nature of the personal data;
- the country or territory of origin of the information contained in the data;
- the country or territory of final destination of that information;
- the purposes for which and period during which the data are intended to be processed;
- the law in force in the country or territory in question;
- the international obligations of that country or territory;
- any relevant codes of conduct or other rules which are enforceable in that country or territory (whether generally or by arrangement in particular cases); and
- any security measures taken in respect of the data in that country or territory.

DPA 1998, Sch 1, Pt II, para 14 provides that the eighth Data Protection Principle does not apply to a transfer falling within any paragraph of Sch 4, except in such circumstances and to such extent as the Secretary of State may by order provide.

DPA 1998, Sch 1, Pt II, para 15(1) provides that where:

- in any proceedings under the DPA any question arises as to whether the requirement of the eighth Data Protection Principle as to an adequate level of protection is met in relation to the transfer of any personal data to a country or territory outside the EEA; and
- an EU Community finding has been made in relation to transfers of the kind in question, that question is to be determined in accordance with that finding.

DPA 1998, Sch 1, Pt II, para 15(2) provides that in sub-para (1) 'Community finding' means a finding of the European Commission, under the procedure provided for in Article 31(2) of the DPD, that a country or territory outside the EEA does, or does not, ensure an adequate level of protection within the meaning of Article 25(2) of the DPD.

Employees and Security

13.05 DPA 1998, Sch 1, Pt II, para 10 provides that the Controller must take reasonable steps to ensure the reliability of any employees of the organisation who have access to the personal data.

Organisations should be aware that they could be held liable, whether with the ICO or in a civil court, in relation to data breaches and data security breaches occasioned by their employees. Organisations may also begin to face claims in relation to online abuse caused, initiated or participated in by their employees while using the organisation's network and devices. Indeed, this applies in relation to their other servants and agents also.

Engaging Data Processors

13.06 Processors[4] also have obligations in relation to processing personal data and security.

DPA 1998, Sch 1, Pt II, para 11 provides that where processing of personal data is carried out by a Processor on behalf of a Controller, the Controller must in order to comply with the seventh principle:

- choose a Processor providing sufficient guarantees in respect of the technical and organisational security measures governing the processing to be carried out; and
- take reasonable steps to ensure compliance with those measures.

Where processing of personal data is carried out by a Processor on behalf of a Controller, then the Controller must have a contract in writing with the Processor, containing certain clauses and obligations.

DPA 1998, Sch 1, Pt II, para 12 provides that where processing of personal data is carried out by a Processor on behalf of a Controller, the Controller is not to be regarded as complying with the seventh principle unless:

- the processing is carried out under a contract,
  - which is made or evidenced in writing; and
  - under which the Processor is to act only on instructions from the Controller, and
- the contract requires the Processor to comply with obligations equivalent to those imposed on a Controller by the seventh principle.

The contracts with Processors must address the following,

- processing must be carried out in pursuance of a contract in writing;

---

4 Note generally, for example, R Morgan, 'Data Controllers, Data Processors and Data Sharers,' SCL *Computers and Law*, 4 March 2011.

- contract must provide that the Processor carries out the processing only on and subject to the instructions of the Controller;
- Processor must comply with the above *security* requirements.

There are also certain other requirements. The Controller:

- must ensure Processors provide sufficient guarantees in respect of the technical security measures and organisational measures governing the processing;
- must take reasonable steps to ensure compliance with these measures.

There are specific requirements where Processors are engaged and relied upon. Where Controllers engage Processors then the Controller must:

- have a contract in writing or other equivalent form which provides that the Processor will act only on instructions of the Controller and that it will comply with the data security measures to which the Controller is subject;
- ensure that the Processor provides sufficient guarantees in respect of the technical security measures and organisational measures it implements;
- takes reasonable steps to ensure compliance with such matters.

What actions should an organisation take if third parties process their organisation's data? Organisations should consider:

- ideally, that an organisation should have advance procedures and policies in place to cater for such an eventuality, for example ensuring that an appropriate senior manager/board member has an assigned role and takes responsibility for date protection compliance, including dealing with breaches, and also having a documented IT security incident handling procedure policy in place. Needless to say, it must be properly policed, implemented, reviewed and updated appropriately;
- once a breach does occur, a proper procedure can assist in containing the breach and recovering from same; assessing the ongoing risk; notify the breach as appropriate; evaluating and reacting to the breach and the risk;
- all of the appropriate personnel within the organisation should be aware of the procedures and consulted as appropriate, including for example managing director, legal, IT, media/press officer;
- a part of the procedure will have a designated list of external contact points, some or all of whom may need to be notified and contacted, as appropriate;
- obviously the nature of organisations, and of breaches themselves, differ and the IT security incident handling procedure policy will

need to be tailored. After all, the cause of a data security breach can be any of a number of potential reasons;

- also, such a policy while covering breaches of data protection and privacy, may well encompass wider issues, such as outsourcing, backups, disaster recovery, business continuity, etc;
- if an organisation does business in other jurisdictions you may need to take additional measures. For example, if you own or have access to personal information of Californian residents then you may have a legal duty to notify those individuals if that information (such as names and credit card details) has been accessed illegally.

Security under the EDPB (previously WP29)

13.07 The influential EDPB (previously WP29) has previously published a document relating to personal data and information security.[5] It refers to the surveillance of employee's electronic communications. In terms of compliance it raises a number of policy concerns for organisations to consider when dealing with their policies and activities regarding such personal data. It suggests that organisations asking if the proposed processing of the employee's personal data is:

- transparent?
- necessary?
- fair?
- proportionate?
- for what purpose?

It also suggests that organisations should consider if each proposed processing activity can be achieved through some other less obtrusive means.

It also refers to informing those outside of the organisation as appropriate in relation to the proposed processing.

It also refers to issues of proportionality in suggesting that an organisation in processing personal data should adopt the minimum processing necessary, and pursuing a strategy of prevention versus detection. Detection leans more towards blanket monitoring of employees, whereas prevention is viewed as more appropriate and employee privacy friendly. Of course, where some issue comes to the organisation's attention, they could then investigate that issue, as opposed to actively monitoring all employees 24/7. An example would be using IT filtering systems, which

---

5   This was published on 29 May 2002.

alert the IT manager that there may be an issue to look at further, rather than the IT manager actively looking at and monitoring all employee communications.

Security and Confidentiality under the DPD

Confidentiality

13.08   Section VIII of the DPD refers to confidentiality and security of processing. Article 16 refers to the confidentiality of processing. It provides that any person acting under the authority of the Controller or of the Processor, including the Processor, who has access to personal data must not process them except on instructions from the Controller, unless required to do so by law.

Security

13.09   Article 17 of the DPD refers to security of processing.

Article 17(1) provides that Member States shall provide that the Controller must implement appropriate technical and organisational measures to protect personal data against accidental or unlawful destruction or accidental loss, alteration, unauthorised disclosure or access, in particular where the processing involves the transmission of data over a network, and against all other unlawful forms of processing. It also provides that having regard to the state of the art and the cost of their implementation, such measures shall ensure a level of security appropriate to the risks represented by the processing and the nature of the data to be protected.

Article 17(2) provides that Member States shall provide that the Controller must, where processing is carried out on his behalf, choose a Processor providing sufficient guarantees in respect of the technical security measures and organisational measures governing the processing to be carried out, and must ensure compliance with those measures.

Article 17(3) provides that the carrying out of processing by way of a Processor must be governed by a contract or legal act binding the Processor to the Controller and stipulating in particular that:

- the Processor shall act only on instructions from the Controller;
- the obligations set out in Article 17(1), as defined by the law of the Member State in,

which the Processor is established, shall also be incumbent on the Processor.

Article 17(4) provides that for the purposes of keeping proof, the parts of the contract or the legal act relating to data protection and the requirements relating to the measures referred to in Article 17(1) shall be in writing or in another equivalent form.

Security under the GDPR

13.10 Security is particularly emphasised as being important under the new data protection regime.

The new GDPR Recitals refer to security as follows: network and information security, Computer Emergency Response Teams (CERTs) and Computer Security Incident Response Teams (CSIRTs); guidance for appropriate measures; appropriate technical and organisational measures; security and risk evaluation; high risk and impact assessments; and impact assessments; and large scale processing operations; consultations; Data breach and data breach notification; Commission delegated acts.

Chapter IV, Section 2 of the new GDPR relates to data security.

Security of Processing

13.11 Taking into account the state of the art, the costs of implementation and the nature, scope, context and purposes as well as the risk of varying likelihood and severity for the rights and freedoms of natural persons, the Controller and the Processor shall implement appropriate technical and organisational measures to ensure a level of security appropriate to the risk, including inter alia, as appropriate:

- the pseudonymisation and encryption of personal data;
- the ability to ensure the ongoing confidentiality, integrity, availability and resilience of processing systems and services;
- the ability to restore the availability and access to personal data in a timely manner in the event of a physical or technical incident;
- a process for regularly testing, assessing and evaluating the effectiveness of technical and organisational measures for ensuring the security of the processing (Article 32(1)).

In assessing the appropriate level of security account shall be taken in particular of the risks that are presented by data processing, in particular from accidental or unlawful destruction, loss, alteration, unauthorised disclosure of, or access to personal data transmitted, stored or otherwise processed (Article 32(2)).

Adherence to an approved code of conduct pursuant to Article 40 or an approved certification mechanism pursuant to Article 42 may be used as an element by which to demonstrate compliance with the requirements set out in Article 32(1) (Article 32(3)).

The Controller and Processor shall take steps to ensure that any person acting under the authority of the Controller or the Processor who has access to personal data shall not process them except on instructions from the Controller, unless they are required to do so by EU or Member State law (Article 32(4)).

Notification of a Data Breach to Supervisory Authority

13.12   In the case of a personal data breach, the Controller shall without undue delay and, where feasible, not later than 72 hours after having become aware of it, notify the personal data breach to the supervisory authority, unless the personal data breach is unlikely to result in a risk for the rights and freedoms of natural persons. Where the notification to the supervisory authority is not made within 72 hours, it shall be accompanied by reasons for the delay (Article 33(1)).

The Processor shall notify the Controller without undue delay after becoming aware of a personal data breach (Article 33(2)).

Contents of Notification

13.13   The notification must at least:

- describe the nature of the personal data breach including where possible, the categories and approximate number of Data Subjects concerned and the categories and approximate number of data records concerned;
- communicate the name and contact details of the DPO or other contact point where more information can be obtained;
- describe the likely consequences of the personal data breach;
- describe the measures taken or proposed to be taken by the Controller to address the personal data breach, including, where appropriate, measures to mitigate its possible adverse effects (Article 33(2)).

Where, and in so far as, it is not possible to provide the information at the same time, the information may be provided in phases without undue further delay (Article 33(4)).

The Controller shall document any personal data breaches, comprising the facts relating to the personal data breach, its effects and the remedial action taken. This documentation must enable the supervisory authority to verify compliance with this Article (Article 33(5)).

Communication of a Data Breach to Data Subject

13.14   When the personal data breach is likely to result in a high risk to the rights and freedoms of individuals the Controller shall communicate the personal data breach to the Data Subject without undue delay (Article 34(1)).[6]

The communication to the Data Subject shall describe in clear and plain language the nature of the personal data breach and contain at least the information and the recommendations provided for in Article 31(3)(b), (d) and (e) (Article 32(2)).

The communication to the Data Subject referred to in Article 32(1) shall not be required if:

- the Controller has implemented appropriate technical and organisational protection measures, and that those measures were applied to the personal data affected by the personal data breach, in particular those that render the data unintelligible to any person who is not authorised to access it, such as encryption; or
- the Controller has taken subsequent measures which ensure that the high risks to the rights and freedoms of Data Subjects referred to in para 1 is no longer likely to materialise; or
- it would involve disproportionate effort. In such a case, there shall instead be a public communication or similar measure whereby the Data Subjects are informed in an equally effective manner (Article 34(3)).

If the Controller has not already communicated the personal data breach to the Data Subject, the supervisory authority, having considered the likelihood of the breach to result in a high risk, may require it to do so or may decide that any of the conditions referred to in Article 34(3) are met (Article 34(4)).

Data Protection Impact Assessment and Prior Consultation

13.15   Chapter IV, Section 3 of the GDPR refers to Impact Assessments and Prior Consultations.

Data Protection Impact Assessment

13.16   Where a type of processing in particular using new technologies, and taking into account the nature, scope, context and purposes of the processing, is likely to result in a high risk for the rights and freedoms of natural persons, the Controller shall, prior to the processing, carry out an assessment of the impact of the envisaged processing operations on the protection of personal data. A single assessment may address a set of similar processing operations that present similar high risks (Article 35(1)).

---

6   Note, for example, P Wainman, 'Data Protection Breaches: Today and Tomorrow,' SCL *Computers and Law*, 30 June 2012. Also see M Dekker, Dr, C Christoffer Karsberg and B Daskala, *Cyber Incident Reporting in the EU* (2012).

The Controller shall seek the advice of the DPO, where designated, when carrying out a data protection impact assessment (Article 35(2)).

A data protection impact assessment shall in particular be required in the following cases:

- a systematic and extensive evaluation of personal aspects relating to natural persons which is based on automated processing, including profiling, and on which decisions are based that produce legal effects concerning the natural person or similarly significantly affect the individual;
- processing on a large scale of special categories of data referred to in Article 9(1), or of personal data relating to criminal convictions and offences referred to in Article 10; or
- a systematic monitoring of a publicly accessible area on a large scale (Article 35(2)).

The supervisory authority shall establish and make public a list of the kind of processing operations which are subject to the requirement for a data protection impact assessment pursuant to Article 35(1). The supervisory authority shall communicate those lists to the EDPB (Article 35(4)).

The supervisory authority may also establish and make public a list of the kind of processing operations which are subject to requirement for a data protection impact assessment. The supervisory authority shall communicate those lists to the EDPB (Article 35(4)).

The supervisory authority may also establish and make public a list of the kind of processing operations for which no data protection impact assessment is required. The supervisory authority shall communicate those lists to the Board.

Prior to the adoption of the lists referred to above, the competent supervisory authority shall apply the consistency mechanism referred to in Article 63 where such lists involve processing activities which are related to the offering of goods or services to Data Subjects or to the monitoring of their behaviour in several Member States, or may substantially affect the free movement of personal data within the EU (Article 35(6)).

Contents of Data Protection Impact Assessment

13.17   The assessment shall contain at least:

- a systematic description of the envisaged processing operations and the purposes of the processing, including where applicable the legitimate interest pursued by the Controller;
- an assessment of the necessity and proportionality of the processing operations in relation to the purposes;

- an assessment of the risks to the rights and freedoms of Data Subjects;
- the measures envisaged to address the risks, including safeguards, security measures and mechanisms to ensure the protection of personal data and to demonstrate compliance with the GDPR taking into account the rights and legitimate interests of Data Subjects and other persons concerned (Article 35(7)).

Compliance with approved codes of conduct referred to in Article 38 by the relevant Controllers or Processors shall be taken into due account in assessing the impact of the processing operations performed by such Controllers or Processors, in particular for the purposes of a data protection impact assessment (Article 35(8)).

Where appropriate, the Controller shall seek the views of Data Subjects or their representatives on the intended processing, without prejudice to the protection of commercial or public interests or the security of the processing operations (Article 35(9)).

Where the processing pursuant to Article 6(1)(c) or (e) has a legal basis in EU law, or the law of the Member State to which the Controller is subject, and such law regulates the specific processing operation or set of operations in question, and a data protection impact assessment has already been carried out as part of a general impact assessment in the context of the adoption of that legal basis, Article 35(1) to (7) shall not apply, unless Member States deem it necessary to carry out such assessment prior to the processing activities (Article 35(10)).

Where necessary, the Controller shall carry out a review to assess if the processing of personal data is performed in compliance with the data protection impact assessment at least when there is a change of the risk represented by the processing operations (Article 35(11)).

Prior Consultation

13.18 The Controller shall consult the supervisory authority prior to the processing of personal data where a data protection impact assessment indicates that the processing would result in a high risk in the absence of measures taken by the Controller to mitigate the risk (Article 36(1)).

Where the supervisory authority is of the opinion that the intended processing referred to in Article 36(2) would infringe the GDPR, in particular where the Controller has insufficiently identified or mitigated the risk, the supervisory authority shall, within a period of up to eight weeks of receipt of the request for consultation give written advice to the Controller, and where applicable the Processor in writing, and may use any of its powers referred to in Article 58. This period may be extended for a further six weeks, taking into account the complexity of the intended processing (Article 36(2)).

When consulting the supervisory authority pursuant to Article 36(1), the Controller shall provide the supervisory authority with:

- where applicable, the respective responsibilities of the Controller, joint Controllers and Processors involved in the processing, in particular for processing within a group of undertakings;
- the purposes and means of the intended processing;
- the measures and safeguards provided to protect the rights and freedoms of Data Subjects pursuant to the GDPR;
- where applicable, the contact details of the DPO;
- the data protection impact assessment provided for; and
- any other information requested by the supervisory authority (Article 36(3)).

Member States shall consult the supervisory authority during the preparation of a proposal for a legislative measure to be adopted by a national parliament, or of a regulatory measure based on such a legislative measure, which relates to processing (Article 36(4)).

Notwithstanding Article 36(1), Member States' law may require Controllers to consult with, and obtain prior authorisation from, the supervisory authority in relation to the processing by a Controller for the performance of a task carried out by the Controller in the public interest, including the processing of such data in relation to social protection and public health (Article 36(5)).

Organisational Security Awareness

13.19 There is an issue of ensuring security awareness within the organisation. Controllers and Processors must take all reasonable steps to ensure that persons employed by them and other persons at the place of work, are aware of and comply with the relevant security measures (note DPA 1998, Sch 1, Pt II, para 10).

Identifying and Controlling Organisational IT Security

13.20 Who needs to be in charge of IT and data security in an organisation? What organisational security measures should be in place?

The DPA does not require that a named individual be appointed with responsibility for security compliance. A titled officer is highly recommended and under the GDPR a formal DPO is now a requirement. There are specific organisational responsibilities, regarding security, which are set out in the DPA and these include a specific requirement that all staff are aware of and comply with the security standards set out in the data protection regime.

These security requirements apply where an organisation collects and processes any personal data. Typically personal data would include information which identifies living individuals such as employees or customers. Accordingly, for most organisations, data protection compliance is likely to be an issue that crosses various aspects of the business such as human resources, IT and customer support. It is not necessarily just an IT function. An organisational decision as to who should be responsible for IT and data security should be made with this in mind.

The security standards set out in the Data Protection Act can be summarised as obliging the organisation to take 'appropriate' security measures to guard against unauthorised access, alteration, disclosure or destruction of any personal data.

In determining what is 'appropriate,' the organisation can have regard to the state of technological development and the cost of implementing the security measures. However, the organisation is obliged to ensure that the measures it decides to adopt provide a level of security appropriate to the harm that might result from a security compromise given the nature of the data concerned. For example, a hospital processing sensitive health data would be expected to adopt a particularly high security standard while a corner shop processing personal data for a paper round might be subject to a less onerous standard.

In light of some high profile cases of data theft or loss, readers should note also that the ICO's office has taken the view that an appropriate level of security for laptop computers used in the financial services and health industries requires the use of encryption in respect of the data stored on the hard drive (over and above the use of user name and password log-in requirements).

In adopting security measures within an organisation, they should note that the legal standard governing personal data is over and above any other legal obligations of confidentiality which could be owed to third parties at common law or under a contract which contains confidentiality provisions.

Appraising Employees

13.21   What guidance should be given to an organisation's employees regarding IT and data security? An organisation might consider these issues.

The overriding principle here is that, for it to be effective, an employee must have clear notice of all aspects of the IT and data security policy. The following might be included.

General Policy: Seek to reserve the right to monitor use of the computer and telephone system, including email. Disclosure of sensitive or confidential information about the company or personal data about any individual without authorisation should be forbidden.

Email: Employees should be made aware that email is an essential business tool but not without its risks. Business communications should be suitable and not too chatty or contain inappropriate material. Personal use of email must be reasonable.

Internet Access: Downloading of any software without approval should be forbidden. No improper or illegal activities (hacking, etc) should be tolerated. Access to certain types of websites (abuse, adult, criminal, hate, violent, etc) should be expressly restricted. Origination or dissemination of inappropriate material should be forbidden.

Mobile Telephones and Devices: Downloading of any software without approval should be forbidden. No improper or illegal activities (hacking, etc) should be tolerated. Access to certain types of websites (adult, criminal, hate, violent, etc) should be expressly restricted. Origination or dissemination of inappropriate material should be forbidden.

Vehicles: Increasingly tracking and other data from vehicles can be related to identified employees. It is important for organisations to consider these personal data issues.

Internet Social Media: Downloading of any software without approval should be forbidden. No improper or illegal activities (hacking, etc) should be tolerated. Access to certain types of websites (adult, criminal, hate, violent, etc) should be expressly restricted. Origination or dissemination of inappropriate material should be forbidden, eg abuse.

Software Installation & Management: Purchase and/or installation of software not approved by you should be forbidden. All software must be required to be tested before installation on the system to ensure that it is free from viruses, malware, etc.

Password Security: Clear guidelines as to the use of passwords should be given including the strength of password required, the importance of keeping one's password confidential, the changing of passwords at regular intervals and (in the light of recent events) the application of password security to laptops, mobile phones and PDAs. At least, in some businesses, stronger encryption may be appropriate and employees should be required to comply with procedures in this regard. Carrying company data on vulnerable media such as memory sticks should be discouraged.

Connecting Hardware: Employees should be required not to connect any hardware (memory sticks, hard drives, etc) without following specified procedures and obtaining appropriate authorisation.

Remote Access: For many businesses, remote access, including web-based remote access, is a vital tool. However, policies should deal with such matter as accessing remotely from insecure locations as internet cafes, etc and emphasise the importance of logging off effectively.

Organisational Security Measures

13.22 What measures should an organisation take? Some suggestions may include:

- ensure that the organisation has the appropriate security equipment and software to protect the systems if granting third party access. If providing access to a third party involves the business opening its systems up to a public network such as the Internet, it is essential that suitable security measures are taken;
- obtain a complete listing of the IT provider personnel who have access to the systems and detail their level, status (full time/ contractor) and ensure that their employment contracts incorporate terms similar to above;

Third parties should be granted access to the systems only when the:

- relevant individuals in the organisation (eg a business manager, in conjunction with IT staff) have agreed that there is a business need for such access to be granted. Access should only be for a temporary period and renewed at regular intervals;
- third party computer accounts should be monitored (subject to legal agreements between the organisation and the third party and in accordance with legal requirements) and disabled as soon as access is no longer required;
- ensure that sensitive files segregated in secure areas/computer systems and available only to qualified persons;
- ensure that the organisation has inventoried the various types of data being stored and classified it according to how important it is and how costly it would be for the company if it were lost or stolen;
- scan computers (especially servers) for unauthorised programs that transmit information to third parties such as hackers;
- programs that have a hidden purpose are known as Trojans. Individuals may have inadvertently or deliberately downloaded free programs from the Internet that send back information such as passwords to hackers or Internet usage information to marketers to build up trends of people's tastes;
- ensure that third parties only have access to information and computer settings on a 'need-to-know' basis;
- the System Administrator for the computer systems should set up computer accounts for third parties so that these third parties do not have access to all information on the systems or have the permission to install non standard software and change computer settings;
- when engaging an external business to destroy records or electronic media, ensure references are checked. Draft a contract setting out the

terms of the relationship. Ensure that destruction is done on-site and require that a certificate of destruction be issued upon completion.

Breach Laws to Consider

13.23   What laws might affect an organisation if an organisation has an IT or data security breach? Suggested legal issues and laws to consider include,

- GDPR;
- DPA 1998;
- DPD;
- ePD;
- Electronic Commerce (EC) Regulations 2002;
- Criminal Damage Act 1971;
- evidence;
- Fraud Act 2006;
- Theft Act 1968;
- civil liability law;
- Protection of Children Act 1978;
- Criminal Justice and Public Order Act 1994;
- European Convention on Human Rights;
- PECR/PECR Amendment.

Other issues to consider include:

- official guidance and current stated positions of regulators and guidance bodies;
- international standards organisations eg technical security standards, etc.

Third Party Security Providers

13.24   What actions should an organisation take if a third party is responsible for IT security or has access to its IT system? Some issues to consider include:

- this is becoming increasingly popular in practice through outsourcing arrangements and vendor agreements;
- it is prudent to understand the security framework and document stakeholder exposure throughout it;
- measures to take with the organisation's IT provider;
- ensure that one engages lawyers to draft appropriate contracts that secure what the IT provider is securing;
- ensure that confidentiality clauses are included to protect all of your intellectual property assets;

- have the IT provider supply a complete security document outlining the hardware, topology, software and methodologies deployed;

- ensure that the IT provider has staff participate in regular training programs to keep abreast of technical and legal issues;

- ensure that the IT provider develops a security breach response plan in the event that your company experiences a data breach; also develop security guidelines for laptops and other portable computing devices when transported off-site;

- have the IT provider ensure that all employees follow strict password and virus protection procedures and develop a mechanism where employees are required to change passwords often, using foolproof methods especially for terminating employees;

- ensure that the IT provider has a records retention/disposal schedule for personally identifiable information, whether stored in paper, micrographic or magnetic/electronic (computer) media.

Council Resolution: Raising Awareness

13.25 An EU Council Resolution[7] indicates the recognition and official concern in relation to the loss of personal data, and the fact that technology has changed significantly since the DPD.

It refers to the dangers of information loss, attacks on organisations, and issues of network and information security for organisations and individuals.

It indicated that EU Member States should engage in information campaigns addressing the issues of security and personal data.

It recognises the need to promote best practice, such as the internationally recognised standards for IT and security set by international and standards setting organisation eg ISO 15408, ISO 27001, ISO 31000 and BS10012:2009.

It also recognises the increase in eGovernment and the need to promote secure eGovernment.

It also notes that in the increase of attacks on the security of personal data though technology, some of the solutions may also come from new technologies. Some of these are referred to as privacy enhancing technologies, or PETs.[8] (See PbD and DPbD, Part 4.)

---

7   EU Council Resolution 2002/C43/02 of 28 January 2002.
8   See, for example, B Beric and G Carlisle, 'Investigating the Legal Protection of Data, Information and Knowledge Under the EU Data Protection Regime,' *International Review of Law, Computers & Technology* (2009) (23) 189–201.

In addition it also refers to the increase of mobile and wireless communications technologies and the need for introducing and enhancing wireless security.

Keeping on top of the increasing threats to information security is an ongoing task. The threats are ever changing, and so equally should be the effort to prevent breaches, and to deal with them if and when they occur. Some of the most current information security threats are highlighted annually by various IT security vendors as well as police and investigative officials. Many security risk reports are published annually.

ICO Guidance

13.26   The ICO has also issued a guide entitled *A Practical Guide to IT Security, Ideal for Small Businesses*[9] which is useful. The ICO has also commented in relation to encryption issues.[10]

The ICO also provides the following tips and suggestions[11] for maintaining and implementing IT security for personal data, namely:

For Computer Security

- Install a firewall and virus-checking on the computers;
- Make sure that the operating system is set up to receive automatic updates;
- Protect the computer by downloading the latest patches or security updates, which should cover vulnerabilities;
- Only allow staff access to the information they need to do their job and do not let them share passwords;
- Encrypt any personal information held electronically that would cause damage or distress if it were lost or stolen;
- Take regular back-ups of the information on your computer system and keep them in a separate place so that if one loses computers, one does not lose the information;
- Securely remove all personal information before disposing of old computers (by using technology or destroying the hard disk);
- Consider installing an anti-spyware tool. Spyware can secretly monitor ones computer activities, etc. Spyware can be unwittingly installed within other file and program downloads, and their use is often malicious. They can capture passwords, banking credentials and credit card details, and then relay them back to fraudsters.

---

9   At https://ico.org.uk.
10   ICO, Our Approach to Encryption, at https://ico.org.uk.
11   ICO, Security Measures, at https://ico.org.uk.

Anti-spyware helps to monitor and protect the computer from spyware threats, and it is often free to use and update.

For Using Emails Securely

- Consider whether the content of the email should be encrypted or password protected. The IT or security team should be able to assist with encryption;
- When starting to type in the name of the recipient, some email software will suggest similar addresses one has used before. If one has previously emailed several people whose name or address starts the same way – eg 'Dave' – the auto-complete function may bring up several 'Dave's.' Make sure to choose the right address before clicking send;
- If one wants to send an email to a recipient without revealing their address to other recipients, make sure to use blind carbon copy (bcc), not carbon copy (cc). When one uses cc every recipient of the message will be able to see the address it was sent to;
- Be careful when using a group email address. Check who is in the group and make sure you really want to send your message to everyone;
- If sending a sensitive email from a secure server to an insecure recipient, security will be threatened. One may need to check that the recipient's arrangements are secure enough before sending the message.

For Using Faxes Securely

- Consider whether sending the information by a means other than fax is more appropriate, such as using a courier service or secure email. Make sure to only send the information that is required;
- Make sure to double check the fax number you are using. It is best to dial from a directory of previously verified numbers;
- Check that you are sending a fax to a recipient with adequate security measures in place. For example, the fax should not be left uncollected in an open plan office;
- If the fax is sensitive, ask the recipient to confirm that they are at the fax machine, they are ready to receive the document, and there is sufficient paper in the machine;
- Ring up or email to make sure the whole document has been received safely;
- Use a cover sheet. This will let anyone know who the information is for and whether it is confidential or sensitive, without them having to look at the contents.

For Other Security

- Shred all your confidential paper waste;
- Check the physical security of your premises;
- Train the staff,
  - so they know what is expected of them;
  - to be wary of people who may try to trick them into giving out personal details;
  - so that they can be prosecuted if they deliberately give out personal details without permission;
  - to use a strong password – these are long (at least seven characters) and have a combination of upper and lower case letters, numbers and the special keyboard characters like the asterisk or currency symbols;
  - not to send offensive emails about other people, their private lives or anything else that could bring your organisation into disrepute;
  - not to believe emails that appear to come from your bank that ask for your account, credit card details or your password (a bank would never ask for this information in this way);
  - not to open Spam – not even to unsubscribe or ask for no more mailings. Tell them to delete the email and either get Spam filters on your computers or use an email provider that offers this service.[12]

ICO and Security Breaches

13.27 The ICO advises that under the revised Regulations (PECR), public electronic communications service providers are required to notify the ICO if a personal data breach occurs.

A personal data breach is defined to mean:

'a breach of security leading the accidental or unlawful destruction, loss, alteration, unauthorised disclosure of, or access to, personal data transmitted, stored or otherwise processed in connection with the provisions of a public electronic communications service.'

---

12 ICO, Security Measures, at https://ico.org.uk.

The ICO advises[13] that the following must be complied with:

Keep a log of personal data breaches

You must keep a record of all personal data breaches in an inventory or log. It must contain:

- the facts surrounding the breach;
- the effects of that breach; and
- remedial action taken.

We have produced a template log to help you record the information you need.

Notify breaches to the ICO

You must notify the ICO of any personal data breaches. This notification must include at least a description of,

- the nature of the breach;
- the consequences of the breach; and
- the measures taken or proposed to be taken by the provider to address the breach.

To make this process easier, we suggest that you send your log to us on a monthly basis. This means one will not have to record the information twice and will meet the organisation's requirement to notify any security breaches without unnecessary delay.

However, if the breach is of a particularly serious nature you need to notify us about the breach as soon as possible, by filling in the security breach notification form (PECR).

When thinking about whether a breach is of a serious nature, we recommend that one considers,

- the type and sensitivity of the data involved;
- the impact it could have on the individual, such as distress or embarrassment; and
- the potential harm, such as financial loss, fraud, theft of identity.

Please email all security breach notifications to us at data security breach@ico.gsi.gov.uk.

Failure to comply with the requirement to submit breach notifications can incur a £1,000 fine.

For more practical information on how to notify us about PECR security breaches please see our guidance for service providers.

---

13   ICO, Security Breaches, at https://ico.org.uk.

Notify breaches to your subscribers

You may also need to tell your subscribers. If the breach is likely to adversely affect their personal data or privacy you need to, without unnecessary delay, notify them of the breach. You need to tell them,

- the nature of the breach;
- contact details for your organisation where they can get more information; and
- how they can mitigate any possible adverse impact of the breach.

You do not need to tell your subscribers about a breach if you can demonstrate that you have measures in place which would render the data unintelligible and that those measures were applied to the data concerned in the breach.

If you don't tell subscribers, the ICO can require you do so, if it considers the breach is likely to have an adverse effect on them.[14]

Disposal of Computer Hardware

13.28 Particular care is needed when considering the disposal of IT hardware, equipment and software. They may still contain personal data files. It may also include commercial or other confidential information relating to the organisation. This can continue to be the case even when it appears that files have been wiped or deleted. It is always advised to take professional legal, IT and or forensic advice.

Disposal can occur from the organisation. However, organisations need to be aware that there can be a security breach as well a breach of the data protection regime if devices and hardware are donated to charity or otherwise given away but there remains corporate and personal data on the devices. Even when it appears data may be deleted, it can sometimes be recovered with the right skills. There have also been instances where equipment is meant to be decommissioned and disposed of but employees or contractors do not fulfil the job, and the devices get into third party hands with data still on them.

This can raise other issues. If an employee leaves, they will be leaving their company laptop, etc behind. This can be reassigned to another employee. However, is the new employee appropriately designated to access to the level and importance of the data on the laptop? Hierarchies of access control need to be considered.

Particular sensitivity also arises if it is intended to recycle or give to charity particular devices. Real consideration should be given to the personal data (and other data) thereon in deciding if and how to so dispose of such devices.

14 ICO, Security Measures, at https://ico.org.uk.

Conclusion

13.29   Security is a legal data protection compliance requirement, as well as best business practice. This is one of the more prominent areas of compliance where time never stands still. The security risks and needs must constantly be appraised and updated. It is also essential to ensure that outsourced data processing activities are also undertaken in an appropriately secure manner. Increasingly the area of appraisals and procedures surrounding security breaches and data loss instances is regulated. If such an event arises, the ICO as well as individual Data Subjects may have to be informed. Liability issues should also be a constant concern for organisations as regards security and risk.

Chapter 14

Outsourcing and Data Processors

Introduction

14.01 While many organisations may feel they do not engage third parties to deal with their personal data, processes and databases, closer inspection often indicates that this is not correct. Many organisations, and across all sectors of activity, engage third parties or outsource certain of their internal processing activities.[1]

One example is where an organisation may find it more convenient to outsource its payroll functions to an organisation specialising in such activities. It is necessary, therefore, that the employee personal data, or certain of it, is transferred to the third party organisation for processing. This third party is a data Processor acting for the organisation. A contract must be in place and appropriate security standards implemented.

Sometime organisations outsource other activities, such as marketing, recruitment, employment of consultants or agents or part time employees. Organisations increasingly outsource market research and customer satisfaction surveys to third parties. These are all Processors where personal data is involved.

If an organisation must transfer or export personal data outside of the EU/EEA and lawfully permit transfers outside of the transfer restriction, it must satisfy, as appropriate, one of the following:

- an export to one of the safe permitted countries; or
- an export to the US under the original EU-US Safe Harbour agreement and the new EU-US Privacy Shield agreement;[2] or

---

1 See generally V Alsenoy, 'Allocating Responsibility Among Controllers, Processors, and "Everything In Between": The Definition of Actors and Roles in Directive 95/46/EC,' *Computer Law & Security Review* (2012) (28) 25–43; R Morgan, 'Data Controllers, Data Processors and Data Sharers,' SCL *Computers and Law*, 04 March 2011.
2 Note that the original Safe Harbour agreement was struck down by the Court of Justice.

- an export pursuant to the accepted standard contractual clauses; or
- an export pursuant to the accepted binding corporate rules (BCRs).

Processors and Security

14.02 Processors also have obligations in relation to processing personal data and security.

Where processing of personal data is carried out by a Processor on behalf of a Controller, then the Controller must have a contract in writing in place with the Processor, containing certain clauses and obligations.

The contracts with Processors must address the following:

- processing must be carried out in pursuance of a contract in writing or another equivalent form;
- contract must provide that the Processor carries out the processing only on and subject to the instructions of the Controller;
- processor must comply with the 'security' requirements (see above).

There are also certain other requirements. The Controller:

- must ensure Processor provides sufficient guarantees in respect of the technical security measures and organisational measures governing the processing;
- must take reasonable steps to ensure compliance with these measures.

Cloud and data security issues also arise to be considered.

Engaging Processors under the DPA 1998

14.03 DPA 1998, Sch 1, Pt II, para 11 provides that where processing of personal data is carried out by a Processor on behalf of a Controller, the Controller in order to comply with the seventh principle must:

- choose a Processor providing sufficient guarantees in respect of the technical and organisational security measures governing the processing to be carried out; and
- take reasonable steps to ensure compliance with those measures.

DPA 1998, Sch 1, Pt II, para 12 provides that where processing of personal data is carried out by a Processor on behalf of a Controller, the Controller is not to be regarded as complying with the seventh principle unless:

- the processing is carried out under a contract,
  - which is made or evidenced in writing; and

○ under which the Processor is to act only on instructions from the Controller, and

● the contract requires the Processor to comply with obligations equivalent to those imposed on a Controller by the seventh principle.

Relying on Third Party Processors

14.04 There are specific requirements where Processors are engaged. Where Controllers engage Processors then the Controller must:

● have a contract in writing or other equipment form which provides that the Processor will act only on instructions of the Controller and that it will comply with the data security measures to which the Controller is subject;

● ensure the Processor provides sufficient guarantees in respect of the technical security measures and organisational measures it implements;

● takes reasonable steps to ensure compliance with such matters.

What actions should an organisation take if third parties process their organisation's data? Organisations should consider:

● advance procedures and policies in place to ensure and cater for such an eventuality;

● ensuring that an appropriate senior manager/board member has an assigned role and takes responsibility for date protection compliance, including dealing with breaches, and also having a documented IT security incident handling procedure policy in place. Needless to say, it must be properly policed, implemented, reviewed and updated appropriately;

● once a breach does occur, a proper procedure can assist in containing the breach and recovering from same; assessing the ongoing risk; notify the breach as appropriate; evaluating and reacting to the breach and the risk;

● all of the appropriate personnel within the organisation should be aware of the procedures and consulted as appropriate, including for example managing director, legal, IT, media/press officer;

● a part of the procedure will have a designated list of external contact points, some or all of whom may need to be notified and contacted, as appropriate;

● obviously the nature of organisations, and of the breaches themselves, differ and the IT security incident handling procedure policy will need to be tailored. After all, the cause of a data security breach can be any of a number of potential reasons;

- also, such a policy while covering breaches of data protection and privacy, may well encompass wider issues, such as outsourcing, backups, disaster recovery, business continuity, etc;
- if doing business in other jurisdictions one may need to take additional measures. For example, if owning or having access to personal information of Californian residents then one may have a legal duty to notify those individuals if that information (such as names and credit card details) has been accessed illegally.

Conclusion

14.05   It is also important that the organisation undertake ongoing assessments and checks regarding the operation of the data processing undertaken by the Processor. This should also include the security and compliance measures. Issues of risk, security breach and data protection compliance must be assessed on an ongoing basis.

Part 2

Inward Facing Organisational DP Obligations

Chapter 15

Processing Employee Personal Data

Introduction

15.01 Organisations sometimes focus on their customer related data compliance issues. It is important for new and existing organisations to look inwards, as there are important inward facing data protection obligations. Personal data includes the personal data of employees also. The employees of the organisation also have Data Subject rights which must be respected.

The variety of inward-facing data protection issues which organisations need to deal with on a daily basis are ever increasing. Some of these include whether to allow employees to bring their own devices (BYOD) into the organisation and to permit them to place organisational data onto such devices. If so permitted, a particular BYOD policy needs to be considered and implemented. If not permitted, this should be expressly specified in a transparent manner.

The ability for organisations to track their employees off-site is also a new consideration. This can include technologies on board vehicles as well as satellite and location technologies. It also includes the organisation's (and employee's BYOD) smart phone (and other) devices.

Clearly, there are many more means by which new and or expanded sets of personal data may be collected and used by an organisation. However, it is equally necessary to consider the data protection compliance issues at the earliest opportunity, and what collections are permissible or which are not.

GDPR New Inward Facing Changes

15.02 Some of the new GDPR changes which apply to inward facing organisational issues include:

- repeal of DPD 95 (Article 94);
- WP29 and European Data Protection Board (Recitals 72, 77, 105, 119, 124, 136, 139, 140, 143, 168; Articles 35, 40–43, 47, 51, 52, 58–62, 64 and 65, 94);
- background and rationale (Recitals 1–8, 11–13);
- context objectives, scope of GDPR (Articles 1, 2 and 3);
- obligations (Recitals 32, 39, 40, 42, 43–47);
- security (Recitals 2, 16, 19, 39, 49, 50, 52, 53, 71, 73, 75, 78, 81, 83, 91, 94, 104, 112; Articles 2, 4, 5, 9, 10, 30, 32, 35, 40, 45, 47);
- processing;
- rights (Recitals 1, 2, 3, 4, 9, 10, 11, 13, 16, 19, 38, 39, 41, 47, 50–54, 57, 59, 63, 65, 66, 68–71, 73–81, 84–86, 89, 91, 94, 98, 102, 104, 108, 109, 111, 113, 114, 116, 122, 129, 137, 139, 141–143, 153–156, 162, 164, 166, 173; Articles 1, 4–7, 9–22);
- proceedings (Recitals 52, 80, 129, 143–147; Articles 23, 40, 78, 79, 81, 82);
- establishment (Recitals 22, 36, 52, 65, 100, 117, 122, 124, 126, 127, 145; Articles 3, 4, 9, 17, 18, 21, 37, 42, 49, 54, 56, 57, 60, 62, 65, 70, 79);
- transfers (Recitals 6, 48, 101–103, 107, 108, 110–114, 153; Articles 4, 3, 14, 15, 23, 28, 30, 40, 42, 44–49, 70, 83, 85, 88, 96);
- new bodies (Recital 142; Articles 9, 80);
- notification/registration replaced (Recital 89);
- exceptions/exemptions (Recitals 14, 15, 17);
- lawful processing and consent (Recital 10, 32, 33, 38–40, 42–46, 49–51, 54, 63, 65, 68, 69, 71, 83, 111, 112, 116, 138, 155, 161, 171; Articles 4–9, 13, 14, 17, 18, 20, 22, 23, 32, 40, 49, 82, 83);
- online identifiers (Recitals 30, 64; Articles 4, 87);
- sensitive and special personal data (Recitals 10, 51, 53, 54, 59, 65, 71, 80, 91, 97; Articles 6, 9, 22, 27, 30, 35, 37, 47);
- health data (Recital 35, 45, 52–54, 63, 65, 71, 73, 75, 91, 112, 155, 159; Articles 4, 9, 17, 23, 36, 88);
- DPR definitions (Article 4);
- new processing rules: obligations (Articles 5–11);
- new (data protection) principles (Article 5);
- lawfulness of processing: legitimate processing conditions (Article 6);
- processing special categories of personal data (Article 9);
- processing re criminal convictions and offences data (Article 10);
- processing not requiring identification (Article 11);

- Controllers and Processors (Chapter IV);
- responsibility of the Controller (Article 24);
- joint Controllers (Article 26);
- Processor (Article 28);
- processing under authority of Controller and Processor (Article 29);
- records of processing activities (Article 30);
- representatives of Controllers not established in EU (Article 27);
- security of processing (Article 32);
- notifying data breach to supervisory authority (Article 33);
- communicating data breach to Data Subject (Article 34);
- data protection impact assessment and prior consultation (Chapter IV, Section 3);
- data protection impact assessment (Article 35);
- prior consultation (Article 36);
- new Data Protection Officer (DPO) (Chapter IV; Section 4; Article 37);
- position (Article 38) and tasks of new DPO (Article 39);
- general principle for transfers (Recitals 6, 48, 101–103, 107, 108, 110–114, 153; Articles 4, 13, 14, 15, 23, 28, 30, 40, 42, 44–49, 70, 83, 85, 88, 96; Article 44);
- transfers via adequacy decision (Article 45);
- transfers via appropriate safeguards (Article 46);
- transfers via binding corporate rules (Article 47);
- transfers or disclosures not authorised by EU law (Article 48);
- derogations for specific situations (Article 49);
- new processing rules: Data Subject rights (Recitals 1–4, 9–11, 13, 16, 19, 38, 39, 41, 47, 50–54, 57, 59, 63, 65, 66, 68–71, 73–81, 84–86, 89, 91, 94, 98, 102, 104, 108, 109, 111, 113, 114, 116, 122, 129, 137, 139, 141–143, 153–156, 162, 164, 166, 173; Articles 1, 4–7, 9–22; Chapter III);
- right to transparency (Recitals 13, 39, 58, 60, 71, 78, 100, 121; Chapter III, Section 1; Articles 5, 12–14, 26, 40–43, 53, 88);
- data access rights (Chapter III, Section 2);
- right to prior information: directly obtained data (Article 13);
- right to prior information: indirectly obtained data (Article 14);
- right of confirmation and right of access (Article 15);
- rectification and erasure (Chapter III, Section 3);
- right to rectification (Article 16);
- right to erasure (Right to be Forgotten) (RtbF) (Article 17);
- right to restriction of processing (Article 18);
- notifications re rectification, erasure or restriction (Article 19);
- right to data portability (Article 20);
- right to object (Article 21);
- rights against automated individual decision making, including profiling (Article 22);

- Data Protection by Design and by Default (DPbD) (Article 25);
- security rights;
- data protection impact assessment and prior consultation;
- communicating data breach to Data Subject (Article 34);
- DPO (contact);
- remedies, liability and sanctions (Chapter VIII);
- right to effective judicial remedy against Controller or Processor (Article 79);
- representation of Data Subjects (Article 80);
- right to compensation and liability (Article 82);
- general conditions for imposing administrative fines (Article 83);
- penalties (Article 84);
- specific data processing situations (Chapter IX);
- processing in employment context (Article 88).

Data Protection Officer (DPO)

15.03 There may have been a traditional view within organisations that the role of the person tasked with dealing with data protection issues was limited to dealing with *outward facing* data protection queries such as access requests, data protection website queries and the like. There may have been an understanding that human resource managers were responsible for dealing with all employee related queries, including references to and copies of employee documentation and personal data.

This is no longer the case. Now there must be a designated DPO appointed in organisations. Furthermore, the role and tasks of the DPO are not limited to outward facing issues. The DPO will also be concerned with inward facing issues. Employees and similar internal facing individuals have data protection rights and will be able to address queries to the DPO quite separate from the human resource functions.

Therefore, organisations must consider DPO issues and the GDPR in terms of internal facing functions. Chapter IV, Section 4 of the new GDPR refers to DPOs and the obligation for organisations to appoint DPOs.

The Controller and the Processor shall designate a DPO in any case where:

- the processing is carried out by a public authority or body, except for courts acting in their judicial capacity; or
- the core activities of the Controller or the Processor consist of processing operations which, by virtue of their nature, their scope and/or their purposes, require regular and systematic monitoring of Data Subjects on a large scale; or

- the core activities of the Controller or the Processor consist of processing on a large scale of special categories of data pursuant to Article 9 and data relating to criminal convictions and offences referred to in Article 10 (Article 37(1)).

A group of undertakings may appoint a single DPO provided that the DPO is easily accessible from each establishment (Article 37(2)).

Where the Controller or the Processor is a public authority or body, a single DPO may be designated for several such authorities or bodies, taking account of their organisational structure and size (Article 37(3)).

In cases other than those referred to in Article 37(1), the Controller or Processor or associations and other bodies representing categories of Controllers or Processors may or, where required by EU or Member State law shall, designate a DPO. The DPO may act for such associations and other bodies representing Controllers or Processors (Article 37(4)).

The DPO shall be designated on the basis of professional qualities and, in particular, expert knowledge of data protection law and practices and the ability to fulfil the tasks referred to in Article 39 (Article 37(5)).

The DPO may be a staff member of the Controller or Processor, or fulfil the tasks on the basis of a service contract (Article 37(6)).

The Controller or the Processor shall publish the contact details of the DPO and communicate these to the supervisory authority (Article 37(7)).

The Controller or the Processor shall ensure that the DPO is involved, properly and in a timely manner, in all issues which relate to the protection of personal data (Article 38(1)).

The Controller or Processor shall support the DPO in performing the tasks referred to in Article 39 by providing resources necessary to carry out these tasks as well as access to personal data and processing operations, and to maintain their expert knowledge (Article 38(2)).

The Controller or Processor shall ensure that the DPO does not receive any instructions regarding the exercise of those tasks. He or she shall not be dismissed or penalised by the Controller or the Processor for performing their tasks. The DPO shall directly report to the highest management level of the Controller or the Processor (Article 38(3)).

Data Subjects may contact the DPO with regard to all issues related to the processing of their personal data and the exercise of their rights under the GDPR (Article 38(4)).

The DPO shall be bound by secrecy or confidentiality concerning the performance of their tasks, in accordance with EU or Member State law (Article 38(5)).

The DPO may fulfil other tasks and duties – which must not result in a conflict of interests (Article 38(6)).

The Controller or Processor shall ensure that any such tasks and duties do not result in a conflict of interests (Article 38(6)).

The DPO shall have at least the following tasks:

- to inform and advise the Controller or the Processor and the employees who carry out processing of their obligations pursuant to the GDPR and to other EU or Member State data protection provisions;
- to monitor compliance with the GDPR, with other EU or Member State data protection provisions and with the policies of the Controller or Processor in relation to the protection of personal data, including the assignment of responsibilities, awareness-raising and training of staff involved in processing operations, and the related audits;
- to provide advice where requested as regards the data protection impact assessment and monitor its performance pursuant to Article 35;
- to cooperate with the supervisory authority;
- to act as the contact point for the supervisory authority on issues related to the processing of personal data, including the prior consultation referred to in Article 36, and to consult, where appropriate, with regard to any other matter (Article 37(1)).

The DPO shall in the performance of their tasks have due regard to the risk associated with the processing operations, taking into account the nature, scope, context and purposes of the processing (Article 39(2)).

Inward Facing Issues

15.04 Organisations must comply with the data protection regime as regards their inward facing personal data. This primarily relates to the employees of the organisation. This raises a number of issues both in terms of whom are the employees, what personal data is being collected and processed, for what purpose or purposes, where is it located, does anyone else obtain the data, etc, and how the organisation ensures that it is data protection compliant in relation to same.

In relation to employee personal data, organisations must ensure compliance with the:

- Data Protection Principles;
- the Legitimate Processing Conditions;
- the Sensitive Personal Data Legitimate Processing Conditions;
- the security requirements;
- risk assessments and privacy impact assessments;

- employee (etc) Data Subject rights;
- new DPO.

Those Covered

15.05 Who is covered by the inward facing organisational data protection obligations? While full time employees are the most obvious example, they are not the only ones. Organisations must consider the inward facing personal data of:

- full time employees;
- part time employees;
- other workers such as temps and casual staff;
- agency staff;
- contractors;
- ex-employees;
- retired employees;
- spouses;
- job applicants, including unsuccessful applicants;
- volunteers;
- apprentices and trainees;
- work experience staff;
- indirectly engaged persons, such as actors (after the Sony film 'The Interview' massive data breach incident – after which the online publication of internal disparaging emails regarding certain actors caused significant reputational damage and potential lawsuits. It also cost key personnel their jobs).

Where an organisation engages with the data of any of the above, it will have to ensure that the data protection regime is complied with.

Compliance with the Data Protection Principles

15.06 In dealing with employee personal data, as well as potential employees and any of the categories outlined above, it is necessary for the organisation to comply with the Data Protection Principles.

The eight Data Protection Principles apply in the work environment as well as elsewhere. Employee personal data must be:

(1) fairly and lawfully processed;
(2) processed for limited purposes;

(3) adequate, relevant and not excessive;
(4) accurate and up to date;
(5) not kept for longer than is necessary;
(6) processed in line with employee data protection rights;
(7) secure; and
(8) not transferred to other countries without adequate protection.[1]

All eight of the principles must be complied with. Compliance with the Data Protection Principles applies to all employee and inward-facing personal data collected and or processed by an organisation. It also applies regardless of registration requirements.

These can be summarised in the new GDPR as:

- processed lawfully, fairly and in a transparent manner ('lawfulness, fairness and transparency');
- for specified, explicit and legitimate purposes and not further processed incompatibly with the purpose; (carveout for archiving purposes in the public interest, scientific and historical research purposes or statistical purposes) ('purpose limitation');
- adequate, relevant and limited to what is necessary for the purposes ('data minimisation');
- accurate and, where necessary, kept up to date; every reasonable step must be taken to ensure that inaccurate personal data, having regard to the purposes for which they are processed, are erased or rectified without delay ('accuracy');
- kept in a form which permits identification of data subjects for no longer than is necessary; (carveout for archiving purposes in the public interest, scientific and historical research purposes or statistical purposes subject to appropriate technical and organisational measures) ('storage limitation');
- appropriate security, including protection against unauthorised or unlawful processing and against accidental loss, destruction or damage, using appropriate technical or organisational measures ('integrity and confidentiality').

The Controller must demonstrate compliance ('accountability').

Ordinary Personal Data Legitimate Processing Conditions

15.07 When dealing with the above inward-facing categories of employees, agents, contractors, etc, the Legitimate Processing

---

1   See DPA 1998, Sch 1, Pt 1, para 1.

Conditions are required to be complied with, *in addition* to the Data Protection Principles.

Schedule 2 of the DPA 1998 contains the general Legitimate Processing Conditions eg employee non sensitive personal data. In order to comply with the general personal data Legitimate Processing Conditions, the organisation must fall within *one* of the following conditions, namely:

- The individual whom the personal data is about has consented to the processing.
- The processing is necessary,
  ○ in relation to a contract which the individual has entered into; or
  ○ because the individual has asked for something to be done so they can enter into a contract.
- The processing is necessary because of a legal obligation that applies to the organisation (except an obligation imposed by a contract);
- The processing is necessary to protect the individual's 'vital interests.' This condition only applies in cases of life or death, such as where an employee's medical history is disclosed to a hospital's A&E department treating them after a serious road accident;
- The processing is necessary for administering justice, or for exercising statutory, governmental, or other public functions;
- The processing is in accordance with the 'legitimate interests' condition.

DPA 1998, Sch 2 contains conditions relevant for the purposes of the first Data Protection Principle, in particular the processing of personal data. It states:

1 The Data Subject has given his consent to the processing.
2 The processing is necessary:
  (a) for the performance of a contract to which the Data Subject is a party, or
  (b) for the taking of steps at the request of the Data Subject with a view to entering into a contract.
3 The processing is necessary for compliance with any legal obligation to which the Controller is subject, other than an obligation imposed by contract.
4 The processing is necessary in order to protect the vital interests of the Data Subject.
5 The processing is necessary:
  (a) for the administration of justice,
  (aa) for the exercise of any functions of either House of Parliament,
  (b) for the exercise of any functions conferred on any person by or under any enactment,

    (c) for the exercise of any functions of the Crown, a Minister of the Crown or a government department, or

    (d) for the exercise of any other functions of a public nature exercised in the public interest by any person.

6 (1) The processing is necessary for the purposes of legitimate interests pursued by the Controller or by the third party or parties to whom the data are disclosed, except where the processing is unwarranted in any particular case by reason of prejudice to the rights and freedoms or legitimate interests of the Data Subject;

    (2) The Secretary of State may by order specify particular circumstances in which this condition is, or is not, to be taken to be satisfied.

There are, therefore, six general Legitimate Processing Conditions. Frequently, an organisation would seek to fall within the legitimate interests condition above. These might be summarised as follows:

- the employee has given explicit consent;
- processing necessary for performance of *contract* to which the employee is a party;
- processing is necessary to take steps at request of the employee prior to entering into contract;
- processing is necessary for compliance with legal obligation (other than contractual obligation);
- necessary to prevent injury or other damage to health of the employee or serious loss or damage to property of the employee or to protect vital interests;
- necessary for the administration of justice, performance of statutory function or function of public nature performed in public interest;
- processing necessary for *legitimate interests* pursued by Controller except where unwarranted.

Legitimate Processing and Organisation's Employees

15.08 Unlike certain other areas, the legitimate processing of employee personal data does not require employee consent. However, many organisations would have originally expected and proceeded on the basis that consent was so required. They would have incorporated (deemed) consent clauses into employment contracts, etc.

    As indicated above, DPA 1998, Sch 2 enables organisations to rely upon the legitimate processing condition that processing is necessary for the purposes of *legitimate interests* pursued by the Controller or by the third party or parties to whom the data are disclosed, except where the processing is unwarranted in any particular case by reason of prejudice to the rights and freedoms or legitimate interests of the Data Subject.

An alternative could be to say that the processing is necessary as part of a contract to which the employee is a party, in particular the employment contract.

Sensitive Personal Data Legitimate Processing Conditions

15.09 Organisations may also feel the need on occasion to store and use sensitive personal data in relation to employees, such as medical and health data. In the case of sensitive personal data, an organisation must in addition to satisfying all of the Data Protection Principles, be able to comply or fall within one of the Sensitive Personal Data Legitimate Processing Conditions.

Schedule 3 to the DPA 1998 sets out conditions relevant for the purposes of the first Data Protection Principle in particular in relation to the processing of Sensitive Personal Data. In the context of employees and inward-facing personal data, it provides:

1   The employee Data Subject has given his or her explicit consent to the processing of the personal data.
2   (1)   The processing is necessary for the purposes of exercising or performing any right or obligation which is conferred or imposed by law on the Controller in connection with employment.
   (2)   The Secretary of State may by order:
     (a)   exclude the application of sub-paragraph (1) in such cases as may be specified, or
     (b)   provide that, in such cases as may be specified, the condition in sub-paragraph (1) is not to be regarded as satisfied unless such further conditions as may be specified in the order are also satisfied.
3   The processing is necessary:
   (a)   in order to protect the vital interests of the employee Data Subject or another person, in a case where:
     (i)   consent cannot be given by or on behalf of the employee Data Subject, or
     (ii)   the Controller cannot reasonably be expected to obtain the consent of the employee Data Subject, or
   (b)   in order to protect the vital interests of another person, in a case where consent by or on behalf of the employee Data Subject has been unreasonably withheld.

4 The processing:
    (a) is carried out in the course of its legitimate activities by any body or association which:
        (i) is not established or conducted for profit, and
        (ii) exists for political, philosophical, religious or trade-union purposes,
    (b) is carried out with appropriate safeguards for the rights and freedoms of Data Subjects,
    (c) relates only to individuals who either are members of the body or association or have regular contact with it in connection with its purposes, and
    (d) does not involve disclosure of the employee personal data to a third party without the consent of the employee Data Subject.

5 The information contained in the personal data has been made public as a result of steps deliberately taken by the employee Data Subject.

6 The processing:
    (a) is necessary for the purpose of, or in connection with, any legal proceedings (including prospective legal proceedings),
    (b) is necessary for the purpose of obtaining legal advice, or
    (c) is otherwise necessary for the purposes of establishing, exercising or defending legal rights.

7 (1) The processing is necessary:
    (a) for the administration of justice,
        (aa) for the exercise of any functions of either House of Parliament,
    (b) for the exercise of any functions conferred on any person by or under an enactment, or
    (c) for the exercise of any functions of the Crown, a Minister of the Crown or a government department.

   (2) The Secretary of State may by order:
    (a) exclude the application of sub-paragraph (1) in such cases as may be specified, or
    (b) provide that, in such cases as may be specified, the condition in sub-paragraph (1) is not to be regarded as satisfied unless such further conditions as may be specified in the order are also satisfied.

7A (1) The processing:
    (a) is either:
        (i) the disclosure of sensitive personal data by a person as a member of an anti-fraud organisation or otherwise in accordance with any arrangements made by such an organisation, or
        (ii) any other processing by that person or another person of sensitive personal data so disclosed, and

        (b) is necessary for the purposes of preventing fraud or a particular kind of fraud.

    (2) In this paragraph 'an anti-fraud organisation' means any unincorporated association, body corporate or other person which enables or facilitates any sharing of information to prevent fraud or a particular kind of fraud or which has any of these functions as its purpose or one of its purposes.

8   (1) The processing is necessary for medical purposes and is undertaken by:

        (a) a health professional, or

        (b) a person who in the circumstances owes a duty of confidentiality which is equivalent to that which would arise if that person were a health professional.

    (2) In this paragraph 'medical purposes' includes the purposes of preventative medicine, medical diagnosis, medical research, the provision of care and treatment and the management of healthcare services.

9   (1) The processing:

        (a) is of sensitive personal data consisting of information as to racial or ethnic origin,

        (b) is necessary for the purpose of identifying or keeping under review the existence or absence of equality of opportunity or treatment between persons of different racial or ethnic origins, with a view to enabling such equality to be promoted or maintained, and

        (c) is carried out with appropriate safeguards for the rights and freedoms of employee Data Subjects.

    (2) The Secretary of State may by order specify circumstances in which processing falling within sub-paragraph (1)(a) and (b) is, or is not, to be taken for the purposes of sub-paragraph (1) (c) to be carried out with appropriate safeguards for the rights and freedoms of Data Subjects.

These Sensitive Personal Data Legitimate Processing conditions may be summarised as follows:

- the employee whom the sensitive personal data is about has given explicit consent to the processing;
- the processing is necessary so that the organisation can comply with employment law;
- the processing is necessary to protect the vital interests of,
  - the employee (in a case where the employee's consent cannot be given or reasonably obtained); or
  - another person (in a case where the individual's consent has been unreasonably withheld);

- the processing is carried out by a not-for-profit organisation and does not involve disclosing personal data to a third party, unless the employee consents. Extra limitations apply to this condition;
- the employee has deliberately made the information public;
- the processing is necessary in relation to legal proceedings, for obtaining legal advice; or otherwise for establishing, exercising or defending legal rights;
- the processing is necessary for administering justice, or for exercising statutory or governmental functions;
- the processing is necessary for medical purposes, and is undertaken by a health professional or by someone who is subject to an equivalent duty of confidentiality;
- the processing is necessary for monitoring equality of opportunity, and is carried out with appropriate safeguards for the rights of individuals.

Furthermore, regulations also set out further obligations in relation to the processing of sensitive personal data.

Sensitive Data Legitimate Processing and Organisation's Employees

15.10 However, where sensitive personal data is involved, the organisation may have to obtain consent, unless otherwise specifically permitted in relation to one of the other particular purpose conditions set out above.

Consent

15.11 If it is the case that none of the condition criteria apply or permit a specific data processing use, then the organisation must obtain appropriate consent.

In considering the legitimising criteria the organisation should pay particular attention to the conditional word 'necessary.' If not strictly necessary, and demonstrably so, in the event that it is ever necessary to justify it when subsequently queried, it means that it may be necessary to fall back to the consent criteria.

Explicit consent, for example, with sensitive personal data usage, can mean having to obtain written consent. There is also a reference to freely given consent. Where employee consent is utilised or required, an issue can sometimes arise as to whether it is voluntarily and freely given. If the employee feels forced into giving consent they, or the ICO, might subsequently say that the consent is invalid, thus compromising the legitimacy of the processing.

Compliance and Policies

15.12 It is essential for all organisations to implement appropriate written policies. These will vary, as there are different types of policy. In addition, each policy will be specifically tailored to meet the needs and circumstances of the particular organisation.

Once finalised, the policy or policies should be properly and effectively communicated to all employees. It may also have to be made available to others who work in or for the organisation eg contractors.

Those in the organisation with responsibility for dealing with personal data also need to be particularly familiarised with the policies, security measures, data protection processes, as well as effectively trained in relation to all aspects of data protection compliance.

As with all legal, business and organisational policies relating to regulatory compliance, data protection policies need to be regularly monitored and updated as requirement dictates. This can be because of legal changes, ICO guideline changes, business and activity changes, changing security and risk requirements, changing technology, etc.

ICO Codes

15.13 It is recommended that the organisation consult the most relevant ICO guidance and codes in terms of implementing, or tailoring, IT data processing and data protection compliance practices.[2]

Responsible Person for Data Protection Compliance

15.14 Organisations will have to appoint a particular identified person in the organisation to deal with and be responsible for all data protection processes and related compliance issues. This includes ensuring that the organisation is data protection compliant in accordance with the DPA and the ICO Employment Practices Code.[3]

In addition to a data protection supervisor or DPO it is also recommended that an individual at Board level be appointed to be responsible for overseeing and dealing with data protection compliance within the organisation. The contemporary importance and significance of data protection ensures that it is now clearly a boardroom issue.

---

2   ICO Employment Practices Code, at https://ico.org.uk.
3   *Ibid.*

Responsibilities include ongoing compliance, policies, strategies, processes, training, monitoring, reviewing and updating, coordinating, engaging appropriate expertise and advices, audits, PbD, education, courses, notification and registration, incident response, etc, as regards data protection.

Personnel Contracts

15.15   The organisation's contracts of employment need to incorporate appropriate notifications, consent clauses (only if appropriate), and references to the organisational policies relevant to data protection, such as corporate communications usage policies, internet policies, devices, security, breaches, etc. There may also be reference to where these policies are located and where the latest and most up to date version will always be available. This might be a staff handbook, intranet, etc.

These documents will all be different depending on the organisation, the sector and the data protection practices ie the types of personal data, what it is used for and why. Issues such as compliance, security and confidentiality should be emphasised.

Training

15.16   Staff induction sessions as well as ongoing staff training should all incorporate guidance in relation to dealing with and handling personal data.

Employee Handbooks

15.17   Most organisations provide an employee handbook to their employees. These handbooks should contain guidance and polices of data protection, corporate communications, usage policies, etc.

Notices, Communications, Internet, Intranet

15.18   All of these provide an opportunity for the organisation to set out and reinforce the organisational requirements regarding the data protection regime. These can be user friendly and instantaneous, and hence provide an easy means of notifying new and urgent changes, notices, etc.

Personnel Department

15.19   While the personnel department or personnel Director will be required to be familiar with data protection, the role and responsibility of operating data protection compliance is not a personnel role. It needs to be someone outside of the employment and personnel function. However, the person responsible for data protection will need to liaise regularly with the personnel department, including training and keeping personnel staff up to date in relation to new developments in data protection compliance.

DPA: Employees and Security

15.20 The security of employee personal data is an essential obligation under the data protection regime.

DPA 1998, Sch 1, Pt II, para 10 provides that the Controller must take reasonable steps to ensure the reliability of any employees of the organisation who have access to the personal data.

Lynda McDonald[4] refers to security indicating that the following would be required to be checked, namely:

- access to buildings, computer rooms and offices where personal data is held;
- access to computer and other equipment where unauthorised access could have a detrimental effect on security;
- that manual records are put away at night in locked filing cabinets before the cleaners arrive;
- that passwords are not written down so that others can access them;
- that strict rules are in force within the business about what personal information can be accessed by which organisations, for example, the information that line managers can access about their staff may be different to (and less than) that which an HR manager can access;
- that there is an efficient and effective security system in place to prevent employees from seeing other employee data;
- that mechanisms are in place to detect any breach of security, and procedures in place to investigate such breaches;
- that all staff have undergone training on the organisation's data protection policy and how it works in practice, either as part of their induction or at specialist sessions which are appropriate to their job role, position and function.[5]

4   L AC MacDonald, *Data Protection: Legal Compliance and Good Practice for Employers* (Tottel, 2008) 11–12.
5   *Ibid.*

Even where an employee is working off-site or at home, or indeed travelling, it is still the organisation's responsibility to ensure appropriate security measures and processes are in place.

These scenarios are increasingly prominent but the organisation should ensure that they occur on a planned and permission basis. Unregulated activities enhance the level of risk as well as increasing the level on unknown, uncontrollable activities.

Access Requests by Employees

15.21 Employees are individuals and are hence able to rely upon their data protection rights, such as requesting a copy of the personal data relating to them. In the instance of an employee access request being made, the organisation should assess the request to see if the appropriate (minimum) fee has been paid and whether any exemptions apply which would prevent a disclosure being made. In addition, while the employee's personal data may have to be disclosed, certain third party personal data should be taken out or redacted. It may also be the case that clarification may have to be obtained to further clarify what particular personal data is being sought. It should not be a mere mechanism to avoid so complying.

The access request must be complied with within forty calendar days.

MacDonald[6] refers to some examples of the types of employee related personal data that may relate to access requests, such as:

- performance reviews or appraisals;
- sickness records;
- warnings or minutes of disciplinary interviews;
- training records;
- statements about pay;
- emails or electronic documents of which they are the subject;
- expressions of opinion regarding eg prospects for promotion.

Information relating to automated individual decisions regarding employees are also relevant and may be requested.

---

6   L AC MacDonald, *Data Protection: Legal Compliance and Good Practice for Employers* (Tottel, 2008), 51.

Conclusion

15.22 Organisations need to actively have considered data protection compliance issues and the recording of compliance even before an employee is engaged. Data protection and personal data arises at recruitment, selection and interview stages. The organisation must also note relevant policies. Unless data protection issues and policy issues are properly incorporated into the employment relationship, the organisation may be non-compliant. In addition, it may not be able to enforce and rely upon particular contract terms, policies, employee obligations, disciplinary rules and such like.

Chapter 16

Employee Data Protection Rights

Introduction

16.01 Just as other parties whose personal data are being collected and processed have data protection rights, employees also have Data Subject rights.

The Data Protection Rights of Employees

16.02 The rights of employees can be summarised as including:

- right of access (DPA 1998, s 7);
- right to establish if personal data exists (DPA 1998, s 7(1)(a));
- right to be informed of the logic in automatic decision taking (DPA 1998, s 7(1)(d));
- right to prevent processing likely to cause damage or distress (DPA 1998, s 18);
- right to prevent processing for direct marketing (DPA 1998, s 11);
- right to prevent automated decision taking (DPA 1998, s 12);
- right to compensation (DPA 1998, s 13);
- right to rectify inaccurate data (DPA 1998, s 14);
- right to rectification, blocking, erasure and destruction (DPA 1998, s 14);
- right to complain to ICO (DPA 1998, s 42);
- right to go to court (DPA 1998, s 15).

Chapter III of the new GDPR refers to the rights of Data Subjects. These include:

- right to transparency (Article 5; Article 12);
- right to prior information: directly obtained data (Article 14);
- right to prior information: indirectly obtained data (Article 14);

- right of confirmation and right of access (Article 15);
- right to be informed of third country safeguards (Article 15(2));
- right to rectification (Article 16);
- right to erasure (Right to be Forgotten) (RtbF) (Article 17);
- right to restriction of processing (Article 18);
- notifications re rectification, erasure or restriction (Article 19);
- right to data portability (Article 18);
- right to object (Article 19);
- rights re automated individual decision making, including profiling (Article 20);
- DPbD (Article 23);
- security rights;
- data protection impact assessment and prior consultation;
- communicating data breach to Data Subject;
- Data Protection Officer (DPO);
- remedies, liability and sanctions (Chapter VIII).

Rights Under the DPA 1998

Employee Access Right

16.03   Part II of the DPA 1998 refers to the rights of Data Subjects and others. In particular, s 7 refers to the right of access to personal data. This applies to employee Data Subjects. It is a Data Subject right.

Section 7(1) provides that subject to the following provisions of this section and to ss 8, 9 and 9A, an employee is entitled:

- to be informed by any Controller whether personal data of which that individual is the employee Data Subject are being processed by or on behalf of that Controller,
- if that is the case, to be given by the Controller a description of,
    - the personal data of which that individual is the employee Data Subject;
    - the purposes for which they are being or are to be processed; and
    - the recipients or classes of recipients to whom they are or may be disclosed,
- to have communicated to them in an intelligible form,
    - the information constituting any personal data of which that individual is the Data Subject; and
    - any information available to the Controller as to the source of those data; and
- where the processing by automatic means of personal data of which that employee is the Data Subject for the purpose of evaluating matters relating to them such as, for example, his performance at work,

his creditworthiness, his reliability or his conduct, has constituted or is likely to constitute the sole basis for any decision significantly affecting them, to be informed by the Controller of the logic involved in that decision-taking.

Therefore, and employee is entitled to the above.

Section 7(2) provides that a Controller is not obliged to supply any information under sub-s (1) unless he has received:

- a request in writing; and
- except in prescribed cases, such fee (not exceeding the prescribed maximum) as he may require.

Section 7(3) provides that where a Controller:

- reasonably requires further information in order to satisfy them as to the identity of the person making a request under this section and to locate the information which that person seeks; and
- has informed them of that requirement,

the Controller is not obliged to comply with the request unless he is supplied with that further information.

Section 7(4) provides that where a Controller cannot comply with the request without disclosing information relating to another individual who can be identified from that information, he is not obliged to comply with the request unless:

- the other individual has consented to the disclosure of the information to the person making the request; or
- it is reasonable in all the circumstances to comply with the request without the consent of the other individual.

Section 7(5) provides that in sub-s (4) the reference to information relating to another individual includes a reference to information identifying that individual as the source of the information sought by the request; and that subsection is not to be construed as excusing a Controller from communicating so much of the information sought by the request as can be communicated without disclosing the identity of the other individual concerned, whether by the omission of names or other identifying particulars or otherwise.

Section 7(6) provides that in determining for the purposes of sub-s (4) (b) whether it is reasonable in all the circumstances to comply with the request without the consent of the other individual concerned, regard shall be had, in particular, to:

- any duty of confidentiality owed to the other individual;
- any steps taken by the Controller with a view to seeking the consent of the other individual;

- whether the other individual is capable of giving consent; and
- any express refusal of consent by the other individual.

Section 7(7) provides that an individual making a request under this section may, in such cases as may be prescribed, specify that his request is limited to personal data of any prescribed description.

Section 7(8) provides that subject to sub-s (4), a Controller shall comply with a request under this section promptly and in any event before the end of the prescribed period beginning with the relevant day.

Section 7(9) provides that if a court is satisfied on the application of any person who has made a request under the foregoing provisions of this section that the Controller in question has failed to comply with the request in contravention of those provisions, the court may order them to comply with the request.

Section 7(10) also provides that in this section:

- 'prescribed' means prescribed by the Secretary of State by regulations;
- 'the prescribed maximum' means such amount as may be prescribed;
- 'the prescribed period' means forty days or such other period as may be prescribed;
- 'the relevant day,' in relation to a request under this section, means the day on which the Controller receives the request or, if later, the first day on which the Controller has both the required fee and the information referred to in sub-s (3).

Section 7(11) provides that different amounts or periods may be prescribed under this section in relation to different cases.

Section 7(12) provides that a person is a relevant person for the purposes of sub-s (4)(c) if he:

- is a person referred to in para 4(a) or (b) or para 8(a) or (b) of Sch 11;
- is employed by an education authority (within the meaning of para 6 of Schedule 11) in pursuance of its functions relating to education and the information relates to them, or he supplied the information in his capacity as such an employee; or
- is the person making the request.

Section 7(12) provides that a person is a relevant person for the purposes of sub-s (4)(c) if he:

- is a person referred to in para 1(p) or (q) of the Schedule to the Data Protection (Subject Access Modification) (Social Work) Order 2000; or
- is or has been employed by any person or body referred to in para 1 of that Schedule in connection with functions which are or have been exercised in relation to the data consisting of the information; or

- has provided for reward a service similar to a service provided in the exercise of any functions specified in para 1(a)(i), (b), (c) or (d) of that Schedule,

and the information relates to them or he supplied the information in his official capacity or, as the case may be, in connection with the provision of that service.

Section 8 refers to provisions supplementary to s 7.

Section 8(1) provides that the Secretary of State may by regulations provide that, in such cases as may be prescribed, a request for information under any provision of subsection (1) of section 7 is to be treated as extending also to information under other provisions of that subsection.

Section 8(2) provides that the obligation imposed by s 7(1)(c)(i) must be complied with by supplying the Data Subject with a copy of the information in permanent form unless:

- the supply of such a copy is not possible or would involve disproportionate effort; or
- the Data Subject agrees otherwise,

and where any of the information referred to in s 7(1)(c)(i) is expressed in terms which are not intelligible without explanation the copy must be accompanied by an explanation of those terms.

Section 8(3) provides that where a Controller has previously complied with a request made under s 7 by an individual, the Controller is not obliged to comply with a subsequent identical or similar request under that section by that individual unless a reasonable interval has elapsed between compliance with the previous request and the making of the current request.

Section 8(4) provides that in determining for the purposes of sub-s (3) whether requests under s 7 are made at reasonable intervals, regard shall be had to the nature of the data, the purpose for which the data are processed and the frequency with which the data are altered.

Section 8(5) provides that s 7(1)(d) is not to be regarded as requiring the provision of information as to the logic involved in any decision-taking if, and to the extent that, the information constitutes a trade secret.

Section 8(6) provides that the information to be supplied pursuant to a request under section 7 must be supplied by reference to the data in question at the time when the request is received, except that it may take account of any amendment or deletion made between that time and the time when the information is supplied, being an amendment or deletion that would have been made regardless of the receipt of the request.

Section 8(7) provides that for the purposes of s 7(4) and (5) another individual can be identified from the information being disclosed if he can be identified from that information, or from that and any other information which, in the reasonable belief of the Controller, is likely to be in, or to come into, the possession of the Data Subject making the request.

Section 9 refers to the application of s 7 where Controller is credit reference agency.

Section 9(1) provides that where the Controller is a credit reference agency, s 7 has effect subject to the provisions of this section.

Section 9(2) provides that an individual making a request under s 7 may limit his request to personal data relevant to his financial standing, and shall be taken to have so limited his request unless the request shows a contrary intention.

Section 9(3) provides that where the Controller receives a request under s 7 in a case where personal data of which the individual making the request is the Data Subject are being processed by or on behalf of the Controller, the obligation to supply information under that section includes an obligation to give the individual making the request a statement, in such form as may be prescribed by the Secretary of State by regulations, of the individual's rights:

- under s 159 of the Consumer Credit Act 1974; and
- to the extent required by the prescribed form, under this Act.

Section 9A relates to unstructured personal data held by public authorities.

Section 9A(1) provides that in this section 'unstructured personal data' means any personal data falling within paragraph (e) of the definition of 'data' in s 1(1), other than information which is recorded as part of, or with the intention that it should form part of, any set of information relating to individuals to the extent that the set is structured by reference to individuals or by reference to criteria relating to individuals.

Section 9A(2) provides that public authority is not obliged to comply with sub-s (1) of s 7 in relation to any unstructured personal data unless the request under that section contains a description of the data.

Section 9A(3) provides that even if the data are described by the Data Subject in his request, a public authority is not obliged to comply with sub-s (1) of s 7 in relation to unstructured personal data if the authority estimates that the cost of complying with the request so far as relating to those data would exceed the appropriate limit.

Section 9A(4) provides that sub-s (3) does not exempt the public authority from its obligation to comply with para (a) of s 7(1) in relation to the unstructured personal data unless the estimated cost of complying with that paragraph alone in relation to those data would exceed the appropriate limit.

Section 9A(5) provides that in sub-s (3) and sub-s (4) 'the appropriate limit' means such amount as may be prescribed by the Secretary of State by regulations, and different amounts may be prescribed in relation to different cases.

Section 9A(6) provides that any estimate for the purposes of this section must be made in accordance with regulations under s 12(5) of the Freedom of Information Act 2000.

Right to Prevent Data Processing Likely to Cause Damage or Distress

16.04 Section 10 of the DPA 1998 refers to the right to prevent processing likely to cause damage or distress.

Section 10(1) provides that subject to sub-s (2), an individual is entitled at any time by notice in writing to a Controller to require the Controller at the end of such period as is reasonable in the circumstances to cease, or not to begin, processing, or processing for a specified purpose or in a specified manner, any personal data in respect of which he is the Data Subject, on the ground that, for specified reasons:

- the processing of those data or their processing for that purpose or in that manner is causing or is likely to cause substantial damage or substantial distress to them or to another; and
- that damage or distress is or would be unwarranted.

Section 10(2) provides that sub-s (1) does not apply,

- in a case where any of the conditions in paras 1 to 4 of Sch 2 is met; or
- in such other cases as may be prescribed by the Secretary of State by order.

Section 10(3) provides that the Controller must within twenty-one days of receiving a notice under sub-s (1) ('the Data Subject notice') give the individual who gave it a written notice:

- stating that he has complied or intends to comply with the Data Subject notice; or
- stating his reasons for regarding the Data Subject notice as to any extent unjustified and the extent (if any) to which he has complied or intends to comply with it.

Section 10(4) provides that if a court is satisfied, on the application of any person who has given a notice under sub-s (1) which appears to the court to be justified (or to be justified to any extent), that the Controller in question has failed to comply with the notice, the court may order them to take such steps for complying with the notice (or for complying with it to that extent) as the court thinks fit.

Section 10(5) provides that the failure by a Data Subject to exercise the right conferred by sub-s (1) or s 11(1) does not affect any other right conferred on them by this part.

Right to Prevent Data Processing for DM

16.05 Section 11 of the DPA 1998 relates to the right to prevent processing for purposes of direct marketing (DM).

Section 11(1) provides that an individual is entitled at any time by notice in writing to a Controller to require the Controller at the end of such period as is reasonable in the circumstances to cease, or not to begin, processing for the purposes of direct marketing personal data in respect of which he is the Data Subject.

Section 11(2) provides that if the court is satisfied, on the application of any person who has given a notice under sub-s (1), that the Controller has failed to comply with the notice, the court may order them to take such steps for complying with the notice as the court thinks fit.

Section 11(2A) provides that this section shall not apply in relation to the processing of such data as are mentioned in para (1) of reg 8 of the Telecommunications (Data Protection and Privacy) Regulations 1999 (processing of telecommunications billing data for certain marketing purposes) for the purposes mentioned in para (2) of that regulation.

Section 11(3) provides that in this section 'direct marketing' means the communication (by whatever means) of any advertising or marketing material which is directed to particular individuals.

Automated Decision Taking/Making Processes

16.06 Controllers may not take decisions which produce legal effects concerning a Data Subject or which otherwise significantly affect a Data Subject and which are based solely on processing by automatic means of personal data and which are intended to evaluate certain personal matters relating to the Data Subject such as, performance at work, credit worthiness, reliability of conduct.

Section 12 provides for the rights in relation to automated decision-taking.

Section 12(1) provides that an individual is entitled at any time, by notice in writing to any Controller, to require the Controller to ensure that no decision taken by or on behalf of the Controller which significantly affects that individual is based solely on the processing by automatic means of personal data in respect of which that individual is the Data Subject for the purpose of evaluating matters relating to them such as, for example, his performance at work, his creditworthiness, his reliability or his conduct.

Section 12(2) provides that where, in a case where no notice under sub-s (1) has effect, a decision which significantly affects an individual is based solely on such processing as is mentioned in sub-s (1):

- the Controller must as soon as reasonably practicable notify the individual that the decision was taken on that basis; and

- the individual is entitled, within twenty-one days of receiving that notification from the Controller, by notice in writing to require the Controller to reconsider the decision or to take a new decision otherwise than on that basis.

Section 12(3) provides that the Controller must, within twenty-one days of receiving a notice under sub-s (2)(b) ('the Data Subject notice') give the individual a written notice specifying the steps that he intends to take to comply with the Data Subject notice.

Section 12(4) provides that a notice under sub-s (1) does not have effect in relation to an exempt decision; and nothing in sub-s (2) applies to an exempt decision.

Section 12(5) provides that in sub-s (4) 'exempt decision' means any decision:

- in respect of which the condition in sub-s (6) and the condition in sub-s (7) are met; or
- which is made in such other circumstances as may be prescribed by the Secretary of State by order.

Section 12(6) provides that the condition in this sub-section is that the decision:

(a) is taken in the course of steps taken,
　　(i) for the purpose of considering whether to enter into a contract with the Data Subject;
　　(ii) with a view to entering into such a contract; or
　　(iii) in the course of performing such a contract, or
(b) is authorised or required by or under any enactment.

Section 12(7) provides that the condition in this sub-section is that either:

- the effect of the decision is to grant a request of the Data Subject; or
- steps have been taken to safeguard the legitimate interests of the Data Subject (for example, by allowing them to make representations).

Section 12(8) provides that if a court is satisfied on the application of a Data Subject that a person taking a decision in respect of them (the 'responsible person') has failed to comply with sub-s (1) or (2)(b), the court may order the responsible person to reconsider the decision, or to take a new decision which is not based solely on such processing as is mentioned in sub-s (1).

Section 12(9) provides that an order under sub-s (8) shall not affect the rights of any person other than the Data Subject and the responsible person.

Section 12 of the DPA 1998 provides Rights in relation to automated decision-taking. It states:

(1) An individual is entitled at any time, by notice in writing to any Controller, to require the Controller to ensure that no decision taken by or on behalf of the Controller which significantly affects that individual is based solely on the processing by automatic means of personal data in respect of which that individual is the Data Subject for the purpose of evaluating matters relating to them such as, for example, his performance at work, his creditworthiness, his reliability or his conduct;

(2) Where, in a case where no notice under sub-s (1) has effect, a decision which significantly affects an individual is based solely on such processing as is mentioned in sub-s (1),

  (a) the Controller must as soon as reasonably practicable notify the individual that the decision was taken on that basis; and

  (b) the individual is entitled, within twenty-one days of receiving that notification from the Controller, by notice in writing to require the Controller to reconsider the decision or to take a new decision otherwise than on that basis.

(3) The Controller must, within twenty-one days of receiving a notice under sub-s (2)(b) ('the Data Subject notice') give the individual a written notice specifying the steps that he intends to take to comply with the Data Subject notice;

(4) A notice under sub-s (1) does not have effect in relation to an exempt decision; and nothing in sub-s (2) applies to an exempt decision;

(5) In sub-s (4) 'exempt decision' means any decision,

  (a) in respect of which the condition in sub-s (6) and the condition in sub-s (7) are met; or

  (b) which is made in such other circumstances as may be prescribed by the Secretary of State by order;

(6) The condition in this sub-section is that the decision,

  (a) is taken in the course of steps taken,

    (i) for the purpose of considering whether to enter into a contract with the Data Subject,

    (ii) with a view to entering into such a contract; or

    (iii) in the course of performing such a contract; or

  (b) is authorised or required by or under any enactment;

(7) The condition in this sub-section is that either,

  (a) the effect of the decision is to grant a request of the Data Subject; or

  (b) steps have been taken to safeguard the legitimate interests of the Data Subject (for example, by allowing them to make representations);

(8) If a court is satisfied on the application of a Data Subject that a person taking a decision in respect of them ('the responsible person') has failed to comply with sub-s (1) or (2)(b), the court may order the responsible person to reconsider the decision, or to take a new decision which is not based solely on such processing as is mentioned in sub-s (1);

(9) An order under sub-s (8) shall not affect the rights of any person other than the Data Subject and the responsible person.

Rectification, Blocking, Erasure and Destruction Rights

16.07　Section 14 of the DPA 1998 provides user rights in relation to rectification, blocking, erasure and destruction.

Section 14(1) provides that if a court is satisfied on the application of a Data Subject that personal data of which the applicant is the subject are inaccurate, the court may order the Controller to rectify, block, erase or destroy those data and any other personal data in respect of which he is the Controller and which contain an expression of opinion which appears to the court to be based on the inaccurate data.

Section 14(2) provides that sub-s (1) applies whether or not the data accurately record information received or obtained by the Controller from the Data Subject or a third party but where the data accurately record such information, then:

- if the requirements mentioned in para 7 of Part II of Sch 1 have been complied with, the court may, instead of making an order under sub-s (1), make an order requiring the data to be supplemented by such statement of the true facts relating to the matters dealt with by the data as the court may approve; and
- if all or any of those requirements have not been complied with, the court may, instead of making an order under that subsection, make such order as it thinks fit for securing compliance with those requirements with or without a further order requiring the data to be supplemented by such a statement as is mentioned in para (a).

Section 14(3) provides that where the court:

- makes an order under sub-s (1); or
- is satisfied on the application of a Data Subject that personal data of which he was the Data Subject and which have been rectified, blocked, erased or destroyed were inaccurate,

it may, where it considers it reasonably practicable, order the Controller to notify third parties to whom the data have been disclosed of the rectification, blocking, erasure or destruction.

Section 14(4) provides that if a court is satisfied on the application of a Data Subject:

- that he has suffered damage by reason of any contravention by a Controller of any of the requirements of the DPA 1998 in respect of any personal data, in circumstances entitling them to compensation under s 13; and
- that there is a substantial risk of further contravention in respect of those data in such circumstances,

the court may order the rectification, blocking, erasure or destruction of any of those data.

Section 14(5) provides that where the court makes an order under sub-s (4) it may, where it considers it reasonably practicable, order the Controller to notify third parties to whom the data have been disclosed of the rectification, blocking, erasure or destruction.

Section 14(6) provides that in determining whether it is reasonably practicable to require such notification as is mentioned in sub-s (3) or (5) the court shall have regard, in particular, to the number of persons who would have to be notified.

Requiring Data Disclosure

16.08 Section 57 of the DPA 1998 prohibits an organisation from forcing or requiring the production by Data Subjects of personal data records to them in relation to recruitment or employment. For example, organisations may be prohibited from forcing employees to disclose genetic data.

Right to Compensation for Data Subjects

16.09 Section 13 of the DPA 1998 refers to compensation for failure to comply with certain requirements.

Section 13(1) provides that an individual who suffers damage by reason of any contravention by a Controller of any of the requirements of the DPA 1998 is entitled to compensation from the Controller for that damage.

Section 13(2) provides that an individual who suffers distress by reason of any contravention by a Controller of any of the requirements of the DPA 1998 is entitled to compensation from the Controller for that distress if:

- the individual also suffers damage by reason of the contravention; or
- the contravention relates to the processing of personal data for the special purposes.

Section 13(3) provides that in proceedings brought against a person by virtue of the section it is a defence to prove that he had taken such care as in all the circumstances was reasonably required to comply with the requirement concerned.

Jurisdiction (Rights)

16.10 Section 15 of the DPA 1998 refers to jurisdiction and procedure.

Section 15(1) provides that the jurisdiction conferred by ss 7 to 14 is exercisable by the High Court or a county court or, in Scotland, by the Court of Session or the sheriff.

Section 15(2) provides that for the purpose of determining any question whether an applicant under sub-s (9) of s 7 is entitled to the information which he seeks (including any question whether any relevant data are exempt from that section by virtue of Part IV) a court may require the information constituting any data processed by or on behalf of the Controller and any information as to the logic involved in any decision-taking as mentioned in s 7(1)(d) to be made available for its own inspection but shall not, pending the determination of that question in the applicant's favour, require the information sought by the applicant to be disclosed to them or his representatives whether by discovery (or, in Scotland, recovery) or otherwise.

Rights Under the DPD

Access Right

16.11 Article 12 of the DPD provides for the right of access, and states, Member States shall guarantee every Data Subject the right to obtain from the Controller:

(a) without constraint at reasonable intervals and without excessive delay or expense,
- confirmation as to whether or not data relating to them are being processed and information at least as to the purposes of the processing, the categories of data concerned, and the recipients or categories of recipients to whom the data are disclosed;
- communication to them in an intelligible form of the data undergoing processing and of any available information as to their source;
- knowledge of the logic involved in any automatic processing of data concerning them at least in the case of the automated decisions referred to in Article 15(1);

(b) as appropriate the rectification, erasure or blocking of data the processing of which does not comply with the provisions of this Directive, in particular because of the incomplete or inaccurate nature of the data;

(c) notification to third parties to whom the data have been disclosed of any rectification, erasure or blocking carried out in compliance with (b), unless this proves impossible or involves a disproportionate effort.

Right Against Automated Individual Decisions

16.12   Article 15 refers to automated individual decisions. Article 15(1) provides that Member States shall grant the right to every person not to be subject to a decision which produces legal effects concerning them or significantly affects them and which is based solely on automated processing of data intended to evaluate certain personal aspects relating to them, such as his performance at work, creditworthiness, reliability, conduct, etc.

Article 15(2) provides that subject to the other Articles of this Directive, Member States shall provide that a person may be subjected to a decision of the kind referred to in Article 15(1) if that decision:

- is taken in the course of the entering into or performance of a contract, provided the request for the entering into or the performance of the contract, lodged by the Data Subject, has been satisfied or that there are suitable measures to safeguard his legitimate interests, such as arrangements allowing them to put his point of view; or
- is authorised by a law which also lays down measures to safeguard the Data Subject's legitimate interests.

Right to Object

16.13   Article 14 of the DPD provides for the Data Subject's right to object. It states that, Member States shall grant the Data Subject the right:

- at least in the cases referred to in Article 7(e) and (f), to object at any time on compelling legitimate grounds relating to his particular situation to the processing of data relating to them, save where otherwise provided by national legislation. Where there is a justified objection, the processing instigated by the Controller may no longer involve those data;
- to object, on request and free of charge, to the processing of personal data relating to them which the Controller anticipates being processed for the purposes of direct marketing, or to be informed before personal data are disclosed for the first time to third parties

or used on their behalf for the purposes of direct marketing, and to be expressly offered the right to object free of charge to such disclosures or uses.

It also provides that Member States shall take the necessary measures to ensure that Data Subjects are aware of the existence of the right.

Rectification, Erasure and Blocking

16.14 Article 12, which relates to the right of access, also provides for rectification, erasure and blocking. It states that Member States shall guarantee every Data Subject the right to obtain from the Controller:

> '(b) as appropriate the rectification, erasure or blocking of data the processing of which does not comply with the provisions of this Directive, in particular because of the incomplete or inaccurate nature of the data;
>
> (c) notification to third parties to whom the data have been disclosed of any rectification, erasure or blocking carried out in compliance with (b), unless this proves impossible or involves a disproportionate effort.'

Rights Under the GDPR

Access Right

16.15 Article 15 of the new GDPR relates to the right of access for the Data Subject. Employees and the other categories of person referred to above are covered by the data access right.

The Data Subject shall have the right to obtain from the Controller confirmation as to whether or not personal data concerning them are being processed, and access to the data and the following information:

- the purposes of the processing;
- the categories of personal data concerned;
- the recipients or categories of recipient to whom the personal data have been or will be disclosed, in particular to recipients in third countries or international organisations;
- where possible, the envisaged period for which the personal data will be stored, or if not possible, the criteria used to determine that period;
- the existence of the right to request from the Controller rectification or erasure of personal data or restriction of processing of personal data concerning the Data Subject or to object to the processing;
- the right to lodge a complaint to a SA;
- where the personal data are not collected from the Data Subject, any available information as to their source;

- the existence of automated decision making including profiling referred to in Article 22(1) and (4) and at least in those cases, meaningful information about the logic involved, as well as the significance and the envisaged consequences of such processing for the Data Subject (Article 15(1)).

Where personal data are transferred to a third country or to an international organisation, the Data Subject shall have the right to be informed of the appropriate safeguards pursuant to Article 46 relating to the transfer (Article 15(2)).

The Controller shall provide a copy of the personal data undergoing processing. For any further copies requested by the Data Subject, the Controller may charge a reasonable fee based on administrative costs. Where the Data Subject makes the request in electronic form, and unless otherwise requested by the Data Subject, the information shall be provided in a commonly used electronic form (Article 15(3)).

The right to obtain a copy referred to in para (3) shall not adversely affect the rights and freedoms of others (Article 15(4)).

Rectification Right

16.16 Chapter III, Section 3 of the GDPR refers to rectification and erasure. The Data Subject shall have the right to obtain from the Controller without undue delay the rectification of inaccurate personal data concerning them. Taking into account the purposes of the processing, the Data Subject shall have the right to have incomplete personal data completed, including by means of providing a supplementary statement (Article 16).

Right to Erasure (Right to be Forgotten)

16.17 The new GDPR states that Data Subject shall have the right to obtain from the Controller the erasure of personal data concerning them without undue delay and the Controller shall have the obligation to erase personal data without undue delay where one of the following grounds applies:

- the personal data are no longer necessary in relation to the purposes for which they were collected or otherwise processed;
- the Data Subject withdraws consent on which the processing is based according to Article 6(1)(a), or Article 9(2)(a), and where there is no other legal ground for the processing;
- the Data Subject objects to the processing pursuant to Article 21(1) and there are no overriding legitimate grounds for the processing, or the Data Subject objects to the processing to Article 21(2);
- the personal data have been unlawfully processed;

- the personal data have to be erased for compliance with a legal obligation in EU or Member State law to which the Controller is subject;
- the data have been collected in relation to the offering of information society services referred to in Article 8(1) (Article 17(1)).

Where the Controller has made the personal data public and is obliged pursuant to Article 17(1) to erase the personal data, the Controller, taking account of available technology and the cost of implementation, shall take reasonable steps, including technical measures, to inform Controllers which are processing the personal data that the Data Subject has requested the erasure by such Controllers of any links to, or copy or replication of, those personal data (Article 17(2)).

Article 17(1) and (2) shall not apply to the extent that processing is necessary:

- for exercising the right of freedom of expression and information;
- for compliance with a legal obligation which requires processing by EU or Member State law to which the Controller is subject or for the performance of a task carried out in the public interest or in the exercise of official authority vested in the Controller;
- for reasons of public interest in the area of public health in accordance with Article 9(2)(h) and (i) as well as Article 9(3);
- for archiving purposes in the public interest, or scientific and historical research purposes or statistical purposes in accordance with Article 89(1) in so far as the right referred to in Article 17(1) is likely to render impossible or seriously impair the achievement of the objectives of that processing; or
- for the establishment, exercise or defence of legal claims (Article 17(3)).

Notification Obligation re Rectification, Erasure or Restriction

16.18 The new GDPR states that the Controller shall communicate any rectification, erasure or restriction of processing carried out in accordance with Articles 16, 17(1) and 18 to each recipient to whom the data have been disclosed, unless this proves impossible or involves disproportionate effort. The Controller shall inform the Data Subject about those recipients if the Data Subject requests it (Article 19).

Right to Restriction of Processing

16.19 Article 18 of the new GDPR refers to the right to restriction of processing. The Data Subject shall have the right to obtain from the

Controller the restriction of the processing where one of the following applies:

- the accuracy of the data is contested by the Data Subject, for a period enabling the Controller to verify the accuracy of the data;
- the processing is unlawful and the Data Subject opposes the erasure of the personal data and requests the restriction of their use instead;
- the Controller no longer needs the personal data for the purposes of the processing, but they are required by the Data Subject for the establishment, exercise or defence of legal claims;
- the Data Subject has objected to processing pursuant to Article 21(1) pending the verification whether the legitimate grounds of the Controller override those of the Data Subject (Article 18(1)).

Where processing has been restricted under Article 18(1), such personal data shall, with the exception of storage, only be processed with the Data Subject's consent or for the establishment, exercise or defence of legal claims or for the protection of the rights of another natural or legal person or for reasons of important public interest of the EU or of a Member State (Article 18(2)).

A Data Subject who has obtained the restriction of processing pursuant to Article 18(1) shall be informed by the Controller before the restriction of processing is lifted (Article 18(3)).

Right to Data Portability

16.20   The new GDPR states that the Data Subject shall have the right to receive the personal data concerning them, which they have provided to a Controller, in a structured, commonly used and machine-readable format and have the right to transmit those data to another Controller without hindrance from the Controller to which the personal data have been provided, where:

- the processing is based on consent pursuant to Article 6(1)(a) or Article 9(2)(a) or on a contract pursuant to Article 6(1)(b); and
- the processing is carried out by automated means (Article 20(1)).

In exercising their right to data portability pursuant to Article 20(1), the Data Subject has the right to have the data transmitted directly from Controller to Controller, where technically feasible (Article 20(2)).

The exercise of the right shall be without prejudice to Article 17. The right shall not apply to processing necessary for the performance of a task carried out in the public interest or in the exercise of official authority vested in the Controller (Article 20(3)).

The right shall not adversely affect the rights and freedoms of others (Article 20(4)).

Automated Individual Decision Making Right

16.21 Chapter III, Section 4 of the new GDPR refers to the right to object and automated individual decision making.

Right to Object

16.22 The new GDPR states that the Data Subject shall have the right to object, on grounds relating to their particular situation, at any time to the processing of personal data concerning them which is based on Article 6(1)(e) or (f), including profiling based on these provisions. The Controller shall no longer process the personal data unless the Controller demonstrates compelling legitimate grounds for the processing which override the interests, rights and freedoms of the Data Subject or for the establishment, exercise or defence of legal claims (Article 21(1)).

Where personal data are processed for direct marketing purposes, the Data Subject shall have the right to object at any time to processing of personal data concerning them for such marketing, which includes profiling to the extent that it is related to such direct marketing (Article 21(2)).

Where the Data Subject objects to processing for direct marketing purposes, the personal data shall no longer be processed for such purposes (Article 21(3)).

At the latest at the time of the first communication with the Data Subject, the right referred to in Article 21(1) and (2) shall be explicitly brought to the attention of the Data Subject and shall be presented clearly and separately from any other information (Article 19(4)).

In the context of the use of information society services, and notwithstanding Directive 2002/58/EC,[1] the Data Subject may exercise their right to object by automated means using technical specifications (Article 21(5)).

Where personal data are processed for scientific and historical research purposes or statistical purposes pursuant to Article 89(1), the Data Subject, on grounds relating to their particular situation, shall have the right to object to processing of personal data concerning them, unless the processing is necessary for the performance of a task carried out for reasons of public interest (Article 21(6)).

Automated Individual Decision Making, Including Profiling

16.23 The new GDPR states that the Data Subject shall have the right not to be subject to a decision based solely on automated processing,

---

1   Directive 2002/58/EC of the European Parliament and of the Council of 12 July 2002 concerning the processing of personal data and the protection of privacy in the electronic communications sector (Directive on privacy and electronic communications).

including profiling, which produces legal effects concerning them or similarly significantly affects them (Article 22(1)).

Article 22(1) shall not apply if the decision:

- is necessary for entering into, or performance of, a contract between the Data Subject and a Controller [a]; or
- is authorised by EU or Member State law to which the Controller is subject and which also lays down suitable measures to safeguard the Data Subject's rights and freedoms and legitimate interests; or
- is based on the Data Subject's explicit consent (Article 22(2)) [c].

In cases referred to in Article 22(2)(a) and (c) the Controller shall implement suitable measures to safeguard the Data Subject's rights and freedoms and legitimate interests, at least the right to obtain human intervention on the part of the Controller, to express their point of view and to contest the decision (Article 22(3)).

Decisions referred to in Article 22(2) shall not be based on special categories of personal data referred to in Article 9(1), unless Article 9(2) (a) or (g) applies and suitable measures to safeguard the Data Subject's rights and freedoms and legitimate interests are in place (Article 22(4)).

Conclusion

16.24   Organisations need to respect the data protection rights of their employees, and even potential employees. In addition, particular care and attention needs to be paid to access requests from employees. Compliance is an ongoing issue as, for example, new changes and business practices will always present new challenges internally.

Chapter 17

Employee Considerations

Introduction

17.01 A large number of issues arise in terms of dealing with employee personal data, both in terms of audits, access, planning and compliance.

Contract

17.02 The starting point for informing and appraising employees of the importance of data protection, confidentiality and security in the organisation, and in relation to the employee's personal data should be to begin with the employment contract. There should be clauses referring to data protection and also to security.

Policies

17.03 There should also be policies relating to data protection furnished to all actual (and prospective) employees. These need to be updated regularly as the issues covered change constantly.

These policies may be separate or may be incorporated into an employee handbook.

Organisations need to be aware that if there is an important change made, unless this is notified and recorded to employees, the organisation may not be able to rely upon the changed clause. For example, if there is a new activity banned or regulated in an updated policy but the new policy is not notified to employees, it may be impossible to use the new policy to disciple an errant employee. They and their lawyers will strongly argue that the new policy was not notified, is not part of the employment relationship, and would be unlawful to apply. There are many examples of this problem occurring in practice.

Data Protection Policy

17.04   In considering what policies to implement, the organisation will have to consider many issues and separate policies, with data protection being just one. Others include health and safety, environmental, etc. The data protection policy will perhaps be the most dynamic given the wide range of data, individuals, processes, activities and technologies involved, and which are ever changing. Someone within the organisation needs to be responsible for examining and implementing ongoing changes as the requirement arises.

Internet Usage Policy

17.05   In addition to a general data protection policy, further specific data protection related policies may be required. The foremost of these relates to the employees' use of the internet on the organisation's systems.

Mobile and Device Usage Policies

17.06   Increasingly, employees use not just desktop computers but also laptops, mobile phones, smart phones, handheld devices, Blackberrys, iPads, etc. Unless explicitly incorporated into one of the above policies, then additional, or extended, policies need to be implemented. One particular issue for an organisation to consider is the employees' own devices, employee devices the bills for which are paid by the organisation, and devices supplied and paid for by the organisation. Somewhat different considerations may need to be applied.

Vehicle Use Policy

17.07   Vehicles must also be considered by organisations in terms of policy and employee usage. Increasingly tracking and other data from vehicles can be related to identified employees. Sometimes this may be as a result of the organisation furnishing a vehicle to the employee for work related business. However, this need not be the case. Even where an employee is using their own vehicle, it is possible for the organisation to be collecting or accessing personal data. In addition, organisations must also be aware that vehicle technology, both in-built and added, can result in greater collections of data, including personal data, being potentially accessible. Tracking, incident and accident reports, etc, are just some examples. It is important for organisations to consider these personal data issues.

Transfers of Undertaking

17.08   Transfers of undertakings or TUPE,[1] as it is known, refers to organisations being transferred to a new owner, whether in whole or in part. Situations like this are an everyday part of the commercial business environment.

The Transfer of Undertakings (Protection of Employment) Regulations 2006[2] provides certain protections for employees where the business is being transferred to a new owner. While primarily directed at the protection of employees' employment related rights, it is also noteworthy in that employee personal data will also be transferred to the new employer or organisation. There are various types of personal data to consider. The same rights, interests, terms, contracts, etc, as applied with the old employer are to apply with the new employer, which included data protection user rights, and possibly corporate communications usage, etc.

Evidence

17.09   Disputes naturally arise between employers and employees from time to time. In such disputes the organisation may need to rely upon documents, information and materials which will contain personal data. While this may fit under the legitimate interests and legal interest provisions, employers should be careful about using less obvious personal data. This might include private emails communications over which an employee may argue privacy and confidentiality. Particular concerns arise in cases where covert monitoring has been used. Before commencing covert activities of this type the organisation should seek advices. Otherwise, any evidence gathered may possibly be ruled inadmissible subsequently.

Organisations also need to be careful in that computer, electronic and mobile data can change, expire and or be amended quickly. It can be important to act quickly. Advance policies, procedures and protocols assist in this regard.

---

1   See generally, L AC MacDonald, *Data Protection: Legal Compliance and Good Practice for Employers* (Tottel, 2008) 44–48.
2   SI 2006/246.

Enforceability

17.10 An important issue for all organisations to consider is that if they ever wish to be able to discipline an errant employee, including up to dismissal, consequent upon their activities regarding personal data, internet usage, security breach, etc, the organisation needs to be able to point to a breach of an explicit contract or policy clause. If the breach is not explicit, or there is not written into the policy and contract, the employee can argue that there is no breach, perhaps regardless of the seriousness of the instant issue arising.

While online abuse is an issue to be dealt with, organisations need to be conscious of reputational damage from such incidents. However, they also need to consider what would happen if any of their employees are involved, whether by way of participation or orchestration, in an incident of abuse. One would have to consider what the contracts and policies say, as well as develop reaction strategies.

Data Breach

17.11 Employee involvement is critical in dealing with – and preparing for – data breach incidents. Various teams of employees will be involved.

Notification of Employee Data Breaches

17.12 However, as employee personal data can also be the subject of a data breach incident, employees may also need to be specifically considered in this context. For example, they may need to be separately informed that there is a breach relating to their personal data and what actions and safeguards are being followed by the organisation to deal with the issue. If the employees need to take specific actions, they may also need to be appraised of this possibility. Potentially liability issues may also arise. For example, employees in the massive Sony data breach incidents may have considered suing Sony for breaches in relation to their data.

Employee Data Organisations

17.13 It is increasingly possible for an organisation to represent Data Subjects, in terms of dealing with particular data protection issues but also in terms of representation and litigation.

While employee unions may represent their members in dealing with data protection issues, it is possible that employers may also have to deal with new organisations in relation to employees' personal data. This may involve breach incidents in particular.

Location

17.14 Increasing technology permits organisations to track devices and hence employees. However, a very careful prior analysis needs to be conducted in advance to consider whether this is strictly needed, desirable, proportionate, transparent and complies with the data protection regime. As with many of these new issues, a question of balance is needed and just because something is technically possible does not equate with it being prudent or lawful.

Conclusion

17.15 These are all issues that need to be addressed well in advance of an incident arising. It may be too late to start implementing policies, etc, after the event.

Employee data protection compliance is a complicated and ongoing obligation for organisations. It also needs to involve the DPOs, appropriate board member, human resources, IT personnel and legal. On occasion, others may also have to become involved also.

Chapter 18

Employee Monitoring Issues

Introduction

18.01 One of the more contentious areas of employee data protection practice relates to the issue of the monitoring of employee email, internet, etc, usage.

One of the reasons is that employers may not be familiar enough with their obligations under the data protection regime. Employers are concerned at certain risks that can arise as result of the activities of employees in the workplace but sometimes proceed without considering data protection.

Sample Legal Issues Arising

18.02 Some examples of the legal issues and concerns that can arise for employers and organisations as a result of the actions of their employees include:

- vicarious liability;
- defamation;
- copyright infringement;
- confidentiality breaches and leaks;
- data protection;
- contract;
- inadvertent contract formation;
- harassment;
- abuse;
- discrimination;
- computer crime;
- interception offences;
- criminal damage;

- data loss;
- data damage;
- computer crime;
- criminal damage;
- eCommerce law;
- arms and dual use good export restrictions;
- non-fatal offences against the person;
- child pornography;
- policies;
- on-site/off-site;
- bring your own device (BYOD), etc;
- online abuse;
- etc.

These are examples of an expanding list of concerns for organisations. Obviously, some of these will be recalibrated in importance depending on the type of organisation, the business sector and what its activities are. Confidentiality, for example, may be critically important for certain organisations, but less important for other organisations.

Employee Misuse of the Email, Internet, etc

18.03 Even before the recent increase in data breach and data loss examples, there is a significant number of examples where problems have arisen for organisations as a result of the activities of certain employees. Increasingly, organisations face the problem that the activity of an errant employee on the internet, television or social networks can go viral instantly on a global scale, with adverse reputational damage for the organisation.

There are many instances where organisations have felt the need to dismiss or otherwise discontinue relationships with employees. Some examples include Norwich EU Healthcare; Lois Franxhi; Royal & Sun Alliance Liverpool (77); C&W Birmingham (6); Rolls Royce Bristol (5); Claire Swire/Bradley Chait; Ford; Weil Gotshal; Sellafield, Target, Sony, etc. As these instances are ever expanding it would be impossible to provide a definitive list.

The frequency and scale of recent breaches of security eg Sony Playstation (70 million individual's personal data[1] and 25 million in another[2])

---

1   See, for example, G Martin, 'Sony Data Loss Biggest Ever,' *Boston Herald*, 27 April 2011.
2   See, for example, C Arthur, 'Sony Suffers Second Data Breach With Theft of 25m More User Details,' *Guardian*, 3 May 2011.

make the topicality and importance of data security compliance ever more important. Even after that, Sony was hacked again in the episode of the film 'The Interview,' which was arguably even more costly and damaging. The largest UK data loss appears to be from Revenue and Customs loss of discs with the names, dates of birth, bank and address details for 25 million individuals.[3] Marks and Spencer was also involved in a data breach as were a number of hotels, and the mobile company TalkTalk.

There are many new UK cases involving substantial fines for data protection breaches. The Brighton and Sussex University Hospitals NHS Trust had a fine of £325,000 imposed by the ICO in relation to a data loss incident.[4] Zurich Insurance was fined £2.3m for losing data in relation to 46,000 individual customers.[5] Sony was fined £250,000.

HP suspended 150 employees in one instance, which is one of the potential actions available.

Prudential was also fined in relation to the mishandling of personal data, while a Barclays employee was fined in court for personal use and access to customer account personal data.

Senior executives at Sony and Target lost their jobs as a result of data breach incidents. Some of the examples where employees have lost their jobs as a result of data breach incidents include senior management as well as IT and tech executives. It is probable that many more junior employees have lost jobs and positions out of the headlines.

In a more creative solution Ford issued a deletion amnesty to 20,000 employees to delete objected to material before a new or amended policy would kick in.

Some of the legal concerns referred to above will now be looked at in greater detail.

Contract

18.04   It is possible for employees to agree and enter into contract via electronic communications. This is increasingly a concern since the legal recognition of electronic contract in the eCommerce legislation.

---

3   See, for example, 'Brown Apologises for Record Loss, Prime Minister Gordon Brown has said he "Profoundly Regrets" the Loss of 25 Million Child Benefit Records,' *BBC*, 21 November 2007, at http://news.bbc.co.uk/2/hi/7104945.stm.

4   See, for example, 'Largest Ever Fine for Data Loss Highlights Need for Audited Data Wiping,' *ReturnOnIt*, at http://www.returnonit.co.uk/largest-ever-fine-for-data-loss-highlights-need-for-audited-data-wiping.php.

5   See, for example, J Oates, 'UK Insurer Hit With Biggest Ever Data Loss Fine,' *The Register*, 24 August 2010, at http://www.theregister.co.uk/2010/08/24/data_loss_fine/. This was imposed by the Financial Services Authority (FSA).

This can include the inadvertent creation of legally binding contracts for the organisation.

In addition, it is possible that an employee may create or agree particular contract terms, delivery dates, etc, electronically which they would not otherwise do.

These can be contracts, or terms, which the organisation would not like to be bound by.

It is also possible that breach of contract issues could arise.

Employment Equality

18.05 It can be illegal to discriminate, or permit discrimination, on grounds of, for example:

- gender;
- race;
- age;
- sexual orientation;
- family status;
- religious beliefs;
- disability;
- member of minority groups.

Instances of such discrimination can occur on the organisations computer systems. Even though the organisation may not be initially aware of the instance, it can still have legal consequences.

Harassment

18.06 Harassment via the organisation's computer systems is also something which could cause consequences for an organisation. Examples could include the circulation of written words, pictures or other material which a person may reasonably regard as offensive. The organisation could be held liable for employees' discriminatory actions unless it took reasonable steps to prevent them, or to deal with them appropriately once they arise. See Protection from Harassment Act 1997 (as amended).

Online Abuse

18.07 This is a growing problem. However, it is also an issue for organisations when their employees are the victims of perpetrators of online abuse. It is only a matter of time before organisations are sued for the actions of their employees using the organisation's systems. Organisations can also assist in tackling these issues, and some indeed have more of an ability to do so than others.

Offline Abuse

18.08   Offline abuse or offline disparagement, defamation, etc can also arise. In the Sony data breach incident regarding the film 'The Interview' there are examples of employee details being published online after the breach. In addition various emails were published where senior employees were at least disparaging others directly or indirectly engaged by the organisations. In instances such as this, as well as being other than best practice for both the employees and the organisation, liability issues can also arise.

Child Pornography

18.09   There is a serious risk and concern for organisations where this could occur on the organisation's computer systems or devices. See, for example, the Protection of Children Act of 1978 (as amended), Criminal Justice Act of 1988 (as amended), and the Criminal Justice and Public Order Act of 1994 (as amended).

Dealing with the Employee Risks

18.10   It is important for all organisations to engage in a process of risk assessment of exposures which can be created as a result of their employee's use of its computer systems and devices.

Organisations should:

- identify the areas of risk;
- assess and evaluate those risks;
- engage in a process to eliminate/reduce the risks identifies as appropriate;
- formalise an overall body of employee corporate communications usage policies;
- implement appropriate and lawful technical solutions appropriate to dealing with the identified risks;
- implement an ongoing strategy to schedule reviews of the new and emerging risks, and to update and or implement appropriate

procedures and policies, including the existing employee corporate communications usage policies;
- security for employee related data;
- risk assessment and indeed impact assessments, particularly where changes happen in relation to employee related data;
- advising all employees of the official policy if and when a breach incident may arise;
- advising and ensuring that the specific employees who might have to deal with breach issues directly are fully aware of and trained on their functions. This will be an ongoing task and will also involve different teams of employees (and others who may be external experts and professional advisors).

Employee Corporate Communications Usage Policies

18.11   Given the general risks, and the risks specific to an organisation identified in a review process, it is critical that the organisation implement appropriate policies in an overall body of employee corporate communications usage policies.

It is important to note that there is no one fixed solution, or one single policy on its own which is sufficient to deal with these issues. Equally, a single policy on its own would not be sufficient to give comfort to the organisation in terms of (a) dealing with the risks and issues, and (b) ensuring that the organisation has implemented sufficient policies that allows it to act appropriately to meet specific risks, including disposal, as they arise.

For example, if an organisation discovers a particular unauthorised activity on its computer systems undertaken by one of its employees, eg illegal file sharing an employee hosting an illegal gambling website on its servers, it may decide that it wishes to dismiss the errant employee. But can it legally dismiss the employee? In the first instance, the organisation should ideally be in the position of being able to point to a specific clause in the employees written contract of employment and a specific breach, or breaches, of one or more of the organisation's employee corporate communications usage policies.

If it can, then the likelihood is that the organisation's legal advisors would be comfortable recommending that the dismissal is warranted, justified and lawful. However, if the answer is no, in that there is no written clause which is clearly breached as a result of the specific activities, even though carried out during the hours of employment, at the organisation's office, on the organisations computer system and utilising the organisation's computer servers, the organisation would not have any legal comfort in dismissing the employee.

The organisation may not be able to obtain pro-dismissal legal advices. If the company decided to proceed with the dismissal in any event it could run the legal risk that the employee may decide to legally challenge the dismissal under employment law. The employee would be assisted in that there is no express written clause which is breached. Unfortunately, the organisation may have to defend such an action on the basis of common law or implied obligations and duties owed by the employee. There may be no guarantee of success.

Focus of Organisational Communications Usage Policies

18.12 Organisations have a need for a comprehensive suite of organisational communications usage policies. This includes use of the organisation's devices, telephone, voicemail, email and Internet. The policies need to address:

- security;
- telephone;
- email;
- text;
- internet;
- mobile and portable devices;
- home and off-site usage;
- vehicle usage;

employee Internet of Things (IoT) usage as it may affect the organisation.

This will involve and ongoing task, not just a one off exercise. It also needs coordinated team responsibility.

Key Issues to Organisational Communications Usage Policies

18.13 The key aspects to consider in relation to the employee corporate communications usage policies, include:

- ownership;
- usage;
- authorisation;
- confidentiality;
- authentication;
- retention and storage;
- viruses;
- disciplinary matters;
- security;
- awareness;

- transparency;
- breach notification;
- DPOs;
- planning and data protection by design.

These will vary depending on each organisation.

From a data protection regime perspective, one of the key issues for an organisation is the ability to monitor employees when needed.

Data Protection and Employee Monitoring

18.14   Organisations may wish to monitor for various reasons. Some of these include:

- continuity of operations during staff illness;
- maintenance;
- preventing/investigating allegations of misuse;
- assessing/verifying compliance with software licensing obligations;
- complying with legal and regulatory requests for information;
- etc.

Organisations may also wish to monitor in order to prevent risks and to identify problems as they arise. When issues arise they will wish to deal appropriately with the employee.

Employers and agencies recruiting for them need to carefully consider the legality of internet and social media monitoring of employees and applicants. It is a growing practice by all accounts, and appears more permissible in the US than the EU. However, organisations should not assume that they are permitted to monitor, records, keep files, and make decisions based upon personal information and personal data gathered online unknown to the individual employee or applicant.[6]

---

6   See, for example, C Brandenburg, 'The Newest Way to Screen Job Applicants: A Social Networker's Nightmare,' *Federal Communications Law Journal* (2007–2008) (60) 597; D Gersen, 'Your Image, Employers Investigate Job Candidates Online More than Ever. What Can You Do to Protect Yourself?' *Student Law* (2007–2008) (36) 24; AR Levinson, 'Industrial Justice: Privacy Protection for the Employed,' *Cornell Journal of Law and Public Policy* (2009) (18) 609–688; I Byrnside, 'Six Degrees of Separation: The Legal Ramifications of Employers Using Social Networking Sites to Research Applicants,' *Vanderbilt Journal of Entertainment and Technology Law* (2008) (2) 445–477; and M Maher, 'You've Got Messages, Modern Technology Recruiting Through Text Messaging and the Intrusiveness of Facebook,' *Texas Review of Entertainment and Sports Law* (2007) (8) 125–151.

The issue of the right to privacy of the employee and the rights and interests of the organisation arise. The issue of the right to privacy is a complex subject beyond the scope of this discussion. However, it is an expanding area, particularly after the introduction of the Human Rights Act 1998 (as amended).[7] Monitoring raises interlinking issues of privacy, human rights and data protection.

Human Right

18.15 The Human Rights Act 1998 (as amended)[8] means that the European Convention for the Protection of Human Rights and Fundamental Freedoms[9] is now incorporated into and applicable in the UK.

This means that Article 8 of European Convention for the Protection of Human Rights and Fundamental Freedoms is an important consideration. It provides that everyone has right to private and family life, and their home and correspondence. It states that:

'(1) Everyone has the right to respect for his private and family life, his home and his correspondence;

(2) There shall be no interference by a public authority with the exercise of this right except such as is in accordance with the law and is necessary in a democratic society in the interests of national security, public safety or the economic wellbeing of the country, for the prevention of disorder or crime, for the protection of health or morals, or for the protection of the rights and freedoms of others.'[10]

The *Halford* case[11] is an example of the interface of human rights and data protection. The Leveson inquiry press hacking is also relevant in commenting on these issues.

Application of Data Protection Regime

18.16 In terms of employee monitoring, employers are entitled to exercise reasonable control and supervision over their employees and their use of organisational resources.

---

7   Human Rights Act 1998, at http://www.legislation.gov.uk/ukpga/1998/42/contents.
8   Human Rights Act 1998, at http://www.legislation.gov.uk/ukpga/1998/42/contents.
9   At http://www.echr.coe.int/Documents/Convention_ENG.pdf. See also Balla, R, 'Constitutionalism – Reform on Data Protection Law and Human Rights,' *Cerentul Juridic* (2011) (47) 61–74.
10   At http://www.echr.coe.int/Documents/Convention_ENG.pdf.
11   *Halford v UK* (1997) IRLR 471, (1997) 24 EHRR 523.

Employers are also entitled to promulgate policies to protect their property and good name and to ensure that they do not become inadvertently liable for the misbehaviour of employees.

Equally, however, employees do retain privacy rights and data protection rights that must be respected by the organisation.

Organisations must consider:

- the culture of organisation;
- whether there is understanding and expectation that employees can use the organisation's computers for personal use;
- whether the organisation accessing the employee's communications without permission would be unfair and unlawful obtaining.

Monitoring involves careful consideration of policy, practice as well as interrelated legal issues of Privacy/Human Rights/Data Protection.

Monitoring or accessing employee emails or tracking of employee web browsing without permission would likely be unfair obtaining. Location issues are increasingly important – for a number of reasons. In terms of employees, particular issue arise as to if and when an organisation can, or should, monitor or record the location of employees eg via their electronic and hardware devices, etc. It is important, therefore, that organisations have appropriate mechanisms and policies to reduce the risks, and then also to deal with issues as they arise. Reactively responding and trying to set up policies once a problem has arisen should be avoided. As pointed out above, if it is not explicitly in place before the incident, then a bad policy (or indeed an outdated policy) cannot be relied upon in invoking particular terms against the employee.

ILO Code

18.17 Organisations should also consider the ILO code recommendations. The ILO Code of Practice on Protection of Workers Personal Data[12] recommends that:

- employees must be informed in advance of reasons, time schedule, methods and techniques used and the personal data collected;
- the monitoring must minimise the intrusion on privacy of employees;
- secret monitoring must be in conformity with legislation or on foot of suspicion of criminal activity or serious wrongdoing;
- continuous monitoring should only occur if required for health and safety or protection of property.

12 At   http://www.ilo.org/wcmsp5/groups/public/---ed_protect/---protrav/---safework/documents/normativeinstrument/wcms_107797.pdf.

EDPB/WP29

Processing in the Employment Context

18.18   The WP29, now replaced by the EDPB, has long been concerned about employee monitoring and surveillance issues in terms of
privacy and personal data. It issued an Opinion in September 2001
entitled Opinion 8/2001 on the Processing of Personal Data in the
Employment Context.[13] It states that 'no business interest may ever
prevail on the principles of transparency, lawful processing, legitimisa-
tion, proportionality, necessity and others contained in data protection
laws.'

WP29 states that when processing workers' personal data, employers
should always bear in mind fundamental data protection principles such
as the following:

- FINALITY: Data must be collected for a specified, explicit and
  legitimate purpose and not further processed in a way incompatible
  with those purposes;
- TRANSPARENCY: As a very minimum, workers need to know
  which data is the employer collecting about them (directly or
  from other sources), which are the purposes of processing operations envisaged or carried out with these data presently or in the
  future. Transparency is also assured by granting the Data Subject
  the right to access to his/her personal data and with the Controllers' obligation of notifying supervisory authorities as provided in
  national law;
- LEGITIMACY: The processing of workers' personal data must be
  legitimate. Article 7 of the Directive lists the criteria making the
  processing legitimate;
- PROPORTIONALITY: The personal data must be adequate, relevant and not excessive in relation to the purposes for which they
  are collected and/or further processed. Assuming that workers have
  been informed about the processing operation and assuming that
  such processing activity is legitimate and proportionate, such a processing still needs to be fair with the worker;
- ACCURACY AND RETENTION OF THE DATA: Employment
  records must be accurate and, where necessary, kept up to date. The
  employer must take every reasonable step to ensure that data inaccurate or incomplete, having regard to the purposes for which they
  were collected or further processed, are erased or rectified;

---

13 Opinion 8/2001 on the processing of personal data in the employment context.
    At http://ec.europa.eu/justice/policies/privacy/docs/wpdocs/2001/wp48en.pdf.

- SECURITY: The employer must implement appropriate technical and organisational measures at the workplace to guarantee that the personal data of his workers is kept secured. Particular protection should be granted as regards unauthorised disclosure or access;
- AWARENESS OF THE STAFF: Staff in charge or with responsibilities in the processing of personal data of other workers need to know about data protection and receive proper training. Without an adequate training of the staff handling personal data, there could never be appropriate respect for the privacy of workers in the workplace.[14]

In relation to consent, the WP29 adds that it has taken the view that where as a necessary and unavoidable consequence of the employment relationship an employer has to process personal data it is misleading if it seeks to legitimise this processing through consent.[15] Reliance on consent as a legitimising mechanism should be confined to cases where the worker has a genuine free choice and is subsequently able to withdraw the consent without detriment.[16] Consent is thus limited, specific, and confined.

Electronic Communications

18.19 The WP29 also issued an opinion on the review of the Directive 2002/58/EC on privacy and electronic communications (ePrivacy Directive).[17] It was entitled Opinion 2/2008 on the review of the Directive 2002/58/EC on privacy and electronic communications (ePrivacy Directive).[18]

Under the heading Data Protection by Design (DPbD) it states that it advocates the application of the principle of *data minimisation* and the deployment of Privacy Enhancing Technologies (PETs) by Controllers. It also calls upon European legislators to make provision for a re-enforcement of said principle, by reiterating Recitals 9 and 30 of the ePrivacy Directive in a new paragraph in Article 1 of this Directive.[19]

---

14 At http://ec.europa.eu/justice/data-protection/article-29/documentation/opinion-recommendation/files/2001/wp48_en.pdf.
15 *Ibid.*
16 *Ibid.*
17 Opinion 2/2008 on the review of the Directive 2002/58/EC on privacy and electronic communications (ePrivacy Directive), at http://ec.europa.eu/justice/policies/privacy/docs/wpdocs/2008/wp150_en.pdf.
18 Adopted on 15 May 2008.
19 Opinion 2/2008 on the review of the Directive 2002/58/EC on privacy and electronic communications (ePrivacy Directive), at http://ec.europa.eu/justice/policies/privacy/docs/wpdocs/2008/wp150_en.pdf, 6.

It also notes that Article 5(1) imposes an obligation to ensure confidentiality of communications irrespective of the nature of the network and whether the communication crosses borders to non-EU member states.[20]

Electronic communications were also considered in WP29 Opinion 8/2006 on the review of the regulatory Framework for Electronic Communications and Services, with focus on the ePrivacy Directive.[21]

The WP29 also issued a working document on the surveillance of electronic communications in the workplace.[22]

It also issued Opinion 4/2007 on the concept of personal data which is also relevant in considering the definition of personal data.[23]

In relation to employee health records it is worth examining Working Document on the processing of personal data relating to health in electronic health records (EHR).[24]

When outsourcing and dealing with Processors it is worth considering Opinion 1/2010 on the concepts of data 'Controller' and data 'Processor.'[25]

In relation to video surveillance, the WP29 issued Opinion 4/2004 on the processing of personal data by means of video surveillance.[26]

Employment Contracts, Terms, Policies

18.20 As indicated above, organisations need to consider:

- whether the contract provision has been properly incorporated?;
- issues of limitation of liability;
- issues of exclusion of warranties;
- disclaimers;
- graduated disclaimers;
- ongoing risk assessment;

---

20 Opinion 2/2008 on the review of the Directive 2002/58/EC.
21 At http://ec.europa.eu/justice/data-protection/article-29/documentation/opinion-recommendation/files/2006/wp126_en.pdf.
22 Working document on the surveillance of electronic communications in the workplace, WP 55, at http://ec.europa.eu/justice/data-protection/article-29/documentation/opinion-recommendation/files/2002/wp55_en.pdf.
23 At http://ec.europa.eu/justice/data-protection/article-29/documentation/opinion-recommendation/files/2007/wp136_en.pdf.
24 At http://ec.europa.eu/justice/data-protection/article-29/documentation/opinion-recommendation/files/2007/wp131_en.pdf.
25 At http://ec.europa.eu/justice/data-protection/article-29/documentation/opinion-recommendation/files/2010/wp169_en.pdf.
26 At http://ec.europa.eu/justice/data-protection/article-29/documentation/opinion-recommendation/files/2004/wp89_en.pdf.

- continual review and updating;
- risk, risk assessment and risk minimisation;
- enforceability;
- etc.

Registration Requirements

18.21 The original data protection regime imposes registration requirements with the ICO. There was a suggestion during the GDPR legislative process that the requirement for registration or notification be replaced instead by greater risk assessment obligations, etc, on organisations. Recital 89 of the new GDPR refers to a replacement of 'general' notification/registration requirement. It remains to be seen how this will fully impact on existing ICO practices. Notification requirements may continue on a national basis; may be discontinued; or only certain risk related activities or organisations may be required to notify.

The ICO sets out the following guidance questions in relation to assessing an organisation's registration requirements, namely:

- Is the organisation processing personal information?
- Is the organisation processing on computer?
- Is the organisation a Controller?
- Is the organisation only processing personal information for personal, family or household affairs (including recreational purposes)?
- Is the organisation processing personal information for any of the following purposes?
- Is the organisation only processing personal information to maintain a public register?
- Is the organisation a not-for-profit organisation?
- As a not-for-profit organisation is all of the processing covered by the following descriptions?
- The organisation may not have to notify if the only processing carried out is for one or more of these purposes,
  - staff administration;
  - advertising, marketing and public relations;
  - accounts and records;
- The organisation does not have to notify if processing for the purpose of judicial functions.[27]

---

27 At http://ec.europa.eu/justice/data-protection/article-29/documentation/opinion-recommendation/files/2004/wp89_en.pdf, 11–26.

The ICO also asks these guidance questions:

- Does the organisation really need this information about an individual?
- Does the organisation know what it is going to use it for?
- Do the employees whose information the organisation has, know that it has got it, and are they likely to understand what it will be used for?
- If the organisation is asked to pass on personal information, would the people about whom the organisation hold information expect the organisation to do this?
- Is the organisation satisfied that the information is being held securely, whether on paper or on computer?
- Is the organisation website secure?
- Does the organisation need to notify the ICO, and if so, is the notification up to date?[28]

The ICO has also issued a useful data protection notification handbook, *A Complete Guide to Notification*.[29] This is available online.

Registration Exemptions

18.22   The ICO advises that the following may have exemption from registration:

- Controllers who only process personal information for,
  - o   staff administration (including payroll);
  - o   advertising, marketing and public relations (in connection with their own business activity); and
  - o   accounts and records;
- some not-for-profit organisations;
- processing personal information for personal, family or household affairs (including recreational purposes);
- maintenance of a public register;
- processing personal information for judicial functions;
- processing personal information without an automated system such as a computer.[30]

However, even if exempt from registration, the other obligations and compliance rules set out in the data protection regime still apply once there is personal data being processed.

---

28   At http://ec.europa.eu/justice/data-protection/article-29/documentaion/opinion-recom-mendation/files/2004/wp89_en.pdf, 29–30.
29   ICO, A Guide to Notification, at https://ico.org.uk.
30   ICO, A Brief Guide to Notification, ICO, p 9, at https://ico.org.uk.

Registration Issues

18.23 Some of the registration, and registration planning, issues to consider are:

- the Controller;
- the legal entity of the Controller;
- the categories of general personal data collected and processed;
- the categories of sensitive personal data collected and processed;
- the purposes and uses for the collection and processing;
- where there are two or more related purposes, separate registration details must be supplied;
- where there are two or more unrelated purposes, separate registrations may be required;
- whether there are any Processors involved;
- location of personal data;
- trans-border data flows with the personal data;
- disclosures of personal data to third parties, if so occurring,
  - security requirements apply;
  - annual renewal;
  - update if there are significant changes.

Processing Compliance Rules

18.24 If an organisation is collecting and processing personal data, it must comply with the DPA 1998 and data protection regime in respect of:

- Data Protection Principles;
- Non-sensitive personal data Legitimate Processing Conditions;
- Sensitive personal data Legitimate Processing Conditions;
- Direct marketing (DM) requirements;
- Security requirements;
- Registration requirements;
- Processor contract requirements;
- Transfer requirements;
  - risk;
  - risk assessment.

Suggested Guidelines

18.25 Some suggested guidelines to consider generally are set out below. However, it is always suggested that appropriate professional legal and technical advice be sought in particular circumstances:

- comply with the processing compliance rules set out above;
- ensure fair obtaining, collecting and processing of personal data;

- compliance must be ensured at the time of data capture NOT subsequently;
- get it right first time;
- the lessons of *British Gas* and other examples are that in a worst case you may have to delete the database and start again from the beginning, or re-do your collection and notification process;
- consider and decide upon opt-in or op-out consent;
- consider the purpose or purposes for the data collection and which must be specified;
- provide information to the Data Subject when collecting;
- consider whether the Data Subject is the source (direct) or whether a third-party is the source (indirect);
- specifying in the registration may not be enough, it may have to be earlier;
- specified and lawful;
- use or purpose to which the data collected will be put must be clear and defined. Otherwise it could be deemed too vague and unfair and ultimately an unfair collection which would undermine the initial consent given;
- if disclosure occurs, it must be specified, clear and defined;
- security measures must be assessed and implemented;
- security includes physical security;
- security also includes technical security;
- measures must be put in place to prevent loss, alteration or destruction;
- other legislation may also apply such as in relation to hacking, criminal damage, etc;
- the personal data must be kept accurate and kept up to date;
- personal data must be kept for no longer than is necessary;
- consider that there are many different types of personal data;
- the organisational or business need requirement must be identified;
- how personal data is collected is must be considered, planned and recorded;
- check Data Protection Principles;
- check Legitimate Processing Conditions;
- explicit consent may be required for collecting and processing sensitive personal data;
- identify and deal with new processes and procedures in advance to ensure data protection compliance. One cannot assume that the organisation can obtain a fair and lawful consent after a go-live;
- identify new contacts, contracts, collections and consents in advance to ensure data protection compliance;
- policy for protecting and securing employee's personal data;
- policy for notifying employees of data breaches involving their personal data;

- insurance issues regarding data breaches;
- risk assessment and planning issues.

The Rights of Employee Data Subjects

18.26 The rights of Data Subjects can be summarised as including:

- right of access (DPA 1998, s 7);
- right to establish if personal data exists (DPA 1998, s 7(1)(a));
- right to be informed of the logic in automatic decision taking (DPA 1998, s 7(1)(d));
- right to prevent processing likely to cause damage or distress (DPA 1998, s 18);
- right to prevent processing for direct marketing (DPA 1998, s 11);
- right to prevent automated decision taking (DPA 1998, s 12);
- right to compensation (DPA 1998, s 13);
- right to rectify inaccurate data (DPA 1998, s 14);
- right to rectification, blocking, erasure and destruction (DPA 1998, s 14);
- right to complain to ICO (DPA 1998, s 42);
- right to go to court (DPA 1998, s 15).

Chapter III of the new GDPR refers to rights of Data Subjects. These include:

- right to transparency (Article 5; Article 12);
- right to prior information: directly obtained data (Article 13);
- right to prior information: indirectly obtained data (Article 14);
- right of confirmation and right of access (Article 15);
- right to rectification (Article 16);
- right to erasure (Right to be Forgotten) (RtbF) (Article 17);
- right to restriction of processing (Article 18);
- notifications re rectification, erasure or restriction (Article 19);
- right to data portability (Article 20);
- right to object (Article 21);
- rights re automated individual decision making, including profiling (Article 22);
- DPbD (Article 25);
- security rights;
- data protection impact assessment and prior consultation;
- communicating data breach to Data Subject (Article 34);
- Data Protection Officer (DPO);
- remedies, liability and sanctions (Chapter VIII).

ECHR Romanian Monitoring Case

18.27 There has been considerable publicity in relation to the recent ECHR case of *Bărbulescu v Romania* (January 2016).[31] This is frequently being reported as holding that employers can monitor employee communications. The ECHR press release heading states: 'Monitoring of an employee's use of the internet and his resulting dismissal was justified'. Popular commentary suggests and implies that all employers can monitor all employee communications including email and internet. A strong and significant word of caution should be noted by organisations. While space prevents a very detailed analysis the following case points should be noted:

- the case does not find on a general basis that employers can monitor all employee email;
- the case does not find on a general basis that employers can monitor all employee internet usage;
- the case does not find on a general basis that employers can monitor all employee communications;
- the case technically related to a claim that national laws are insufficient, it is not a case per se between the employee and the employer;
- there is a significant dissent encompassed within the judgment – which some will feel is a more correct assessment of the law – and provides better guidance to employers;
- the majority decision acknowledges difficult legal and factual issues and certain matters missing from the claim file from the respective sides;
- the employer had accessed two online communications' accounts of the employee, one ostensibly for business and one personal;
- notwithstanding that the personal account was clearly personal and private, and there being various apparent issues, the majority seemed to ignore this clear breach by the employer;
- details of one or both accounts were then disclosed to other employees in the organisation and discussed by them openly – this further breach by the employer was also ignored by the majority;
- in terms of the account established ostensibly for business purposes and which was accessed by the employer, this contained personal data and sensitive personal data;
- the employer was not able to establish any reason or suspicion of wrongdoing to trigger a wish to access or monitor this account;
- as such, a considered analysis would suggest that there was no basis for general monitoring in this instance, and seems to lead to the conclusion that there is also a breach by the employer here;

---

31 *Bărbulescu v Romania*, ECHR, Case No 61496/08, 12 January 2016.

- this important point is ignored in the majority decision;
- it is well established and recognised that employees do not give up their privacy and data protection rights at the door of the employer. The majority decision appears to ignore and not take into account that employers must have some genuine reason or suspicion in the specific case to go beyond the employee's rights to monitor and access online communications. The issue related to Yahoo Messenger accounts, not the official company email;
- it does not appear that specific warnings to employees beyond a general communications policy (which did not refer to monitoring issues) was issued, or issued to the employee in question, or at least this was not established. For some the majority decision ignores this important point. Again, this leans strongly towards there being an employer breach.

It might be speculated whether a different result would have been achieved before the EU Court of Justice in this instance.

On balance, employers should remain cautious against global employee monitoring in the UK and EU. Employees, supervisory authorities, WP29/EDPB and others might suggest the decision is regressive not progressive, or is simply wrong or must be interpreted cautiously and confined to unusual facts and an unusual decision. The logic of the majority decision could be criticised as being in contrast to the established body of law and legal understanding in relation to these issues. The majority suggests a logic which means that the result justifies the means and issues of law, rights and process are irrelevant. The majority do not point to any lawful basis for employer monitoring and access prior to any problem issue being raised with the employee. It has to be cautioned that organisations may better be guided by the dissent analysis than the frequently misunderstood blanket monitoring headline of the case.

Conclusion

18.28 Organisations at different times may feel a tension to engage in monitoring of employees. No matter how tempting, this needs to be checked in order to see if it is possible and to remain data protection compliant. While there are naturally risks and issues to deal with, the starting point will always be one of proportionate responses which ensure data protection compliance. The need, or more limited circumstance, of notification with the ICO will need to be fully considered by organisations.

Outward Facing Organisational DP Obligations

Part 3
Outward Facing Organisational
Obligations

Chapter 19

Outward Facing Issues

Introduction

19.01 Beyond the inward facing employee related sphere, organisations also need to consider the outward facing sphere. For many organisations the outward facing data protection issues frequently dominate more. They can also be the most contentious. These issues raise significant data protection concerns and compliance issues to be dealt with.

Some of the queries that can arise include:

- Designated Data Protection Officers (DPOs);
- What are the forms of outward facing personal data to consider?
- How to comply with the data protection regime when dealing with existing customers?
- How do organisations contact potential customers yet remain data protection compliant?
- Can an organisation engage in direct marketing (DM)?
- Is profiling possible generally, or even in more limited circumstances?
- Do users who are not customers raise additional issues?
- Do security considerations still arise?
- Are there even more security issues to consider?
- Are there higher security obligations for customers and users?
- How does the deletion and Right to be Forgotten regime work?
- What are the new risk assessment and impact assessment provisions?

The general increase in internet usage, profiling, advertising, marketing and social media are also important issues to consider. Abuse whether online or via social media or related websites is increasingly recognised as a problem to be dealt with. Civil sanctions and actions are likely to increase in the instances where it needs to be invoked. In some instances and in some jurisdictions organisations may also need to consider criminal law sanctions.

GDPR New Outward Facing Changes

19.02 Some of the new GDPR changes which apply to outward facing organisational issues include:

- repeal of DPD 95 (Article 94);
- WP29 and European Data Protection Board (Recitals 72, 77, 105, 119, 124, 136, 140, 143, 168; Articles 35, 40–43, 47, 51, 52, 58–62, 64, and 65);
- background and rationale (Recitals 1, 8, 11, 13);
- context objectives, scope of GDPR (Articles 1, 2 and 3);
- obligations (Recitals 32, 39, 40, 42, 43–47);
- security (Recitals 2, 16, 19, 39, 49, 50, 52, 53, 71, 73, 75, 78, 81, 83, 91, 94, 104, 112; Articles 2, 4, 5, 9, 10, 30, 32, 35, 40, 47);
- processing;
- rights (Recitals 1, 2, 4, 9, 10, 11, 13, 16, 19, 38, 39, 41, 47, 50–54, 57, 63, 65, 66, 68–71, 73–81, 84–86, 89, 91, 94, 98, 102, 104, 108, 109, 111, 113, 114, 116, 122, 129, 137, 139, 141–143, 153–156, 162, 164, 166, 173; Articles 1, 4–7, 9–22);
- proceedings (Recitals 52, 80, 129, 143, 147; Articles 23, 40, 78, 79, 81, 82);
- establishment (Recitals 22, 36, 52, 65, 100, 117, 122, 124, 126, 127; Articles 3, 4, 9, 17, 18, 21, 37, 42, 49, 54, 56, 57, 60, 62, 65, 70, 79);
- transfers (Recitals 6, 48, 101–103, 107, 108, 110–114, 153; Articles 4, 13–15, 23, 28, 30, 40, 42, 44–49, 70, 83, 85, 88, 96);
- ICO, etc;
- new bodies (Recital 142; Articles 9, 80);
- notification/registration replaced (Recital 89);
- exceptions/exemptions (Recitals 14, 15, 17);
- lawful processing and consent (Recitals 10, 32, 33, 38–40, 42–46, 49–51, 54, 63, 65, 68, 69, 71, 83, 111, 112, 116, 138, 155, 161, 171; Articles 4–9, 13, 14, 17, 18, 20, 22, 23, 32, 40, 49, 82, 83);
- online identifiers (Recitals 30, 64; Articles 4, 87);
- sensitive and special personal data (Recitals 10, 51, 53, 54, 59, 65, 71, 80, 91, 97; Articles 6, 9, 22, 27, 30, 35, 37, 47);
- children (Recital 38);
- health data (Recitals 35, 45, 52–54, 63, 65, 71, 73, 75, 91, 112, 155, 159; Article 4, 9, 17, 23, 36, 88);
- DPR definitions (Article 4);
- new processing rules: obligations (Articles 5–11);
- new (data protection) principles (Article 5);
- lawfulness of processing: legitimate processing conditions (Article 6);
- child's consent;
- processing special categories of personal data (Article 9);
- processing re criminal convictions and offences data (Article 10);

- processing not requiring identification (Article 11);
- Controllers and Processors (Chapter IV);
- responsibility of the Controller (Article 24);
- joint Controllers (Article 26);
- Processor (Article 28);
- processing under authority of Controller and Processor (Article 29);
- records of processing activities (Article 30);
- representatives of Controllers not established in EU (Article 27);
- co-operation with supervisory authority;
- security of processing (Article 32);
- notifying data breach to supervisory authority (Article 33);
- communicating data breach to Data Subject (Article 34);
- data protection impact assessment and prior consultation (Chapter IV, Section 3);
- data protection impact assessment (Article 35);
- prior consultation (Article 36);
- new DPO (Chapter IV; Section 4; Article 37);
- position (Article 38) and tasks of new DPO (Article 39);
- general principle for transfers (Recitals 6, 48, 101–103, 107, 108, 110–114, 153; Articles 4, 13–15, 23, 28, 30, 40, 42, 44–49, 70, 83, 85, 88, 96; Articles 44);
- transfers via adequacy decision (Article 45);
- transfers via appropriate safeguards (Article 46);
- transfers via binding corporate rules (Article 47);
- transfers or disclosures not authorised by EU law (Article 48);
- derogations for specific situations (Article 49);
- new processing rules: Data Subject rights (Recitals 1–4, 9–11, 13, 16, 19, 38, 39, 41, 47, 50–54, 57, 59, 63, 65, 66, 68–71, 73–81, 84–86, 89, 91, 94, 98, 102, 104, 108, 109, 111, 113, 114, 116, 122, 129, 137, 141–143, 153–156, 162, 164, 166, 173; Articles 1, 4–7, 9–22; Chapter III);
- right to transparency (Recitals 13, 39, 58, 60, 71, 78, 100, 121; Articles 5; Chapter III, Section 1; Articles 12–14, 26, 40–43, 53, 88);
- data access rights (Chapter III, Section 2);
- right to prior information: directly obtained data (Article 13);
- right to prior information: indirectly obtained data (Article 14);
- right of confirmation and right of access (Article 15);
- rectification and erasure (Section 3);
- right to rectification (Article 16);
- right to erasure (Right to be Forgotten) (RtbF) (Article 17);
- right to restriction of processing (Article 18);
- notifications re rectification, erasure or restriction (Article 19);
- right to data portability (Article 20);
- right to object (Article 21);

- rights against automated individual decision making, including profiling (Article 22);
- Data Protection by Design and by Default (DPbD) (Article 25);
- security rights;
- data protection impact assessment and prior consultation;
- communicating data breach to Data Subject (Article 34);
- DPO (contact details);
- remedies, liability and sanctions (Chapter VIII);
- right to judicial remedy against supervisory authority;
- right to effective judicial remedy against Controller or Processor (Article 79);
- representation of Data Subjects (Article 80);
- suspension of proceedings (Article 81);
- right to compensation and liability (Article 82);
- codes of conduct and certification;
- general conditions for imposing administrative fines (Article 83);
- penalties (Article 84);
- specific data processing situations (Chapter IX);
- safeguards and derogations: public Interest/scientific/historical research/statistical archiving processing;
- obligations of secrecy (Article 90).

Data Protection Officer

19.03   Chapter IV, Section 4 of the new GDPR refers to Data Protection Officers (DPOs) and the obligation for organisations to appoint DPOs.

The Controller and the Processor shall designate a DPO in any case where:

- the processing is carried out by a public authority or body, except for courts acting in their judicial capacity;
- the core activities of the Controller or the Processor consist of processing operations which, by virtue of their nature, their scope and/or their purposes, require regular and systematic monitoring of Data Subjects on a large scale; or
- the core activities of the Controller or the Processor consist of processing on a large scale of special categories of data pursuant to Article 9 and data relating to criminal convictions and offences referred to in Article 10 (Article 37(1)).

A group of undertakings may appoint a single DPO provided that a DPO is easily accessible from each establishment (Article 37(2)).

Where the Controller or the Processor is a public authority or body, a single DPO may be designated for several such authorities or bodies, taking account of their organisational structure and size (Article 37(3)).

In cases other than those referred to in Article 37(1), the Controller or Processor or associations and other bodies representing categories of Controllers or Processors may or, where required by EU or Member State law shall, designate a DPO. The DPO may act for such associations and other bodies representing Controllers or Processors (Article 37(4)).

The DPO shall be designated on the basis of professional qualities and, in particular, expert knowledge of data protection law and practices and the ability to fulfil the tasks referred to in Article 39 (Article 37(5)).

The DPO may be a staff member of the Controller or Processor, or fulfil the tasks on the basis of a service contract (Article 37(6)).

The Controller or the Processor shall publish the contact details of the DPO and communicate them to the supervisory authority (Article 37(7)).

The Controller or the Processor shall ensure that the DPO is involved, properly and in a timely manner, in all issues which relate to the protection of personal data (Article 38(1)).

The Controller or Processor shall support the DPO in performing the tasks referred to in Article 39 by providing resources necessary to carry out those tasks and access to personal data and processing operations, and to maintain their expert knowledge (Article 38(2)).

The Controller or Processor shall ensure that the DPO does not receive any instructions regarding the exercise of those tasks. He or she shall not be dismissed or penalised by the Controller or the Processor for performing their tasks. The DPO shall directly report to the highest management level of the Controller or the Processor (Article 38(3)).

Data Subjects may contact the DPO on all issues related to the processing of the Data Subject's data and the exercise of their rights under the GDPR (Article 38(4)).

The DPO shall be bound by secrecy or confidentiality concerning the performance of their tasks, in accordance with EU or Member State law (Article 38(5)).

The DPO may fulfil other tasks and duties. The Controller or Processor shall ensure that any such tasks and duties do not result in a conflict of interests (Article 38(6)).

The DPO shall have at least the following tasks:

- to inform and advise the Controller or the Processor and the employees who are processing personal data of their obligations pursuant to the GDPR and to other EU or Member State data protection provisions;

- to monitor compliance with the GDPR, with other EU or Member State data protection provisions and with the policies of the Controller or Processor in relation to the protection of personal data, including the assignment of responsibilities, awareness-raising and training of staff involved in the processing operations, and the related audits;
- to provide advice where requested as regards the data protection impact assessment and monitor its performance pursuant to Article 33;
- to cooperate with the supervisory authority;
- to act as the contact point for the supervisory authority on issues related to the processing, including the prior consultation referred to in Article 36, and consult, where appropriate, with regard to any other matter (Article 39(1)).

The DPO shall in the performance of their tasks have due regard to the risk associated with the processing operations, taking into account the nature, scope, context and purposes of processing (Article 39(2)).

Data Protection by Design

19.04   There are new obligations for organisations. This applies particularly as regards the introduction of outward facing uses and changes which involve personal data (see details below).

Types of Outward Facing Personal Data

Customers, Prospects and Users

19.05   What forms of outward facing personal data must organisations be concerned with? The types of personal data which are considered related to:

- current customers;
- past customers;
- prospective customers;
- users whom may not be registered customers;
- distinguishing adults and children.

Organisations will be often concerned with collecting personal preferences, account details, etc, from customers and leads. Direct marketing (DM) and additional avenues for commercialisation are also a frequent business imperative. Increasingly commercial organisations may be tempted by profiling technologies. Retailers may also be tempted by increasing sophistication in camera and visual recognition technology for commercial uses.[1]

In addition, there may be individuals who access the organisations website but who are not actual customers. Indeed, they may never become customers. Yet certain personal data may still be collected by the organisation. In this instance, it is also necessary for the organisation to comply with the Data Protection Principles and related obligations.

How to be Outward Facing Compliant

Customers, Prospects and Users

19.06 How can an organisation focus on the elements that will ensure data protection compliance when dealing with the personal data of customers, prospects and/or users. In terms of personal data collected and processed relating to the above categories, the following must be complied with, namely, the:

- prior information requirements;
- Data Protection Principles;
- Legitimate Processing Conditions;
- Sensitive Personal Data Legitimate Processing Conditions;
- security requirements;
- notification requirements (note potential changes in this regard);
- risk and risk assessments, particularly as regards new processes and activities.

Particular considerations can also arise in relation to users whom may not be customers in the normal and contractual sense.

What Prior Information Requirements?

19.07 The organisation is obliged to inform customers, etc, in a fair and transparent manner that it is intending to collect and process their personal data. It must identify exactly whom the Controller is, ie the legal entity collecting and processing the personal data. The categories

---

1   This issue arose for consideration in the first data protection audit of Facebook by the Irish supervisory authority. See also, for example, S Monteleone, 'Privacy and Data Protection at the time of Facial Recognition: Towards a New Right to Digital Identity?' *European Journal of Law and Technology* (2012) (3:3).

of personal data being collected must be outlined, as well as the purposed linked to the categories of personal data. If any third parties will be involved in processing the personal data, these must be referred to and identified, at least by category, when the personal data is being collected. Particular information must also be produced where it is envisaged that the personal data may be transferred outside of the EU/EEA.

Compliance with the Outward Facing Data Protection Principles

19.08 In dealing with customer personal data, as well as potential customers, etc, it is necessary for the organisation to comply with the Data Protection Principles.

The eight data protection principles are:

(1) fairly and lawfully processed;
(2) processed for limited purposes;
(3) adequate, relevant and not excessive;
(4) accurate and up to date;
(5) not kept for longer than is necessary;
(6) processed in line with employee, etc, rights;
(7) secure; and
(8) not transferred to other countries without adequate protection.

Chapter II of the new GDPR refers to the Data Protection Principles in Article 5 as follows.

Personal data must be:

(a) processed lawfully, fairly and in a transparent manner in relation to the Data Subject ('lawfulness, fairness and transparency');
(b) collected for specified, explicit and legitimate purposes and not further processed in a manner incompatible with those purposes; further processing for archiving purposes in the public interest, scientific or historical research purposes or statistical purposes shall, in accordance with Article 89(1), not be considered incompatible with the initial purposes ('purpose limitation');
(c) adequate, relevant and limited to what is necessary in relation to the purposes for which they are processed ('data minimisation');
(d) accurate and, where necessary, kept up to date; every reasonable step must be taken to ensure that personal data that are inaccurate, having regard to the purposes for which they are processed, are erased or rectified without delay ('accuracy');
(e) kept in a form which permits identification of Data Subjects for no longer than is necessary for the purposes for which the personal

data are processed; personal data may be stored for longer periods insofar as the data will be processed solely for archiving purposes in the public interest, scientific or historical research purposes or statistical purposes in accordance with Article 89(1) subject to implementation of the appropriate technical and organisational measures required by the Regulation in order to safeguard the rights and freedoms of the Data Subject ('storage limitation');

(f) processed in a manner that ensures appropriate security of the personal data, including protection against unauthorised or unlawful processing and against accidental loss, destruction or damage, using appropriate technical or organisational measures ('integrity and confidentiality') (Article 5(1)).

The Controller shall be responsible for and be able to demonstrate compliance with Article 5(1) ('accountability' principle) (Article 5(2)).

These can be summarised as:

- processed lawfully, fairly and transparently ('lawfulness, fairness and transparency');
- for specified, explicit and legitimate purposes and not further processed incompatibly with the purpose ('purpose limitation');
- adequate, relevant and limited to what is necessary for the purposes ('data minimisation');
- accurate and, where necessary, kept up to date ('accuracy');
- kept in a form which permits identification for no longer than is necessary ('storage limitation');
- appropriate security, including protection against unauthorised or unlawful processing and against accidental loss, destruction or damage, using appropriate technical or organisational measures ('integrity and confidentiality').

The Controller must demonstrate compliance ('accountability').

Compliance with the Data Protection Principles applies to all customers, etc, personal data collected and or processed by an organisation. It also applies regardless of registration notification requirements.

This requires that each of the Data Protection Principles must be considered separately and individually assessed by the organisation to ensure that is can, and will continue to be in compliance if and when it collects and processes personal data of customers, etc.

This will involve particular consideration of the contacting model with customers, how contracts are formed, the instant that they are formed and how records are maintained in the event that these need to be examined and evidenced subsequently. Integral to this contract model process is how the data protection elements, data protection policies, data protection clauses, data protection prior information requirements and customers consent, as appropriate, are complied with. Is the organisation proposing to ask questions which are not strictly required for the provision of the service or goods? Are questions being asked which are wholly unrelated to the actual service or product? If so, the third Data Protection Principle may be breached. If the product or service is time limited, and no further product or service is envisaged, it would be difficult for the organisation to permanently keep the personal data. This could conflict with the second, third and or fifth Data Protection Principles.

Depending on the type of service, products and or relationship with customers etc, whether physical and online, can mean that even more particular attention needs to be paid to fulfilling compliance with certain Data Protection Principles.

Customers, etc, and Ordinary Personal Data Legitimate Processing Conditions

19.09 What are the Legitimate Processing Conditions when an organisation is processing personal data regarding customers, etc? The Legitimate Processing Conditions are required to be complied with, in addition to the Data Protection Principles. Schedule 2 of the DPA 1998 contains the general Legitimate Processing Conditions. In order to collect and process personal data, in addition to complying with the above Data Protection Principles, organisations must comply or fall within one of the following general personal data Legitimate Processing Conditions in dealing with customer, etc, personal data:

- the customer, etc, whom the personal data is about has consented to the processing;
- the processing is necessary,
  - o in relation to a contract which the customers, etc, has entered into; or
  - o because the customers, etc, has asked for something to be done so they can enter into a contract;
- the processing is necessary because of a legal obligation that applies to the organisation (except an obligation imposed by a contract);
- the processing is necessary to protect the customers, etc, 'vital interests.' This condition only applies in cases of life or death, such as where an individual's medical history is disclosed to a hospital's A&E department treating them after a serious road accident;
- the processing is necessary for administering justice, or for exercising statutory, governmental, or other public functions;
- the processing is in accordance with the 'legitimate interests' condition.

Organisations prior to collecting and processing customer, etc, personal data should identify what personal data it is seeking, why, and which of the Legitimate Processing Conditions it will be complying with. This will differ according to the organisation, sector and particular activity envisaged.

Frequently, organisations may wish to rely upon the consent option. In that instance, there should be documented policies and or contact whereby the customer is informed and appraised of the proposed data processing and freely consents to same. The manner of consent should be recorded. If it is not recorded, it could present difficulties subsequently where it is needed to be proven that consent was obtained for a particular customer or for a whole database of customers.

A further issue arises. Many organisations over a long period of time will make changes to its business activities. There may also be changes to the contract and transaction models which can mean changes to the processing activities and contacts, policies, etc, relating to data protection and consent. The data of the changeover, the nature of the changes, and means of recording and maintaining a record of the consent also needed to be maintained by the organisation in an easily accessible manner.

These issues can be more pronounced for organisations which change their business models and processed more frequently. Many internet companies will, therefore, have frequent additional challenges.

Schedule 2 of the DPA 1998 also contains the Legitimate Processing Conditions relevant for the purposes of the first Data Protection Principle, as relevant to the processing of customers, etc personal data. It refers as follows:

1   The customers, etc, has given their consent to the processing.
2   The processing is necessary:
    (a)   for the performance of a contract to which the customers, etc, are a party; or
    (b)   for the taking of steps at the request of the customers, etc, with a view to entering into a contract.
3   The processing is necessary for compliance with any legal obligation to which the Controller is subject, other than an obligation imposed by contract.
4   The processing is necessary in order to protect the vital interests of the customers, etc.
5   The processing is necessary:
    (a)   for the administration of justice;
    (aa) for the exercise of any functions of either House of Parliament;
    (b)   for the exercise of any functions conferred on any person by or under any enactment;

    (c)   for the exercise of any functions of the Crown, a Minister of the Crown or a government department; or

    (d)   for the exercise of any other functions of a public nature exercised in the public interest by any person;

6 (1)   The processing is necessary for the purposes of legitimate interests pursued by the organisation or by the third party or parties to whom the data are disclosed, except where the processing is unwarranted in any particular case by reason of prejudice to the rights and freedoms or legitimate interests of the customers, etc.

    (2)   The Secretary of State may by order specify particular circumstances in which this condition is, or is not, to be taken to be satisfied.

These compliance conditions might be summarised as follows:

- customer, etc, gives consent;
- processing necessary for performance of contract to which the customer, etc, is a party;
- processing is necessary to take steps at request of the Data Subject prior to entering into contract;
- processing is necessary for compliance with legal obligation (other than contractual obligation);
- necessary to prevent injury or other damage to health of Data Subject or serious loss or damage to property of the customer, etc, or to protect vital interests;
- necessary for the administration of justice, performance of statutory function or function of public nature performed in public interest;
- processing necessary for legitimate interests pursued by the organisation except where unwarranted.

As noted above, frequently, an organisation would seek to fall within the contract consent or legitimate interests condition above in relation to customers, etc.

However, an organisation may seek to maintain compliance based on the legitimate interests condition. This could mean, on occasion, that an organisation seeks to legitimise processing activities by saying the customer has entered a contact and that the processing is a legitimate and necessary consequence of that. However, organisations seeking to adopt this model should seek professional advice beforehand. It is quite easy for an organisation to feel that it is compliant, but then for additional activities, commercialisation and or direct marketing to occur which may not be transparent, fair or warranted.

In any event, the Data Protection Principles must be complied with regardless of the particular Legitimate Processing Condition.

Customers, etc, Sensitive Personal Data Legitimate Processing Conditions

19.10 Organisations generally, or more frequently organisation involved in particular sectors, may wish to know certain information which falls within the sensitive personal data categories eg health data; sexual data. In the case of customers, etc, sensitive personal data, an organisation must, in addition to the Data Protection Principles, be able to comply or fall within one of the Sensitive Personal Data Legitimate Processing Conditions.

Schedule 3 of the DPA 1998 sets out conditions relevant for the purposes of the first Data Protection Principle in particular in relation to the Sensitive Personal Data Legitimate Processing Conditions. It refers as follows:

1 The customers have given explicit consent to the processing of the personal data.

2 (1) The processing is necessary for the purposes of exercising or performing any right or obligation which is conferred or imposed by law on the Controller in connection with employment.

   (2) The Secretary of State may by order:
      (a) exclude the application of sub-para (1) in such cases as may be specified; or
      (b) provide that, in such cases as may be specified, the condition in sub-para (1) is not to be regarded as satisfied unless such further conditions as may be specified in the order are also satisfied.

3 The processing is necessary:
   (a) in order to protect the vital interests of the Data Subject or another person, in a case where:
      (i) consent cannot be given by or on behalf of the Data Subject; or
      (ii) the Controller cannot reasonably be expected to obtain the consent of the Data Subject; or
   (b) in order to protect the vital interests of another person, in a case where consent by or on behalf of the Data Subject has been unreasonably withheld.

4 The processing:
   (a) is carried out in the course of its legitimate activities by any body or association which;
      (i) is not established or conducted for profit; and
      (ii) exists for political, philosophical, religious or trade-union purposes;

    (b)   is carried out with appropriate safeguards for the rights and freedoms of Data Subjects;

    (c)   relates only to individuals who either are members of the body or association or have regular contact with it in connection with its purposes; and

    (d)   does not involve disclosure of the personal data to a third party without the consent of the Data Subject.

5   The information contained in the personal data has been made public as a result of steps deliberately taken by the Data Subject.

6   The processing:

    (a)   is necessary for the purpose of, or in connection with, any legal proceedings (including prospective legal proceedings);

    (b)   is necessary for the purpose of obtaining legal advice; or

    (c)   is otherwise necessary for the purposes of establishing, exercising or defending legal rights.

7   (1)   The processing is necessary:

       (a)   for the administration of justice;

       (aa) for the exercise of any functions of either House of Parliament;

       (b)   for the exercise of any functions conferred on any person by or under an enactment; or

       (c)   for the exercise of any functions of the Crown, a Minister of the Crown or a government department;

    (2)   The Secretary of State may by order:

       (a)   exclude the application of sub-para (1) in such cases as may be specified; or

       (b)   provide that, in such cases as may be specified, the condition in sub-para (1) is not to be regarded as satisfied unless such further conditions as may be specified in the order are also satisfied;

7A (1)   The processing:

       (a)   is either;

          (i)   the disclosure of sensitive personal data by a person as a member of an anti-fraud organisation or otherwise in accordance with any arrangements made by such an organisation; or

          (ii) any other processing by that person or another person of sensitive personal data so disclosed; and

       (b)   is necessary for the purposes of preventing fraud or a particular kind of fraud.

    (2)   In this paragraph 'an anti-fraud organisation' means any unincorporated association, body corporate or other person which enables or facilitates any sharing of information to prevent

fraud or a particular kind of fraud or which has any of these functions as its purpose or one of its purposes.

8 (1) The processing is necessary for medical purposes and is undertaken by:

    (a) a health professional; or

    (b) a person who in the circumstances owes a duty of confidentiality which is equivalent to that which would arise if that person were a health professional.

  (2) In this paragraph 'medical purposes' includes the purposes of preventative medicine, medical diagnosis, medical research, the provision of care and treatment and the management of healthcare services.

9 (1) The processing:

    (a) is of sensitive personal data consisting of information as to racial or ethnic origin;

    (b) is necessary for the purpose of identifying or keeping under review the existence or absence of equality of opportunity or treatment between persons of different racial or ethnic origins, with a view to enabling such equality to be promoted or maintained; and

    (c) is carried out with appropriate safeguards for the rights and freedoms of Data Subjects;

  (2) The Secretary of State may by order specify circumstances in which processing falling within sub-para (1)(a) and (b) is, or is not, to be taken for the purposes of sub-para (1)(c) to be carried out with appropriate safeguards for the rights and freedoms of Data Subjects.

These customers, etc, Sensitive Personal Data Legitimate Processing Conditions may be summarised as follows:

- The customers, etc, whom the sensitive personal data is about, has given explicit consent to the processing;
- The processing is necessary so that the organisation can comply with employment law;
- The processing is necessary to protect the vital interests of,
  - the customer, etc (in a case where the customers, etc's, consent cannot be given or reasonably obtained); or
  - another person (in a case where the customers, etc's, consent has been unreasonably withheld);
- The processing is carried out by a not-for-profit organisation and does not involve disclosing personal data to a third party, unless the customer, etc's, consents. Extra limitations apply to this condition;
- The customers, etc, has deliberately made the information public;

- The processing is necessary in relation to legal proceedings; for obtaining legal advice; or otherwise for establishing, exercising or defending legal rights;
- The processing is necessary for administering justice, or for exercising statutory or governmental functions;
- The processing is necessary for medical purposes, and is undertaken by a health professional or by someone who is subject to an equivalent duty of confidentiality;
- The processing is necessary for monitoring equality of opportunity, and is carried out with appropriate safeguards for the rights of individuals.

Furthermore, regulations enacted also set out further obligations in relation to the processing of sensitive personal data.

It should be noted that the ability of an organisation to actually come within one of the Sensitive Personal Data Legitimate Processing Conditions is more restricted that the general personal data conditions. This is because the data protection regime considers that organisations have less legitimate interest in the processing of sensitive personal data. It also recognises the greater importance that legislators and individuals attach to the sensitive categories of personal data.

Customers, etc, and Security Requirements

19.11 What security issues arise for customer, etc, related personal data? Customers, etc, will be concerned to ensure that their personal data is not inadvertently accessed, disclosed or used in a manner which they have not consented to and are unaware of. This is a legal requirement under the data protection regime. Appropriate security measures must also be established. These obligations are becoming ever more present with examples of unauthorised access, disclosure, hacks, etc such as Talk Talk, Sony, Ashley Madison, Vtech (the children's toy manufacturer), Hyatt hotels, etc.

In the case of outward facing personal data, such categories will generally present significant differences to employee related personal data. Generally there will be more customer, etc, related personal data. It will also be more widely accessible within the organisation. Fewer people within an organisation need to have access to employee files and personal data. Customers, etc, personal data tends to be spread across more than one single location or database. Frequently, the personal data are obtained through a variety of sources, and which are more diverse than inward facing personal data. This all means that there are greater security issues and access issues to be considered by the organisation.

Increasingly, attacks and breaches that come to public attention tend to relate to outward facing personal data. This means that there is greater reason to maintain and or enhance these security measures to avoid the consequences of publicity, official enquiries, enforcement proceedings, or complaints and or proceedings from Data Subjects.

Security is also an issue to carefully consider in relation to the new and developing areas of cloud computing, outsourcing, and new models and categories of data processing.

Organisations should be aware of the importance of maintaining separate databases and maintaining these in a non accessible or open manner. Encryption, access restrictions, separate locations, etc are just some of the security precautions to be considered.

Notification Requirements

19.12 Organisations collecting and processing customer, etc, personal data will also have to consider notification requirement issues. The notification registration details will have to specify the categories of customer, etc, personal data being collected, for what purposes and activities, and also whether there are any third party recipients and transfers (TBDFs). The notification also needs to outline details of the security measures. These of course may change over time, and notifications, policies, etc, may equally need to reflect these changes.

Direct Marketing (DM)

19.13 Most commercial organisations will wish to engage in direct marketing (DM). For some organisations this will be an important core activity. Section 11(3) of the DPA 1998 provides that 'direct marketing' means the communication (by whatever means) of any advertising or marketing material which is directed to particular individuals.

The data protection regime has extensive provisions dealing with direct marketing. There are requirements to inform the Data Subject that they may object by a written request and free of charge to their personal data being used for direct marketing (DM) purposes.

If the Controller anticipates that personal data kept by it will be processed for purposes of direct marketing it must inform the persons to whom the data relates that they may object by means of a request in writing to the Controller and free of charge.

However, s 11 of the DPA 1998 provides a right to prevent processing for purposes of direct marketing. A customer is entitled at any time by notice in writing to a Controller to require the Controller at the end of such period (as is reasonable in the circumstances) to cease, or not to begin, processing for the purposes of direct marketing (DM) personal data in respect of which he is the Data Subject (s 11(1)).

If a court is satisfied, on the application of any person who has given a notice under sub-s (1), that the Controller has failed to comply with the notice, the court may order them to take such steps for complying with the notice as the court thinks fit (s 11(2)).[2]

Two individuals were fined £440,000 by the ICO for sending unsolicited marketing Spam messages.[3]

Consequences of Non-Compliance

19.14 If the organisation fails to assess and organise compliance procedures in advance of undertaking the collection and processing of personal data of customers, etc, it will inevitable be operating in breach of the data protection regime. Any personal data collected will be illicit.

Equally, if originally compliant but during operation one of the Data Protection Principles, Legitimate Processing Conditions, and/or security requirements are breached, the personal data processed will be questionable, particularly if new personal data is involved or has new activities and uses.

What are the consequences? The collection and/or processing are illegal. The organisation, as the Controller, can be the subject of complaints, investigations and enforcement proceedings from the ICO. Depending on the severity of the non-compliance, prosecutions can also involve the directors and employees of the organisation, in addition to the organisation itself.

If convicted, the organisation could face significant fines. These will be in addition to the bad publicity and media attention which a prosecution can bring.

There can be other consequences too. If the organisation relies heavily on direct marketing (DM), or is a particular type of internet company, the customer database of personal data can be one of the most significant assets of the organisation. If the database is collected in

---

2   Section 11(2A) of the DPA 1998 provides that this section shall not apply in relation to the processing of such data as are mentioned in para (1) of reg 8 of the Telecommunications (Data Protection and Privacy) Regulations 1999 (processing of telecommunications billing data for certain marketing purposes) for the purposes mentioned in para (2) of that regulation.

3   *ICO v Niebel* and *ICO v McNeish* at https//:ico.org.uk. Note, case was appealed.

breach of the data protection regime, the organisation will not be able to establish compliant data collections and consents. It could, therefore, be ordered to delete the database.

Alternatively, an organisation may wish to sell its business or to seek investors for the business. This is frequently the case in the technology sector. However, as part of a potential purchaser or investor assessing whether to proceed, it will undertake a due diligence examination of the processes, procedures and documentation of the organisation. It will request to see documented evidence of data protection compliance and that the valuable database, etc, are fully data protection compliant. If this cannot be established, serious question marks will arise and the transaction may not proceed.

Users Versus Customers

19.15 Do separate issues arise for users and their personal data? Where someone is a customer, there is more direct contact and therefore more direct means for the organisation to engage with the customer in a measured contract formation process. Consequently, it is possible to ensure compliance though a considered and documented data protection compliance process and to engage consent appropriately at an early stage from the individual customer or potential customer.

Users, however, may not be customers. Therefore, customer contact models which incorporate consent or other data protection legitimising procedures for customers may leave a gap where non customer users are not presented with the same documentation, notices and sign up document sets. Organisations therefore need to consider users as separate from normal customers. They must assess where the organisation interacts with such users, physically or online, and what personal data may be collected. Where personal data is collected from users, the organisation needs to ensure compliance. This may mean that the organisation needs to have a separate additional set of notices, policies and consent documentation in relation to users.

Conclusion

19.16 When organisations begin to look outwards, a separate range of data collection possibilities will arise. The avenues for data collection are more diverse. In addition, the intended uses to which the organisation will put this type of personal data will be potentially greater. The Data Protection Principles and Legitimate Processing Conditions require particular consideration and configuration to the intended data processing activities of customer, etc personal data. Different security and enforcement risks can arise and need to be protected against. It cannot be assumed that everyone that the organisation may wish to collect personal data from will be an actual customer. Therefore, organisations need to consider how to ensure separate consent and notifications to this category of person. An example of this may be cookies which may obtain personal data (see later).

Chapter 20

Data Protection and Privacy by Design

Introduction

20.01 It has been suggested that 'law should play a more active role in establishing best practices for emerging online trends.'[1] Data Protection by Design (DPbD) and data protection by default are prime examples. One of the most important and developing practical areas of data protection is the concept of DPbD as referred to in the GDPR. Originally developed as a follow on from the data protection legal regime, it is now being recognised more widely, and is also being explicitly referred to and recognised in primary legislation itself.

DPbD/PbD and data protection by default are important for organisations both in terms of being a legal obligation but also commercially in terms of being a competitive advantage.[2]

Background

20.02 The concept of PbD is complementary to data protection law and regulation. The idea is acknowledged to have started with Dr Ann Cavoukian, the Information and Privacy Commissioner for Ontario, Canada. She states that:

'the increasing complexity and interconnectedness of information technologies [requires] building privacy right into system design ... the concept

---

1 W McGeveran, 'Disclosure, Endorsement, and Identity in Social Marketing,' *Illinois Law Review* (2009)(4) 1105–1166, at 1105.
2 See, for example, A Mantelero, 'Competitive Value of Data Protection: The Impact of Data Protection Regulation on Online Behaviour,' *International Data Privacy Law* (2013) (3:4) 229.

of Privacy by Design (PbD), … describe[s] the philosophy of embedding privacy proactively into technology itself – making it the default.'[3]

Principles of PbD

20.03   The Information and Privacy Commissioner for Ontario refers to seven principles of PbD.[4] These are set out below.

1   Proactive not Reactive; Preventative not Remedial

The Privacy by Design (PbD) approach is characterised by proactive rather than reactive measures. It anticipates and prevents privacy invasive events before they happen. PbD does not wait for privacy risks to materialise, nor does it offer remedies for resolving privacy infractions once they have occurred – it aims to prevent them from occurring. In short, PbD comes before-the-fact, not after.

2   Privacy as the Default Setting

One point is certain – the default rules PbD seek to deliver the maximum degree of privacy by ensuring that personal data are automatically protected in any given IT system or business practice. If an individual does nothing, their privacy still remains intact. No action is required on the part of the individual to protect their privacy – it is built into the system, by default.

3   Privacy Embedded into Design

PbD is embedded into the design and architecture of IT systems and business practices. It is not bolted on as an add-on, after the fact. The result is that privacy becomes an essential component of the core functionality being delivered. Privacy is integral to the system, without diminishing functionality.

4   Full Functionality – Positive-Sum, not Zero-Sum

PbD seeks to accommodate all legitimate interests and objectives in a positive-sum 'win-win' manner, not through a dated, zero-sum approach, where unnecessary trade-offs are made. PbD avoids the pretence of false dichotomies, such as privacy vs security, demonstrating that it is possible to have both.

---

3   At http://privacybydesign.ca/about/.
4   At http://www.privacybydesign.ca/content/uploads/2009/08/7foundational principles. pdf.

5   End-to-End Security – Full Lifecycle Protection

PbD, having been embedded into the system prior to the first element of information being collected, extends securely throughout the entire lifecycle of the data involved – strong security measures are essential to privacy, from start to finish. This ensures that all data are securely retained, and then securely destroyed at the end of the process, in a timely fashion. Thus, PbD ensures cradle to grave, secure lifecycle management of information, end-to-end.

6   Visibility and Transparency – Keep it Open

PbD seeks to assure all stakeholders that whatever the business practice or technology involved, it is in fact, operating according to the stated promises and objectives, subject to independent verification. Its component parts and operations remain visible and transparent, to users and providers alike. Remember, trust but verify.

7   Respect for User Privacy – Keep it User-Centric

Above all, PbD requires architects and operators to keep the interests of the individual uppermost by offering such measures as strong privacy defaults, appropriate notice, and empowering user-friendly options. Keep it user-centric.[5]

DPD

20.04   DPD Recital 46 states that whereas the protection of the rights and freedoms of Data Subjects with regard to the processing of personal data requires that appropriate technical and organisational measures be taken, both at the time of the design of the processing system and at the time of the processing itself, particularly in order to maintain security and thereby to prevent any unauthorised processing; whereas it is incumbent on the Member States to ensure that Controllers comply with these measures; whereas these measures must ensure an appropriate level of security, taking into account the state of the art and the costs of their implementation in relation to the risks inherent in the processing and the nature of the data to be protected.

---

5   At http://www.privacybydesign.ca/content/uploads/2009/08/7foundational principles.
     pdf.

Specific Processing Risks

20.05 DPD Recital 53 states that whereas, however, certain processing operations are likely to pose specific risks to the rights and freedoms of Data Subjects by virtue of their nature, their scope, or their purposes, such as that of excluding individuals from a right, benefit or a contract, or by virtue of the *specific use of new technologies*; whereas it is for Member States, if they so wish, to specify such risks in their legislation.

DPD Recital 54 states that whereas with regard to all the processing undertaken in society, the amount posing such specific risks should be very limited; whereas Member States must provide that the SA, or the data protection official in cooperation with the authority, check such processing prior to it being carried out; whereas following this prior check, the SA may, according to its national law, give an opinion or an authorisation regarding the processing; whereas such checking may equally take place in the course of the preparation either of a measure of the national parliament or of a measure based on such a legislative measure, which defines the nature of the processing and lays down appropriate safeguards.

GDPR

Data Protection by Design (DPbD)

20.06 The Commission proposed an enhanced data protection regime including DPbD.[6] Article 25 of the GDPR refers to data protection by design and by default. This is an increasingly important area in data protection.

Data Subject's rights and freedoms and legitimate interests and compliance increasingly require planning and pre-problem solving.

Data Protection by Design and by Default (DPbD)

20.07 Article 25 of the new GDPR refers to DPbD and by default. (Note also the related concept of Privacy by Design (PbD). In some ways PbD is the impetus for the current DPbD rules.)

Taking into account the state of the art, the cost of implementation and the nature, scope, context and purposes of the processing as well as

---

6   See GDPR, S Spiekermann, 'The Challenges of Privacy by Design,' *Communications of the ACM* (2012) (55) 38–40; S Spiekermann and LF Cranor, 'Engineering Privacy,' *IEEE Transactions on Software Engineering* (2009) (35) 67–82; L Tielemans and M Hildebrandt, 'Data Protection by Design and Technology Neutral Law,' *Computer Law and Security Review* (2013) (29:5) 509.

the risks of varying likelihood and severity for rights and freedoms of natural persons posed by the processing, the Controller shall, both at the time of the determination of the means for processing and at the time of the processing itself, implement appropriate technical and organisational measures, such as pseudonymisation, which are designed to implement data protection principles, such as data minimisation, in an effective manner and to integrate the necessary safeguards into the processing in order to meet the requirements of the GDPR and protect the rights of Data Subjects (Article 25(1)).

The Controller shall implement appropriate technical and organisational measures for ensuring that, by default, only personal data which are necessary for each specific purpose of the processing are processed. This applies to the amount of data collected, the extent of their processing, the period of their storage and their accessibility. In particular, such measures shall ensure that by default personal data are not made accessible without the individual's intervention to an indefinite number of natural persons (Article 25(2)).

An approved certification mechanism pursuant to Article 42 may be used as an element to demonstrate compliance with the requirements set out in this Article.

Prior to the new GDPR, the ICO has issued recommendations in relation to privacy notices, namely:

- Privacy Impact Assessment Code of Practice (see below).

This now needs to be read in light of the GDPR changes.

ICO

20.08   PbD is embraced by the ICO in the UK. The ICO refers to DPbD by saying that 'Privacy by Design is an approach whereby privacy and data protection compliance is designed into systems holding information right from the start, rather than being bolted on afterwards or ignored, as has too often been the case.'[7]

It provides[8] the following documents and guidance:

- Privacy by Design report;[9]
- Privacy by Design implementation plan;[10]

---

7   ICO, *Privacy by Design* at https://ico.org.uk.
8   *Ibid.*
9   *Ibid.*
10 ICO, *PbD ICO Implementation Plan*, at https://ico.org.uk.

- Privacy Impact Assessment (PIA) handbook;[11]
- ICO technical guidance note on Privacy Enhancing Technologies (PETs);[12]
- Enterprise Privacy Group paper on PETs;
- HIDE (Homeland security, biometric Identification and personal Detection Ethics);
- Glossary of privacy and data protection terms;
- Privacy Impact Assessments – international study (Loughborough University).

Privacy by Design Report

20.09 The ICO report on Privacy by Design was launched in November 2008. The Commission in the Foreword notes that:

> 'The capacity of organisations to acquire and use our personal details has increased dramatically since our data protection laws were first passed. There is an ever increasing amount of personal information collected and held about us as we go about our daily lives ... we have seen a dramatic change in the capability of organisations to exploit modern technology that uses our information to deliver services, this has not been accompanied by a similar drive to develop new effective technical and procedural privacy safeguards. We have seen how vulnerable our most personal of details can be and these should not be put at risk.'[13]

In the report, Toby Stevens, Director, of the Enterprise Privacy Group, adds that:

> 'This report is the first stage in bridging the current gap in the development and adoption of privacy-friendly solutions as part of modern information systems. It aims to address the current problems related to the handling of personal information and put into place a model for privacy by design that will ensure privacy achieves the same structured and professional recognition as information security has today.'[14]

The report describes PbD as follows:

> 'The purpose of privacy by design is to give due consideration to privacy needs prior to the development of new initiatives – in other words, to consider the impact of a system or process on individuals' privacy and to do this throughout the systems lifecycle, thus ensuring that appropriate controls are implemented and maintained.'[15]

---

11 ICO, *Privacy Impact Assessment*, at https://ico.org.uk.
12 ICO, *Privacy by Design, An Overview of Privacy Enhancing Technologies*, 26 November 2008. At https://ico.org.uk.
13 ICO, *Privacy by Design* (2008). At https://ico.org.uk.
14 *Ibid*, 2.
15 *Ibid*, 7.

The report refers to the various lifecycles that arise in an organisation.[16] These can be products, services, systems and processes:

> 'For a privacy by design approach to be effective, it must take into account the full lifecycle of any system or process, from the earliest stages of the system business case, through requirements gathering and design, to delivery, testing, operations, and out to the final decommissioning of the system.
>
> This lifetime approach ensures that privacy controls are stronger, simpler and therefore cheaper to implement, harder to by-pass, and fully embedded in the system as part of its core functionality.
>
> However, neither current design practices in the private and public sectors, nor existing tools tend to readily support such an approach. Current privacy practices and technologies are geared towards 'spot' implementations and 'spot' verifications to confirm that privacy designs and practices are correct at a given moment within a given scope of inspection.'[17]

ICO Recommendations

20.10   The ICO report makes a number of recommendations in relation to PbD practice in the UK.[18] These are set out below:

> 'Working with industry bodies to build an **executive mandate for privacy by design**, supported by sample business cases for the costs, benefits and risks associated with the processing of personal information, and promotion of executive awareness of key privacy and identity concepts so that privacy is reflected in the business cases for new systems.
>
> Encouraging widespread use of **privacy impact assessments throughout the systems lifecycle**, and ensuring that these assessments are both maintained and published where appropriate to demonstrate transparency of privacy controls.
>
> Supporting the development of **cross-sector standards for data sharing** both within and between organisations, so that privacy needs are harmonised with the pressures on public authorities and private organisations to share personal information.
>
> Nurturing the development of **practical privacy standards** that will help organisations to turn the legal outcomes mandated under data protection laws into consistent, provable privacy implementations.

---

16   ICO, *Privacy by Design*, (2008).
17   ICO, *Privacy by Design*, (2008). At https://ico.org.uk, at 7–8.
18   *Ibid*, summarised at 3, and in detail at 22–31.

Promoting current and future research into PETs that deliver commercial products to manage consent and revocation, privacy-friendly identification and authentication, and prove the effectiveness of privacy controls.

Establishing more rigorous compliance and enforcement mechanisms by assigning responsibility for privacy management within organisations to nominated individuals, urging organisations to demonstrate greater clarity in their personal information processing, and empowering and providing the ICO with the ability to investigate and enforce compliance where required.

The government, key industry representatives and academics, and the ICO are urged to consider, prioritise and set in motion plans to deliver these recommendations and hence make privacy by design a reality.'[19]

The report highlights the need and context for PbD in relation to the many instances of data loss in the UK (and internationally). It states that:

'Consumer trust in the ability of public authorities and private organisations to manage personal information is at an all-time low ebb. A stream of high-profile privacy incidents in the UK over the past year has shaken confidence in the data sharing agenda for government with associated impacts on high-profile data management programmes, and businesses are having to work that much harder to persuade customers to release personal information to them.'[20]

PbD is part of the solution whereby 'the evolution of a new approach to the management of personal information that ingrains privacy principles into every part of every system in every organisation.'[21]

Organisations need to address many key privacy and data protection issues, such as:

'assessing information risks from the individual's perspective; adopting transparency and data minimisation principles; exploiting opportunities for differentiation through enhanced privacy practices; and ensuring that privacy needs influence their identity management agenda (since identity technologies are invariably needed to deliver effective privacy approaches).'[22]

Commercial Adoption

20.11   Many multinationals and other organisations are embracing PbD and DPbD. Microsoft, for example, has endorsed PbD for a number of years now. At one particular stage Google rolled out a major privacy

19 ICO, *Privacy by Design*, (2008), note emphasis in original.
20 ICO, *Privacy by Design*, (2008). At https://ico.org.uk, at 6.
21 *Ibid.*
22 *Ibid.*

policy change regarding users' personal data. It decided to combine the policies for over 60 separate and discrete products and services of Google (and other companies and brand names).

The data protection authorities of the EU, as well as elsewhere around the world (including various officials in the US), requested Google to not go-ahead or in the case of the EU, to delay it until officials could consider it further.

The EU data protection authorities, under WP29 and the French data protection authority (CNIL) carried out an investigation of the new privacy policy and its implications. In *WP29 and Data Protection Authorities/Google*[23] the new Google policy change was found to be in breach of data protection law. Various changes are required. However, one of these included that Google incorporate the policy of DPbD into its products and services. In addition to mandated DPbD per the new GDPR, it may be that specific DPbD requirements or recommendations come to be included in individual decisions of SAs when dealing with audits, complaints and investigations.

Conclusion

20.12 An organisation must be proactive and not reactive. Data protection considerations need to be considered and built in from the earliest stage in processes which potentially impact data protection. They must be transparent and visible. Problem issues are addressed and solutions incorporated into the process design and process cycle so that pre-problem solving is achieved for personal data. DPbD needs to be built in, not merely added or considered once a problem arises at the end or after go-live. However, PbD and DPbD means incorporating these considerations into the whole life cycle and not just at the beginning and or the end. It is also incorporated into engineering processes and not just system consideration and data categories. PbD and DPbD is now a key concept and requirement under the new GDPD. There is increasing emphasis on privacy engineering as a part of the mechanisms needed to achieve DPbD.

DPbD is one of the more important innovations in data protection generally. This is reflected in the GDPR. All organisations will need to appraise themselves of the concept and the regulatory compliance issues. The above Google requirement to implement DPbD is also timely and

---

23 See WP29 Letter to Google: http://www.cnil.fr/fileadmin/documents/en/20121016-letter_google-article_29-FINAL.pdf; Appendix: http://www.cnil.fr/fileadmin/documents/en/GOOGLE_PRIVACY_POLICY-_RECOMMENDATIONS-FINAL-EN.pdf; French DP regulator (CNIL) statement: http://www.cnil.fr/english/news-and-events/news/article/googles-new-privacy-policy-incomplete-information-and-uncontrolled-combination-of-data-across-ser/.

reflects the importance that enterprise, both large and small, needs to engage the benefits, as well as the requirements, of DPbD.

Privacy impact assessments[24] are also referred to in the GDPR and may also be relevant in the context of DPbD. DPbD, privacy impact assessments are also relevant in the context of developing cloud services.[25] Cloud services also raise important data protection and security considerations and these should be carefully considered by customers as well as providers.[26] The WP29 has also commented in relation to Cloud issues,[27] big data issues,[28] Internet of Things (IoT),[29] drones,[30] apps on smart devices,[31] cookies,[32] device fingerprinting,[33] anonymisation and pseudonomisation techniques,[34] purpose limitation,[35] smart devices,[36] etc.

---

24 Wright, D, 'The State of the Art in Privacy Impact Assessments,' *Computer Law & Security Review* (2012) (28) 54–61.

25 Cloud and data protection reliability and compliance issues are referred to in R Clarke 'How Reliable is Cloudsourcing? A Review of Articles in the Technical Media 2005–11,' *Computer Law & Security Review* (2012) (28) 90–95. King and Raja also research the area of the protections of sensitive personal data and cloud computing, see NJ King and VT Raja 'Protecting the Privacy and Security of Sensitive Customer Data in the Cloud,' *Computer Law & Security Review* (2012) (28) 308–319; J Peng, 'A New Model of Data Protection on Cloud Storage,' *Journal of Networks* (03/2014) (9:3) 666.

26 See, for example ICO, *Guidance on the Use of Cloud Computing*, at https://ico.org. uk. WP29, *Opinion 05/2012 on Cloud Computing*, WP 196, 1 July 2012; P Lanois, 'Caught in the Clouds: The Web 2.0, Cloud Computing, and Privacy?,' *Northwestern Journal of Technology and Intellectual Property* (2010) (9) 29–49; FM Pinguelo and BW Muller 'Avoid the Rainy Day: Survey of US Cloud Computing Caselaw,' *Boston College Intellectual Property & Technology Forum* (2011) 1–7; IR Kattan, 'Cloudy Privacy Protections: Why the Stored Communications Act Fails to Protect the Privacy of Communications Stored in the Cloud,' *Vandenburg Journal of Entertainment and Technology Law* (2010–2011) (13) 617–656.

27 WP29, Opinion 02/2015 on C-SIG Code of Conduct on Cloud Computing; and Opinion 05/2012 on Cloud Computing.

28 WP29, Statement on Statement of the WP29 on the impact of the development of big data on the protection of individuals with regard to the processing of their personal data in the EU, 2014. The ICO also issued guidance on big data and data protection issues prior to the new GDPD in 2014.

29 WP29, Opinion 8/2014 on the Recent Developments on the Internet of Things.

30 WP29, Opinion 01/2015 on Privacy and Data Protection Issues relating to the Utilisation of Drones.

31 WP29, Opinion 02/2013 on apps on smart devices.

32 WP29, Cookie sweep combined analysis 2015; Opinion 04/2012 on Cookie Consent Exemption.

33 WP29, Opinion 9/2014 on the application of Directive 2002/58/EC to device fingerprinting.

34 WP29, Opinion 05/2014 on Anonymisation Techniques. The ICO has previously issued guidance on anonymisation techniques prior to the GDPD in an anonymisation code of practice (2012).

35 WP29, Opinion 03/2013 on purpose limitation.

36 WP29, Opinion 02/2013 on apps on smart devices.

Chapter 21

Cookies and Electronic Communications

Introduction

21.01   Cookies are software files used to speed up interactions with websites. However, they can also be used to monitor individuals, create profiles and assist direct marketing (DM) to individuals.[1] There are, therefore, obvious concerns in relation to privacy and data protection.

The use of cookies is sometimes controversial. This is because cookies can be covert and non-transparent. Policymakers are therefore concerned that the use of cookies should be regulated by the data protection regime to protect internet users.

The ePD was amended by Directive 2009/136/EC, in particular Article 5(3), to ensure that the use of cookies would be predicated upon user consent and transparent.

The new GDPR states that it shall not impose additional obligations on natural or legal persons in relation to the processing of personal data in connection with the provision of publicly available electronic communications services in public communication networks in the EU in relation to matters for which they are subject to specific obligations with the same objective set out in Directive 2002/58/EC[2] (Article 89).

---

1   See, for example, A Newson, A Duffy and C Cheng, 'Cookies Compliance: The Practicalities,' SCL *Computers and Law*, 29 February 2012.
2   Directive 2002/58/EC of the European Parliament and of the Council of 12 July 2002 concerning the processing of personal data and the protection of privacy in the electronic communications sector (Directive on privacy and electronic communications).

Cookie Amendment

21.02   The concern in relation to cookies and data protection has led to Article 5.3 of ePD[3] being amended by Directive 2009/136/EC[4] in relation to how cookies can be used. The amended Article 5.3 reads:

> 'Member States shall ensure that the storing of information, or the gaining of access to information already stored, in the terminal equipment of a subscriber or user is only allowed on condition that the subscriber or user concerned has given his or her consent, having been provided with clear and comprehensive information, in accordance with [the DPD], inter alia, about the purposes of the processing. This shall not prevent any technical storage or access for the sole purpose of carrying out the transmission of a communication over an electronic communications network, or as strictly necessary in order for the provider of an information society service explicitly requested by the subscriber or user to provide the service.'

The Privacy and Electronic Communications (EC Directive) (Amendment) Regulations 2011 (the PECR Amendment Regulations) introduce these changes in the UK.

ICO

Guidance

21.03   The ICO updated the guidance in relation to cookies in May 2012, entitled *Privacy and Electronic Communications Regulations, Guidance on the Rules on Use of Cookies and Similar Technologies.*[5]

It states, that the PECR[6] covers the use of cookies and similar technologies for storing information, and accessing information stored, on a user's equipment such as their computer or mobile device.

The PECR apply to cookies, and similar technologies, for storing information.[7] The PECR implements the ePD regarding the protection of

---

3   Directive 2002/58/EC, the ePrivacy Directive.

4   Directive 2009/136/EC of the European Parliament and of the Council of 25 November 2009 amending Directive 2002/22/EC on universal service and users' rights relating to electronic communications networks and services, Directive 2002/58/EC concerning the processing of personal data and the protection of privacy in the electronic communications sector and Regulation (EC) No 2006/2004 on cooperation between national authorities responsible for the enforcement of consumer protection laws.

5   ICO, *Privacy and Electronic Communications Regulations, Guidance on the Rules on Use of Cookies and Similar Technologies.* At https://ico.org.uk.

6   Privacy and Electronic Communications (EC Directive) Regulations 2003.

7   ICO, *Privacy and Electronic Communications Regulations, Guidance on the Rules on Use of Cookies and Similar Technologies.* At https://ico.org.uk.

privacy in the electronic communications sector. Users must be informed about cookies and given choices as regards cookie monitoring.[8] In 2009, the ePD was amended by Directive 2009/136/EC. This includes changes to Article 5(3) of the ePD requiring consent for the storage or access to information stored on a user's equipment. The UK amendments were introduced through the Privacy and Electronic Communications (EC Directive)(Amendment) Regulations 2011 (the PECR Amendment Regulations).[9]

The new rules protect the privacy of internet users. The changes are prompted by concerns about online tracking of internet users eg online monitoring, tracking, accessing the devices of users, spyware, etc. The new rules prevent cookies being used without the knowledge, consent or agreement of users.[10] Organisations must now obtain consent to use cookies and similar technologies.[11]

Implementing the Rules

21.04   The ICO report also emphasises the importance of auditing cookies and websites using cookies, to ensure that users are provided with transparent information in advance relating to cookies and that organisations obtain user consent. New websites need to apply the new rules. Existing websites need to be reviewed and reconfigured to ensure user consent is obtained in order to use cookies.[12]

Definitions

21.05   The PECR Amendment Regulations apply not just to cookies but also to similar technologies used for collecting and storing user information, eg Local Shared Objects/'Flash Cookies,' web beacons or bugs.[13] There are also different types of cookies. For example, cookies can expire at the end of a browser session or can last for longer. The new PECR apply to both. Some of the PECR definitions are:

---

8   ICO, *Privacy and Electronic Communications Regulations, Guidance on the Rules on Use of Cookies and Similar Technologies.* At https://ico.org.uk.
9   *Ibid.*
10   *Ibid.*
11   *Ibid.*
12   *Ibid.*
13   *Ibid.*

Session cookies:	allow websites to link the actions of a user during a browser session. They may be used for a variety of purposes such as remembering what a user has put in their shopping basket as they browse around a site. They could also be used for security when a user is accessing internet banking or to facilitate use of webmail. These session cookies expire after a browser session so would not be stored long term. For this reason session cookies may sometimes be considered less privacy intrusive than persistent cookies;
Persistent cookies:	are stored on a users' device in between browser sessions which allows the preferences or actions of the user across a site (or in some cases across different websites) to be remembered. Persistent cookies may be used for a variety of purposes including remembering users' preferences and choices when using a site or to target advertising;
First and third party cookies:	Whether a cookie is 'first' or 'third' party refers to the website or domain placing the cookie. First party cookies in basic terms are cookies set by a website visited by the user – the website displayed in the URL window. Third party cookies are cookies that are set by a domain other than the one being visited by the user. If a user visits a website and a separate company sets a cookie through that website this would be a third party cookie;
Subscriber:	This means a person who is a party to a contract with a provider of public electronic communications services for the supply of such services. In this context the person who pays the bill for the internet connection (that is, the person legally responsible for the charges);
User:	This means any individual using a public electronic communications service. In this context a user would be the person sat at a computer or using a mobile device to browse the internet;
Terminal equipment:	The device a cookie is placed on, usually a computer or mobile device.[14]

---

14 ICO, *Privacy and Electronic Communications Regulations, Guidance on the Rules on Use of Cookies and Similar Technologies*. At https://ico.org.uk.

Consent

21.06   The PECR Amendment Regulations require organisations to obtain user consent in order to use cookies. The DPD defines 'the Data Subject's consent' as:

> 'any freely given specific and informed indication of his wishes by which the Data Subject signifies his agreement to personal data relating to them being processed.'[15]

Consent must involve some form of communication where the individual knowingly indicates their acceptance. Hence, the prior information requirement. This may involve eg clicking an icon, sending an email or subscribing to a service. Users must be fully and transparently informed in advance, in order that they are able to fully understand the issues surrounding cookies and consent to cookies.[16]

'Prior' Consent

21.07   The ICO indicated that 'prior' consent means that consent be obtained prior to the cookie being used.[17]

The use of cookies should be delayed until users have had the opportunity to understand cookies and decide. The prior information should be clear and comprehensive.[18]

If users make a one-off visit to a website, a persistent cookie should not be needed. Organisations should shorten the lifespan of cookies or even make them temporary session cookies.[19]

Implied Consent Basis for PECR Compliance

21.08   The ICO indicates that explicit consent provides the best certainty. Organisations collecting sensitive personal data, eg health data, always require explicit consent.[20]

Consent (implied or express) must be freely given, specific and informed. For implied consent, there has to be some action taken by the consenting individual from which their consent can be inferred. This might, for example, be visiting a website, moving from one page to another or clicking a particular button. In this instance, the individual

15   ICO, *Privacy and Electronic Communications Regulations, Guidance on the Rules on Use of Cookies and Similar Technologies*. At https://ico.org.uk.
16   *Ibid.*
17   *Ibid.*
18   *Ibid.*
19   *Ibid.*
20   *Ibid.*

has to have a reasonable understanding that by doing so they are agreeing to cookies.[21]

'Specific and Informed'

21.09   However, merely visiting a website is not sufficient consent.[22] A user cannot 'give' consent if they are not aware that their actions are being interpreted as consent. If the user is not informed, there is no valid consent.[23]

If seeking to rely upon implied consent for cookies, it is important that the organisation seeking consent satisfy themselves that the user's actions are not only an explicit request for content or services but there is also an expression of the user's agreement that the organisation may use cookies.[24]

Clear and relevant information must be readily available to users, explaining what is likely to happen while the user is accessing the website and what choices the user has in terms of controlling what happens with cookies.[25] The ICO indicates that important factors may include the following:

- *The nature of the intended audience of the website*

  Websites might be aimed at a tech savvy audience who understand what is going on. These websites would not necessarily need to provide very basic information about what cookies, are but may still need to give users detailed explanations of how the organisation uses cookies and similar technology.[26]

- *The way in which users expect to receive information from and on the website*
  The more the information about cookies fits with the rest of the website, the more likely users are to read it. In turn, the more likely the website operator is able to assume that users understand and accept how the website works.[27]

- *The language used must be appropriate for the audience*

  The ICI refers to the advice of the International Chambers of Commerce.[28]

---

21   ICO, *Privacy and Electronic Communications Regulations, Guidance on the Rules on Use of Cookies and Similar Technologies.* At https://ico.org.uk.
22   *Ibid.*
23   *Ibid.*
24   *Ibid.*
25   *Ibid*
26   *Ibid.*
27   *Ibid.*
28   *Ibid.*

'Indication of Wishes'

21.10   Consent in the offline world can be given orally, in writing or it might be implied via a particular course of action.[29]

User actions can only give an indication if there is a shared understanding of what is happening. Without a clear notice, it is difficult to assume that the user was happy for cookies to be set. The ICO stresses the importance of providing more and better information to users about cookies.[30]

The ICO recognises that gaining explicit opt-in consent for analytics cookies is difficult. Implied consent might be the most practical and user-friendly option.[31] The key to valid implied consent in this context is increasing user knowledge.[32]

User or Subscriber Consent

21.11   The PECR Amendment Regulations require that cookie consent should be obtained from the user or subscriber.[33]

The rules require the following:

'A person shall not store or gain access to information stored, in the terminal equipment of a subscriber or user unless the requirements of paragraph (2) are met.

(2)   The requirements are that the subscriber or user of that terminal equipment,
   (a)   is provided with clear and comprehensive information about the purposes of the storage of, or access to, that information; and
   (b)   has given his or her consent.' (PECR Regulation 6).[34]

Organisations (and website designers) must:

- inform users that the cookies are there;
- explain what the cookies are doing; and
- obtain user consent to store a cookie on the user's device.[35]

Since 2003, organisations using cookies are required to provide clear information to users. The revised PECR Amendment Regulations require clear prior information about the cookies and user consent to the cookie.[36]

---

29   ICO, *Privacy and Electronic Communications Regulations, Guidance on the Rules on Use of Cookies and Similar Technologies*. At https://ico.org.uk.
30   *Ibid.*
31   *Ibid.*
32   *Ibid.*
33   *Ibid.*
34   *Ibid.*
35   *Ibid.*
36   *Ibid.*

Exception

21.12   There is an exception to the requirement to provide information about cookies and to obtain consent. This is where the use of the cookie is:

- for the sole purpose of carrying out the transmission of a communication over an electronic communications network; or
- where such storage or access is strictly necessary for the provision of an information society service requested by the subscriber or user.[37]

'Strictly necessary' means that the storage or access must be essential, rather than reasonably necessary, for the exemption to apply. It must be essential to provide the service requested by the user, rather than merely essential for other uses the organisation may wish to make of that data. There may also be other legal requirements eg security required by the seventh Data Drotection Principle.[38]

Potential examples of the exception are cookies for the 'add to basket'/'proceed to checkout' button, so the website 'remembers' what the user chose on a previous page. This cookie is strictly necessary to provide the service the user requests (taking the purchase to the checkout). In this exception no consent is required.[39]

The ICO adds that the intention of the legislation is clearly that this exemption is viewed narrowly.[40]

Compliance Responsibility

21.13   The person setting the cookie is responsible for compliance. Where third party cookies are on a website, both parties will have a responsibility for ensuring users are clearly informed about the cookies and for obtaining user consent.[41]

Placing contractual obligations into agreements with web publishers may be advisable.[42]

---

37   *Ibid.* In defining an 'information society service' the Electronic Commerce (EC Directive) Regulations 2002 refer to 'any service normally provided for remuneration, at a distance, by means of electronic equipment for the processing (including digital compression) and storage of data, and at the individual request of a recipient of a service.'
38   *Ibid.*
39   ICO, *Privacy and Electronic Communications Regulations, Guidance on the Rules on Use of Cookies and Similar Technologies.* At https://ico.org.uk.
40   *Ibid.*
41   *Ibid.*
42   *Ibid.*

Website designers must also consider the PECR Amendment Regulations. The development of new software, or upgrades, must be compliant with the new data protection requirements. Data Protection by Design (DPbD) can assist in compliance. This means that privacy and data protection compliance are designed into systems right from the start, not merely bolted on afterwards.[43] (See also Part 4.)

UK organisations are subject to the new requirements even if the website is hosted abroad. The ICO adds that organisations outside of Europe, but whose websites target the European market or provide products or services to customers in Europe, should expect to comply.[44]

Browser Settings

21.14 The Directive and Regulations suggest browser settings may be one means of obtaining consent if they allow the subscriber to indicate their agreement to cookies.[45] However, relying solely on browser settings may not be sufficient.[46]

Practical Advice

21.15 It is not enough simply to continue to comply with the old 2003 prior information requirements and allow an opt out. The ICO states that the new law must be fully complied with.[47]

First Steps

21.16 Organisations should:

- check what type of cookies (and similar technologies) they use and how they use them;
- assess how intrusive the organisation cookies are;
- where the organisation needs consent – decide what solution is best to obtain consent.[48]

43 ICO, *Privacy and Electronic Communications Regulations, Guidance on the Rules on Use of Cookies and Similar Technologies*. At https://ico.org.uk.
44 *Ibid.*
45 *Ibid.*
46 *Ibid.*
47 *Ibid.*
48 *Ibid.*

Check Cookie Types and How Used

21.17 Organisations should audit their website[49] to analyse which cookies are strictly necessary, and also therefore which may not need consent.[50]

Assess Cookie Intrusiveness

21.18 The more intrusive the use of cookies, the more consideration is required.[51]

Some cookies create detailed user browsing profiles.[52] This can be very intrusive. The more privacy intrusive the cookie activity, the more important is the consent.[53] Privacy neutral cookies are at one end of the scale and more intrusive uses of the technology at the other. More information and detailed choices are required as the level of intrusiveness increases.[54]

Decide Consent Solution

21.19 Once the organisation knows what it does, how, and for what purpose, it needs to consider the best method for gaining consent. The more privacy intrusive the activity, the greater the need for meaningful consent.[55]

Conducting a Cookies Audit

21.20 An audit of cookies could involve the following:

- identify which cookies are operating on the organisation's website;
- confirm the purpose(s) of each cookies;
- confirm whether the organisation links cookies to other information held about users – such as usernames;
- identify what data each cookie holds;
- confirm the type of cookie – session or persistent;
- if a persistent cookie, the length of the lifespan;
- whether it is a first or third party cookie;
- if it is a third party cookie, who has set it;
- check that the privacy policy/statement provides accurate and clear information about each cookie.[56]

---

49 ICO, *Privacy and Electronic Communications Regulations, Guidance on the Rules on Use of Cookies and Similar Technologies*. At https://ico.org.uk.
50 *Ibid.*
51 *Ibid.*
52 *Ibid.*
53 *Ibid.*
54 *Ibid.*
55 *Ibid.*
56 *Ibid.*

Providing Information about Cookies

21.21   The information should be sufficiently full and intelligible to allow users to clearly understand the potential consequences of allowing cookies. This compares with the transparency requirements of the first Data Protection Principle.[57]

Getting Consent in Practice

21.22   Appropriate cookie consent depends on what the cookie is doing and the relationship with users.[58]

Pop Ups and Similar Techniques

21.23   Pop-ups, message bars and header bars may be an option for compliance if asking the user directly if they agree to the website putting something on their computer and if they click yes, this may be the consent.[59] The information must make the position absolutely clear to users.[60]

Terms and Conditions

21.24   Consent for the cookies may be gained online using the terms of use or terms and conditions to which the user agrees when they register or sign up.[61]

However, changing the terms of use alone, to include consent for cookies would not be sufficient. Consent has to be specific and informed. To satisfy the rules on cookies, organisations must make users aware of the changes and specifically that the changes refer to the use of cookies. Organisations need a positive indication that users understand and agree to the changes. This may include asking the user to tick a box to indicate that they consent to the new terms.[62]

Organisations must gain consent by giving the user specific information about what they are agreeing to and providing a way to show their acceptance. The ICO states that any attempt to gain consent that relies on users' ignorance about what they are agreeing to is unlikely to be compliant.[63]

---

57   ICO, *Privacy and Electronic Communications Regulations, Guidance on the Rules on Use of Cookies and Similar Technologies*. At https://ico.org.uk.
58   *Ibid.*
59   *Ibid.*
60   *Ibid.*
61   *Ibid.*
62   *Ibid.*
63   *Ibid.*

Settings-led Consent

21.25 Some cookies are deployed when a user makes a choice about how the website works or will be configured. Consent could be gained as part of the process by which the user confirms what they want to do or how they want the website to work for them.[64] Agreement for a language setting cookie could be integrated with the choice the user is already making if choosing a language.[65]

Feature-led Consent

21.26 Some objects are stored when a user chooses to use a particular feature of the website and or to personalise the content which the user is served by the website. If the user is clicking a button or agreeing to the functionality being 'switched on' – one can also ask for their consent to set a cookie at this point. It must be clear to the user that by choosing to take a particular action, then certain things will happen, the organisation may interpret this as consent. The more complex or intrusive the activity, the more prior information, and clearer information, will have to be provided to the user.[66]

If a feature is provided by a third party, users must be made aware of this and given information on how the third party might use cookies (and similar technologies) so that the user is able to make an informed choice.[67] Apps, for example, are increasingly contentious.

Functional and Analytical Uses

21.27 Organisations may collect information about how people access and use the website, without the request of the user. Organisations must ensure that information provided is prominent. Users must make fully informed choices.[68]

Organisations should put in place a mechanism to obtain consent for analytical and functional cookies at the point the user logs in.[69]

For users browsing and whom have no relationship with the organisation, websites should ensure the information provided to users about

---

64 ICO, *Privacy and Electronic Communications Regulations, Guidance on the Rules on Use of Cookies and Similar Technologies*. At https://ico.org.uk.
65 *Ibid.*
66 *Ibid.*
67 *Ibid.*
68 *Ibid.*
69 *Ibid.*

cookies is absolutely clear and is highlighted in a prominent place (not merely through a privacy policy/statement link). It must highlight the use of cookies and obtain agreement to set these cookies.[70]

If information about website use is passed to a third party, this must be absolutely clear to the user. Organisations should review what the third party does with the information about website visitors. Users must be able to alter their account settings to limit the sharing of visitor information. User options must be prominent, not hidden away.[71]

Third Party Cookies

21.28   Some websites allow third parties to use cookies. The process of consent for these cookies is more complex.[72]

Consent Mechanisms

21.29   The ICO[73] sets out possible mechanisms for gaining consent:

Relationship with the user or subscriber	Cookie type	Possible means of consent
Registered user of online banking	First party analytical cookies (session) and first party cookies used to tailor advertising on log in pages (persistent)	Highlighting the cookies and asking for consent from the user as they log into their account. Once this consent is obtained the option will not have to be provided on subsequent visits.
Occasional visitor to online magazine	Cookie to remember and tailor preferences for viewing and set up of the site (persistent)	The mechanism for the user to select or tailor their preferences 'Would you like us to remember your ...' is amended to specifically flag that this process involves agreeing to a cookie. If the user selects the option to request that their preferences are remembered – having clearly had highlighted the role of the cookie in that process – the consent requirements would be satisfied.

70   ICO, *Privacy and Electronic Communications Regulations, Guidance on the Rules on Use of Cookies and Similar Technologies*. At https://ico.org.uk.
71   *Ibid.*
72   *Ibid.*
73   *Ibid.*

User wishing to download game or App	First party cookie used to person-alise the gaming experience (persistent)	In most cases the user will already be agreeing to terms and conditions to download the game or app. The way in which cookies are used is clearly and specifically highlighted in a prominent place in the process of agreement to these conditions (for example next to the 'I agree' box). Once this consent is obtained the option will not have to be provided each time the game is used.

Adapted from ICO *Privacy and Electronic Communications Regulations, Guidance on the Rules on Use of Cookies and Similar Technologies.*

Sometimes a combination of solutions is required.[74]

Cookie Consent for More than One Website

21.30   An organisation with several connected websites could obtain consent for cookies on each website in one place, eg when the user logged in on one website/the first website. It would have to be absolutely clear which websites the cookies relate to and what the cookies are used for and what the user is agreeing to.[75]

Changes to Cookie Use after Consent

21.31   If the purposes of the cookies change significantly after consent, organisations need to make users aware of the changes and allow them to make new choices. Users can provide consent to multiple cookies performing a set of functions.[76]

Withdrawing Cookie Consent

21.32   Users can choose to withdraw consent at any time. Organisations must provide information about how consent can be withdrawn. In this instance, cookies that have already been set must be removed. Organisations may explain the consequences of withdrawing consent, eg functionality impact.[77]

---

74   ICO, *Privacy and Electronic Communications Regulations, Guidance on the Rules on Use of Cookies and Similar Technologies.* At https://ico.org.uk.
75   *Ibid.*
76   *Ibid.*
77   *Ibid.*

Alternatives to Cookies and Privacy

21.33 Sometimes functions performed by a cookie can be achieved through other means eg 'device fingerprinting'. Organisations must still inform users what is collected and how it is used.[78]

Cookies and Personal Data

21.34 Organisations need to make sure they comply with the additional requirements of the DPA[79] in addition to cookie compliance.

Enforcement and Penalties

21.35 If organisations refuse or fail to comply, the ICO can take action.[80] These options[81] include:

Information notice: requiring organisations to provide the ICO with specified information within a certain time period;

Undertaking: fixing the organisation to a particular course of action to improve its compliance;

Enforcement notice: compelling the organisation to take specified action to bring ensure compliance with the Regulations. Failure to comply with an enforcement notice can be a criminal offence;

Monetary penalty notice: a monetary penalty notice requires an organisation to pay a monetary penalty as determined by the ICO, up to a maximum of £500,000. This power can be used in the most serious of cases and if specific criteria are met, if any person has seriously contravened the PECR and if the contravention was of a kind likely to cause substantial damage or substantial distress. The contravention must be deliberate or the person must have known or ought to have known that there was a risk that a contravention would occur and failed to take reasonable steps to prevent it.[82]

Enforcement of Cookie Rules

21.36 Enforcement will involve in most cases the ICO asking the organisation to respond to the complaint. It will explain what steps need to be taken to comply with the rules.[83]

---

78 ICO, *Privacy and Electronic Communications Regulations, Guidance on the Rules on Use of Cookies and Similar Technologies*. At https://ico.org.uk.
79 *Ibid.*
80 *Ibid.*
81 *Ibid.*
82 *Ibid.*
83 *Ibid.*

Formal action is considered if the organisation refuses. Further guidance is set out in the ICO Data Protection Regulatory Action Policy and Guidance on the issuing of monetary penalties.[84]

Organisations will need to be able to demonstrate they have taken sensible, measured action to move to compliance.[85]

Monetary penalties will be reserved for the most serious of breaches of the PECR rules.[86]

Do These Rules Apply to Intranets?

21.37 The ICO currently considers that the new rules do not apply in the same way to internal intranet systems.[87]

Can an Organisation Do Nothing?

21.38 No. It is the law. Compliance is required. The UK Regulations, and EU Directive of 2009, cannot be selectively ignored.[88]

Does the Same Apply for Mobile Devices?

21.39 Yes. The new requirements also apply to cookies set on mobile devices and other terminal equipment eg internet enabled televisions, games consoles, etc.[89]

Awareness

21.40 Organisations must educate consumers and users about cookies generally.[90]

Analytical Cookies

21.41 The Regulations do not distinguish between analytical cookies and cookies used for other purposes. Analytical cookies do not fall within the 'strictly necessary' exception criteria. Organisations need to inform users about analytical cookies and obtain consent.[91]

However, the ICO appears less likely to take enforcement action in relation to purely analytical cookies.[92]

84 ICO, *Privacy and Electronic Communications Regulations, Guidance on the Rules on Use of Cookies and Similar Technologies*. At https://ico.org.uk.
85 *Ibid.*
86 *Ibid.*
87 *Ibid.*
88 *Ibid.*
89 *Ibid.*
90 *Ibid.*
91 *Ibid.*
92 *Ibid.*

Online Behavioural Advertising WP29 Opinion

21.42 WP29 (now replaced by the EDPB) adopted an Opinion[93] on online behavioural advertising ('OBA'). OBA also entails tracking users internet activities and the building of profiles about them. These are later used to provide advertising matching their interests. These practices must not be carried out at the expense of individuals' rights to privacy and data protection, according to WP29.

The data protection regime safeguards must be respected. The Opinion refers to such safeguards.

Organisations are bound by Article 5(3) of ePD. Placing cookies or similar devices on users' terminal equipment or obtaining information through such devices is only allowed with the informed consent of the users. Organisations must create prior opt-in mechanisms requiring an affirmative action by users indicating their willingness to receive cookies and to the monitoring of their surfing behaviour for the purposes of serving tailored advertising. Organisations should: (i) limit in time the scope of the consent; (ii) offer the possibility to revoke it easily; and (iii), create visible tools to be displayed where the monitoring takes place.[94]

OBA enables the creation of very detailed user profiles which, in most cases, are deemed personal data. The DPD generally is also applicable, eg rights of access, rectification, erasure, retention, etc. Users must be provided with 'clear and comprehensive information.'[95]

The Opinion invites industry to undertake a dialogue with the WP29 with the view to put forward technical and other means to comply with the new rules.[96]

Issues

21.43 The Opinion states that online advertising and behavioural advertising raises important data protection and privacy concerns. User behaviour online is analysed in order to build extensive profiles about Data Subjects and their interests. Such profiles can be used to provide tailored advertising.

OBA is increasingly based on the use of tracking cookies (and similar devices). It is highly privacy intrusive.

The Opinion clarifies the legal framework applicable to behavioural advertising. It also invites industry to suggest technical and other solutions.

---

93 WP29, *Opinion 2/2010 on Online Behavioural Advertising* (WP 171).
94 *Ibid.*
95 *Ibid.*
96 *Ibid.*

Online Behavioural Advertising

21.44 A broad range of methods are being used to create so called 'more relevant' advertisements to users. There are several methods, including contextual advertising, segmented advertising and behavioural advertising.

Behavioural advertising is advertising that is based on tracking user behaviour online. It tracks repeated site visits, interactions, keywords, online content production, order of visits and views, length of viewing, etc to develop a specific user profile and tailored adverts to match these inferred interests of the user.

Behavioural advertising involves: (a) advertising networks providers (also referred to as 'ad network providers'), who distribute behavioural advertising; (b) advertisers; and (c) publishers who are the website owners looking for revenues by selling space to display ads on their website(s).

Tracking Technologies

21.45 Most tracking for behavioural advertising uses information from the user's browser and computer terminal equipment. The main tracking technology used is cookies.

Tracking website visits and repeated visits enable the ad network provider to build a profile of the visitor to deliver personalised advertising. Cookies can have different life spans. 'Persistent cookies' either have a precise expiry date far in the future or until manually deleted.

Most internet browsers offer the possibility to block third party cookies. Some browsers support 'private' browsing sessions that will automatically destroy (some) cookies on closing the browser.

Flash cookies, however, cannot be deleted through the traditional privacy settings of a web browser.

Building Profiles, Types of Identifiers

21.46 Predictive profiles are established by observing user behaviour over time, eg monitoring visited pages and ads viewed/clicked. Explicit profiles are created from personal data that Data Subjects themselves provide to a web service, eg by registering. Ad networks construct predictive profiles with a combination of tracking techniques, cookies and data mining software. Gender and age range can be deduced by analysing the pages the Data Subject visits and the ads viewed. Cookie data can be enriched with aggregated data derived from the behaviour of Data Subjects who exhibit similar behavioural patterns in other contexts. The location of the Data Subject is also a source of target profiling, obtained from eg user IP address.

Legal Framework Introduction

21.47   Article 5(1) of Directive 2002/58 protects the confidentiality of communications in general.

The protection of the confidentiality of communications in the case of cookies is provided in Article 5(3). Recital 66, adopted when the ePD was amended[97] and Recital 24 and 25 of the ePD are also relevant.

The Opinion also notes that the DPD applies to matters not covered by the ePD whenever personal data are processed.

Scope of Article 5(3) and DPD

21.48   Advertisers should consider Article 5(3) of the ePD and also the DPD.

Substantive Scope of Article 5(3)

21.49   Article 5(3) requires obtaining informed consent to lawfully store information or to gain access to information stored in the user's equipment. Tracking cookies are 'information' stored in the Data Subject's equipment. They are accessed by advertising network providers when Data Subjects visit a partner website. Article 5(3) is therefore fully applicable. Hence, any storage of cookies or similar devices (irrespective of type) and any subsequent use of previously stored cookies to gain access to Data Subjects' information will have to comply with Article 5(3).

Article 5(3) applies to 'information.' It is not a prerequisite that this information is personal data within the meaning of the DPD. Recital 24 notes that 'terminal equipment of users … and any information stored on such equipment are part of the private sphere of these users requiring protection under the European Convention.' The protection of the private sphere of the Data Subject triggers the obligations in Article 5 (3). WP29 Opinion 1/2008 confirms that Article 5(3) is a

---

97   In 2009.

general provision, applicable to electronic communication services but also any other services when these techniques are used. Article 5(3) applies irrespectively of whether the entity placing the cookie is a Controller or a Processor.

Scope of DPD

21.50 If the cookie information collected is personal data then, in addition to Article 5(3), the DPD is also applicable.

Behavioural advertising often processes personal data (per Article 2 DPD). For example, it normally collects user IP addresses which allows the tracking of users of a specific computer.

Users are 'singled out,' even if their names are not known. Furthermore, the information collected relates to, (ie is about) a person's characteristics or behaviour and is used to influence that particular person.

Interplay Between Two Directives

21.51 Recital 10 of ePD states that the DPD applies, 'to all matters concerning protection of fundamental rights and freedoms which are not specifically covered by the provisions of this Directive, including the obligations on the Controller and the rights of individuals.'

Article 5 (3) of the ePD and consent will be directly applicable. The DPD will be fully applicable (except for provisions specifically addressed in the ePD, which mainly correspond to Article 7 of the DPD on the legal grounds for data processing). The remaining provisions of the DPD including the principles, Data Subject rights (such as access, erasure, right to object), confidentiality, security and international data transfers are fully applicable.

Territorial Scope of Article 5(3) and DPD

21.52 The territorial scope of application of the above framework is determined by a combination of both Article 3 (1) of the ePD and Article 4.1 (a) and (c) of the DPD. Earlier WP29 Opinions give guidance on the concept of establishment and the use of equipment referred to in Article 4(1)(a) and (c) respectively as determinants for the applicability of the DPD. This also applies to advertising.

Roles and Responsibilities

21.53 Behavioural advertising involves ad network providers, publishers and advertisers. The role they play can establish their obligations.

Ad Network Providers

21.54 Article 5(3) applies regardless of whether the entity placing or reading the cookie is a Controller or a Processor. The obligation to obtain informed consent applies to ad network providers.

When personal data is involved, the ad network providers also act as Controller. Additional obligations arise from the DPD. The ad network providers control the purposes and means of processing.

The Opinion notes that they 'rent' space from publishers' web sites to place adverts; they set and/read cookie related information, collect IP addresses, use the information gathered on user surfing behaviour to build profiles and to select and deliver the ads to be displayed on the basis of this profile. They act as Controllers.

Publishers

21.55 Publishers rent out space on their websites for ad networks to place adverts.

The WP29 Opinion states that publishers have responsibility for the initial part of the data processing, namely the transfer of the IP address that takes place when individuals visit their websites. The publishers facilitate such transfer and co-determine the purposes for which it is carried out, ie to serve visitors with tailored advertising. Publishers will have some, but not all, responsibility as Controllers.

Publishers do not hold personal information; so it may not make sense to apply all DPD obligations, such as access right. However, the obligation to inform users of the data processing is applicable to publishers.

In addition, publishers are joint Controllers if they collect and transmit personal data regarding users, such as name, address, age, location, etc to the ad network provider. The publishers are therefore bound by the obligations of the DPD regarding the part of the data processing under their control. In the ad network providers and publishers 'shall ensure that the complexity and the technicalities of the behavioural advertising system do not prevent them from finding appropriate ways to comply with data Controllers' obligations and to ensure Data Subjects' rights.'

Service agreements between publishers and ad network providers should outline the roles and responsibilities of both parties.

Advertisers

21.56 When a user clicks an ad and visits the advertisers' website, the advertiser can track which campaign resulted in the click-through. If the advertiser captures the targeting information and combines it with the Data Subject's onsite surfing behaviour or registration data, then the advertiser is an independent Controller for this data processing.

Prior Informed Consent Obligation

21.57 The general rule contained in the first paragraph of Article 5 (3). The ePD was amended in 2009. The changes reinforce the need for users' informed prior consent.

Prior Consent for Behavioural Advertising

21.58 Pursuant to Article 5 (3), an ad network provider who wishes to store or gain access to information stored in a user's terminal equipment must: (i) provide the user with clear and comprehensive information in accordance with the DPD, inter alia, about the purposes of the processing; and (ii) it has obtained the user's consent to the storage of or access to information on their terminal equipment, after providing the information requested under (i).

Consent must be obtained before the cookie is placed and/or information stored in the user's terminal equipment is collected, referred to as prior consent. Informed consent can only be obtained if prior information about the sending and purposes of the cookie has been given to the user. For consent to be valid whatever the circumstances in which it is given, it must be freely given, specific and constitute an informed indication of the Data Subject's wishes. Consent must be obtained before the personal data are collected, as a necessary measure to ensure that Data Subjects can fully appreciate that they are consenting and what they are consenting to. Consent is also revocable.

Consent via Browser Settings

21.59 Publishers and ad network providers often provide information in their general terms and conditions and/or privacy policies about third party cookies used for behavioural advertising. However, this does not meet the requirements of Article 5(3) amended, which places emphasis on providing prior information and obtaining prior consent (prior to the starting of the processing).

Recital 66 of the amended ePD indicates that the user consent may be expressed by using the appropriate settings of a browser or other application, 'where it is technically possible and effective, in accordance with the relevant provisions of [the DPD].' Consent can be given in different ways – where technically possible, effective and in accordance with the other relevant requirements for valid consent.

When may browser settings meet the requirements of the DPD, and thus constitute a valid consent 'in accordance with [the DPD]?' WP29 considers that this will happen rarely.

The definition and requirements for valid consent per Article 2(h) of the DPD, means users cannot be deemed to have consented simply because they acquired/used a browser or other application which by default allows the collection and processing of their information. Average users are not aware of the tracking of their online behaviour, the purposes of the tracking, how to use browser settings to reject cookies, etc. User inaction cannot provide a clear and unambiguous indication of wishes.

WP29 Opinion 1/2008 states that 'The responsibility for [cookie] processing cannot be reduced to the responsibility of the user for taking or not taking certain precautions in his browser settings.' For browser settings to be able to deliver informed consent, it should not be possible to 'bypass' the choice made by the user in setting the browser (such as the 're-spawned' practice).

Consent in bulk for any future processing without knowing the circumstances surrounding the processing cannot be valid consent.

Therefore, in order for browsers or any other application to be able to 'deliver' valid consent, they must deal with the following:

- browsers which by default reject third party cookies and which require users to engage in an affirmative action to accept both the setting of and continued transmission of information contained in cookies by specific websites may be able to deliver valid and effective consent. (If the browser settings were predetermined to accept all cookies, such consent would not comply with Article 5 (3). Such consent cannot constitute a true indication of the Data Subject wishes. Such consent would not be specific nor prior (to the processing);
- browsers should convey clear, comprehensive and fully visible information in order to ensure that consent is fully informed. To meet the requirements of the DPD browsers should convey, on behalf of the ad network provider, the relevant information about the purposes of the cookies and the further processing. Generic warnings without explicit references to the ad network placing the cookie, are unsatisfactory.

The WP29 is of the view that unless the above requirements are met, providing information and facilitating user ability to reject cookies, cannot be informed consent per Article 5(3) of the ePD and in light of Article 2(h) of the DPD.

Browsers should require users to go through a privacy wizard when they first install or update the browser and provide for an easy way of exercising choice during use.

Consent and Opt-Out Options

21.60 Cookie opt-out mechanisms are welcomed by WP29 but it is noted that such opt-out mechanisms do not in principle deliver user consent. This mechanism is not an adequate mechanism to obtain average users informed consent. General users lack the basic understanding of the collection of any data, its uses, how the technology works and more importantly how and where to opt-out.

WP29 considers that cookie-based opt-out mechanisms do not provide average users with the effective means to consent to receive behavioural advertisement. They fail the requirements of Article 5(3).

Prior Opt-In Consent Better For Informed Consent

21.61 WP29 prefers prior opt-in mechanisms, which require an affirmative user action to indicate consent before the cookie is sent to the Data Subject. Implicit consent does not always lead to unambiguous consent (as required by Article 7(a) of the DPD). In a previous Opinion, WP29 recommends the use of specific messages: 'In the case of cookies, the user should be informed when a cookie is intended to be received, stored or sent ... The message should specify, in generally understandable language, which information is intended to be stored in the cookie, for what purpose as well as the period of validity of the cookie.' After receiving such information, the user should be offered the possibility to indicate whether they want to be profiled for behavioural advertising. However, in accordance with Recital 25 of the ePD ('the right to refuse (cookies) may be offered once for the use of various devices to be installed on the user's terminal equipment ... during subsequent connections'), user acceptance of a cookie could be understood to be valid not only for the sending of the cookie but also for subsequent collection of data arising from such a cookie. This can mean, the consent obtained to place the cookie and use the information to send targeting advertising would cover subsequent 'readings' of the cookie that take place when the user visits a website partner of the ad network provider which placed the cookie.

However, taking into account that: (i) this practice would mean that individuals accept to be monitored 'once for ever'; and (ii) individuals might simply 'forget' that, for example, a year ago, they agreed to be monitored; WP29 considers that safeguards are needed.

First, organisations should limit the scope of the consent in terms of time. Consent to be monitored should not be 'for ever' but it should be valid for a limited period of time, for example, one year. After this period, ad network providers would need to obtain a new consent. Cookies can have a limited lifespan.

Second, risks should be further mitigated with additional information practices.

Third, consent can always be revoked. Data Subjects should be offered the possibility to easily revoke their consent to monitoring for behavioural advertising. In this regard, the need to provide clear information about this possibility and how to exercise it is essential.

Informed Consent and Children

21.62   In Opinion 2/2009 the WP29 addresses the personal data of children. One problem relates to obtaining informed consent. In some cases, children's consent must be provided by parent or guardian. Ad network providers would need to provide notice to parents about the collection and the use of children's information and obtain their consent before collecting and further using their information for behavioural targeting of children.

In the light of the above and the vulnerability of children, WP29 feels that ad network providers should not offer interest categories intended to serve behavioural advertising or influence children.

Obligation to Provide Information for Online Behavioural Advertising (OBA)

21.63   Transparency is a key condition for users to be able to consent to data collection and processing. Users may not know or understand the technology that supports behavioural advertising or that advertising is being targeted at them. Effective information must be provided to internet users. Only if users are adequately informed, will they be in a position to exercise their consent choices.

What Information Provided by Whom?

21.64   Article 5(3) states that the user must be provided with information, 'in accordance with [the DPD], inter alia about the purposes of the processing.' Article 10 of the DPD refers to the provision of this information.

With regard to behavioural advertising, Data Subjects should be informed about the identity of the advertising network provider and the purposes of the processing. The user should be clearly informed that cookies will allow the advertising provider to collect information about their visits to other websites, the advertisements they have been shown, which ones they have clicked on, timing, etc.

There should be a simple explanation on the uses of the cookie to create profiles to target advertising. Recital 25 of the ePD requires notices to be provided in a 'clear and comprehensive' manner. The Opinion notes that statements such as 'advertisers and other third parties may also use their own cookies or action tags' are clearly not sufficient.

Recital 25 requires the prior information to be 'as user friendly as possible.' The WP29 considers that providing a minimum of information directly on the screen, interactively, easily visible and understandable, would be the most effective way to comply. The information must be easily accessible and highly visible. It must not be hidden in general terms and conditions and/or privacy policies/statements.

Given the possibility for users to accept the monitoring once, to cover subsequent future readings of the cookie, it is essential for ad network providers to find ways to inform users periodically that monitoring is taking place. Unless users are given clear and unambiguous reminders, by easy means, of the monitoring, problems can arise. A monitoring symbol would be helpful to remind users of the monitoring but also to control whether they want to continue or even revoke their consent. Under Article 5 (3) of ePD, the obligation to provide the necessary prior (and post) information and obtain Data Subjects' consent ultimately lies with the entity that sends and reads the cookie. In most cases, this is the ad network provider. When publishers are joint-controllers, they are also bound by the obligation to provide information. Publishers have certain obligations from the DPD. They are bound by the obligation to provide information to users about the data processing that takes place as a result of the re-directing of their browser and also about the purposes for which the information will be used later on by ad network providers. The information should refer not only to the transfer of IP address for the purposes of displaying acts but also to further data processing carried out by the ad network providers, including setting up of cookies. Data Protection Authorities are to consider appropriate awareness raising measures.

Other Obligations from DPD

21.65   In addition to Article 5(3), Controllers must ensure compliance with all the DPD obligations (which do not overlap with Article 5(3)).

Obligations and Special Data Categories

21.66   Targeting users based on sensitive personal data opens the possibility of abuse. It can also lead to awkward situations which may arise if individuals receive advertising that reveals, for example, sexual preferences or political activity. Using interest categories that reveal sensitive data should be discouraged according to the WP29.

To use sensitive personal data, ad network providers must comply with Article 8 of the DPD. The only available legal ground that would legitimise such processing would be explicit, separate prior opt-in consent per Article 8(2)(a). An opt-out consent mechanism would not meet the requirement of the law. Such consent could not be obtained thorough browser settings. Explicit prior consent would be needed.

Compliance with Data Protection Principles

21.67   Article 6 of the DPD must be respected by Controllers.

Behavioural advertising profiles could potentially be used for purposes other than advertising.

However, Article 6(1)(b) contains the purpose limitation principle. This prohibits processing which is not compatible with the purposes that legitimised the initial collection. Incompatible secondary uses contradict Art 6(b) of the DPD. Also, ad networks cannot enrich the information gathered for the purposes of behavioural advertisement with other information.

Secondary incompatible uses need additional legal grounds to do so per Article 7 of DP. Hence, they will need to inform Data Subjects and, in most cases, obtain consent per Article 7(a).

Article 6(1)(e) requires data to be deleted when no longer necessary for the purpose for which the data were collected (retention principle). Compliance means limiting the storage of information. Organisations must specify and respect express time limits under which data will be retained.

Policies must ensure that information collected each time a cookie is read is immediately deleted or anonymised once the necessity for retaining it has expired. Each Controller needs to be able to justify the necessity for a given retention period.

When a user asks for a deletion of their profile or if they exercise their right to withdraw consent, this requires the ad network provider to erase or delete promptly the Data Subject's information.

Data Subjects Rights

21.68   Users and Data Subjects have rights of access, rectification, erasure and to object (Articles 12 and 14 of the DPD).

The WP29 refers to initiatives offering access to interest categories that Data Subjects have been labelled with based on the cookie ID number. These new tools may enable users not only to access the interest categories that related to them but also modify them and erase them.

These tools should be as visible as possible to users.

Other Obligations

21.69   Article 17 of the Directive imposes the obligation upon Controllers and Processors to apply technical and organisational measures to protect personal data against accidental or unlawful destruction, loss, disclosure, and other forms of unlawful processing. Compliance with the security obligations require ad network providers to implement state of the art technical and organisational measures to ensure the security and confidentiality of the information.

Pursuant to Article 18 of the DPD, Controllers may have to notify the processing of personal data to data protection authorities, unless exempted.

If the data is transferred outside the EU, for example, to servers located in third countries, ad network providers must ensure compliance with the provisions on transfers of personal data to third countries (Articles 25 and 26 the DPD).

WP29 Recommendations

21.70 Individuals are often unaware that behavioural advertising and cookies enable advertisers to track them online, to build profiles and to serve tailored advertising. It is very doubtful whether users are aware of, much less that they consent to, being monitored for tailored advertising.

Notices in general terms and conditions and/or privacy policies, often in obscure language, fall short of the requirements of data protection legislation. Organisations need to improve compliance efforts for the new rules.

The Opinion recommends as follows.

Applicable Laws

21.71 The EU legal framework for cookies is primarily Article 5(3) of the ePD.

Article 5(3) applies whenever 'information' such as a cookie is stored or retrieved from terminal equipment of an internet user. It is not a prerequisite that this information be personal data.

In addition, the DPD applies to matters not specifically covered by the ePrivacy Directive whenever personal data are processed. Behavioural advertising is based on the use of identifiers that enable the creation of very detailed user profiles which, in most cases, are personal data.

Jurisdiction, Territorial Issues, Establishment

21.72 The DPD applies to the data processing that takes place when publishers and ad network providers engage in behavioural advertising, eg Article 4(1)(a) and (c) of the DPD and eg Article 3 of the ePD.

There is other WP29 guidance also relevant.

Roles and Responsibilities

21.73   Ad network providers are bound by Article 5(3) of the ePD as they place cookies and/or retrieve information from cookies already stored in users' terminal equipment. They are also Controllers as they determine the purposes and the essential means of the processing of data.

Publishers have certain Controller related responsibilities regarding processing in the first phase of the processing, ie, when they set up their websites to trigger the transfer of the IP address to ad network providers (which enables further processing). If publishers transfer directly identifiable personal data to ad network providers themselves, they will be deemed joint Controllers.

Obligations and Rights re Ad Network Providers

21.74   Article 5(3) of the ePD requires prior informed consent by ad network providers.

Browser settings may only deliver consent in very limited circumstances. The browser must either alone or in combination with other means effectively convey clear, comprehensive and fully visible information about the processing.

Ad network providers should encourage and work with browser manufacturers/developers to implement Data Protection by Design (DPbD) in browsers.

Cookie-based opt out mechanisms in general do not constitute an adequate mechanism to obtain informed user consent. In most cases user consent is implied if they do not opt out. However, few people exercise the opt-out option, not because they have made an informed decision to accept behavioural advertising, but because they do not realise that the processing is taking place, nor how to exercise the opt out.

Ad network providers need to 'swiftly' move away from opt out mechanisms and create prior opt in mechanisms. Informed, valid consent requires an affirmative action by the Data Subject indicating their willingness to receive cookies and subsequent monitoring of their online surfing behaviour for the purposes of tailored advertising.

A users' acceptance to receive a cookie could also entail acceptance for the subsequent readings of the cookie, and hence for the monitoring of internet browsing (Recital 25 ePD). It would not be necessary to request consent for each reading of the cookie. However, to ensure that Data Subjects remain aware of the monitoring over time, ad network providers should:

- limit in time the scope of the consent;
- offer the possibility to easily revoke their consent to being monitored for behavioural advertising; and

- create a symbol or other tools which should be visible in all the websites where the monitoring takes place (the website partners of the ad network provider). This symbol would remind individuals of the monitoring but also help them to control whether they want to continue being monitored or wish to revoke their consent.

Network providers should ensure compliance with the obligations that arise from the DPD which do not directly overlap with Article 5(3), namely, the purpose limitation principle, and security obligations.

Ad network providers should enable individuals to exercise their rights of access and rectification and erasure. The WP29 welcomes the practice of some ad network providers to offer Data Subjects the possibility to access and modify the interest categories in which they have been classified.

Ad network providers should implement retention policies which ensure that information collected each time that a cookie is read is automatically deleted after a set period of time (necessary for the purposes of the processing). This also applies for alternative tracking technologies eg JavaScript installed in the user's browser.

Ad Network Providers and Publishers

21.75   Providing highly visible information is a precondition for consent to be valid. Mentioning the practice of behavioural advertising in general terms and conditions and/or privacy policies can never suffice. Ad network providers/publishers must provide information to users in compliance with Article 10 of the DPD. They should ensure that individuals are told, at a minimum, who (ie which entity) is responsible for serving the cookie and collecting the related information. In addition, they should be informed in simple ways that (a) the cookie will be used to create profiles; (b) what type of information will be collected to build such profiles; (c) the fact that the profiles will be used to deliver targeted advertising and (d) that the cookie will enable the user identification across multiple websites.

Network providers and publishers should provide the information directly on the screen, interactively, if needed, through layered notices. It should be easily accessible and highly visible.

Icons placed on the publisher's website, around advertising, with links to additional information, can assist.

WP29 Opinions

Opinion 16/2011 on OBA

21.76 WP29 Opinion 16/2011 on EASA/IAB Best Practice Recommendation on Online Behavioural Advertising (WP 188) was adopted on 08 December 2011.

Directive 2009/136/EC revised the ePD. One of the key changes concerns the mechanisms for implanting information in the user's terminal device eg cookies. The existing opt-out regime, where a user can object to the processing of information collected via terminal equipment (such as cookies) was rejected.

Instead, the standard became informed consent. These changes are important for the online behavioural advertising (OBA) industry relies heavily on cookies and similar technologies.

The consent rule reflects a growing concern amongst citizens, politicians, data protection authorities, consumer organisations and policy-makers that the technical possibilities to track individual internet behaviour over time, across different websites is increasing. Soon after the change, WP29 adopted Opinion 2/2010 on Online Behavioural Advertising (OBA). The opinion describes the roles and responsibilities of the different actors engaged in online behavioural advertising, and clarifies the applicable legal framework. The opinion focuses on the tracking of internet behaviour over time, across different websites as the source of the most important data protection concerns with regard to OBA.

In April 2011 the European Advertising Standards Alliance (EASA) and the Internet Advertising Bureau Europe (IAB), adopted a self-regulatory Best Practice Recommendation on online behavioural advertising ('EASA/IAB Code'). WP29 comments on this. It states that the EASA/IAB Code per se is not adequate to ensure compliance with data protection regime.

ePD Cookie Amendment

21.77 The WP29 issued *Opinion 04/2012 on Cookie Consent Exemption*.[98]

WP29 states that the new amendment has:

'reinforced the protection of users of electronic communication networks and services by requiring informed consent before information is stored or accessed in the user's (or subscriber's) terminal device. The requirement applies to all

---

98 WP29, *Opinion 04/2012 on Cookie Consent Exemption*, at http://ec.europa.eu/justice/data-protection/article-29/documentation/opinion-recommendation/files/2012/wp194_en.pdf.

types of information stored or accessed in the user's terminal device although the majority of discussion has centred on the usage of cookies.'[99]

Generally customer, etc, informed consent is required. However, now under Article 5(3), exemptions from requiring informed consent can apply to cookies if either:

- the cookie is used 'for the sole purpose of *carrying out the transmission* of a communication over an electronic communications network' (Condition A); *OR*
- the cookie is '*strictly necessary* in order for the provider of an information society service explicitly requested by the subscriber or user to *provide the service*' (Condition B).[100]

Condition A

21.78 The phrase 'sole purpose' in Condition A limits the types of processing using cookies. Simply using a cookie to assist, speed up or regulate the transmission over an electronic communications network is not sufficient. The transmission 'must *not be possible without* the use of the cookie.'[101]

Three issues arise, namely:

- the ability to route the information over the network, notably by identifying the communication endpoints;
- the ability to exchange data items in their intended order, notably by numbering data packets;
- the ability to detect transmission errors or data loss.[102]

Condition A 'encompasses cookies that fulfil at least one of the properties defined above for Internet communications.'[103]

Condition B

21.79 The Condition B exemption criteria are high.[104] A cookie matching CRITERION B has to pass two tests simultaneously, namely:

- the information society service is explicitly requested by the user: the user (or subscriber) by positive action requested a service with a clearly defined perimeter;

---

99 WP29, *Opinion 04/2012 on Cookie Consent Exemption*. The Opinion explains how revised Article 5.3 impacts on the use of cookies but and potentially similar technologies.
100 WP29, *Opinion 04/2012 on Cookie Consent Exemption*.
101 *Ibid*.
102 *Ibid*.
103 *Ibid*.
104 WP29, *Opinion 04/2012 on Cookie Consent Exemption* at http://ec.europa.eu/justice/data-protection/article-29/documentation/opinion-recommendation/files/

- the cookie is strictly needed to enable the information society service: if cookies are disabled, the service will not work.[105]

Recital 66 of Directive 2009/136/EC underlines that 'Exceptions to the obligation to provide information and offer the right to refuse should be limited to those situations where the technical storage or access is strictly necessary for the legitimate purpose of enabling the use of a specific service explicitly requested by the subscriber or user.' The Opinion states that there has to be a clear link between the strict necessity of a cookie and the delivery of the service explicitly requested by the user for the exemption to apply.

A cookie matching Condition B would need to pass the following tests:

- a cookie is necessary to provide a specific functionality to the user (or subscriber): if cookies are disabled, the functionality will not be available;
- this functionality has been explicitly requested by the user (or subscriber), as part of an information society service.[106]

Characteristics of a Cookie

21.80   Cookies are, according to the Opinion, often categorised according to whether they are 'session cookies' or 'persistent cookie';[107] or whether they are 'third party cookies' or not.[108]

A cookie exempted from consent should have a lifespan in direct relation to the original purpose used for, and must be set to expire once not needed, reflecting the reasonable expectations and consent of users.

'Third party' cookies are usually not 'strictly necessary' and relate to a service distinct from the service 'explicitly requested' by the user. Therefore, 'first party' session cookies are more likely exempted from consent than 'third party' persistent cookies. The Opinion states that ultimately, the purpose and the specific processing will determine whether or not a cookie can be exempted from consent according to Condition

---

2012/wp194_en.pdf. The Opinion explains how revised Article 5.3 impacts on the use of cookies but and potentially similar technologies.

105 *Ibid.*
106 *Ibid.*
107 A 'session cookie' is a cookie that is automatically deleted when the user closes his browser. A 'persistent cookie' is a cookie that remains stored in the user's terminal device until it reaches a defined expiration date (which can be minutes, days or several years in the future).
108 The Opinion uses the term 'third party cookie' to describe cookies that are set by data controllers that do not operate the website currently visited by the user.

A or B. Permanently cookies on the user's computer are unlikely to be exempted.

Multipurpose Cookies

21.81   A cookie for several purposes may only be exempted from consent if all the distinct purposes for which the cookie is used are individually exempted from consent.

Tracking is unlikely to meet Condition A or B. A website would need to seek user consent for the tracking purpose.

If a website uses several, a single point of information and consent can be sufficient.

The Opinion gives examples of cookie use, such as:

- user-input cookies;
- authentication cookies;
- field code changed;
- user centric security cookies;
- multimedia player session cookies;
- field code changed;
- UI customisation cookies;
- social plug-in content sharing cookies.[109]

Non-Exempted Cookies

21.82   Some cookie uses do not fall into the Condition A or B exemptions. Examples include:

- social plug-in tracking cookies;
- third party advertising;
- first party analytics.

Social plug-in tracking cookies can also be used to track individuals, both members and non-members, with third party cookies for additional purposes such as behavioural advertising, analytics, market research, etc. These cookies are not 'strictly necessary' to provide functionality explicitly requested by the user. Such tracking cookies cannot be exempt under Condition B. Without consent, there is unlikely to be a legal basis for social media websites collecting data through social plug-ins about

---

109 WP29, *Opinion 04/2012 on Cookie Consent Exemption*, 7 June 2012, at http://ec.europa.eu/justice/data-protection/article-29/documentation/opinion-recommendation/files/2012/wp194_en.pdf. The Opinion explains how revised Article 5.3 impacts on the use of cookies but and potentially similar technologies.

non-members of their network. By default, social plug-ins should thus not set a third party cookie in pages displayed to non-members.[110]

With regard to third party advertising, the Opinion states that third party cookies used for behavioural advertising are not exempted from consent.[111] Consent is required for all related third party operational cookies.[112]

Opinion Summary and Guidelines

21.83   The Opinion provides the following guide of cookies which can be exempted from informed consent under certain conditions and if they are not used for additional purposes:

- user input cookies (session-id), for the duration of a session or persistent cookies limited to a few hours in some cases;
- authentication cookies, used for authenticated services, for the duration of a session;
- user centric security cookies, used to detect authentication abuses, for a limited persistent duration;
- multimedia content player session cookies, such as flash player cookies, for the duration of a session;
- load balancing session cookies, for the duration of session;
- UI customisation persistent cookies, for the duration of a session (or slightly more);
- third party social plug-in content sharing cookies, for logged in members of a social network.[113]

In relation to social media websites, the WP29 notes that the use of third party social plug-in cookies for other purposes than to provide a functionality explicitly requested by their own members requires consent, notably if these purposes involve tracking users across websites.[114]

The WP29 notes[115] that third party advertising cookies cannot be exempted from consent, and further clarifies that consent would also be needed for operational purposes related to third party advertising such as frequency capping, financial logging, ad affiliation, click fraud detection, research and market analysis, product improvement and debugging.

While some operational purposes may distinguish one user from another, in principle these purposes do not justify the use of unique

---

110   WP29, *Opinion 04/2012 on Cookie Consent Exemption.*
111   This is already noted in Opinion 2/2010 and Opinion 16/2011.
112   *Ibid.*
113   This is already noted in Opinion 2/2010 and Opinion 16/2011.
114   *Ibid.*
115   *Ibid.*

identifiers. There are discussions regarding the implementation of Do Not Track standard in Europe.[116]

Some primary guidelines offered by the Opinion include:

- when applying Condition B, it is important to examine what is strictly necessary from the point of view of the user, not the service provider;
- if a cookie is used for several purposes, it can only benefit from an exemption to informed consent, if each distinct purpose individually benefits from such an exemption;
- first party session cookies are far more likely to be exempted from consent than third party persistent cookies. However, the purpose of the cookie should always be the basis for evaluating if the exemption can be successfully applied, rather than a technical feature of the cookie.[117]

It is important to verify carefully if it fulfils one of the two exemption criteria in Article 5(3) as modified by Directive 2009/136/EC. If substantial doubts remain on whether or not an exemption criterion applies, websites should closely examine if there is an opportunity to gain consent from users in a simple clear way, thus avoiding legal uncertainty.[118]

ICO

21.84 In relation to cookies and the new PECR Amendment Regulations the ICO recommends that organisations:

- check what type of cookies and similar technologies the organisation uses and how it uses them;
- assess how intrusive the organisation cookies are;
- where the organisation needs consent, decide what solution to obtain consent will be best in the circumstances.[119]

The ICO has issued guidance in terms of:

- Guide to Privacy and Electronic Communications;[120]

---

116 WP29, *Opinion 04/2012 on Cookie Consent Exemption.*
117 *Ibid.*
118 *Ibid.*
119 ICO, *Privacy and Electronic Communications Regulations, Guidance on the Rules on Use of Cookies and Similar Technologies*, at https://ico.org.uk.
120 ICO, *The Guide to Privacy and Electronic Communications*, at https://ico.org.uk.

- Privacy and Electronic Communications Regulations, Guidance on the Rules on Use of Cookies and Similar Technologies.[121]

In Opinion 2/2010, the WP29 notes that behavioural advertising must not be carried out at the expense of individuals' rights to privacy and data protection. The data protection regime sets forth specific safeguards which must be respected.

The advertising industry needs to comply with the precise requirements of the ePD.

Conclusion

21.85 While the technicalities of cookies can be a little complex, and it is sometimes easy for organisations to look straight at the potential data available via the use of cookies, it is critical for organisations to consider the new rules. Some cookie use may be permitted, but clearly some is not. Organisations and those responsible for web development need to reassess their current online practices to ensure full compliance. It may mean a period of adjustment as organisations, and developers, come to grips with understanding what personal data is required and what may be gathered legitimately by permitted cookies.

As a result of reviews after the new GDPR there may be further changes to the cookie and OBA legal regime.

---

121 ICO, *Privacy and Electronic Communications Regulations, Guidance on the Rules on Use of Cookies and Similar Technologies*, at https://ico.org.uk.

Chapter 22

Enforcement Powers

Introduction

22.01 What happens if an organisation does not comply with the data protection regime when dealing with customers, etc, personal data?

When things go wrong, there can be legal and publicity consequences for the organisation. The impact of a data protection breach can mean an immediate cross team effort to deal with the data protection breach.

In dealing with an incident, and in planning for compliance with customer, etc personal data, organisations should be aware of the various ICO enforcement powers. These emphasise the importance of consequences for non-compliance. Enforcement proceedings can be issued by the ICO. Significant fines and penalties can result. Potentially also, individual customers may decide to sue for damage, loss and breach of their personal data rights.

Data protection compliance is also an important due diligence issue when organisations are reviewed at time of sale and purchase, and indeed at other times also. It can affect a sale or purchase as well as the value involved. In some instances where there is non-compliance, a customer database, which in some instances is the most valuable asset of a commercial organisation, may have to be deleted. That is a real cost of non compliance and not getting things right from day one.

Enforcement Notices

22.02 In terms of the ICO, Part V of the DPA 1998 refers to enforcement actions. Section 40 provides that the ICO may issue enforcement notices to organisations. Under s 40(1), if the ICO is satisfied that a Controller has contravened or is contravening any of the Data Protection Principles, in relation to the use of customer, etc personal data, the

ICO may serve a notice (referred to as 'an enforcement notice'). The enforcement notice will require compliance by the organisation with the Data Protection Principles, or principle in question:

- to take within such time as may be specified in the notice, or to refrain from taking after such time as may be so specified, such steps as are so specified; and or
- to refrain from processing any personal data, or any personal data of a description specified in the notice, or to refrain from processing them for a purpose so specified or in a manner so specified, after such time as may be so specified.

The enforcement notice is, therefore, very wide in terms of what the ICO can require. It can encompass all types of non-compliance or breach in relation to customer, etc personal data. The ICO considers whether the contravention has caused or is likely to cause personal damage or distress, in deciding whether to serve an enforcement notice (s 40(2)). This would encompass non-compliance in terms of collecting and processing customer, etc personal data. However, the ICO may reserve such notices for more serious instances of non-compliance or breach. It may be argued that an actual data breach or data loss instance is naturally a serious incident and therefore may lean towards investigation and enforcement. This might be particularly the case if the breach has not been remedied by the time of notification of the breach to the ICO.

Section 40(3) provides an enforcement notice in respect of a contravention of the fourth Data Protection Principle (which requires the Controller to rectify, block, erase or destroy any inaccurate data) may also require the Controller to rectify, block, erase or destroy any other data held by it and containing an expression of opinion which appears to the ICO to be based on the inaccurate data.

Section 40(4) provides that an enforcement notice in respect of a contravention of the fourth Data Protection Principle, in the case of data which accurately record information received or obtained by the Controller from the Data Subject or a third party, may require the Controller either:

- to rectify, block, erase or destroy any inaccurate data and any other data held by it and containing an expression of opinion as mentioned in s 40(3); or
- to take such steps as are specified in the notice for securing compliance with the requirements specified in para 7 of Part II of Sch 1 and, if the ICO thinks fit, for supplementing the data with such statement of the true facts relating to the matters dealt with by the data as the ICO may approve.

Section 40(5) provides that where:

- an enforcement notice requires the Controller to rectify, block, erase or destroy any personal data; or
- the ICO is satisfied that personal data which have been rectified, blocked, erased or destroyed had been processed in contravention of any of the data protection principles,

an enforcement notice may require the Controller to notify third parties to whom the data have been disclosed of the rectification, blocking, erasure or destruction.

Section 40(8) provides that if by reason of special circumstances the ICO considers that an enforcement notice should be complied with as a matter of urgency, it may include a statement to that effect; and in that event ss 40(7) shall not apply but the notice must not require the provisions of the notice to be complied with before the end of the period of seven days beginning with the day on which the notice is served.

Section 40(9) provides that notification regulations (as defined by s 16(2)) may make provision as to the effect of the service of an enforcement notice on any entry in the register maintained under s 19 which relates to the person on whom the notice is served. Section 40(10) provides that this section has effect subject to s 46(1).

Assessment Notices

22.03 Organisations also need to be aware of assessment notices that may be issued by the ICO. Section 41 relates to assessment notices. Section 40(1) provides that the ICO may serve a Controller within s 41(2) with a notice (referred to as an 'assessment notice') for the purpose of enabling the ICO to determine whether the Controller has complied or is complying with the data protection principles.

Section 40(2) provides that a Controller comes within this subsection if a:

- government department;
- public authority designated for the purposes of this section by an order made by the Secretary of State; or
- person of a description designated for the purposes of this section by such an order.

Section 40(3) provides that an assessment notice is a notice which requires the Controller to do all, or any, of the following:

- permit the ICO to enter any specified premises;

- direct the ICO to any documents on the premises that are of a specified description;
- assist the ICO to view any information of a specified description that is capable of being viewed using equipment on the premises;
- comply with any request from the ICO for:
  - a copy of any of the documents to which the ICO is directed;
  - a copy (in such form as may be requested) of any of the information which the ICO is assisted to view;
- direct the ICO to any equipment or other material on the premises which is of a specified description;
- permit the ICO to inspect or examine any of the documents, information, equipment or material to which the ICO is directed or which the ICO is assisted to view;
- permit the ICO to observe the processing of any personal data that takes place on the premises;
- make available for interview by the ICO a specified number of persons of a specified description who process personal data on behalf of the Controller (or such number as are willing to be interviewed).

An assessment notice must, in relation to each requirement imposed by the notice, specify the time at which the requirement is to be complied with; or the period during which the requirement is to be complied with (s 40(5)). Section 40(6) provides that an assessment notice must also contain particulars of the rights of appeal conferred by s 48. Section 40(7) provides that the ICO may cancel an assessment notice. Section 40(8), (9), (10), (1) and (1) refer to the Secretary of State and provisions that may be made in relation to public authorities, which certain organisations may also have to consult.

Limitations

22.04　Section 41B refers to assessment notices and limitations. Section 41B(1) provides that a time specified in an assessment notice under s 41A(5) in relation to a requirement must not fall, and a period so specified must not begin, before the end of the period within which an appeal can be brought against the notice, and if such an appeal is brought the requirement need not be complied with pending the determination or withdrawal of the appeal.

Section 41B(2) provides that if by reason of special circumstances the ICO considers that it is necessary for the Controller to comply with a requirement in an assessment notice as a matter of urgency, the ICO may include in the notice a statement to that effect and a statement of the reasons for that conclusion; and in that event sub-s (1) applies in relation to the requirement as if for the words from 'within' to the end there were substituted of seven days beginning with the day on which the notice is served.

Section 41B(3) provides that a requirement imposed by an assessment notice does not have effect in so far as compliance with it would result in the disclosure of:

- any communication between a professional legal adviser and the adviser's client in connection with the giving of legal advice with respect to the client's obligations, liabilities or rights under the DPA 1998; or
- any communication between a professional legal adviser and the adviser's client, or between such an adviser or the adviser's client and any other person, made in connection with or in contemplation of proceedings under or arising out of DPA 1998 (including proceedings before the Tribunal) and for the purposes of such proceedings.

Section 41B(4) provides that in sub-s (3) references to the client of a professional legal adviser include references to any person representing such a client.

Section 41B(5) provides that nothing in s 41A authorises the ICO to serve an assessment notice on:

- a judge;
- a body specified in s 23(3) of the Freedom of Information Act 2000 (bodies dealing with security matters); or
- the Office for Standards in Education, Children's Services and Skills in so far as it is a Controller in respect of information processed for the purposes of functions exercisable by Her Majesty's Chief Inspector of Education, Children's Services and Skills by virtue of s 5(1)(a) of the Care Standards Act 2000.

Section 41B(6) provides that in this section 'judge' includes:

(a) a justice of the peace (or, in Northern Ireland, a lay magistrate);
(b) a member of a tribunal; and
(c) a clerk or other officer entitled to exercise the jurisdiction of a court or tribunal;

and in this subsection 'tribunal' means any tribunal in which legal proceedings may be brought.

Code of Practice about Assessment Notices

22.05 Section 41C refers to codes of practice about assessment notices. Section 41C(1) provides that the ICO must prepare and issue a code of practice as to the manner in which the ICO's functions under and in connection with s 41A are to be exercised.

Section 41C(2) provides that the code must in particular:

- specify factors to be considered in determining whether to serve an assessment notice on a Controller;
- specify descriptions of documents and information that:
  - are not to be examined or inspected in pursuance of an assessment notice; or
  - are to be so examined or inspected only by persons of a description specified in the code;
- deal with the nature of inspections and examinations carried out in pursuance of an assessment notice;
- deal with the nature of interviews carried out in pursuance of an assessment notice;
- deal with the preparation, issuing and publication by the Commissioner of assessment reports in respect of Controllers that have been served with assessment notices.

Section 41C(3) provides that the provisions of the code made by virtue of s 41C(2)(b) must, in particular, include provisions that relate to:

- documents and information concerning an individual's physical or mental health;
- documents and information concerning the provision of social care for an individual.

Section 41C(4) provides that an assessment report is a report which contains:

- a determination as to whether a Controller has complied or is complying with the data protection principles;
- recommendations as to any steps which the Controller ought to take, or refrain from taking, to ensure compliance with any of those principles; and
- such other matters as are specified in the code.

Section 41C(5) provides that the ICO may alter or replace the code.

Request for Assessment

22.06 Section 42 refers to a request for an assessment. Section 42(1) provides that a request may be made to the ICO by or on behalf of any person who is, or believes themselves to be, directly affected by any processing of personal data for an assessment as to whether it is likely or unlikely that the processing has been or is being carried out in compliance with the provisions of the DPA 1998.

On receiving a request under this section, the ICO shall make an assessment in such manner as appears to it to be appropriate, unless it has not been supplied with such information as it may reasonably require in order to, satisfy it as to the identity of the person making the request, and enable it to identify the processing in question (s 42(2)).

Section 42(3) provides that the matters to which the ICO may have regard in determining in what manner it is appropriate to make an assessment include:

- the extent to which the request appears to it to raise a matter of substance;
- any undue delay in making the request; and
- whether or not the person making the request is entitled to make an application under s 7 in respect of the personal data in question.

Section 42(1) provides that where the ICO has received a request under this section it shall notify the person who made the request:

- whether it has made an assessment as a result of the request; and
- to the extent that it considers appropriate, having regard in particular to any exemption from s 7 applying in relation to the personal data concerned, of any view formed or action taken as a result of the request.

Information Notices

22.07   Section 43 refers to information notices. Section 43(1) provides that if the ICO:

- has received a request under s 42 in respect of any processing of personal data; or
- reasonably requires any information for the purpose of determining whether the Controller has complied or is complying with the Data Protection Principles,

it may serve the Controller with a notice ('an information notice') requiring the Controller, to furnish the ICO with specified information relating to the request or to compliance with the principles.

Section 43(1A) provides that in s 43(1) 'specified information' means information:

- specified, or described, in the information notice; or
- falling within a category which is specified, or described, in the information notice.

Section 43(1B) provides that the ICO may also specify in the information notice:

- the form in which the information must be furnished;
- the period within which, or the time and place at which, the information must be furnished.

Section 43(2) provides that an information notice must contain:

(a) in a case falling within sub-s (1)(a), a statement that the ICO has received a request under s 42 in relation to the specified processing; or

(b) in a case falling within sub-s (1)(b), a statement that the ICO regards the specified information as relevant for the purpose of determining whether the Controller has complied, or is complying, with the data protection principles and his reasons for regarding it as relevant for that purpose.

Section 43(3) provides that an information notice must also contain particulars of the rights of appeal conferred by s 48.

Section 43(4) provides that subject to sub-s (5), a period specified in an information notice under sub-s (1B)(b) must not end, and a time so specified must not fall, before the end of the period within which an appeal can be brought against the notice and, if such an appeal is brought, the information need not be furnished pending the determination or withdrawal of the appeal.

Section 43(5) provides that if by reason of special circumstances the ICO considers that the information is required as a matter of urgency, it may include in the notice a statement to that effect and a statement of its reasons for reaching that conclusion; and in that event sub-s (4) shall not apply, but the notice shall not require the information to be furnished before the end of the period of seven days beginning with the day on which the notice is served.

Section 43(6) provides that a person shall not be required by virtue of this section to furnish the ICO with any information in respect of:

(a) any communication between a professional legal adviser and his client in connection with the giving of legal advice to the client with respect to his obligations, liabilities or rights under the DPA 1998; or

(b) any communication between a professional legal adviser and his client, or between such an adviser or his client and any other person, made in connection with or in contemplation of proceedings under or arising out of this Act (including proceedings before the Tribunal) and for the purposes of such proceedings.

Section 43(8) provides that a person shall not be required by virtue of this section to furnish the ICO with any information if the furnishing of that information would, by revealing evidence of the commission of any offence, other than an offence under the DPA 1998 or an offence within sub-s (8A), expose them to proceedings for that offence.

Section 43(8A) provides that the offences mentioned in sub-s (8) are:

● an offence under s 5 of the Perjury Act 1911 (false statements made otherwise than on oath);

● an offence under s 44(2) of the Criminal Law (Consolidation) (Scotland) Act 1995 (false statements made otherwise than on oath); or

● an offence under Article 10 of the Perjury (Northern Ireland) Order 1979 (false statutory declarations and other false unsworn statements).

Section 43(8B) provides that any relevant statement provided by a person in response to a requirement under this section may not be used in evidence against that person on a prosecution for any offence under the DPA 1998 (other than an offence under s 47) unless in the proceedings,

● in giving evidence the person provides information inconsistent with it; and

● evidence relating to it is adduced, or a question relating to it is asked, by that person or on that person's behalf.

Section 43(8C) provides that in sub-s (8B) 'relevant statement,' in relation to a requirement under this section, means an oral statement, or a written statement made for the purposes of the requirement.

Section 43(9) provides that the ICO may cancel an information notice.[1]

Special Information Notices

22.08 Section 44 refers to special information notices. Section 44(1) provides that if the ICO:

(a) has received a request under s 42 in respect of any processing of personal data; or

(b) has reasonable grounds for suspecting that, in a case in which proceedings have been stayed under s 32, the personal data to which the proceedings relate:

(i) are not being processed only for the special purposes; or

---

1 Section 43(10) provides that this section has effect subject to s 46(3).

(ii) are not being processed with a view to the publication by any person of any journalistic, literary or artistic material which has not previously been published by the Controller,

it may serve the Controller with a notice ('special information notice') requiring the Controller to furnish the ICO with specified information for the purpose specified in sub-s (2).

Section 44(1A) provides that in sub-s (1) 'specified information' means information:

- specified, or described, in the special information notice; or
- falling within a category which is specified, or described, in the special information notice.

Section 44(1B) provides that the ICO may also specify in the special information notice:

- the form in which the information must be furnished;
- the period within which, or the time and place at which, the information must be furnished.

Section 44(2) provides that purpose is the purpose of ascertaining:

- whether the personal data are being processed only for the special purposes; or
- whether they are being processed with a view to the publication by any person of any journalistic, literary or artistic material which has not previously been published by the Controller.

Section 44(3) provides that a special information notice must contain:

- in a case falling within paragraph (a) of sub-s (1), a statement that the ICO has received a request under s 42 in relation to the specified processing; or
- in a case falling within paragraph (b) of that sub-section, a statement of the Commissioner's grounds for suspecting that the personal data are not being processed as mentioned in that paragraph.

Section 44(4) provides that a special information notice must also contain particulars of the rights of appeal conferred by s 48.

Section 44(5) provides that subject to sub-s (6), a period specified in a special information notice under sub-s (1B)(b) must not end, and a time so specified must not fall, before the end of the period within which an appeal can be brought against the notice and, if such an appeal is brought, the information need not be furnished pending the determination or withdrawal of the appeal.

Section 44(6) provides that if by reason of special circumstances the ICO considers that the information is required as a matter of urgency, he may include in the notice a statement to that effect and a statement of his reasons for reaching that conclusion; and in that event sub-s (5) shall not apply, but the notice shall not require the information to be furnished before the end of the period of seven days beginning with the day on which the notice is served.

Section 44(7) provides that a person shall not be required by virtue of this section to furnish the ICO with any information in respect of:

- any communication between a professional legal adviser and his client in connection with the giving of legal advice to the client with respect to his obligations, liabilities or rights under the DPA 1998; or
- any communication between a professional legal adviser and his client, or between such an adviser or his client and any other person, made in connection with or in contemplation of proceedings under or arising out of the DPA 1998 (including proceedings before the Tribunal) and for the purposes of such proceedings.

Section 44(8) provides that in sub-s (7) references to the client of a professional legal adviser include references to any person representing such a client.

Section 44(9) provides that a person shall not be required by virtue of this section to furnish the ICO with any information if the furnishing of that information would, by revealing evidence of the commission of any offence, other than an offence under the DPA 1998 or an offence within sub-s (9A), expose them to proceedings for that offence.

Section 44(9A) provides that the offences mentioned in sub-s (9) are:

- an offence under s 5 of the Perjury Act 1911 (false statements made otherwise than on oath);
- an offence under s 44(2) of the Criminal Law (Consolidation) (Scotland) Act 1995 (false statements made otherwise than on oath); or
- an offence under Article 10 of the Perjury (Northern Ireland) Order 1979 (false statutory declarations and other false unsworn statements).

Section 44(9B) provides that any relevant statement provided by a person in response to a requirement under this section may not be used in evidence against that person on a prosecution for any offence under this Act (other than an offence under s 47) unless in the proceedings:

- in giving evidence the person provides information inconsistent with it; and
- evidence relating to it is adduced, or a question relating to it is asked, by that person or on that person's behalf.

Section 44(9C) provides that in sub-s (9B) 'relevant statement,' in relation to a requirement under this section, means an oral statement; or a written statement made for the purposes of the requirement.

Section 44(10) provides that the ICO may cancel a special information notice.

ICO Determination of Special Purposes

22.09   Section 45 refers to a determination by the ICO as to the special purposes. Section 45(1) provides that where at any time it appears to the ICO (whether as a result of the service of a special information notice or otherwise) that any personal data:

- are not being processed only for the special purposes; or
- are not being processed with a view to the publication by any person of any journalistic, literary or artistic material which has not previously been published by the Controller,

it may make a determination in writing to that effect.

Section 45(2) provides that notice of the determination shall be given to the Controller; and the notice must contain particulars of the right of appeal conferred by s 48.

Section 45(3) provides that a determination under s 45(1) shall not take effect until the end of the period within which an appeal can be brought and, where an appeal is brought, shall not take effect pending the determination or withdrawal of the appeal.

Restriction on Enforcement for Special Purposes Processing

22.10   Section 46 refers to the restriction on enforcement in case of processing for the special purposes. Section 46(1) provides that the ICO may not at any time serve an enforcement notice on a Controller with respect to the processing of personal data for the special purposes unless:

- a determination under s 45(1) with respect to those data has taken effect; and
- the court has granted leave for the notice to be served.

Section 46(2) provides that the court shall not grant leave for the purposes of s 46(1)(b) unless it is satisfied:

- that the ICO has reason to suspect a contravention of the data protection principles which is of substantial public importance; and

- except where the case is one of urgency, that the Controller has been given notice, in accordance with rules of court, of the application for leave.

Section 46(3) provides that the ICO may not serve an information notice on a Controller with respect to the processing of personal data for the special purposes unless a determination under s 45(1) with respect to those data has taken effect.

Failure to Comply with Notice

22.11 Section 47 refers to the failure to comply with notice. Section 47(1) provides that a person who fails to comply with an enforcement notice, an information notice or a special information notice is guilty of an offence.

Section 47(2) provides that a person who, in purported compliance with an information notice or a special information notice:

- makes a statement which he knows to be false in a material respect; or
- recklessly makes a statement which is false in a material respect,

is guilty of an offence.

Section 47(3) provides that it is a defence for a person charged with an offence under s 47(1) to prove that he exercised all due diligence to comply with the notice in question.

Appeal

22.12 Section 48 refers to rights of appeal. Section 48(1) provides that a person on whom an enforcement notice, an assessment notice, an information notice or a special information notice has been served may appeal to the (Data Protection) Tribunal against the notice.

Section 48(2) provides that a person on whom an enforcement notice has been served may appeal to the Tribunal against the refusal of an application under s 41(2) for cancellation or variation of the notice.

Section 48(3) provides that where an enforcement notice, an assessment notice, an information notice or a special information notice contains a statement by the ICO in accordance with ss 40(8), 41B(2), 43(5) or 44(6) then, whether or not the person appeals against the notice, he may appeal against:

- the ICO's decision to include the statement in the notice; or
- the effect of the inclusion of the statement as respects any part of the notice.

Section 48(4) provides that a Controller in respect of whom a determination has been made under s 45 may appeal to the Tribunal against the determination.

Section 48(6) provides that sch 6 has effect in relation to appeals under this section and the proceedings of the Tribunal in respect of any such appeal.

Unlawful Obtaining Etc of Personal Data

22.13   Section 55 refers to unlawful obtaining etc, of personal data. Section 55(1) provides that a person must not knowingly or recklessly, without the consent of the Controller:

- obtain or disclose personal data or the information contained in personal data; or
- procure the disclosure to another person of the information contained in personal data.

Section 55(2) provides that s 55(1) does not apply to a person who shows:

(a) that the obtaining, disclosing or procuring:
    (i)   was necessary for the purpose of preventing or detecting crime; or
    (ii)   was required or authorised by or under any enactment, by any rule of law or by the order of a court,
(b) that they acted in the reasonable belief that they had in law the right to obtain or disclose the data or information or, as the case may be, to procure the disclosure of the information to the other person;
(c) that they acted in the reasonable belief that they would have had the consent of the Controller if the Controller had known of the obtaining, disclosing or procuring and the circumstances of it; or
(d) that in the particular circumstances the obtaining, disclosing or procuring was justified as being in the public interest.

Section 55(3) provides that a person who contravenes s 55(1) is guilty of an offence.

Section 55(4) provides that a person who sells personal data is guilty of an offence if they had obtained the data in contravention of s 55(1).

Section 55(5) provides that a person who offers to sell personal data is guilty of an offence if,

- they had obtained the data in contravention of s 55(1); or
- they subsequently obtain the data in contravention of that subsection.

Section 55(6) provides that for the purposes of sub-s (5), an advertisement indicating that personal data are or may be for sale is an offer to sell the data.

Section 55(7) provides that s 1(2) does not apply for the purposes of this section; and for the purposes of s 55(4) to (6), 'personal data' includes information extracted from personal data.

Section 55(8) provides that references in this section to personal data do not include references to personal data which by virtue of ss 28 or 33A are exempt from this section.

Power of ICO to Impose Monetary Penalty

22.14   Section 55A refers to the power of the ICO to impose monetary penalty. Section 55A(1) provides that the ICO may serve a Controller with a monetary penalty notice if the ICO is satisfied that:

- there has been a serious contravention of s 4(4) by the Controller;
- the contravention was of a kind likely to cause substantial damage or substantial distress; and
- s 55A(2) or (3) applies.

Section 55A(2) provides that this subsection applies if the contravention was deliberate.

Section 55A(3) provides that this subsection applies if the Controller:

(a) knew or ought to have known:
    (i)   that there was a risk that the contravention would occur; and
    (ii) that such a contravention would be of a kind likely to cause substantial damage or substantial distress, but
(b) failed to take reasonable steps to prevent the contravention.

Section 55A(3A) provides that the ICO may not be satisfied as mentioned in sub-s (1) by virtue of any matter which comes to the ICO's attention as a result of anything done in pursuance of:

- an assessment notice;
- an assessment under s 51(7).

Section 55A(4) provides that a monetary penalty notice is a notice requiring the Controller to pay to the ICO a monetary penalty of an amount determined by the ICO and specified in the notice.

Section 55A(5) provides that the amount determined by the ICO must not exceed the prescribed amount.

Section 55A(6) provides that the monetary penalty must be paid to the ICO within the period specified in the notice.

Section 55A(7) provides that the notice must contain such information as may be prescribed.

Section 55A(8) provides that any sum received by the ICO by virtue of this section must be paid into the Consolidated Fund.

Section 55A(9) provides that in this section:

- 'data Controller' does not include the Crown Estate Commissioners or a person who is a data Controller by virtue of s 63(3);
- 'prescribed' means prescribed by regulations made by the Secretary of State.

See table of ICO penalties (above), which indicate that substantial fines and penalties can be imposed on organisations and, importantly, upon individuals also. Court prosecutions can also arise.

Monetary Penalty Notices

Procedural Rights

22.15 Section 55B refers to monetary penalty notices and procedural rights. Section 55B(1) provides that before serving a monetary penalty notice, the ICO must serve the Controller with a notice of intent.

Section 55B(2) provides that (2)A notice of intent is a notice that the ICO proposes to serve a monetary penalty notice. Section 55B(3) provides that a notice of intent must:

- inform the Controller that it may make written representations in relation to the ICO's proposal within a period specified in the notice; and
- contain such other information as may be prescribed.

Section 55B(4) provides that the ICO may not serve a monetary penalty notice until the time within which the Controller may make representations has expired.

Section 55B(5) provides that a person on whom a monetary penalty notice is served may appeal to the Tribunal against:

- the issue of the monetary penalty notice;
- the amount of the penalty specified in the notice.

Section 55B(6) provides that in this section, 'prescribed' means prescribed by regulations made by the Secretary of State.

Guidance

22.16   Section 55C refers to guidance about monetary penalty notices. Section 55C(1) provides that the ICO must prepare and issue guidance on how he proposes to exercise his functions under ss 55A and 55B.

Section 55C(2) provides that the guidance must, in particular, deal with:

- the circumstances in which it would consider it appropriate to issue a monetary penalty notice; and
- how it will determine the amount of the penalty.

Section 55C(3) provides that the ICO may alter or replace the guidance. Section 55C(4) provides that if the guidance is altered or replaced, the ICO must issue the altered or replacement guidance. Section 55C(5) provides that the ICO may not issue guidance under this section without the approval of the Secretary of State. Section 55C(6) provides that the ICO must lay any guidance issued under this section before each House of Parliament.

Section 55C(7) provides that the ICO must arrange for the publication of any guidance issued under this section in such form and manner as it considers appropriate.

Section 55C(8) provides that in sub-s (5) to (7), 'guidance' includes altered or replacement guidance.

Enforcement

22.17   Section 55D refers to monetary penalty notices: enforcement. Section 55D(1) provides that this section applies in relation to any penalty payable to the ICO by virtue of s 55A.

Section 55D(2) provides that in England and Wales, the penalty is recoverable:

- if a county court so orders, as if it were payable under an order of that court;
- if the High Court so orders, as if it were payable under an order of that court.

Section 55D(3) provides that in Scotland, the penalty may be enforced in the same manner as an extract registered decree arbitral bearing a warrant for execution issued by the sheriff court of any sheriffdom in Scotland.

Section 55D(4) provides that in Northern Ireland, the penalty is recoverable:

- if a county court so orders, as if it were payable under an order of that court;

- if the High Court so orders, as if it were payable under an order of that court.

Notices under Sections 55A and 55B: Supplemental Provisions

22.18 Section 55E refers to notices under ss 55A and 55B (ie ICO monetary penalty notice) and contains supplemental provisions. Section 55E(1) provides that the Secretary of State may by order make further provision in connection with monetary penalty notices and notices of intent.

Section 55E(2) provides that an order under this section may in particular:

(a) provide that a monetary penalty notice may not be served on a Controller with respect to the processing of personal data for the special purposes except in circumstances specified in the order;

(b) make provision for the cancellation or variation of monetary penalty notices;

(c) confer rights of appeal to the Tribunal against decisions of the ICO in relation to the cancellation or variation of such notices;

(d) [amended];

(e) make provision for the determination of appeals made by virtue of para (c);

(f) [amended];

(3) An order under this section may apply any provision of the DPA with such modifications as may be specified in the order;

(4) An order under this section may amend the DPA.

Prohibition of Requirement as to Production of Certain Records

22.19 Section 56 refers to a prohibition of requirement as to production of certain records. Section 56(1) provides that a person must not, in connection with:

- the recruitment of another person as an employee;
- the continued employment of another person; or
- any contract for the provision of services to them by another person,

require that other person or a third party to supply them with a relevant record or to produce a relevant record to them.

Section 56(2) provides that a person concerned with the provision (for payment or not) of goods, facilities or services to the public or a section of the public must not, as a condition of providing or offering to provide any goods, facilities or services to another person, require that other person or a third party to supply them with a relevant record or to produce a relevant record to them.

Section 56(1) provides that s 56(1) and (2) do not apply to a person who shows:

- that the imposition of the requirement was required or authorised by or under any enactment, by any rule of law or by the order of a court; or
- that in the particular circumstances the imposition of the requirement was justified as being in the public interest.

Section 56(4) provides that having regard to the provisions of Part V of the Police Act 1997 (certificates of criminal records etc), the imposition of the requirement referred to in s 56(1) or (2) is not to be regarded as being justified as being in the public interest on the ground that it would assist in the prevention or detection of crime.

Section 56(5) provides that a person who contravenes s 56(1) or (2) is guilty of an offence.

Section 56(6) provides that in this section 'a relevant record' means any record which:

- has been or is to be obtained by a Data Subject from any Controller specified in the first column of the Table below in the exercise of the right conferred by s 7; and
- contains information relating to any matter specified in relation to that Controller in the second column,

and includes a copy of such a record or a part of such a record.

Formal undertaking agreements can also arise, whereby the organisation agrees to do or not do certain things.

Tasks

22.20 Without prejudice to other tasks set out under the GDPR, each supervisory authority shall on its territory:

- monitor and enforce the application of the GDPR;
- promote public awareness and understanding of the risks, rules, safeguards and rights in relation to processing. Activities addressed specifically to children shall receive specific attention;

- advise, in accordance with national law, the national parliament, the government, and other institutions and bodies on legislative and administrative measures relating to the protection of natural person's rights and freedoms with regard to processing;
- promote the awareness of Controllers and Processors of their obligations under the GDPR;
- upon request, provide information to any Data Subject concerning the exercise of their rights under the GDPR and, if appropriate, co-operate with the supervisory authorities in other Member States to this end;
- handle complaints lodged by a Data Subject, or by a body, organisation or association in accordance with Article 80, and investigate, to the extent appropriate, the subject matter of the complaint and inform the complainant of the progress and the outcome of the investigation within a reasonable period, in particular if further investigation or coordination with another supervisory authority is necessary;
- co-operate with, including sharing information and provide mutual assistance to other supervisory authorities with a view to ensuring the consistency of application and enforcement of the GDPR;
- conduct investigations on the application of the GDPR, including on the basis of information received from another supervisory authority or other public authority;
- monitor relevant developments, insofar as they have an impact on the protection of personal data, in particular the development of information and communication technologies and commercial practices;
- adopt standard contractual clauses referred to in Article 28(8) and 46(2)(d);
- establish and maintain a list in relation to the requirement for data protection impact assessment pursuant to Article 35(4);
- give advice on the processing operations referred to in Article 36(2);
- encourage the drawing up of codes of conduct pursuant to Article 40(1) and give an opinion and approve such codes of conduct which provide sufficient safeguards, pursuant to Article 40(5);
- encourage the establishment of data protection certification mechanisms and of data protection seals and marks pursuant to Article 42(1), and approve the criteria of certification pursuant to Article 42(5);
- where applicable, carry out a periodic review of certifications issued in accordance with Article 42(7);
- draft and publish the criteria for accreditation of a body for monitoring codes of conduct pursuant to Article 41 and of a certification body pursuant to Article 43;

- conduct the accreditation of a body for monitoring codes of conduct pursuant to Article 41 and of a certification body pursuant to Article 43;
- authorise contractual clauses and provisions referred to in Article 46(3);
- approve binding corporate rules pursuant to Article 47;
- contribute to the activities of the EDPB;
- keep internal records of breaches of the GDPR and of measures taken in accordance with Article 58(2);
- fulfil any other tasks related to the protection of personal data (Article 57(1)).

Each supervisory authority shall facilitate the submission of complaints referred to in Article 57(1)(f), by measures such as a complaint submission form which can also be completed electronically, without excluding other means of communication (Article 57(2)).

The performance of the tasks of each supervisory authority shall be free of charge for the Data Subject and, where applicable, for the DPO (Article 57(3)).

Where requests are manifestly unfounded or excessive, in particular because of their repetitive character, the supervisory authority may charge a reasonable fee based on administrative costs, or refuse to act on the request. The supervisory authority shall bear the burden of demonstrating the manifestly unfounded or excessive character of the request (Article 57(4)).

Powers

22.21 Pursuant to the new GDPR, each supervisory authority shall have the following investigative powers:

- to order the Controller and the Processor, and, where applicable, the Controller's or the Processor's representative to provide any information it requires for the performance of its tasks;
- to carry out investigations in the form of data protection audits;
- to carry out a review on certifications issued pursuant to Article 42(7);
- to notify the Controller or the Processor of an alleged infringement of the GDPR;
- to obtain, from the Controller and the Processor, access to all personal data and to all information necessary for the performance of its tasks;
- to obtain access to any premises of the Controller and the Processor, including to any data processing equipment and means, in accordance with EU law or Member State procedural law (Article 58(1)).

Each supervisory authority shall have the following corrective powers:

- to issue warnings to a Controller or Processor that intended processing operations are likely to infringe provisions of the GDPR;
- to issue reprimands to a Controller or a Processor where processing operations have infringed provisions of the GDPR;
- to order the Controller or the Processor to comply with the Data Subject's requests to exercise their rights pursuant to the GDPR;
- to order the Controller or Processor to bring processing operations into compliance with the provisions of the GDPR, where appropriate, in a specified manner and within a specified period;
- to order the Controller to communicate a personal data breach to the Data Subject;
- to impose a temporary or definitive limitation including a *ban on processing*;
- to order the rectification or erasure of data pursuant to Articles 16, 17 and 18 and the notification of such actions to recipients to whom the personal data have been disclosed pursuant to Articles 17(2) and 19;
- to withdraw a certification or to order the certification body to withdraw a certification issued pursuant to Articles 42 and 43, or to order the certification body not to issue certification if the requirements for the certification are not or no longer met;
- to impose an administrative fine pursuant to Articles 83, in addition to, or instead of measures referred to in this paragraph, depending on the circumstances of each individual case;
- to order the suspension of data flows to a recipient in a third country or to an international organisation (Article 58(2)).

Each supervisory authority shall have the following authorisation and advisory powers:

- to advise the Controller in accordance with the prior consultation procedure referred to in Article 36;
- to issue, on its own initiative or on request, opinions to the national parliament, the Member State government or, in accordance with national law, to other institutions and bodies as well as to the public on any issue related to the protection of personal data;
- to authorise processing referred to in Article 36(5), if the law of the Member State requires such prior authorisation;
- to issue an opinion and approve draft codes of conduct pursuant to Article 40(5);
- to accredit certification bodies pursuant to Article 43;
- to issue certifications and approve criteria of certification in accordance with Article 42(5);

- to adopt standard data protection clauses referred to in Article 28(8) and in Article 43(2)(d);
- to authorise contractual clauses referred to in Article 46(3)(a);
- to authorise administrative agreements referred to in Article 46(3)(b);
- to approve binding corporate rules pursuant to Article 47 (Article 58(3)).

The exercise of the powers conferred on the supervisory authority pursuant to this Article shall be subject to appropriate safeguards, including effective judicial remedy and due process, set out in EU and Member State law in accordance with the Charter of Fundamental Rights of the EU (Article 58(4)).

Each Member State shall provide by law that its supervisory authority shall have the power to bring infringements of the GDPR to the attention of the judicial authorities and where appropriate, to commence or engage otherwise in legal proceedings, in order to enforce the provisions of the GDPR (Article 58(5)).

Each Member State may provide by law that its supervisory authority shall have additional powers to those referred to in Article 58(1), (2) and (3). The exercise of these powers shall not impair the effective operation of Chapter VII (Article 58(6)).

General Conditions for Imposing Administrative Fines

22.22   The new GDPR provides that each supervisory authority shall ensure that the imposition of administrative fines pursuant to the GDPR referred to in Article 83(4), (5) and (6) shall in each individual case be effective, proportionate and dissuasive (Article 83(1)).

Administrative fines shall, depending on the circumstances of each individual case, be imposed in addition to, or instead of, measures referred to in Article 83(a) to (h) and (j). When deciding whether to impose an administrative fine and deciding on the amount of the administrative fine in each individual case due regard shall be given to the following:

- the nature, gravity and duration of the infringement taking into account the nature, scope or purpose of the processing concerned as well as the number of Data Subjects affected and the level of damage suffered by them;
- the intentional or negligent character of the infringement;
- action taken by the Controller or Processor to mitigate the damage suffered by Data Subjects;

- the degree of responsibility of the Controller or Processor taking into account technical and organisational measures implemented by them pursuant to Articles 25 and 32;
- any relevant previous infringements by the Controller or Processor;
- the degree of co-operation with the supervisory authority, in order to remedy the infringement and mitigate the possible adverse effects of the infringement;
- the categories of personal data affected by the infringement;
- the manner in which the infringement became known to the supervisory authority, in particular whether, and if so to what extent, the Controller or Processor notified the infringement;
- where measures referred to Article 58(2), have previously been ordered against the Controller or Processor concerned in regard to the same subject-matter, compliance with these measures;
- adherence to approved codes of conduct pursuant to Article 40 or approved certification mechanisms pursuant to Article 42; and
- any other aggravating or mitigating factor applicable to the circumstances of the case, such as financial benefits gained, or losses avoided, directly or indirectly, from the infringement (Article 83(2)).

If a Controller or Processor intentionally or negligently, for the same or linked processing operations, infringes several provisions of the GDPR, the total amount of the administrative fine shall not exceed the amount specified for the gravest infringement (Article 83(3)).

Infringements of the following provisions shall, in accordance with Article 83(2), be subject to administrative fines up to 10,000,000 EUR, or in case of an undertaking, up to two percent of the total worldwide annual turnover of the preceding financial year, whichever is higher:

- the obligations of the Controller and the Processor pursuant to Articles 8, 11, 25–39 and 42 and 43;
- the obligations of the certification body pursuant to Articles 42 and 43;
- the obligations of the monitoring body pursuant to Article 41(4) (Article 83(4)).

Infringements of the following provisions shall, in accordance with Article 83(2), be subject to administrative fines up to 20,000,000 EUR, or in case of an undertaking, up to four percent of the total worldwide annual turnover of the preceding financial year, whichever is higher:

- the basic principles for processing, including conditions for consent, pursuant to Articles 5, 6, 7 and 9;
- the Data Subjects' rights pursuant to Articles 12–22;

- the transfers of personal data to a recipient in a third country or an international organisation pursuant to Articles 44–49;
- any obligations pursuant to Member State laws adopted under Chapter IX;
- non-compliance with an order or a temporary or definite limitation on processing or the suspension of data flows by the supervisory authority pursuant to Article 58(2) or does not provide access in violation of Article 53(1) (Article 83(5)).

Non-compliance with an order by the supervisory authority as referred to in Article 58(2) shall, in accordance with Article 83(2), be subject to administrative fines up to 20,000,000 EUR, or in case of an undertaking, up to four percent of the total worldwide annual turnover of the preceding financial year, whichever is higher (Article 83(6)).

Without prejudice to the corrective powers of supervisory authorities pursuant to Article 58(2), each Member State may lay down the rules on whether and to what extent administrative fines may be imposed on public authorities and bodies established in that Member State (Article 83(7)).

The exercise by the supervisory authority of its powers under this Article shall be subject to appropriate procedural safeguards in conformity with EU law and Member State law, including effective judicial remedy and due process (Article 83(8)).

Where the legal system of the Member State does not provide for administrative fines, Article 83 may be applied in such a manner that the fine is initiated by the competent supervisory authority and imposed by competent national courts, while ensuring that these legal remedies are effective and have an equivalent effect to the administrative fines imposed by supervisory authorities. In any event, the fines imposed shall be effective, proportionate and dissuasive. Those Member States shall notify to the Commission the provisions of their laws which they adopt pursuant to this paragraph by 25 May 2018 and, without delay, any subsequent amendment law or amendment affecting them (Article 83(9)).

Penalties

22.23 The new GDPR provides that Member States shall lay down the rules on penalties applicable to infringements of the GDPR in particular for infringements which are not subject to administrative fines pursuant to Article 83, and shall take all measures necessary to ensure that they are implemented. Such penalties shall be effective, proportionate and dissuasive (Article 84(1)).

Each Member State shall notify to the Commission those provisions of its law which it adopts pursuant to Article 84(1), by 25 May 2018 and, without delay, any subsequent amendment affecting them (Article 84(2)).

Conclusion

22.24 Data protection is important. Personal data is considered important and sensitive to customers. This should be respected by organisations. Organisations are not permitted to collect nor process customer, etc, personal data without being data protection compliant. It is in this context that there can be severe consequences for organisations for non-compliance, whether in collecting personal data initially, or in the subsequent processing of the personal data. The ICO can impose penalties financially, or can prosecute for non-compliance. Alternatively, enforcement notices can be imposed which specify certain actions that must be implemented by the organisation. Certain types of organisation can be the recipient of separate types of notices, namely assessment notices. In any of these events, customers, etc will be particularly concerned that their personal data has been collected, is being processed in a certain manner and or may have been subject to a breach event. This can have its own consequences. Overall, it should also be noted that the consequences of breach or non-compliance are becoming increasingly important as enforcement actions and penalties are increasing, in frequency, number and financial scale. The new GDPR regime also further changes the enforcement rules (see below).

Chapter 23

Trans Border Data Flows/ Transfers of Personal Data

Introduction

23.01 Organisations are under ever increasing pressure to reduce costs. This can sometimes involve consideration of outsourcing to countries outside of the EEA. Any transfers of personal data, unless specifically exempted, are restricted.

In addition, the global nature of commercial activities means that organisations as part of normal business processes may seek to transfer particular sets of personal data to group entities whom may be located outside of the EEA. There can be similar situations where an organisation wishes to make trans border data flows to agents, partners or outsourced Processors.

The data protection regime controls and regulates the transfers of personal data[1] from the UK to jurisdictions outside of the EEA. The transfer of personal data outside of the EU/EEA are known as trans border data flows (TBDFs).[2] Frequently organisations would have transferred personal data to other sections within their international organisation, such as banks. This could be personal data in relation to

---

1 See A Nugter, *Transborder Flow of Personal Data within the EC* (Kluwer Law and Taxation Publishers, 1990).
2 CT Beling, 'Transborder Data Flows: International Privacy Protection and the Free Flow of Information,' *Boston College International and Comparative Law Review* (1983)(6) 591–624; 'Declaration on Transborder Data Flows,' *International Legal Materials* (1985)(24) 912–913; Council Recommendation Concerning Guidelines Governing the Protection of Privacy and Transborder Flows of Personal Data,' *International Legal Materials* (1981)(20) 422–450; 'Draft Recommendation of the Council Concerning Guidelines the Protection of Privacy and Transborder Flows of Personal Data,' *International Legal Materials* (1980)(19) 318–324.

customers as well as employees (eg where the HR or payroll section may be in a different country). This too is included in the default ban, unless specifically exempted.

This trend of TDBFs has increased, however, as more and more activity is carried out online, such as eCommerce and social media. Personal data is frequently transferred or mirrored on computer servers in more than one country as a matter of apparent technical routine.

However, organisations need to be aware that any transfer of personal data of EU citizens needs to be in compliance with the EU data protection regime. One of the obligations is that TBDFs of personal data may not occur.[3] This default position can be derogated from if one of a limited number of criteria are satisfied. If none of the exemption criteria apply, the default position in the data protection regime applies and the transfer cannot take place.

Transfer Ban

23.02 Article 25 of the DPD prohibits the transfer of data outside of the EEA unless:

- The third country ensures appropriate levels of protection (Article 25); or
- the transfer can come within one of the exemptions (Article 26).

The regime created under the DPD means that transfers are prohibited per se. The focus is directed upon the privacy protection elsewhere and the dangers of uncontrolled transfers of personal data.

The DPA sets out in the eight Data Protection Principle that:

'Personal data shall not be transferred to a country or territory outside the European Economic Area [EEA] unless that country or territory ensures an adequate level of protection for the rights and freedoms of Data Subjects in relation to the processing of personal data.'

Data protection compliance practice for organisations means that they will have to include a compliance assessment as well as an assessment of the risks associated with transfers of personal data outside of the EEA. This applies to transfers from parent to subsidiary or to a branch office in the same way as a transfer to an unrelated company or entity. However, different exemptions can apply in different scenarios.

---

3   For one article noting the difficulties that the data protection regime creates in terms of trans border data flows, see L Kong, 'Data Protection and Trans Border Data Flow in the European and Global Context,' *European Journal of International Law* (2010) (21) 441–456.

DPA: Adequate Protection Exception

23.03   If the recipient country has already been deemed by the UK or EU to already have an adequate level of protection for personal data, then the transfer is permitted.

The DPA 1998, Sch 1, Pt II, refers to the eighth Data Protection Principle and provides that an adequate level of protection is one which is adequate in all the circumstances of the case, having regard in particular to:

- the nature of the personal data;
- the country or territory of origin of the information contained in the data;
- the country or territory of final destination of that information;
- the purposes for which and period during which the data are intended to be processed;
- the law in force in the country or territory in question;
- the international obligations of that country or territory;
- any relevant codes of conduct or other rules which are enforceable in that country or territory (whether generally or by arrangement in particular cases); and
- any security measures taken in respect of the data in that country or territory.

It is also provided that a transfer can occur where there has been a positive Community finding in relation to the type of transfer proposed. A Community finding means a finding of the European Commission (under the procedure provided for in Article 31(2) of the DPD), that a country or territory outside the European Economic Area does, or does not, ensure an adequate level of protection within the meaning of Article 25(2) of the Directive.

Therefore, if there has been a positive community finding in relation to a named country outside of the EEA, this means that that country is deemed to have a level of protection in its laws comparable to the EU data protection regime. This then makes it possible for organisations to make transfers to that specific country.

The EU Commission provides a list of Commission decisions on the adequacy of the protection of personal data in named third countries.[4] The EU Commission has thus far recognised that Switzerland, Canada, Argentina, Guernsey, Isle of Man, the US Department of Commerce's Safe Harbour Privacy Principles (if signed up and adhered to), and the

---

4   At http://ec.europa.eu/justice/data-protection/international-transfers/adequacy/index_ en.htm.

transfer of air passenger name record to the United States Bureau of Customs and Border Protection (as specified) as providing adequate protection for personal data. This list will expand over time.

Exceptions

23.04 If the recipient country's protection for personal data is not adequate, or not ascertainable, but it is intended that TBDFs are still commercially desired, the organisation should ascertain if the transfer is comes within one of the excepted categories. Transfers of personal data from the UK to outside of the EEA cannot occur unless it falls within one of the transfer exemptions.

The exemptions from the transfer restrictions are:

- the Data Subject has given consent;
- the transfer is necessary for performance of contract between Data Subject and Controller;
- the transfer is necessary for taking steps at the request of the Data Subject with a view to entering into a contract with the Controller;
- the transfer is necessary for conclusion of a contract between Controller and a person other than Data Subject that is entered into at request of Data Subject and is in the interests of the Data Subject;
- the transfer is necessary for the performance of such a contract;
- the transfer is required or authorised under any enactment or instrument imposing international obligation on UK;
- the transfer is necessary for reasons of substantial public interest;
- the transfer is necessary for purposes of or in connection with legal proceedings or prospective legal proceedings;
- the transfer is necessary in order to prevent injury or damage to the health of the Data Subject or serious loss of or damage to the property of the Data Subject or otherwise to protect vital interests;
- subject to certain conditions the transfer is only part of personal data on a register established by or under an enactment;
- the transfer has been authorised by data protection commissioners where the Controller adduces adequate safeguards;
- the transfer is made to a country that has been determined by the EU Commission as having 'adequate levels of [data] protection' ie a Community finding (see above);
- the transfer is made to a US entity that has signed up to the EU/US 'safe harbour' arrangements (although less have signed up than originally envisaged);
- EU Commission contract provisions: the Model Contracts (the EU has set out model contracts which if incorporated into the

data exporter – data importer/recipient relationship can act as an exemption thus permitting the transfer to occur.

In determining whether a third country ensures an adequate level of protection one factor taken into account includes:

- 'any security measures taken in respect of the data in that country or territory';
- the transfer is necessary for obtaining legal advice or in connection with legal proceedings or prospective proceedings;
- (subject to certain conditions) it is necessary in order to prevent injury or damage to the health or property of the Data Subject, or in order to protect his or her vital interests;
- the transfer is required or authorised by law;
- the ICO has authorised the transfer where the Controller has given or adduced adequate safeguards; or
- the contract relating to the transfer of the data embodies appropriate contract clauses as specified in a 'Community finding.'

Other potential exempted categories are where:

- the transfers substantially in the public interest;
- the transfers made in connection with any (legal) claim;
- the transfers in the vital interests of the Data Subject;
- there are public protesters;
- the transfer is necessary for the performance of a contract. (This will depend on the nature of the goods or services provided under the contract. The transfer must be necessary for the benefit of the transferee and not just convenient for the organisation.)

For example, where a customer books a hotel in New York through an agent in London and it is necessary for the ultimate performance of the contract for the personal data to be transferred to the hotel in New York from the UK. The transfer of the personal data is permitted.

However, when a UK company in processing its employee payroll personal data sends it to a US parent company, such a transfer is for the convenience of the company and is not strictly necessary for the performance of a contract.

Creating Adequacy

Through Consent

23.05 One of the possible transfer solutions is 'creating adequacy' through consent.

Under Article 26 of the DPD, transfers can be made to a non-EEA country where the unambiguous consent of the Data Subject to that transfer is obtained. This will involve establishing sufficient prior information being provided to the Data Subject and appropriate consent then being given to the organisation.

Through Contract

23.06 One of the other exemptions relates to transfers permitted as a result of adopting the EU model contracts into the legal relationship between the data exporter and the data importer/recipient.

Transfers of data to a third country may be made even though there is not adequate protection in place in the third country, if the Controller secures the necessary level of protection through contractual obligations.

These contractual protections are the model contract clauses emanating from Commission. The Commission has issued what it considers to be adequate clauses which are incorporated into the contract relationship of the data exporter and data importer as then provide an adequate level of consent.

Obtaining consent of pre-existing customers may pose a problem so in some cases may not be possible or practical. For example, it may not be possible to retrospectively change existing contracts and terms.

However, going forward it may be possible to include 'transfer' issues in any data protection compliance and related models.

Binding Corporate Rules

23.07 The Commission and the WP29[5] (now the EDPB) also developed a policy of recognising adequate protection of the policies of multinational organisations transferring personal data whom satisfy the determined binding corporate rules (BCR), pursuant to the DPD Article 26 (2).[6] This relates to transfers internally between companies

---

5   WP29, Recommendation 1/2007 on the Standard Application for Approval of Binding Corporate Rules for the Transfer of Personal Data; Working Document setting up a table with the elements and principles to be found in Binding Corporate Rules, WP 153 (2008); Working Document Setting up a framework for the structure of Binding Corporate Rules, WP154 (2008); Working Document on Frequently Asked Questions (FAQs) related to Binding Corporate Rules, WP155 (2008).

6   See http://ec.europa.eu/justice/data-protection/international-transfers/binding-corporate-rules/index_en.htm; L Moerel, *Binding Corporate Rules, Corporate Self-Regulation of Global Data Transfers* (OUP, 2012).

within a related group of large multinational companies. It therefore, differs from the model contract clauses above which generally relate to non-related companies, rather than group companies.

Organisations which have contracts, policies and procedure which satisfy the BCR and are so accepted as doing so after a review process with the Commission or one of the national Data Protection Authorities can transfer personal data outside of the EU within the group organisation.

The WP29 has issued the following documents in relation to the BCR, namely:

- Working Document on Transfers of personal data to third countries: Applying Article 26 (2) of the EU Data Protection Directive to Binding Corporate Rules for International Data Transfers, 3 June 2003, WP 74;
- Model Checklist, Application for approval of Binding Corporate Rules, 25 November 2004, WP 102;
- Working Document Setting Forth a Co-Operation Procedure for Issuing Common Opinions on Adequate Safeguards Resulting From Binding Corporate Rules, 14 April 2005, WP 107;
- Working Document Establishing a Model Checklist Application for Approval of Binding Corporate Rules, 14 April 2005, WP 108;
- Recommendation 1/2007 on the Standard Application for Approval of Binding Corporate Rules for the Transfer of Personal Data;
- Working Document setting up a table with the elements and principles to be found in Binding Corporate Rules, 24 June 2008, WP 153;
- Working Document Setting up a framework for the structure of Binding Corporate Rules, 24 June 2008, WP 154;
- Working Document on Frequently Asked Questions (FAQs) related to Binding Corporate Rules, 24 June 2008.

The BCR[7] appear to be increasingly popular to large multinational organisation in relation to their data processing and data transfer compliance obligations. The ICO also refers to the BCR at:

- https://co.org.uk

It is envisaged that the popularity of the BCR option for exemption from the data protection regime transfer restrictions will increase. However,

---

7   See also L Moerel, *Binding Corporate Rules, Corporate Self-Regulation and Global Data Transfers* (OUP, 2012).

the review process with the Commission or one of the national Data Protection Authorities (such as the ICO) can take some time given the complexity involved.

DPD: Transfer Ban in Detail

23.08 DPD Article 25 refers to the principles. Article 25(1) provides that the Member States shall provide that the transfer to a third country of personal data which are undergoing processing or are intended for processing after transfer may take place only if, without prejudice to compliance with the national provisions, the third country in question ensures an adequate level of protection.

Article 25 (2) provides that the adequacy of the level of protection afforded by a third country shall be assessed in the light of all the circumstances surrounding a data transfer operation or set of data transfer operations. Particular consideration shall be given to the nature of the data, the purpose and duration of the proposed processing operation or operations, the country of origin and country of final destination, the rules of law, both general and sectoral, in force in the third country in question and the professional rules and security measures which are complied with in that country.

Article 25(3) provides that the Member States and the Commission shall inform each other of cases where they consider that a third country does not ensure an adequate level of protection within the meaning of Article 25(2).

Article 25 (4) provides that where the Commission finds, under the procedure provided for in Article 31(2), that a third country does not ensure an adequate level of protection within the meaning of Article 25(2), Member States shall take the measures necessary to prevent any transfer of data of the same type to the third country in question.

Article 25 (4) provides that at the appropriate time, the Commission shall enter into negotiations with a view to remedying the situation resulting from the finding made pursuant to Article 25(4).

Article 25(6) provides that the Commission may find, in accordance with the procedure referred to in Article 31(2), that a third country ensures an adequate level of protection within the meaning of Article 25(2), by reason of its domestic law or of the international commitments it has entered into, particularly upon conclusion of the negotiations referred to in Article 25(5), for the protection of the private lives and basic freedoms and rights of individuals. In addition, Member States shall take the measures necessary to comply with the Commission's decision.

GDPR: The New Transfers Regime

Transfers Restricted

23.09 Cross border data transfers are referred to in Recitals 6, 48, 101–103, 107, 108, 110–115, 153.

Data Chapter V of the new GDPR refers to data transfers and transfer of personal data to third countries or international organisations.

Any transfer of personal data which are undergoing processing or are intended for processing after transfer to a third country or to an international organisation shall only take place if, subject to the other provisions of the GDPR, the conditions laid down in this Chapter are complied with by the Controller and Processor, including for onward transfers of personal data from the third country or an international organisation to another third country or to another international organisation. All provisions in this Chapter shall be applied in order to ensure that the level of protection of natural persons guaranteed by the GDPR is not undermined (Article 44).

Transfers Restricted on Adequacy Decision

23.10 A transfer of personal data to a third country or an international organisation may take place where the Commission has decided that the third country, a territory or one or more specified sectors within that third country, or the international organisation in question ensures an adequate level of protection. Such transfer shall not require any specific authorisation (Article 45(1)).

When assessing the adequacy of the level of protection, the Commission shall, in particular, take account of the following elements:

- the rule of law, respect for human rights and fundamental freedoms, relevant legislation, both general and sectoral, including concerning public security, defence, national security and criminal law and the access of public authorities to personal data, as well as the implementation of such legislation, data protection rules, professional rules and security measures, including rules for onward transfer of personal data to another third country or international organisation, which are complied with in that country or international organisation, case law, as well as effective and enforceable Data Subject rights and effective administrative and judicial redress for the Data Subjects whose personal data are being transferred;
- the existence and effective functioning of one or more independent supervisory authorities in the third country or to which an international organisation is subject, with responsibility for ensuring and

enforcing compliance with the data protection rules, including adequate enforcement powers, for assisting and advising the Data Subjects in exercising their rights and for co-operation with the supervisory authorities of the Member States; and

- the international commitments the third country or international organisation concerned has entered into, or other obligations arising from legally binding conventions or instruments as well as from its participation in multilateral or regional systems, in particular in relation to the protection of personal data (Article 45(2)).

The Commission, after assessing the adequacy of the level of protection, may decide, by means of implementing act, that a third country, a territory or one or more specified sectors within a third country, or an international organisation ensures an adequate level of protection within the meaning of Article 45(3). The implementing act shall provide for a mechanism for a periodic review, at least every four years, which shall take into account all relevant developments in the third country or international organisation. The implementing act shall specify its territorial and sectorial application and, where applicable, identify the supervisory authority or authorities referred to in Article 45(2)(b). The implementing act shall be adopted in accordance with the examination procedure referred to in Article 93(2) (Article 45(3)).

The Commission shall, on an on-going basis, monitor developments in third countries and international organisations that could affect the functioning of decisions adopted pursuant to para 3 and decisions adopted on the basis of Article 25(6) of the DPD (Article 45(4)).

The Commission shall, where available information reveals, in particular following the review referred to in Article 45(3), that a third country, a territory or one or more specified sectors within a third country, or an international organisation no longer ensures an adequate level of protection within the meaning of Article 45(2), to the extent necessary, repeal, amend or suspend the decision referred to in Article 45(3) without retro-active effect. Those implementing acts shall be adopted in accordance with the examination procedure referred to in Article 87(2), or, in cases of extreme urgency, in accordance with the procedure referred to in Article 93(2) (Article 45(5)). On duly justified imperative grounds of urgency, the Commission shall adopt immediately applicable implementing acts in accordance with the procedure referred to in Article 93(3) (Article 45(5)).

The Commission shall enter into consultations with the third country or international organisation with a view to remedying the situation giving rise to the decision made pursuant to Article 45(5) (Article 45(6)).

A decision pursuant to paragraph 5 is without prejudice to transfers of personal data to the third country, territory or one or more specified sectors within that third country, or the international organisation in question pursuant to Articles 46 to 49 (Article 45(7)).

The Commission shall publish in the Official Journal of the EU and on its website a list of those third countries, territories and specified sectors within a third country and international organisations for which it has decided that an adequate level of protection is or is no longer ensured (Article 45(8)).

Decisions adopted by the Commission on the basis of Article 25(6) of the DPD shall remain in force until amended, replaced or repealed by a Commission Decision adopted in accordance with Article 45(3) or (5) (Article 45(9)).

Transfers Subject to Appropriate Safeguards

23.11 In the absence of a decision pursuant to Article 45(3), a Controller or Processor may transfer personal data to a third country or an international organisation only if the Controller or Processor has provided appropriate safeguards, and on condition that enforceable Data Subject rights and effective legal remedies for Data Subjects are available (Article 46(1)).

The appropriate safeguards referred to in Article 46(1) may be provided for, without requiring any specific authorisation from a supervisory authority, by:

- a legally binding and enforceable instrument between public authorities or bodies;
- binding corporate rules in accordance with Article 47;
- standard data protection clauses adopted by the Commission in accordance with the examination procedure referred to in Article 93(2); or
- standard data protection clauses adopted by a supervisory authority and approved by the Commission pursuant to the examination procedure referred to in Article 93(2); or
- an approved code of conduct pursuant to Article 40 together with binding and enforceable commitments of the Controller or Processor in the third country to apply the appropriate safeguards, including as regards Data Subjects' rights; or
- an approved certification mechanism pursuant to Article 42 together with binding and enforceable commitments of the Controller or Processor in the third country to apply the appropriate safeguards, including as regards Data Subjects' rights (Article 46(2)).

Subject to the authorisation from the competent supervisory authority, the appropriate safeguards referred to in Article 46(1) may also be provided for, in particular, by:

- contractual clauses between the Controller or Processor and the Controller, Processor or the recipient of the personal data in the third country or international organisation; or
- provisions to be inserted into administrative arrangements between public authorities or bodies which include enforceable and effective Data Subject rights (Article 46(3)).

The supervisory authority shall apply the consistency mechanism referred to in Article 63 in the cases referred to in Article 46(3) (Article 46(4)).

Authorisations by a Member State or supervisory authority on the basis of Article 26(2) of the DPD shall remain valid until amended, replaced or repealed, if necessary, by that supervisory authority. Decisions adopted by the Commission on the basis of Article 26(4) of the DPD shall remain in force until amended, replaced or repealed, if necessary, by a Commission Decision adopted in accordance with Article 46(2) (Article 42(5)).

Binding Corporate Rule

23.12 The competent supervisory authority shall approve binding corporate rules (BCR) in accordance with the consistency mechanism set out in Article 63, provided that they:

- are legally binding and apply to and are enforced by every member concerned of the group of undertakings or groups of enterprises engaged in a joint economic activity, including their employees;
- expressly confer enforceable rights on Data Subjects with regard to the processing of their personal data;
- fulfil the requirements laid down in Article 47(2) (Article 47(1)).

The binding corporate rules shall specify at least:

- the structure and contact details of the concerned group of undertakings or group of enterprises engaged in a joint economic activity and of each of its members;
- the data transfers or set of transfers, including the categories of personal data, the type of processing and its purposes, the type of Data Subjects affected and the identification of the third country or countries in question;
- their legally binding nature, both internally and externally;
- the application of the general data protection principles, in particular purpose limitation, data minimisation, limited storage periods, data

quality, data protection by design and by default (DPbD), legal basis for the processing, processing of special categories of personal data, measures to ensure data security, and the requirements in respect of onward transfers to bodies not bound by the binding corporate rules [d];

- the rights of Data Subjects in regard to processing and the means to exercise these rights, including the right not to be subject to decisions based solely on automated processing, including profiling in accordance with Article 22, the right to lodge a complaint before the competent supervisory authority and before the competent courts of the Member States in accordance with Article 79, and to obtain redress and, where appropriate, compensation for a breach of the binding corporate rules [e];

- the acceptance by the Controller or Processor established on the territory of a Member State of liability for any breaches of the binding corporate rules by any member concerned not established in the EU; the Controller or the Processor shall be exempted from this liability, in whole or in part, only if it proves that that member is not responsible for the event giving rise to the damage[f];

- how the information on the binding corporate rules, in particular on the provisions referred to in this Article 47(2)(d), (e) and (f) is provided to the Data Subjects in addition to Articles 13 and 14;

- the tasks of any DPO designated in accordance with Article 37 or any other person or entity in charge of the monitoring compliance with the binding corporate rules within the group of undertakings, or group of enterprises engaged in a joint economic activity, as well as monitoring the training and complaint handling;

- the complaint procedures;

- the mechanisms within the group of undertakings, or group of enterprises engaged in a joint economic activity, for ensuring the verification of compliance with the binding corporate rules. Such mechanisms shall include data protection audits and methods for ensuring corrective actions to protect the rights of the Data Subject. Results of such verification should be communicated to the person or entity referred under point (h) and to the board of the controlling undertaking or of the group of enterprises engaged in a joint economic activity, and should be available upon request to the competent supervisory authority [i];

- the mechanisms for reporting and recording changes to the rules and reporting these changes to the supervisory authority;

- the co-operation mechanism with the supervisory authority to ensure compliance by any member of the group of undertakings, or group of enterprises engaged in a joint economic activity, in particular by making available to the supervisory authority the results of verifications of the measures referred to in this Article 47(2)(j);

- the mechanisms for reporting to the competent supervisory authority any legal requirements to which a member of the group of undertakings, or group of enterprises engaged in a joint economic activity is subject in a third country which are likely to have a substantial adverse effect on the guarantees provided by the binding corporate rules; and
- the appropriate data protection training to personnel having permanent or regular access to personal data (Article 47(2)).

There may be future changes and requirements too. The Commission may specify the format and procedures for the exchange of information between Controllers, Processors and supervisory authorities for binding corporate rules. Those implementing acts shall be adopted in accordance with the examination procedure set out in Article 93(2) (Article 48(3)).

Transfers Not Authorised By EU Law

23.13   Any judgment of a court or tribunal and any decision of an administrative authority of a third country requiring a Controller or Processor to transfer or disclose personal data may only be recognised or enforceable in any manner if based on an international agreement, such as a mutual legal assistance treaty, in force between the requesting third country and the EU or a Member State, without prejudice to other grounds for transfer pursuant to this Chapter (Article 48).

Derogations

23.14   In the absence of an adequacy decision pursuant to Article 45(3), or of appropriate safeguards pursuant to Article 46, including binding corporate rules, a transfer or a set of transfers of personal data to a third country or an international organisation shall take place only on one of the following conditions:

- the Data Subject has explicitly consented to the proposed transfer, after having been informed of the possible risks of such transfers for the Data Subject due to the absence of an adequacy decision and appropriate safeguards; [a]
- the transfer is necessary for the performance of a contract between the Data Subject and the Controller or the implementation of pre-contractual measures taken at the Data Subject's request; [b]
- the transfer is necessary for the conclusion or performance of a contract concluded in the interest of the Data Subject between the Controller and another natural or legal person; [c]
- the transfer is necessary for important reasons of public interest;

- the transfer is necessary for the establishment, exercise or defence of legal claims;
- the transfer is necessary in order to protect the vital interests of the Data Subject or of other persons, where the Data Subject is physically or legally incapable of giving consent;
- the transfer is made from a register which according to EU or Member State law is intended to provide information to the public and which is open to consultation either by the public in general or by any person who can demonstrate a legitimate interest, but only to the extent that the conditions laid down in EU or Member State law for consultation are fulfilled in the particular case. [g]

Where a transfer could not be based on a provision in Articles 45 or 46, including the provision of binding corporate rules, and none of the derogations for a specific situation pursuant to para (1) is applicable, a transfer to a third country or an international organisation may take place only if the transfer is not repetitive, concerns only a limited number of Data Subjects, is necessary for the purposes of compelling legitimate interests pursued by the Controller which are not overridden by the interests or rights and freedoms of the Data Subject, and the Controller has assessed all the circumstances surrounding the data transfer and has on the basis of that assessment provided suitable safeguards with respect to the protection of personal data. The Controller shall inform the supervisory authority of the transfer. The Controller shall in addition to the information referred to in Article 13 and Article 14, inform the Data Subject about the transfer and on the compelling legitimate interests pursued by the Controller (Article 49(1)). [h]

A transfer pursuant to paragraph Article 49(1)(g) shall not involve the entirety of the personal data or entire categories of the personal data contained in the register. Where the register is intended for consultation by persons having a legitimate interest, the transfer shall be made only at the request of those persons or if they are to be the recipients (Article 49(2)).

Article 49(1)(a), (b) and(c) and para (2) shall not apply to activities carried out by public authorities in the exercise of their public powers (Article 49(3)).

The public interest referred to in Article 49(1)(g) shall be recognised in EU law or in the law of the Member State to which the Controller is subject (Article 49(5)).

In the absence of an adequacy decision, EU law or Member State law may, for important reasons of public interest, expressly set limits to the transfer of specific categories of personal data to a third country or an international organisation. Member States shall notify such provisions to the Commission (Article 49(5)).

The Controller or Processor shall document the assessment as well as the suitable safeguards referred to in Article 49(1)(second subparagraph) in the records referred to in Article 30 (Article 44(6)).

International Cooperation

23.15 In relation to third countries and international organisations, the Commission and supervisory authorities shall take appropriate steps to:

- develop international co-operation mechanisms to facilitate the effective enforcement of legislation for the protection of personal data;
- provide international mutual assistance in the enforcement of legislation for the protection of personal data, including through notification, complaint referral, investigative assistance and information exchange, subject to appropriate safeguards for the protection of personal data and other fundamental rights and freedoms;
- engage relevant stakeholders in discussion and activities aimed at furthering international co-operation in the enforcement of legislation for the protection of personal data;
- promote the exchange and documentation of personal data protection legislation and practice, including on jurisdictional conflicts with third countries (Article 50).

DPD

Derogations

23.16 Article 26 of the DPD refers to derogations. Article 26(1) provides that by way of derogation from Article 25, Member States shall provide that a transfer or a set of transfers of personal data to a third country which does not ensure an adequate level of protection within the meaning of Article 25(2) may take place on condition that:

- the Data Subject has given their consent unambiguously to the proposed transfer; or
- the transfer is necessary for the performance of a contract between the Data Subject and the Controller or the implementation of pre-contractual measures taken in response to the Data Subject's request; or
- the transfer is necessary for the conclusion or performance of a contract concluded in the interest of the Data Subject between the Controller and a third party; or

- the transfer is necessary or legally required on important public interest grounds, or for the establishment, exercise or defence of legal claims; or
- the transfer is necessary in order to protect the vital interests of the Data Subject; or
- the transfer is made from a register which according to laws or regulations is intended to provide information to the public and which is open to consultation either by the public in general or by any person who can demonstrate legitimate interest, to the extent that the conditions laid down in law for consultation are fulfilled in the particular case.

Article 26(2) provides that without prejudice to Article 26(1), a Member State may authorise a transfer or a set of transfers of personal data to a third country which does not ensure an adequate level of protection within the meaning of Article 25(2), where the Controller adduces adequate safeguards with respect to the protection of the privacy and fundamental rights and freedoms of individuals and as regards the exercise of the corresponding rights. Such safeguards may in particular result from appropriate contractual clauses.

Article 26(3) provides that the Member State shall inform the Commission and the other Member States of the authorisations it grants pursuant to Article 26(2). If a Member State or the Commission objects on justified grounds involving the protection of the privacy and fundamental rights and freedoms of individuals, the Commission shall take appropriate measures in accordance with the procedure laid down in Article 31(2). Member States shall take the necessary measures to comply with the Commission's decision.

Article 26(4) provides that where the Commission decides, in accordance with the procedure referred to in Article 31(2), that certain standard contractual clauses offer sufficient safeguards as required by Article 26(2), Member States shall take the necessary measures to comply with the Commission's decision.

GDPR

23.17 Chapter III, Section 5 of the new GDPR refers to Restrictions. EU or Member State law to which the Controller or Processor is subject may restrict by way of a legislative measure the scope of the obligations and rights provided for in Articles 12 to 22 and Article 34, as well as Article 5 in so far as its provisions correspond to the rights and obligations provided for in Articles 12 to 20, when such a restriction respects the essence of the fundamental rights and freedoms and is a necessary and proportionate measure in a democratic society to safeguard:

- national security [a];
- defence [b];
- public security [c];
- the prevention, investigation, detection or prosecution of criminal offences or the execution of criminal penalties, including the safe-guarding against and the prevention of threats to public security [d];
- other important objectives of general public interests of EU or of a Member State, in particular an important economic or financial interest of EU or of a Member State, including monetary, budgetary and taxation matters, public health and social security [e];
- the protection of judicial independence and judicial proceedings;
- the prevention, investigation, detection and prosecution of breaches of ethics for regulated professions [g];
- a monitoring, inspection or regulatory function connected, even occasionally, to the exercise of official authority in cases referred to in (a) to (e) and (g);
- the protection of the Data Subject or the rights and freedoms of others;
- the enforcement of civil law claims (Article 23(1)).

In particular, any legislative measure referred to in Article 23(1) shall contain specific provisions at least, where relevant, as to:

- the purposes of the processing or categories of processing;
- the categories of personal data;
- the scope of the restrictions introduced;
- the safeguards to prevent abuse or unlawful access or transfer;
- the specification of the Controller or categories of Controllers;
- the storage periods and the applicable safeguards taking into account the nature, scope and purposes of the processing or categories of processing;
- the risks for the rights and freedoms of Data Subjects; and
- the right of Data Subjects to be informed about the restriction, unless this may be prejudicial to the purpose of the restriction (Article 23(2)).

Issues

23.18   Certain issues may arise in relation to:

- What is a 'transfer'? Is there a difference between transfer versus transit?

- 'Data' and anonymised data, is there a restriction on TBDFs of anonymised data? For example, can certain anonymised data fall outside the definition of personal data?
- 'Third country' currently includes the EU countries and EEA countries of Iceland, Norway, Liechtenstein. The EU countries are expanding over time. In addition, the list of permitted additional third countries is also expanding over time, for example, safe harbour.
- How the Safe Harbour transfer problem will be resolved after the Court of Justice struck down the original EU–US Safe Harbour data transfer agreement, and the proposed EU-US Privacy Shield replacement.[8] Many organisations used this as the legitimising basis for the lawful transfer of personal data from the EU to the US.

Establishing if the Ban Applies

23.19   Assessing if the export ban applies, includes asking the following questions:

- Does the organisation wish to transfer personal data?
- Is there a transfer to a 'third country'?
- Does that third country have an adequate level of protection?
- Does it involve transfers to the US – Privacy Shield/Safe Harbour or other transfer mechanism?
- Does it involve white list countries?
- What constitutes adequacy?
- What is the nature of the data?
- How is it to be used?
- What laws and practices are in place in the third country?
- Is it a transfer by Controller to Processor? Under Article 7 of the DPD such a transfer requires a contract to be put in place relating to security measures to date. The Controller retains control of the personal data so that the risk to the Data Subject is minimal. Contracts may still be required;
- Are they transfers within an international or multinational company or group of companies where an internal privacy code or agreement is in place?
- Are they transfers within a consortium established to process international transactions, for example, banking?

---

8   *Digital Rights Ireland and Seitlinger and Others*, Joined Cases C-293/12 and C-594/12, Court of Justice, 8 April 2014.

- Are they transfers between professionals such as lawyers or accountants where a clients business has on international dimension?
- The European Commission has identified core principles which must be present in the foreign laws or codes of practice or regulations in order to achieve the requisite standard of 'adequacy' in third party countries – are these principles present?
- Has the personal data been processed for a specific purpose?
- Is the personal data accurate and up to date?
- Has the Data Subject been provided with adequate information in relation to the transfer?
- Have technical and organisational security measures been taken by the Controller?
- Is there a right of access to the data by the Data Subject?
- Is there a prohibition on onward transfer of data?
- Is there an effective procedure or mode of enforcement?

Contracts, consent and binding corporate rules take on a new significance as the concepts of permissibility and adequacy receive renewed scrutiny. Given the controversy and striking out of the EU-US Safe Harbour arrangement, all Controllers engaged in processing, and those considering transfers, should very carefully consider all of the implications, current changes and the potential for change and additional measures in the short to medium term. For example, while official policymakers have agreed proposals for the EU-US Privacy Shield, the WP29 suggests further clarity, if not amendment. The Commission, and WP29 or the new EDPB, are likely to consider transfer legitimising mechanisms in future.

Checklist for Compliance

23.20 Organisations should consider the following queries:

- Does the organisation transfer customer, etc personal data outside of that EEA?
- Is there a transfer to the US? If so, is the recipient of the data a safe harbour recipient? If yes, then the organisation can transfer the data. If not, the organisation needs to: (i) assess the adequacy of the protection measures in place; (ii) see if that transfer is exempted; (iii) create adequacy through consent or appropriate contract.
- Is the recipient country a Commission permitted white list country? If so, transfer is permitted.
- Are there data protection rules in place or codes of practice and if so did they incorporate the adequate and equivalent protections?

- If there is inadequate protection is it practical to obtain the consent of the Data Subject?
- If not, then is it practical to enter into an appropriate contract with the recipient?
- Are the Commission model data contract clauses is available?

The ICO also asks:

1. Does the organisation need to transfer personal data abroad?
2. Is the organisation transferring the personal data to a country outside of the EEA or will it just be in transit through a non-EEA country?
3. Has the organisation complied with all the other Data Protection Principles?
4. Is the transfer to a country on the EU Commission's white list of countries or territories (per a Community finding) accepted as providing adequate levels of protection for the rights and freedoms of Data Subjects in connection with the processing of their personal data?
5. If the transfer is to the US, has the US recipient of the personal data signed up to the EU-US Department of Commerce Safe Harbour scheme [or the replacement EU-US Privacy Shield or any alternative mechanism]?
6. Is the personal data passenger name record information (PNR)? If so, particular rules may apply.
8. Can the organisation assess that the level of protection for Data Subjects' rights as 'adequate in all the circumstances of the case'?.
9. If not, can the organisation put in place adequate safeguards to protect the rights of the Data Subjects whose data is to be transferred?
10. Can the organisation rely on another exception from the restriction on international transfers of personal data?

Conclusion

23.21 Data protection compliance practice for organisations means that they will have to include a compliance assessment, as well as an assessment of associated risks, in relation to potential transfers of personal data outside of the EEA. This applies to transfers from parent to subsidiary or to a branch office as well as transfers to any unrelated company or entity.

The ICO also provides useful guidance in relation to:

- Assessing Adequacy;
- Model Contract Clauses;

- Binding Corporate Rules; and
- Outsourcing.

There is also the following ICO guidance which can be a useful reference for organisations, namely, the:

Data Protection Act 1998,
The Eighth Data Protection Principle and International Data Transfers,
The Information Commissioner's Recommended Approach to Assessing Adequacy Including Consideration of the Issue of Contractual Solutions, Binding Corporate Rules and Safe Harbour.

Organisations should be aware that if they wish to transfer personal data outside of the EEA, that additional considerations arise and that unless there is a specific exemption, then the transfer may not be permitted. Once a transfer possibility arises, the organisation should undertake a compliance exercise to assess if the transfer can be permitted, and if so, how. Additional compliance documentation and contracts may be required.

The increasing locations and methods by which personal data may be collected by organisations, in particular internet, communications and social media, will increasingly be scrutinised in terms of transparency, consent and compliance. Equally, cloud computing is receiving particular data protection attention. Apps are also being considered as is the developing area of the Internet of Things (IoT) and related data protection compliance issues.

Chapter 24

ePrivacy and Electronic Communications

Introduction

24.01 There is increasing use of electronically transmitted personal data. This is protected and regulated, in certain respects, separate from the general data protection regime under the DPD (and forthcoming GDPR).

While originally the regulation of telecommunications related personal data centred on telecoms companies, it is now recognised as encompassing telecoms companies and certain companies engaged in activities involving the collection or transmission of particular personal data over electronic communications networks, including the internet.

Organisations concerned with compliance relating to marketing, email marketing, text marketing, telephone marketing, fax marketing, the use of location based data, cookies, identification regarding telephone calls and other telephone issues need to consider the additional data protection rules.

The GDPR indicates that it shall not impose additional obligations on natural or legal persons in relation to the processing of personal data in connection with the provision of publicly available electronic communications services in public communication networks in the EU in relation to matters for which they are subject to specific obligations with the same objective set out in Directive 2002/58/EC[1] (Article 89).

However, other Directives may be reviewed in terms of amendments required in order to smoothly comply with the GDPR.

---

1   Directive 2002/58/EC of the European Parliament and of the Council of 12 July 2002 concerning the processing of personal data and the protection of privacy in the electronic communications sector (Directive on privacy and electronic communications).

Background

24.02 There has been a separation between the data protection of general personal data, in the DPD, and the regulation of personal data in (tele)communications networks. The later were legislated for in the Data Protection Directive of 1997.[2] This was later replaced with the ePrivacy Directive (ePD). More recently, the ePD was amended by Directive 2006/24/EC and Directive 2009/136/EC.

ePD[3] concerns the processing and protection of personal data and privacy in the electronic communications sector. It is also known as the Directive on privacy and electronic communications, hence ePD. One of the concerns has been how electronic communications and electronic information are increasingly used for profiling for marketing purposes, including by electronic means.[4] (Indeed, this is also reflected in the new cookie rules mentioned earlier).

Scope of the ePD

24.03 The ePD broadly relates to and encompasses the following, namely:

* definitions;
* security;
* confidentiality;
* traffic data;
* non itemised bills;
* call and connected line identification;
* location data;
* exceptions;
* directories;
* unsolicited communications;
* technical features.

It also provides rules in relation to:

* email marketing;
* text marketing;
* telephone marketing;
* fax marketing;
* cookies, etc (see above also, Chapter 21).

---

2   Directive 97/66/EC.
3   Directive 2002/58/EC of 12 July 2002.
4   See, for example, W McGeveran, 'Disclosure, Endorsement, and Identity in Social Marketing,' *University of Illinois Law Review* (2009) (4) 1105–1166.

Marketing

24.04 How should organisations go about ensuring data protection compliance for direct marketing (DM)? When is DM permitted? All organisations should carefully assess compliance issues when considering any direct marketing activities. Getting it wrong can be costly and can have ICO enforcement and investigation consequences as well as penalties.

Article 13 of the ePD refers to unsolicited communications. Article 13(1) in particular provides that the use of the following, namely:

- automated calling systems without human intervention (automatic calling machines);
- facsimile machines (fax); or
- electronic mail,

for the purposes of direct marketing may *only* be allowed in respect of subscribers who have given their *prior consent*.

This means that there is a default rule prohibiting DM without prior consent. Many marketing orientated organisations may be surprised, if not dismayed by this.

Existing Customers' Email

24.05 However, in the context of existing customers, there is a possibility to direct market using emails. Article 13(2) of the ePD provides that notwithstanding Article 13(1), where an organisation obtains from its customers their electronic contact details for email, in the context of the sale of a product or a service, in accordance with the DPD, the organisation may use these electronic contact details for DM of its own similar products or services provided that customers clearly and distinctly are given the opportunity to object, free of charge and in an easy manner, to such use of electronic contact details when they are collected and on the occasion of each message in case the customer has not initially refused such use.

Therefore, once the email details are obtained at the time of a product or service transaction, it will be possible to use that email for direct marketing purposes. Conditions or limitations apply however. Firstly, the organisation is only permitted to market and promote similar products or services. This, therefore, rules out unrelated, non-identical and non-similar products and services. Secondly, at the time of each subsequent act of DM, the customer must be given the opportunity in an easy manner to opt-out or cancel the DM. Effectively, they must be taken off the DM list.

National Opt-out Registers

24.06 Article 13(3) of ePD provides that Member States shall take appropriate measures to ensure that, free of charge, unsolicited communications for purposes of direct marketing, in cases other than those referred to in paras 1 and 2, are not allowed either without the consent of the subscribers concerned or in respect of subscribers who do not wish to receive these communications, the choice between these options to be determined by national legislation. This means that each Member State must determine and provide a means for individuals to opt-out of receiving DM in advance.[5]

Marketing Emails Must Not Conceal Their Identity

24.07 Article 13(4) of ePD provides that the practice of sending electronic mail for purposes of DM disguising or concealing the identity of the sender on whose behalf the communication is made shall be prohibited. This means that organisations cannot conceal their identity if permitted to engage in direct marketing. If these are not complied with, what might otherwise be permissible DM can be deemed to be impermissible. Complaints, investigations or enforcement proceedings can thus arise.

Marketing Emails Must Have an Opt-Out

24.08 In addition, Article 13(4) of ePD provides that the practice of sending electronic mail for purposes of DM without a valid address to which the recipient may send a request that such communications cease, shall be prohibited. This means that organisations must also include an easy contact address or other details at which the recipient can contact if they wish to object to receiving any further DM. If these are not complied with, what might otherwise be permissible DM can be deemed to be impermissible. Complaints, investigations or enforcement proceedings can thus also arise.

Marketing Protection for Organisations: ePD

24.09 Article 13(5) of ePD provides that Article 13(1) and (3) shall apply to subscribers who are natural persons. Member States shall also ensure, in the framework of EU law and applicable national legislation, that the legitimate interests of subscribers other than natural persons with regard to unsolicited communications are sufficiently protected.

---

5   See ICO, *Marketing*, at https://ico.org.uk.

This means that protection from unsolicited DM can also be extended to organisations.

Background

24.10 As with the DPD, the Recitals provide background, purpose and interpretation of the Directive. This includes:

- requiring respect of fundamental rights and the Charter of Fundamental Rights of the EU (Recital 2);
- guaranteeing the confidentiality of communications (Recital 3);
- the internet, new possibilities for users and new risks for personal data and privacy (Recital 6);
- specific legal, regulatory and technical provisions to protect fundamental rights and freedoms of natural persons and legitimate interests of legal persons, in particular with regard to increasing capacity for automated data storage and processing of subscriber and user data (Recital 7);
- protection of the fundamental rights of natural persons (particularly privacy, and the legitimate interests of legal persons) (Recital 12);
- location data (Recital 14);
- consent (Recital 17);
- value added services (VAS) (Recital 18);
- appropriate security measures; informing subscribers of any special risks of a security breach; informing subscribers and users of existing security risks; informing users and subscribers of measures they can take to protect the security of their communications (eg specific types of software or encryption); and which does not discharge a service provider of the obligation to take, at its own costs, appropriate and immediate measures to remedy any new, unforeseen security risks and restore the normal security level of the service (Recital 20);
- measures to prevent unauthorised access (Recital 21);
- prohibition of storage of communications and the related traffic data (Recital 22);
- confidentiality of communications and lawful business practice (Recital 23);
- spyware, web bugs, hidden identifiers and other similar devices (Recital 24);
- 'cookies' (Recital 25);
- data relating to subscribers processed within electronic communications networks to establish connections and to transmit or contain information on the private life of natural persons and recognising concern for the right to respect for their correspondence and concern the legitimate interests of legal persons (ie companies) and that data may only be stored to the extent that is necessary for the provision

of the service for the purpose of billing and for interconnection payments, and for a limited time (any further processing, for marketing or value added services, may only be allowed if the subscriber has agreed to this on the basis of accurate and full information given by the provider about the types of further processing and the subscriber's right not to give or to withdraw his/her consent – traffic data used for marketing communications services or for the provision of value added services should also be erased or made anonymous after the provision of the service); service providers should always keep subscribers informed of the types of data they are processing and the purposes and duration for which this is done (Recital 26);

- consent to be obtained (Recital 31);
- subcontracting (Recital 32);
- call line identification (Recital 34);
- mobile location data (Recital 35);
- safeguards (Recital 37);
- directories (Recitals 38, 39, 40);
- limited offering of similar products or services (Recital 41);
- other forms of direct marketing (Recital 42);
- unsolicited messages for direct marketing (Recital 43);
- opt-out registers (Recital 45);
- the protection of personal data and the privacy of the user (Recital 46);
- where the rights of users and subscribers are not respected, national legislation should provide for judicial remedies. Penalties should be imposed for failure to comply (Recital 47).

Scope

24.11 ePD Article 1 refers to the scope and aim of the Directive. Article 1(1) provides that the Directive harmonises the provisions of the Member States to ensure an equivalent level of protection of fundamental rights and freedoms, and in particular the right to privacy, with respect to the processing of personal data in the electronic communication sector and to ensure the free movement of such data and of electronic communication equipment and services in the EU.

Article 1(2) provides that the provisions of the Directive particularise and complement Directive 95/46/EC for the purposes mentioned in Article 1(1). Moreover, they provide for protection of the legitimate interests of subscribers who are legal persons.

Article 1(3) provides that the ePD shall not apply to activities which fall outside the scope of the Treaty establishing the European Community, such as those covered by Titles V and VI of the Treaty on

EU, and in any case to activities concerning public security, defence, State security (including the economic well-being of the State when the activities relate to State security matters) and the activities of the State in areas of criminal law.

Definitions

24.12 Article 2 of the ePD refers to definitions. The definitions in the DPD and in the ePD shall apply. The following additional definitions shall also apply:

'user'	means any natural person using a publicly available electronic communications service, for private or business purposes, without necessarily having subscribed to this service;
'traffic data'	means any data processed for the purpose of the conveyance of a communication on an electronic communications network or for the billing thereof;
'location data'	means any data processed in an electronic communications network, indicating the geographic position of the terminal equipment of a user of a publicly available electronic communications service;
'communication'	means any information exchanged or conveyed between a finite number of parties by means of a publicly available electronic communications service. This does not include any information conveyed as part of a broadcasting service to the public over an electronic communications network except to the extent that the information can be related to the identifiable subscriber or user receiving the information;
'call'	means a connection established by means of a publicly available telephone service allowing two-way communication in real time;
'consent'	by a user or subscriber corresponds to the Data Subject's consent in the DPD;
'value added service'	means any service which requires the processing of traffic data or location data other than traffic data beyond what is necessary for the transmission of a communication or the billing thereof;
'electronic mail'	means any text, voice, sound or image message sent over a public communications network which can be stored in the network or in the recipient's terminal equipment until it is collected by the recipient.

Services

24.13 Article 3 relates to the services concerned. Article 3(1) provides that the ePD shall apply to the processing of personal data in connection with the provision of publicly available electronic communications services in public communications networks in the EU.

Article 3(2) provides that Articles 8, 10 and 11 shall apply to subscriber lines connected to digital exchanges and, where technically possible and if it does not require a disproportionate economic effort, to subscriber lines connected to analogue exchanges.

Article 3(3) provides that cases where it would be technically impossible or require a disproportionate economic effort to fulfil the requirements of Articles 8, 10 and 11 shall be notified to the Commission by the Member States.

Unsolicited Communications

24.14 Article 13 refers to unsolicited communications. Article 13(1) provides that the use of automated calling systems without human intervention (automatic calling machines), facsimile machines (fax) or electronic mail for the purposes of direct marketing may only be allowed in respect of subscribers who have given their prior consent.

Article 13(2) provides that notwithstanding Article 13(1), where a natural or legal person obtains from its customers their electronic contact details for electronic mail, in the context of the sale of a product or a service, in accordance with the DPD, the same natural or legal person may use these electronic contact details for direct marketing of its own similar products or services provided that customers clearly and distinctly are given the opportunity to object, free of charge and in an easy manner, to such use of electronic contact details when they are collected and on the occasion of each message in case the customer has not initially refused such use.

Article 13(3) provides that Member States shall take appropriate measures to ensure that, free of charge, unsolicited communications for purposes of direct marketing, in cases other than those referred to in Article 13(1) and (2), are not allowed either without the consent of the subscribers concerned or in respect of subscribers who do not wish to receive these communications, the choice between these options to be determined by national legislation.

Article 13(4) provides that in any event, the practice of sending electronic mail for purposes of direct marketing disguising or concealing the identity of the sender on whose behalf the communication is made, or without a valid address to which the recipient may send a request that such communications cease, shall be prohibited.

Article 13(5) provides that Article 13(1) and (3) shall apply to subscribers who are natural persons. Member States shall also ensure, in the framework of EU law and applicable national legislation, that the legitimate interests of subscribers other than natural persons with regard to unsolicited communications are sufficiently protected.

Security

24.15 Article 4 relates to security. Article 4(1) provides that the provider of a publicly available electronic communications service must take appropriate technical and organisational measures to safeguard security of its services, if necessary in conjunction with the provider of the public communications network with respect to network security. Having regard to the state of the art and the cost of their implementation, these measures shall ensure a level of security appropriate to the risk presented. Obviously, these can change over time as risks and as technology change.

Article 4(2) provides that in case of a particular risk of a breach of the security of the network, the provider of a publicly available electronic communications service must inform the subscribers concerning such risk and, where the risk lies outside the scope of the measures to be taken by the service provider, of any possible remedies, including an indication of the likely costs involved.

Confidentiality

24.16 Article 5 refers to confidentiality of the communications. Article 5(1) provides that Member States shall ensure the confidentiality of communications and the related traffic data by means of a public communications network and publicly available electronic communications services, through national legislation. In particular, they shall prohibit listening, tapping, storage or other kinds of interception or surveillance of communications and the related traffic data by persons other than users, without the consent of the users concerned, except when legally authorised to do so in accordance with Article 15(1). This paragraph shall not prevent technical storage which is necessary for the conveyance of a communication without prejudice to the principle of confidentiality.

Article 5(2) provides that para 1 shall not affect any legally authorised recording of communications and the related traffic data when carried out in the course of lawful business practice for the purpose of providing evidence of a commercial transaction or of any other business communication.

Article 5(3) provides that Member States shall ensure that the use of electronic communications networks to store information or to gain access to information stored in the terminal equipment of a subscriber or user is only allowed on condition that the subscriber or user concerned is provided with clear and comprehensive information in accordance with the DPD, inter alia about the purposes of the processing, and is offered the right to refuse such processing by the Controller. This shall not prevent any technical storage or access for the sole purpose of carrying out or facilitating the transmission of a communication over an electronic communications network, or as strictly necessary in order to provide an information society service explicitly requested by the subscriber or user.

Traffic Data

24.17 Article 6 refers to traffic data. Article 6(1) provides that traffic data relating to subscribers and users processed and stored by the provider of a public communications network or publicly available electronic communications service must be erased or made anonymous when it is no longer needed for the purpose of the transmission of a communication without prejudice to Article 6(2), (3) and (5) and Article 15(1).

Article 6(2) provides that traffic data necessary for the purposes of subscriber billing and interconnection payments may be processed. Such processing is permissible only up to the end of the period during which the bill may lawfully be challenged or payment pursued.

Article 6(3) provides that for the purpose of marketing electronic communications services or for the provision of value added services, the provider of a publicly available electronic communications service may process the data referred to in Article 6(1) to the extent and for the duration necessary for such services or marketing, if the subscriber or user to whom the data relate has given his/her consent. Users or subscribers shall be given the possibility to withdraw their consent for the processing of traffic data at any time.

Article 6(3) provides that the service provider must inform the subscriber or user of the types of traffic data which are processed and of the duration of such processing for the purposes mentioned in Article 6(2) and, prior to obtaining consent, for the purposes mentioned in Article 6(3).

Article 6(3) provides that processing of traffic data, in accordance with Article 6(1), (2), (3) and (4), must be restricted to persons acting under the authority of providers of the public communications networks and publicly available electronic communications services handling billing or traffic management, customer enquiries, fraud detection, marketing electronic communications services or providing a value added service, and must be restricted to what is necessary for the purposes of such activities.

Article 6(6) provides that Articles 6(1), (2), (3) and (5) shall apply without prejudice to the possibility for competent bodies to be informed of traffic data in conformity with applicable legislation with a view to settling disputes, in particular interconnection or billing disputes.

Non-Itemised Billing

24.18 Article 7 relates to itemised billing. Article 7(1) provides that subscribers shall have the right to receive non-itemised bills. Article 7(2) provides that Member States shall apply national provisions in order to reconcile the rights of subscribers receiving itemised bills with the right to privacy of calling users and called subscribers, for example by ensuring that sufficient alternative privacy enhancing methods of communications or payments are available to such users and subscribers.

Calling and Connected Line Identification

24.19 Article 8 relates to presentation and restriction of calling and connected line identification. Article 8(1) provides that where presentation of calling line identification is offered, the service provider must offer the calling user the possibility, using a simple means and free of charge, of preventing the presentation of the calling line identification on a per-call basis. The calling subscriber must have this possibility on a per-line basis.

Article 8(2) provides that where presentation of calling line identification is offered, the service provider must offer the called subscriber the possibility, using a simple means and free of charge for reasonable use of this function, of preventing the presentation of the calling line identification of incoming calls.

Article 8(3) provides that where presentation of calling line identification is offered and where the calling line identification is presented prior to the call being established, the service provider must offer the called subscriber the possibility, using a simple means, of rejecting incoming calls where the presentation of the calling line identification has been prevented by the calling user or subscriber.

Article 8(4) provides that where presentation of connected line identification is offered, the service provider must offer the called subscriber the possibility, using a simple means and free of charge, of preventing the presentation of the connected line identification to the calling user.

Article 8(5) provides that Article 8(1) shall also apply with regard to calls to third countries originating in the EU. Paragraphs (2), (3) and (4) shall also apply to incoming calls originating in third countries.

Article 8(6) provides that Member States shall ensure that where presentation of calling and/or connected line identification is offered, the providers of publicly available electronic communications services inform the public thereof and of the possibilities set out in paras (1), (2), (3) and (4).

Location Data other than Traffic Data

24.20 Article 9 of the ePD relates to location data other than traffic data. Article 9(1) provides that where location data other than traffic data, relating to users or subscribers of public communications networks or publicly available electronic communications services, can be processed, such data may only be processed when they are made anonymous, or with the *consent* of the users or subscribers to the extent and for the duration necessary for the provision of a value added service. The service provider must inform the users or subscribers, prior to obtaining their consent, of the type of location data other than traffic data which will be processed, of the purposes and duration of the processing and whether the data will be transmitted to a third party for the purpose of providing the value added service. Users or subscribers shall be given the possibility to withdraw their consent for the processing of location data other than traffic data at any time.

This is increasingly important as more and more smart phones and electronic devices permit the capture of location based data relating to individuals and/or their personal equipment.

Article 9(1) provides that where consent of the users or subscribers has been obtained for the processing of location data other than traffic data, the user or subscriber must continue to have the possibility, using a simple means and free of charge, of temporarily refusing the processing of such data for each connection to the network or for each transmission of a communication.

Article 9(1) provides that processing of location data other than traffic data in accordance with Articles 9(1) and (2) must be restricted to persons acting under the authority of the provider of the public communications network or publicly available communications service or of the third party providing the value added service, and must be restricted to what is necessary for the purposes of providing the value added service.

Exceptions

24.21 Article 10 relates to exceptions. Member States shall ensure that there are transparent procedures governing the way in which a provider of a public communications network and/or a publicly available electronic communications service may override:

- the elimination of the presentation of calling line identification, on a temporary basis, upon application of a subscriber requesting the tracing of malicious or nuisance calls. In this case, the data containing the identification of the calling subscriber will be stored and be made available by the provider of a public communications network and/or publicly available electronic communications service;

- the elimination of the presentation of calling line identification and the temporary denial or absence of consent of a subscriber or user for the processing of location data, on a per-line basis for organisations dealing with emergency calls and recognised as such by a Member State, including law enforcement agencies, ambulance services and fire brigades, for the purpose of responding to such calls.

Article 11 refers to automatic call forwarding. It provides that Member States shall ensure that any subscriber has the possibility, using a simple means and free of charge, of stopping automatic call forwarding by a third party to the subscriber's terminal.

Directories

24.22 Article 12 refers to directories of subscribers. Article 12(1) provides that Member States shall ensure that subscribers are informed, free of charge and before they are included in the directory, about the purpose(s) of a printed or electronic directory of subscribers available to the public or obtainable through directory enquiry services, in which their personal data can be included and of any further usage possibilities based on search functions embedded in electronic versions of the directory.

Article 12(2) provides that Member States shall ensure that subscribers are given the opportunity to determine whether their personal data are included in a public directory, and if so, which, to the extent that such data are relevant for the purpose of the directory as determined by the provider of the directory, and to verify, correct or withdraw such data. Not being included in a public subscriber directory, verifying, correcting or withdrawing personal data from it shall be free of charge.

Article 12(3) provides that Member States may require that for any purpose of a public directory other than the search of contact details of persons on the basis of their name and, where necessary, a minimum of other identifiers, additional consent be asked of the subscribers.

Article 12(4) provides that Articles 12(1) and (2) shall apply to subscribers who are natural persons. Member States shall also ensure, in the framework of EU law and applicable national legislation, that the legitimate interests of subscribers other than natural persons with regard to their entry in public directories are sufficiently protected.

Technical Features

24.23 ePD Article 14 refers to technical features and standardisation. Article 14(1) provides that in implementing the provisions of this

Directive, Member States shall ensure, subject to Articles 14(2) and (3), that no mandatory requirements for specific technical features are imposed on terminal or other electronic communication equipment which could impede the placing of equipment on the market and the free circulation of such equipment in and between Member States.

Article 14(2) provides that where provisions of this Directive can be implemented only by requiring specific technical features in electronic communications networks, Member States shall inform the Commission in accordance with the procedure provided for by Directive 98/34/EC laying down a procedure for the provision of information in the field of technical standards and regulations and of rules on information society services.

Article 14(3) provides that where required, measures may be adopted to ensure that terminal equipment is constructed in a way that is compatible with the right of users to protect and control the use of their personal data, in accordance with Directive 1999/5/EC and Council Decision 87/95/EEC on standardisation in the field of information technology and communications.

ePD and DPD

24.24   Article 15 refers to application of certain provisions of the DPD. Article 15(1) provides that Member States may adopt legislative measures to restrict the scope of the rights and obligations provided for in Article 5, Article 6, Article 8(1), (2), (3) and (4), and Article 9 of the ePD when such restriction constitutes a necessary, appropriate and proportionate measure within a democratic society to safeguard national security (ie State security), defence, public security, and the prevention, investigation, detection and prosecution of criminal offences or of unauthorised use of the electronic communication system, as referred to in Article 13(1) of the DPD. To this end, Member States may, inter alia, adopt legislative measures providing for the retention of data for a limited period justified on the grounds laid down in this paragraph. All the measures referred to in this paragraph shall be in accordance with the general principles of EU law, including those referred to in Article 6(1) and (2) of the Treaty on EU.

Article 15(1) provides that the provisions of Chapter III on judicial remedies, liability and sanctions of the DPD shall apply with regard to national provisions adopted pursuant to this Directive and with regard to the individual rights derived from this Directive.

Article 15(3) provides that the WP29 shall also carry out the tasks laid down in Article 30 of that Directive with regard to matters covered by the ePD, namely the protection of fundamental rights and freedoms and of legitimate interests in the electronic communications sector.

epD Amended by Directive 2006/24/EC

24.25 The ePD was amended by Directive 2006/24/EC of 15 March 2006 on the retention of data generated or processed in connection with the provision of publicly available electronic communications services or of public communications networks and amending the ePD.

Directive 2006/24/EC: Background

24.26 Recital 3 notes that Articles 5, 6 and 9 of the ePD lay down the rules applicable to the processing by network and service providers of traffic and location data generated by using electronic communications services. Such data must be erased or made anonymous when no longer needed for the purpose of the transmission of a communication, except for the data necessary for billing or interconnection payments. Subject to consent, certain data may also be processed for marketing purposes and the provision of value-added services.

Recital 4 notes that Article 15(1) of the ePD sets out the conditions under which Member States may restrict the scope of the rights and obligations provided for in Article 5, Article 6, Article 8(1), (2), (3) and (4), and Article 9 of that Directive. Any such restrictions must be necessary, appropriate and proportionate within a democratic society for specific public order purposes, ie to safeguard national security (ie State security), defence, public security or the prevention, investigation, detection and prosecution of criminal offences or of unauthorised use of the electronic communications systems.

It also refers to:

- data retention measures (Recital 5) – they are contentious and have on occasion been struck down. Furthermore, the *DRI* case[6] struck down the Data Retention Directive;

---

6   Judgment in Joined Cases C-293/12 and C-594/12, *Digital Rights Ireland* and *Seitlinger and Others*, Court of Justice, 8 April 2014. Directive 2006/24/EC of the European Parliament and of the Council of 15 March 2006 on the retention of data generated or processed in connection with the provision of publicly available electronic communications services or of public communications networks and amending Directive 2002/58/EC (OJ 2006 L105, p 54). Rauhofer and Mac Sithigh, 'The Data Retention Directive Never Existed,' *SCRIPTed* (2014) (11:1) 118.

- the use of electronic communications as a tool in the prevention, investigation, detection and prosecution of criminal offences, in particular organised crime (Recital 7);
- the Declaration on Combating Terrorism[7] (Recital 8);
- Article 8 ECHR; public authorities; national security or public safety, for the prevention of disorder or crime, or for the protection of the rights and freedoms of others; data retention; investigative law enforcement tool in several Member States, and in particular re serious matters such as organised crime and terrorism (Recital 9);
- retaining traffic and location data for the investigation, detection, and prosecution of criminal offences (Recital 11);
- the traffic data does not relate to content data (Recital 13);
- sanctions for infringements; ePD; Council Framework Decision 2005/222/JHA on attacks against information systems; criminal offence (Recital 18);
- the right of any person who has suffered damage as a result of an unlawful processing operation or of any act incompatible with national provisions adopted pursuant to the DPD to receive compensation, which derives from Article 23 of that Directive, applies also in relation to the unlawful processing of any personal data pursuant to this Directive (Recital 19);
- Council of Europe Convention on Cybercrime and the Council of Europe Convention for the Protection of Individuals with Regard to Automatic Processing of Personal Data (Recital 20);
- harmonising obligations on providers to retain certain data and to ensure that those data are available for the purpose of the investigation, detection and prosecution of serious crime, as defined; the principle of proportionality (Recital 21);
- the obligations should be proportionate – this Directive is not intended to harmonise the technology for retaining data, the choice of which is a matter to be resolved at national level (Recital 23);
- power of Member States to adopt legislative measures concerning the right of access to, and use of, data by national authorities; the scope of EU law; national law; such laws or action must fully respect fundamental rights as they result from the common constitutional traditions of the Member States and as guaranteed by the ECHR. Per Article 8 ECHR interference by public authorities with privacy rights must meet the requirements of necessity and proportionality and must therefore serve specified, explicit and legitimate purposes and be exercised in a manner that is adequate, relevant and not excessive in relation to the purpose of the interference (Recital 25).

7 Adopted by the European Council on 25 March 2004.

Scope

24.27 Article 1 refers to subject matter and scope. Article 1(1) provides that the Directive aims to harmonise Member States' provisions concerning the obligations of the providers of publicly available electronic communications services or of public communications networks with respect to the retention of certain data which are generated or processed by them, in order to ensure that the data are available for the purpose of the investigation, detection and prosecution of serious crime, as defined by each Member State in its national law.

Article 1(2) provides that the Directive shall apply to traffic and location data on both legal entities and natural persons and to the related data necessary to identify the subscriber or registered user. It shall not apply to the content of electronic communications, including information consulted using an electronic communications network.

Definitions

24.28 Article 2 of Directive 2006/24/EC refers to definitions. The definitions in the DPD, Directive 2002/21/EC (Framework Directive), and in ePD shall apply.

Article 2(1) of Directive 2006/24/EC provides that for the purpose of the Directive:

'data'	means traffic data and location data and the related data necessary to identify the subscriber or user;
'user'	means any legal entity or natural person using a publicly available electronic communications service, for private or business purposes, without necessarily having subscribed to that service;
'telephone service'	means calls (including voice, voicemail and conference and data calls), supplementary services (including call forwarding and call transfer) and messaging and multi-media services (including short message services, enhanced media services and multi-media services);
'user ID'	means a unique identifier allocated to persons when they subscribe to or register with an internet access service or Internet communications service;
'cell ID'	means the identity of the cell from which a mobile telephony call originated or in which it terminated;
'unsuccessful call Attempt'	means a communication where a telephone call has been successfully connected but not answered or there has been a network management intervention.

Obligation to Retain Data

24.29 Article 3 of Directive 2006/24/EC refers to an obligation
to retain data. Article 3(1) provides that by way of derogation from
Articles 5, 6 and 9 of ePD, Member States shall adopt measures to
ensure that the data specified in Article 5 of this Directive are retained
in accordance with the provisions thereof, to the extent that those data
are generated or processed by providers of publicly available electronic
communications services or of a public communications network within
their jurisdiction in the process of supplying the communications services concerned.

Article 3(2) provides that the obligation to retain data provided for in
Article 3(1) shall include the retention of the data specified in Article 5
relating to unsuccessful call attempts where those data are generated or
processed, and stored (as regards telephony data) or logged (as regards
Internet data), by providers of publicly available electronic communications services or of a public communications network within the jurisdiction of the Member State concerned in the process of supplying the
communication services concerned. This Directive shall not require data
relating to unconnected calls to be retained.

Access

24.30 Article 4 of Directive 2006/24/EC refers to access to data. It
provides that Member States shall adopt measures to ensure that data
retained in accordance with this Directive are provided only to the
competent national authorities in specific cases and in accordance with
national law. The procedures to be followed and the conditions to be
fulfilled in order to gain access to retained data in accordance with necessity and proportionality requirements shall be defined by each Member
State in its national law, subject to the relevant provisions of EU law or
public international law, and in particular the ECHR as interpreted by the
European Court of Human Rights.

Data Categories

24.31 Article 5 of Directive 2006/24/EC refers to categories of data to
be retained. Article 5(1) provides that:

> '1. Member States shall ensure that the following categories of data are
> retained under this Directive:
> (a) data necessary to trace and identify the source of a communication;
> (1) concerning fixed network telephony and mobile telephony:
> (i) the calling telephone number;
> (ii) the name and address of the subscriber or registered user;
> (2) concerning Internet access, Internet email and Internet
> telephony:

   (i) the user ID(s) allocated;

   (ii) the user ID and telephone number allocated to any communication entering the public telephone network;

   (iii) the name and address of the subscriber or registered user to whom an Internet Protocol (IP) address, user ID or telephone number was allocated at the time of the communication;

(b) data necessary to identify the destination of a communication;

  (1) concerning fixed network telephony and mobile telephony:

   (i) the number(s) dialled (the telephone number(s) called), and, in cases involving supplementary services such as call forwarding or call transfer, the number or numbers to which the call is routed;

   (ii) the name(s) and address(es) of the subscriber(s) or registered user(s);

  (2) concerning Internet e-mail and Internet telephony:

   (i) the user ID or telephone number of the intended recipient(s) of an Internet telephony call;

   (ii) the name(s) and address(es) of the subscriber(s) or registered user(s) and user ID of the intended recipient of the communication;

(c) data necessary to identify the date, time and duration of a communication:

  (1) concerning fixed network telephony and mobile telephony, the date and time of the start and end of the communication;

  (2) concerning Internet access, Internet email and Internet telephony:

   (i) the date and time of the log-in and log-off of the Internet access service, based on a certain time zone, together with the IP address, whether dynamic or static, allocated by the Internet access service provider to a communication, and the user ID of the subscriber or registered user;

   (ii) the date and time of the log-in and log-off of the Internet email service or Internet telephony service, based on a certain time zone;

(d) data necessary to identify the type of communication:

  (1) concerning fixed network telephony and mobile telephony: the telephone service used;

  (2) concerning Internet email and Internet telephony: the Internet service used;

(e) data necessary to identify users' communication equipment or what purports to be their equipment:

  (1) concerning fixed network telephony, the calling and called telephone numbers;

  (2) concerning mobile telephony:

   (i) the calling and called telephone numbers;

   (ii) the International Mobile Subscriber Identity (IMSI) of the calling party;

            (iii)   the International Mobile Equipment Identity (IMEI) of the calling party;

            (iv)   the IMSI of the called party;

            (v)   the IMEI of the called party;

            (vi)   in the case of pre-paid anonymous services, the date and time of the initial activation of the service and the location label (Cell ID) from which the service was activated;

      (3)   concerning Internet access, Internet email and Internet telephony:

            (i)   the calling telephone number for dial-up access;

            (ii)   the digital subscriber line (DSL) or other end point of the originator of the communication;

   (f)   data necessary to identify the location of mobile communication equipment:

      (1)   the location label (Cell ID) at the start of the communication;

      (2)   data identifying the geographic location of cells by reference to their location labels (Cell ID) during the period for which communications data are retained.

2.   No data revealing the content of the communication may be retained pursuant to this Directive.'

Periods of Retention

24.32   Article 6 of Directive 2006/24/EC refers to periods of retention. Member States shall ensure that the categories of data specified in Article 5 are retained for periods of not less than six months and not more than two years from the date of the communication.

Security

24.33   Article 7 of Directive 2006/24/EC refers to data protection and data security. It provides that without prejudice to the provisions adopted pursuant to DP and Directive 2002/58/EC, each Member State shall ensure that providers of publicly available electronic communications services or of a public communications network respect, as a minimum, the following data security principles with respect to data retained in accordance with this Directive:

- the retained data shall be of the same quality and subject to the same security and protection as those data on the network;
- the data shall be subject to appropriate technical and organisational measures to protect the data against accidental or unlawful destruction, accidental loss or alteration, or unauthorised or unlawful storage, processing, access or disclosure;

- the data shall be subject to appropriate technical and organisational measures to ensure that they can be accessed by specially authorised personnel only; and
- the data, except those that have been accessed and preserved, shall be destroyed at the end of the period of retention.

Storage Requirements for Retained Data

24.34 Article 8 of Directive 2006/24/EC refers to storage requirements for retained data. It provides that Member States shall ensure that the data specified in Article 5 are retained in accordance with this Directive in such a way that the data retained and any other necessary information relating to such data can be transmitted upon request to the competent authorities without undue delay.

ICO

24.35 Article 9 of Directive 2006/24/EC refers to the national supervisory authority. Each Member State shall designate one or more public authorities to be responsible for monitoring the application within its territory of the provisions adopted by the Member States pursuant to Article 7 regarding the security of the stored data. Those authorities may be the same authorities as those referred to in Article 28 of the DPD. The authorities referred to in Article 9(1) shall act with complete independence in carrying out the monitoring referred to in that paragraph.

Statistics on Retention

24.36 Article 10 of Directive 2006/24/EC refers to statistics. Article 10(1) provides that Member States shall ensure that the Commission is provided on a yearly basis with statistics on the retention of data generated or processed in connection with the provision of publicly available electronic communications services or a public communications network. Such statistics shall include:

- the cases in which information was provided to the competent authorities in accordance with applicable national law;
- the time elapsed between the date on which the data were retained and the date on which the competent authority requested the transmission of the data;
- the cases where requests for data could not be met.

Article 10(2) provides that such statistics shall not contain personal data.

ePD Amendment

24.37 Article 11 of Directive 2006/24/EC refers to amendment of ePD. The following paragraph shall be inserted in Article 15 of ePD:

> '1a. Paragraph 1 shall not apply to data specifically required by Directive 2006/24/EC of the European Parliament and of the Council of 15 March 2006 on the retention of data generated or processed in connection with the provision of publicly available electronic communications services or of public communications networks [] to be retained for the purposes referred to in Article 1(1) of that Directive.'

Future Measures

24.38 Article 12 of Directive 2006/24/EC refers to future measures. Article 12(1) provides that a Member State facing particular circumstances that warrant an extension for a limited period of the maximum retention period referred to in Article 6 may take the necessary measures. That Member State shall immediately notify the Commission and inform the other Member States of the measures taken under this Article and shall state the grounds for introducing them.

Remedies, Liability and Penalties

24.39 Article 13 of Directive 2006/24/EC refers to remedies, liability and penalties. Article 13(1) provides that each Member State shall take the necessary measures to ensure that the national measures implementing Chapter III of the DPD providing for judicial remedies, liability and sanctions are fully implemented with respect to the processing of data under this Directive.

Article 13(2) of Directive 2006/24/EC provides that each Member State shall, in particular, take the necessary measures to ensure that any intentional access to, or transfer of, data retained in accordance with the Directive that is not permitted under national law adopted pursuant to the Directive is punishable by penalties, including administrative or criminal penalties, that are effective, proportionate and dissuasive.

Conclusion

24.40 Originally envisaged as relating to telecoms type data only, this secondary aspect data protection regime has expanded in substance, scope and detail. While much of it is still specific to telecoms companies and entities involved in the transfer of electronic communications, certain issues are more generally applicable. The ePD as amended applies to all organisations who wish to engage in direct marketing through a variety of means. Compliance is necessary and needs to be planned in advance. If not specifically exempted from the default rule it is difficult to envisage permissible direct marketing (DM).

Chapter 25

Electronic Direct Marketing and Spam

Introduction

25.01   Direct marketing (DM) tends to be one of the most contentious areas of data protection practice. It also receives probably most attention, with the possible exceptions of data breach/data loss and internet/social media data protection issues.

Most organisations need to engage in (DM) at some stage, some more heavily than others. Many organisations may even go so far as to say that DM is an essential ingredient of continued commercial success.

However, DM is sometimes viewed as spam and unsolicited commercial communications which are unwanted and also unlawful. The data protection regime (and eCommerce legal regime) refers to permissible DM and sets out various obligatory requirements while at the same time setting a default position of prohibiting non-exempted or non-permitted electronic direct marketing.

The GDPR does not impose additional obligations on natural or legal persons in relation to the processing of personal data in connection with the provision of publicly available electronic communications services in public communication networks in the EU in relation to matters for which they are subject to specific obligations with the same objective set out in Directive 2002/58/EC[1] (Article 95 of GDPR). There may be a review to ensure that the ePrivacy Directive (ePD) fully complements and does not conflict with the GDPR, and if so, amendments may be required.

---

1   Directive 2002/58/EC of the European Parliament and of the Council of 12 July 2002 concerning the processing of personal data and the protection of privacy in the electronic communications sector (Directive on privacy and electronic communications).

Direct Marketing (DM)

25.02   If the organisation anticipates that personal data kept by it will be processed for the purposes of DM, it must inform the persons to whom the data relates that they may object by means of a request in writing to the Controller and free of charge.[2]

Unsolicited Communications in the ePD

25.03   Article 13 of the ePD refers to unsolicited communications. Article 13(1) provides that the use of automated calling systems without human intervention (automatic calling machines), facsimile machines (fax) or electronic mail for the purposes of direct marketing may only be allowed in respect of subscribers who have given their prior consent.

Article 13(2) provides that notwithstanding Article 13(1), where a natural or legal person obtains from its customers their electronic contact details for email, in the context of the sale of a product or a service, in accordance with the DPD, the same natural or legal person may use these electronic contact details for direct marketing of its own similar products or services provided that customers clearly and distinctly are given the opportunity to object, free of charge and in an easy manner, to such use of electronic contact details when they are collected and on the occasion of each message in case the customer has not initially refused such use.

Article 13(3) provides that Member States shall take appropriate measures to ensure that, free of charge, unsolicited communications for purposes of DM, in cases other than those referred to in Article 13(1) and (2), are not allowed either without the consent of the subscribers concerned or in respect of subscribers who do not wish to receive these communications, the choice between these options to be determined by national legislation.

Article 13(4) provides that in any event, the practice of sending electronic mail for purposes of DM disguising or concealing the identity of the sender on whose behalf the communication is made, or without a valid address to which the recipient may send a request that such communications cease, shall be prohibited.

Article 13(5) provides that Article 13(1) and (3) shall apply to subscribers who are natural persons. Member States shall also ensure that the legitimate interests of subscribers other than natural persons with regard to unsolicited communications are sufficiently protected.

---

2   See, for example, L Edwards, 'Consumer Privacy Law 1: Online Direct Marketing,' and L Edwards and J Hatcher, 'Consumer Privacy Law: Data Collection, Profiling and Targeting,' each in L Edwards and C Waelde, eds, *Law and the Internet* (Hart, 2009) 489 et seq, and 511 *et seq* respectively.

Marketing Default Position

25.04   How should organisations go about data protection compliance DM? When is DM permitted? All organisations should carefully assess compliance issues when considering any DM activities. Getting it wrong can be costly and can have ICO enforcement and investigation consequences, not to mention penalties Indeed, a penalty of £440,000 was recently imposed in relation to spam DM (see ICO cases chart).

Article 13 of the ePD provides a number of rules in relation to unsolicited communications. Article 13(1) provides that:

- automated calling systems without human intervention (automatic calling machines);
- facsimile machines (fax); or
- electronic mail,

for the purposes of DM may *only* be allowed in respect of subscribers who have given their *prior consent*.

Therefore, there is a default rule prohibiting the forms of DM referred to above *without* prior consent. Many marketing orientated organisation may consider this a hindrance to what may have been considered legitimate marketing and business activities.

Limited Direct Marketing Permitted

25.05   Limited direct marketing is permitted, namely, of subscribers or customers whom have given their prior consent. This implies consent in advance of receiving the DM or simultaneous to the DM.

However, in terms of DM by email, this is further restricted.

Direct Marketing to Existing Customers' Email

25.06   In the context of existing customers, there is a possibility to DM using emails. Article 13(2) of the ePD provides that where an organisation obtains from its customers their electronic contact details for email, in the context of the sale of a product or a service, in accordance with the DPD, the organisation may use these electronic contact details for DM of its own similar products or services provided that customers clearly and distinctly are given the opportunity to object, free of charge and in an easy manner, to such use of electronic contact details when they are collected and on the occasion of each message in case the customer has not initially refused such use.

Therefore, once the email details are obtained at the time of a product or service transaction, it will be possible to use that email for direct marketing purposes. Conditions or limitations apply however. Firstly, the organisation is only permitted to market and promote similar products or services. This, therefore, rules out unrelated, non-identical and non-similar products and services. Secondly, at the time of each subsequent act of DM, the customer must be given the opportunity in an easy and accessible manner to opt out or cancel the DM. Effectively, they must be taken off of the organisation's DM list.

National Marketing Opt-out Registers

25.07 Article 13(3) of ePD provides that Member States shall take appropriate measures to ensure that, free of charge, unsolicited communications for purposes of direct marketing, in cases other than those referred to in Article 13(1) and (2), are not allowed either without the consent of the subscribers concerned or in respect of subscribers who do not wish to receive these communications, the choice between these options to be determined by national legislation. This means that each Member State must determine and provide a means for individuals to opt-out of receiving DM in advance.[3]

Deceptive Emails: Marketing Emails Must Not Conceal Identity

25.08 Article 13(4) of ePD provides that the practice of sending email for purposes of DM disguising or concealing the identity of the sender on whose behalf the communication is made shall be prohibited. This means that organisations cannot conceal their identity if permitted to engage in direct marketing. If these are not complied with, what might otherwise be permissible DM can be deemed to be impermissible. Complaints, investigations or enforcement proceedings can thus arise.

Marketing Emails Must Provide Opt-Out

25.09 In addition, Article 13(4) of ePD provides that the practice of sending email for purposes of DM without a valid address to which the recipient may send a request that such communications cease, shall be prohibited. This means that organisations must also include an easy contact address or other details at which the recipient can contact if they wish to object to receiving any further DM. If these are not complied with, what might otherwise be permissible DM can be deemed to be impermissible. Complaints, investigations or enforcement proceedings can thus also arise.

Marketing Protection for Organisations

25.10 Article 13 (5) of the ePD provides that Article 13(1) and (3) shall apply to subscribers who are natural persons. Member States shall

---

3   See ICO, *Marketing*, at https://ico.org.uk.

also ensure, in the framework of EU law and applicable national legislation, that the legitimate interests of subscribers other than natural persons with regard to unsolicited communications are sufficiently protected. This means that protection from unsolicited DM can also be extended to organisations.

PECR

25.11 Detailed provisions governing direct marketing by electronic communications are set out in the PECR (Privacy and Electronic Communications (EC Directive) Regulations 2003[4]), implementing the ePD in the UK.

It provides rules in relation to automated calling machine; fax; email; unsolicited call by automated calling machine or fax; unsolicited telephone call; disguising or concealing identity; contact address; opt in/opt out; and 'soft opt in.'

PECR is also interesting in that it applies to both legal and natural persons. Generally, rights are not recognised for organisations in the data protection regime.

The PECR refers to the implementation of the rules regarding electronic communications and direct marketing DM). Regulations 22 and 23 refer to email marketing.[5]

Regulation 22 of the PECR provides as follows:

'(1) This regulation applies to the transmission of unsolicited communications by means of electronic mail to individual subscribers.

(2) Except in the circumstances referred to in paragraph (3), a person shall neither transmit, nor instigate the transmission of, unsolicited communications for the purposes of direct marketing by means of electronic mail unless the recipient of the electronic mail has previously notified the sender that he consents for the time being to such communications being sent by, or at the instigation of, the sender.

(3) A person may send or instigate the sending of electronic mail for the purposes of direct marketing where:

(a) that person has obtained the contact details of the recipient of that electronic mail in the course of the sale or negotiations for the sale of a product or service to that recipient;

(b) the direct marketing is in respect of that person's similar products and services only; and

(c) the recipient has been given a simple means of refusing (free of charge except for the costs of the transmission of the refusal) the

---

4   SI 2003/2426.
5   Privacy and Electronic Communications (EC Directive) Regulations 2003, at http://www.legislation.gov.uk/uksi/2003/2426/contents/made.

use of his contact details for the purposes of such direct market-ing, at the time that the details were initially collected, and, where he did not initially refuse the use of the details, at the time of each subsequent communication.

(4) A subscriber shall not permit his line to be used in contravention of paragraph (2).'

Regulation 23 of the PECR provides as follows:

'A person shall neither transmit, nor instigate the transmission of, a communi-cation for the purposes of direct marketing by means of electronic mail:

(a) where the identity of the person on whose behalf the communication has been sent has been disguised or concealed; or

(b) where a valid address to which the recipient of the communication may send a request that such communications cease has not been provided.'

Regulation 24 of the PECR is also relevant in that it provides the information which must be furnished with the direct marketing so that the recipient may contact the organisation to opt-out, namely:

- the name of the organisation; and
- either the address of the person or a telephone number on which he can be reached free of charge.

Regulation 19 of the PECR prohibits the use of automated calling machines for the purposes of direct marketing.

The use of fax machines for the purposes of direct marketing is restricted in reg 20 of the PECR.

Regulation 21 of the PECR provides restrictions in relation to direct marketing by unsolicited telephone calls. An organisation cannot under-take such direct marketing if the called line is previously notified that such calls should not be made to that line; or if the called line is listed on an opt out register (referred to under reg 26 of the PECR).

ICO PECR Guidance

25.12 The ICO guidance states as follows:

'The Regulations define electronic mail as "any text, voice, sound, or image message sent over a public electronic communications network which can be stored in the network or in the recipient's terminal equipment until it is collected by the recipient and includes messages sent using a short message service" (Regulation 2 "Interpretation" applies).

In other words, email, text, picture and video marketing messages are all considered to be "electronic mail". Marketing transmitted in WAP messages is considered to be "electronic mail". WAP Push allows a sender to send a specially formatted SMS message to a handset which, when received, allows a recipient through a single click to access and view content stored online, through the browser on the handset.

We consider this rule also applies to voicemail and answerphone messages left by marketers making marketing calls that would otherwise be "live". So there are stricter obligations placed on you if you make live calls but then wish to leave messages on a person's voicemail or answerphone.

Faxes are not considered to be "electronic mail". Fax marketing is covered elsewhere in the Regulations. These regulations also do not cover so-called silent calls or calls where a fax or other electronic signal is transmitted; this is because no marketing material is transmitted during these calls.'[6]

It adds that:

'This is what the law requires:

- You cannot transmit, or instigate the transmission of, unsolicited marketing material by electronic mail to an individual subscriber unless they have previously notified you, the sender, that they consent, for the time being, to receiving such communications. There is an exception to this rule which has been widely referred to as the soft opt in (Regulation 22 (2) refers).
- You cannot transmit, or instigate the transmission of, any marketing by electronic mail (whether solicited or unsolicited) to any subscriber (whether corporate or individual) where:
  - Your identity has been disguised or concealed; or
  - You have not provided a valid address to which the recipient can send an opt-out request.
  - That electronic mail would contravene regulations 7 or 8 of the Electronic Commerce (EC Directive) Regulations 2002 (SI 2002/2013); or
  - That electronic mail encourages recipients to visit websites which contravene those regulations (Regulation 23 refers).
- A subscriber must not allow their line to be used to breach Regulation 22 (2) (Regulation 22 (4) refers).'[7]

DPA: Offences by Direct Marketers under PECR

25.13 Offences arise in relation to activities referred to under PECR. These include:

- sending unsolicited marketing messages to individuals by fax, SMS, email or automated dialling machine;

---

6   ICO, *Electronic Mail*, at https://ico.org.uk.
7   *Ibid.*

- sending unsolicited marketing by fax, SMS, email or automated dialling machine to a business if it has objected to the receipt of such messages;
- marketing by telephone where the subscriber has objected to the receipt of such calls;
- failing to identify the caller or sender or failing to provide a physical address or a return email address;
- failing to give customers the possibility of objecting to future email and SMS marketing messages with each message sent;
- concealing the identity of the sender on whose behalf the marketing communication was made.

Fines can be significant. Organisations can be fined up to £500,000 by the ICO for unwanted marketing phone calls and emails in accordance with the updated amended PECR. It is also envisaged that fines will increase significantly in potential under the proposed GDPR.

ICO Monetary Penalties

25.14 The ICO is also empowered under the Criminal Justice and Immigration Act 2008 (CJIA 2008) to impose penalties of a monetary variety. Section 77 of the CJIA 2008 provides power to alter penalty for unlawfully obtaining etc personal data, as follows:

(1) The Secretary of State may by order provide for a person who is guilty of an offence under s 55 of the DPA (unlawful obtaining etc of personal data) to be liable:

    (a) on summary conviction, to imprisonment for a term not exceeding the specified period or to a fine not exceeding the statutory maximum or to both;

    (b) on conviction on indictment, to imprisonment for a term not exceeding the specified period or to a fine or to both;

(2) In subsection (1)(a) and (b) 'specified period' means a period provided for by the order but the period must not exceed:

    (a) in the case of summary conviction, 12 months (or, in Northern Ireland, 6 months); and

    (b) in the case of conviction on indictment, two years;

(3) The Secretary of State must ensure that any specified period for England and Wales which, in the case of summary conviction, exceeds 6 months is to be read as a reference to 6 months so far as it relates to an offence committed before the commencement of s 282(1) of the Criminal Justice Act 2003 (increase in sentencing powers of magistrates' courts from 6 to 12 months for certain offences triable either way);

(4) Before making an order under this section, the Secretary of State must consult:
   (a) the Information Commissioner;
   (b) such media organisations as the Secretary of State considers appropriate; and
   (c) such other persons as the Secretary of State considers appropriate;
(5) An order under this section may, in particular, amend the DPA 1998.

Civil Sanctions under the DPA

25.15 Individual Data Subjects can also sue for compensation under the DPA 1998. Where a person suffers damage as a result of a failure by a Controller or Processor to meet their data protection obligations, then the Controller or Processor may be subject to civil sanctions by the person affected. Damage suffered by a Data Subject will include damage to reputation, financial loss and mental distress.

Section 13 of the DPA 1998 provides as follows:

- an individual who suffers damage by reason of any contravention by a Controller of any of the requirements of this Act is entitled to compensation from the Controller for that damage;
- an individual who suffers distress by reason of any contravention by a Controller of any of the requirements of this Act is entitled to compensation from the Controller for that distress if,
   ○ the individual also suffers damage by reason of the contravention; or
   ○ the contravention relates to the processing of personal data for the special purposes;
- in proceedings brought against a person by virtue of this section it is a defence to prove that one had taken such care as in all the circumstances was reasonably required to comply with the requirement concerned.

While there are certain conditions, the primary clause refers to 'any contravention' by the organisation. In terms of the defence, in order to be able to avail of it, an organisation will have to establish that it has 'taken such care as in all the circumstances was reasonably required.' This will vary from organisation to organisation, sector to sector, the type of personal data involved, the risks of damage, loss, etc, the nature of the security risks, the security measures and procedures adopted, the history of risk, loss and damage in the organisation and sector.

Certain types of data will convey inherent additional risks over others, such as loss of financial personal data. This can be argued to require higher obligations for the organisation.

One interesting area to consider going forward is online damage, such as viral abuse, publication, defamation, bulletin boards, discussion forums and websites (or sections of websites), and social media websites. Where damage occurs as a result of misuse or loss of personal data or results in defamation, abuse and threats, liability could arise for the individual tortfeasors as well as the website.

While there are eCommerce defences in the eCommerce Directive, one should recall that the data protection regime (and its duty of care and liability provisions) are separate and stand alone from the eCommerce Directive legal regime. Indeed, even in terms of the eCommerce defences one should also recall that (a) an organisation must first fall within an eCommerce defence, and not lost that defence, in order to avail of it; and (b) there is no automatic entitlement to an internet service provider (ISP) or website to a global eCommerce defence, as in fact there in not one eCommerce defence but three specific defences relating to specific and technical activities. Not all or every ISP activity will fall into one of these defences. Neither will one activity fall into all three defences.

It is also possible to conceive of a website which has no take down procedures, inadequate take down defences, or non-expeditious take down procedures or remedies, and which will face potential liability under privacy and data protection as well as eCommerce liability. For example, an imposter social media profile which contains abuse, personal data and defamatory material could attract liability for the website operator under data protection, and under normal liability if none of the eCommerce defences were unavailable or were lost. The later could occur if, for example, the false impersonating profile was notified to the website (or it was otherwise aware) but it did not do anything.[8]

PECR implemented ePD (also known as the ePrivacy Directive) regarding the protection of privacy in the electronic communications sector. In 2009 ePD was amended by Directive 2009/136/EC. This included changes to Article 5(3) of ePD requiring consent for the storage or access to information stored on a subscriber or users terminal equipment ie a requirement for organisations to obtain consent for cookies and similar technologies.[9]

---

8   This is a complex and developing area of law, common law, civil law, Directive, forthcoming Regulation (DPR) and case law, both in the UK and internationally. A full detailed analysis is beyond this current work.

9   The same comments apply, *ibid.*

The government introduced the amendments on 25 May, 2011 through the Privacy and Electronic Communications (EC Directive) (Amendment) Regulations 2011 (the PECR Amendment Regulations).[10]

Call and Fax Opt Out Registers

25.16   The Telephone Preference Service (TPS) and Fax Preference Service (FPS), operated by the Direct Marketing Association, are registers that allow people to register their numbers and their preference to opt out of receiving unsolicited calls or faxes. Therefore, organisation proposing to use call or fax for DM, must first consult these registers to ensure that no contact details are used which are already registered on these registers.

The Spam Problem

25.17   Spam is just one of a number of names taken to describe the problem of unsolicited electronic commercial marketing materials. The Spam name comes originally from a Monty Python comic sketch. However, electronic Spam is far from comic and costs industry hundreds of millions of pounds each year in employee lost time and resources, in lost bandwidth, in reduced capacity and network speed, as well as other problems.

Spam Internationally

25.18   The growing recognition of the problems caused by Spam, such as scams, viruses, lost productivity and bandwidth, has meant an increasing number of local and national laws specifically dedicated to preventing Spam.

In the US for example there a large number of local state laws[11] and national federal laws dedicated to tackling Spam. These include both news specific laws and Spam specific amendments to pre-existing laws. A US federal Spam act known as the CANSPAM Act was introduced.[12]

---

10   *Ibid.*
11   See www.spamlaws.com.
12   See VJ Reid, 'Recent Developments in Private Enforcement of the Can-Spam Act,' *Akron Intellectual Property Journal* (2010) (4) 281–307.

Related Issues

25.19   Certain related issues also arise, which are beyond detailed analysis presently but which may be used for specific organisations to consider further.

One example is the increasingly controversial area of profiling, advertising and direct marketing in relation to children.[13]

Online behavioural advertising (OBA) and the behavioural targeting of internet advertising is increasingly debated[14]

Commentators, and media, often focus on the issue of threats to privacy, data protection and reputation rights caused by web 2.0 activities such as social media, search engine services, etc. The query arises as to whether revenue versus privacy is better respected by certain online services providers?[15]

Cases

25.20   There are many official cases, prosecutions and fines in relation to Spam. See examples in table at para **12.41** above.

Conclusion

25.21   Few organisation will not be interested in DM and advertising. The key is to get it right. The consequences of sending unlawful electronic communications can amount to offences, prosecutions official enforcement and investigations as well as being sued or prosecuted. This is one of the areas which is consistently an area of focus from ICO investigation. These issues become more important as: (a) increased competition puts pressure on organisations to engage, or increase, marketing and profiling efforts; and (b) the software, devices and technologies available to facilitate such efforts are increasing in significance. Over time, cost efforts also decrease in terms of adopting these new tools. As always, however, organisations are cautioned to ensure data

---

13   U Munukutla-Parker, 'Unsolicited Commercial E-mail, Privacy Concerns Related to Social Network Services, Online Protection of Children, and Cyberbullying,' *I/S: A Journal of Law and Policy* (2006) (2) 628–650.

14   Deane-Johns, 'Behavioural Targeting of Internet Advertising,' *Computers and Law* (2009) (20) 22.

15   L Edwards and C Waelde, eds, *Law and the Internet* (Oxford: Hart, 2009) 539.

protection compliance. They might also, on occasion, pause to question general ethical consideration in certain instances. Depending on the sector, there may also be an obligation to consider and comply with certain third party organisational rules, particularly as regards direct marketing issues. Indeed, the new GDPR also provides the impetus for representative organisations to increasingly consider industry-wide data protection Codes of Conduct. These are encouraged by the ICO and the new GDPR.

Part 4
New EU Regime

Chapter 26

New Regime

Introduction

26.01 The EU data protection regime is fundamentally updated and expanded.[1] Many things have changed since the introduction of the DPD. Data processing activities have changed as well as increases in scale and complexity. New data processing activities and issues are constantly evolving. The EU undertook a formal review of the data protection regime. Partly on foot of the review, it was decided to update the DPD, ultimately via the new EU Regulation, namely the GDPR.

Formal Nature of Regulations and Directives

26.02 As noted above, the DPD is replaced by a Regulation, the GDPR. The final version of the GDPR was agreed in April 2016. However, it is important to note that an EU Regulation differs from a Directive under formal EU law.[2] A Regulation is immediately directly effective in all EU Member States – without the need for national implementing laws. A Directive requires national implementing measures, whereas a Regulation does not. The GDPR Regulation applies in the UK as in other EU countries. It changes the UK data protection regime as well

---

1   European Commission – Press release, 'Agreement on Commission's EU Data Protection Reform Will Boost Digital Single Market,' Brussels (15 December 2015), available at http://europa.eu/rapid/press-release_IP-15-6321_en.htm; R Graham, 'Prepare for European Data Protection Reform,' *SCL Computer and Law*, 30 November 2011.
2   Generally see, for example, A Biondi and P Eeckhout, eds, *EU Law after Lisbon* (2012); N Foster, *Foster on EU Law* (2011); O'Neill, A, *EU Law for UK Lawyers* (2011); Steiner, J, *EU Law* (2011). Also, HCFJA de Waele, 'Implications of Replacing the Data Protection Directive by a Regulation. A Legal Perspective,' *Privacy & Data Protection* (2012) (12) 3.

as commercial practice. The reforms introduced are described as being 'comprehensive.'[3]

Review Policy

26.03   The Commission and others have recognised that technology and commercial changes have meant that the data protection regime required updating.[4] Indeed, the Council of Europe Convention on data protection[5] which pre-dates the DPD and which was incorporated into the national law of many EU (and other states) prior to the DPD, is also in the process of being updated.[6] The WP29 also refers to the need for future data protection measures in its Opinion regarding *The Future of Privacy*.[7] Indeed, there have also been calls for greater political activism in relation to particular data protection issues.[8] Others[9] have also highlighted new problematic developments in relation to such things as location data and location based services, which need to be dealt with.[10] Online abuse and offline abuse issues are other issues which need to be addressed. Rebecca Wong refers to some of the areas of concern which the GDPR proposes to address.[11] These include:

- the data protection regime in the online age;
- social media;
- cloud computing;

---

3   In Brief, *Communications Law* (2012) (17) 3.

4   For example, see also from a US perspective, N Roethlisberger, 'Someone is Watching: The Need for Enhanced Data Protection, *Hastings Law Journal* (2011) (62:6) 1793.

5   Convention for the Protection of Individuals with regard to Automatic Processing of Personal Data, Council of Europe (1982), at http://conventions.coe.int/Treaty/en/Treaties/Html/108.htm.

6   See S Kierkegaard et al, '30 Years On – The Review of the Council of Europe Data Protection Convention 108,' *Computer Law & Security Review* (2011) (27) 223–231.

7   The Future of Privacy, WP29, referred to in R Wong, 'Data Protection: The Future of Privacy,' *Computer Law & Security Review* (2011) (27) 53–57.

8   A Ripoll Servent and A MacKenzie, 'Is the EP Still a Data Protection Champion? The Case of SWIFT,' *Perspectives on European Politics & Society* (2011) (12) 390–406.

9   C Cuijpers and M Pekarek, 'The Regulation of Location-Based Services: Challenges to the European Union Data Protection Regime,' *Journal of Location Based Services* (2011) (5) 223–241.

10 See, for example, M Hildebandt, 'Location Data, Purpose Binding and Contextual Integrity: What's the Meggase,' in L Florida, ed, *Protection of Information and the Right to Privacy – A New Equilibrium* (Springer 2014) 31.

11 R Wong, 'The Data Protection Directive 95/46/EC: Idealisms and Realisms,' *International Review of Law, Computers & Technology* (2012) (26) 229–244.

- minimum/maximum standards;
- the Data Protection Principles.[12]

The Commission states[13] that the policy in reviewing the data protection regime is to:

- modernise the EU legal system for the protection of personal data, in particular to meet the challenges resulting from globalisation and the use of new technologies;
- strengthen individuals' rights, and at the same time reduce administrative formalities to ensure a free flow of personal data within the EU and beyond;
- improve the clarity and coherence of the EU rules for personal data protection and achieve a consistent and effective implementation and application of the fundamental right[14] to the protection of personal data in all areas of the EU's activities.[15]

It is also to enhance consumer confidence in eCommerce.[16] In addition, it should also bring comprehensive savings to organisations as the compliance obligations of complying with somewhat differing national data protection regimes will be reduced if not eliminated.[17]

The review[18] summarises the need for new data protection rules, as follows:

'The current EU data protection rules date from 1995. Back then, the internet was virtually unknown to most people. Today, 250 million people use the internet daily in Europe.

Think how that has changed our personal data landscape through the explosion of ecommerce, social networks, online games and cloud computing.

---

12 See *ibid*.
13 Reform of Data Protection Legal Framework, Commission, Justice Directorate, at http://ec.europa.eu/justice/data-protection/index_en.htm.
14 In relation to data protection as a fundamental right, see, for example S Rodata, 'Data Protection as a Fundamental Right,' in S Gutwirth, Y Poullet, P de Hert, C de Terwangne and S Nouwt, *Reinventing Data Protection?* (Springer, 2009) 77. A Mantelero notes that 'If legislators consider data protection as a fundamental right, it is necessary to reinforce its protection in order to make it effective and not conditioned by the asymmetries which characterize the relationship between Data Subject and data controllers,' A Mantelero, 'Competitive Value of Data Protection: The Impact of Data Protection Regulation on Online Behaviour,' *International Data Privacy Law* (11/2013) (3:4) 98.
15 Reform of Data Protection legal Framework, Commission, Justice Directorate, at http://ec.europa.eu/justice/data-protection/index_en.
16 In Brief, *Communications Law* (2012) (17) 3.
17 See *ibid*.
18 See details of some of the steps and consultations, at http://ec.europa.eu/justice/data-protection/index_en.htm.

The European Commission has therefore adopted proposals for updating data protection rules to meet the challenges of the digital age. In particular, the proposals will strengthen protection of your personal data online.'

These proposals were debated in some detail.[19] Commentators describe the new GDPR as 'a long (and ambitious) text'.[20] In addition, the process which has arrived at this stage is described as being herculean.[21] The details of the changes were agreed in December 2015, and finalised and enacted in April 2016.

Importance

26.04 Costa and Poullet indicate that once the GDPR 'comes into force, the document will be the new general legal framework of data protection, repealing [the DPD] more than twenty-seven years after its adoption.'[22] The GDPR, as well as Article 8(1) of the EU Charter of fundamental rights of 2000 and Article 16(1) of the Lisbon Treaty, reassert the importance of privacy and data protection 'as a fundamental right'.[23] '[E]ffective and more coherent protection' is required[24] (see below).

In terms of policy as between modernising via a Directive or via a Regulation 'in order to ensure a full consistent and high level of protection equivalent in all the EU member states, a Regulation was judged as the adequate solution to ensure full harmonisation'[25] throughout the EU. The Commission may also oversee and monitor the national supervisory authorities.[26]

Individuals are rarely aware about how their data are collected and processed while they are surfing on the internet at home, using their cell phones, walking down a video-surveyed street or with an RFID tag embedded in their clothes, and so on.[27] There is a need for greater

---

19 See Commission, *Why Do We Need New Data Protection Rules Now?*, at http://ec. europa.eu/justice/data-protection/document/review2012/factsheets/1_en.pdf.
20 P De Hert and V Papakonstantinou, 'The Proposed Data Protection Regulation Replacing Directive 95/46/EC: A Sound System for the Protection of Individuals,' *Computer Law & security Review* (2012) (28) 130–142. Note also, IN Walden and RN Savage, 'Data Protection and Privacy Laws: Should Organisations be Protected?,' *International and Comparative Law Quarterly* (1988) (37) 337–347.
21 *Ibid.*
22 L Costa and Y Poullet, 'Privacy and the Regulation of 2012,' *Computer Law & Security Review* (2012) (28) 254–262, at 254.
23 *Ibid*, 254.
24 *Ibid.*
25 *Ibid*, 255.
26 *Ibid.*
27 *Ibid*, 256.

transparency. As regards data processing, 'transparency translates the widening of the knowledge about information systems ... coupled with fairness.'[28]

Fundamental Right

26.05 Personal data protection is now recognised as a fundamental right for individuals, both in the new GDPR and the EU Charter of Fundamental Rights of 2000, Lisbon Treaty (Treaty on the Functioning of the European Union) and the Council of Europe Convention.

'**EU Charter (Article 8(1))**

Protection of Personal Data

Everyone has the right to the protection of personal data concerning him or her.'

'**EU Lisbon Treaty (Article 16(1))**

Everyone has the right to the protection of personal data concerning them.'

Innovations

26.06 Commentators have indicated that parts of the GDPR contain particular 'legislative innovation.'[29] Some examples of this innovation are indicated to be the:

- Data Protection Principles;
- Data Subjects' rights;
- Controllers' and Processors' obligations;
- Regulation issues regarding technologies.[30]

It has been noted that while the DPD emphasises protection for the fundamental right and freedoms of individuals 'and in particular their right to privacy,' the GDPR in Articles 1 and 2 stresses the need to protect the fundamental right and freedoms of individuals 'and in particular their right to the protection of personal data.'[31] Further references also emphasise data protection as a stand-alone concept from privacy, such

---

28 L Costa and Y Poullet, 'Privacy and the Regulation of 2012,' *Computer Law & Security Review* (2012) (28) 254–292.
29 *Ibid.*
30 *Ibid.*
31 *Ibid*, 255.

as data protection risk assessments and pre-problem solving via data protection by design (DPbD) and by default.

There is a new consistency mechanism whereby the national data protection authorities are obliged to cooperate with each other and with the Commission.[32] Two examples given include: data protection assessments; and the obligation of notifying Data Subjects in relation to data breaches.[33]

The obligations in terms of insufficient security and data breaches are more detailed in the GDPR than previously.[34] The obligations are now more detailed than those in relation to telcos and ISPs in the ePD.[35] Data breaches are referred to in the GDPR. In the event of a data breach the Controller must notify the ICO. In addition the Controller must also communicate to the Data Subjects if there is a risk of harm to their privacy or personal data.

Data portability is a newly expressed right. It 'implies the right of Data Subjects to obtain from the Controller a copy of their personal data in a structured and commonly used format ... data portability is a kind of right to backup and use personal information under the management of the data Controller. Second, data portability grants the right to transmit personal data and other information provided by the Data Subject from one automated processing system to another one ... therefore the right to take personal data and leave.'[36]

The DPD stated that Controller must not process personal data excessively. However, this is now more limited. The GDPR states that data collection and processing must be transparent, fair and limited to the minimum.

Broader parameters are contained in the GDPR in relation to consent. The definition and conditions are broader than previously. The inclusion of the words freely given, specific, informed and unambigious appears more specific than the previous 'unambiguously' consented.

The DPD Article 15 protection in relation to automated individual decisions 'is considerably enlarged'[37] regarding profiling in GDPR. The use of, *inter alia*, the word 'measure' in the GDPR as opposed to

---

32 Chapter VII, section 10, see L Costa and Y Poullet, 'Privacy and the Regulation of 2012,' *Computer Law & Security Review* (2012) (28) 254–262, at 255.

33 *Ibid.*

34 L Costa and Y Poullet, 'Privacy and the Regulation of 2012,' *Computer Law & Security Review* (2012) (28) 254–262, at 256.

35 *Ibid.*

36 *Ibid*, at 256.

37 *Ibid*, at 258. Also see Council of Europe Recommendation regarding profiling (25 November 2010).

'decision' in the DPD now makes the category of activity encompassed within the obligation much wider.[38] There is greater Data Subject protection. While there were previously two exemptions, in terms of contract and also a specific law, the GDPR adds a third in terms of consent from the Data Subject. However, Controllers will need to ensure a stand alone consent for profiling separate from any consent for data collection and processing per se.[39]

The GDPR also moves significantly further than the DPD in terms of creating obligations, responsibility and liability on Controllers.[40] Appropriate policies must be implemented by Controllers, as well as complaint data processing, secure data processing, the undertaking of data protection impact assessments, shared liability as between joint Controllers, appointing representatives within the EU where the Controllers are located elsewhere and provisions regarding Processors.[41]

While the DPD imposed compensation obligations on Controllers in the case of harm to Data Subjects, the GDPR extends liability to Processors.[42] In addition, where harm is suffered by Data Subjects any joint Controller and or Processors shall be 'jointly and severally liable for the entire amount of the damage.'[43]

The concepts of data protection by design (DPbD), data protection by default and impact assessments all emphasise the ability of the data protection regime to become involved in standards setting and the regulation of particular technologies and technical solutions.[44] The Ontario Data Protection Commissioner, Anne Cavoukian, refers to PbD (the precursor to DPbD).[45] The GDPR describes it as follows, by indicating that:

> '[h]aving regard to the state of the art and the cost of implementation and taking account of the nature, scope, context and purposes of the processing as well as the risks of varying likelihood and severity for rights and freedoms of individuals posed by the processing, the Controller shall, both at the time of the determination of the means for processing and at the time of the processing itself, implement appropriate technical and organisational measures,

---

38 L Costa and Y Poullet, 'Privacy and the Regulation of 2012,' *Computer Law & Security Review* (2012) (28) 254–262, at 258–259.
39 *Ibid*, at 258. Also see Council of Europe Recommendation regarding profiling (25 November 2010) 259.
40 *Ibid*.
41 *Ibid*.
42 *Ibid*.
43 *Ibid*.
44 *Ibid*.
45 For example, Anne Cavoukian, DPA Ontario, Privacy Guidelines for RFID Information Systems, at www.ipc.on.ca, says the privacy and security must be built into the solution from the outset, at the design stage. Referred to *ibid*.

such as pseudonymisation, which are designed to implement data protection principles, such as data minimisation, in an effective way and to integrate the necessary safeguards into the processing in order to meet the requirements of [the GDPR] and protect the rights of Data Subjects.' (Article 23(1)).

Data protection by default is referred to and defined as follows:

'The Controller shall implement mechanisms for ensuring that, by default, only those personal data are processed which are necessary for each specific purpose of the processing and are especially not collected or retained beyond the minimum necessary for those purposes, both in terms of the amount of the data and the time of their storage. In particular, those mechanisms shall ensure that by default personal data are not made accessible to an indefinite number of individuals' (Article 23(2)).

These accord with the general principle of data minimisation, whereby non-personal data should be processed first and where the collection and processing of personal data is required, it must be the minimum data as opposed to the minimum data which is so processed. This is referred to in Article 5(1)(c).

Data Subjects have more control over their personal data. In the context of social networks, 'individual profiles should be kept private from others by default.'[46]

The concept of DPbD and data protection by default as provided in the GDPR are predicted to soon impact upon organisational contracts and contracting practices relating to data processing activities.[47]

As mentioned above, one of the new areas is the obligation to engage in data protection impact assessments. Article 35(1) provides that that:

'[w]here a type of processing in particular using new technologies, and taking into account the nature, scope, context and purposes of the processing, is likely to result in a high risk for the rights and freedoms of natural persons, the Controller shall, prior to the processing, carry out an assessment of the impact of the envisaged processing operations on the protection of personal data. A single assessment may address a set of similar processing operations that present similar high risks.'

This is particularly so where the envisaged processing could give rise to specific risks.

A further addition is the possibility of mass group claims or claims through representative organisations. This is referred to as 'collective

---

46 L Costa and Y Poullet, 'Privacy and the Regulation of 2012,' *Computer Law & Security Review* (2012) (28) 254–262, at 260, and referring to European data Protection Supervisor on the Communications from Commission to the European Parliament, the Council, the Economic and Social Committee and the Committee of the Regions, 'A Comprehensive Approach on Personal Data Protection in the European Union,' at 23.
47 *Ibid*, 260.

redress' and allows data protection and privacy NGOs to complain to both the ICO and to the courts (see Recital 143 and Article 80).[48] 'Civil procedure rules'[49] may also need to be introduced.

The regime as regards trans-border data flows or TBDFs will be 'significantly altered.'[50] These are included in Articles 44–50.

Enhanced Provisions and Changes

26.07 One of the more important extensions and enhancements relates to the expanded Right to be Forgotten. The 'right to be forgotten and to erasure, which consists of securing from the Controller the erasure of personal data as well prevention of any further dissemination of his data.'[51] (It is also said to interface with the new right to data portability[52]).

The Right to be Forgotten is even more enhanced in instances where the personal data was originally disclosed when the Data Subject was a child. Some commentators refer to the option of an entire 'clean slate.'[53]

'The use of data from social networks in employment contexts is a representative example. Personal data such as photos taken in private contexts have been used to refuse job positions and fire people. But forgetfulness is larger. It is one dimension of how people deal with their own history, being related not only to leaving the past behind but also to living in the present without the threat of a kind of "Miranda" warning, where whatever you say can be used against you in the future. In this sense the right to be forgotten is closely related to entitlements of dignity and self-development. Once again, privacy appears as the pre-requisite of our liberties, assuring the possibility to freely express ourselves and move freely on the street ...'[54]

The Right to be Forgotten is most clearly associated and related to the following in particular:

- where the personal data is no longer necessary in relation to the purposes for which they were originally collected and processed (and the associated finality principle);

---

48 See also Commission on a common framework for collective redress, at http://ec.europa.eu/consumers/redress_cons/collective_redress_en.htm.
49 L Costa and Y Poullet, 'Privacy and the Regulation of 2012,' *Computer Law & Security Review* (2012) (28) 254–262, at 261.
50 *Ibid.*
51 *Ibid*, at 256.
52 *Ibid.*
53 *Ibid*, at 257.
54 *Ibid.*

- where the Data Subject has withdrawn their consent for processing;
- where Data Subjects object to the processing of the personal data concerning them;
- where the processing of the personal data does not comply with the GDPR.[55]

The GDPR and the Right to be Forgotten 'amplifies the effectiveness of data protection principles and rules.'[56]

Data Subjects can have their data erased under the right to be forgotten when there is no compliance, in addition to instances where they simply withdraw their consent.[57] User control and Data Subject control are, therefore, enhanced.

The GDPR and Right to be Forgotten create the following compliance obligations, namely:

- erasing personal data and not processing it further;
- informing third parties that the Data Subject has requested the deletion of the personal data;
- taking responsibility for publication by third parties under the Controller's authority[58] (Articles 17, 2 and 8).

The GDPR also enhances and expands the various powers of the national supervisory authorities, such as the ICO.[59]

Some of the key changes are referred to below. In some respects, these could also be seen as advantages of the new GDPR data protection regime:

- administrative costs are to be reduced with a single EU wide set of rules and obligations;
- there may be less need to interact with the ICO, as more responsibility and accountability is passed to the organisational level;
- the consent requirement is clarified as to mean explicit consent (whereas previously there were references to different categories of consent);
- rights are improved with easier access to personal data, as well as its transferability;
- the enhanced Right to be Forgotten will improve the position of Data Subjects and the ability to delete data;
- the EU data protection regime will apply to non-EU entities operating with regard to EU personal data and EU citizens;

---

55 L Costa and Y Poullet, 'Privacy and the Regulation of 2012,' *Computer Law & Security Review* (2012) (28) 254–262.
56 *Ibid.*
57 *Ibid*, at 257.
58 *Ibid.*
59 *Ibid*, at 260.

- the national authorities will be able to impose fines based on a percent of global turnover[60] (see below).

The ICO welcomes the GDPR, stating:

> 'it strengthens the position of individuals, recognises important concepts such as privacy by design and privacy impact assessments and requires organisations to be able to demonstrate that they have measures in place to ensure personal information is properly protected.'[61]

The EU Commission's press statement dated 15 December 2015 issued once the new GDPR text was agreed notes that the GDPR 'will enable people to better control their personal data. At the same time modernised and unified rules will allow businesses to make the most of the opportunities of the Digital Single Market by cutting red tape and benefiting from reinforced consumer trust.'[62]

The Commission also refers to the benefits of the changes. It states:

> 'The reform will allow people to regain control of their personal data. Two-thirds of Europeans (67%), according to a recent Eurobarometer survey, stated they are concerned about not having complete control over the information they provide online. Seven Europeans out of ten worry about the potential use that companies may make of the information disclosed. The data protection reform will strengthen the right to data protection, which is a fundamental right in the EU, and allow them to have trust when they give their personal data.

> The new rules address these concerns by strengthening the existing rights and empowering individuals with more control over their personal data. Most notably, these include,

- **easier access to your own data**: individuals will have more information on how their data is processed and this information should be available in a clear and understandable way;
- **a right to data portability**: it will be easier to transfer your personal data between service providers;
- **a clarified "Right to be Forgotten"**: when you no longer want your data to be processed, and provided that there are no legitimate grounds for retaining it, the data will be deleted;
- **the right to know when your data has been hacked:** For example, companies and organisations must notify the national supervisory authority of serious data breaches as soon as possible so that users can take appropriate measures.

---

60 In Brief, *Communications Law* (2012) (17) 3.
61 Referred to in In Brief, *Communications Law* (2012) (17) 3.
62 European Commission – Press release, 'Agreement on Commission's EU Data Protection Reform Will Boost Digital Single Market,' Brussels (15 December 2015), available at http://europa.eu/rapid/press-release_IP-15-6321_en.htm.

Clear modern rules for businesses

In today's digital economy, personal data has acquired enormous economic significance, in particular in the area of big data. By unifying Europe's rules on data protection, lawmakers are creating a business opportunity and encouraging innovation.

One continent, one law: The regulation will establish one single set of rules which will make it simpler and cheaper for companies to do business in the EU.

One-stop-shop: businesses will only have to deal with one single supervisory authority. This is estimated to save €2.3 billion per year.

European rules on European soil: companies based outside of Europe will have to apply the same rules when offering services in the EU.

Risk-based approach: the rules will avoid a burdensome one-size-fits-all obligation and rather tailor them to the respective risks.

Rules fit for innovation: the regulation will guarantee that data protection safeguards are built into products and services from the earliest stage of development (Data protection by Design (DPbD)). Privacy-friendly techniques such as pseudonomysation will be encouraged, to reap the benefits of big data innovation while protecting privacy.

Benefits for big and small alike

The data protection reform will stimulate economic growth by cutting costs and red tape for European business, especially for small and medium enterprises (SMEs). The EU's data protection reform will help SMEs break into new markets. Under the new rules, SMEs will benefit from four reductions in red tape:

- **No more notifications**: Notifications to supervisory authorities are a formality that represents a cost for business of €130 million every year. The reform will scrap these entirely.
- **Every penny counts**: Where requests to access data are manifestly unfounded or excessive, SMEs will be able to charge a fee for providing access.
- **Data Protection Officers**: SMEs are exempt from the obligation to appoint a data protection officer insofar as data processing is not their core business activity.
- **Impact Assessments**: SMEs will have no obligation to carry out an impact assessment unless there is a high risk.

...

Better protection of citizens' data

Individuals' personal data will be better protected, when processed for any law enforcement purpose including prevention of crime. It will protect everyone – regardless of whether they are a victim, criminal or witness. All law enforcement processing in the Union must comply with the principles of necessity, proportionality and legality, with appropriate safeguards for the individuals. Supervision is ensured by independent national data protection authorities, and effective judicial remedies must be provided.

The Data Protection Directive for Police and Criminal Justice Authorities provides clear rules for the transfer of personal data by law enforcement authorities outside the EU, to ensure that the level of protection of individuals guaranteed in the EU is not undermined.'[63]

In one survey, 72 percent of internet users were concerned that they gave away too much personal data.[64] However, red tape reduction and economic growth are also commercial issues considered under the new regime. New technological changes are also recognised and encompassed. European harmonisation issues are also a central consideration.

The New Data Protection Regime

Introducing the New GDPR Changes

26.08 Some of the new headline changes include:

- new and updated fundamental principles, such as fairness and legality, processing conditions, prior information, consent, transparency, accuracy, lawfulness of processing, definitions;
- DPOs;
- special rules concerning children in relation to information society services;
- expanded rights including subject access rights;
- new enforcement and sanctions provisions;
- Right to be Forgotten;
- right to data portability;
- new security and breach provisions;
- provisions regarding single supervisory authority or one-stop-shop;
- risk based approach, risk minimisation, consultations and reporting.

Some of the new detailed changes include:

- repeal of DPD 95 (Article 94);
- WP29 and European Data Protection Board (Articles 35, 40–43, 51, 52, 58–63, 64, 65 and 94);

---

63 European Commission – Press release, 'Agreement on Commission's EU Data Protection Reform will Boost Digital Single Market,' Brussels (15 December 2015) available at http://europa.eu/rapid/press-release_IP-15-6321_en.htm.
64 Eurobarometer, 'Attitudes on Data Protection and Electronic Identity in the EU' (June 2011).

- background and rationale (Recitals 1, 8, 11, 13);
- context objectives, scope of GDPR (Articles 1, 2 and 3);
- obligations (Recitals 32, 39, 40, 42, 43–47);
- security (Articles 2, 4, 5, 9, 10, 30, 32, 35, 40, 45 and 47);
- processing;
- rights (Articles 1, 4–7, 9–22);
- proceedings (Articles 23, 40, 78, 79, 81 and 82);
- establishment (Articles 3, 4, 9, 17, 18, 21, 37, 42, 49, 54, 56, 57, 60, 62, 65, 70 and 79);
- transfers (Articles 44–50);
- ICO, etc;
- new bodies (Recital 142; Articles, 9 and 80);
- notification/registration replaced (Recital 89);
- exceptions/exemptions (Article 23);
- lawful processing and consent (Articles 4–9, 13, 14, 17, 18, 20, 22, 23, 32, 40, 49, 82, 83);
- online identifiers (Recital 30; Articles 4, 87);
- sensitive and special personal data (Articles 6, 9, 22, 27, 30, 35, 37, 47);
- children (Articles 6, 8, 12, 40, 57);
- health data (Articles 4, 9, 17, 23, 36, 88);
- DPR definitions (Article 4);
- new processing rules: obligations (Articles 5–11);
- new (data protection) principles (Article 5);
- lawfulness of processing: legitimate processing conditions (Article 6);
- child's consent: conditions for information society services (Article 8);
- processing special categories of personal data (Article 9);
- processing re criminal convictions and offences data (Article 10);
- processing not requiring identification (Article 11);
- Controllers and Processors (Chapter IV);
- responsibility of the Controller (Article 24);
- joint Controllers (Article 26);
- Processor (Article 28);
- processing under authority of Controller and Processor (Article 29);
- records of processing activities (Article 30);
- representatives of Controllers not established in EU (Article 27);
- co-operation with supervisory authority;
- security of processing (Article 32);
- notifying data breach to supervisory authority (Article 33);
- communicating data breach to Data Subject (Article 34);

- data protection impact assessment and prior consultation (Chapter IV, Section 3);
- data protection impact assessment (Article 35);
- prior consultation (Article 36);
- new Data Protection Officer (DPO) (Chapter IV, Section 4; Article 37);
- position (Article 38) and tasks of new DPO (Article 39);
- general principle for transfers (Article 44);
- transfers via adequacy decision (Article 45);
- transfers via appropriate safeguards (Article 46);
- transfers via binding corporate rules (Article 47);
- transfers or disclosures not authorised by EU law (Article 48);
- derogations for specific situations (Article 49);
- new processing rules: Data Subject rights (Chapter III);
- right to transparency (Article 5; Chapter III, Section 1; Articles 12–14, 26, 40–43, 88);
- data access rights (Chapter III, Section 2);
- right to prior information: directly obtained data (Article 13);
- right to prior information: indirectly obtained data (Article 14);
- right of confirmation and right of access (Article 15);
- rectification and erasure (Chapter III, Section 3).
- right to rectification (Article 16);
- right to erasure (Right to be Forgotten) (RtbF) (Article 17);
- right to restriction of processing (Article 18);
- notifications re rectification, erasure or restriction (Article 19);
- right to data portability (Article 20);
- right to object (Article 21);
- rights against automated individual decision making, including profiling (Article 22);
- Data protection by design (DPbD) and by default (Article 25).
- security rights;
- data protection impact assessment and prior consultation;
- communicating data breach to Data Subject (Article 34);
- Data Protection Officer (DPO) (contact);
- remedies, liability and sanctions (Chapter VIII);
- right to lodge complaint with supervisory authority (Article 77);
- right to judicial remedy against supervisory authority (Article 78);
- right to effective judicial remedy against Controller or Processor (Article 79);
- representation of Data Subjects (Article 80);
- suspension of proceedings (Article 81);
- right to compensation and liability (Article 82);

- codes of conduct and certification (Chapter IV, Section 5; Articles 40–43);
- international co-operation on personal data (Articles 50, 60);
- Supervisory Authorities (Chapter VI, Section 1; Article 81);
- general conditions for imposing administrative fines (Article 83);
- penalties (Article 84);
- specific data processing situations (Chapter IX);
- processing and freedom of expression and information (Article 85);
- processing and public access to official documents (Article 86);
- processing national identification numbers (Article 87);
- processing in employment context (Article 88);
- safeguards and derogations: public interest/scientific/historical research/statistical processing (Article 89);
- obligations of secrecy (Article 90);
- churches and religious associations (Article 91);
- delegated acts and implementing acts (Chapter X);
- exercise of the delegation (Article 92);
- relationship to Directive 2002/58/EC (Article 95);
- relationship to previously concluded agreements (Article 96);
- review of other EU data protection instruments (Article 98);
- restrictions.

New GDPR Definitions

26.09 Article 4 of the new GDPR sets out the definitions for the new data protection regime. (See para 3.04 for details of particular definitions.)

Prior to the new GDPR, the ICO has issued recommendations in relation to personal data, definitions, etc, namely:

- Determining What is Personal Data;
- What is 'Data' for the Purposes of the DPA?;
- What is Personal Data? – A Quick Reference Guide.

These now need to be read in light of the GDPR changes.

GDPR Recitals

26.10 The Recitals to the new GDPR are also instructive in relation to the purposes and themes covered. They include reference to, for example: the DPD being repealed; WP29/EDPB; background and rationale; obligations; security; processing; rights; proceedings; establishment; transfers; supervisory authorities; new bodies; lawful processing and consent; online identifiers; sensitive personal data; children; and health data (see para **4.07** for details of the Recitals in greater detail). The importance of data protection and health data is also referred to by the OECD.[65]

Main Provisions and Changes of GDPR

26.11   The main new GDPR provisions and changes are referred to below.

Repeal of DPD 95

26.12   The DPD of 1995 is repealed. It is repealed with effect from 25 May 2018 (Article 94(1)). References to the repealed DPD shall be construed as references to the GDPR (Article 94(2)).

WP29 and European Data Protection Board

26.13   A new European Data Protection Board (EDPB) is established. This effectively replaces the WP29. References to the previous WP29 shall be construed as references to the EDPB established by the GDPR (Article 94(2)). Chapter IV, Section 3 of the GDPR provides for the EDPB. The EDPB is established as body of the EU and shall have legal personality (Article 68(1)). The EDPB shall be composed of the head of one supervisory authority of each Member State and of the European Data Protection Supervisor, or their respective representatives (Article 68(3)). The EDPB shall act independently when performing its tasks or exercising its powers pursuant to Articles 70 and 71 (Article 69(1)).

Context of GDPR

26.14   The initial provisions refer to the context of the GDPR, namely, the subject matter and objectives (Article 1); material scope (Article 2); and territorial scope (Article 3).

GDPR Definitions

26.15   Article 4 of the new GDPR sets out the important definitions for the new data protection regime, as more particularly detailed in para **3.04** above.

---

65   *Strengthening Health Information Infrastructure for Health Care Quality Governance: Good Practices, New Opportunities, and Data Privacy Protection Challenges*, OECD (2013).

New Processing Rules: Obligations

26.16 The new processing rules as set out in the new GDPR regime are set out below.

The Recitals refer to the following: data processing must be lawful and fair (Recital 39); processing necessary for a contract (Recital 40); processing for a legal obligation (Recital 40); processing necessary to protect life (Recital 46); the legitimate interests of the Controller (Recital 47).

(Data Protection) Principles

26.17 Article 5 of the GDPR sets out the new principles relating to data protection. Personal data must be:

- processed lawfully, fairly and in a transparent manner in relation to the Data Subject ('lawfulness, fairness and transparency');
- collected for specified, explicit and legitimate purposes and not further processed in a manner that is incompatible with those purposes; further processing for archiving purposes in the public interest, scientific or historical research purposes or statistical purposes shall, in accordance with Article 89(1), not be considered to be incompatible with the initial purposes ('purpose limitation');
- adequate, relevant and limited to what is necessary in relation to the purposes for which they are processed ('data minimisation');
- accurate and, where necessary, kept up to date; every reasonable step must be taken to ensure that personal data that are inaccurate, having regard to the purposes for which they are processed, are erased or rectified without delay ('accuracy');
- kept in a form which permits identification of Data Subjects for no longer than is necessary for the purposes for which the personal data are processed; personal data may be stored for longer periods insofar as the personal data will be processed solely for archiving purposes in the public interest, scientific or historical research purposes or statistical purposes in accordance with Article 89(1) subject to implementation of the appropriate technical and organisational measures required by the GDPR in order to safeguard the rights and freedoms of the Data Subject ('storage limitation');
- processed in a way that ensures appropriate security of the personal data, including protection against unauthorised or unlawful processing and against accidental loss, destruction or damage, using appropriate technical or organisational measures ('integrity and confidentiality').

The Controller must be responsible for and be able to demonstrate compliance with the above ('accountability').

These can be summarised as:

- processed lawfully, fairly and transparently ('lawfulness, fairness and transparency');
- for specified, explicit and legitimate purposes and not further processed incompatibly with the purpose; (with a carveout) ('purpose limitation');
- adequate, relevant and limited to what is necessary for the purposes ('data minimisation');
- accurate and, where necessary, kept up to date; every reasonable step must be taken to ensure that personal data that are inaccurate, having regard to the purposes for which they are processed, are erased or rectified without delay ('accuracy');
- kept in a form which permits identification for no longer than is necessary; (with a carveout) ('storage limitation');
- appropriate security, including protection against unauthorised or unlawful processing and against accidental loss, destruction or damage, using appropriate technical or organisational measures ('integrity and confidentiality').

The Controller must demonstrate compliance ('accountability').

Lawfulness of Processing: Legitimate Processing Conditions

26.18 Article 6 of the GDPR sets out the new provisions in relation to the lawfulness of processing. Processing of personal data shall be lawful only if and to the extent that at least one of the following applies:

- the Data Subject has given *consent* to the processing of their personal data for one or more specific purposes (see section below at para **26.19** and also Article 7);
- processing is necessary for the performance of a contract to which the Data Subject is party or in order to take steps at the request of the Data Subject prior to entering into a contract;
- processing is necessary for compliance with a legal obligation to which the Controller is subject;
- processing is necessary in order to protect the vital interests of the Data Subject or of another natural person;
- processing is necessary for the performance of a task carried out in the public interest or in the exercise of official authority vested in the Controller;
- processing is necessary for the purposes of the legitimate interests pursued by the Controller or by a third party, except where such interests are overridden by the interests or fundamental rights and freedoms of the Data Subject which require protection of personal data, in particular where the Data Subject is a child. This shall not

apply to processing carried out by public authorities in the performance of their tasks (Article 6(1)).

Member States may maintain or introduce more specific provisions to adapt the application of the rules of the GDPR with regard to the processing of personal data for compliance with Article 6(1)(c) and (e) by determining more precisely specific requirements for the processing and other measures to ensure lawful and fair processing including for other specific processing situations as provided for in Chapter IX (Article 6(2)). The basis for the processing referred to in Article 6(1)(c) and (e) must be laid down by EU law, or Member State law to which the Controller is subject.

The purpose of the processing shall be determined in this legal basis or as regards the processing referred to in Article 6(1)(e), shall be necessary for the performance of a task carried out in the public interest or in the exercise of official authority vested in the Controller. This legal basis may contain specific provisions to adapt the application of rules of the GDPR, *inter alia* the general conditions governing the lawfulness of processing by the Controller, the type of data which are subject to the processing, the Data Subjects concerned; the entities to, and the purposes for which the data may be disclosed; the purpose limitation; storage periods and processing operations and processing procedures, including measures to ensure lawful and fair processing, such as those for other specific processing situations as provided for in Chapter IX. EU law or the Member State law must meet an objective of public interest and be proportionate to the legitimate aim pursued (Article 6(3)).

Where the processing for another purpose than the one for which the data have been collected is not based on the Data Subject's consent or on EU or Member State law which constitutes a necessary and proportionate measure in a democratic society to safeguard the objectives referred to in Article 23(1), the Controller shall, in order to ascertain whether processing for another purpose is compatible with the purpose for which the personal data are initially collected, take into account, *inter alia*:

- any link between the purposes for which the data have been collected and the purposes of the intended further processing;
- the context in which the personal data have been collected, in particular regarding the relationship between Data Subjects and the Controller;
- the nature of the personal data, in particular whether special categories of personal data are processed, pursuant to Article 9 or whether personal data related to criminal convictions and offences are processed, pursuant to Article 10;

- the possible consequences of the intended further processing for Data Subjects;
- the existence of appropriate safeguards, which may include encryption or pseudonymisation (Article 7(4)).

Prior to the new GDPD, the ICO has issued recommendations in relation to marketing personal data issues, namely:

- Direct Marketing;
- Direct Marketing Checklist – Ideal for Small Businesses;
- Companies Receiving Unwanted Marketing;
- Guidance on Political Campaigning.

These now need to be read in light of the GDPR changes.

Consent for Processing: Conditions for Consent

26.19   Consent is an important issue under the new GDPR.[66] Lawful processing and consent are referred to in Recital 40. The WP29 also refers to consent issues.[67]

Article 7 of the GDPR refers to conditions for consent as follows. Where processing is based on consent, the Controller shall be able to demonstrate that the Data Subject has consented to the processing of their personal data (Article 7(1)).

If the Data Subject's consent is given in the context of a written declaration which also concerns other matters, the request for consent must be presented in a manner which is *clearly distinguishable* from other matters, in an *intelligible and easily accessible form*, using *clear and plain language*. Any part of such a declaration which constitutes an infringement of the GDPR shall not be binding (Article 7(2)).

The Data Subject shall have the *right to withdraw his or her consent at any time*. The withdrawal of consent shall not affect the lawfulness of processing based on consent before its withdrawal. Prior to giving consent, the Data Subject shall be informed thereof. It shall be as easy to withdraw consent as to give consent (Article 7(3)).

When assessing whether consent is freely given, utmost account shall be taken of the fact whether, *inter alia*, the performance of a service, is conditional on consent to the processing of personal data that is not necessary for the performance of this contract (Article 7(4)).

---

66 JP Vandenbroucke and J Olsen, 'Informed Consent and the New EU Regulation on Data Protection,' *International Journal of Epidemiology* (2013) (42: 6) 1891.
67 WP29 Opinion 15/2011 Consent; Working Document 02/2013 providing guidance on obtaining consent for cookies, 201; Opinion 04/2012 on Cookie Consent Exemption.

Children

26.20 The issue of children in the data protection regime have been steadily rising. The increased use of social media and Web 2.0 services enhance the exposures and risks for children and the uninitiated.[68]

This has included children's groups, regulators and also the EDPB (previously the WP29). WP29 issued Opinion 2/2009 on the Protection of Children's Personal Data (General Guidelines and the Special Case of Schools) in 2009 and also Working Document 1/2008 on the Protection of Children's Personal Data (General Guidelines and the Special Case of Schools) in 2008. Schools are being encouraged to be proactive and to have appropriate codes and policies for children's social media and internet usage.[69]

There is now going to be an explicit acknowledgement of children's interest in the EU data protection regime, unlike with the DPD which contained no explicit reference. The GDPR refers to a 'child' including as below the age of 16 years. This is significant amongst other things in relation consent, contracting, etc. It is also significant for social networks which have significant numbers of children. Up until now it was common for certain social networks to purport to accept users only over the age of 13. A child was defined in the first and final version of the GDPR as up to 18 years of age. Therefore, the potential implications will require careful assessment. This includes, for example, social contracts, consent, notices, terms of use, contract terms, payment and purchase issues, related process models, sign-ups, social media, internet, etc.

Article 8 of the original proposal for the GDPR contained provisions in relation to the processing of personal data of a child. The final version of Article 8(1) provided that where Article 6(1)(a) applies, in relation to the offer of information society services directly to a child, the processing of the personal data of a child shall be lawful where the child is at least 16 years old. Where the child is below the age of 16 years, such processing shall be lawful only if and to the extent that consent is given or authorised by the holder of parental responsibility over the child. The original Article 8(1) proposal provided that Article 8(1) shall not affect

---

68 See, for example, D Gourlay and G Gallagher, 'Collecting and Using Children's Information Online: the UK/US Dichotomy,' SCL *Computers and Law*, 12 December 2011.

69 Note generally, for example, JS Groppe, 'A Child's Playground or a Predator's Hunting Ground? – How to Protect Children on Internet Social Networking Sites,' *CommLaw Conspectus* (2007)(16) 215–245; EP Steadman, 'MySpace, But Who's Responsibility? Liability of Social Networking Websites When Offline Sexual Assault of Minors Follows Online Interaction,' *Villanova Sports and Entertainment Law Journal* (2007) (14) 363–397; DC Beckstrom, 'Who's Looking at Your Facebook Profile? The Use of Student Conduct Codes to Censor College Students' Online Speech,' *Willamette Law Review* (2008) 261–312.

the general contract law of Member States, such as the rules on the validity, formation or effect of a contract in relation to a child. Under the original Article 8(3) the Commission is empowered to adopt delegated acts in accordance with Article 86 for the purpose of further specifying the criteria and requirements for the methods to obtain verifiable consent referred to in Article 8(1). In doing so, the Commission shall consider specific measures for micro, small and medium-sized enterprises (original draft Article 8(3)). In addition, the Commission under may lay down standard forms for specific methods to obtain verifiable consent referred to in Article 8(1). Those implementing acts shall be adopted in accordance with the examination procedure referred to in Article 87(2) (original draft Article 8(4)).

The explicit reference to children is new, and some would argue overdue. Increasingly, the activities of children on the internet and on social media, poses risks and concerns.[70] This has been further emphasised of late with tragic events involving online abuse, in particular cyber bullying. Risks arise obviously from their activities online (eg inappropriate content, cyber bullying, but also from the collection and use of their personal data online and collected online, sometimes without their knowledge or consent). Their personal data and privacy is more vulnerable than that of older people.

It is important for organisation to note the 'child' provisions in the GDPR. This will have implications in how organisations:

- consider the interaction with children and what personal data may be collected and processed;
- ensure that there is appropriate compliance for such collection and processing for children as distinct from adults.

Child's Consent: Conditions for Information Society Services

26.21 Processing of children's personal data are referred to in Recital 38.

Article 8 of the GDPR makes new provisions in relation to conditions for children's consent for Information Society services. Where Article 6(1)(a) applies, in relation to the offer of information society services directly to a child, the processing of personal data of *a child shall be lawful where the child is at least 16* years old. Where the child is *below the age of 16 years*, such processing shall only be lawful if and to the extent that consent is given or authorised by the holder of *parental responsibility* over the child (Article 8(1)).

---

70 See, for example, L McDermott, 'Legal Issues Associated with Minors and Their Use of Social Networking Sites,' *Communications Law* (2012) (17) 19–24.

The Controller shall make reasonable efforts to verify in such cases that consent is given or authorised by the holder of parental responsibility over the child, taking into consideration available technology (Article 8(2)). This shall not affect the general contract law of Member States such as the rules on the validity, formation or effect of a contract in relation to a child (Article 8(3)).

Processing Special Categories of Personal Data

26.22   Sensitive personal data are referred to in Recitals 10 and 51 and special categories of personal data are referred to in Recitals 10, 51, 52, 53, 54, 71, 80, 91 and 97.

Article 9 refers to the processing of special categories of personal data. The processing of personal data, revealing racial or ethnic origin, political opinions, religious or philosophical beliefs, or trade-union membership, and the processing of genetic data, biometric data for the purpose of uniquely identifying a natural person, data concerning health or data concerning a natural person's sex life and sexual orientation shall be *prohibited* (Article 9(1)).[71]

The above shall not apply if one of the following applies:

- the Data Subject has given *explicit consent* to the processing of those personal data for one or more specified purposes, except where EU law or Member State law provide that the above prohibition may not be lifted by the Data Subject;
- processing is necessary for the purposes of carrying out the obligations and exercising specific rights of the Controller or of the Data Subject in the field of employment and social security and social protection law in so far as it is authorised by EU law or Member State law or a collective agreement pursuant to Member State law providing for adequate safeguards for the fundamental rights and the interests of the Data Subject;
- processing is necessary to protect the vital interests of the Data Subject or of another natural person where the Data Subject is physically or legally incapable of giving consent;
- processing is carried out in the course of its legitimate activities with appropriate safeguards by a foundation, association or any other not-for-profit-seeking body with a political, philosophical, religious or trade union aim and on condition that the processing

---

71   In relation to genetic data generally, see for example D Hallinan, PJA de Hert and M Friedewald, 'Genetic Data and the Data Protection Regulation: Anonymity, Multiple Subjects, Sensitivity and a Prohibitionary Logic Regarding Genetic Data?,' *Computer Law and Security Review* (2013) (29: 4) 317.

relates solely to the members or to former members of the body or to persons who have regular contact with it in connection with its purposes and that the personal data are not disclosed outside that body without the consent of the Data Subjects;

- processing relates to personal data which are manifestly made public by the Data Subject;
- processing is necessary for the establishment, exercise or defence of legal claims or whenever courts are acting in their judicial capacity;
- processing is necessary for reasons of substantial public interest, on the basis of EU or Member State law which shall be proportionate to the aim pursued, respect the essence of the right to data protection and provide for suitable and specific measures to safeguard the fundamental rights and the interests of the Data Subject;
- processing is necessary for the purposes of preventive or occupational medicine, for the assessment of the working capacity of the employee, medical diagnosis, the provision of health or social care or treatment or the management of health or social care systems and services on the basis of EU law or Member State law or pursuant to contract with a health professional and subject to the conditions and safeguards referred to in Article 9(3); [h] or
- processing is necessary for reasons of public interest in the area of public health, such as protecting against serious cross-border threats to health or ensuring high standards of quality and safety of health care and of medicinal products or medical devices, on the basis of EU law or Member State law which provides for suitable and specific measures to safeguard the rights and freedoms of the Data Subject, in particular professional secrecy;
- processing is necessary for archiving purposes in the public interest, scientific or historical research purposes or statistical purposes in accordance with Article 89(1) based on EU or Member State law which shall be proportionate to the aim pursued, respect the essence of the right to data protection and provide for suitable and specific measures to safeguard the fundamental rights and the interests of the Data Subject (Article 9(2)).

Personal data referred to in Article 9(1) may be processed for the purposes referred to in Article 9(2)(h) when those data are processed by or under the responsibility of a professional subject to the obligation of professional secrecy under EU or Member State law or rules established by national competent bodies or by another person also subject to an obligation of secrecy under EU or Member State law or rules established by national competent bodies (Article 9(3)).

Member States may maintain or introduce further conditions, including limitations, with regard to the processing of genetic data, biometric data or health data (Article 9(5)).

Health Research

26.23 The issue of health research was just one of the matters which proved to be of some controversy during the discussions for the GDPR. The final provisions include the following. The sensitive data processing prohibition in Article 9(1) shall not apply in the following health research instances:

- processing is necessary for the purposes of preventive or occupational medicine, for the assessment of the working capacity of the employee, medical diagnosis, the provision of health or social care or treatment or the management of health or social care systems and services on the basis of EU or Member State law or pursuant to contract with a health professional and subject to the conditions and safeguards referred to in paragraph 3 (Article 9(2)(h));
- processing is necessary for reasons of public interest in the area of public health, such as protecting against serious cross-border threats to health or ensuring high standards of quality and safety of health care and of medicinal products or medical devices, on the basis of EU or Member State law which provides for suitable and specific measures to safeguard the rights and freedoms of the data subject, in particular professional secrecy (Article 9(2)(i)).

Personal data referred to in Article 9(1) may be processed for the purposes referred to in Article 9(2)(h) when those data are processed by or under the responsibility of a professional subject to the obligation of professional secrecy under Union or Member State law or rules established by national competent bodies or by another person also subject to an obligation of secrecy under EU or Member State law or rules established by national competent bodies (Article 9(3)).

Processing re Criminal Convictions and Offences Data

26.24 Article 10 refers to processing of data relating to criminal convictions and offences. Processing of personal data relating to criminal convictions and offences or related security measures based on Article 6(1) shall be carried out only under the control of official authority or when the processing is authorised by EU law or Member State law providing for adequate safeguards for the rights and freedoms of Data Subjects. Any comprehensive register of criminal convictions may be kept only under the control of official authority.

Processing Not Requiring Identification

26.25 Article 11 refers to processing not requiring identification. If the purposes for which a Controller processes personal data *do not or do no longer require* the identification of a Data Subject by the Controller, the Controller shall not be obliged to maintain, acquire or process additional information in order to identify the Data Subject for the sole purpose of complying with the GDPR (Article 11(1)).

Where, in such cases the Controller is able to demonstrate that it is not in a position to identify the Data Subject, the Controller shall inform the Data Subject accordingly, if possible. In such cases, Articles 15 to 20 shall not apply except where the Data Subject, for the purpose of exercising their rights under these articles, provides additional information enabling their identification (Article 11(2)).

Controllers and Processors

26.26 Chapter IV of the GDPR refers to Controllers and Processors. Chapter IV, Section 1 refers to general obligations. The WP29 also refers to Controller and Processor issues.[72]

Responsibility of the Controller

26.27 Taking into account the nature, scope, context and purposes of the processing as well as the risks of varying likelihood and severity for the rights and freedoms of individuals, the Controller shall implement appropriate technical and organisational measures to ensure and be able to demonstrate that the processing of personal data is performed in compliance with the GDPR. Those measures shall be reviewed and updated where necessary (Article 24(1)).

Where proportionate in relation to the processing activities, the measures referred to in Article 24(1) shall include the implementation of appropriate data protection policies by the Controller (Article 24(2)).

Adherence to approved codes of conduct pursuant to Article 40 or an approved certification mechanism pursuant to Article 42 may be used as an element to demonstrate compliance with the obligations of the Controller (Article 24(3)).

Joint Controllers

26.28 Where two or more Controllers jointly determine the purposes and means of the processing of personal data, they are joint Controllers. They shall, in a transparent manner, determine their respective responsibilities for compliance with the obligations under the GDPR,

---

72 WP29 Opinion 1/2010 on the concepts of 'controller' and 'processor.'

in particular as regards the exercising of the rights of the Data Subject and their respective duties to provide the information referred to in Articles 13 and 14, by means of an arrangement between them unless, and in so far as, the respective responsibilities of the Controllers are determined by EU or Member State law to which the Controllers are subject. The arrangement may designate a point of contact for Data Subjects (Article 26(1)).

The arrangement shall duly reflect the joint Controllers' respective effective roles and relationships vis-à-vis Data Subjects. The essence of the arrangement shall be made available for the Data Subject (Article 26(2)).[73]

Irrespective of the terms of the arrangement referred to in Article 24(1), the Data Subject may exercise their rights under the GDPR in respect of and against each of the Controllers (Article 24(3)).

Processor

26.29   Where a processing is to be carried out on behalf of a Controller, the Controller shall use only Processors providing sufficient guarantees to implement appropriate technical and organisational measures in such a manner that the processing will meet the requirements of the GDPR and ensure the protection of the rights of the Data Subject (Article 28(1)).

The Processor shall not engage another Processor without the prior specific or general written authorisation of the Controller. In the case of general written authorisation, the Processor shall inform the Controller on any intended changes concerning the addition or replacement of other Processors, thereby giving the Controller the opportunity to object to such changes (Article 28(2)).

The carrying out of processing by a Processor shall be governed by a contract or other legal act under EU or Member State law, that is binding the Processor with regard to the Controller and that sets out the subject-matter and duration of the processing, the nature and purpose of the processing, the type of personal data and categories of Data Subjects and the obligations and rights of the Controller. The contract or other legal act shall stipulate, in particular, that the Processor:

- process the personal data only on documented instructions from the Controller, including with regard to transfers of personal data to a third country or an international organisation, unless required to do so by EU or Member State law to which the Processor is subject; in

---

73   Generally see J Mäkinen, 'Data Quality, Sensitive Data and Joint Controllership as Examples of Grey Areas in the Existing Data Protection Framework for the Internet of Things,' *Information & Communications Technology Law* (2015) (24:3) 262.

such a case, the Processor shall inform the Controller of that legal requirement before processing the data, unless that law prohibits such information on important grounds of public interest;

- ensure that persons authorised to process the personal data have committed themselves to confidentiality or are under an appropriate statutory obligation of confidentiality;
- take all measures required pursuant to Article 32;
- respect the conditions referred to in Article 28(2) and (4) for engaging another Processor;
- taking into account the nature of the processing, assist the Controller by appropriate technical and organisational measures, insofar as this is possible, for the fulfilment of the Controller's obligation to respond to requests for exercising the Data Subject's rights laid down in Chapter III;
- assist the Controller in ensuring compliance with the obligations pursuant to Articles 32 to 36 taking into account the nature of processing and the information available to the Processor;
- at the choice of the Controller, deletes or returns all the personal data to the Controller after the end of the provision of services relating to processing, and deletes existing copies unless EU or Member State law requires storage of the personal data;
- make available to the Controller all information necessary to demonstrate compliance with the obligations laid down in this Article and allow for and contribute to audits, including inspections, conducted by the Controller or another auditor mandated by the Controller. (With regard to this point, the Processor shall immediately inform the Controller if, in its opinion, an instruction breaches the GDPR or EU or Member State data protection provisions) (Article 28(3)).

Where a Processor engages another Processor for carrying out specific processing activities on behalf of the Controller, the same data protection obligations as set out in the contract or other legal act between the Controller and the Processor as referred to in Article 28(3) shall be imposed on that other Processor by way of a contract or other legal act under EU or Member State law, in particular providing sufficient guarantees to implement appropriate technical and organisational measures in such a manner that the processing will meet the requirements of the GDPR. Where that other Processor fails to fulfil its data protection obligations, the initial Processor shall remain fully liable to the Controller for the performance of that other Processor's obligations (Article 28(4)).

Adherence of the Processor to an approved code of conduct pursuant to Article 40 or an approved certification mechanism pursuant to Article 42 may be used as an element to demonstrate sufficient guarantees referred to in Article 28(1) and (4) (Article 28(5)).

Without prejudice to an individual contract between the Controller and the Processor, the contract or the other legal act referred to in Article 26(3) and (4) may be based, in whole or in part, on standard contractual clauses referred to in Article 28(7) and (8), including when they are part of a certification granted to the Controller or Processor pursuant to Articles 42 and 43 (Article 28(6)).

The Commission may lay down standard contractual clauses for the matters referred to in Article 28(3) and (4) and in accordance with the examination procedure referred to in Article 93(2) (Article 28(7)).

A supervisory authority may adopt standard contractual clauses for the matters referred to in Article 28(3) and (4) and in accordance with the consistency mechanism referred to in Article 63 (Article 28(8)).

The contract or the other legal act referred to in Article 28(3) and (4) shall be in writing, including in an electronic form (Article 28(9)).

Without prejudice to Articles 82, 83 and 84, if a Processor infringes the GDPR by determining the purposes and means of data processing, the Processor shall be considered to be a Controller in respect of that processing (Article 28(10)).

Organisations acting as Processors should recall that while they may indeed be Processors, they can also at the same time be Controllers in relation to different sets of personal data.

Processing Under Authority of Controller and Processor

26.30   The Processor and any person acting under the authority of the Controller or of the Processor who has access to personal data shall not process them except on instructions from the Controller, unless required to do so by EU or Member State law (Article 29).

Records of Processing Activities

26.31   Each Controller and where applicable the Controller's representative, shall maintain a record of processing activities under its responsibility. This record shall contain all of the following information:

- the name and contact details of the Controller and where applicable the joint Controller, the Controller's representative and the DPO;
- the purposes of the processing;
- a description of categories of Data Subjects and of the categories of personal data;
- the categories of recipients to whom the personal data have been or will be disclosed including recipients in third countries or international organisations;
- where applicable, transfers of data to a third country or an international organisation, including the identification of that third country

or international organisation and, in case of transfers referred to in Article 49(1), the documentation of suitable safeguards;
- where possible, the envisaged time limits for erasure of the different categories of data;
- where possible, a general description of the technical and organisational security measures referred to in Article 32(1) (Article 30(1)).

Each Processor and, where applicable, the Processor's representative shall maintain a record of all categories of processing activities carried out on behalf of a Controller, containing:

- the name and contact details of the Processor or Processors and of each Controller on behalf of which the Processor is acting, and where applicable of the Controller's or the Processor's representative, and the DPO;
- the categories of processing carried out on behalf of each Controller;
- where applicable, transfers of data to a third country or an international organisation, including the identification of that third country or international organisation and, in case of transfers referred to in Article 49(1), the documentation of suitable safeguards;
- where possible, a general description of the technical and organisational security measures referred to in Article 32(1) (Article 30(2)).

The records referred to in Article 30(1) and (2) shall be in writing, including in an electronic form (Article 30(3)).

The Controller and the Processor and, where applicable, the Controller's or the Processor's representative, shall make the record available to the supervisory authority on request (Article 30(4)).

The obligations referred to in Article 30(1) and (2) shall not apply to an enterprise or an organisation employing fewer than 250 persons unless the processing it carries out is likely to result in a risk to the rights and freedoms of Data Subject, the processing is not occasional, or the processing includes special categories of data as referred to in Article 9(1) or personal data relating to criminal convictions and offences referred to in Article 10 (Article 30(5)).

Representatives of Controllers Not Established in EU

26.32 Where Article 3(2) applies, the Controller or the Processor shall designate in writing a representative in the EU (Article 27(1)).

This obligation shall not apply to:

- processing which is occasional, does not include, on a large scale, processing of special categories of data as referred to in Article 9(1) or processing of personal data relating to criminal convictions and offences referred to in Article 10, and is unlikely to result in a risk

for the rights and freedoms of natural persons, taking into account
the nature, context, scope and purposes of the processing; or

- a public authority or body (Article 27(2)).

The representative shall be established in one of the Member States
where the Data Subjects whose personal data are processed in relation to the offering of goods or services to them, or whose behaviour is
monitored, are (Article 27(3)).

The representative shall be mandated by the Controller or the Processor to be addressed in addition to or instead of the Controller or the Processor by, in particular, supervisory authorities and Data Subjects, on all
issues related to the processing, for the purposes of ensuring compliance
with the GDPR (Article 27(4)).

The designation of a representative by the Controller or the Processor shall be without prejudice to legal actions which could be initiated
against the Controller or the Processor themselves (Article 28(5)).

Cooperation with Supervisory Authority

26.33 The Controller and the Processor and, where applicable, their
representatives, shall co-operate, on request, with the supervisory authority in the performance of its tasks (Article 31).

Data Protection by Design (DPbD) and by Default

26.34 Article 25 refers to data protection by design and by default.
Note also the related concept, or precursor concept, of Privacy by
Design (PbD). In some ways PbD is the impetus for the current DPbD
rules.

Taking into account the state of the art and the cost of implementation
and the nature, scope, context and purposes of the processing as well as
the risks of varying likelihood and severity for rights and freedoms of
natural persons posed by the processing, the Controller shall, both at the
time of the determination of the means for processing and at the time of
the processing itself, implement appropriate technical and organisational
measures, such as pseudonymisation, which are designed to implement
data protection principles, such as data minimisation, in an effective
manner and to integrate the necessary safeguards into the processing in
order to meet the requirements of the GDPR and protect the rights of
Data Subjects (Article 25(1)).

The Controller shall implement appropriate technical and organisational measures for ensuring that, by default, only personal data which
are necessary for each specific purpose of the processing are processed.
That obligation applies to the amount of data collected, the extent of their
processing, the period of their storage and their accessibility. In particular, such measures shall ensure that by default personal data are not made

accessible without the individual's intervention to an indefinite number of natural persons (Article 27(2)).

An approved certification mechanism pursuant to Article 42 may be used as an element to demonstrate compliance with the requirements set out in Article 25(1) and (2) (Article 25(3)).

Rectification and Erasure

26.35 See details of obligations below.

Security

26.36 The Recitals refer to: network and information security, Computer Emergency Response Teams (CERTs) and Computer Security Incident Response Teams (CSIRTs); appropriate technical and organisational measures; security and risk evaluation; high risk and impact assessments; and impact assessments; and large scale processing operations; consultations; data breach and data breach notification; Commission delegated acts.

Chapter IV, Section 2 of the GDPR refers to security in detail.

Security of Processing

26.37 Having regard to the state of the art and the costs of implementation and taking into account the nature, scope, context and purposes of the processing as well as the risk of varying likelihood and severity for the rights and freedoms of natural persons, the Controller and the Processor shall implement appropriate technical and organisational measures, to ensure a level of security appropriate to the risk, including, *inter alia*, as appropriate:

- the pseudonymisation and encryption of personal data;
- the ability to ensure the ongoing confidentiality, integrity, availability and resilience of processing systems and services;
- the ability to restore the availability and access to data in a timely manner in the event of a physical or technical incident;
- a process for regularly testing, assessing and evaluating the effectiveness of technical and organisational measures for ensuring the security of the processing (Article 32(1)).

In assessing the appropriate level of security account shall be taken in particular of the risks that are presented by processing, in particular from accidental or unlawful destruction, loss, alteration, unauthorised disclosure of, or access to personal data transmitted, stored or otherwise processed (Article 32(2)).

Adherence to an approved code of conduct pursuant to Article 40 or an approved certification mechanism pursuant to Article 42 may be used as an element to demonstrate compliance with the requirements set out in Article 32(1) (Article 32(3)).

The Controller and Processor shall take steps to ensure that any natural person acting under the authority of the Controller or the Processor who has access to personal data shall not process them except on instructions from the Controller, unless he or she is required to do so by EU or Member State law (Article 32(4)).

Prior to the new GDPD, the ICO has issued recommendations in relation security issues, namely:

- A Practical Guide to IT Security: Ideal for the Small Business;
- Guidance on Data Security Breach Management;
- Notification of Data Security Breaches to the Information Commissioner's Office;
- Notification of Privacy and Electronic Communications Security Breaches.

These now need to be read in light of the GDPR changes.

Notifying Data Breach to Supervisory Authority

26.38   In the case of a personal data breach, the Controller shall without undue delay and, where feasible, not later than 72 hours after having become aware of it, notify the personal data breach to the supervisory authority competent in accordance with Article 55, unless the personal data breach is unlikely to result in *a* risk for the rights and freedoms of natural persons. Where the notification to the supervisory authority is not made within 72 hours, it shall be accompanied by a reason for the delay (Article 33(1)).

The Processor shall notify the Controller without undue delay after becoming aware of a personal data breach (Article 33(2)).

The notification referred to in Article 33(1) must at least:

- describe the nature of the personal data breach including where possible, the categories and approximate number of Data Subjects concerned and the categories and approximate number of data records concerned;
- communicate the name and contact details of the DPO or other contact point where more information can be obtained;
- describe the likely consequences of the personal data breach;
- describe the measures taken or proposed to be taken by the Controller to address the personal data breach, including, where appropriate, measures to mitigate its possible adverse effects (Article 33(2)).

Where, and in so far as, it is not possible to provide the information at the same time, the information may be provided in phases without undue further delay (Article 33(4)).

The Controller shall document any personal data breaches, comprising the facts relating to the personal data breach, its effects and the remedial action taken. This documentation must enable the supervisory authority to verify compliance with this Article (Article 33(5)).

Organisations should obviously review their security procedures. However, in accordance with the GDPR obligations and in accordance with planned preparedness, organisations should have procedures for how and when they notify the ICO. (Depending on the organisation and sector, other regulators may also need to be notified.)

Each organisation should have a prepared notification procedure and letter for the ICO in the event that it is needed. This may be incorporated into an overall data breach procedure for the organisation.

WP29 also refers to breach and breach notification issues in one of its official documents.[74]

Communicating Data Breach to Data Subject

26.39 When the personal data breach is likely to result in a high risk to the rights and freedoms of natural persons, the Controller shall communicate the personal data breach to the Data Subject without undue delay (Article 34(1)).

The communication to the Data Subject referred to in Article 34(1) shall describe in clear and plain language the nature of the personal data breach and contain at least the information and measures referred to in Article 33(3)(b), (c) and (d) (Article 34(2)).

The communication to the Data Subject shall not be required if:

- the Controller has implemented appropriate technical and organisational protection measures, and that those measures were applied to the data affected by the personal data breach, in particular those that render the data unintelligible to any person who is not authorised to access it, such as encryption;
- the Controller has taken subsequent measures which ensure that the high risk for the rights and freedoms of Data Subjects referred to in Article 34(3) is no longer likely to materialise;
- it would involve disproportionate effort. In such a case, there shall instead be a public communication or similar measure, whereby the Data Subjects are informed in an equally effective manner (Article 34(3)).

---

74 WP29, Opinion 03/2014 on Personal Data Breach Notification. Also see WP29; Working Document 01/2011 on the current EU personal data breach framework and recommendations for future policy developments; Opinion 06/2012 on the draft Commission Decision on the measures applicable to the notification of personal data breaches under Directive 2002/58/EC on privacy and electronic communications.

If the Controller has not already communicated the personal data breach to the Data Subject, the supervisory authority, having considered the likelihood of the personal data breach resulting in a high risk, may require it to do so or may decide that any of the conditions referred to in Article 34(3) are met (Article 34(4)).

Each organisation should have a prepared Data Subject notification procedure and letter/email for the Data Subject in the event that it is needed. This may be incorporated into an overall data breach procedure for the organisation.

Data Protection Impact Assessment and Prior Consultation

26.40 Chapter IV, Section 3 of the GDPR refers to impact assessments and prior consultations. The WP29 also refers to impact assessments.[75]

Data Protection Impact Assessment

26.41 Where a type of processing in particular using new technologies, and taking into account the nature, scope, context and purposes of the processing, is likely to result in a high risk for the rights and freedoms of natural persons, the Controller shall, prior to the processing, carry out an assessment of the impact of the envisaged processing operations on the protection of personal data. A single assessment may address a set of similar processing operations that present similar high risks (Article 35(1)).

The Controller shall seek the advice of the DPO, where designated, when carrying out a data protection impact assessment (Article 35(2)).

A data protection impact assessment referred to in Article 35(1) shall in particular be required in the case of:

- a systematic and extensive evaluation of personal aspects relating to natural persons which is based on automated processing, including

---

75 WP29 Opinion 03/2014 on Personal Data Breach Notification; Opinion 07/2013 on the Data Protection Impact Assessment Template for Smart Grid and Smart Metering Systems ('DPIA Template') prepared by Expert Group 2 of the Commission's Smart Grid Task Force; Opinion 04/2013 on the Data Protection Impact Assessment Template for Smart Grid and Smart Metering Systems ('DPIA Template') prepared by Expert Group 2 of the Commission's Smart Grid Task Force; Opinion 9/2011 on the revised Industry Proposal for a Privacy and Data Protection Impact Assessment Framework for RFID Applications (and Annex: Privacy and Data Protection Impact Assessment Framework for RFID Applications); Opinion 5/2010 on the Industry Proposal for a Privacy and Data Protection Impact Assessment Framework for RFID Applications; Statement on the role of a risk-based approach in data protection legal framework, 2014.

profiling, and on which decisions are based that produce legal effects concerning the individual person or similarly significantly affect the natural person;

- processing on a large scale of special categories of data referred to in Article 9(1), or of personal data relating to criminal convictions and offences referred to in Article 10;
- a systematic monitoring of a publicly accessible area on a large scale (Article 35(3)).

The supervisory authority shall establish and make public a list of the kind of processing operations which are subject to the requirement for a data protection impact assessment pursuant to Article 35(1). The supervisory authority shall communicate those lists to the EDPB (Article 35(4)).

The supervisory authority may also establish and make public a list of the kind of processing operations for which no data protection impact assessment is required. The supervisory authority shall communicate those lists to the EDPB (Article 35(5)).

Prior to the adoption of the lists referred to in Article 35(4) and (5) the competent supervisory authority shall apply the consistency mechanism referred to in Article 63 where such lists involve processing activities which are related to the offering of goods or services to Data Subjects or to the monitoring of their behaviour in several Member States, or may substantially affect the free movement of personal data within the EU (Article 35(6)).

The assessment shall contain at least:

- a systematic description of the envisaged processing operations and the purposes of the processing, including where applicable the legitimate interest pursued by the Controller;
- an assessment of the necessity and proportionality of the processing operations in relation to the purposes;
- an assessment of the risks to the rights and freedoms of Data Subjects referred to in Article 35(1); and
- the measures envisaged to address the risks, including safeguards, security measures and mechanisms to ensure the protection of personal data and to demonstrate compliance with the GDPR taking into account the rights and legitimate interests of Data Subjects and other persons concerned (Article 35(7)).

Compliance with approved codes of conduct referred to in Article 40 by the relevant Controllers or Processors shall be taken into due account in assessing the impact of the processing operations performed by such Controllers or Processors, in particular for the purposes of a data protection impact assessment (Article 35(8)).

Where appropriate, the Controller shall seek the views of Data Subjects or their representatives on the intended processing, without prejudice to the protection of commercial or public interests or the security of the processing operations (Article 35(9)).

Where the processing pursuant to Article 6(1)(c) or (e) has a legal basis in EU law, or the law of the Member State to which the Controller is subject, that law regulates the specific processing operation or set of operations in question, and a data protection impact assessment has already been carried out as part of a general impact assessment in the context of the adoption of that legal basis, Article 35(1)–(7) shall not apply, unless Member States deem it to be necessary to carry out such an assessment prior to the processing activities (Article 35(10)).

Where necessary, the Controller shall carry out a review to assess if the processing is performed with the data protection impact assessment at least when there is a change of the risk represented by the processing operations (Article 35(11)).

Organisations must assess their obligations in terms of implementing procedures for, and undertaking of, DPIAs.[76]

Prior Consultation

26.42 The Controller shall consult the supervisory authority prior to the processing where a data protection impact assessment as provided for in Article 35 indicates that the processing would result in a high risk in the absence of measures taken by the Controller to mitigate the risk (Article 36(1)).

Where the supervisory authority is of the opinion that the intended processing referred to in Article 36(2) would infringe the GDPR, in particular where the Controller has insufficiently identified or mitigated the risk, it shall within a maximum period of eight weeks following the request for consultation provide written advice to the Controller and, where applicable to the Processor, and may use any of its powers referred to in Article 58. This period may be extended by six weeks, taking into account the complexity of the intended processing. The supervisory authority shall inform the Controller and, where applicable, the Processor, of any such extension within one month of receipt of the request for consultation together with the reasons for the delay. Those periods may be suspended until the supervisory authority has obtained information it has requested for the purposes of the consultation. (Article 36(2)).

---

76 Generally note D Wright and P de Hert, eds, *Privacy Impact Assessment* (Springer 2012).

When consulting the supervisory authority pursuant to Article 36(3), the Controller shall provide the supervisory authority with:

- where applicable, the respective responsibilities of Controller, joint Controllers and Processors involved in the processing, in particular for processing within a group of undertakings;
- the purposes and means of the intended processing;
- the measures and safeguards provided to protect the rights and freedoms of Data Subjects pursuant to the GDPR;
- where applicable, the contact details of the DPO;
- the data protection impact assessment provided for in Article 35; and
- any other information requested by the supervisory authority (Article 36(3)).

Member States shall consult the supervisory authority during the preparation of a proposal for a legislative measure to be adopted by a national parliament or of a regulatory measure based on such a legislative measure, which relates to the processing (Article 36(7)).

Notwithstanding Article 36(1), Member States' law may require Controllers to consult with, and obtain prior authorisation from, the supervisory authority in relation to the processing by a Controller for the performance of a task carried out by the Controller in the public interest, including processing in relation to social protection and public health (Article 36(5)).

Data Protection Officer

26.43 See obligations below (at para **26.71**).

Data Transfers

26.44 Recitals 101–115 refer to cross border data transfers. The WP29 also refers to transfers.[77]

Chapter V of the GDPR refers to data transfers and transfer of personal data to third countries or international organisations.

---

77 WP29 Statement on the implementation of the judgement of the Court of Justice of the European Union of 6 October 2015 in the *Maximilian Schrems v Data Protection Commissioner case* (C-362/14); Recommendation 1/2012 on the Standard Application form for Approval of Binding Corporate Rules for the Transfer of Personal Data for Processing Activities; Opinion 3/2009 on the Draft Commission Decision on standard contractual clauses for the transfer of personal data to processors established in third countries, under Directive 95/46/EC (data controller to data processor); FAQs in order to address some issues raised by the entry into force of the EU Commission Decision 2010/87/EU of 5 February 2010 on standard contractual clauses for the transfer of personal data to processors established in third countries under Directive 95/46/EC 2010; Recommendation 1/2007 on the Standard Application for Approval of Binding Corporate Rules for the Transfer of Personal Data.

Prior to the new GDPR, the ICO has issued recommendations in relation to personal data transfer issues, namely:

- Assessing Adequacy;
- International Transfers – Legal Guidance;
- Model Contract Clauses;
- Outsourcing – A Guide for Small and Medium-Sized Businesses.

These now need to be read in light of the GDPR changes.

General Principle for Transfers

26.45   Any transfer of personal data which are undergoing processing or are intended for processing after transfer to a third country or to an international organisation shall take place only if, subject to the other provisions of the GDPR, the conditions laid down in this Chapter are complied with by the Controller and Processor, including for onward transfers of personal data from the third country or an international organisation to another third country or to another international organisation. All provisions in this Chapter shall be applied in order to ensure that the level of protection of natural persons guaranteed by the GDPR are not undermined (Article 44).

Transfers via Adequacy Decision

26.46   A transfer of personal data to a third country or an international organisation may take place where the Commission has decided that the third country, a territory or one or more specified sectors within that third country, or the international organisation in question ensures an adequate level of protection. Such transfer shall not require any specific authorisation (Article 45(1)).

When assessing the adequacy of the level of protection, the Commission shall, in particular, take account of the following elements:

- the rule of law, respect for human rights and fundamental freedoms, relevant legislation, both general and sectoral, including concerning public security, defence, national security and criminal law and the access of public authorities to personal data, as well as the implementation of this legislation, data protection rules, professional rules and security measures, including rules for onward transfer of personal data to another third country or international organisation, which are complied with in that country or international organisation, case law, as well as effective and enforceable Data Subject rights and effective administrative and judicial redress for the Data Subjects whose personal data are being transferred;
- the existence and effective functioning of one or more independent supervisory authorities in the third country or to which an international

organisation is subject, with responsibility for ensuring and enforcing compliance with the data protection rules, including adequate enforcement powers for assisting and advising the Data Subjects in exercising their rights and for assisting and advising the Data Subjects in exercising their rights and for co-operation with the supervisory authorities of the Member States; and

- the international commitments the third country or international organisation concerned has entered into, or other obligations arising from legally binding conventions or instruments as well as from its participation in multilateral or regional systems, in particular in relation to the protection of personal data (Article 45(2)).

The Commission, after assessing the adequacy of the level of protection, may decide by means of implementing act, that a third country, or a territory or one or more specified sectors within that third country, or an international organisation ensures an adequate level of protection within the meaning of Article 45(3).

The Commission shall, on an on-going basis, monitor developments in third countries and international organisations that could affect the functioning of decisions adopted pursuant to Article 45(3) and decisions adopted on the basis of Article 25(6) of the DPD (Article 45(4)).

The Commission shall publish in the Official Journal of the EU and on its website a list of those third countries, territories and specified sectors within a third country and international organisations where it has decided that an adequate level of protection is or is no longer ensured (Article 45(8)).

Decisions adopted by the Commission on the basis of Article 25(6) of the DPD shall remain in force until amended, replaced or repealed by a Commission Decision adopted in accordance with Article 45(3) or (5) (Article 45(9)).

Note that the EU-US Safe Harbour data transfer regime was struck down by the Court of Justice in the *Schrems* case.[78] The Safe Harbour regime was held to be invalid. Notwithstanding the GDPR, the previous Safe Harbour regime will have to be replaced. Negotiations between the EU Commission and the US authorities are ongoing. It has been hoped

---

78 *Schrems v Commissioner*, Court of Justice, Case C-362/14, 6 October 2015, at http://curia.europa.eu/juris/document/document.jsf?text=&docid=169195&pageIndex=0&doclang=en&mode=req&dir=&occ=first&part=1&cid=113326. The case technically related to Prism and Facebook Europe and transfers to the US. However, the wider import turned out to be the entire EU-US Safe Harbour Agreement and data transfers to the US. Note WP29 statement on the case, Statement on the implementation of the judgement of the Court of Justice of the European Union of 6 October 2015 in the *Maximilian Schrems v Data Protection Commissioner case* (C-362/14).

that agreement may be reached and a new agreement implemented in early 2016. The replacement is entitled EU-US Privacy Shield.

It should be noted also that there have been some concerns that the same or similar reasons for the striking down of the Safe Harbour regime may cause concerns for some of the other transfer legitimising mechanisms. It remains to be seen if further challenges or concerns will arise.

Transfers via Appropriate Safeguards

26.47 In the absence of a decision pursuant to Article 45(3), a Controller or Processor may transfer personal data to a third country or an international organisation only if the Controller or Processor has provided appropriate safeguards, and on condition that enforceable Data Subject rights and effective legal remedies for Data Subjects are available (Article 46(1)).

The appropriate safeguards referred to in Article 46(1) may be provided for, without requiring any specific authorisation from a supervisory authority, by:

- a legally binding and enforceable instrument between public authorities or bodies;
- binding corporate rules in accordance with Article 47;
- standard data protection clauses adopted by the Commission in accordance with the examination procedure referred to in Article 93(2);
- standard data protection clauses adopted by a supervisory authority and approved by the Commission pursuant to the examination procedure referred to in Article 93(2);
- an approved code of conduct pursuant to Article 40 together with binding and enforceable commitments of the Controller or Processor in the third country to apply the appropriate safeguards, including as regards Data Subjects' rights; or
- an approved certification mechanism pursuant to Article 42 together with binding and enforceable commitments of the Controller or Processor in the third country to apply the appropriate safeguards, including as regards Data Subjects' rights (Article 46(2)).

Subject to the authorisation from the competent supervisory authority, the appropriate safeguards referred to in Article 46(1) may also be provided for, in particular, by:

- contractual clauses between the Controller or Processor and the Controller, Processor or the recipient of the personal data in the third country or international organisation; or

- provisions to be inserted into administrative arrangements between public authorities or bodies which include enforceable and effective Data Subject rights (Article 46(3)).

The supervisory authority shall apply the consistency mechanism referred to in Article 63 in the cases referred to in Article 46(3) (Article 46(4)).

Authorisations by a Member State or supervisory authority on the basis of Article 26(2) of the DPD shall remain valid until amended, replaced or repealed, if necessary, by that supervisory authority. Decisions adopted by the Commission on the basis of Article 26(4) of the DPD shall remain in force until amended, replaced or repealed, if necessary, by a Commission Decision adopted in accordance with Article 46(2) (Article 46(5)).

Transfers via Binding Corporate Rules

26.48 The competent supervisory authority shall approve binding corporate rules in accordance with the consistency mechanism set out in Article 63, provided that they:

- are legally binding and apply to and are enforced by every member concerned of the group of undertakings or groups of enterprises engaged in a joint economic activity, including their employees;
- expressly confer enforceable rights on Data Subjects with regard to the processing of their personal data; and
- fulfil the requirements laid down in Article 47(2) (Article 47(1)).

The binding corporate rules shall specify at least:

- the structure and contact details of the group of enterprises engaged in a joint economic activity and of each of its members;
- the data transfers or set of transfers, including the categories of personal data, the type of processing and its purposes, the type of Data Subjects affected and the identification of the third country or countries in question;
- their legally binding nature, both internally and externally;
- the application of the general data protection principles, in particular purpose limitation, data minimisation, limited storage periods, data quality, data protection by design (DPbD) and by default, legal basis for the processing, processing of special categories of personal data, measures to ensure data security, and the requirements in respect of onward transfers to bodies not bound by the binding corporate rules [d];
- the rights of Data Subjects in regard to processing and the means to exercise these rights, including the right not to be subject to decisions based solely on automated processing, including profiling in accordance with Article 22, the right to lodge a complaint with the

competent supervisory authority and before the competent courts of the Member States in accordance with Article 79, and to obtain redress and, where appropriate, compensation for a breach of the binding corporate rules [e];

- the acceptance by the Controller or Processor established on the territory of a Member State of liability for any breaches of the binding corporate rules by any member concerned not established in the EU; the Controller or the Processor shall be exempted from this liability, in whole or in part, only if it proves that that member is not responsible for the event giving rise to the damage [f];

- how the information on the binding corporate rules, in particular on the provisions referred to in this Article 47(2)(d), (e) and (f) is provided to the Data Subjects in addition to Articles 13 and 14;

- the tasks of any DPO designated in accordance with Article 37 or any other person or entity in charge of monitoring compliance with the binding corporate rules within the group of undertakings, or group of enterprises engaging in a joint economic activity, as well as monitoring training and complaint handling;

- the complaint procedures;

- the mechanisms within the group of undertakings, or group of enterprises engaging in a joint economic activity for ensuring the verification of compliance with the binding corporate rules. Such mechanisms shall include data protection audits and methods for ensuring corrective actions to protect the rights of the Data Subject. Results of such verification should be communicated to the person or entity referred under point (h) and to the board of the controlling undertaking or of the group of enterprises engaged in a joint economic activity, and should be available upon request to the competent supervisory authority;

- the mechanisms for reporting and recording changes to the rules and reporting those changes to the supervisory authority;

- the co-operation mechanism with the supervisory authority to ensure compliance by any member of the group of undertakings, or group of enterprises engaging in a joint economic activity, in particular by making available to the supervisory authority the results of verifications of the measures referred to in this Article 47(2)(j);

- the mechanisms for reporting to the competent supervisory authority any legal requirements to which a member of the group of undertakings, or group of enterprises engaging in a joint economic activity is subject in a third country which are likely to have a substantial adverse effect on the guarantees provided by the binding corporate rules; and

- the appropriate data protection training to personnel having permanent or regular access to personal data (Article 47(2)).

The Commission may specify the format and procedures for the exchange of information between Controllers, Processors and supervisory authorities for binding corporate rules. Those implementing acts shall be adopted in accordance with the examination procedure set out in Article 93(2) (Article 47(4)).

Given that the EU-US Safe Harbour data transfer regime was struck down by the Court of Justice in the *Schrems* case,[79] there have been some concerns that a similar strike down problem could arise for other transfer legitimising mechanisms, including BCRs. The WP29 also refers to BCR issues, including the *Schrems* case.[80]

Transfers or Disclosures Not Authorised by EU Law

26.49 Any judgment of a court or tribunal and any decision of an administrative authority of a third country requiring a Controller or Processor to transfer or disclose personal data may only be recognised or enforceable in any manner if based on an international agreement, such as a mutual legal assistance treaty, in force between the requesting third country and the EU or a Member State, without prejudice to other grounds for transfer pursuant to this Chapter (Article 48).

---

79 *Schrems v Commissioner*, Court of Justice, Case C-362/14, 6 October 2015, at http://curia.europa.eu/juris/document/document.jsf?text=&docid=169195&pageIndex=0&doclang=en&mode=req&dir=&occ=first&part=1&cid=113326. The case technically related to Prism and Facebook Europe and transfers to the US. However, the wider import turned out to be the entire EU-US Safe Harbour Agreement and data transfers to the US. Note WP29 statement on the case, Statement on the implementation of the judgement of the Court of Justice of the European Union of 6 October 2015 in the *Maximilian Schrems v Data Protection Commissioner case* (C-362/14).

80 WP29 Statement on the implementation of the judgement of the Court of Justice of the European Union of 6 October 2015 in the *Maximilian Schrems v Data Protection Commissioner case* (C-362/14); Explanatory Document on the Processor Binding Corporate Rules, Revised version May 2015 – WP 204; Opinion 02/2014 on a Referential for requirements for Binding Corporate Rules submitted to national Data Protection Authorities in the EU and Cross Border Privacy Rules submitted to APEC CBPR Accountability Agents; Opinion 07/2013 on the Data Protection Impact Assessment Template for Smart Grid and Smart Metering Systems ('DPIA Template') prepared by Expert Group 2 of the Commission's Smart Grid Task Force; Opinion 04/2013 on the Data Protection Impact Assessment Template for Smart Grid and Smart Metering Systems ('DPIA Template') prepared by Expert Group 2 of the Commission's Smart Grid Task Force; Working Document 02/2012 setting up a table with the elements and principles to be found in Processor Binding Corporate Rules; Recommendation 1/2012 on the Standard Application form for Approval of Binding Corporate Rules for the Transfer of Personal Data for Processing Activities; Opinion 5/2010 on the Industry Proposal for a Privacy and Data Protection Impact Assessment Framework for RFID Applications.

Derogations for Specific Situations

26.50 In the absence of an adequacy decision pursuant to Article 45(3), or of appropriate safeguards pursuant to Article 46, including binding corporate rules, a transfer or a set of transfers of personal data to a third country or an international organisation shall take place only on one of the following conditions:

- the Data Subject has explicitly consented to the proposed transfer, after having been informed of the possible risks of such transfers for the Data Subject due to the absence of an adequacy decision and appropriate safeguards; [a]
- the transfer is necessary for the performance of a contract between the Data Subject and the Controller or the implementation of pre-contractual measures taken at the Data Subject's request; [b]
- the transfer is necessary for the conclusion or performance of a contract concluded in the interest of the Data Subject between the Controller and another natural or legal person; [c]
- the transfer is necessary for important reasons of public interest;
- the transfer is necessary for the establishment, exercise or defence of legal claims;
- the transfer is necessary in order to protect the vital interests of the Data Subject or of other persons, where the Data Subject is physically or legally incapable of giving consent;
- the transfer is made from a register which according to EU or Member State law is intended to provide information to the public and which is open to consultation either by the public in general or by any person who can demonstrate a legitimate interest, but only to the extent that the conditions laid down in EU or Member State law for consultation are fulfilled in the particular case. [g]

Where a transfer could not be based on a provision in Article 45 or 46, including the provisions on binding corporate rules, and none of the derogations for a specific situation referred to in the first subparagraph of this paragraph is applicable, a transfer to a third country or an international organisation may take place only if the transfer is not repetitive, concerns only a limited number of data subjects, is necessary for the purposes of compelling legitimate interests pursued by the Controller which are not overridden by the interests or rights and freedoms of the Data Subject, and the Controller has assessed all the circumstances surrounding the data transfer and has on the basis of that assessment provided suitable safeguards with regard to the protection of personal data. The Controller shall inform the supervisory authority of the transfer. The Controller shall, in addition to providing the information referred to in Articles 13 and 14, inform the Data

Subject of the transfer and on the compelling legitimate interests pursued (Article 49(1)).

A transfer pursuant to Article 49(1)(g) shall not involve the entirety of the personal data or entire categories of the personal data contained in the register. Where the register is intended for consultation by persons having a legitimate interest, the transfer shall be made only at the request of those persons or if they are to be the recipients (Article 49(2)).

Article 47(1)(a), (b), (c) and the second subparagraph shall not apply to activities carried out by public authorities in the exercise of their public powers (Article 49(3)).

The public interest referred to in Article 47(1)(d) must be recognised in EU law or in the law of the Member State to which the Controller is subject (Article 49(4)).

In the absence of an adequacy decision, EU law or Member State law may, for important reasons of public interest, expressly set limits to the transfer of specific categories of personal data to a third country or an international organisation. Member States shall notify such provisions to the Commission (Article 49(5)).

The Controller or Processor shall document the assessment as well as the suitable safeguards referred to in Article 49(1) in the records referred to in Article 30 (Article 49(6)).

Data Subject Rights

26.51   The Recitals refer to: Data Subject rights; principles of fair and transparent processing; prior information requirements; right of access; right of rectification and right to be forgotten (RtbF); right to complain to single supervisory authority; automated processing.

Chapter III of the GDPR refers to the rights of Data Subjects. These include:

- right to transparency (Article 5; Article 12);
- right to prior information: directly obtained data (Article 13);
- right to prior information: indirectly obtained data (Article 14);
- right of confirmation and right of access (Article 15);
- right to rectification (Article 16);
- right to erasure (Right to be Forgotten) (RtbF) (Article 17);
- right to restriction of processing (Article 18);
- notifications re rectification, erasure or restriction (Article 19);
- right to data portability (Article 20);
- right to object (Article 21);
- rights re automated individual decision making, including profiling (Article 22);
- DPbD (Article 25);
- security rights;

- data protection impact assessment and prior consultation;
- communicating data breach to data subject;
- Data Protection Officer (DPO);
- remedies, liability and sanctions (Chapter VIII).

Transparency

26.52   Article 5 of the GDPR provides that personal data shall be 'processed ... in a transparent manner in relation to the Data Subject.' Transparency:

> 'require[s] greater awareness among citizens about the processing going on: its existence, its content and the flows generated in and out by using terminals.
>
> Transparency also relates to security of data and risk management.'[81]

Some commentators have suggested the GDPR could go further. It has been suggested that 'the greater the flow of information systems the more opaque it becomes in modern information systems and with new ICT applications. In that case the right to transparency must increase alongside these new processes.'[82]

Article 5 of the new GDPR in the Data Protection Principles first principle now reads that personal data shall be:

> 'processed lawfully, fairly and in a transparent manner in relation to the Data Subject ("lawfulness, fairness and transparency").'

Article 12 refers to transparent information, communication and modalities for exercising the rights of the Data Subject.

The Controller shall take appropriate measures to provide any information referred to in Articles 13 and 14 and any communication under Articles 15–22, and 34 relating to processing to the Data Subject in a concise, transparent, intelligible and easily accessible form, using clear and plain language, in particular for any information addressed specifically to a child. The information shall be provided in writing, or by other means, where appropriate, by electronic form. When requested by the Data Subject, the information may be provided orally, provided that the identity of the Data Subject is proven by other means (Article 12(1)).

The Controller shall facilitate the exercise of Data Subject rights under Articles 15–22. In cases referred to in Article 11(2) the Controller shall

---

81 L Costa and Y Poullet, 'Privacy and the Regulation of 2012,' *Computer Law & Security Review* (2012) (28) 254–262, at 256.

82 *Ibid*, at 256.

not refuse to act on the request of the Data Subject for exercising their rights under Articles 15–22, unless the Controller demonstrates that it is not in a position to identify the Data Subject (Article 12(2)).

The Controller shall provide information on action taken on a request under Articles 15–22 to the Data Subject without undue delay and in any event within one month of receipt of the request. That period may be extended by two further months when necessary, taking into account the complexity and the number of the requests. The Controller shall inform the Data Subject of any such extension within one month of receipt of the request, together with the reasons for the delay. Where the Data Subject makes the request by electronic means, the information shall be provided by electronic means where possible, unless otherwise requested by the Data Subject (Article 12(3)).

If the Controller does not take action on the request of the Data Subject, the Controller shall inform the Data Subject without delay and at the latest within one month of receipt of the request of the reasons for not taking action and on the possibility of lodging a complaint to a supervisory authority and seeking a judicial remedy (Article 12(4)).

Information provided under Articles 13 and 14 and any communication and any actions taken under Articles 15–22 and 34 shall be provided free of charge. Where requests from a Data Subject are manifestly unfounded or excessive, in particular because of their repetitive character, the Controller may either charge a reasonable fee taking into account the administrative costs for providing the information or the communication or taking the action requested; or refuse to act on the request. The Controller shall bear the burden of demonstrating the manifestly unfounded or excessive character of the request (Article 12(4)).

Without prejudice to Article 11, where the Controller has reasonable doubts concerning the identity of the natural person making the request referred to in Articles 15–21, the Controller may request the provision of additional information necessary to confirm the identity of the Data Subject (Article 12(6)).

The information to be provided to Data Subjects pursuant to Articles 13 and 14 may be provided in combination with standardised icons in order to give in an easily visible, intelligible and clearly legible manner, a meaningful overview of the intended processing. Where the icons are presented electronically they shall be machine-readable (Article 12(7)).

The Commission shall be empowered to adopt delegated acts in accordance with Article 92 for the purpose of determining the information to be presented by the icons and the procedures for providing standardised icons (Article 12(8)).

Prior to the new GDPR, the ICO has issued recommendations in relation privacy notices, namely:

- Getting It Right: Collecting Information about Your Customers;
- Privacy Notices Code of Practice.

These now need to be read in light of the GDPR changes.

Data Access Rights

26.53   Chapter III, Section 2 of the GDPR refers to data access. It should be noted that the prior information requirements might have previously been viewed as Controller compliance obligations. However, they are now reformulated as part of the Data Subject rights. This therefore is a change in emphasis.

Right to Prior Information: Directly Obtained Data

26.54   Article 13 refers to information to be provided where the data are collected from the Data Subject. Where personal data relating to a Data Subject are collected from the Data Subject, the Controller shall, at the time when personal data are obtained, provide the Data Subject with the following information:

- the identity and the contact details of the Controller and, where applicable, of the Controller's representative;
- the contact details of the DPO, where applicable;
- the purposes of the processing for which the personal data are intended as well as the legal basis for the processing;
- where the processing is based on Article 6(1)(f), the legitimate interests pursued by the Controller or by a third party;
- the recipients or categories of recipients of the personal data, if any;
- where applicable, the fact that the Controller intends to transfer personal data to a third country or international organisation and the existence or absence of an adequacy decision by the Commission, or in the case of transfers referred to in Articles 46 or 47, or the second subparagraph of Article 49(1), reference to the appropriate or suitable safeguards and the means by which to obtain a copy of them or where they have been made available (Article 13(1)).

In addition to the information referred to in Article 13(1), the Controller shall, at the time when personal data are obtained, provide the Data Subject with the following further information necessary to ensure fair and transparent processing:

- the period for which the personal data will be stored, or if that is not possible, the criteria used to determine that period;

- the existence of the right to request from the Controller access to and rectification or erasure of personal data or restriction of processing concerning the Data Subject or to object to the processing as well as the right to data portability;
- where the processing is based on Article 6(1)(a) or Article 9(2)(a), the existence of the right to withdraw consent at any time, without affecting the lawfulness of processing based on consent before its withdrawal;
- the right to lodge a complaint to a supervisory authority;
- whether the provision of personal data is a statutory or contractual requirement, or a requirement necessary to enter into a contract, as well as whether the Data Subject is obliged to provide the data and of the possible consequences of failure to provide such data;
- the existence of automated decision making including profiling referred to in Article 22(1) and (4) and at least in those cases, meaningful information about the logic involved, as well as the significance and the envisaged consequences of such processing for the Data Subject (Article 13(2)).

Where the Controller intends to further process the data for a purpose other than that for which the personal data were collected, the Controller shall provide the Data Subject prior to that further processing with information on that other purpose and with any relevant further information as referred to in Article 13(2) (Article 13(2)).

Article 13(1), (2) and (3) shall not apply where and insofar as the Data Subject already has the information (Article 13(4)).

Right to Prior Information: Indirectly Obtained Data

26.55   Article 14 refers to information to be provided where the data have not been obtained from the Data Subject. Where personal data have not been obtained from the Data Subject, the Controller shall provide the Data Subject with the following information:

- the identity and the contact details of the Controller and, where applicable, of the Controller's representative;
- the contact details of the DPO, where applicable;
- the purposes of the processing for which the personal data are intended as well as the legal basis of the processing;
- the categories of personal data concerned;
- the recipients or categories of recipients of the personal data, if any;
- where applicable, that the Controller intends to transfer personal data to a recipient in a third country or international organisation and the existence or absence of an adequacy decision by the

Commission, or in case of transfers referred to in Article 46 or 47, or the second subparagraph of Article 49(1), reference to the appropriate or suitable safeguards and the means to obtain a copy of them or where they have been made available (Article 14(1)).

In addition to the information referred to in Article 14(1), the Controller shall provide the Data Subject with the following information necessary to ensure fair and transparent processing in respect of the Data Subject:

- the period for which the personal data will be stored, or if this is not possible, the criteria used to determine that period;
- where the processing is based on Article 6(1)(f), the legitimate interests pursued by the Controller or by a third party;
- the existence of the right to request from the Controller access to and rectification or erasure of personal data or restriction of processing concerning the Data Subject and to object to processing as well as the right to data portability;
- where processing is based on Article 6(1)(a) or Article 9(2)(a), the existence of the right to withdraw consent at any time, without affecting the lawfulness of processing based on consent before its withdrawal;
- the right to lodge a complaint to a supervisory authority;
- from which source the personal data originate, and if applicable, whether it came from publicly accessible sources;
- the existence of automated decision making including profiling referred to in Article 22(1) and (4) and at least in those cases, meaningful information about the logic involved, as well as the significance and the envisaged consequences of such processing for the Data Subject (Article 14(2)).

The Controller shall provide the information referred to in Article 14(1) and (2),

- within a reasonable period after obtaining the data, but at the latest within one month, having regard to the specific circumstances in which the data are processed; or
- if the data are to be used for communication with the Data Subject, at the latest at the time of the first communication to that Data Subject; or
- if a disclosure to another recipient is envisaged, at the latest when the data are first disclosed (Article 14(3)).

Where the Controller intends to further process the data for a purpose other than the one for which the data were obtained, the Controller shall provide the Data Subject prior to that further processing with information on that other purpose and with any relevant further information as referred to in Article 14(2) (Article 14(4)).

Article 14(1) to (4) shall not apply where and insofar as:

- the Data Subject already has the information;
- the provision of such information proves impossible or would involve a disproportionate effort, in particular for processing for archiving purposes in the public interest, scientific or historical research purposes or statistical purposes subject to the conditions and safeguards referred to in Article 89(1) or in so far as the obligation referred to in Article 14(1) is likely to render impossible or seriously impair the achievement of the objectives of that processing. In such cases the Controller shall take appropriate measures to protect the Data Subject's rights and freedoms and legitimate interests, including making the information publicly available;
- obtaining or disclosure is expressly laid down by EU or Member State law to which the Controller is subject and which provides appropriate measures to protect the Data Subject's legitimate interests; or
- where the data must remain confidential subject to an obligation of professional secrecy regulated by EU or Member State law, including a statutory obligation of secrecy (Article 14(5)).

Right of Confirmation and Right of Access

26.56 The Data Subject shall have the right to obtain from the Controller confirmation as to whether or not personal data concerning them are being processed, and where that is the case, access to the personal data and the following information:

- the purposes of the processing;
- the categories of personal data concerned;
- the recipients or categories of recipients to whom the personal data have been or will be disclosed, in particular recipients in third countries or international organisations;
- where possible, the envisaged period for which the personal data will be stored, or if possible, this the criteria used to determine that period;
- the existence of the right to request from the Controller rectification or erasure of personal data or restriction of the processing of personal data concerning the Data Subject or to object to the processing;
- the right to lodge a complaint to a supervisory authority;
- where the personal data are not collected from the Data Subject, any available information as to their source;

- the existence of automated decision making including profiling referred to in Article 22(1) and (4) and at least in those cases, meaningful information about the logic involved, as well as the significance and the envisaged consequences of such processing for the Data Subject (Article 15(1)).

Where personal data are transferred to a third country or to an international organisation, the Data Subject shall have the right to be informed of the appropriate safeguards pursuant to Article 46 relating to the transfer (Article 15(2)).

The Controller shall provide a copy of the personal data undergoing processing. For any further copies requested by the Data Subject, the Controller may charge a reasonable fee based on administrative costs. Where the Data Subject makes the request by electronic means, and unless otherwise requested by the Data Subject, the information shall be provided in a commonly used electronic form (Article 15(3)).

The right to obtain a copy referred to in Article 15(3) shall not adversely affect the rights and freedoms of others (Article 15(4)).

Prior to the new GDPD, the ICO has issued recommendations in relation data access issues, namely:

- Access to Information Held in Complaint Files;
- Enforced Subject Access (section 56);
- How to Disclose Information Safely – Removing Personal Data from Information Requests and Datasets;
- Regulatory Activity Exemption;
- Subject Access: Code of Practice;
- Subject Access: Responding to a Request Checklist.

These now need to be read in light of the GDPR changes.

Right to be Informed of Third Country Safeguards

26.57 Where personal data are transferred to a third country or to an international organisation, the Data Subject shall have the right to be informed of the appropriate safeguards pursuant to Article 46 relating to the transfer (Article 15(2)). This has added relevance as part of the potential ripples from the *Schrems* Court of Justice decision.

Rectification and Erasure

26.58 Chapter III, Section 3 of the GDPR refers to rectification and erasure. This was already an important and topical issue and is now even more important on foot of the *Google Spain* case (see below) and also issues such as online abuse.

Right to Rectification

26.59   The Data Subject shall have the right to obtain from the Controller without undue delay the rectification of inaccurate personal data concerning them. Taking into account the purposes of the processing, the Data Subject shall have the right to have incomplete personal data completed, including by means of providing a supplementary statement (Article 16).

Right to Erasure (Right to be Forgotten) (RtbF)

26.60   The Data Subject shall have the right to obtain from the Controller the erasure of personal data concerning them without undue delay where one of the following grounds applies:

- the personal data are no longer necessary in relation to the purposes for which they were collected or otherwise processed;
- the Data Subject withdraws consent on which the processing is based according to Article 6(1)(a), or Article 9(2)(a), and where there is no other legal ground for the processing;
- the Data Subject objects to the processing of personal data pursuant to Article 21(1) and there are no overriding legitimate grounds for the processing, or the Data Subject objects to the processing of personal data pursuant to Article 21(2);
- the personal data have been unlawfully processed;
- the personal data have to be erased for compliance with a legal obligation in EU or Member State law to which the Controller is subject;
- the data have been collected in relation to the offer of information society services referred to in Article 8(1) (Article 17(1)).

Where the Controller has made the personal data public and is obliged pursuant to Article 17(1) to erase the personal data, the Controller, taking account of available technology and the cost of implementation, shall take reasonable steps, including technical measures, to inform Controllers which are processing the personal data that the Data Subject has requested the erasure by such Controllers of any links to, or copy or replication of those personal data (Article 17(2)).

Article 17(1) and (2) shall not apply to the extent that processing is necessary:

- for exercising the right of freedom of expression and information;
- for compliance with a legal obligation which requires processing of personal data by EU or Member State law to which the Controller is subject or for the performance of a task carried out in the public interest or in the exercise of official authority vested in the Controller;

- for reasons of public interest in the area of public health in accordance with Article 9(2)(h) and (i) as well as Article 9(3);
- for archiving purposes in the public interest, or scientific and historical research purposes or statistical purposes in accordance with Article 89(1) in so far as the right referred to in Article 17(1) is likely to render impossible or seriously impair the achievement of the objectives of that processing; or
- for the establishment, exercise or defence of legal claims (Article 17(3)).[83]

In the *Google Spain* case, the Court of Justice held that:

'Article 2(b) and (d) of [the DPD] ... are to be interpreted as meaning that, first, the activity of a search engine consisting in finding information published or placed on the internet by third parties, indexing it automatically, storing it temporarily and, finally, making it available to internet users according to a particular order of preference must be classified as "processing of personal data" within the meaning of Article 2(b) when that information contains personal data and, second, the operator of the search engine must be regarded as the "controller" in respect of that processing, within the meaning of Article 2(d).

Article 4(1)(a) of [the DPD] is to be interpreted as meaning that processing of personal data is carried out in the context of the activities of an establishment of the controller on the territory of a Member State, within the meaning of that provision, when the operator of a search engine sets up in a Member State a branch or subsidiary which is intended to promote and sell advertising space offered by that engine and which orientates its activity towards the inhabitants of that Member State.'[84]

The WP29 also refers to RtbF issues as well as the *Google Spain* case.[85] This includes WP29 'Guidelines on the implementation of the

---

83 In relation to the original draft, etc, see for example, G Sartor, 'The Right to be Forgotten in the Draft Data Protection Regulation,' *International Data Privacy Law* (2015) (5;1) 64. Also A Mantelero, 'The EU Proposal for a general data protection regulation and the roots of the "right to be forgotten,"' *Computer Law and Security Report* (2013) (29:3) 229.

84 *Google Spain SL and Google Inc v Agencia Española de Protección de Datos (AEPD) and Mario Costeja González*, Case C-131/12, 13 May 2014. Also see, for example, P Lambert, *International Handbook of Social Media Laws* (Bloomsbury 2014); P Lambert, *Social Networking: Law, Rights and Policy* (Clarus Press 2014); V Mayer-Schönberger, *Delete: the Virtue of Forgetting in the Digital Age* (Princeton, 2009).

85 WP29 Guidelines on the implementation of the Court of Justice of the European Union judgment on 'Google Spain and Inc v Agencia Española de Protección de Datos (AEPD) and Mario Costeja González' C-131/121; Opinion 8/2010 on applicable law (WP29 adds as follows: 'In its judgment in Google Spain the Court of Justice of the European Union decided upon certain matters relating to the territorial

Court of Justice of the European Union judgment on "Google Spain and Inc v Agencia Española de Protección de Datos (AEPD) and Mario Costeja González.'"

Right to Restriction of Processing

26.61   Article 18 refers to the right to restriction of processing. The Data Subject shall have the right to obtain from the Controller the restriction of the processing where one of the following applies:

- the accuracy of the personal data is contested by the Data Subject, for a period enabling the Controller to verify the accuracy of the personal data;
- the processing is unlawful and the Data Subject opposes the erasure of the personal data and requests the restriction of their use instead;
- the Controller no longer needs the personal data for the purposes of the processing, but they are required by the Data Subject for the establishment, exercise or defence of legal claims;
- the data subject has objected to processing pursuant to Article 21(1) pending the verification whether the legitimate grounds of the Controller override those of the Data Subject (Article 18(1)).

Where processing of personal data has been restricted under Article 18(1), such personal data shall, with the exception of storage, only be processed with the Data Subject's consent or for the establishment, exercise or defence of legal claims or for the protection of the rights of another natural or legal person or for reasons of important public interest of the EU or of a Member State (Article 18(2)).

A Data Subject who obtained the restriction of processing pursuant to Article 18(1) shall be informed by the Controller before the restriction of processing is lifted (Article 18(3)).

Notifications re Rectification, Erasure or Restriction

26.62   The Controller shall communicate any rectification or erasure of personal data or restriction of processing carried out in accordance with Articles 16, 17(1) and 18 to each recipient to whom the personal data have been disclosed, unless this proves impossible or involves disproportionate effort. The Controller shall inform the Data Subject about those recipients if the Data Subject requests this (Article 19).

---

scope of Directive 95/46/EC. The WP29 commenced an internal analysis of the potential implications of this judgment on applicable law and may provide further guidance on this issue during the course of 2015, including, possibly, additional examples.').

Right to Data Portability

26.63   The Data Subject shall have the right to receive the personal data concerning him or her, which he or she has provided to a Controller, in a structured, commonly used, machine-readable format and have the right to transmit those data to another Controller without hindrance from the Controller to which the personal data have been provided, where:

- the processing is based on consent pursuant to Article 6(1)(a) or Article 9(2)(a) or on a contract pursuant to Article 6(1)(b); and
- the processing is carried out by automated means (Article 20(1)).

In exercising his or her right to data portability pursuant to Article 20(1), the Data Subject has the right to obtain that the data is transmitted directly from Controller to Controller where technically feasible (Article 20(2)).

The exercise of this right shall be without prejudice to Article 17. The right shall not apply to processing necessary for the performance of a task carried out in the public interest or in the exercise of official authority vested in the Controller (Article 20(3)).

The right shall not adversely affect the rights and freedoms of others (Article 20(4)).

Right Against Automated Individual Decision Making

26.64   Chapter III, Section 4 of the GDPR refers to the right to object and automated individual decision making.

Right to Object

26.65   The Data Subject shall have the right to object, on grounds relating to his or her particular situation, at any time to the processing of personal data concerning him or her which is based on Article 6(1)(e) or (f), including profiling based on these provisions. The Controller shall no longer process the personal data unless the Controller demonstrates compelling legitimate grounds for the processing which override the interests, rights and freedoms of the Data Subject or for the establishment, exercise or defence of legal claims (Article 21(1)).

Where personal data are processed for direct marketing purposes, the Data Subject shall have the right to object at any time to the processing of personal data concerning him or her for such marketing, which includes profiling to the extent that it is related to such direct marketing (Article 20(2)).

Where the Data Subject objects to the processing for direct marketing purposes, the personal data shall no longer be processed for such purposes (Article 21(3)).

At the latest at the time of the first communication with the Data Subject, the right referred to in Article 21(1) and (2) shall be explicitly brought to the attention of the Data Subject and shall be presented clearly and separately from any other information (Article 21(4)).

In the context of the use of information society services, and notwithstanding Directive 2002/58/EC,[86] the Data Subject may exercise his or her right to object by automated means using technical specifications (Article 21(5)).

Where personal data are processed for scientific or historical research purposes or statistical purposes pursuant to Article 89(1), the Data Subject, on grounds relating to his or her particular situation, shall have the right to object to processing of personal data concerning him or her, unless the processing is necessary for the performance of a task carried out for reasons of public interest (Article 21(6)).

Rights re Automated Individual Decision Making, Including Profiling

26.66   There is often a wide concern as to the data protection impact of increased profiling techniques.[87]

The new GDPR provides that the Data Subject shall have the right not to be subject to a decision based solely on automated processing, including profiling,[88] which produces legal effects concerning him or her or similarly significantly affects him or her (Article 22(1)).

Article 22(1) shall not apply if the decision:

- is necessary for entering into, or performance of, a contract between the Data Subject and a Controller [a];
- is authorised by EU or Member State law to which the Controller is subject and which also lays down suitable measures to safeguard the Data Subject's rights and freedoms and legitimate interests; or
- is based on the Data Subject's explicit consent (Article 22(1)) [c].

In cases referred to in Article 22(2)(a) and (c) the Controller shall implement suitable measures to safeguard the Data Subject's rights and freedoms and legitimate interests, at least the right to obtain human intervention on the part of the Controller, to express his or her point of view and to contest the decision (Article 22(3)).

---

86   Directive 2002/58/EC of the European Parliament and of the Council of 12 July 2002 concerning the processing of personal data and the protection of privacy in the electronic communications sector (Directive on privacy and electronic communications).

87   This is in the EU as well as the US (and elsewhere). From a US perspective, see N Roethlisberger, 'Someone is Watching: The Need for Enhanced Data Protection,' *Hastings Law Journal* (2011) (62:6) 1793.

88   See, for example, M Hildebrandt, 'Who is Profiling Who? Invisible Visibility,' in S Gutwirth, Y Poullet, P de Hert, C de Terwange and S Nouwt, *Reinventing Data Protection?* (Springer, 2009) 239.

Decisions referred to in Article 22(2) shall not be based on special categories of personal data referred to in Article 9(1), unless Article 9(2) (a) or (g) applies and suitable measures to safeguard the Data Subject's rights and freedoms and legitimate interests are in place (Article 22(4)).

Data Protection by Design and by Default

26.67 Article 25 refers to data protection by design and by default. Note also the related concept of Privacy by Design (PbD). In some ways PbD is the impetus or precursor for the current DPbD rules.

Taking into account the state of the art and the nature, scope, context and purposes of the processing as well as the risks of varying likelihood and severity for rights and freedoms of natural persons posed by the processing, the Controller shall, both at the time of the determination of the means for processing and at the time of the processing itself, implement appropriate technical and organisational measures, such as pseudonymisation, which are designed to implement data protection principles, such as data minimisation, in an effective way and to integrate the necessary safeguards into the processing in order to meet the requirements of the GDPR and protect the rights of Data Subjects (Article 25(1)).

The Controller shall implement appropriate technical and organisational measures for ensuring that, by default, only personal data which are necessary for each specific purpose of the processing are processed. That obligation applies to the amount of data collected, the extent of their processing, the period of their storage and their accessibility. In particular, such measures shall ensure that by default personal data are not made accessible without the individual's intervention to an indefinite number of natural persons (Article 23(2)).

An approved certification mechanism pursuant to Article 42 may be used as an element to demonstrate compliance with the requirements set out in Article 25(1) and (2) (Article 25(3)).

Security Rights

26.68 See above (paras **26.36** and **26.37**).

Data Protection Impact Assessment and Prior Consultation

Data Protection Impact Assessment

26.69 Chapter IV, Section 3 of the GDPR refers to Impact Assessments and Prior Consultations.

Where a type of processing in particular using new technologies, and taking into account the nature, scope, context and purposes of the processing, is likely to result in a high risk for the rights and freedoms of natural persons, the Controller shall, prior to the processing, carry out an assessment of the impact of the envisaged processing operations on the protection of personal data. A single assessment may address a set of similar processing operations that present similar high risks (Article 35(1)).

The Controller shall seek the advice of the DPO, where designated, when carrying out a data protection impact assessment (Article 35(2)).

A data protection impact assessment referred to in Article 35(1) shall in particular be required in the case of:

- a systematic and extensive evaluation of personal aspects relating to natural persons which is based on automated processing, including profiling, and on which decisions are based that produce legal effects concerning the natural person or similarly significantly affect the natural person;
- processing on a large scale of special categories of data referred to in Article 9(1), or of personal data relating to criminal convictions and offences referred to in Article 10; or
- a systematic monitoring of a publicly accessible area on a large scale (Article 35(3)).

The supervisory authority shall establish and make public a list of the kind of processing operations which are subject to the requirement for a data protection impact assessment pursuant to Article 35(1). The supervisory authority shall communicate those lists to the EDPB (Article 35(4)).

The supervisory authority may also establish and make public a list of the kind of processing operations for which no data protection impact assessment is required. The supervisory authority shall communicate those lists to the EDPB (Article 35(5)).

Prior to the adoption of the lists referred to in Article 35(4) and (5) the competent supervisory authority shall apply the consistency mechanism referred to in Article 63 where such lists involve processing activities which are related to the offering of goods or services to Data Subjects or to the monitoring of their behaviour in several Member States, or may substantially affect the free movement of personal data within the EU (Article 35(6)).

The assessment shall contain at least:

- a systematic description of the envisaged processing operations and the purposes of the processing, including where applicable the legitimate interest pursued by the Controller;
- an assessment of the necessity and proportionality of the processing operations in relation to the purposes;
- an assessment of the risks to the rights and freedoms of Data Subjects referred to in Article 35(1);

- the measures envisaged to address the risks, including safeguards, security measures and mechanisms to ensure the protection of personal data and to demonstrate compliance with the GDPR taking into account the rights and legitimate interests of Data Subjects and other persons concerned (Article 35(7)).

Compliance with approved codes of conduct referred to in Article 40 by the relevant Controllers or Processors shall be taken into due account in assessing the impact of the processing operations performed by such Controllers or Processors, in particular for the purposes of a data protection impact assessment (Article 35(8)).

Where appropriate, the Controller shall seek the views of Data Subjects or their representatives on the intended processing, without prejudice to the protection of commercial or public interests or the security of the processing operations (Article 35(9)).

Where the processing pursuant to Article 6(1)(c) or (e) has a legal basis in EU law or the law of the Member State to which the Controller is subject, that law regulates the specific processing operation or set of operations in question, and a data protection impact assessment has already been carried out as part of a general impact assessment in the context of the adoption of this legal basis, Article 35(1)–(7) shall not apply, unless Member States deem it necessary to carry out such assessment prior to the processing activities (Article 35(10)).

Where necessary, the Controller shall carry out a review to assess if the processing is performed in compliance with the data protection impact assessment at least when there is a change of the risk represented by the processing operations (Article 35(11)).

Prior Consultation

26.70 The Controller shall consult the supervisory authority prior to the processing where a data protection impact assessment as provided for in Article 33 indicates that the processing would result in a high risk in the absence of measures taken by the Controller to mitigate the risk (Article 36(1)).

Where the supervisory authority is of the opinion that the intended processing referred to in Article 36(1) would infringe the GDPR, in particular where the Controller has insufficiently identified or mitigated the risk, it shall within a period of up to eight weeks of receipt of the request for consultation, provide written advice to the Controller and, where applicable the Processor, and may use any of its powers referred to in Article 58. That period may be extended for six weeks, taking into account the complexity of the processing. The supervisory authority shall inform the Controller, and where applicable the Processor of any such extension within one month of receipt of the request for consultation together with the reasons for the delay. Those periods may be suspended until the supervisory authority has obtained any information it has requested for the purposes of the consultation (Article 36(2)).

When consulting the supervisory authority pursuant to Article 36(1), the Controller shall provide the supervisory authority with:

- where applicable, the respective responsibilities of Controller, joint Controllers and Processors involved in the processing, in particular for processing within a group of undertakings;
- the purposes and means of the intended processing;
- the measures and safeguards provided to protect the rights and freedoms of Data Subjects pursuant to the GDPR;
- where applicable, the contact details of the DPO;
- the data protection impact assessment provided for in Article 35; and
- any other information requested by the supervisory authority (Article 36(3)).

Member States shall consult the supervisory authority during the preparation of a proposal for a legislative measure to be adopted by a national parliament or of a regulatory measure based on such a legislative measure, which relates to the processing (Article 36(4)).

Notwithstanding Article 36(1), Member States' law may require Controllers to consult with, and obtain prior authorisation from, the supervisory authority in relation to the processing by a Controller for the performance of a task carried out by the Controller in the public interest, including processing in relation to social protection and public health (Article 36(5)).

Communicating Data Breach to Data Subject

26.71 Individual data subjects are to be notified in the event of a data breach. Further details are set out above in para **26.39**.

Data Protection Officer

26.72 Section 4 of the new GDPR refers to Data Protection Officers (DPOs) and the obligation for organisations to appoint DPOs. See Chapter 32 and para **26.114** for particular details.

Remedies, Liability and Sanctions

26.73 Chapter VIII refers to remedies, liability issues and sanctions regarding data protection.

The Recitals refer to proceedings against Controllers, Processors and jurisdiction; damages and compensation; the prevention, investigation, detection or prosecution of criminal offences or the execution of criminal penalties, including public security.

Right to Lodge Complaint with Supervisory Authority

26.74 Without prejudice to any other administrative or judicial remedy, every Data Subject shall have the right to lodge a complaint with a supervisory authority, in particular in the Member State of his or her habitual residence, place of work or place of the alleged infringement if the Data Subject considers that the processing of personal data relating to him or her infringes the GDPR (Article 77(1)).

The supervisory authority with which the complaint has been lodged shall inform the complainant on the progress and the outcome of the complaint including the possibility of a judicial remedy pursuant to Article 78 (Article 77(2)).

Right to Judicial Remedy Against Supervisory Authority

26.75 Without prejudice to any other administrative or non-judicial remedy, each natural or legal person shall have the right to an effective judicial remedy against a legally binding decisions of a supervisory authority concerning them (Article 78(1)).

Without prejudice to any other administrative or non-judicial remedy, each Data Subject shall have the right to an effective judicial remedy where the supervisory authority which is competent in accordance with Article 55 and Article 56 does not handle a complaint or does not inform the Data Subject within three months on the progress or outcome of the complaint lodged under Article 77 (Article 78(2)).

Proceedings against a supervisory authority shall be brought before the courts of the Member State where the supervisory authority is established (Article 78(3)).

Where proceedings are brought against a decision of a supervisory authority which was preceded by an opinion or a decision of the EDPB in the consistency mechanism, the supervisory authority shall forward that opinion or decision to the court (Article 78(4)).

Right to Effective Judicial Remedy Against Controller or Processor

26.76 Without prejudice to any available administrative or non-judicial remedy, including the right to lodge a complaint with a supervisory authority pursuant Article 77, each Data Subject shall have the right to an effective judicial remedy where they consider that their rights under this GDPR have been infringed as a result of the processing of their personal data in non-compliance with the GDPR (Article 79(1)).

Proceedings against a Controller or a Processor shall be brought before the courts of the Member State where the Controller or Processor has an establishment. Alternatively, such proceedings may be brought before the courts of the Member State where the Data Subject has his or her habitual residence, unless the Controller or Processor is a public authority of a Member State acting in the exercise of its public powers (Article 79(2)).

Representation of Data Subjects

26.77 The Data Subject shall have the right to mandate a not-for-profit body, organisation or association, which has been properly constituted according to the law of a Member State, has statutory objectives which are in the public interest and is active in the field of the protection of Data Subject's rights and freedoms with regard to the protection of their personal data to lodge the complaint on his or her behalf, to exercise the rights referred to in Articles 77, 78 and 79 on his or her behalf and to exercise the right to receive compensation referred to in Article 82 on his or her behalf where provided for by Member State law (Article 80(1)).

Member States may provide that any body, organisation or association referred to in Article 80(1), independently of a Data Subject's mandate, has the right to lodge, in that Member State, a complaint with the supervisory authority competent in accordance with Article 77 and to exercise the rights referred to in Articles 78 and 79 if it considers that the rights of a Data Subject under the GDPR have been infringed as a result of the processing (Article 80(2)).

Suspension of Proceedings

26.78 Where a court has information on proceedings, concerning the same subject matter, as regards processing by the same Controller or Processor that are pending in a court in another Member State, it shall contact that court in the other Member State to confirm the existence of such proceedings (Article 81(1)).

Where proceedings concerning the same subject matter as regards processing of the same Controller or Processor are pending in a court in another Member State, any competent court other than the court first seized may suspend its proceedings (Article 81(2)).

Where those proceedings are pending at first instance, any court other than the court first seized may also, on the application of one of the parties, decline jurisdiction if the court first seized has jurisdiction over the actions in question and its law permits the consolidation thereof (Article 81(3)).

Right to Compensation and Liability

26.79 Any person who has suffered material or non-material damage as a result of an infringement of the GDPR shall have the right to receive compensation from the Controller or Processor for the damage suffered (Article 82(1)).

Any Controller involved in the processing shall be liable for the damage caused by the processing which infringes the GDPR. A Processor shall be liable for the damage caused by the processing only where it has not complied with obligations of the GDPR specifically directed to Processors or where it has acted outside or contrary to lawful instructions of the Controller (Article 82(2)).

A Controller or Processor shall be exempt from liability under Article 82(2) if it proves that it is not in any way responsible for the event giving rise to the damage (Article 82(3)).

Where more than one Controller or Processor or both a Controller and a Processor are involved in the same processing and, where they are, in accordance with Article 82(2) and (3), responsible for any damage caused by the processing, each Controller or Processor shall be held liable for the entire damage, in order to ensure effective compensation of the Data Subject (Article 82(4)).

Where a Controller or Processor has, in accordance with Article 82(4), paid full compensation for the damage suffered, that Controller or Processor shall be entitled to claim back from the other Controllers or Processors involved in the same processing that part of the compensation corresponding to their part of responsibility for the damage in accordance with the conditions set out in Article 82(2) (Article 82(5)).

Court proceedings for exercising the right to receive compensation shall be brought before the courts competent under the law of the Member State referred to in Article 79(2) (Article 82(6)).

Codes of Conduct and Certification

26.80 Chapter IV, Section 5 of the GDPR refers to Codes of Conduct and Certification.

Codes of Conduct

26.81 The Member States, the supervisory authorities, the EDPB and the Commission shall encourage the drawing up of codes of conduct intended to contribute to the proper application of the GDPR, taking account of the specific features of the various data processing sectors and the specific needs of micro, small and medium-sized enterprises (Article 40(1)).

Associations and other bodies representing categories of Controllers or Processors may prepare codes of conduct, or amend or extend such codes, for the purpose of specifying the application of the GDPR, such as:

- fair and transparent data processing;
- the legitimate interests pursued by Controllers in specific contexts;
- the collection of data;
- the pseudonymisation of personal data;
- the information of the public and of Data Subjects;
- the exercise of the rights of Data Subjects;
- the information provided to, and the protection of children and the manner in which the consent of the holders of parental responsibility over children to be obtained;
- the measures and procedures referred to in Articles 24 and 24 and measures to ensure security of processing referred to in Article 32;
- the notification of personal data breaches to supervisory authorities and the communication of such personal data breaches to Data Subjects;
- transfer of personal data to third countries or international organisations; or
- out-of-court proceedings and other dispute resolution procedures for resolving disputes between Controllers and Data Subjects with regard to the processing, without prejudice to the rights of the Data Subjects pursuant to Articles 75 and 79 (Article 40(2)).

In addition to adherence by Controller or Processor subject to the Regulation, codes of conduct approved pursuant to Article 40(5) and having general validity pursuant to Article 40(9) may also be adhered to by Controllers or Processors that are not subject to this Regulation pursuant to Article 3 in order to provide appropriate safeguards within the framework of personal data transfers to third countries or international organisations under the terms referred to in Article 46(2)(e). Such Controllers or Processors shall make binding and enforceable commitments, via contractual or other legally binding instruments, to apply those appropriate safeguards including with regard to the rights of Data Subjects (Article 40(3)).

Such a code of conduct shall contain mechanisms which enable the body referred to in Article 41(1) to carry out the mandatory monitoring of compliance with its provisions by the Controllers or Processors which undertake to apply it, without prejudice to the tasks and powers of the supervisory authority competent pursuant to Article 55 or 56 (Article 40(4)).

Associations and other bodies referred to in Article 40(2) which intend to prepare a code of conduct or to amend or extend an existing code, shall submit the draft code, amendment or extension to the supervisory authority which is competent pursuant to Article 55. The supervisory authority shall provide an opinion on whether the draft code, or amendment or extension complies with the GDPR and shall approve such draft code, or amendment or extension if it finds that it provides sufficient appropriate safeguards (Article 40(5)).

Where the draft code, or amendment or extension is approved, and where the code of conduct concerned does not relate to processing activities in several Member States, the supervisory authority shall register and publish the code (Article 40(6)).

Where a draft code of conduct relates to processing activities in several Member States, the supervisory authority which is competent shall, before approving the draft code, amendment or extension, submit it to the EDPB which shall provide an opinion on whether the draft code, amendment or extension complies with the GDPR or, in the situation referred to in Article 40(3), provides appropriate safeguards (Article 40(7)).

Where the opinion referred to in Article 40(7) confirms that the draft code, amendment or extension complies with the GDPR, or, in the situation referred to in Article 40(3), provides appropriate safeguards, the EDPB shall submit its opinion to the Commission (Article 40(8)).

The Commission may by way of implementing acts decide that the approved codes of conduct, amendments or extensions submitted to it pursuant to Article 40(3) have general validity within the EU. Those implementing acts shall be adopted in accordance with the examination procedure set out in Article 93(2) (Article 40(9)).

The Commission shall ensure appropriate publicity for the approved codes which have been decided as having general validity in accordance with Article 40(9) (Article 40(10)).

The EDPB shall collate all approved codes of conduct, amendments and extensions in a register and shall make them publicly available by way of appropriate means (Article 40(11)).

Monitoring of Approved Codes of Conduct

26.82 Without prejudice to the tasks and powers of the competent supervisory authority under Articles 57 and 58, the monitoring of compliance with a code of conduct pursuant to Article 40, may be carried out by a body which has an appropriate level of expertise in relation to the subject-matter of the code and is accredited for this purpose by the competent supervisory authority (Article 41(1)).

A body referred to in Article 41(2) may be accredited to monitor compliance with a code of conduct where that body has:

- demonstrated its independence and expertise in relation to the subject-matter of the code to the satisfaction of the competent supervisory authority;
- establishes procedures which allow it to assess the eligibility of Controllers and Processors concerned to apply the code, to monitor their compliance with its provisions and to periodically review its operation;
- establishes procedures and structures to handle complaints about infringements of the code or the manner in which the code has been, or is being, implemented by a Controller or Processor, and to make those procedures and structures transparent to Data Subjects and the public;
- demonstrated to the satisfaction of the competent supervisory authority that its tasks and duties do not result in a conflict of interests (Article 41(2)).

The competent supervisory authority shall submit the draft criteria for accreditation of a body to the EDPB (Article 41(3)).

Without prejudice to the tasks and powers of the competent supervisory authority and the provisions of Chapter VIII, a body referred to in Article 41(1) shall, subject to adequate safeguards, take appropriate action in cases of infringement of the code by a Controller or Processor, including suspension or exclusion of the Controller or Processor concerned from the code. It shall inform the competent supervisory authority of such actions and the reasons for taking them (Article 41(4)).

The competent supervisory authority shall revoke the accreditation of a body referred to in Article 41(1) if the conditions for accreditation are not, or are no longer, met or actions taken by the body infringe the GDPR (Article 41(5)).

This article shall not apply to processing of personal data carried out by public authorities and bodies (Article 41(6)).

Certification

26.83 The Member States, the supervisory authorities, the EDPB and the Commission shall encourage, in particular at EU level, the establishment of data protection certification mechanisms and of data protection seals and marks, for the purpose of demonstrating compliance with the GDPR of processing operations by Controllers and Processors. The specific needs of micro, small and medium-sized enterprises shall be taken into account (Article 42(1)).

In addition to adherence by Controllers or Processors subject to the GDPR, data protection certification mechanisms, seals or marks approved pursuant to Article 42(5) may be established for the purpose of demonstrating the existence of appropriate safeguards provided by Controllers or Processors that are not subject to the GDPR according to Article 3 within the framework of personal data transfers to third countries or international organisations under the terms referred to in Article 46(2)(f). Such Controllers or Processors shall make binding and enforceable commitments, via contractual or other legally binding instruments, to apply those appropriate safeguards, including with regard to the rights of Data Subjects (Article 42(2)).

The certification shall be voluntary and available via a process that is transparent (Article 42(3)).

A certification pursuant to this Article does not reduce the responsibility of the Controller or the Processor for compliance with the GDPR and is without prejudice to the tasks and powers of the supervisory authorities which are competent pursuant to Article 55 or 56 (Article 42(4)).

A certification pursuant to this Article shall be issued by the certification bodies referred to in Article 43, or by the competent supervisory authority on the basis of the criteria approved by that competent supervisory authority pursuant to Article 58(3), or by the EDPB. Where the criteria approved by the EDPB this may result in a common certification, the European Data Protection Seal (Article 42(5)).

The Controller or Processor which submits its processing to the certification mechanism shall provide the certification body, the competent supervisory authority, with all information and access to its processing activities which are necessary to conduct the certification procedure (Article 42(6)).

The certification shall be issued to a Controller or Processor for a maximum period of three years and may be renewed under the same conditions, provided that the relevant requirements continue to be met. Certification shall be withdrawn, as applicable, by the certification bodies referred to in Article 43, or by the competent supervisory authority where the requirements for the certification are not or no longer met (Article 42(7)).

The EDPB shall collate all certification mechanisms and data protection seals and marks in a register and shall make them publicly available by any appropriate means (Article 42(8)).

Certification Body and Procedure

26.84 Without prejudice to the tasks and powers of the competent supervisory authority under Articles 57 and 58, certification bodies which have an appropriate level of expertise in relation to data protection shall, after informing the supervisory authority in order to allow it to exercise its powers pursuant to Article 58(2)(h) where necessary, issue and renew certification. Member States shall ensure that those certification bodies are accredited by one or both of the following:

- the supervisory authority which is competent according to Article 55 or 56; and/or
- the national accreditation body named in accordance with Regulation (EC) 765/2008 of the European Parliament and the Council in accordance with EN-ISO/IEC 17065/2012 and with the additional requirements established by the supervisory authority which is competent pursuant to Article 55 or 56 (Article 43(1)).

The certification body referred to in Article 43(1) may be accredited in accordance with that paragraph only where they have:

- demonstrated their independence and expertise in relation to the subject-matter of the certification to the satisfaction of the competent supervisory authority;
- undertaken to respect the criteria referred to in Article 42(5) and approved by the supervisory authority which is competent according to Article 55 or 56 or by the EDPB pursuant to Article 63;
- established procedures for the issuing, periodic review and withdrawal of data protection certification, seals and marks;
- established procedures and structures to handle complaints about infringements of the certification or the manner in which the certification has been, or is being, implemented by the Controller or Processor, and to make these procedures and structures transparent to Data Subjects and the public; and
- demonstrated to the satisfaction of the competent supervisory authority that their tasks and duties do not result in a conflict of interests (Article 43(2)).

The accreditation of the certification bodies shall take place on the basis of criteria approved by the supervisory authority which is competent according to Article 55 or 56 or the EDPB. In case of an accreditation pursuant to Article 43(1)(b), those requirements shall complement those envisaged in Regulation 765/2008 and the technical rules that describe the methods and procedures of the certification bodies (Article 43(3)).

The certification body referred to in Article 43(1) shall be responsible for the proper assessment leading to the certification or the withdrawal of such certification without prejudice to the responsibility of the Controller or Processor for compliance with the GDPR. The accreditation is issued for a maximum period of five years and can be renewed on the same conditions provided the certification body meets the requirements set out in this Article (Article 43(4)).

The certification body shall provide the competent supervisory authority with the reasons for granting or withdrawing the requested certification (Article 43(5)).

The requirements referred to in Article 43(3) and the criteria referred to in Article 42(5) shall be made public by the supervisory authority in an easily accessible form. The supervisory authorities shall also transmit those and criteria to the EDPB. The EDPB shall collate all certification mechanisms and data protection seals in a register and shall make them publicly available by any appropriate means (Article 43(6)).

Without prejudice to Chapter VIII, the competent supervisory authority or the National Accreditation Body shall revoke the accreditation of a certification body pursuant to Article 43(1) where the conditions for accreditation are not, or are no longer, met or where actions taken by the body infringe the GDPR (Article 43(7)).

The Commission shall be empowered to adopt delegated acts in accordance with Article 92, for the purpose of specifying the requirements to be taken into account for the data protection certification mechanisms referred to in Article 42(1) (Article 43(8)).

The Commission may adopt implementing acts laying down technical standards for certification mechanisms and data protection seals and marks and mechanisms to promote and recognise those certification mechanisms, seals and marks. Those implementing acts shall be adopted in accordance with the examination procedure set out in Article 93(2) (Article 43(9)).

International Co-operation on Personal Data

26.85   In relation to third countries and international organisations, the Commission and supervisory authorities shall take appropriate steps to:

- develop international co-operation mechanisms to facilitate the effective enforcement of legislation for the protection of personal data;
- provide international mutual assistance in the enforcement of legislation for the protection of personal data, including through notification, complaint referral, investigative assistance and information exchange, subject to appropriate safeguards for the protection of personal data and other fundamental rights and freedoms;
- engage relevant stakeholders in discussion and activities aimed at furthering international co-operation in the enforcement of legislation for the protection of personal data;

- promote the exchange and documentation of personal data protection legislation and practice, including on jurisdictional conflicts with third countries (Article 50).

Supervisory Authorities

Independent Supervisory Authorities

26.86 Supervisory authorities such as the ICO (previously called data protection authorities (DPAs) and the complete independence of supervisory authorities are referred to in Recitals 13, 20, 36, 79, 80, 81, 82, 84, 85, 86, 87, 89, 91, 94, 95, 96, 108, 109, 112–113, 116–139, 141–144, 148, 150, 151, 153, 164, 168, 171.

Chapter VI, Section 1 of the GDPR refers to their 'independent status'.

Each Member State shall provide that one or more independent public authorities to be responsible for monitoring the application of the GDPR, in order to protect the fundamental rights and freedoms of natural persons in relation to the processing and to facilitate the free flow of personal data within the EU (Article 51(1)).

Each supervisory authority shall contribute to the consistent application of the GDPR throughout the EU. For that purpose, the supervisory authorities shall cooperate with each other and the Commission in accordance with Chapter VII (Article 51(2)).

Where more than one supervisory authority is established in a Member State, that Member State shall designate the supervisory authority which is to represent those authorities in the EDPB and shall set out the mechanism to ensure compliance by the other authorities with the rules relating to the consistency mechanism referred to in Article 63 (Article 51(3)).

Each Member State shall notify to the Commission those provisions of its law which it adopts pursuant to this Chapter, by 25 May 2018 and, without delay, any subsequent amendment affecting them (Article 51(4)).

Supervisory Authority Independence

26.87 Each supervisory authority shall act with complete independence in performing its tasks and exercising the powers in accordance with the GDPR (Article 52(1)).

The member or members of each supervisory authority shall, in the performance of their tasks and exercise of their powers in accordance with the GDPR, remain free from external influence, whether direct or indirect and shall neither seek nor take instructions from anybody (Article 52(2)).

Member or members of each supervisory authority shall refrain from any action incompatible with their duties and shall not, during their term of office, engage in any incompatible occupation, whether gainful or not (Article 52(3)).

Each Member State shall ensure that each supervisory authority is provided with the human, technical and financial resources, premises and infrastructure necessary for the effective performance of its tasks and exercise of its powers, including those to be carried out in the context of mutual assistance, co-operation and participation in the EDPB (Article 52(4)).

Each Member State shall ensure that each supervisory authority chooses and has its own staff which shall be subject to the exclusive direction of the member or members of the supervisory authority concerned (Article 52(5)).

Member States shall ensure that each supervisory authority is subject to financial control which shall not affect its independence and that it has separate, public, annual budgets, which may be part of the overall state or national budget (Article 52(6)).

There have been a number of cases taken in relation to ensuring that supervisory authorities are sufficiently independent in their roles as required under EU law.[89]

General Conditions for Supervisory Authority Members

26.88   Member States shall provide that each member of their supervisory authority to be appointed by means of a transparent procedure by:

- the parliament;
- government;
- their head of State; or
- an independent body entrusted with the appointment Member State law (Article 53(1)).

---

89   For example, *Commission v Germany*, Case C-518/07 (9 March 2010); *Commission v Austria*, Case C-614/10 (16 October 2012). There is also a recent case filed in Ireland by Digital Rights Ireland. Note, for example, P Schütz, 'Comparing Formal Independence of Data Protection Authorities in Selected EU Member States,' Fourth Biennial ECPR Standing Group for Regulatory Governance Conference (2012); A Balthasar, '"Complete Independence" of National Data Protection Supervisory Authorities – Second Try: Comments on the Judgement of the CJEU of 16 October 2012, Case C-614/10 (*European Commission v Austria*), With Due Regard to its Previous Judgement of 9 March 2010, C-518/07 (*European Commission v Germany*),' *Utrecht Law Review* (2013) (9:3) 26.

Each member shall have the qualifications, experience and skills, in particular in the area of protection of personal data, required to perform its duties and exercise its powers (Article 53(2)).

Rules on Establishment

26.89 Each Member State shall provide by law for all of the following:

- the establishment of each supervisory authority;
- the qualifications and eligibility conditions required to be appointed as member of each supervisory authority;
- the rules and procedures for the appointment of the member or members of each supervisory authority;
- the duration of the term of the member or members of each supervisory authority of no less than four years, except for the first appointment after 24 May 2016, part of which may take place for a shorter period where that is necessary to protect the independence of the supervisory authority by means of a staggered appointment procedure;
- whether and, if so, for how many terms the member or members of each supervisory authority is eligible for reappointment;
- the conditions governing the obligations of the member or members and staff of each supervisory authority, prohibitions on actions, occupations and benefits incompatible therewith during and after the term of office and rules governing the cessation of employment (Article 54(1)).

The member or members and the staff of each supervisory authority shall, in accordance with EU or Member State law, be subject to a duty of professional secrecy both during and after their term of office, with regard to any confidential information which has come to their knowledge in the course of the performance of their tasks or exercise of their powers. During their term of office, this duty of professional secrecy shall in particular apply to reporting by natural persons of infringements of the GDPR (Article 54(2)).

Competence

26.90 Each supervisory authority shall be competent for the performance of the tasks assigned to and the exercise of the powers conferred on it in accordance with the GDPR on the territory of its own Member State (Article 55(1)).

Where processing is carried out by public authorities or private bodies acting on the basis of Article 6(1)(c) or (e), the supervisory authority of the Member State concerned shall be competent. In such cases Article 56 does not apply (Article 55(2)).

Supervisory authorities shall not be competent to supervise processing operations of courts acting in their judicial capacity (Article 55(3)).

Competence of Lead Supervisory Authority

26.91 Without prejudice to Article 55, the supervisory authority of the main establishment or of the single establishment of the Controller or Processor shall be competent to act as lead supervisory authority for the cross-border processing of this Controller or Processor in accordance with the procedure provided in Article 60 (Article 56(1)).

By derogation from Article 56(1), each supervisory authority shall be competent to handle a complaint lodged with it or a possible infringement of the GDPR, if the subject matter relates only to an establishment in its Member State or substantially affects Data Subjects only in its Member State (Article 56(2)).

In the cases referred to in Article 56(2), the supervisory authority shall inform the lead supervisory authority without delay on this matter. Within a period of three weeks after being informed the lead supervisory authority shall decide whether or not it will deal with the case in accordance with the procedure provided in Article 60, taking into account whether or not there is an establishment of the Controller or Processor in the Member State of which the supervisory authority informed it (Article 56(3)).

Where the lead supervisory authority decides to deal with the case, the procedure provided in Article 60 shall apply. The supervisory authority which informed the lead supervisory authority may submit to the lead supervisory authority a draft for a decision. The lead supervisory authority shall take utmost account of that draft when preparing the draft decision (Article 56(4)).

Where the lead supervisory authority decides not to handle the case, the supervisory authority which informed the lead supervisory authority shall handle it according to Articles 61 and 62 (Article 56(5)).

The lead supervisory authority shall be the sole interlocutor of the Controller or Processor for the cross-border processing carried out by that Controller or Processor (Article 56(6)).

Supervisory Authority Tasks

26.92 Without prejudice to other tasks set out under the GDPR, each supervisory authority shall on its territory:

- monitor and enforce the application of the GDPR;
- promote public awareness and understanding of the risks, rules, safeguards and rights in relation to the processing. Activities addressed specifically to children shall receive specific attention;

- advise, in accordance with national law, the national parliament, the government, and other institutions and bodies on legislative and administrative measures relating to the protection of natural persons' rights and freedoms with regard to the processing;
- promote the awareness of Controllers and Processors of their obligations under the GDPR;
- upon request, provide information to any Data Subject concerning the exercise of their rights under the GDPR and, if appropriate, co-operate with the supervisory authorities in other Member States to that end;
- handle complaints lodged by a Data Subject, or by a body, organisation or association in accordance with Article 80, and investigate, to the extent appropriate, the subject matter of the complaint and inform the complainant of the progress and the outcome of the investigation within a reasonable period, in particular if further investigation or coordination with another supervisory authority is necessary;
- co-operate with, including sharing information and provide mutual assistance to other supervisory authorities with a view to ensuring the consistency of application and enforcement of the GDPR;
- conduct investigations on the application of the GDPR, including on the basis of information received from another supervisory authority or other public authority;
- monitor relevant developments, insofar as they have an impact on the protection of personal data, in particular the development of information and communication technologies and commercial practices;
- adopt standard contractual clauses referred to in Article 28(8) and 46(2)(d);
- establish and maintain a list in relation to the requirement for data protection impact assessment pursuant to Article 35(4);
- give advice on the processing operations referred to in Article 36(2);
- encourage the drawing up of codes of conduct pursuant to Article 40(1) and give an opinion and approve such codes of conduct which provide sufficient safeguards, pursuant to Article 40(5);
- encourage the establishment of data protection certification mechanisms and of data protection seals and marks pursuant to Article 42(1), and approve the criteria of certification pursuant to Article 42(5);
- where applicable, carry out a periodic review of certifications issued in accordance with Article 42(7);
- draft and publish the criteria for accreditation of a body for monitoring codes of conduct pursuant to Article 41 and of a certification body pursuant to Article 43;

- conduct the accreditation of a body for monitoring codes of conduct pursuant to Article 41 and of a certification body pursuant to Article 43;
- authorise contractual clauses and provisions referred to in Article 46(3);
- approve binding corporate rules pursuant to Article 47;
- contribute to the activities of the EDPB;
- to keep internal records of breaches of the GDPR and of measures taken in accordance with Article 58(2); and
- fulfil any other tasks related to the protection of personal data (Article 57(1)).

Each supervisory authority shall facilitate the submission of complaints referred to in Article 57(1)(f), by measures such as a complaint submission form, which can be completed also electronically, without excluding other means of communication (Article 57(2)).

The performance of the tasks of each supervisory authority shall be free of charge for the Data Subject and where applicable for the DPO (Article 57(3)).

Where requests are manifestly unfounded or excessive, in particular because of their repetitive character, the supervisory authority may charge a reasonable fee based on administrative costs, or refuse to act on the request. The supervisory authority shall bear the burden of demonstrating the manifestly unfounded or excessive character of the request (Article 57(4)).

Supervisory Authority Powers

Investigative Powers

26.93 Each supervisory authority shall have all of the following investigative powers:

- to order the Controller and the Processor, and, where applicable, the Controller's or the Processor's representative to provide any information it requires for the performance of its tasks;
- to carry out investigations in the form of data protection audits;
- to carry out a review on certifications issued pursuant to Article 42(7);
- to notify the Controller or the Processor of an alleged infringement of the GDPR;
- to obtain, from the Controller and the Processor, access to all personal data and to all information necessary for the performance of its tasks;

- to obtain access to any premises of the Controller and the Processor, including to any data processing equipment and means, in conformity with EU law or Member State procedural law (Article 58(1)).

Corrective Powers

26.94 Each supervisory authority shall have all of the following corrective powers:

- to issue warnings to a Controller or Processor that intended processing operations are likely to infringe provisions of the GDPR;
- to issue reprimands to a Controller or a Processor where processing operations have infringed provisions of the GDPR;
- to order the Controller or the Processor to comply with the Data Subject's requests to exercise his or her rights pursuant to the GDPR;
- to order the Controller or Processor to bring processing operations into compliance with the provisions of the GDPR, where appropriate, in a specified manner and within a specified period;
- to order the Controller to communicate a personal data breach to the Data Subject;
- to impose a temporary or definitive limitation including a ban on processing;
- to order the rectification or erasure of personal data or restriction of processing pursuant to Articles 16, 17 and 18 and the notification of such actions to recipients to whom the personal data have been disclosed pursuant to Article 17(2) and Article 19;
- to withdraw a certification or to order the certification body to withdraw a certification issued pursuant to Article 42 and 43, or to order the certification body not to issue certification if the requirements for the certification are not or no longer met;
- to impose an administrative fine pursuant to Articles 83, in addition to, or instead of measures referred to in this paragraph, depending on the circumstances of each individual case;
- to order the suspension of data flows to a recipient in a third country or to an international organisation (Article 58(2)).

Authorisation and Advisory Powers

26.95 Each supervisory authority shall have all of the following authorisation and advisory powers:

- to advise the Controller in accordance with the prior consultation procedure referred to in Article 36;
- to issue, on its own initiative or on request, opinions to the national parliament, the Member State government or, in accordance with

national law, to other institutions and bodies as well as to the public on any issue related to the protection of personal data;

- to authorise processing referred to in Article 36(5), if the law of the Member State requires such prior authorisation;
- to issue an opinion and approve draft codes of conduct pursuant to Article 40(5);
- to accredit certification bodies pursuant to Article 43;
- to issue certifications and approve criteria of certification in accordance with Article 42(5);
- to adopt standard data protection clauses referred to in Article 28(8) and in Article 46(2)(d);
- to authorise contractual clauses referred to in Article 46(3)(a);
- to authorise administrative agreements referred to in Article 46(3)(b);
- to approve binding corporate rules pursuant to Article 47 (Article 58(3)).

The exercise of the powers conferred on the supervisory authority pursuant to this Article shall be subject to appropriate safeguards, including effective judicial remedy and due process, set out in EU and Member State law in accordance with the Charter (Article 58(4)).

Each Member State shall provide by law that its supervisory authority shall have the power to bring infringements of the GDPR to the attention of the judicial authorities and where appropriate, to commence or engage otherwise in legal proceedings, in order to enforce the provisions of the GDPR (Article 58(5)).

Each Member State may provide by law that its supervisory authority shall have additional powers than those referred to in Article 58(1), (2) and (3). The exercise of these powers shall not impair the effective operation of Chapter VII (Article 58(6)).

Activity Report

26.96   Each supervisory authority shall draw up an annual report on its activities, which may include a list of types of infringements notified and the types of measures taken in accordance with Article 58(2). The reports shall be transmitted to the national parliament, the government and other authorities as designated by national law. It shall be made available to the public, the Commission and the EDPB (Article 59).

Cooperation, etc

26.97   There are provisions in relation to cooperation between the lead supervisory authority and other supervisory authorities concerned (Article 60).

There are also provisions in relation to mutual assistance (Article 61).

Joint operations of supervisory authorities are also referred to (Article 62).

There is a consistency mechanism (Chapter VIII, Section 2, Chapter 63).

There is also reference to opinions of the EDPR (Article 64).

General Conditions for Administrative Fines

26.98 Each supervisory authority shall ensure that the imposition of administrative fines pursuant to this Article in respect of infringements of the GDPR referred to in Article 83(4), (5) and (6) shall in each individual case be effective, proportionate and dissuasive (Article 83(1)).

Administrative fines shall, depending on the circumstances of each individual case, be imposed *in addition* to, or instead of, measures referred to in Article 58(2)(a)–(h) and (j). When deciding whether to impose an administrative fine, and deciding on the amount of the administrative fine in each individual case, due regard shall be given to the following:

- the nature, gravity and duration of the infringement taking into account the nature scope or purpose of the processing concerned as well as the number of Data Subjects affected and the level of damage suffered by them;
- the intentional or negligent character of the infringement;
- action taken by the Controller or Processor to mitigate the damage suffered by Data Subjects;
- the degree of responsibility of the Controller or Processor taking into account technical and organisational measures implemented by them pursuant to Articles 25 and 32;
- any relevant previous infringements by the Controller or Processor;
- the degree of cooperation with the supervisory authority, in order to remedy the infringement and mitigate the possible adverse effects of the infringement;
- the categories of personal data affected by the infringement;
- the manner in which the infringement became known to the supervisory authority, in particular whether, and if so to what extent, the Controller or Processor notified the infringement;
- where measures referred to Article 53(2), have previously been ordered against the Controller or Processor concerned with regard to the same subject-matter, compliance with those measures;
- adherence to approved codes of conduct pursuant to Article 40 or approved certification mechanisms pursuant to Article 42; and

- any other aggravating or mitigating factor applicable to the circumstances of the case, such as financial benefits gained, or losses avoided, directly or indirectly, from the infringement (Article 83(2)).

If a Controller or Processor intentionally or negligently, for the same or linked processing operations, violates several provisions of the GDPR, the total amount of the fine may not exceed the amount specified for the gravest infringement (Article 83(3)).

Infringements of the following provisions shall, in accordance with Article 83(2), be subject to administrative fines up to 10,000,000 EUR, or in case of an undertaking, up to two percent of the total worldwide annual turnover of the preceding financial year, whichever is higher:

- the obligations of the Controller and the Processor pursuant to Articles 8, 11, 23, 25–39, 42 and 43;
- the obligations of the certification body pursuant to Articles 42 and 43;
- the obligations of the monitoring body pursuant to Article 41(4) (Article 83(4)).

Infringements of the following provisions shall, in accordance with Article 83(2), be subject to administrative fines up to 20,000,000 EUR, or in case of an undertaking, up to four percent of the total worldwide annual turnover of the preceding financial year, whichever is higher:

- the basic principles for processing, including conditions for consent, pursuant to Articles 5, 6, 7 and 9;
- the Data Subjects' rights pursuant to Articles 12–22;
- the transfers of personal data to a recipient in a third country or an international organisation pursuant to Articles 40–49;
- any obligations pursuant to Member State law adopted under Chapter IX;
- non-compliance with an order or a temporary or definite limitation on processing or the suspension of data flows by the supervisory authority pursuant to Article 53(2) or failure to provide access in violation of Article 58(1) (Article 83(5)).

Non-compliance with an order by the supervisory authority as referred to in Article 58(2) shall, in accordance with Article 83(2), be subject to administrative fines up to 20,000,000 EUR, or in case of an undertaking, up to four percent of the total worldwide annual turnover of the preceding financial year, whichever is higher (Article 83(6)).

Without prejudice to the corrective powers of supervisory authorities pursuant to Article 58(2), each Member State may lay down the rules on whether and to what extent administrative fines may be imposed on public authorities and bodies established in that Member State (Article 83(7)).

The exercise by the supervisory authority of its powers under this Article shall be subject to appropriate procedural safeguards in conformity with EU law and Member State law, including effective judicial remedy and due process (Article 83(8)).

Where the legal system of the Member State does not provide for administrative fines, this Article may be applied in such a manner that the fine is initiated by the competent supervisory authority and imposed by competent national courts, while ensuring that these legal remedies are effective and have an equivalent effect to the administrative fines imposed by supervisory authorities. In any event, the fines imposed shall be effective, proportionate and dissuasive. Those Member States shall notify to the Commission those provisions of their laws which they adopt pursuant to this paragraph by 25 May 2018 and, without delay, any subsequent amendment law or amendment affecting them (Article 83(9)).

Penalties

26.99 Member States shall lay down the rules on other penalties applicable to infringements of the GDPR in particular for infringements which are not subject to administrative fines pursuant to Article 83, and shall take all measures necessary to ensure that they are implemented. Such penalties shall be effective, proportionate and dissuasive (Article 84(1)).

Each Member State shall notify to the Commission those provisions of its law which it adopts pursuant to paragraph 1, by 25 May 2018 and, without delay, any subsequent amendment affecting them (Article 84(2)).

Specific Data Processing Situations

26.100 Chapter IX of the GDPR refers to provisions regarding specific data processing situations.

Processing and Freedom of Expression and Information

26.101 Member States shall by law reconcile the right to the protection of personal data pursuant to the GDPR with the right to freedom of expression and information, including the processing of personal data for journalistic purposes and the purposes of academic, artistic or literary expression (Article 85(1)).

For processing carried out for journalistic purposes or the purpose of academic artistic or literary expression, Member States shall provide for exemptions or derogations from the provisions in Chapter II (Principles), Chapter III (Rights of the Data Subject), Chapter IV (Controller and Processor), Chapter V (transfer of personal data to third countries or international organisations), Chapter VI (independent supervisory authorities), Chapter VII (cooperation and consistency) and Chapter IX (specific data processing situations) if they are necessary to reconcile the right to the protection of personal data with the freedom of expression and information (Article 85(2)).

Each Member State shall notify to the Commission those provisions of its law which it has adopted pursuant to Article 85(2) and, without delay, any subsequent amendment law or amendment affecting them (Article 85(3)).

Processing and Public Access to Official Documents

26.102 Personal data in official documents held by a public authority or a public body or a private body for the performance of a task carried out in the public interest may be disclosed by the authority or body in accordance with EU law or Member State law to which the public authority or body is subject in order to reconcile public access to official documents with the right to the protection of personal data pursuant to the GDPR (Article 86).

Processing National Identification Numbers

26.103 Member States may further determine the specific conditions for the processing of a national identification number or any other identifier of general application. In that case the national identification number or any other identifier of general application shall be used only under appropriate safeguards for the rights and freedoms of the Data Subject pursuant to the GDPR (Article 87).

Processing in Employment Context

26.104 Issues related to employee personal data are continuing to grow in importance.[90]

The new GDPR provides that Member States may, by law or by collective agreements, provide for more specific rules to ensure the protection of the rights and freedoms in respect of the processing of employees' personal data in the employment context, *in particular* for the purposes of the recruitment, the performance of the contract of employment, including discharge of obligations laid down by law or by collective agreements, management, planning and organisation of work, equality and diversity in the workplace, health and safety at work, protection of employer's or customer's property and for the purposes of the exercise

90 See, for example, Chapters 16–19 and Article 82 of the GDPR.

and enjoyment, on an individual or collective basis, of rights and benefits related to employment, and for the purpose of the termination of the employment relationship (Article 88(1)).

These rules shall include suitable and specific measures to safeguard the Data Subject's human dignity, legitimate interests and fundamental rights, with particular regard to the transparency of processing, the transfer of data within a group of undertakings or group of enterprises engaged in a joint economic activity and monitoring systems at the work place (Article 88(2)).

Each Member State shall notify to the Commission those provisions of its law which it adopts pursuant to Article 88(1), by 25 May 2018 and, without delay, any subsequent amendment affecting them (Article 88(3)).

Prior to the new GDPR, the ICO has issued recommendations in relation to personal data employment issues, namely:

- Employment Practices Code;
- Employment Practices Code – A Quick Guide;
- Employment Practices Code – Supplementary Guidance;
- Disclosure of Employee Information under TUPE;
- Getting it Right: A brief Guide to Data Protection for Small Businesses;
- Monitoring under Section 75 of the Northern Ireland Act 1998.

These now need to be read in light of the GDPR changes.

Safeguards and Derogations: Public Interest/Scientific/Historical Research/ Statistical Archiving Processing

26.105 There are also provisions in relation to safeguards and derogations for processing personal data for archiving purposes in the public interest, scientific or historical research purposes or statistical purposes.

Processing for archiving purposes in the public interest, scientific or historical research purposes or statistical purposes, shall be subject to appropriate safeguards for the rights and freedoms of the Data Subject. These safeguards shall ensure that technical and organisational measures are in place in particular in order to ensure the respect of the principle of data minimisation. These measures may include pseudonymisation, provided that those purposes can be fulfilled in that manner. Where those purposes can be fulfilled by further processing which does not permit or no longer permits the identification of Data Subjects these purposes shall be fulfilled in that manner (Article 89(1)).

Where personal data are processed for scientific and historical research purposes or statistical purposes, EU or Member State law may provide for derogations from the rights referred to in Articles 15, 16, 18 and 21 subject to the conditions and safeguards referred to in Article 89(1) in so far as such rights are likely to render impossible or seriously impair the achievement of the specific purposes, and such derogations are necessary for the fulfilment of those purposes (Article 89(2)).

Where personal data are processed for archiving purposes in the public interest, EU or Member State law may provide for derogations from the rights referred to in Articles 15, 16, 18, 19, 20 and 21 subject to the conditions and safeguards referred to in Article 89(1) in so far as such rights are likely to render impossible or seriously impair the achievement of the specific purposes, and such derogations are necessary for the fulfilment of these purposes (Article 89(3)).

Where processing referred to in Article 89(2) and (3) serves at the same time another purpose, the derogations shall apply only to processing for the purposes referred to in those paragraphs (Article 89(4)).

Obligations of Secrecy

26.106 Member States may adopt specific rules to set out the powers by the supervisory authorities laid down in Article 58(1)(e) and (f) in relation to Controllers or Processors that are subject, under EU or Member State law or rules established by national competent bodies to an obligation of professional secrecy or other equivalent obligations of secrecy where this is necessary and proportionate to reconcile the right of the protection of personal data with the obligation of secrecy. Those rules shall only apply with regard to personal data which the Controller or Processor has received as a result of, or has obtained in, an activity covered by that obligation of secrecy (Article 90(1)).

Each Member State shall notify to the Commission the rules adopted pursuant to Article 90(1), by 25 May 2018 and without delay, any subsequent amendment affecting them (Article 90(2)).

Churches and Religious Associations

26.107 Where in a Member State, churches and religious associations or communities apply, at the time of entry into force of the GDPR, comprehensive rules relating to the protection of natural persons with regard to the processing, such rules may continue to apply, provided that they are brought in line with the provisions of the GDPR (Article 91(1)).

Churches and religious associations which apply comprehensive rules in accordance with Article 91(1), shall be subject to the supervision of an independent supervisory authority which may be specific, provided that it fulfils the conditions laid down in Chapter VI of the GDPR (Article 91(2)).

Delegated Acts and Implementing Acts

26.108   Chapter X of the GDPR refers to delegated acts and implementing acts.

Exercise of the Delegation

26.109   The power to adopt delegated acts is conferred on the Commission subject to the conditions laid down in Article 92.

The delegation of power referred to in Article 12(8) and Article 43(8) shall be conferred on the Commission for an indeterminate period of time from 24 May 2016 (Article 92(2)).

The delegation of power referred to in Article 12(8) and Article 43(8) may be revoked at any time by the European Parliament or by the Council. A decision of revocation shall put an end to the delegation of power specified in that decision. It shall take effect the day following the publication of the decision in the Official Journal of the EU or at a later date specified therein. It shall not affect the validity of any delegated acts already in force (Article 92(3)).

As soon as it adopts a delegated act, the Commission shall notify it simultaneously to the European Parliament and to the Council (Article 92(4)).

A delegated act adopted pursuant to Article 12(8) and Article 43(8) shall enter into force only if no objection has been expressed either by the European Parliament or the Council within a period of three months of notification of that act to the European Parliament and the Council or if, before the expiry of that period, the European Parliament and the Council have both informed the Commission that they will not object. That period shall be extended by three months at the initiative of the European Parliament or the Council (Article 92(5)).

Relationship to Directive 2002/58/EC

26.110   The GDPR shall not impose additional obligations on natural or legal persons in relation to the processing in connection with the provision of publicly available electronic communications services in public communication networks in the EU in relation to matters for which they are subject to specific obligations with the same objective set out in Directive 2002/58/EC[91] (Article 95).

---

91 Directive 2002/58/EC of the European Parliament and of the Council of 12 July 2002 concerning the processing of personal data and the protection of privacy in the electronic communications sector (Directive on privacy and electronic communications).

Relationship to Previously Concluded Agreements

26.111   International agreements involving the transfer of personal data to third countries or international organisations which were concluded by Member States prior 24 May 2016, and which comply with EU law as applicable prior to that date, shall remain in force until amended, replaced or revoked (Article 96).

Review of Other EU Data Protection Instruments

26.112   The Commission shall, if appropriate, submit legislative proposals with a view to amending other EU legal instruments on the protection of personal data, in order to ensure uniform and consistent protection of natural persons with regard to the processing of personal data. This shall in particular concern the rules relating to the protection of natural persons with regard to the processing of personal data by EU institutions, bodies, offices and agencies and on the free movement of such data (Article 98).

Restrictions

26.113   The GDPR does not address national security; the GDPR should not apply to data processing by a natural person in the course of a purely personal or household activity and thus without a connection with a professional or commercial activity; without prejudice to eCommerce Directive[92] in particular eCommerce defences of Articles 12–15; the GDPR does not apply to the data of the deceased.

Chapter III, Section 5 of the GDPR refers to Restrictions. EU or Member State law to which the Controller or Processor is subject may restrict by way of a legislative measure the scope of the obligations and rights provided for in Articles 12–22 and Article 34, as well as Article 5 in so far as its provisions correspond to the rights and obligations provided for in Articles 12–22, when such a restriction respects the essence of the fundamental rights and freedoms and is a necessary and proportionate measure in a democratic society to safeguard:

- national security;
- defence;
- public security;
- the prevention, investigation, detection or prosecution of criminal offences or the execution of criminal penalties, including the safeguarding against and the prevention of threats to public security;

92   Directive 2000/31/EC.

- other important objectives of general public interests of the EU or of a Member State, in particular an important economic or financial interest of the EU or of a Member State, including monetary, budgetary and taxation matters, public health and social security;
- the protection of judicial independence and judicial proceedings;
- the prevention, investigation, detection and prosecution of breaches of ethics for regulated professions;
- a monitoring, inspection or regulatory function connected, even occasionally, to the exercise of official authority in cases referred to in (a)–(e), and (g);
- the protection of the Data Subject or the rights and freedoms of others;
- the enforcement of civil law claims (Article 23(1)).

In particular, any legislative measure referred to in Article 23(1) shall contain specific provisions at least, where relevant, as to:

- the purposes of the processing or categories of processing;
- the categories of personal data;
- the scope of the restrictions introduced;
- the safeguards to prevent abuse or unlawful access or transfer;
- the specification of the Controller or categories of Controllers;
- the storage periods and the applicable safeguards taking into account the nature, scope and purposes of the processing or categories of processing;
- the risks for the rights and freedoms of Data Subjects; and
- the right of Data Subjects to be informed about the restriction, unless this may be prejudicial to the purpose of the restriction (Article 23(2)).

New Data Protection Officer Obligation

Introduction

26.114 Now organisations need to have a designated Data Protection Officer (DPO) to deal with the data protection compliance obligations, dealing with Data Subject access requests, etc. That is not to say that board and management responsibility for data protection compliance is in any way diminished.

DPO

26.115 Chapter IV, Section 4 of the new GDPR refers to DPOs and the obligation for organisations to appoint DPOs.

The Controller and the Processor shall designate a DPO in all cases specified by the GDPR, in particular in Article 35. (For further details see Chapter 23.)

Position of DPO

26.116   The Controller or the Processor shall ensure that the DPO is involved, properly and in a timely manner in all issues which relate to the protection of personal data (Article 38(1)).

The Controller or Processor shall support the DPO in performing the tasks referred to in Article 39 by providing resources necessary to carry out those tasks as well as access to personal data and processing operations, and to maintain his or her expert knowledge (Article 38(2)).

The Controller or Processor shall ensure that the DPO does not receive any instructions regarding the exercise of the tasks. He or she shall not be dismissed or penalised by the Controller or the Processor for performing the tasks. The DPO shall directly report to the highest management level of the Controller or the Processor (Article 38(3)).

Data Subjects may contact the DPO with regard to all issues relating to the processing of their personal data and to the exercise of their rights under the GDPR (Article 38(4)).

The DPO shall be bound by secrecy or confidentiality concerning the performance of their tasks, in accordance with EU or Member State law (Article 38(5)).

The DPO may fulfil other tasks and duties. The Controller or Processor shall ensure that any such tasks and duties do not result in a conflict of interests (Article 38(6)).

Tasks of DPO

26.117   The DPO shall have at least the following tasks:

- to inform and advise the Controller or the Processor and the employees who carry out processing of their obligations pursuant to the GDPR and to other EU or Member State data protection provisions;
- to monitor compliance with the GDPR, with other EU or Member State data protection provisions and with the policies of the Controller or Processor in relation to the protection of personal data, including the assignment of responsibilities, awareness-raising and training of staff involved in processing operations, and the related audits;
- to provide advice where requested as regards the data protection impact assessment and monitor its performance pursuant to Article 39;
- to cooperate with the supervisory authority;
- to act as the contact point for the supervisory authority on issues related to the processing, including the prior consultation referred to in Article 36, and consult, where appropriate, on any other matter (Article 39(1)).

The DPO shall in the performance of his or her tasks have due regard to the risk associated with the processing operations, taking into account the nature, scope, context and purposes of processing (Article 39(2)).

Importance

26.118   The new profession and new mandated requirement for a DPO will prove to be one of the game changes in data protection practice and protection for personal data. While the DPO will be promoting data protection compliance, adherence to the new data protection regime, pre-problem solving (such as data protection by design and by default) and the understanding of data protection throughout the organisation, the protection of the DPO's independence will ensure that the temptation by some in an organisation to ignore or downgrade data protection in favour of (new) collections and processing, and maximum use compared to proportionate and limited data use, can be more robustly resisted. The independence of the DPO is also protected by ensuring that they report directly to the highest level which will generally be a board member. This will assist in eliminating the possibility of junior managers or others seeking to adversely influence, ignore or overrule the DPO in the proper performance of their functions and role.

Conclusion

26.119   All organisations need to become very familiar with the GDPR. While in some instances the current compliance mechanisms are continued, there are many new requirements to compliance. Organisations need to start now in terms of ensuring preparation and compliance. Indeed, the most prudent organisations will continually be adopting best practice, and data protection compliance is an area where best practice has positive benefits above and beyond mere compliance.

Part 5
Particular Issues

Chapter 27

Data Breach

Introduction

27.01 The new GDPR defines 'personal data breach' as a 'breach of security leading to the accidental or unlawful destruction, loss, alteration, unauthorised disclosure of, or access to, personal data transmitted, stored or otherwise processed'. The importance attached to dealing with data breaches and data breach incidents is highlighted in the GDPR. Now data breaches must be notified to the supervisory authority and the Data Subjects. (Bear in mind that employees can also be Data Subjects.) Data Subjects can suffer loss and damage if there has been a data breach, and particularly so if they are unaware of it and are not notified when the organisation becomes aware in order that, for example, remedial measures can be undertaken by the Data Subject. For example they may wish to change passwords or cancel credit cards, depending on the nature of the breach. Indeed, in some instances organisations may need to recommend remedial or safety measures to Data Subjects after a data breach.

Data Breach Incidents in Context

27.02 The issue and frequency of data breaches and data breach incidents are highlighted in Part 1. In addition, it is clear that national supervisory authorities take data breaches very seriously. Significant fines are now regularly levelled at organisations, including large organisations and public organisations, in relation to data breaches. Similarly, even smaller organisations have been fined.

The ICO, and other supervisory authorities, can carry out audits and inspections of organisations, which can include security and data breach preparedness, as well as the implications which result from a recent data breach incident. In fact, many data breaches result in media publicity for the organisation, in which case the ICO is likely to contact the organisation.

Notification of a Data Breach to Supervisory Authority

27.03 In the case of a personal data breach, the new GDPR requires that the Controller shall without undue delay and, where feasible, not later than 72 hours after having become aware of it, notify the personal data breach to the supervisory authority competent in accordance with Article 33, unless the personal data breach is unlikely to result in a risk for the rights and freedoms of natural persons. Where the notification to the supervisory authority is not made within 72 hours, it shall be accompanied by reasons for delay (Article 35(1)).

The Processor shall notify the Controller without undue delay after becoming aware of a personal data breach (Article 33(2)).

The notification referred to in Article 33(1) must at least:

- describe the nature of the personal data breach including where possible, the categories and approximate number of Data Subjects concerned and the categories and approximate number of data records concerned;
- communicate the name and contact details of the DPO or other contact point where more information can be obtained;
- describe the likely consequences of the personal data breach;
- describe the measures taken or proposed to be taken by the Controller to address the personal data breach, including, where appropriate, to mitigate its possible adverse effects (Article 33(3)).

Where, and in so far as, it is not possible to provide the information at the same time, the information may be provided in phases without undue further delay (Article 33(4)).

The Controller shall document any personal data breaches, comprising the facts relating to the personal data breach, its effects and the remedial action taken. This documentation shall enable the supervisory authority to verify compliance with this Article (Article 33(5)).

Communication of a Data Breach to Data Subject

27.04 When the personal data breach is likely to result in a high risk to the rights and freedoms of natural persons the Controller shall communicate the personal data breach to the Data Subject without undue delay (Article 34(1)).[1]

The communication to the Data Subject referred to in Article 34(2) shall describe in clear and plain language the nature of the personal data breach and contain at least the information and measures referred to in Article 33(3)(b), (c) and (d) (Article 34(2)).

The communication to the Data Subject referred to in Article 34(1) shall not be required if:

- the Controller has implemented appropriate technical and organisational protection measures, and that those measures were applied to the personal data affected by the personal data breach, in particular those that render the personal data unintelligible to any person who is not authorised to access it, such as encryption;
- the Controller has taken subsequent measures which ensure that the high risk for the rights and freedoms of Data Subjects referred to in para 1 is no longer likely to materialise;
- it would involve disproportionate effort. In such cases, there shall instead be a public communication or similar measure whereby the Data Subjects are informed in an equally effective manner (Article 34(3)).

If the Controller has not already communicated the personal data breach to the Data Subject, the supervisory authority, having considered the likelihood of the personal data breach resulting in a high risk, may require it to do so or may decide that any of the conditions referred to in Article 34(4) are met (Article 34(4)).

Employee Data Breaches

27.05 Employee involvement is critical in dealing with – and preparing for – data breach incidents. Various teams of employees will be involved.

However, as employee personal data can also be the subject of a data breach incident, employees may need to be specifically considered in this context also. For example, they may need to be separately informed that there is a breach relating to their personal data and what actions and safeguards are being followed by the organisation to deal with the issue.

---

1   Note, for example, P Wainman, 'Data Protection Breaches: Today and Tomorrow,' SCL *Computers and Law*, 30 June 2012. Also see M Dekker, Dr, C Christoffer Karsberg and B Daskala, *Cyber Incident Reporting in the EU* (2012).

If the employees need to take specific actions, they may also need to be appraised of this possibility. Potentially liability issues may also arise. For example, employees in the massive Sony data breach incidents may have considered suing Sony for breaches in relation to their data.

Notification Timelines

27.06 Organisations will need to assess the categories of personal data they have that may be involved in a data breach. They also need to assess what type of organisation or sector they are involved in. These factors may dictate how the data protection regime may impose time limits for respective notification of breaches.

Notification Processes

27.07 DPOs and organisations need to develop, and update as appropriate, breach notification procedures. There needs to be an appropriate response plan for the different types of breach incidents, ICO, other regulators if appropriate or required, Data Subjects and other organisations, whether partners, Processors, outsource security, etc.

Contracts and agreements should also be reviewed to ensure appropriate breach, notification and security provisions.

Security Standards

27.08 The requirement to comply with the new GDPR regime, to maintain security and to prevent and to deal with data breaches increasingly directs attention to detailed standards and implementation measures. One example is compliance with ISO 27001 international standard for confidentiality and security. In particular it refers to:

- security policies;
- organisational information security;
- HR security issues (including employees, families, contractors previously and currently);
- asset identification and control
- encryption;
- physical and environmental security factors;
- operational security;
- communications security;

- acquisition, development and maintenance of systems;
- supplier relations;
- security incident management;
- security issues and business continuity;
- compliance with internal policies and external issues such as a data protection regime and other laws.

Also consider ISO 31000 on international risk management standards, and BS10012:2009 a standard for personal information management systems.

Organisations, including Processors, must implement appropriate security measures, considering:

- PIAs;
- anonymising data;
- deleting after use purpose;
- confidentiality;
- integrity;
- availability;
- access controls and restrictions;
- Approved Codes of Conduct and Certification;
- separating, segregating and securing different data sets;
- encryption.

Incident Response

27.09 Some of the incident response and action points include, and not in order of priority:

- incident detection and reporting;
- incident notification to organisation (eg notification or demand from hacker, posting online, etc);
- internal notification(s);
- team notifications;
- risk assessment;
- PIAs;
- disciplinary action;
- hacker relation action;
- supervisory authority external breach notification;
- Data Subject breach notification;
- customer breach notification.

Conclusion

27.10 Data breach issues should be considered in conjunction with the various risk reduction mechanisms referred to under the new GDPR regime, such as impact assessments, Data Protection by Design and by default, mandatory breach reporting, mandatory prior consultations with the supervisory authority in the case of identified high risks, codes of conduct and certification mechanisms.

Chapter 28

Data Protection Impact Assessment

Data Protection Impact Assessment and Prior Consultation

28.01 Chapter IV, Section 3 of the GDPR refers to data protection impact assessments (DPIAs) (sometimes also referred to as privacy impact assessments (PIAs)) and prior consultations. As a result of the new GDPR regime there is now a mandatory data protection impact assessment regime. These assessments must be undertaken when data processing activities involve specific data protection and privacy risks. In particular when new products and services, or other changes to existing products and services arise, the organisation should ensure that these activities are the subject of a data protection impact assessment (DPIA).

These impact assessments will help organisations to identify and understand current and new risks in their processing activities, or indeed to their processing activities. Considerations include:

- identifying when a project involves the collection of new information about individuals;
- identifying whether information about individuals will be disclosed to organisations or people who have not previously had routine access to the information;
- identifying whether the project involves the use of new technology which may raise privacy and data protection issues, such as over-reach or privacy intrusion;
- identifying whether the personal data raises issues or concerns or is in some way objectionable.

Data Protection Impact Assessment

The New Requirement

28.02   Where a type of processing in particular using new technologies, and taking into account the nature, scope, context and purposes of the processing, is likely to result in a high risk for the rights and freedoms of natural persons, the Controller shall, prior to the processing, carry out an assessment of the impact of the envisaged processing operations on the protection of personal data. A single assessment may address a set of similar processing operations that present similar high risks (Article 35(1)).

The Controller shall seek the advice of the data protection officer (DPO), where designated, when carrying out a data protection impact assessment (Article 35(2)).

A DPIA referred to in Article 35(1) shall in particular be required in the following cases:

- a systematic and extensive evaluation of personal aspects relating to natural persons which is based on automated processing, including profiling, and on which decisions are based that produce legal effects concerning the natural person or similarly significantly affect the natural person;
- processing on a large scale of special categories of data referred to in Article 9(1), or of personal data relating to criminal convictions and offences referred to in Article 10;
- a systematic monitoring of a publicly accessible area on a large scale (Article 35(3)).

The supervisory authority shall establish and make public a list of the kind of processing operations which are subject to the requirement for a DPIA pursuant to Article 35(1). The supervisory authority shall communicate those lists to the EDPB (Article 35(4)).

The supervisory authority may also establish and make public a list of the kind of processing operations for which no DPIA is required. The SA shall communicate those lists to the EDPB (Article 35(5)).

Prior to the adoption of the lists referred to in Article 35(4) and (5) the competent supervisory authority shall apply the consistency mechanism referred to in Article 57 where such lists involve processing activities which are related to the offering of goods or services to Data Subjects or to the monitoring of their behaviour in several Member States, or may substantially affect the free movement of personal data within the EU (Article 35(6)).

The assessment shall contain at least:

- a systematic description of the envisaged processing operations and the purposes of the processing, including where applicable the legitimate interest pursued by the Controller;

- an assessment of the necessity and proportionality of the processing operations in relation to the purposes;
- an assessment of the risks to the rights and freedoms of Data Subjects referred to in Article 35(1);
- the measures envisaged to address the risks, including safeguards, security measures and mechanisms to ensure the protection of personal data and to demonstrate compliance with the GDPR taking into account the rights and legitimate interests of Data Subjects and other persons concerned (Article 35(7)).

Compliance with approved codes of conduct referred to in Article 40 by the relevant Controllers or Processors shall be taken into due account in assessing the impact of the processing operations performed by such Controllers or Processors, in particular for the purposes of a DPIA (Article 35(8)).

Where appropriate, the Controller shall seek the views of Data Subjects or their representatives on the intended processing, without prejudice to the protection of commercial or public interests or the security of the processing operations (Article 35(9)).

Where the processing pursuant to Article 6(1)(c) or (e) has a legal basis in EU law, or the law of the Member State to which the Controller is subject, that law regulates the specific processing operations in question, and a DPIA has already carried out as part of a general impact assessment in the context of the adoption of this legal basis, Article 35(1)–(7) shall not apply, unless Member States deem it necessary to carry out such assessment prior to the processing activities (Article 35(10)).

Where necessary, the Controller shall carry out a review to assess if processing is performed in accordance with the DPIA at least when there is a change of the risk represented by processing operations (Article 35(11)).

Reasons for Assessment

28.03   Vodafone refer to the following reasons for assessments:

- *accountability*: to demonstrate that the assessment process was performed appropriately and in accordance with the programme of assessments agreed with the board sponsor for privacy;
- *provides basis for post implementation review*: to ensure any privacy risks identified are allocated a business owner and a timetable for delivery mitigation actions, therefore providing the DPO with a mechanism for ensuring that the agreed actions are delivered within agreed timescales;
- *provides a basis for audit*: Vodafone distinguishes between a review which is undertaken by the DPO who is responsible for ensuring it is implemented and the controls required are delivered, and the

audit which is an objective and neutral assessment undertaken by the group or local audit function or any other suitably qualified audit function that is not part of delivering the overall Privacy Risk Management System;

- *provides corporate memory*: ensuring the information gained is available to those completing new assessments if original staff have left or use a part of a subsequent assessment of the same business or commercial unit or activity;
- enables the experience gained during the project to be shared with the future assessment teams and others outside the organisation.[1]

Nokia also give reasons for undertaking assessments:

- 'to measure the implementation of privacy requirements, to get an understanding of the current status (risk, controls, root causes, etc)';[2]
- the assessment is part of technical and organisational measures. It assists to find out if new projects follow the privacy requirements; project management; communicate fulfilment of requirements; help to generate status reports for management teams; an effective tool for assigning responsibility and fixing problems;
- the [D]PIA assessment serves as 'a repository for information requests from authorities and consumers. Consumers might ask Nokia where and for how long their data is stored. A data protection authority might, for example, ask how consumers are informed about privacy practices or who the controller of the data is. Privacy assessment might also be used to prepare notifications for data protection authorities';[3]
- 'a means to improve general awareness. The assessment process ... builds up competencies and privacy awareness, as it offers an extensive set of questions that might be relevant for privacy compliance.'[4]

Key Elements of Assessment Report

28.04   Some key elements of an assessment report are -as follows:

- the scope of the assessment undertaken;
- summary of the consultative process undertaken;

1   S Deadman and A Chandler, 'Vodafone's Approach to Privacy Impact Assessments,' in D Wright and P de Hert, eds, *Privacy Impact Assessment* (Springer, 2012) 298.
2   T Brautigam, 'PIA: Cornerstone of Privacy Compliance in Nokia,' in D Wright and P de Hert, eds, *Privacy Impact Assessment* (Springer, 2012) 260–261.
3   *Ibid.*
4   *Ibid.*

- the project background paper(s) provided to those consulted (appendices);
- analysis of the privacy issues and risks arising from the assessment;
- the business case justifying privacy intrusion and implications, treatment or mitigating action, together with timelines for implementation;
- references to relevant laws, codes and guidelines, including internal Vodafone local group policies.[5]

Assessment Characteristics

28.05 Common characteristics of impact assessments:

- *Statement of problem*: Is government intervention both necessary and desirable?
- *Definition of alternative remedies*: these include different approaches, such as the use of economic incentives or voluntary approaches;
- *Determination of physical effects of each alternative, including potential unintended consequences*: the net should be cast wide. Generally speaking, regulations or investments in many areas of public policy can have social, environmental and other implications that must be kept in mind;
- *Estimation of benefits and costs of each alternative*: benefits should be quantified and where possible monetised. Costs should be true opportunity and not simply expenditures;
- *Assessment of other economic impacts*: including effects on competition, effects on small firms, international trade implications;
- *Identification of winners and losers*: those in the community who stand to gain and lose from each alternative and, if possible, the extent of their gains and losses;
- *Communication with the interested public, including the following activities*: notification of intent to regulate, request for compliance costs and other data, public disclosure of regulatory proposals and supporting analysis, and consideration of and response to public comments;
- A *clear choice of the preferred alternative*, plus a statement defending that choice;
- *Provision of a plan for ex post analysis of regulatory outcomes*: it is important to establish a benchmark against which to measure

---

5   S Deadman and A Chandler, above, 299.

performance. Planning is needed to ensure that procedures are in place for the collection of date to permit such benchmarking.[6]

Some assessment characteristics distinguishing it from other privacy related processes include:

- an assessment focuses on a particular initiative or project;
- an assessment is performed at depth, through the project life cycle, and involves engagement with stakeholders;
- an assessment assesses a project against the needs, expectations and concerns of all stakeholders, including but not limited to legal requirements;
- an assessment assesses all aspects of privacy and data protection;
- an assessment adopts a multi-perspective approach, taking into account the costs and benefits as perceived by all stakeholders;
- an assessment adopts a multi perspective approach, taking into account the risks as perceived by all stakeholders;
- an assessment is a process used to establish what undertakings an organisation needs to give;
- an assessment is the process that identifies the problems and identifies solutions to them;
- an assessment is conducted before and in parallel with a project, and ensures that harmful and expensive problems that an audit would later expose are involved, and that unavoidable negative impacts on privacy are minimised and harms mitigated.[7]

Key Steps and Methodologies

28.06   The key steps and methodologies in an assessment include:

- identifying all of the personal data related to a programme or service and looking at how it will be used;
- mapping where personal data is sent after collection;
- identifying privacy and data protection risks and the level of the risks;
- finding methods to eliminate or reduce the risks.[8]

---

6   OECD, 'Regulatory Performance: Ex Post Evaluation of Regulatory Tools and Institutions,' Working Party on Regulatory Management and Reform, Draft Report by the Secretariat, OECD, Paris (2004), 7; referred to in D Parker, '(Regulatory) Impact Assessment and Better Regulation,' in D Wright and P de Hert, eds, *Privacy Impact Assessment* (Springer, 2012) 80.

7   R Clarke, 'PIAs in Australia: A Work-In-Progress Report,' in D Wright and P de Hert, eds, *Privacy Impact Assessment* (Springer, 2012) 121.

8   Office of the Privacy Commissioner of Canada, Fact Sheet on Privacy Impact Assessment. Also note OIPC of Alberta, 'Commissioner Accepts Privacy Impact assessment for the Alberta Security Screening Directive,' press release, 16 January 2003.

Some Assessment Issues

28.07 Organisations might consider issues such as the following:

- preparation;
- undertaking of the assessment;
- the timing of the assessment;
- cost and resourcing the assessment;
- whom the report is for;
- issues and problems raised;
- independence of those undertaking the assessment;
- any constraints;
- legal professional privilege and confidentiality;
- after undertaking the assessment, draft report/comments/final report;
- whether the assessment is a one off or an ongoing assessment in a (rolling) series?

Prior Consultation

28.08 The Controller shall consult the supervisory authority *prior to* processing where a DPIA as provided for in Article 35 indicates that the processing would result in a high risk in the absence of measures taken by the Controller to mitigate the risk (Article 36(1)).

Where the supervisory authority is of the opinion that the intended processing referred to in Article 36(1) would infringe the GDPR, in particular where the Controller has insufficiently identified or mitigated the risk, it shall within a period of up to eight weeks of receipt of the request for consultation, provide written advice to the Controller and, where applicable the Processor, and may use any of its powers referred to in Article 53. That period may be extended for a further six weeks, taking into account the complexity of the intended processing. The supervisory authority shall inform the Controller and, where applicable, the Processor, of any uch extension within one month of receipt of the request for consultation together with the reasons for the delay. Those periods may be suspended until the supervisory authority has obtained information it may have requested for the purposes of the consultation (Article 36(2)).

When consulting the supervisory authority pursuant to Article 36(1), the Controller shall provide the supervisory authority with:

- where applicable, the respective responsibilities of the Controller, joint Controllers and Processors involved in the processing, in particular for processing within a group of undertakings;
- the purposes and means of the intended processing;

- the measures and safeguards provided to protect the rights and freedoms of Data Subjects pursuant to the GDPR;
- where applicable, the contact details of the DPO;
- the DPIA provided for in Article 35; and
- any other information requested by the supervisory authority (Article 36(3)).

Member States shall consult the supervisory authority during the preparation of a proposal for a legislative measure to be adopted by a national parliament, or of a regulatory measure based on such a legislative measure, which relates to processing (Article 37(4)).

Notwithstanding Article 36(1), Member States' law may require Controllers to consult with, and obtain prior authorisation from, the supervisory authority in relation to the processing of personal data by a Controller for the performance of a task carried out by the Controller in the public interest, including processing in relation to social protection and public health (Article 36(5)).

Conclusion

28.09 Carrying out impact assessments and the like helps to not only identify privacy and data protection problems, which can then be addressed, but also helps to raise these at the earliest stage possible. Therefore, the least expensive and least problematic time to make remedial changes is engaged. Carrying out such assessments is not a requirement under the new GDPR regime. This is especially so for high risk activities and when sensitive personal data may be involved. These assessments ensure organisations understand the data they hold, and the problem issues likely to arise. The organisation, its processes, and the ultimate customer relationship, will all be improved. Impact assessments are ultimately one of the mechanisms under the new GDPR for assessing, and thus minimising, risk in the personal data environment.

Organisations must now be proactive and assess when processing activities are likely to raise risks in relation to personal data and processing. The DPO and other relevant parties/teams must be involved. Assessments must be more systematic. Risk identification and evaluation are now key considerations. Measures to mitigate and address risks must be considered and documented, including risk assessments. In situations where there are substantial risk issues, it may be necessary to consult with the ICO.

Chapter 29

Social Media

Introduction

29.01 New technologies 'permit easy dissemination and using of information. Current ICT allows individuals to share [sometimes unknowingly] their personal preferences and behaviour information on an unprecedented scale. This could lead to people losing control of personal information.'[1] Web 2.0 is an increasing part of our daily lives. One of its more popular examples is social media. What are the legal implications of social media?[2] One of the most controversial issues in relation to social media websites is their data processing and respect for privacy and personal data.[3] This is only part of the story. There are many discrete issues, such as:

- employers using social networks to vet and screen job applicants;[4]
- employers monitoring their employees' social media;[5]

1   T Stanimir, 'Personal Data Protection and the New Technologies,' *Proceedings of the International Conference on Information Technologies* (2011) 333–344.
2   S Nelson, J Simek and J Foltin, 'The Legal Implications of Social Networking,' *Regent University Law Review*, (2009–2010) (22) 1–34. Also, P Viscounty, J Archie, F Alemi and J Allen, 'Social Networking and the Law,' *Business Law Today* (2008–009) (58) 18.
3   See, for example, P Roth, 'Data Protection Meets Web 2.0: Two Ships Passing in the Night,' *UNSW Law Journal* (2010) (33) 532–561. NJ Slabbert, 'Orwell's Ghost: How Teletechnology is Reshaping Civil Society,' *CommLaw Conspectus* (2007–2008) (16) 349–359.
4   C Brandenburg, 'The Newest Way to Screen Job Applicants: A Social Networker's Nightmare,' *Federal Communications Law Journal* (2007–2008) (60) 597. D Gersen, 'Your Image, Employers Investigate Job Candidates Online More than Ever. What can You Do to Protect Yourself?' *Student Law* (2007–2008) (36) 24; I Byrnside, 'Six Degrees of Separation: The Legal Ramifications of Employers Using Social Networking Sites to Research Applicants,' *Vanderbilt Journal of Entertainment and Technology Law* (2008) (2) 445–477.
5   AR Levinson, 'Industrial Justice: Privacy Protection for the Employed,' *Cornell Journal of Law and Public Policy* (2009) (18) 609–688.

- recruiting through social media;[6]
- universities monitoring student usage of social media;
- universities using social media websites to vet applicants;
- new forms of digital evidence, both criminal and civil.

One example of note is the Facebook investigation of particular data protection issues by one of the EU national supervisory authorities. The Facebook Beacon settlement, albeit in the US, can also be viewed as significant as it involves a significant financial settlement in relation to privacy, data protection and online marketing without user consent. LinkedIn has also been audited in the EU.

Prior to the new GDPR, the ICO has issued recommendations in relation to online and computing personal data issues, namely:

- Bring Your Own Device (BYOD) guidance;
- Cloud Computing;
- IT Asset Disposal;
- Personal Information Online Code of Practice;
- Personal Information Online: Small Business Checklist;
- Privacy in Mobile Apps: Guidance for App Developers;
- Social Media and Online Forums – When Does the DPA apply?

These now need to be read in light of the GDPR changes.

Investigations

29.02 Social media organisations can be officially investigated and audited much like any other organisations can. One audit,[7] for example, reviewed certain specific aspects of social media data protection compliance. This arose after a number of complaints regarding specific aspects of an organisation. The following issues were looked at, namely:

- privacy policies;
- advertising;
- access requests;
- retention;
- cookies/social plug-ins;
- third part apps;
- disclosures to third parties;

---

6   M Maher, 'You've Got Messages, Modern Technology Recruiting Through Text Messaging and the Intrusiveness of Facebook,' *Texas Review of Entertainment and Sports Law* (2007) (8) 125–151.
7   Facebook Ireland Limited, *Report of Re-Audit, Data Protection Commissioner*, 21 September 2012.

- facial recognition/tag suggest;
- data security;
- deletion of accounts;
- friend finder;
- tagging;
- posting on other profiles;
- credits;
- pseudonymous profiles;
- abuse reporting;
- compliance management/governance.

That is not to suggest that every potential data protection issue was considered. It was not. Other issues and complaints can arise in future, as well as further investigations.[8]

The audit investigation forced the social media organisation to make particular changes to particular aspects of its data protection practices. These are referred to in the reports. The entity in the EU, the entity which was investigated, is responsible for its data protection compliance for everywhere outside of the US and Canada. Therefore, these changes should see an impact even beyond the EU. In addition it is noted that the controversial use of facial recognition technology by the organisation has had to be turned off for users in the EU. This is a direct result of the complaints and the official audit investigation.

Originally, it did not permit users to delete their accounts. However, it has now been made clear to the organisation that it must permit users the right and functional ability to delete their accounts. It will be recalled that one of the Data Protection Principles refers to personal data being held no longer than is necessary. User consent to processing can also be withdrawn.

The organisation settled litigation in the US relating to an advertising feature which it had launched and later cancelled. The case is meant to have been settled for approximately $20m. Note, also that there was

---

8   The *Europe Against Facebook* group also point out that there are particular issues and complaints outstanding. See http://www.europe-v-facebook.org/EN/en.html. There was also a group created in the US by MoveOn.org called *Petition: Facebook, Stop Invading My Privacy*, similarly objecting to certain practices of the social media website. A Morganstern, 'In the Spotlight: Social Network Advertising and the Right of Publicity,' *Intellectual Property Law Bulletin* (2007–2008) (1) 181–198; R Podolny, 'When "Friends" Become Adversaries: Litigation in the Age of Facebook,' *Manitoba Law Journal* (2009) (33) 391–408; Y Hashemi, 'Facebook's Privacy Policy and Its Third-Party Partnerships: Lucrativity and Liability,' *BU Journal of Science & Technology Law* (2009) (15) 140–161. Also P Nyoni and M Velempini, 'Data Protection Laws and Privacy on Facebook,' *SA Journal of Information Management* (2015) (17:1) 1

a strong dissenting judgement criticising the settlement as, *inter alia*, too low.[9]

Social Media and Leveson

29.03 Amongst the many witnesses at the *Leveson Inquiry* were Facebook, Google and Twitter. One of the headline issues relates to what activities and services they engage in, respectively, and what they can and cannot do in terms of specific content. These are controversial and evolving issues in terms of both data protection compliance as well as take downs and liability for material on (and via) their websites. This is an area which will continue to expand. Already it is a critical area of contention in litigation (and policy discussion). Sony has been fined £250,000 by the ICO and Google is being sued by UK Apple users.[10]

Social Media Data Transfers: Processors

29.04 Any social media organisation may quite legitimately need to engage third parties or outsource particular tasks. However, it is not always clear that the website will have ensured that an appropriate written contract is in place and that appropriate security measures are in place with the outsourced Processor as regards the personal data received and processed by it. Users should also be informed of such outsourcing and be assured of the security measures. Consent, transparency and prior information are equally important compliance issues.

Apps: Social Media Data Transfers

29.05 Increasingly, social networks provide and facilitate third party apps or applications on their websites.[11] Frequently, as part of this practice, personal data is disclosed to the third party companies operating or developing the apps. Unfortunately, there appears to be an overly loose

---

9   The Beacon advertising feature. See appeal and lower court in the case of *McCall v Facebook*. The appeal case is *McCall v Facebook*, US Court of Appeals for the Ninth Circuit. At http://cdn.ca9.uscourts.gov/datastore/opinions/2012/09/20/10–16380.pdf. See also, for example, W McGeveran, 'Disclosure, Endorsement, and Identity in Social Marketing,' *Illinois Law Review* (2009) (4) 1105–1166.

10   See *Google Inc v Vidal-Hall* [2015] EWCA Civ 311 (27 March 2015).

11   See, for example, Y Hashemi, 'Facebook's Privacy Policy and its Third-Party Partnerships: Lucrativity and Liability,' *BUJ Science & Technology Law* (2009) (15) 140–161.

compliance relationship as regards the transfer and protection of users' personal data. Sometimes, data would be accessible or transferred without regard to users' personal data rights, user knowledge, contracts and security. In addition, there could sometimes be no restriction on the apps developers using the personal data for more than one purpose and for activities unrelated to the initial intended purpose.

The new GDPR also recognises that apps raise data protection issues.

Awareness

29.06   Increasingly potential employers, schools and universities use social media profile information in making assessments on applications regarding specific individuals. Unfortunately, one of the issues relates to the consequence of this for individuals, sometimes adverse consequences.[12] In addition, many users, and particularly those of a younger age, will not (fully) appreciate that such activities and consequences can arise from their social media.

There is arguably more to be done by social networks in terms of informing and appraising users of the issues which can arise. This is particularly emphasised when children and teenagers are concerned.

WP29 in its Opinion regarding social media, recognises the dangers arising from apps.[13] Compliance with the DPD must be ensured. There is also a UK Home Office Good Practice Guidance for the Providers of Social Networks.[14] Arguably, these could be updated. This is an area where significant ongoing research is needed.

Tagging

29.07   It is possible that people are visible online in photographs uploaded to social networks which they would not want, may be unaware of, and also have not consented to.

In addition, social media websites can permit people to be tagged and labelled in uploaded photographs, without their consent.

These concerns are even more enhanced as Facebook has recently announced enhanced capacity to index and reveal information and photographs from its website. (Facebook Graph Search tool as well as new facial recognition applications.)

---

12   See discussion at L Edwards and C Waelde, eds, above, 481.
13   WP29, Opinion 5/2009 on online social networking, at http://ec.europa.eu/justice/policies/privacy/docs/wpdocs/2009/wp163_en.pdf.
14   At   https://www.gov.uk/government/uploads/system/uploads/attachment_data/file/251456/industry_guidance_social_networking.pdf.

Transparency and User Friendly Tools

29.08   Social media frequently appear to value membership numbers over fully transparent, obvious and user friendly privacy protection and complaint tools. The on-site tools (when present) are 'frequently unobvious or difficult to use. The cynical might imagine that this is because ... the revenue stream from the SNS comes from third parties – advertisers – having access to as much data, on as many profiles, as possible.'[15]

One part solution is to have privacy and friend restricted access as the default model for social media websites. This is suggested particularly in relation to children by the Home Office code of conduct for social networks.[16]

WP29 in the context of online behavioural advertising indicates that an icon in itself can be insufficient. In that context it was particularly concerned with consent issues. However, significant research remains to be undertaken in order to properly assess the adequacy of icons, notices, tools, information, information notices, report buttons, reports processes, report teams, response times, resolutions times, etc, in relation to online abuse and social media websites. There is as yet a distinct shortage of research and literature on this topic. This is despite the media reports of online abuse and many examples of tragic consequences.

Abuse, Attacks, Threats, Trolling, Victims

29.09   It is clear that these problem issues are significant and appear to be increasing. Pierre Trudel, for example, notes that the risks to individuals increase from many online activities, including in relation to data protection, safety, etc.[17]

Popular social media websites, such as Twitter and Reddit, are recognising that more needs to be done to address issues of online abuse and have been progressing changes to assist in dealing with the problem.

The Olympics in London brought to the fore the disadvantages of social media, where social networks such as Twitter, Facebook, etc, can be used for abuse.[18] There is a growing and troubling number of

---

15 L Edwards and C Waelde, eds, *Law and the Internet* (Hart, 2009) 483.

16 In 2008. At https://www.gov.uk/government/uploads/system/uploads/attachment_data/file/251456/industry_guidance_social_networking.pdf.

17 P Trudel, 'Privacy Protection on the Internet: Risk Management and Networked Normativity,' in S Gutwirth, Y Poullet, P de Hert, C de Terwange and S Nouwt, *Reinventing Data Protection?* (Springer, 2009) 317.

18 J Rosenberg, 'Tom Daley, Twitter Abuse and the Law,' *Guardian*, 31 July 2012; S James, 'Man Cautioned After Mark Halsey Twitter Abuse,' *Guardian*, 27 September

instances of suicides arising as a result of abuse and threats occurring on social media websites. Social networks, and other websites, also contain controversial material in relation to self-harm.

YouTube and Google also embrace policies to 'real name' posting policies (in part). Such policies may assist in reducing trolling and attacks online, as well as the unfortunate consequences thereof.[19]

The problem of cyber bullying is incontrovertible, with increasing high-profile suicides recently. If anyone is still unclear about the devastation caused to victims and families, the video posted by Canadian teenager Amanda Todd is required viewing. Indeed it should be required viewing for parents, educators and policymakers.

The cyberbullying of teenagers is just one facet of online abuse, which can range from threats to defamation, harassment to stalking, grooming and breaches of privacy and data protection. There are also overlaps. The cyberbullying of children can involve harassment, threats, verbal abuse and defamation, or in the case of Amanda Todd, privacy and data-protection breaches later expanding to threats. The solutions are multifaceted. Much of the recent commentary points to education, educators and parents. While this is correct, it is only one aspect.

One point missing from the current discussion is that it is legally possible to find anonymous abusers. Victims and the police can apply to court for the disclosure of user details from relevant websites and service providers. These are frequently known as Norwich Pharmacal orders. Online abusers can face civil as well as criminal consequences, even if they are children or teenagers. It goes without saying the police must properly follow up reports. It is clear from recent media commentary that the UK police are proactive and considered in this area.

Much of this abuse occurs on social media websites, but it does also occur via mobile telephones and smartphones. An article in the Guardian states that the 'Mobile internet is now just the internet.'[20] Some social media sites provide 'tools' or 'reporting processes.' However, many of them, and indeed other Web 2.0 websites, do not do all they could to deal with these issues. Even some of the largest social networks have been slower to implement reporting procedures for certain forms of abuse than should be the case. Some websites also have particular tools available which they use for certain activities, but are reluctant to extend to abuse victims.

2012; LL Baughmanm, 'Friend Request or Foe? Confirming the Misuse of Internet and Social Networking Sites by Domestic Violence Perpetrators,' *Widener Law Journal* (2010) (19) 933–966. Generally, also see JJ Ator, 'Got Facebook?' *GPSolo* (March, 2009) 4–5.

19 Generally note, for example, B Kane, 'Balancing Anonymity, Popularity, & Micro-Celebrity: The Crossroads of Social Networking & Privacy,' *Albany Law Journal of Science and Technology* (2010) (20) 327–363.

20 J Naughton, Mobile internet is Now Just the Internet,' *Guardian*, 27 December 2015.

But no matter how many 'report buttons' there are on a given website, they are entirely useless without protocols, policies and procedures behind the scenes to follow through on reports that are made. A complaints procedure is meaningless unless there are enough people investigating abuse reports.

It would be interesting to examine and compare the number of people employed in abuse investigation teams across various social media websites. Should there be a minimum number of employees assigned per number of users of a social media website? Or should there be a minimum number of employees per amount of abuse reports made? The turnover of such websites could easily absorb hiring more staff.

A further point arises regarding social media and related websites. Some are happy to publish statistics about the level of reports and complaints received relating to copyright infringement. This appears commercially driven. There is significantly less 'transparency' as regards the level of abuse reports and complaints made to social media websites, and around how, and how quickly, these abuse reports are resolved.

As much as we are presently shocked by the dark side of internet abuse, cyberbullying and the terrible consequences, it may be that we would be further shocked at the scale of abuse being reported, when the facility is available to do so. That may be a useful line of pursuit for anyone who is officially concerned about this issue. It is also worth considering that whatever a website may say at first blush may not always be the whole picture.

We are now beginning to realise that, on occasion, social media and other websites can have a dark side.

Unfortunately, there are large gaps in our knowledge, research and understanding of these developing issues. More research is needed to appraise ourselves of all potential solutions and policy decisions as well as assisting websites to fully engage their own (corporate, moral and legal) responsibilities and functional capabilities.

There are also business case advantages. The EU Commission and websites have recently announced a new code of conduct initiative for online hate takedowns.

Employment and Social Media

29.10 Employers are increasingly considering access to employees' social media materials.[21] A general policy of such monitoring is not

---

21 A Blank, 'On the Precipe of e-Discovery: Can Litigants Obtain Employee Social Networking Web Site Information Through Employers?' *CommLaw Conspectus* (2009–2010) (18) 487–516. Also, I Byrnside, 'Six Clicks of Separation: The Legal

permitted under EU data protection law. Nor can employees be forced to disclose or permit access to their social media accounts by way of enforced access. However, it is the case that social media evidential material is increasingly frequent in employment disputes and employment litigation. Organisations should seek legal advice in advance of seeking to utilise or rely upon such materials, otherwise potential litigation, dismissals or disciplinary actions can be deemed to be illegal.[22]

Digital Evidence

29.11 There are growing digital evidence opportunities for litigation, which can include personal data.[23] These can include service of documents[24] and civil discovery.[25] Social media have been described as digital footprints.[26] This can also include employees' social media activity.[27]

Ramifications of Employers using Social Networking Sites to Research Applicants,' *Vanderbilt Journal of Entertainment and Technology Law* (2008) (10) 445–477.

22 See also M Maher, 'You've Got Messages: Modern technology Recruiting Through Text-Messaging and the Intrusiveness of Facebook,' *Texas Review of Entertainment & Sports Law*, (2007) (8) 125–151; C Brandenburg, 'The Newest Way to Screen Job Applicants: A Social Networker's Nightmare,' *Federal Communications Law Journal* (2007–2008) (60) 597–626.

23 K Minotti, 'The Advent of Digital Diaries: Implications of Social Networking Web Sites for the Legal Profession,' *South Carolina Law Review* (2009) (60) 1057–1074; JS Wilson, 'MySpace, Your Space or Our Space? New Frontiers in Electronic Evidence,' *Oregon Law Review* (2007) (86) 1201–1240; AC Payne, 'Twitigation: Old Rules in a New World,' *Washburn Law Journal* (2010) (49) 842–870.

24 AL Shultz, AL, 'Superpoked and Served: Service of Process via Social Networking Sites,' 43 *University Richmond Law Review* (2008–2009) (43) 1497–1528. RJ Hedges, Rashbaum and AC Losey, 'Electronic Service of Process at Home and Abroad: Allowing Domestic Electronic Service of Process in Federal Courts,' *Federal Courts Law Review* (2010) (4) 54–76.

25 SC Bennett, 'Civil Discovery of Social Networking Information,' *Southwestern Law Review* (2009–2010) (39) 413–431. Also, DS Witte, 'Your Opponent Does Not Need a Friend Request to See Your Page: Social Networking Sites and Electronic Discovery,' *McGeorge Law Review* (2009–2010) (41) 891–903; RA Ward, 'Discovering Facebook: Social Network Subpoenas and the Stored Communications Act,' *Harvard Journal of Law & Technology* (2011) (24) 563–588.

26 EM Marsico, Jr , 'Social Networking Websites: Are Myspace and Facebook the Fingerprints of the Twenty-first Century?' *Widener Law Journal* (2010) (19) 967–976. Also, EE North, 'Facebook Isn't Your Space Anymore: Discovery of Social Networking Website,' *University of Kansa Law Review* (2009–2010) (58) 1279–1309; TM Williams, 'Facebook: Ethics, Traps, and Reminders,' *Litigation News* (2009–2010) (35) 4.

27 For example, see, L Thomas, 'Social Networking in the Workplace: Are Private Employers Prepared to Comply With Discovery Requests for Posts and Tweets?' *SMU Law Review* (2010) (63) 1373–1402.

The Rights of Data Subjects

29.12 It is noted that '[o]ne aspect of privacy and data protection is a remedy against intrusiveness and loss of control of the circulation of a person's informational image.'[28] In addition, '[s]uch intrusiveness and its loss do not only exist when someone is or can be identified; for instance, the acts of being observed and being traced are privacy threats, even without knowing the name of the observed or traced person.'[29]

Even with social media, the rights of Data Subjects remain. The rights of Data Subjects, including for social media, can be summarised as including:

- right of access (DPA 1998, s 7);
- right to establish if personal data exists (DPA 1998, s 7(1)(a));
- right to be informed of the logic in automatic decision taking (DPA 1998, s 7(1)(d));
- right to prevent processing likely to cause damage or distress (DPA 1998, s 18);
- right to prevent processing for direct marketing (DPA 1998, s 11);
- right to prevent automated decision taking (DPA 1998, s 12);
- right to compensation (DPA 1998, s 13);
- right to rectify inaccurate data (DPA 1998, s 14);
- right to rectification, blocking, erasure and destruction (DPA 1998, s 14);
- right to complain to ICO (DPA 1998, s 42);
- right to go to court (DPA 1998, s 15).

These expand under the GDPR. Chapter III of the GDPR refers to the rights of Data Subjects. These include:

- right to transparency (Article 5; Article 12);
- right to prior information: directly obtained data (Article 13);
- right to prior information: indirectly obtained data (Article 14);
- right of confirmation and right of access (Article 15);
- right to rectification (Article 16);
- right to erasure (Right to be Forgotten) (RtbF) (Article 17);
- right to restriction of processing (Article 18);
- notifications re rectification, erasure or restriction (Article 19);
- right to data portability (Article 20);
- right to object (Article 21);
- rights re automated individual decision making, including profiling (Article 22);

---

28 L Costa and Y Poullet, 'Privacy and the Regulation of 2012,' *Computer Law & Security Review* (2012) (28) 254–262, at 256.
29 *Ibid.*

- DPbD (Article 25);
- security rights;
- data protection impact assessment and prior consultation;
- communicating data breach to Data Subject;
- Data Protection Officer;
- remedies, liability and sanctions (Chapter VIII).

Consent and Social Media

29.13 It is noted that social media websites:

> 'are of course data Controllers, and so under [data protection] law they must, in pursuit of "fair processing," gain the consent of their users to process their personal data – and indeed, "explicit consent" in the case of sensitive personal data (which abounds on SNA [social networking service] – on almost every Facebook profile a user reveals his or her race, politics, sexuality or religious beliefs, since these predetermined fields in the user profile, which most users fill in without much thought).'[30]

Frequently, social media websites seek to comply with the consent requirement by providing that it is 'required as part of registration before "admission" to the site is granted. Consent is usually obtained by displaying a privacy policy [or privacy statement] on the site and asking the user to accede to them by ticking a box. As there is no chance to negotiate, and little or no evidence that users either read or understand these conditions, it is hard to see how this consent is "free and informed" ... yet business practice for the entire sector seems to regard this consent is satisfactory.'[31]

There are other difficulties.

> 'A further problem arises where SNS users display facts or images about other users – eg commonly, photographs featuring multiple persons. Such users rarely seek prior consent and such software tools as are made available usually only facilitate post factum removal, for example, of "tags" on Facebook.'[32]

> 'Also, the question arises as to whether ordinary users should be subject to the full panopoly of [data protection] obligations vis-a-vis their peers, and if they are not, how invasions of privacy by users rather than the site itself should be controlled. One suggestion has been that sites should be subject to liability for invasion of privacy if they do not take down expediently on complaint.'[33]

---

30 L Edwards and C Waelde, eds, *Law and the Internet* (Hart, 2009) 479.
31 *Ibid.*
32 *Ibid.*
33 *Ibid.*

Consent is an important issue under the new GDPR.[34] Lawful processing and consent are referred to in Recitals 32 and 40. The WP29 also refers to consent issues.[35]

Article 7 of the GDPR refers to conditions for consent as follows. Where processing is based on consent, the Controller shall be able to demonstrate that the Data Subject has consented to processing of their personal data (Article 7(1)).

If the Data Subject's consent is given in the context of a written declaration which also concerns other matters, the request for consent must be presented in a manner which is *clearly distinguishable* from the other matters, in an *intelligible and easily accessible form*, using *clear and plain language.* Any part of the declaration which constitutes an infringement of the GDPR shall not be binding (Article 7(2)).

The Data Subject shall have the *right to withdraw his or her consent at any time.* The withdrawal of consent shall not affect the lawfulness of processing based on consent before its withdrawal. Prior to giving consent, the Data Subject shall be informed thereof. It shall be as easy to withdraw consent as to give it (Article 7(3)).

When assessing whether consent is freely given, utmost account shall be taken of whether, inter alia, the performance of a contract, including the provision of a service, is conditional on the consent to the processing of data that is not necessary for the performance of that contract (Article 7(4)).

The issue of children in the data protection regime has been steadily rising. The increased use of social media and Web 2.0 services enhance the exposures and risks for children and the uninitiated.[36]

This has included children's groups, regulators and also the EDPB (previously the WP29). WP29 issued Opinion 2/2009 on the Protection of Children's Personal Data (General Guidelines and the Special Case of Schools) in 2009 and also Working Document 1/2008 on the Protection of Children's Personal Data (General Guidelines and the Special Case of Schools) in 2008. Schools are being encouraged to be proactive and to have appropriate codes and policies for children's social media and internet usage.[37]

---

34 JP Vandenbroucke and J Olsen, 'Informed Consent and the New EU Regulation on Data Protection,' *International Journal of Epidemiology* (2013) (42: 6) 1891.

35 WP29 Opinion 15/2011 Consent; Working Document 02/2013 providing guidance on obtaining consent for cookies, 201; Opinion 04/2012 on Cookie Consent Exemption.

36 See, for example, D Gourlay and G Gallagher, 'Collecting and Using Children's Information Online: the UK/US Dichotomy,' SCL *Computers and Law*, 12 December 2011.

37 Note generally, for example, JS Groppe, 'A Child's Playground or a Predator's Hunting Ground? – How to Protect Children on Internet Social Networking Sites,' *CommLaw Conspectus* (2007) (16) 215–245; EP Steadman, 'MySpace, But Who's Responsibility? Liability of Social Networking Websites When Offline Sexual Assault

There is now going to be an explicit acknowledgement of children's interest in the EU data protection regime, unlike with the DPD which contained no explicit reference. The GDPR expressly refers to a 'child' for the first time. This is significant amongst other things in relation to consent, contracting, etc. It is also significant for social networks which have significant numbers of children. Up until now it was common for certain social networks to purport to accept users only over the age of 13. Now that the age of a child in the context of information society services is considered by the GDPR to be at least 16 years old, it may require careful assessment in relation to social media contracts, terms, processes, sign ups, etc. (Note, Member States may additionally make provisions in relation to the age of children in this regard in addition to the above, for example, not below the age of 13 years old (see Article 8).)

The explicit reference to children is new, and some would argue overdue. Increasingly, the activities of children on the internet and on social media poses risks and concerns.[38] This has been further emphasised of late with tragic events involving online abuse, in particular cyber bullying. Risks arise obviously from their activities online (eg inappropriate content, cyber bullying, but also from the collection and use of their personal data online and collected online, sometimes without their knowledge or consent). Their personal data and privacy is more vulnerable than that of older people.

It is important for organisations to note the definition of 'child' in the GDPR. This will have implications in how organisations;

- consider the interaction with children and what personal data may be collected and processed;
- ensure that there is appropriate compliance for such collection and processing for children as distinct from adults.

Processing of children's personal data are referred to in Recitals 58, 65, 71 and 75.

The German Federal court has recently affirmed lower courts holding unlawful Facebook's 'friend finder' function which accesses users' email lists and promoted/advertised to these contacts even if not members of the website.[39]

---

of Minors Follows Online Interaction,' *Villanova Sports and Entertainment Law Journal* (2007) (14) 363–397; DC Beckstrom, 'Who's Looking at Your Facebook Profile? The Use of Student Conduct Codes to Censor College Students' Online Speech,' *Willamette Law Review* (2008) 261–312.

38 See, for example, L McDermott, 'Legal Issues Associated with Minors and Their Use of Social Networking Sites,' *Communications Law* (2012) (17) 19–24.

39 *Federation of German Consumer Organisations (VZBV) v Facebook*, German Federal Court of Justice, 14 January 2016.

Website Discretion, Liability and Obligations

29.14   On occasion certain websites will argue that they are not responsible for certain activities occurring on their websites. A particular example is user generated content. One frequent argument relates to the issue of the limited ISP defences of *caching, hosting* and *mere conduit* in the ECD.[40] There is also an argument raised by certain websites that they can target and deal with European consumers and users, yet are not responsible in relation to the collection and processing of users' personal data. This later point is based on the argument that if the website company is based outside of the EU, even though the users are in the EU, they do not have to comply with the data protection regime. There is an irony here. These website companies seek to avail of EU law as regards EU law defences of mere conduit, caching and hosting, yet then argue their preferred policy of ignoring EU data protection law. Are such websites immune to the EU data protection regime? Can websites pick and choose one set of EU laws to benefit them, but ignore entirely other laws which create rights for their users?

These issues in relation to websites, social media and jurisdiction are commented upon later.

Third Party Controllers and EU Data Subjects

29.15   DPD Recital 20 states that the fact that the processing of data is carried out by a person established in a third country must not stand in the way of the protection of individuals provided for in this Directive. In these cases, the processing should be governed by the law of the Member State in which the means used are located, and there should be guarantees to ensure that the rights and obligations provided for in this Directive are respected in practice.

Specific Processing Risks

29.16   DPD Recital 53 states that certain processing operations are likely to pose specific risks to the rights and freedoms of Data Subjects by virtue of their nature, their scope or their purposes, such as that of excluding individuals from a right, benefit or a contract, or by virtue of

---

40   Directive 2000/31/EC of the European Parliament and of the Council of 8 June 2000 on certain legal aspects of information society services, in particular electronic commerce, in the Internal Market ('Directive on electronic commerce').

the *specific use of new technologies*; it is for Member States, if they so wish, to specify such risks in their legislation.

DPD Recital 54 states that with regard to all the processing undertaken in society, the amount posing such specific risks should be very limited. Member States must provide that the supervisory authority, or the data protection official in cooperation with the authority, check such processing prior to it being carried out. Following this prior check, the supervisory authority may, according to its national law, give an opinion or an authorisation regarding the processing. Such checking may equally take place in the course of the preparation either of a measure of the national parliament or of a measure based on such a legislative measure, which defines the nature of the processing and lays down appropriate safeguards.

DPA 1998

Right to Prevent Data Processing Likely to Cause Damage or Distress

29.17   Section 10 of the DPA 1998 refers to the right to prevent processing likely to cause damage or distress. This can also be considered relevant to social media.

Section 10(1) provides that subject to s 10(2), an individual is entitled at any time by notice in writing to a Controller to require the Controller at the end of such period as is reasonable in the circumstances to cease, or not to begin, processing, or processing for a specified purpose or in a specified manner, any personal data in respect of which he is the Data Subject, on the ground that, for specified reasons:

- the processing of those data or their processing for that purpose or in that manner is causing or is likely to cause substantial damage or substantial distress to them or to another; and
- that damage or distress is or would be unwarranted.

Section 10(2) provides that s 10(1) does not apply:

- in a case where any of the conditions in paras 1 to 4 of Sch 2 are met; or
- in such other cases as may be prescribed by the Secretary of State by order.

Section 10(3) provides that the Controller must within 21 days of receiving a notice under s 10(1) ('the Data Subject notice') give the individual who gave it a written notice:

- stating that he has complied or intends to comply with the Data Subject notice; or
- stating his reasons for regarding the Data Subject notice as to any extent unjustified and the extent (if any) to which he has complied or intends to comply with it.

Section 10(4) provides that if a court is satisfied, on the application of any person who has given a notice under s 10(1) which appears to the court to be justified (or to be justified to any extent), that the Controller in question has failed to comply with the notice, the court may order them to take such steps for complying with the notice (or for complying with it to that extent) as the court thinks fit.

Section 10(5) provides that the failure by a Data Subject to exercise the right conferred by s 10(1) or s 11(1) does not affect any other right conferred on them by this Part.

Right to Prevent Data Processing for DM

29.18   Section 11 of the DPA 1998 relates to the right to prevent processing for purposes of direct marketing. This can also be considered relevant to social media.

Section 11(1) provides that an individual is entitled at any time by notice in writing to a Controller to require the Controller at the end of such period as is reasonable in the circumstances to cease, or not to begin, processing for the purposes of direct marketing personal data in respect of which he is the Data Subject.

Section 11(2) provides that if the court is satisfied, on the application of any person who has given a notice under s 11(1), that the Controller has failed to comply with the notice, the court may order them to take such steps for complying with the notice as the court thinks fit.

Section 11(2A) provides that this section shall not apply in relation to the processing of such data as are mentioned in para (1) of reg 8 of the Telecommunications (Data Protection and Privacy) Regulations 1999 (processing of telecommunications billing data for certain marketing purposes) for the purposes mentioned in para (2) of that regulation.

Section 11(3) provides that in this section 'direct marketing' means the communication (by whatever means) of any advertising or marketing material which is directed to particular individuals.

Compensation for Data Subjects

29.19 Section 13 of the DPA 1998 refers to compensation for failure to comply with certain requirements. This can be relevant to social media.

Section 13(1) provides that an individual who suffers damage by reason of any contravention by a Controller of any of the requirements of the DPA 1998 is entitled to compensation from the Controller for that damage.

Section 13(2) provides that an individual who suffers distress by reason of any contravention by a Controller of any of the requirements of the DPA 1998 is entitled to compensation from the Controller for that distress if:

- the individual also suffers damage by reason of the contravention; or
- the contravention relates to the processing of personal data for the special purposes.

Section 13(3) provides that in proceedings brought against a person by virtue of the section it is a defence to prove that he had taken such care as in all the circumstances was reasonably required to comply with the requirement concerned.

Rectification, Blocking, Erasure and Destruction Rights

29.20 Section 14 of the DPA 1998 provides user rights in relation to rectification, blocking, erasure and destruction. This can also be relevant to social media.

Section 14(1) provides that if a court is satisfied on the application of a Data Subject that personal data of which the applicant is the subject are inaccurate, the court may order the Controller to rectify, block, erase or destroy those data and any other personal data in respect of which he is the Controller and which contain an expression of opinion which appears to the court to be based on the inaccurate data.

Section 14(2) provides that s 14(1) applies whether or not the data accurately record information received or obtained by the Controller from the Data Subject or a third party but where the data accurately record such information, then:

- if the requirements mentioned in Sch 1, Pt II, para 7 have been complied with, the court may, instead of making an order under s 14(1), make an order requiring the data to be supplemented by such statement of the true facts relating to the matters dealt with by the data as the court may approve; and
- if all or any of those requirements have not been complied with, the court may, instead of making an order under that subsection, make such order as it thinks fit for securing compliance with those

requirements with or without a further order requiring the data to be supplemented by such a statement as is mentioned in the above bullet.

Section 14(3) provides that where the court:

- makes an order under s 14(1); or
- is satisfied on the application of a Data Subject that personal data of which he was the Data Subject and which have been rectified, blocked, erased or destroyed were inaccurate,

it may, where it considers it reasonably practicable, order the Controller to notify third parties to whom the data have been disclosed of the rectification, blocking, erasure or destruction.

Section 14(4) provides that if a court is satisfied on the application of a Data Subject:

- that he has suffered damage by reason of any contravention by a Controller of any of the requirements of the DPA 1998 in respect of any personal data, in circumstances entitling them to compensation under s 13; and
- that there is a substantial risk of further contravention in respect of those data in such circumstances,

the court may order the rectification, blocking, erasure or destruction of any of those data.

Section 14(5) provides that where the court makes an order under s 14(4) it may, where it considers it reasonably practicable, order the Controller to notify third parties to whom the data have been disclosed of the rectification, blocking, erasure or destruction.

Section 14(6) provides that in determining whether it is reasonably practicable to require such notification as is mentioned in s 14(3) or (5) the court shall have regard, in particular, to the number of persons who would have to be notified.

Automated Decision Taking/Making Processes

29.21 Automated decision taking/making processes can also be considered in the social media context. Controllers may not take decisions which produce legal effects concerning a Data Subject or which otherwise significantly affect a Data Subject and which are based solely on processing by automatic means of personal data and which are intended to evaluate certain personal matters relating to the Data Subject such as, performance at work, credit worthiness, reliability of conduct.

Section 12 of the DPA 1998 provides for the rights in relation to automated decision-taking.

Section 12(1) provides that an individual is entitled at any time, by notice in writing to any Controller, to require the Controller to ensure that no decision taken by or on behalf of the Controller which significantly affects that individual is based solely on the processing by automatic means of personal data in respect of which that individual is the Data Subject for the purpose of evaluating matters relating to them such as, for example, his performance at work, his creditworthiness, his reliability or his conduct.

Section 12(2) provides that where, in a case where no notice under s 12(1) has effect, a decision which significantly affects an individual is based solely on such processing as is mentioned in s 12(1):

- the Controller must as soon as reasonably practicable notify the individual that the decision was taken on that basis; and
- the individual is entitled, within 21 days of receiving that notification from the Controller, by notice in writing to require the Controller to reconsider the decision or to take a new decision otherwise than on that basis.

Section 12(3) provides that the Controller must, within 21 days of receiving a notice under s 12(2)(b) ('the Data Subject notice') give the individual a written notice specifying the steps that he intends to take to comply with the Data Subject notice.

Section 12(4) provides that a notice under s 12(1) does not have effect in relation to an exempt decision; and nothing in s 12(2) applies to an exempt decision.

Section 12(5) provides that in s 12(4) 'exempt decision' means any decision:

- in respect of which the condition in s 12(6) and the condition in s 12(7) are met; or
- which is made in such other circumstances as may be prescribed by the Secretary of State by order.

Section 12(6) provides that the condition in this subsection is that the decision:

- is taken in the course of steps taken,
  - ○ for the purpose of considering whether to enter into a contract with the Data Subject;
  - ○ with a view to entering into such a contract; or
  - ○ in the course of performing such a contract; or
- is authorised or required by or under any enactment.

Section 12(7) provides that the condition in this subsection is that either:

- the effect of the decision is to grant a request of the Data Subject; or

- steps have been taken to safeguard the legitimate interests of the Data Subject (for example, by allowing them to make representations).

Section 12(8) provides that if a court is satisfied on the application of a Data Subject that a person taking a decision in respect of them (the 'responsible person') has failed to comply with s 12(1) or (2)(b), the court may order the responsible person to reconsider the decision, or to take a new decision which is not based solely on such processing as is mentioned in s 12(1).

Section 12(9) provides that an order under s 12(8) shall not affect the rights of any person other than the Data Subject and the responsible person.

Section 12 of the DPA 1998 provides rights in relation to automated decision-taking. It states:

(1) An individual is entitled at any time, by notice in writing to any Controller, to require the Controller to ensure that no decision taken by or on behalf of the Controller which significantly affects that individual is based solely on the processing by automatic means of personal data in respect of which that individual is the Data Subject for the purpose of evaluating matters relating to them such as, for example, his performance at work, his credit worthiness, his reliability or his conduct;

(2) Where, in a case where no notice under s 12(1) has effect, a decision which significantly affects an individual is based solely on such processing as is mentioned in s 12(1),

    (a) the Controller must as soon as reasonably practicable notify the individual that the decision was taken on that basis; and

    (b) the individual is entitled, within 21 days of receiving that notification from the Controller, by notice in writing to require the Controller to reconsider the decision or to take a new decision otherwise than on that basis;

(3) The Controller must, within 21 days of receiving a notice under s 12(2)(b) ('the Data Subject notice') give the individual a written notice specifying the steps that he intends to take to comply with the Data Subject notice;

(4) A notice under s 12(1) does not have effect in relation to an exempt decision; and nothing in s 12(2) applies to an exempt decision;

(5) In s 12(4) 'exempt decision' means any decision,

    (a) in respect of which the condition in s 12(6) and the condition in s 12(7) are met; or

    (b) which is made in such other circumstances as may be prescribed by the Secretary of State by order;

(6) The condition in the subsection is that the decision:
   (a) is taken in the course of steps taken;
      (i) for the purpose of considering whether to enter into a contract with the Data Subject;
      (ii) with a view to entering into such a contract; or
      (iii) in the course of performing such a contract; or
   (b) is authorised or required by or under any enactment;
(7) The condition in the subsection is that either:
   (a) the effect of the decision is to grant a request of the Data Subject; or
   (b) steps have been taken to safeguard the legitimate interests of the Data Subject (for example, by allowing them to make representations);
(8) If a court is satisfied on the application of a Data Subject that a person taking a decision in respect of them ('the responsible person') has failed to comply with s 12(1) or (2)(b), the court may order the responsible person to reconsider the decision, or to take a new decision which is not based solely on such processing as is mentioned in s 12(1);
(9) An order under s 12(8) shall not affect the rights of any person other than the Data Subject and the responsible person.

DPD

Right Against Automated Individual Decisions

29.22   Article 15 of the DPD provides for the right against automated individual decisions. This can also be considered relevant to social media. Article 15(1) states that Member States shall grant the right to every person not to be subject to a decision which produces legal effects concerning them or significantly affects them and which is based solely on automated processing of data intended to evaluate certain personal aspects relating to them, such as his performance at work, creditworthiness, reliability, conduct, etc.

Article 15(2) states that subject to the other Articles of the Directive, Member States shall provide that a person may be subjected to a decision of the kind referred to in Article 15(1) if that decision:

- is taken in the course of the entering into or performance of a contract, provided the request for the entering into or the performance of the contract, lodged by the Data Subject, has been satisfied or that there are suitable measures to safeguard his legitimate interests, such as arrangements allowing them to put his point of view; or
- is authorised by a law which also lays down measures to safeguard the Data Subject's legitimate interests.

Right to Object

29.23   Section VII refers to the Data Subject's right to object. This can also be considered relevant to social media. Article 14 of the DPD provides for the Data Subject's right to object. It states that, Member States shall grant the Data Subject to the right:

- at least in the cases referred to in Article 7(e) and (f), to object at any time on compelling legitimate grounds relating to his particular situation to the processing of data relating to them, save where otherwise provided by national legislation. Where there is a justified objection, the processing instigated by the Controller may no longer involve those data;
- to object, on request and free of charge, to the processing of personal data relating to them which the Controller anticipates being processed for the purposes of direct marketing, or to be informed before personal data are disclosed for the first time to third parties or used on their behalf for the purposes of direct marketing, and to be expressly offered the right to object free of charge to such disclosures or uses.

It also provides that Member States shall take the necessary measures to ensure that Data Subjects are aware of the existence of the right.

GDPR

Definitions and Social Media

29.24   The GDPR is relevant to social media. The GDPR definitions include:

'personal data breach'	means a breach of security leading to the accidental or unlawful destruction, loss, alteration, unauthorised disclosure of, or access to, personal data transmitted, stored or otherwise processed;
'main establishment'	means: • as regards a Controller with establishments in more than one Member State, the place of its central administration in the EU, unless the decisions on the purposes and means of the processing of personal data are taken in another establishment of the Controller in the EU and the latter establishment has the power to have such decisions implemented, in which case the establishment having taken such decisions is to be considered to be the main establishment;

- as regards a Processor with establishments in more than one Member State, the place of its central administration in the EU, or, if the Processor has no central administration in the EU, the establishment of the Processor in the EU where the main processing activities in the context of the activities of an establishment of the Processor take place to the extent that the Processor is subject to specific obligations under the GDPR.

'representative'	means any natural or legal person established in the EU who, designated by the Controller or Processor in writing pursuant to Article 27, represents the Controller or Processor, with regard to their respective obligations under the GDPR;
'enterprise'	means any natural or legal person engaged in an economic activity, irrespective of its legal form, including partnerships or associations regularly engaged in an economic activity;
'group of undertakings'	means a controlling undertaking and its controlled undertakings.

The originally proposed definition of a child appears deleted in the final version of the GDPR.

However, see reference to children below.

Right to Object, Profiling and Social Media

29.25 Electronic identity or eID's are also an area being considered.[41]

Transparency

29.26 Article 12 refers to transparent information, communication and modalities for exercising the rights of the Data Subject. The Controller shall take appropriate measures to provide any information referred to in Articles 15–22 and 34 relating to the processing to the Data Subject in a concise, transparent, intelligible and easily accessible form, using clear and plain language, in particular for any information addressed specifically to a child. When requested by the Data Subject, the information may be provided orally, as long as the identity of the Data Subject is proven by other means (Article 12(1)).

---

41 See, for example, Norberto Nuno Gomes de Ardrade, 'Regulating Electronic Identity in the European Union: An Analysis of the Lisbon Treaty's Competences and Legal Basis for eID,' *Computer Law and Security Review* (2012) (28) 153–162, at 153. European Commission, *Communication from the Commission – a Digital Agenda for Europe* (Brussels: European Commission 2010) 11.

The Controller shall facilitate the exercise of Data Subject rights under Articles 15–22. In cases referred to in Article 11(2), the Controller shall not refuse to act on the request of the Data Subject for exercising their rights under Articles 15–22, unless the Controller demonstrates that it is not in a position to identify the Data Subject (Article 12(2)).

The Controller shall provide information on action taken on a request under Articles 15–22 to the Data Subject without undue delay and in any event within one month of receipt of the request. This period may be extended by two further months where necessary, taking into account the complexity of the request and the number of the requests. The Controller shall inform the Data Subject of any extensions within one month of receipt of the request, together with the reasons for the delay. Where the Data Subject makes the request in electronic form means, the information shall be provided in electronic form where possible, unless otherwise requested by the Data Subject (Article 12(3)).

If the Controller does not take action on the request of the Data Subject, the Controller shall inform the Data Subject without delay and at the latest within one month of receipt of the request of the reasons for not taking action and on the possibility of lodging a complaint to a supervisory authority and seeking a judicial remedy (Article 12(4)).

Information provided under Articles 13 and 14 and any communication and any actions taken under Articles 15–22 and 34 shall be provided free of charge. Where requests from a Data Subject are manifestly unfounded or excessive, in particular because of their repetitive character, the Controller may either charge a reasonable fee taking into account the administrative costs of providing the information or communication or taking the action requested; or, refuse to act on the request. In these cases, the Controller shall bear the burden of demonstrating the manifestly unfounded or excessive character of the request (Article 12(5)).

Without prejudice to Article 11, where the Controller has reasonable doubts concerning the identity of the individual making the request referred to in Articles 15–21, the Controller may request the provision of additional information necessary to confirm the identity of the Data Subject (Article 12(6)).

The information to be provided to Data Subjects pursuant to Articles 13 and 14 may be provided in combination with standardised icons in order to give in an easily visible, intelligible and clearly legible manner a meaningful overview of the intended processing. Where the icons are presented electronically they shall be machine-readable (Article 12(7)).

The Commission shall be empowered to adopt delegated acts in accordance with Article 92 for the purpose of determining the information to be presented by the icons and the procedures for providing standardised icons (Article 12(8)).

Child's Consent: Conditions for Information Society Services

29.27   Processing of children's personal data are referred to in Recital 38. Article 8 of the GDPR makes provisions in relation to conditions for children's consent for information society services. Where Article 6(1)(a) applies, in relation to the offer of information society services directly to a child, the processing of personal data of a child shall be lawful where the child is at least 16 years old. Where the child is below the age of 16 years, such processing shall be lawful only if and to the extent that such consent is given or authorised by the holder of parental responsibility over the child (Article 8(1)). (Member States may provide by law for a lower age for those purposes provided that such lower age is not below 13 years (Article 8(1)).) The Controller shall make reasonable efforts to verify in such cases that consent is given or authorised by the holder of parental responsibility over the child, taking into consideration available technology (Article 8(2)). This shall not affect the general contract law of Member States such as the rules on the validity, formation or effect of a contract in relation to a child (Article 8(3)).

Data Access Rights

29.28   Chapter III, Section 2 of the GDPR refers to data access. It should be noted that the prior information requirements might have previously been viewed as Controller compliance obligations. However, they are now reformulated as part of the Data Subject information and access rights. This would therefore be a change in emphasis.

Right to Prior Information: Directly Obtained Data

29.29   Article 13 refers to information to be provided where the data are collected from the Data Subject. Where personal data relating to a Data Subject are collected from the Data Subject, the Controller shall, at the time when personal data are obtained, provide the Data Subject with *all* of the following information:

- the identity and the contact details of the Controller and, where applicable, of the Controller's representative;
- the contact details of the DPO, where applicable;
- the purposes of the processing for which the personal data are intended as well as the legal basis of the processing;
- where the processing is based on Article 6(1)(f), the legitimate interests pursued by the Controller or by a third party;
- the recipients or categories of recipients of the personal data, if any;
- where applicable, the fact that the Controller intends to transfer personal data to a third country or international organisation and the

existence or absence of an adequacy decision by the Commission, or in case of transfers referred to in Article 46 or 47, or Article 49(1) (second subparagraph), reference to the appropriate or suitable safeguards and the means by which to obtain a copy of them or where they have been made available (Article 13(1)).

In addition to the information referred to in Article 13(1), the Controller shall, at the time when personal data are obtained, provide the Data Subject with the following further information necessary to ensure fair and transparent processing:

- the period for which the personal data will be stored, or if this is not possible, the criteria used to determine this period;
- the existence of the right to request from the Controller access to and rectification or erasure of personal data or restriction of processing concerning the Data Subject or to object to the processing as well as the right to data portability;
- where the processing is based on Article 6(1)(a) or Article 9(2)(a), the existence of the right to withdraw consent at any time, without affecting the lawfulness of processing based on consent before its withdrawal;
- the right to lodge a complaint with a supervisory authority;
- whether the provision of personal data is a statutory or contractual requirement, or a requirement necessary to enter into a contract, as well as whether the Data Subject is obliged to provide the data and of the possible consequences of failure to provide such data;
- the existence of automated decision making, including profiling, referred to in Article 22(1) and (4) and at least in those cases, meaningful information about the logic involved, as well as the significance and the envisaged consequences of such processing for the Data Subject (Article 13(2)).

Where the Controller intends to further process the personal data for a purpose other than the one for which the data were collected, the Controller shall provide the Data Subject prior to that further processing with information on that other purpose and with any relevant further information as referred to in Article 13(2) (Article 13(3)).

Article 13(1), (2) and (3) shall not apply where and insofar as the Data Subject already has the information (Article 13(4)).

Right to Prior Information: Indirectly Obtained Data

29.30   Article 14 refers to information to be provided where the personal data have not been obtained from the Data Subject. Where personal data have not been obtained from the Data Subject, the Controller shall provide the Data Subject with the following information:

- the identity and the contact details of the Controller and, where applicable, of the Controller's representative;
- the contact details of the DPO, where applicable;
- the purposes of the processing for which the personal data are intended as well as the legal basis of the processing;
- the categories of personal data concerned;
- the recipients or categories of recipients of the personal data, if any;
- where applicable, that the Controller intends to transfer personal data to a recipient in a third country or international organisation and the existence or absence of an adequacy decision by the Commission, or in case of transfers referred to in Article 46 or 47, or the second subparagraph of Article 49(1), reference to the appropriate or suitable safeguards and the means to obtain a copy of them or where they have been made available (Article 14(1)).

In addition to the information referred to in Article 14(1), the Controller shall provide the Data Subject with the following information necessary to ensure fair and transparent processing in respect of the Data Subject:

- the period for which the personal data will be stored, or if this is not possible, the criteria used to determine that period;
- where the processing is based on Article 6(1)(f), the legitimate interests pursued by the Controller or by a third party;
- the existence of the right to request from the Controller access to and rectification or erasure of the personal data or restriction of processing of data concerning the Data Subject and to object to the processing as well as the right to data portability;
- where processing is based on Article 6(1)(a) or Article 9(2)(a), the existence of the right to withdraw consent at any time, without affecting the lawfulness of processing based on consent before its withdrawal;
- the right to lodge a complaint to a supervisory authority;
- from which source the personal data originate, and if applicable, whether it came from publicly accessible sources;
- the existence of automated decision making including profiling referred to in Article 22(1) and (4) and at least in those cases, meaningful information about the logic involved, as well as the significance and the envisaged consequences of such processing for the Data Subject (Article 14(2)).

The Controller shall provide the information referred to in Article 14(1) and (2):

- within a reasonable period after obtaining the personal data, but at the latest within one month, having regard to the specific circumstances in which the personal data are processed;
- if the personal data are to be used for communication with the Data Subject, at the latest at the time of the first communication to that Data Subject; or
- if a disclosure to another recipient is envisaged, at the latest when the personal data are first disclosed (Article 14(3)).

Where the Controller intends to further process the personal data for a purpose other than that for which the data were obtained, the Controller shall provide the Data Subject prior to that further processing with information on that other purpose and with any relevant further information as referred to in Article 14(2) (Article 14(4)).

Article 14(1)–(4) shall not apply where and insofar as:

- the Data Subject already has the information;
- the provision of such information proves impossible or would involve a disproportionate effort, in particular for processing for archiving purposes in the public interest, scientific or historical research purposes or statistical purposes, subject to the conditions and safeguards referred to in Article 89(1) or in so far as the obligation referred to in Article 14(1) is likely to render impossible or seriously impair the achievement of the objectives of that processing. In such cases the Controller shall take appropriate measures to protect the Data Subject's rights and freedoms and legitimate interests, including making the information publicly available;
- obtaining or disclosure is expressly laid down by EU or Member State law to which the Controller is subject and which provides appropriate measures to protect the Data Subject's legitimate interests; or
- where the personal data must remain confidential subject to an obligation of professional secrecy regulated by EU or Member State law, including a statutory obligation of secrecy (Article 14(5)).

Right of Confirmation and Right of Access

29.31 The Data Subject shall have the right to obtain from the Controller confirmation as to whether or not personal data concerning them are being processed, and where that is the case, access to the personal data and the following information:

- the purposes of the processing;

- the categories of personal data concerned;
- the recipients or categories of recipients to whom the personal data have been or will be disclosed, in particular recipients in third countries or international organisations;
- where possible, the envisaged period for which the personal data will be stored, or if not possible, the criteria used to determine that period;
- the existence of the right to request from the Controller rectification or erasure of personal data or restriction of processing of personal data concerning the Data Subject or to object to such processing;
- the right to lodge a complaint to a supervisory authority;
- where the personal data are not collected from the Data Subject, any available information as to their source;
- the existence of automated decision making including profiling referred to in Article 22(1) and (4) and at least in those cases, meaningful information about the logic involved, as well as the significance and the envisaged consequences of such processing for the Data Subject (Article 15(1)).

Where personal data are transferred to a third country or to an international organisation, the Data Subject shall have the right to be informed of the appropriate safeguards pursuant to Article 46 relating to the transfer (Article 15(2)).

The Controller shall provide a copy of the personal data undergoing processing. For any further copies requested by the Data Subject, the Controller may charge a reasonable fee based on administrative costs. Where the Data Subject makes the request by electronic means, and unless otherwise requested by the Data Subject, the information shall be provided in a commonly used electronic form (Article 15(3)).

The right to obtain a copy referred to in Article 15(3) shall not adversely affect the rights and freedoms of others (Article 15(4)).

Prior to the new GDPD, the ICO has issued recommendations in relation to data access, namely:

- Access to Information Held in Complaint Files;
- Enforced Subject Access (section 56);
- How to Disclose Information Safely – Removing Personal Data from Information Requests and Datasets;
- Regulatory Activity Exemption;
- Subject Access: Code of Practice;
- Subject Access: Responding to a Request Checklist.

These now need to be read in light of the GDPR changes.

Rectification and Erasure

29.32 Chapter III, Section 3 of the GDPR refers to rectification and erasure.

Prior to the new GDPD, the ICO has issued recommendations in relation to personal data deletion issues, namely:

* Deleting Personal Data.

This now needs to be read in light of the GDPR changes.

Right to Rectification

29.33 The Data Subject shall have the right to obtain from the Controller without undue delay the rectification of personal data concerning them. Taking into account the purposes of the processed, the Data Subject shall have the right to obtain completion of incomplete personal data completed, including by means of providing a supplementary statement (Article 16).

Right to Erasure (Right to be Forgotten) (RtbF)

29.34 The Data Subject shall have the right to obtain from the Controller the erasure of personal data concerning them without undue delay and the Controller shall have the obligation to erase personal data without undue delay where one of the following grounds applies:

* the data are no longer necessary in relation to the purposes for which they were collected or otherwise processed;
* the Data Subject withdraws consent on which the processing is based according to Article 6(1)(a), or Article 9(2)(a), and where there is no other legal ground for the processing;
* the Data Subject objects to the processing pursuant to Article 21(1) and there are no overriding legitimate grounds for the processing, or the Data Subject objects to the processing pursuant to Article 21(2);
* the personal data have been unlawfully processed;
* the data have to be erased for compliance with a legal obligation in EU or Member State law to which the Controller is subject;
* the personal data have been collected in relation to the offer of information society services referred to in Article 8(1) (Article 17(1)).

Where the Controller has made the personal data public and is obliged pursuant to Article 17(1) to erase the personal data, the Controller, taking account of available technology and the cost of implementation, shall take reasonable steps, including technical measures, to inform Controllers which are processing the personal data that the Data Subject has requested the erasure by such Controllers of any links to, or copy or replication of, that personal data (Article 17(2)).

Article 17(1) and (2) shall not apply to the extent that processing is necessary:

- for exercising the right of freedom of expression and information;
- for compliance with a legal obligation which requires processing of personal data by EU or Member State law to which the Controller is subject or for the performance of a task carried out in the public interest or in the exercise of official authority vested in the Controller;
- for reasons of public interest in the area of public health in accordance with Article 9(2)(h) and (i) as well as Article 9(3);
- for archiving purposes in the public interest, scientific or historical research purposes or statistical purposes in accordance with Article 89(1) in so far as the right referred to in Article 17(1) is likely to render impossible or seriously impair the achievement of the objectives of that processing; or
- for the establishment, exercise or defence of legal claims (Article 17(3)).

Right to Restriction of Processing

29.35 Article 18 refers to the right to restriction of processing. The Data Subject shall have the right to obtain from the Controller the restriction of the processing where one of the following applies:

- the accuracy of the data is contested by the Data Subject, for a period enabling the Controller to verify the accuracy of the data;
- the processing is unlawful and the Data Subject opposes the erasure of the personal data and requests the restriction of their use instead;
- the Controller no longer needs the personal data for the purposes of the processing, but they are required by the Data Subject for the establishment, exercise or defence of legal claims;
- the Data Subject has objected to processing pursuant to Article 21(1) pending the verification whether the legitimate grounds of the Controller override those of the Data Subject (Article 18(1)).

Where processing has been restricted under Article 18(1), such personal data shall, with the exception of storage, only be processed with the Data Subject's consent or for the establishment, exercise or defence of legal claims or for the protection of the rights of another natural or legal person or for reasons of important public interest of the EU or of a Member State (Article 18(2)).

A Data Subject who obtained the restriction of processing pursuant to Article 18(1) shall be informed by the Controller before the restriction of processing is lifted (Article 18(3)).

Notification re Rectification, Erasure or Restriction

29.36   The Controller shall communicate any rectification or erasure of personal data or restriction of processing carried out in accordance with Articles 16, 17(1) and 18 to each recipient to whom the personal data have been disclosed, unless this proves impossible or involves disproportionate effort. The Controller shall inform the Data Subject about those recipients if the Data Subject requests it (Article 19).

Right to Data Portability

29.37   The Data Subject shall have the right to receive the personal data concerning them, which they have provided to a Controller, in a structured and commonly used and machine-readable format and have the right to transmit those data to another Controller without hindrance from the Controller to which the data have been provided, where:

- the processing is based on consent pursuant to Article 6(1)(a) or Article 9(2)(a) or on a contract pursuant to Article 6(1)(b); and
- the processing is carried out by automated means (Article 20(2)).

In exercising their right to data portability pursuant to Article 20(1), the Data Subject has the right to have the data transmitted directly from Controller to Controller where technically feasible (Article 20(2)).

The exercise of this right shall be without prejudice to Article 17. That right shall not apply to processing necessary for the performance of a task carried out in the public interest or in the exercise of official authority vested in the Controller (Article 20(3)).

The right referred to in Article 20(4) shall not adversely affect the rights and freedoms of others (Article 20(4)).

Right Against Automated Individual Decision Making

29.38   Chapter III, Section 4 of the GDPR refers to the right to object and automated individual decision making.

Right to Object

29.39   The Data Subject shall have the right to object, on grounds relating to their particular situation, at any time to processing of personal data concerning them which is based on Article 6(1)(e) or (f), including profiling based on these provisions. The Controller shall no longer process the personal data unless the Controller demonstrates compelling legitimate grounds for the processing which override the interests, rights and freedoms of the Data Subject or for the establishment, exercise or defence of legal claims (Article 21(1)).

Where personal data are processed for direct marketing purposes, the Data Subject shall have the right to object at any time to the processing of personal data concerning them for such marketing, which includes profiling to the extent that it is related to such direct marketing (Article 21(2)).

Where the Data Subject objects to the processing for direct marketing purposes, the personal data shall no longer be processed for such purposes (Article 21(3)).

At the latest at the time of the first communication with the Data Subject, the right referred to in Article 21(1) and (2) shall be explicitly brought to the attention of the Data Subject and shall be presented clearly and separately from any other information (Article 21(4)).

In the context of the use of information society services, and notwithstanding Directive 2002/58/EC,[42] the Data Subject may exercise their right to object by automated means using technical specifications (Article 21(5)).

Where personal data are processed for scientific or historical research purposes or statistical purposes pursuant to Article 89(1), the Data Subject, on grounds relating to their particular situation, shall have the right to object to processing of personal data concerning them, unless the processing is necessary for the performance of a task carried out for reasons of public interest (Article 21(6)).

Rights re Automated Individual Decision Making, Including Profiling

29.40   The Data Subject shall have the right not to be subject to a decision based solely on automated processing, including profiling, which produces legal effects concerning them or similarly significantly affects them (Article 22(1)).

Article 22(1) shall not apply if the decision:

- is necessary for entering into, or performance of, a contract between the Data Subject and a Controller [a];
- is authorised by EU or Member State law to which the Controller is subject and which also lays down suitable measures to safeguard the Data Subject's rights and freedoms and legitimate interests; or
- is based on the Data Subject's explicit consent (Article 22(1)) [c].

In cases referred to in Article 22(2) (a) and (c) the Controller shall implement suitable measures to safeguard the Data Subject's rights and freedoms and legitimate interests, at least the right to obtain human

---

42   Directive 2002/58/EC of the European Parliament and of the Council of 12 July 2002 concerning the processing of personal data and the protection of privacy in the electronic communications sector (Directive on privacy and electronic communications).

intervention on the part of the Controller, to express his or her point of view and to contest the decision (Article 22(3)).

Decisions referred to in Article 22(4) shall not be based on special categories of personal data referred to in Article 9(1), unless Article 9(2)(a) or (g) applies and suitable measures to safeguard the Data Subject's rights and freedoms and legitimate interests are in place (Article 22(4)).

Communicating Data Breach to Data Subject

29.41   When a personal data breach is likely to result in a high risk to the rights and freedoms of natural persons, the Controller shall communicate the personal data breach to the Data Subject without undue delay (Article 34(1)).

The communication to the Data Subject shall describe in clear and plain language the nature of the personal data breach and contain at least the information referred to in Article 33(3)(b), (c) and (d) (Article 34(2)).

The communication to the Data Subject shall not be required if:

- the Controller has implemented appropriate technical and organisational protection measures, and those measures were applied to the personal data affected by the personal data breach, in particular those that render the personal data unintelligible to any person who is not authorised to access it, such as encryption;
- the Controller has taken subsequent measures which ensure that the high risk for the rights and freedoms of Data Subjects referred to in Article 34(1) is no longer likely to materialise;
- it would involve disproportionate effort. In such cases, there shall instead be a public communication or similar measure whereby the Data Subjects are informed in an equally effective manner (Article 34(3)).

If the Controller has not already communicated the personal data breach to the Data Subject, the supervisory authority, having considered the likelihood of the breach to result in a high risk, may require it to do so or may decide that any of the conditions referred to in Article 34(3) are met (Article 34(4)).

Security of Processing

29.42   Taking into account the state of the art, the costs of implementation and the nature, scope, context and purposes of the processing as well as the risk of varying likelihood and severity for the rights and freedoms of natural persons, the Controller and the Processor shall implement appropriate technical and organisational measures, to ensure a level of security appropriate to the risk, including inter alia, as appropriate:

- the pseudonymisation and encryption of personal data;

- the ability to ensure the ongoing confidentiality, integrity, availability and resilience of processing systems and services;
- the ability to restore the availability and access to personal data in a timely manner in the event of a physical or technical incident;
- a process for regularly testing, assessing and evaluating the effectiveness of technical and organisational measures for ensuring the security of the processing (Article 32(1)).

In assessing the appropriate level of security account shall be taken in particular of the risks that are presented by data processing, in particular from accidental or unlawful destruction, loss, alteration, unauthorised disclosure of, or access to personal data transmitted, stored or otherwise processed (Article 32(2)).

Adherence to an approved code of conduct pursuant to Article 40 or an approved certification mechanism pursuant to Article 39 may be used as an element to demonstrate compliance with the requirements set out in Article 32(1) (Article 32(3)).

The Controller and Processor shall take steps to ensure that any natural person acting under the authority of the Controller or the Processor who has access to personal data shall not process them except on instructions from the Controller, unless he or she is required to do so by EU or Member State law (Article 32(4)).

Representatives of Controllers Not Established in EU

29.43   Where Article 3(2) applies, the Controller or the Processor shall designate in writing a representative in the EU (Article 27(1)).

This obligation shall not apply to:

- processing which is occasional, does not include, on a large scale, processing of special categories of data as referred to in Article 9(1) or processing of personal data relating to criminal convictions and offences referred to in Article 10, and is unlikely to result in a risk for the rights and freedoms of natural persons, taking into account the nature, context, scope and purposes of the processing; or
- a public authority or body (Article 27(2)).

The representative shall be established in one of the Member States where the Data Subjects whose personal data are processed in relation to the offering of goods or services to them, or whose behaviour is monitored (Article 27(3)).

The representative shall be mandated by the Controller or the Processor to be addressed in addition to or instead of the Controller or the Processor by, in particular, supervisory authorities and Data Subjects, on all issues related to the processing, for the purposes of ensuring compliance with the GDPR (Article 27(4)).

The designation of a representative by the Controller or the Processor shall be without prejudice to legal actions which could be initiated against the Controller or the Processor themselves (Article 27(5)).

Chapter IV, Section 3 of the GDPR refers to Impact assessments and Prior Consultations.

Data Protection Impact Assessment

29.44 Where a type of processing in particular using new technologies, and taking into account the nature, scope, context and purposes of the processing, is likely to result in a high risk for the rights and freedoms of natural persons, the Controller shall, prior to the processing, carry out an assessment of the impact of the envisaged processing operations on the protection of personal data. A single assessment may address a set of similar processing operations that present similar high risks (Article 35(1)).

The Controller shall seek the advice of the DPO, where designated, when carrying out a data protection impact assessment (Article 35(2)).

A data protection impact assessment referred to in Article 35(1) shall in particular be required in the case of:

- a systematic and extensive evaluation of personal aspects relating to natural persons which is based on automated processing, including profiling, and on which decisions are based that produce legal effects concerning the individual or similarly significantly affect the individual;
- processing on a large scale of special categories of data referred to in Article 9(1), or of data relating to criminal convictions and offences referred to in Article 10;
- a systematic monitoring of a publicly accessible area on a large scale (Article 35(3)).

The supervisory authority shall establish and make public a list of the kind of processing operations which are subject to the requirement for a data protection impact assessment pursuant to Article 35(1). The supervisory authority shall communicate those lists to the EDPB (Article 68(4)).

The supervisory authority may also establish and make public a list of the kind of processing operations for which no data protection impact assessment is required. The supervisory authority shall communicate those lists to the EDPB (Article 35(5)).

Prior to the adoption of the lists referred to above the competent supervisory authority shall apply the consistency mechanism referred to in Article 63 where such lists involve processing activities which are related to the offering of goods or services to Data Subjects or to the monitoring of their behaviour in several Member States, or may substantially affect the free movement of personal data within the EU (Article 35(6)).

The assessment shall contain at least:

- a systematic description of the envisaged processing operations and the purposes of the processing, including where applicable the legitimate interest pursued by the Controller;
- an assessment of the necessity and proportionality of the processing operations in relation to the purposes;
- an assessment of the risks to the rights and freedoms of Data Subjects referred to in Article 35(1); and
- the measures envisaged to address the risks, including safeguards, security measures and mechanisms to ensure the protection of personal data and to demonstrate compliance with the GDPR taking into account the rights and legitimate interests of Data Subjects and other persons concerned (Article 35(7)).

Compliance with approved codes of conduct referred to in Article 40 by the relevant Controllers or Processors shall be taken into due account in assessing the impact of the processing operations performed by such Controllers or Processors, in particular for the purposes of a data protection impact assessment (Article 35(8)).

Where appropriate, the Controller shall seek the views of Data Subjects or their representatives on the intended processing, without prejudice to the protection of commercial or public interests or the security of the processing operations (Article 35(9)).

Where the processing pursuant to Article 6(1)(c) or (e) has a legal basis in EU law, or the law of the Member State to which the Controller is subject, that law regulates the specific processing operation or set of operations in question, and a data protection impact assessment has already been carried out as part of a general impact assessment in the context of the adoption of this legal basis, Article 35(1) to (7) shall not apply unless Member States deem it to be necessary to carry out such an assessment prior to the processing activities (Article 35(10)).

Where necessary, the Controller shall carry out a review to assess if the processing is performed in accordance with the data protection impact assessment at least when there is a change of the risk represented by the processing operations (Article 35(11)).

Prior Consultation

29.45 The Controller shall consult the supervisory authority prior to the processing where a data protection impact assessment as provided for in Article 35 indicates that the processing would result in a high risk in the absence of measures taken by the Controller to mitigate the risk (Article 36(1)).

Where the supervisory authority is of the opinion that the intended processing referred to in Article 36(1) would infringe the GDPR, in particular where the Controller has insufficiently identified or mitigated the risk, it shall within a maximum period of eight weeks following the request for consultation give written advice to the Controller and, where applicable the Processor, and may use any of its powers referred to in Article 58. This period may be extended by six weeks, taking into account the complexity of the intended processing. The supervisory authority shall inform the Controller and, where applicable, the Processor, of any such extension within one month of receipt of the request for consultation together with the reasons for the delay. These periods may be suspended until the supervisory authority has obtained any information it has requested for the purposes of the consultation (Article 36(2)).

When consulting the supervisory authority pursuant to Article 36(1), the Controller shall provide the supervisory authority with:

- where applicable, the respective responsibilities of Controller, joint Controllers and Processors involved in the processing, in particular for processing within a group of undertakings;
- the purposes and means of the intended processing;
- the measures and safeguards provided to protect the rights and freedoms of Data Subjects pursuant to the GDPR;
- where applicable, the contact details of the DPO;
- the data protection impact assessment provided for in Article 35; and
- any other information requested by the supervisory authority (Article 36(3)).

Member States shall consult the supervisory authority during the preparation of a proposal for a legislative measure to be adopted by a national parliament, or of a regulatory measure based on such a legislative measure, which relates to the processing (Article 36(4)).

Notwithstanding Article 36(1), Member States' law may require Controllers to consult with, and obtain prior authorisation from, the supervisory authority in relation to the processing by a Controller for the performance of a task carried out by the Controller in the public interest, including processing in relation to social protection and public health (Article 36(5)).

Chapter 30

Jurisdiction and Social Media

30.01 One of the developing and more contentious areas of internet liability relates to issues of service provider liability. There is a claim often advanced by some service providers, that they are not liable to the EU data protection regime if the companies and or parent companies are located in the US. Effectively, they are claiming to be exempt from having to comply with EU law in relation to EU citizens in Europe, and the personal data of those citizens. Other companies, however, are happy to indicate a willingness to comply with EU data protection rules. Facebook, for example, indicated that Facebook in Dublin is responsible for Facebook privacy and data protection in Europe and elsewhere (apart from the US and Canada). This position is not universal with other multinationals however.

DPA: Jurisdiction

30.02 Section 15 of the DPA 1998 refers to jurisdiction and procedure. Section 15(1) provides that the jurisdiction conferred by ss 7 to 14 is exercisable by the High Court or a county court or, in Scotland, by the Court of Session or the sheriff. Section 15(2) provides that for the purpose of determining any question whether an applicant under sub-s (9) of s 7 is entitled to the information which he seeks (including any question whether any relevant data are exempt from that section by virtue of Part IV) a court may require the information constituting any data processed by or on behalf of the Controller and any information as to the logic involved in any decision-taking as mentioned in s 7(1)(d) to be made available for its own inspection but shall not, pending the determination of that question in the applicant's favour, require the information sought by the applicant to be disclosed to them or his representatives whether by discovery (or, in Scotland, recovery) or otherwise. Certain internet companies, however, seek to avoid liability to the UK and EU data protection regimes by segregating services and seeking to suggest that the entire service and surrounding infrastructure is located outside of the UK and EU. These are ongoing issues of contention. There is a Spanish case being referred to the ECJ relating to some of these multinational arguments (see below).

DPD: Member States/Jurisdiction

30.03 DPD Recital 18 states that in order to ensure that individuals are *not deprived of the protection to which they are entitled under the DPD*, any processing of personal data in the EU must be carried out in accordance with the law of one of the Member States (emphasis added). In this connection, processing carried out under the responsibility of a Controller who is established in a Member State should be governed by the law of that State. This is where certain internet multinationals take issue. They seek to argue that a particular segregated service or activity is not located or undertaken in the EU, notwithstanding that it involves UK citizens, UK personal data, the activities of UK citizens located in the UK and personal data collected in the UK. If there are ongoing services or activities these are also used and operated by UK citizens in the UK. Yet, certain internet multinationals would claim to be exempted from EU data protection, service provider and content liability rules in the UK, Ireland and EU.

DPD Recital 19 states that establishment on the territory of a Member State implies the effective and real exercise of activity through stable arrangements; whereas the legal form of such an establishment, whether simply branch or a subsidiary with a legal personality, is not the determining factor in this respect. When a single Controller is established on the territory of several Member States, particularly by means of subsidiaries, they must ensure, in order to avoid any circumvention of national rules, that each of the establishments fulfils the obligations imposed by the national law applicable to its activities.

Some internet multinationals argue that a segregated service is operated by a segregated legal entity which is not an 'establishment on the territory of a Member State.' This seeks to ignore that the core nexus of the Data Subject, the personal data, the collection, the use and activity by the individual are all UK/EU related. As indicated above, these are issues which are being litigated and disputed contentiously at present.

In addition, it is noted that there are ongoing development which, at the time of writing, indicates that EU data protection regulators have found that Google is in breach of EU data protection law in its unilaterally changed privacy policies in March 2011.[1] This change occurred despite EU regulators officially requesting Google to delay the go-live of the new policy pending an official examination and review. Google refused to comply. This will be an interesting, as well as an important, issue to watch as it develops.

GDPR: Recitals and Social Media

Location/Jurisdiction/Processing

30.04   Recital 22 states that any processing of personal data in the context of the activities of an establishment of a Controller or a Processor in the EU should be carried out in accordance with the Regulation, *regardless of whether the processing itself takes place within the EU.* Establishment implies the effective and real exercise of activity through stable arrangements. The legal form of such arrangements, whether through a branch or a subsidiary with a legal personality, is not the determining factor in this respect (emphasis added).

This reiterates, if that was needed, that EU citizens and the personal data of EU citizens must be respected and UK/EU laws complied with. Similarly, the following Recitals also enhance this position.

Recital 23 states that in order *to ensure that natural persons are not deprived of the protection* to which they are entitled under the GDPR, the processing of personal data of data subjects who are in the EU by a Controller or a Processor *not established in the EU should be subject to the GDPR* where the processing activities are related to offering goods or services to such Data Subjects irrespective of whether connected to a payment. In order to determine whether such a Controller or Processor is offering goods or services to data subjects who are in the EU, it should be ascertained whether it is apparent that the Controller or Processor envisages offering services to Data Subjects in one or more Member States in the EU. Whereas the mere accessibility of the Controller's, Processor's or an intermediary's website in the EU, of an email address or of other contact details, or the use of a language generally used in the third country where the Controller is established, is insufficient to ascertain such intention, factors such as the use of a language or a currency

---

1   See, for example, B Pancevski and S Duke, 'Google to Face Legal Threats, The Internet Giant May Be Forced to Pay Compensation for Breach of Privacy Law,' *Sunday Times*, 14 October 2012; C Arthur, 'Google's privacy policy: EU data protection chiefs to act within days EU data protection commissioners are believed to have determined that pooling of data by Google breaches privacy laws,' *Guardian*, 8 October 2012.

generally used in one or more Member States with the possibility of ordering goods and services in that other language, or the mentioning of customers or users who are in the EU, may make it apparent that the Controller envisages offering goods or services to Data Subjects in the EU (emphasis added).

Establishment

30.05 Recital 36 states that the main establishment of a Controller in the EU should be the place of its central administration in the EU, unless the decisions on the purposes and means of the processing of personal data are taken in another establishment of the Controller in the EU, in which case that other establishment should be considered to be the main establishment. The main establishment of a Controller in the Union should be determined according to objective criteria and should imply the effective and real exercise of management activities determining the main decisions as to the purposes and means of processing through stable arrangements. That criterion should not depend on whether the processing of personal data is carried out at that location. The presence and use of technical means and technologies for processing personal data or processing activities do not, in themselves, constitute a main establishment and are therefore not determining criteria for a main establishment. The main establishment of the Processor should be the place of its central administration in the EU or, if it has no central administration in the EU, the place where the main processing activities take place in the EU. In cases involving both the Controller and the Processor, the competent lead supervisory authority should remain the supervisory authority of the Member State where the Controller has its main establishment, but the supervisory authority of the Processor should be considered to be a supervisory authority concerned and that supervisory authority should participate in the cooperation procedure provided for by the GDPR. In any case, the supervisory authorities of the Member State or Member States where the Processor has one or more establishments should not be considered to be supervisory authorities concerned where the draft decision concerns only the Controller. Where the processing is carried out by a group of undertakings, the main establishment of the controlling undertaking should be considered to be the main establishment of the group of undertakings, except where the purposes and means of processing are determined by another undertaking.

Group Companies

30.06 Recital 37 states that group of undertakings should cover a controlling undertaking and its controlled undertakings, whereby the controlling undertaking should be the undertaking which can exert a dominant influence over the other undertakings by virtue, for example, of ownership, financial participation or the rules which govern it or the power to have personal data protection rules implemented. An undertaking which controls the processing of personal data in undertakings affiliated to it should be regarded, together with those undertakings, as a group of undertakings.

Third Country Controllers Must Appoint Representative in EU

30.07   Recital 80 states that where a Controller or a Processor not established in the EU is processing personal data of Data Subjects who are in the EU whose processing activities are related to the offering of goods or services, irrespective of whether a payment of the Data Subject is required, to such data subjects in the EU, or to the monitoring of their behaviour as far as their behaviour takes place within the EU, the Controller or the Processor should designate a representative, unless the processing is occasional, does not include processing, on a large scale, of special categories of personal data or the processing of personal data relating to criminal convictions and offences, and is unlikely to result in a risk to the rights and freedoms of natural persons, taking into account the nature, context, scope and purposes of the processing or if the Controller is a public authority or body. The representative should act on behalf of the Controller or the Processor and may be addressed by any supervisory authority. The representative should be explicitly designated by a written mandate of the Controller or of the Processor to act on its behalf with regard to its obligations under the GDPR. The designation of such a representative does not affect the responsibility or liability of the Controller or of the Processor under the GDPR. Such a representative should perform its tasks according to the mandate received from the Controller or Processor, including cooperating with the competent supervisory authorities with regard to any action taken to ensure compliance with the GDPR. The designated representative should be subject to enforcement proceedings in the event of non-compliance by the Controller or Processor.

Public International Law

30.08   Recital 22 states that where the national law of a Member State applies by virtue of public international law, the Regulation should also apply to a Controller not established in the EU, such as in a Member State's diplomatic mission or consular post.

GDPR Covers Social Media

30.09 In the GDPR, 'main establishment' is defined to mean as regards the Controller with establishments in more than one Member State, the place of its central administration in the EU, unless the decisions on the purposes and means of the processing of personal data are taken in another establishment of the Controller in the EU and the latter establishment has the power to have such decisions implemented, in which case the establishment having taken such decisions is to be considered to be the main establishment. As regards the Processor, 'main establishment' as regards a Processor with establishments in more than one Member State, the place of its central administration in the EU, or, if the Processor has no central administration in the EU, the establishment of the Processor in the Union where the main processing activities in the context of the activities of an establishment of the Processor take place to the extent that the Processor is subject to specific obligations under the GDPR.

In the GDPR also the concept of 'representative' is defined to mean a natural or legal person established in the EU who, designated by the Controller or Processor in writing, represents the Controller or Processor acts and may be addressed by any SA and other bodies in the EU instead of the Controller, with regard to the obligations of the Controller under the GDPR.

GDPR Recital 22 states that any processing of personal data in the context of the activities of an establishment of a Controller or a Processor in the EU should be carried out in accordance with the Regulation, *regardless* of whether the processing itself takes place within the EU. (Emphasis added). Establishment implies the effective and real exercise of activity through stable arrangements. The legal form of such arrangements, whether through a branch or a subsidiary with a legal personality, is not the determining factor in that respect.

GDPR Recital 23 states that in order to *ensure that natural persons are not deprived of the protection* to which they are entitled under the GDPR, the processing of personal data of Data Subjects who are in the EU by a Controller or a Processor not established in the EU should be subject to the GDPR where the processing activities are related to the offering of goods or services to such Data Subjects irrespective of whether connected to a payment. (Emphasis added.) Further details are also specified as regards the offering of services to Data Subjects.

Recital 36 states that the main establishment of a Controller in the EU should be the place of its central administration in the EU, unless the decisions on the purposes and means of the processing of personal data are taken in another establishment of the Controller in the EU, in which case that other establishment should be considered to be the main establishment. Further details such as objective criteria are also referred to.

Third country Controllers must appoint a Representative in EU. GDPR Recital 80 states that where a Controller not established in the EU is processing personal data of Data Subjects residing in the EU whose processing activities are related to the offering of goods or services to such Data Subjects, or to the monitoring their behaviour, the Controller should designate a representative.

It is also noted that there is no exception made in the GDPR for UGC or user generated content.

Article 3 of the GDPR provides that the GDPR applies to the processing of personal data in the context of the activities of an establishment of a Controller or a Processor in the EU, regardless of whether the processing takes place in the EU or not.

The GDPR applies to the processing of personal data of Data Subjects who are in the EU by a Controller or Processor not established in the EU, where the processing activities are related to,

- the offering of goods or services, irrespective of whether payment of the Data Subject is required, to such Data Subjects in the EU; or
- the monitoring of their behaviour as far as their behaviour takes place within the EU.

The GDPR applies to the processing of personal data by a Controller not established in the EU, but in a place where Member State applies by virtue of public international law.

Spanish Case

30.10 An important case may be *Google Spain and Google Case* C-131/12 in the ECJ. This is a reference for a preliminary ruling from the Audiencia Nacional (Spain).

It specifically relates to the following:

- interpretation of Arts 2(b) and (d), 4(1)(a) and (c), 12(b) and 14(a) of the DPD; and
- Art 8 of the Charter of Fundamental Rights of the EU (OJ 2000 C 364, p 1);
- concept of establishment on the territory of a Member State;
- relevant criteria;
- concept of 'use of equipment ... situated on the territory of a Member State';
- temporary storage of information indexed by internet search engines;
- right to erasure and blocking of data.

The first edition of this work predicted that answers to some of these questions may have important implications for online business models as well as the rights of UK citizens. The first edition also predicted that the answers may have been partly answered by the provisions and confirmations of the DPD even before the GDPR. This contrasts with the surprise reaction of many commentators to the ultimate Court of Justice decision against Google. The Court of Justice held that:

> 'Article 2(b) and (d) of Directive 95/46/EC ... are to be interpreted as meaning that, first, the activity of a search engine consisting in finding information published or placed on the internet by third parties, indexing it automatically, storing it temporarily and, finally, making it available to internet users according to a particular order of preference must be classified as "processing of personal data" within the meaning of Article 2(b) when that information contains personal data and, second, the operator of the search engine must be regarded as the "controller" in respect of that processing, within the meaning of Article 2(d).
>
> *Article 4(1)(a) of Directive 95/46 is to be interpreted as meaning that processing of personal data is carried out in the context of the activities of an establishment of the controller on the territory of a Member State, within the meaning of that provision, when the operator of a search engine sets up in a Member State a branch or subsidiary which is intended to promote and sell advertising space offered by that engine and which orientates its activity towards the inhabitants of that Member State.'[2]*

The field of deletion of online materials will continue to gather pace. One aspect of this relates to the deletion of personal data. While the *Google Spain* case has received a lot of attention,[3] both academic and media, this merely reflects existing law under the DPD, not the forthcoming GDPR. Arguably the GDPR expands this deletion or RtbF requirement. However, given the existing DPD, one can query the level of surprise at the decision. There is also merit in querying the pursuit of moonshot (or speculative) litigation in this instance. Moonshot litigation does not always work and can sometimes backfire. While corporates do indeed face difficult questions from time to time and litigation might sometimes be necessary, certain litigation should also be avoided. The contentious and non-contentious messages coming from corporates in this space can sometimes be more positive, nuanced and improved.

---

2   Emphasis added. *Google Spain SL and Google Inc v Agencia Española de Protección de Datos (AEPD) and Mario Costeja González*, Case C-131/12, 13 May 2014, available at http://curia.europa.eu/juris/liste.jsf?pro=&nat=or&oqp=&dates=&lg=&langua ge=en&jur=C%2CT%2CF&cit=none%252CC%252CCJ%252CR%252C2008E%25 2C%252C%252C%252C%252C%252C%252C%252C%252C%252Ctrue%252Cfals e%252Cfalse&td=%3BALL&pcs=Oor&avg=&page=1&mat=or&parties=google%2 Bspain&jge=&for=&cid=511372, accessed 2 January 2015.
3   J Jones, 'Control-Alter-Delete: The "Right to be forgotten" – Google Spain SL, Google Inc v Agencia Espanola de Proteccion de Datos,' *EIPR* (2014) (36) 595.

Weltimmo Case

30.11   The recent *Weltimmo*[4] case also refers to jurisdiction issues, holding that a SA can sometimes have jurisdiction even over organisations located elsewhere. DPD Article 28(6) provides:

'Each supervisory authority is competent, whatever the national law applicable to the processing in question, to exercise, on the territory of its own Member State, the powers conferred on it in accordance with paragraph 3. Each authority may be requested to exercise its powers by an authority of another Member State.'

DPD Article 4 states:

'Each Member State shall apply the national provisions it adopts pursuant to this Directive to the processing of personal data where:
(a) the processing is carried out in the context of the activities of an establishment of the controller on the territory of the Member State; when the same controller is established on the territory of several Member States, he must take the necessary measures to ensure that each of these establishments complies with the obligations laid down by the national law applicable.'

The Court of Justice held that:

'1. Article 4(1)(a) of the DPD must be interpreted as permitting the application of the law on the protection of personal data of a Member State other than the Member State in which the controller with respect to the processing of those data is registered, in so far as that controller exercises, through stable arrangements in the territory of that Member State, a real and effective activity – even a minimal one – in the context of which that processing is carried out.

In order to ascertain, in circumstances such as those at issue in the main proceedings, whether that is the case, the referring court may, in particular, take account of the fact (i) that the activity of the controller in respect of that processing, in the context of which that processing takes place, consists of the running of property dealing websites concerning properties situated in the territory of that Member State and written in that Member State's language and that it is, as a consequence, mainly or entirely directed at that Member State, and (ii) that that controller has a representative in that Member State, who is responsible for recovering the debts resulting from that activity and for representing the controller in the administrative and judicial proceedings relating to the processing of the data concerned.

---

4   *Weltimmo sro v Nemzeti Adatvédelmi és Információszabadság Hatóság*, Court of Justice, Case C-230/14, 1 October 2015.

By contrast, the issue of the nationality of the persons concerned by such data processing is irrelevant.

2. Where the supervisory authority of a Member State, to which complaints have been submitted in accordance with Article 28(4) of DPD, reaches the conclusion that the law applicable to the processing of the personal data concerned is not the law of that Member State, but the law of another Member State, Article 28(1), (3) and (6) of that directive must be interpreted as meaning that that supervisory authority will be able to exercise the effective powers of intervention conferred on it in accordance with Article 28(3) of that directive only within the territory of its own Member State. Accordingly, it cannot impose penalties on the basis of the law of that Member State on the controller with respect to the processing of those data who is not established in that territory, but should, in accordance with Article 28(6) of that directive, request the supervisory authority within the Member State whose law is applicable to act.

3. DPD must be interpreted as meaning that the term "adatfeldolgozás" (technical manipulation of data), used in the Hungarian version of that directive, in particular in Articles 4(1)(a) and 28(6) thereof, must be understood as having the same meaning as that of the term "adatkezelés" (data processing).'

The new GDPR also refers to jurisdictional issues and assists the Data Subject further.

Policies

30.12   In March 2012 Google controversially combined over 60 separate and discrete products and services of Google (and other companies and brand names). Data protection authorities of the EU, as well as elsewhere around the world (including officials in the US), requested Google not to go-ahead or in the case of the EU, to delay it until officials could consider it further. Google refused.

The EU data protection authorities, under WP29 and the French data protection authority (CNIL) carried out an investigation of the new privacy policy and its implications. In *WP29 and Data Protection Authorities/Google*[5] it found various breaches and problems with the new policy. Google has been required to change the policy as well as to develop new tools for users and their personal data.

---

5   See   Appendix: http://www.cnil.fr/fileadmin/documents/en/GOOGLE_PRIVACY_
    POLICY-_RECOMMENDATIONS-FINAL-EN.pdf; French DP regulator (CNIL)
    statement: http://www.cnil.fr/english/news-and-events/news/article/googles-new-
    privacy-policy-incomplete-information-and-uncontrolled-combination-of-data-
    across-ser/

As regards jurisdictional issues the above WP29 complaint on the Google policy notes and confirms that EU data protection law applies to G (see WP29 Appendix, para 1, page 2). Footnote 1 to the complaint notes that the Google EU headquarters is located in Dublin, Ireland. It further notes that Google companies are located in the EU, such as in the UK, Ireland, and France. Footnote 1 also notes that Google uses computer servers in the EU, such as in Belgium and Finland. It also has a data centre in Ireland. It seems clear, therefore, EU law and jurisdiction could apply to Google and these products and services.

Recall also the DPD also refers to jurisdiction issues. Article 4 refers to the national law applicable. (See text of Article 4 in the preceding paragraph.)

Some non-EU entities will sometimes argue not as they are non-in EU and or are US based, they do not have to comply with EU data protection law – even despite having millions of users and customers in Europe. It is worth considering (c) above. The DPD states that EU law applies if the service provider uses equipment in the EU. WP29 above confirms Google, for example, uses servers in EU. Google also has a new data centre in Dublin. So we can see that 1(c) above applies. Therefore, EU law and jurisdiction apply to Google and its related products and services. In any event, Google has various legal entities in the EU, so EU law would in any event applies. It is understood that some of the official unease has resulted in greater transparency in relation to collections and policies. The new GDPR also advances the principle of transparency.

Conclusion

30.13 The intersection of data protection and social media is one of the most controversial issues in contemporary data protection practice. Users are concerned as to what personal data is being collected and what it will be used for. Naturally, social networks will seek to commercialise and use profile information for advertising and marketing purposes. This tension remains. Furthermore, the tension is elevated when the individuals using social media websites are children. Various tragic events create a new level of sensitivity and importance. While the GDPR is a welcome advancement, additional research is also needed, and on an ongoing basis.

The frequency of change in social media and new ways to collect and process new categories of personal data during social media activities means that the mechanics of complying with access requests will have to continually evolve. There is also an issue remaining with certain social networks currently as to whether they are fully or only partially compliant in terms of responding to data access requests.

These issues are critically important, given the number of UK citizens using the internet and social networks in particular. Yet, many will be unfamiliar with these issues given that they are often overlooked in general summaries of data protection law. General compliance and data loss/data breach incidents are more frequently highlighted instead. However, increasingly users are becoming aware of their rights, including access rights.

Chapter 31

Leveson, the Press and Data Protection

Introduction

31.01   The UK Leveson Report deals with (certain) data protection issues in detail, namely the recommendations relating to data protection and journalism. The evidence and issues are more fully described in Part H, 5 of the Report.

DPA 1998, s 32

31.02   The current s 32 of the DPA 1998 refers to journalism activities. It provides:

'(1)   Personal data which are processed only for the special purposes are exempt from any provision to which this subsection relates if—
  (a)   the processing is undertaken with a view to the publication by any person of any journalistic, literary or artistic material,
  (b)   the data Controller reasonably believes that, having regard in particular to the special importance of the public interest in freedom of expression, publication would be in the public interest, and
  (c)   the data controller reasonably believes that, in all the circumstances, compliance with that provision is incompatible with the special purposes.
(2)   Subsection (1) relates to the provisions of—
  (a)   the data protection principles except the seventh data protection principle,
  (b)   section 7,
  (c)   section 10,
  (d)   section 12, and
  (e)   section 14(1) to (3).

(3)   In considering for the purposes of subsection (1)(b) whether the belief of a data Controller that publication would be in the public interest was or is a reasonable one, regard may be had to his compliance with any code of practice which—

(a)   is relevant to the publication in question, and

(b)   is designated by the [Secretary of State] by order for the purposes of this subsection.

(4)   Where at any time ('the relevant time') in any proceedings against a data Controller under section 7(9), 10(4), 12(8) or 14 or by virtue of section 13 the data Controller claims, or it appears to the court, that any personal data to which the proceedings relate are being processed—

(a)   only for the special purposes, and

(b)   with a view to the publication by any person of any journalistic, literary or artistic material which, at the time twenty-four hours immediately before the relevant time, had not previously been published by the data Controller,

the court shall stay the proceedings until either of the conditions in subsection (5) is met.

(5)   Those conditions are—

(a)   that a determination of the Commissioner under section 45 with respect to the data in question takes effect, or

(b)   in a case where the proceedings were stayed on the making of a claim, that the claim is withdrawn.

(6)   For the purposes of this Act 'publish', in relation to journalistic, literary or artistic material, means make available to the public or any section of the public.'

Lord Lester of Herne Hill is referred to in the Report (p 1067) as having 'warned at length that, as drafted and because of cl 31, the DPA failed to implement the Directive and authorised interference by the press with the right to privacy in breach of Art 8 of the ECHR.'

At page 1068 of the Report, it refers to:

'Mr Coppel's arguments ... would be that on the current state of the UK authorities, s 32 fails to implement the Directive from which it derives, and is inconsistent with the relevant parts of the ECHR to which it is intended to give effect, because the relationship between privacy and expression rights has got out of balance. A proper balance is a fundamental obligation. The UK is therefore positively *required* to change the law to restore the balance. That is indeed Mr Coppel's own contention: that UK data protection law currently fails to implement our obligations, and that Lord Lester's concerns had proved to be prescient.'

The Report itself then states:

'2.11 Without going so far as that, even if the current balance were within the spectrum permitted by our international obligations, the argument could be expressed in terms that it is at an extreme end of that spectrum, and the

UK can as a matter of law, and should as a matter of policy, restore a more even-handed approach, not least given the asymmetry of risks and harms as between the individual and the press.

2.12 Put at its very lowest, the point could be made that the effect of the development of the case law has been to push personal privacy law in media cases out of the data protection regime and into the more open seas of the Human Rights Act. This has happened for no better reason than the slowness of the legal profession to assimilate data protection law and, in the case of the judiciary, its greater familiarity with (and, he suggests, perhaps a preference for) the latitude afforded by the human rights regime over the specificity of data protection. But this, the argument goes, is undesirable because the data protection regime is much more predictable, detailed and sophisticated in the way it protects and balances rights, and significantly reduces the risks, uncertainties and expense of litigation concomitant on more open-textured law dependent on a court's discretion. Where the law has provided specific answers, the fine-nibbed pen should be grasped and not the broad brush. The balancing of competing rights in a free democracy is a highly sophisticated exercise; appropriate tools have been provided for the job and should be used.'

Leveson Recommendations

To the Ministry of Justice

31.03 The Leveson Report makes the following recommendations, namely:

'48. The exemption in section 32 of the Data Protection Act 1998 should be amended so as to make it available only where:49 (a) the processing of data is necessary for publication, rather than simply being in fact undertaken with a view to publication; (b) the data Controller reasonably believes that the relevant publication would be or is in the public interest, with no special weighting of the balance between the public interest in freedom of expression and in privacy; and (c) objectively, that the likely interference with privacy resulting from the processing of the data is outweighed by the public interest in publication.

49. The exemption in section 32 of the Data Protection Act 1998 should be narrowed in scope, so that it no longer allows, by itself, for exemption from:50 (a) the requirement of the first data protection principle to process personal data fairly (except in relation to the provision of information to the Data Subject under paragraph 2(1)(a) of Part II Schedule 1 to the 1998 Act) and in accordance with statute law; (b) the second data protection principle (personal data to be obtained only for specific purposes and not processed incompatibly with those purposes); (c) the fourth data protection principle (personal data to be accurate and kept up to date); (d) the sixth data protection principle (personal data to be processed in accordance with the rights of

individuals under the Act); (e) the eighth data protection principle (restrictions on exporting personal data); and (f) the right of subject access. The recommendation on the removal of the right of subject access from the scope of section 32 is subject to any necessary clarification that the law relating to the protection of journalists' sources is not affected by the Act.

50. It should be made clear that the right to compensation for distress conferred by section 13 of the Data Protection Act 1998 is not restricted to cases of pecuniary loss, but should include compensation for pure distress.

51. The procedural provisions of the Data Protection Act 1998 with special application to journalism in: (a) section 32(4) and (5) (b) sections 44 to 46 inclusive should be repealed.

52. In conjunction with the repeal of those procedural provisions, consideration should be given to the desirability of including in the Data Protection Act 1998 a provision to the effect that, in considering the exercise of any powers in relation to the media or other publishers, the Information Commissioner's Office should have special regard to the obligation in law to balance the public interest in freedom of expression alongside the public interest in upholding the data protection regime.

53. Specific provision should be made to the effect that, in considering the exercise of any of its powers in relation to the media or other publishers, the Information Commissioner's Office must have regard to the application to a data Controller of any relevant system of regulation or standards enforcement which is contained in or recognised by statute.

54. The necessary steps should be taken to bring into force the amendments made to section 55 of the Data Protection Act 1998 by section 77 of the Criminal Justice and Immigration Act 2008 (increase of sentence maxima) to the extent of the maximum specified period; and by section 78 of the 2008 Act (enhanced defence for public interest journalism).

55. The prosecution powers of the Information Commissioner should be extended to include any offence which also constitutes a breach of the data protection principles.

56. A new duty should be introduced (whether formal or informal) for the Information Commissioner's Office to consult with the Crown Prosecution Service in relation to the exercise of its powers to undertake criminal proceedings.

57. The opportunity should be taken to consider amending the Data Protection Act 1998 formally to reconstitute the Information Commissioner's Office as an Information Commission, led by a Board of Commissioners with suitable expertise drawn from the worlds of regulation, public administration, law and business, and active consideration should be given in that context to the desirability of including on the Board a Commissioner from the media sector.'

To the ICO

31.04   The Leveson Report also makes recommendation to the ICO. These are:

'58. The Information Commissioner's Office should take immediate steps to prepare, adopt and publish a policy on the exercise of its formal regulatory functions in order to ensure that the press complies with the legal requirements of the data protection regime.

59. In discharge of its functions and duties to promote good practice in areas of public concern, the Information Commissioner's Office should take immediate steps, in consultation with the industry, to prepare and issue comprehensive good practice guidelines and advice on appropriate principles and standards to be observed by the press in the processing of personal data. This should be prepared and implemented within six months from the date of this Report.

60. The Information Commissioner's Office should take steps to prepare and issue guidance to the public on their individual rights in relation to the obtaining and use by the press of their personal data, and how to exercise those rights.

61. In particular, the Information Commissioner's Office should take immediate steps to publish advice aimed at individuals (Data Subjects) concerned that their data have or may have been processed by the press unlawfully or otherwise than in accordance with good practice.

62. The Information Commissioner's Office, in the Annual Report to Parliament which it is required to make by virtue of section 52(1) of the Act, should include regular updates on the effectiveness of the foregoing measures, and on the culture, practices and ethics of the press in relation to the processing of personal data.

63. The Information Commissioner's Office should immediately adopt the Guidelines for Prosecutors on assessing the public interest in cases affecting the media, issued by the Director of Public Prosecutions in September 2012.

64. The Information Commissioner's Office should take immediate steps to engage with the Metropolitan Police on the preparation of a long-term strategy in relation to alleged media crime with a view to ensuring that the Office is well placed to fulfil any necessary role in this respect in the future, and in particular in the aftermath of Operations Weeting, Tuleta and Elveden.

65. The Information Commissioner's Office should take the opportunity to review the availability to it of specialist legal and practical knowledge of the application of the data protection regime to the press, and to any extent necessary address it.

66. The Information Commissioner's Office should take the opportunity to review its organisation and decision-making processes to ensure that large-scale issues, with both strategic and operational dimensions (including the relationship between the culture, practices and ethics of the press in relation to personal information on the one hand, and the application of the data protection regime to the press on the other) can be satisfactorily considered and addressed in the round.'

Increased Sentencing for Data Breach

31.05   The Leveson Report also makes other law recommendations. These are:

'67. On the basis that the provisions of s 77–78 of the Criminal Justice and Immigration Act 2008 are brought into effect, so that increased sentencing powers are available for breaches of s 55 of the Data Protection Act 1998.

68. The Secretary of State for Justice should use the power vested in him by s 124(1)(a)(i) of the Coroners and Justice Act 2009 to invite the Sentencing Council of England and Wales to prepare guidelines in relation to data protection offences (including computer misuse).'

Comparison

31.06   A comparison of the DPA 1998 and the Leveson comments is set out below.

DPA 1998 (s 32)	Leveson
(1) Personal data which are processed only for the special purposes are exempt from any provision to which this subsection relates if— (a) the processing is undertaken with a view to the publication by any person of any journalistic, literary or artistic material, (b) the data Controller reasonably believes that, having regard in particular to the special importance of the public interest in freedom of expression, publication would be in the public interest, and (c) the data Controller reasonably believes that, in all the circumstances, compliance with that provision is incompatible with the special purposes.	48 The exemption in s 32 of the Data Protection Act 1998 should be amended so as to make it available only where:(a) the processing of data is necessary for publication, rather than simply being in fact undertaken with a view to publication; (b) the data Controller reasonably believes that the relevant publication would be or is in the public interest, with no special weighting of the balance between the public interest in freedom of expression and in privacy; and (c) objectively, that the likely interference with privacy resulting from the processing of the data is outweighed by the public interest in publication.

(2) Sub-s (1) relates to the provisions of—
  (a) the data protection principles except the seventh data protection principle,
  (b) s 7,
  (c) s 10,
  (d) s 12, and
  (e) s 14(1) to (3).
(3) In considering for the purposes of sub-s (1)(b) whether the belief of a data Controller that publication would be in the public interest was or is a reasonable one, regard may be had to his compliance with any code of practice which—
  (a) is relevant to the publication in question, and
  (b) is designated by the[Secretary of State]by order for the purposes of this sub-section.
(4) Where at any time ('the relevant time') in any proceedings against a data Controller under s 7(9), 10(4), 12(8) or 14 or by virtue of s 13 the data Controller claims, or it appears to the court, that any personal data to which the proceedings relate are being processed—
  (a) only for the special purposes, and
  (b) with a view to the publication by any person of any journalistic, literary or artistic material which, at the time twenty-four hours immediately before the relevant time, had not previously been published by the data Controller, the court shall stay the proceedings until either of the conditions in sub-s (5) is met.
(5) Those conditions are—
  (a) that a determination of the Commissioner under s 45 with respect to the data in question takes effect, or
  (b) in a case where the proceedings were stayed on the making of a claim, that the claim is withdrawn.
(6) For the purposes of this Act 'publish', in relation to journalistic, literary or artistic material, means make available to the public or any section of the public.
	49 The exemption in s 32 of the Data Protection Act 1998 should be narrowed in scope, so that it no longer allows, by itself, for exemption from: (a) the requirement of the first data protection principle to process personal data fairly (except in relation to the provision of information to the Data Subject under paragraph 2(1) (a) of Part II Schedule 1 to the 1998 Act) and in accordance with statute law; (b) the second data protection principle (personal data to be obtained only for specific purposes and not processed incompatibly with those purposes); (c) the fourth data protection principle (personal data to be accurate and kept up to date); (d) the sixth data protection principle (personal data to be processed in accordance with the rights of individuals under the Act); (e) the eighth data protection principle (restrictions on exporting personal data); and (f) the right of subject access. The recommendation on the removal of the right of subject access from the scope of s 32 is subject to any necessary clarification that the law relating to the protection of journalists' sources is not affected by the Act.
	50 It should be made clear that the right to compensation for distress conferred by s 13 of the Data Protection Act 1998 is not restricted to cases of pecuniary loss, but should include compensation for pure distress.
	51 The procedural provisions of the Data Protection Act 1998 with special application to journalism in: (a) s 32(4) and (5); (b) ss 44 – 46 inclusive should be repealed.

	52	In conjunction with the repeal of those procedural provisions, consideration should be given to the desirability of including in the Data Protection Act 1998 a provision to the effect that, in considering the exercise of any powers in relation to the media or other publishers, the Information Commissioner's Office should have special regard to the obligation in law to balance the public interest in freedom of expression alongside the public interest in upholding the data protection regime.
	53	Specific provision should be made to the effect that, in considering the exercise of any of its powers in relation to the media or other publishers, the Information Commissioner's Office must have regard to the application to a data controller of any relevant system of regulation or standards enforcement which is contained in or recognised by statute.

Conclusion

31.07 The recommendations of the Leveson Report were initially accepted at a political level in the UK. The exact nature of the amendments to be introduced need to be finalised. It remains to be seen precisely what effect this will have. There has been some criticism that more recent political developments have slowed these amendments.

Chapter 32

Data Protection Officer

Introduction

32.01 Organisations are now required to have a Data Protection Officer (DPO). In addition, the role and task requirements are now more explicit. The DPO must also have an appropriate independence in their activities and cannot be compromised or dictated to in a manner which undermines their role and duties in relation to personal data. It is now clear that the profession of the independent and expert DPO has arrived.

New Role of DPO

32.02 Chapter IV, Section 4 of the new GDPR refers to the new role and requirement of DPOs and the obligation for organisations to appoint DPOs.

The Controller and the Processor shall designate a DPO in any case where:

- the processing is carried out by a public authority or body, except for courts acting in their judicial capacity;
- the core activities of the Controller or the Processor consist of processing operations which, by virtue of their nature, their scope and/or their purposes, require regular and systematic monitoring of Data Subjects on a large scale;
- the core activities of the Controller or the Processor consist of processing on a large scale of special categories of data pursuant to Article 9 and personal data relating to criminal convictions and offences referred to in Article 10 (Article 37(1)).

Tasks and Role

32.03 The Controller or the Processor shall ensure that the DPO is involved, properly and in a timely manner in all issues which relate to the protection of personal data (Article 38(1)).

The DPO shall have at least the following tasks:

- to inform and advise the Controller or the Processor and the employees who carry out processing of their obligations pursuant to the GDPR and to other EU or Member State data protection provisions;
- to monitor compliance with the GDPR, with other EU or Member State data protection provisions and with the policies of the Controller or Processor in relation to the protection of personal data, including the assignment of responsibilities, awareness-raising and training of staff involved in the processing operations, and the related audits;
- to provide advice where requested as regards the data protection impact assessment and monitor its performance pursuant to Article 35;
- to cooperate with the supervisory authority;
- to act as the contact point for the supervisory authority on issues related to the processing, including the prior consultation referred to in Article 34, and consult, as appropriate, on any other matter (Article 39(1)).

The DPO shall in the performance of their tasks have due regard to the risk associated with the processing operations, taking into account the nature, scope, context and purposes of the processing (Article 39(2)).

The DPO may fulfil other tasks and duties. The Controller or Processor shall ensure that any such tasks and duties do not result in a conflict of interests (Article 38(6)).

The DPO will also supervise, advise and/or assist in relation to PIAs and monitor performance and make recommendations. They will also monitor and deal with any requests from the supervisory authority and also be the designated contact for the supervisory authority.

It is important that the DPO has regard to the risks that may arise specific to the organisation in relation to personal data and processing issues (including security issues). Depending on the sector, there may also be a Code of Conduct and/or certification issues for the DPO to be also concerned with. Data protection seals and certification are meant to help organisations demonstrate compliance.

Group DPO

32.04   A group of undertakings may appoint a single DPO provided that a DPO is easily accessible from each establishment (Article 37(2)).

Where the Controller or the Processor is a public authority or body, a single DPO may be designated for several such authorities or bodies, taking account of their organisational structure and size (Article 37(3)).

In cases other than those referred to in Article 37(1), the Controller or Processor or associations and other bodies representing categories of Controllers or Processors may or, where required by EU or Member State law shall, designate a DPO. The DPO may act for such associations and other bodies representing Controllers or Processors (Article 37(4)).

Qualifications and Expertise of DPO

32.05   The DPO shall be designated on the basis of professional qualities and, in particular, expert knowledge of data protection law and practices and the ability to fulfil the tasks referred to in Article 39 (Article 37(5)).

The DPO may be a staff member of the Controller or Processor, or fulfil the tasks on the basis of a service contract (Article 37(6)).

Contact Details

32.06   The Controller or the Processor shall publish the contact details of the DPO and communicate these to the supervisory authority (Article 37(7)).

Data Subjects may contact the DPO on all issues related to the processing of the Data Subject's personal data and the exercise of their rights under the GDPR (Article 38(4)).

Reporting

32.07   The DPO shall directly report to the highest management level of the Controller or the Processor (Article 38(3)).

Independent in Role and Tasks

32.08   The Controller or Processor shall ensure that the DPO does not receive any instructions regarding the exercise of their tasks. He or she shall not be dismissed or penalised by the Controller or the Processor for performing their tasks (Article 38(3)).

Resources

32.09 The Controller or Processor shall support the DPO in performing the tasks referred to in Article 39 by providing resources necessary to carry out those tasks and access to personal data and processing operations, and to maintain his or her expert knowledge (Article 38(2)).

Summary

32.10 In summary, organisations must designate a DPO to:

- monitor internal compliance with the GDPR regime and rules;
- ensure governance of the organisation's data management;
- draft and update compliant data protection policies;
- implement systems, changes and functions in terms of being compliant.

The DPO should be qualified and have particular expertise in data protection law and practice. They need to be able to fulfil their tasks in compliance and conformity with the GDPR. It appears they may be an employee or a contractor.

The DPO details must be made available publicly and the supervisory authority (such as the ICO) should be notified.

The organisation must involve the DPO in a timely manner in relation to all issues in relation to the protection of personal data and Data Subject issues. Proper and adequate resources must be supplied to the DPO by the organisation in order that they can undertake their tasks. There is an obligation that the DPO has independence in their role and functions, and that they cannot be controlled or micromanaged or instructed in relation to their tasks.

The DPO will report to the Board or highest management level as appropriate. This also emphasises the increasing importance attached to data protection understanding and compliance.

The DPO advises the organisation and employees in relation to their data protection obligations under national law and the GDPR. They will also monitor compliance with the data protection legal regime as well as internal policies. They will also be involved in assigning responsibilities, raising awareness and staff education and training.

DPOs should be highlighting the changes and the new GDPR to the organisation. Key issues need to be identified to appropriate management. New and ongoing change and compliance issues need appropriate resourcing. The DPO should assess what personal data the organisation collects and processes, for what purpose, and where it is located and secured. Particular attention is needed with regard to outsourcing issues and contracts with Processors. Contracts, including service level agreements in relation to IT systems, cloud, etc may be assessed. The various IT hardware, software and systems that employees use need to be considered.

The structure of the organisation needs to be considered, as well as jurisdiction and location issues. The life cycles, storage and disposal of personal data is also an important consideration for the new DPO.

The processes, policies and documentation must be maintained by the organisation, which places particular obligations on the DPO to consider the different documentation sets.

Chapter 33

Other Data Protection Issues

Introduction

33.01 Data protection covers many separate but important topics. Many of these are directly relevant to many organisations. Unfortunately, all of these cannot be adequately covered in a book such as this. However, it may assist to briefly refer to some of these.

Medical and Health Data

33.02 Medical and health data comprise one of the categories of sensitive personal data. Hence, there are greater conditions and compliance obligations. There is also a greater need for higher security measures. The concerns in relation to medical and health data increase once such data is held in electronic form and electronic databases. There is a need for enhanced practical and security procedures.[1]

There are various and increasing forms of recording personal health and related data regarding individuals, held in databases or biobanks.[2] One of the concerns is also the increasing possibility for profiling individuals from bio-informatic and genetic data.[3] The issue of consent in relation to bio data and biobanks is an issue of increasing concern.[4]

---

1 I Sandea, 'Analysis of the Legal Aspects Concerning Data Protection in Electronic Medical Registry,' *Applied Medical Informatics* (2009) (25) 16–20.
2 LA Bygrave, 'The Body as Data? Biobank Regulation via the "Back door" of Data Protection Law,' *Law, Innovation & Technology* (2010) (2) 1–25.
3 IM Azmi, 'Bioinformatics and Genetic Privacy: The Impact of the Personal Data Protection Act 2010,' *Computer Law & Security Review* (2011) (27) 394–401.
4 See, for example, J Taupitz and J Weigel, 'The Necessity of Broad Consent and Complementary Regulations for the Protection of Personal Data in Biobanks: What Can We Learn from the German Case?' *Public Health Genomics* (2012) (15) 263–271.

There is presently controversy in relation to the apparent transfer of sensitive medical health data relating to 1.6 million patients. This involves current, historical and live feed patient data. The transfer is being made by the Royal Free NHS Trust to DeepMind and or Google UK Limited and or a third party, the details of which are redacted in an Information Sharing Agreement signed by one party on 29 September 2015. The exact details are somewhat unclear. It is clear, however, that serious questions arise as to how the arrangement could be a data protection complaint based on the details currently available, including lack of transparency in particular to the patients whose sensitive personal data is involved. There does not appear to have been any opportunity or mechanism for patients to opt-in or to opt-out before any proposed data transfers. The purpose of the transfer and the details leading up to the transfer and arrangement are also unclear, which also undermines the possibility of fair, complaint processing. Fundamentally, the entire project relates to a new secondary use in relation to the medical data in question, as this required proper consideration and data protection compliance, which is not evident from the documentation thus far available. The data referred to is also of such a nature as to appear to go beyond the purported purpose thus far disclosed. One would expect any medical data being transferred – in particular names, address and other non-necessary information – to be redacted and or pseudononymised prior to transfer, which does not appear to have happened and which is not required in the Information Sharing Agreement. While Big Data health projects can have benefits, and such projects can be worth the endeavour even without a successful resulting health benefit, they all need to be data protection complaint. Serious questions remain in relation to this project, and thus far compliance has not been demonstrated. In fact, the information disclosed in the Data Sharing agreement and an official NHS Q&A document raise more questions than answers. It appears at this stage and on the basis of these documents to be non-data protection complaint.

Genome Data

33.03 A related and growing area is genomic,[5] genome research and the implications for individuals' privacy and personal data. Individual may be concerned with what happens with their own DNA gene sequence, information regarding predispositions to diseases, how this

---

5   L Curren et al, 'Identifiability, Genomics, and UK Data Protection Law,' *European Journal of Health Law* (2010) (17) 329–344.

may affect them, and how doctors, employers, insurers, and government may access and use such personal data. One recent text relating to this area is *The Governance of Genetic Information, Who Decides?* by Widdows and Mulle.[6]

Body Scanners

33.04   The introduction of body scanning technology in airports has been controversial.[7] While the prime argument in favour relates to airline security and terrorism, not everyone is convinced, and those challenged to produce evidence of successful attacks prevented, have been less forthcoming.

The main controversy centres on the ability of the body scanners to provide a complete, graphic, internal and intrusive image of a person's naked body once they walk through the scanner. There are of course different types and different settings. However, the introduction of body scanners is a perfect example of the introduction of a new technology without considering the privacy and data protection implications in advance. Later versions of body scanners have been developed which produce a line image drawing, not a biological naked image. They are equally capable of highlighting contraband material. Privacy designed body scanners can be equally effective.

Investigation, Discovery and Evidence

33.05   The issue of electronic evidence is important and critical, whether for the organisation or the Data Subject wishing to use such evidence. It is recommended that organisations consider these issues proactively in advance rather than hoping to be able to deal with them adequately in a reactive manner.

Cloud

33.06   The popularity of cloud computing and virtualisation services with users, enterprise and increasingly official organisations is ever

---

6   H Widdows and C Mullen, eds, 'Frontmatter, The Governance of Genetic Information, Who Decides?' *Cambridge Law, Medicine and Ethics* (2009).
7   See, for example, O Mironenko, 'Body Scanners Versus Privacy and Data Protection,' *Computer Law & Security Review* (2011) (27) 232–244.

increasing. However, there are real concerns in relation to privacy, data protection, data security,[8] continuity, discovery, liability, record keeping, etc.[9] One commentator refers to cloud computing as 'the privacy storm on the horizon.'[10] Any organisation considering cloud services needs to carefully consider the advantages, disadvantages, assessments and contract assurances that will be required. Such organisations, as well as the service operators, also need to assure themselves as to how they ensure data protection compliance.

New Hardware Devices, New Software

33.07 The arrival of new devices, from smartphones, combined devices and even communications devices on devices (such as RFID tags), emphasise that organisations need to be much more aware and considered in their policies and risk assessments under the data protection regime. Gaming and new headset devices (eg OR) will increase and will raise many new issues, including for personal rights, consent, representations and personal data.

Internet of Things

33.08 The beginning of the so called Internet of Things (IoT) or connected devices, of old and new devices, is now well heralded. However, the full consideration of the data protection implications are yet to be fully appreciated. Organisations need to appreciate the implications for employees, users and also their compliance systems. Manufacturers

8   See for example, C Soghoian, 'Caught in the Cloud: Privacy, Encryption, and Government Back Doors in the Web 2.0 Era,' *Journal of Telecommunications & High Technology Law* (2010) (8) 359–424. Also note U Pagallo, 'Robots in the Cloud with Privacy: A new Threat to Data Protection?' *Computer Law & Security Report* (2013) (29:5) 501.

9   ICO, *Guidance on the Use of Cloud Computing*, at https://ico.org.uk; Article 29 Working Party, *Opinion 05/2012 on Cloud Computing*, WP 196, 1 July 2012; P Lanois, 'Caught in the Clouds: The Web 2.0, Cloud Computing, and Privacy?' *Northwestern Journal of Technology and Intellectual Property* (2010) (9) 29–49; FM Pinguelo and BV Muller, 'Avoid the Rainy Day: Survey of US Cloud Computing Caselaw,' *Boston College Intellectual Property & Technology Forum* (2011) 1–7; IR Kattan, 'Cloudy Privacy Protections: Why the Stored Communications Act Fails to Protect the Privacy of Communications Stored in the Cloud,' *Vandenburg Journal of Entertainment and Technology Law* (2010–2011) (13) 617–656.

10 AC DeVere, 'Cloud Computing: Privacy Storm on the Horizon?' *Albany Law Journal* (2010) (20) 365–373.

are assisted in identifying and reducing these risks by the new risk and assessment tools of the GDPR.

On-Site/Off-Site

33.09 Organisations have to tackle the issues presented by employees not just working on-site, but also travelling and working at home or other locations off-site. This can impact, for example, the security and security risks regarding the personal data collected and processed by the organisation. It also means that devices may be taken off-site and or that third party devices may exist and which are utilised to access the organisation's systems remotely.

Online Abuse

33.10 The increasingly evident problem of online abuse such as cyberbullying, trolling, defamation copying and utilising personal data to abuse and blackmail children, teenagers, etc, are issues which need to be considered by all organisations, as well as policymakers. Pierre Trudel, for example, notes that the risks to individuals increase from many online activities, including in relation to data protection, safety, etc.[11]

New Regime

33.11 The new GDPR overhauls and modernises the data protection regime throughout the EU (and elsewhere). UK organisations will be affected and will have to prepare for the upcoming regime. What will the new data protection regime under the forthcoming EU GDPR do? Some of the specific changes and updates for organisations are highlighted in Part 4 of the book.

The whole area of transfers of personal data outside of the EEA (TBDFs) is regularly changing, for example, as new countries are added to a white list of permitted export countries after having been examined on behalf of the EU Commission. There are also other changes such as contractual clauses and binding corporate rules (BCR) (and noting related updates in relation to safe harbour, and the debate as to whether

---

11 P Trudel, 'Privacy Protection on the Internet: Risk Management and Networked Normativity,' in S Gutwirth, Y Poullet, P de Hert, C de Terwange and S Nouwt, *Reinventing Data Protection?* (Springer, 2009) 317.

there are knock on consequences for contractual clauses and BCRs). If an organisation needs to consider the possibility of data transfer exports to non-EEA countries, the current most up to data transfer rules should be assessed, as well as appropriate professional advice. It may be necessary to have specific legal contracts in place. These rules may also be sector specific for certain industries eg airlines flying to US from Europe. The EDPB (previously WP29) is also an important resource for organisations.

Further topical issues are regularly being analysed by the EDPB (previously WP29). These issues may be consulted at, http://ec.europa.eu/justice/data-protection/article-29/index_en.htm.

Drones

33.12   As much as there is a new GDPR data protection regime, there are also new rules and regulations being developed in relation to drones. Drones now have to be registered in more and more jurisdictions, However, the privacy and data protection implications, while being highlighted in general discussion, are not yet adequately encompassed in express privacy and data protection rules. There will be increasing calls to do so, as well as increasing examples of why such an accommodation is needed.

Increasing Actions

33.13   There will be increasing enforcement and fines facing organisations when compliance goes wrong and also when data breach incidents arise. In addition to the actions of regulators such as the ICO, there will also be increasing actions from individual Data Subjects, class actions and representative organisations. While this might occur most frequently where financial data or sensitive data is concerned, it will not be limited to these areas. For example, there are already examples of data breach and data loss in relation to Internet of Things devices and services which open up new areas of exposure.

Data Ethics

33.14   The government has just announced that it agrees to a proposal from the Science and Technology Committee to establish a 'Council of Data Science Ethics'. The government is developing an 'ethical framework for government data science'. The Committee issued a report entitled 'Report: The Big Data Dilemma' in February 2016, to which the government issued a response.

In addition, the government also indicates that it will not presently introduce criminal penalties for serious data breaches, and will consider developments, including the new GDPR. The ICO had previously called for criminal sanctions on a number of occasions previously.

The government also confirms that it will not introduce compulsory data protection audits of local authorities, as there is already ongoing progress in that area.

Nicola Blackwood, MP, the Chair of the Committee states that:

> 'Big Data has enormous potential to improve public services and business productivity, but there are also justified privacy concerns when personal data is used in new applications, services and research. Getting the balance between the benefits and the risks right is vital.

> I am pleased therefore that the Government has accepted our call to set up a "Council of Data Science Ethics" to address the growing legal and ethical challenges associated with balancing privacy, anonymisation of data, security and public benefit.'[12]

The government response was published on 26 April 2016.

Conclusion

33.15 Data protection compliance is never a one size fits all or a single one time policy document. The nature of what amounts to personal data and the activities to which such data can be processed for are ever changing. Those within an organisation, therefore, need to be constantly alert to compliance issues and changes. Organisations also need to be constantly alert to new issues and dangers.

---

12 'Government Agree to set up "Council of Data Ethics,"' The Science and Technology Committee, available at http://www.parliament.uk/business/committees/committees-a-z/commons-select/science-and-technology-committee/news-parliament-2015/big-data-dilemma-government-response-15-16/. The report is at http://www.publications.parliament.uk/pa/cm201516/cmselect/cmsctech/468/468.pdf; the government response is at http://www.publications.parliament.uk/pa/cm201516/cmselect/cmsctech/992/99202.htm. The report is officially titled *House of Commons Science and Technology Committee, The Big Data Dilemma*, Fourth Report of Session 2015–16.

Appendices

Reference Links

Information Commissioner's Office:
https://ico.org.uk/

Article 29 Working Party:
http://ec.europa.eu/justice/data-protection/article-29/documentation/opinion-recommendation/index_en.htm

European Data Protection Board:
[not yet available]

Society of Computers and Law:
http://www.scl.org

Legislative Links

Data Protection Act 1998:
http://www.legislation.gov.uk/ukpga/1998/29/contents

Data Protection Directive 1995:
http://eur-lex.europa.eu/legal-content/EN/TXT/PDF/?uri=CELEX:31995L0046&from=en

Proposed General Data Protection Regulation (Commission original version):
http://ec.europa.eu/justice/data-protection/document/review2012/com_2012_11_en.pdf

Final Agreed version of General Data Protection Regulation:
http://static.ow.ly/docs/Regulation_consolidated_text_EN_47uW.pdf

Appendices

General Data Protection Regulation (Official Journal published final text):
http://ec.europa.eu/justice/data-protection/reform/files/regulation_oj_en.pdf

Forms and Document Links

ICO section on notifications:
https://ico.org.uk/for-organisations/register/

Notification self assessment guides:
https://ico.org.uk/for-organisations/register/self-assessment/

ICO online notification form:
https://ico.org.uk/registration/new

Complying with Data Protection

All organisations collect and process at least some personal data as defined under the DPA and the data protection regime. Therefore, an organisation must ensure it only collects and processes personal data if complying with,

- The obligation to only collect and process personal data if in compliance with the DPA;
- the updated Data Protection Principles;
- the updated Legitimate Processing Conditions;
- the updated Sensitive Personal Data Legitimate Processing Conditions;
- the separate consideration to the processing of children's personal data;
- the security and risk conditions;
- the notification and registration conditions as and where still applicable;
- the data breach notification conditions and incident management;
- the new Data Protection by Design obligations;
- the new accountability obligations;
- data protection impact assessment and risk assessment;
- the personal data outsourcing and data processor conditions;
- the personal data transfer ban or trans border data flow restrictions and standards;
- the individual data subject rights, including access, deletion, right to be forgotten, etc.

- queries, audits and investigation orders from the ICO;
- the time limits for undertaking various tasks and obligations.

Data Protection Principles

All organisations with personal data must comply with the following Data Protection Principles, namely,

- Personal data shall be obtained only for one or more specified and lawful purposes, and shall not be further processed in any manner incompatible with that purpose or those purposes;
- Personal data shall be adequate, relevant and not excessive in relation to the purpose or purposes for which they are processed;
- Personal data shall be accurate and, where necessary, kept up to date;
- Personal data processed for any purpose or purposes shall not be kept for longer than is necessary for that purpose or those purposes;
- Personal data shall be processed in accordance with the rights of data subjects under this Act;
- Appropriate technical and organisational measures shall be taken against unauthorised or unlawful processing of personal data and against accidental loss or destruction of, or damage to, personal data;
- Personal data shall not be transferred to a country or territory outside the EEA unless that country or territory ensures an adequate level of protection for the rights and freedoms of data subjects in relation to the processing of personal data.

The eight Data Protection Principles can be summarised as,

1. fairly and lawfully processed;
2. processed for limited purposes;
3. adequate, relevant and not excessive;
4. accurate and up to date;
5. not kept for longer than is necessary;
6. processed in line with individual data subject rights;
7. secure; and
8. not transferred to other countries without adequate protection.

All eight of the principled must be complied with. Compliance with the Data Protection Principles applies to all employee and inward-facing personal data collected and or processed by an organisation. It also applied regardless of registration requirements. Noting of course the updates and clarifications of the new GDPR.

Ordinary Personal Data Legitimate Processing Conditions

When dealing with the above inward-facing categories of employees, agents, contractors, etc., the Legitimate Processing Conditions are required to be complied with, *in addition* to the Data Protection Principles.

Schedule 2 of the DPA contains the general Legitimate Processing Conditions eg employee non sensitive personal data. In order to comply with the general personal data Legitimate Processing Conditions, the organisation must fall within *one* of the following conditions, namely:

- The individual who the personal data is about has consented to the processing.
- The processing is necessary,
  - in relation to a contract which the individual has entered into; or
  - because the individual has asked for something to be done so they can enter into a contract.
- The processing is necessary because of a legal obligation that applies to the organisation (except an obligation imposed by a contract);
- The processing is necessary to protect the individual's 'vital interests.' This condition only applies in cases of life or death, such as where an employee's medical history is disclosed to a hospital's A&E department treating them after a serious road accident;
- The processing is necessary for administering justice, or for exercising statutory, governmental, or other public functions;
- The processing is in accordance with the 'legitimate interests' condition.

DPA Schedule 2 of the DPA contains conditions relevant for the purposes of the first Data Protection Principle, in particular the processing of personal data. It states:

1 The data subject has given his consent to the processing;
2 The processing is necessary,
   (a) for the performance of a contract to which the data subject is a party; or
   (b) for the taking of steps at the request of the data subject with a view to entering into a contract;
3 The processing is necessary for compliance with any legal obligation to which the data controller is subject, other than an obligation imposed by contract;
4 The processing is necessary in order to protect the vital interests of the data subject;

5   The processing is necessary,
   (a) for the administration of justice;
   (aa) for the exercise of any functions of either House of Parliament;
   (b) for the exercise of any functions conferred on any person by or under any enactment;
   (c) for the exercise of any functions of the Crown, a Minister of the Crown or a government department; or
   (d) for the exercise of any other functions of a public nature exercised in the public interest by any person.

6(1) The processing is necessary for the purposes of legitimate interests pursued by the data controller or by the third party or parties to whom the data are disclosed, except where the processing is unwarranted in any particular case by reason of prejudice to the rights and freedoms or legitimate interests of the data subject;

(2) The Secretary of State may by order specify particular circumstances in which this condition is, or is not, to be taken to be satisfied.

There are, therefore, six general Legitimate Processing Conditions. Frequently, an organisation would seek to fall within the legitimate interests condition above. These might be summarised as follows:

- The employee has given explicit consent;
- Processing necessary for performance of *contract* to which the employee is a party;
- Processing is necessary to take steps at request of the employee prior to entering into contract;
- Processing is necessary for compliance with legal obligation (other than contractual obligation);
- Necessary to prevent injury or other damage to health of the employee or serious loss or damage to property of the employee or to protect vital interests;
- Necessary for the administration of justice, performance of statutory function or function of public nature performed in public interest;
- Processing necessary for *legitimate interests* pursued by data controller except where unwarranted.

Unlike certain other areas, the legitimate processing of employee personal data does not require employee consent. However, many organisations would have originally expected and proceeded on the basis that consent was so required. They would have incorporated (deemed) consent clauses into employment contracts, etc.

As indicated above, Schedule 2 of the DPA enables organisations to rely upon the legitimate processing condition that processing is necessary for the purposes of *legitimate interests* pursued by the data controller or by the third party or parties to whom the data are disclosed, except where the processing is unwarranted in any particular case by reason of prejudice to the rights and freedoms or legitimate interests of the data subject.

An alternative would be to say that the processing is necessary as part of a contract to which the employee is a party, in particular the employment contract.

Noting of course the updates and clarifications of the new GDPR.

Sensitive Personal Data Legitimate Processing Conditions

Organisation may also feel the need on occasion to store and use sensitive personal data in relation to employees, such as medical and health data. In the case of sensitive personal data, an organisation must in addition to satisfying all of the Data Protection Principles, be able to comply or fall within *one* of the Sensitive Personal Data Legitimate Processing Conditions.

Schedule 3 of the DPA sets out conditions relevant for the purposes of the first Data Protection Principle in particular in relation to the processing of Sensitive Personal Data. In the context of employees and inward-facing personal data, it provides:

1   The employee data subject has given his or her explicit consent to the processing of the personal data;

2(1) The processing is necessary for the purposes of exercising or performing any right or obligation which is conferred or imposed by law on the data controller in connection with employment;

(2) The Secretary of State may by order,
   (a) exclude the application of sub-paragraph (1) in such cases as may be specified; or
   (b) provide that, in such cases as may be specified, the condition in sub-paragraph (1) is not to be regarded as satisfied unless such further conditions as may be specified in the order are also satisfied;

3   The processing is necessary,
   (a) in order to protect the vital interests of the employee data subject or another person, in a case where,
      (i) consent cannot be given by or on behalf of the employee data subject; or
      (ii) the data controller cannot reasonably be expected to obtain the consent of the employee data subject; or
   (b) in order to protect the vital interests of another person, in a case where consent by or on behalf of the employee data subject has been unreasonably withheld;

4   The processing,
    (a) is carried out in the course of its legitimate activities by any body or association which,
      (i) is not established or conducted for profit; and
      (ii) exists for political, philosophical, religious or trade-union purposes;
    (b) is carried out with appropriate safeguards for the rights and freedoms of data subjects;
    (c) relates only to individuals who either are members of the body or association or have regular contact with it in connection with its purposes; and
    (d) does not involve disclosure of the employee personal data to a third party without the consent of the employee data subject;

5   The information contained in the personal data has been made public as a result of steps deliberately taken by the employee data subject;

6   The processing,
    (a) is necessary for the purpose of, or in connection with, any legal proceedings (including prospective legal proceedings);
    (b) is necessary for the purpose of obtaining legal advice; or
    (c) is otherwise necessary for the purposes of establishing, exercising or defending legal rights;

7(1) The processing is necessary,
    (a) for the administration of justice;
    (aa) for the exercise of any functions of either House of Parliament;
    (b) for the exercise of any functions conferred on any person by or under an enactment; or
    (c) for the exercise of any functions of the Crown, a Minister of the Crown or a government department;

(2) The Secretary of State may by order,
    (a) exclude the application of sub-paragraph (1) in such cases as may be specified; or
    (b) provide that, in such cases as may be specified, the condition in sub-paragraph (1) is not to be regarded as satisfied unless such further conditions as may be specified in the order are also satisfied;

7A(1) The processing,
    (a) is either,
      (i) the disclosure of sensitive personal data by a person as a member of an anti-fraud organisation or otherwise in accordance with any arrangements made by such an organisation; or
      (ii) any other processing by that person or another person of sensitive personal data so disclosed; and

(b) is necessary for the purposes of preventing fraud or a particular kind of fraud;

(2) In this paragraph 'an anti-fraud organisation' means any unincorporated association, body corporate or other person which enables or facilitates any sharing of information to prevent fraud or a particular kind of fraud or which has any of these functions as its purpose or one of its purposes;

8(1) The processing is necessary for medical purposes and is undertaken by,

(a) a health professional; or

(b) a person who in the circumstances owes a duty of confidentiality which is equivalent to that which would arise if that person were a health professional;

(2) In this paragraph 'medical purposes' includes the purposes of preventative medicine, medical diagnosis, medical research, the provision of care and treatment and the management of healthcare services;

9(1) The processing,

(a) is of sensitive personal data consisting of information as to racial or ethnic origin;

(b) is necessary for the purpose of identifying or keeping under review the existence or absence of equality of opportunity or treatment between persons of different racial or ethnic origins, with a view to enabling such equality to be promoted or maintained; and

(c) is carried out with appropriate safeguards for the rights and freedoms of employee data subjects;

(2) The Secretary of State may by order specify circumstances in which processing falling within sub-paragraph (1)(a) and (b) is, or is not, to be taken for the purposes of sub-paragraph (1)(c) to be carried out with appropriate safeguards for the rights and freedoms of data subjects.

These Sensitive Personal Data Legitimate Processing conditions may be summarised as follows,

- The employee whom the sensitive personal data is about has given explicit consent to the processing;
- The processing is necessary so that the organisation can comply with employment law;
- The processing is necessary to protect the vital interests of,
  - the employee (in a case where the employee's consent cannot be given or reasonably obtained); or
  - another person (in a case where the individual's consent has been unreasonably withheld);

- The processing is carried out by a not-for-profit organisation and does not involve disclosing personal data to a third party, unless the employee consents. Extra limitations apply to this condition;
- The employee has deliberately made the information public;
- The processing is necessary in relation to legal proceedings, for obtaining legal advice; or otherwise for establishing, exercising or defending legal rights;
- The processing is necessary for administering justice, or for exercising statutory or governmental functions;
- The processing is necessary for medical purposes, and is undertaken by a health professional or by someone who is subject to an equivalent duty of confidentiality;
- The processing is necessary for monitoring equality of opportunity, and is carried out with appropriate safeguards for the rights of individuals.

Furthermore, regulations also set out further obligations in relation to the processing of sensitive personal data. Noting of course the updates and clarifications of the new GDPR.

Access Request Flows

Morgan and Boardman[1] refer to the access request. The following flow description is a further adapted of same.

Objections to Marketing

Jay[2] provides the following suggestions for organisations when dealing with access requests/marketing objections, namely,

- Does the objection relate to marketing or another form or processing?
- Does it relate to direct marketing within the definition?
- Is it in writing or sent electronically or oral?
- If it is not in writing or electronic is it appropriate to deal with it as sent or should the individual be require to put it in writing or send it by electronic means?

---

1 Morgan, R,. and Boardman, R., *Data Protection Strategy, Implementing Data Protection Compliance*, (London: Sweet and Maxwell, 2012), p. 335.
2 Jay and Hamilton, *Data Protection: Law and Practice*, (London: Sweet and Maxwell, 2007), pp. 436–437.

- At which branch or office was it received?
- On what date was the request received?
- Has the individual making the request given an intelligible name and address to which the controller can respond?
- When does the period for response expire?
- What time scale has the individual specified to stop marketing processing on a notice?
- What marketing processing is affected?
- Is more time needed to comply with the requirement?
- How is the marketing data held? Is it manual or automated or some of both?
- Does the objection apply to manual or automated?
- Has the individual described the data?
- Has the individual described the processing?
- Has the individual explained why unwarranted damage and distress would be caused?
- On what grounds are the data being processing?
- Can one of the primary grounds be claimed?
- Does the notice amount to a revocation of an existing consent?
- Is it possible to comply with the objection?
- Is processing about others affected?
- Would compliance mean system changes?

Audit Checklist

Morgan and Boardman[3] refer to the audits. There checklists include for example:

Extent of Audit

- What parts of the organisation and its files and systems have been audits and for what reason?
- Are they likely to be sufficient to give an indication of the organisation's overall data protection compliance or not?

Classes of Personal Data Audited

- Computer?
- Email?
- Other letter/memo files?

---

3   Morgan, R, and Boardman, R, *Data Protection Strategy, Implementing Data Protection Compliance*, (London: Sweet and Maxwell, 2012), pp 78 *et seq*.

- Internet?
- Intranet?
- Manual (relevant filing system)
- Video (scanned images, CCTV, photographic, film)
- Audio (contract, training, voicemail)
- Biometric
- Other categories of personal data (eg tachograph)
- Types of Personal Data
- Is there personal data or not?
- If yes, is the personal data sensitive personal data?
- Or accessible personal data?
- Is any of the personal data confidential? Eg medical/financial? If so, what are the consequences of this and what are individuals told about this?
- Is there any automatic or automated processing of personal data? If so, what are the consequences of this and what are individuals told about this?
- Are there any cookies? If so, how are they used?

Types of Data Subject

- Staff
- Retires Staff
- Staff spouses or other family members
- Members of the public
- Customers
- Prospective customers
- Business contacts, which may include,
  - Sole traders or partnerships, who are identifiable individuals and so data subjects; or
  - Managers or other individual office holders in those bodies the organisation has contracts with?

'Owner' of Personal Data

- Who?
- Any 'private' files?
- How are private emails handled?
- What, if any, of the data is processed by a data processor?
- What personal data is received from another organisation?
- What personal data is shared with one or more other organisations?
- Does the organisation process data itself on behalf of others, as a data processor?

Appendices

Purposes of Processing

- How and why is the personal data collected?
- What information is given to individuals about this, how and when?
- How well does the data's use match the purposes for which it is collected?
- Does the organisation carry out direct marketing? If so, how?
- Does it subscribe to 'preference' service?
- What or whom ensures that the personal data are accurate?
- What are the consequences if the personal data is inaccurate?
- How long is it kept?
- What happens to it when it is no longer used?
- What are the criteria for its destruction?
- Is it in fact destroyed: if so, who does this and how do they do it?

Contracts

- Data processing contracts
- Data sharing contracts
- Contracts involving personal data outside of the EEA
- Fair obtaining warranties

Security of Personal Data

- Physical security
- Staff security
- What standards accreditation does the organisation have?
- System security – eg passwords, firewalls, etc
- What about portable media eg Laptops, memory sticks, CDs, etc?
- Procedures for sending secure faxes – and emails – for sensitive personal data?
- Is there any use of wireless transmission wi-fi?
- Security with data processors
- How were they selected?
- Was their security checked?
- How is it guaranteed by the data processor and documented?
- Is there any ongoing review processing?

Sending Outside EEA?

- Files?
- Emails?
- Internet material?
- Intranet material?

Cookies

- Which?

- From where?
- How intrusive?

Noting also of course the updates and clarifications of the new GDPR require separate additional audit and record processes for the privacy impact and risk impact assessments.

Procedures

Morgan and Boardman[4] refer to processes and procedures in relation compliance and ongoing compliance. The queries checklist includes for example:

Procedures and Procedures

- What industry/trade association guidance is available?
- What published processed and procedures are there in respect of personal data?
- How are they brought to the attention of staff others?
- How enforced?
- How updated?
- Who is responsible for this?
- How does he/she fit into the organisations structure?

Data Protection Notification/Registration

- Has the organisation notified?
- If not, why does it consider itself exempt?
- Is the notification consistent with the personal data identified by the audit?
- Purposes?
- Is the notification up to date?
- How is the notification kept up to date?

Data Subjects' Rights

- What Procedures are in place to deal with requests in connection with data subjects rights?
- How has it worked so far?
- Any problems with identifying a particular individual in the personal data?
- Are the Information Commissioner's Codes (eg CCTV, employment practice, data sharing) followed?

---

4   Morgan, R, and Boardman, R, *Data Protection Strategy, Implementing Data Protection Compliance*, (London: Sweet and Maxwell, 2012), pp 80 *et seq.*

Appendices

People

- Who is in charge of data protection?
- What resources does he/she have?
- How is he/she supported by senior management?
- What if any disciplinary action has been taken in respect of data protection?

Information Commissioner Office (ICO)

- Apart from notification/registration, has the organisation ever had any dealings with the ICO? If so, what and when and with what particular results?

Obviously in future risk issues and risk assessments will be very important.

Index

[All references are to paragraph number]

A

Abuse
employee monitoring, and, 18.07
generally, 33.10
social media, and, 29.09

Accuracy
overview, 1.19

Ad network providers
DPD, 21.54
WP29 recommendations, 21.74–21.75

'Add to basket' buttons
cookies, 21.12

Adequate protection
transfer of personal data, 23.03

Advertisers
cookies, 21.56

Anonymised data
transfer of personal data, 23.18

Appeals
enforcement powers, 22.12

Assessment notices
appeals, 22.12
Code of Practice, 22.05
generally, 22.03
limitations, 22.04
request, 22.06

Audits
cookies, 21.20

Automated decision taking
data protection rights, 16.06
generally, 9.13
social media, 29.21

B

Behavioural advertising (OBA)
consent obligations, 21.58
WPA Opinion 2/2010
contextual, 21.44
generally, 21.42
issues, 21.43

Behavioural advertising (OBA) – *contd*
WPA Opinion 2/2010 – *contd*
meaning, 21.44
predictive profiles, 21.46
tracking technology, 21.45
types, 21.44
WPA Opinion 16/2011, 21.76
WPA Opinion 04/2012
characteristics of cookie,
21.80
Condition A, 21.78
Condition B, 21.79
generally, 21.77
guidelines, 21.83
multipurpose cookies, 21.81
non-exempted cookies, 21.82
summary, 21.83

Binding corporate rules
definition, 3.04
transfer of personal data, 23.07

Biometric data
definition, 3.04

Blocking
data protection rights, 16.07
generally, 9.17
social media, 29.20

Blogs
sources of law, 2.16

Body scanners
generally, 33.04

Breach of preliminary assessment
offences under DPA, 12.07

Breaches of rules
data processing activities,
12.03
generally, 12.02
other consequences, 12.04

Browser settings
and see **Cookies**
consent obligations, 21.59
generally, 21.14

Index

Index

Index

Index

Index

Index

Index

Index

Index

Index

Index

Index

Index

Index

Medical data
GDPR, and, 4.07
generally, 33.02
Mere conduit
social media, and, 29.14
Message bars
cookies, 21.23
Microsoft
privacy by design, 20.11
Misuse of electronic communications
entering into contracts, 18.04
generally, 18.03
Mobile devices
cookies, 21.39
Monetary penalty notices
enforcement, 22.17
generally, 22.14
guidance, 22.16
power to impose, 22.14
procedural rights, 22.15
supplemental provisions, 22.18
Monitoring employees
application of data protection regime,
18.16
child pornography, 18.09
conclusion, 18.28
contracts of employment, and,
18.20
corporate communications usage policy
content, 18.12
generally, 18.11
key issues, 18.13
data protection, and, 18.14
data subjects rights, 18.26
EDPB Opinion, 18.18
email misuse
entering into contracts, 18.04
generally, 18.03
equality, 18.05
guidelines, 18.25
harassment, 18.06
human rights, 18.15
Internet misuse
entering into contracts, 18.04
generally, 18.03
ILO Code, 18.17
introduction, 18.01
issues arising, 18.02
misuse of electronic communications
entering into contracts, 18.04
generally, 18.03
offline abuse, 18.08
online abuse, 18.07

Monitoring employees – *contd*
policies
corporate communications,
18.11–18.13
processing compliance rules,
18.24
purpose, 18.14
registration, and
exemptions, 18.22
general requirement, 18.21
issues, 18.23
risk assessment
generally, 18.10
policies, 18.11–18.13
Romanian/ECHR case, 18.27
WP29 Opinion, 18.19
Multinationals
privacy by design, 20.11
Multipurpose cookies
generally, 21.81

N

National Identification Numbers
GDPR, and, 26.103
National laws
DPD, and, 4.10
National security
GDPR, and, 4.07
Non-compliance
enforcement and penalties
civil sanctions, 12.20
conclusion, 12.34
director liability, 12.21
DPA, under, 12.02–12.14,
12.15–12.22, 12.32
DPD, under, 12.23–12.15
GDPR, under, 12.16–12.19,
12.26–12.27
ICO, and, 12.15, 12.28–12.31,
12.33
introduction, 12.01
processors, 12.22
Notification
see also **Registration**
changes, of, 10.04
conclusion, 10.07
GDPR, and, 4.07
introduction, 10.01
register, 10.03
regulations, 10.06
Notification of data breach
contents, 13.13

Index

Index

Index

Index

Index

Index

Index